Trade and Growth of the Advanced Developing Countries in the Pacific Basin

Papers and Proceedings of The Eleventh
Pacific Trade and Development Conference

Wontack Hong and
Lawrence B. Krause
Editors

1 9 8 1

KOREA DEVELOPMENT INSTITUTE

Seoul, Korea

All Rights Reserved by
THE KOREA DEVELOPMENT INSTITUTE
P.O. Box 113, Cheong Ryang, Seoul, Korea

Distributed Outside Korea by
The University Press of Hawaii

ISBN 0-8248-0791-X

FOREWORD

It is a great honor for both our country and this Institute to have the opportunity to host the 11th Pacific Trade and Development Conference. The theme of this conference, trade and growth of the advanced developing countries under the new international economic order, is especially relevant as the world stands at the threshold of the 1980s. This issue is of particular importance to us because many countries in the Pacific region have already emerged or are in the process of emerging as advanced developing countries.

I believe this conference will provide an excellent forum to discuss the problems facing these countries, and to search for ways to overcome the problems. It is my hope that this conference will be beneficial to all participants as well as to all the countries represented.

Mahn Je Kim
President,
Korea Development Institute

TABLE OF CONTENTS

v

vi

vii

PREFACE

This book encompasses the papers and proceedings of the Eleventh Pacific Trade and Development Conference, held at the Korea Development Institute in Seoul, Korea in September 1980.

The conference was devoted to certain advanced developing countries in the Pacific basin. The rapid growth of Korea, Taiwan, Hong Kong and Singapore, that has been made possible through export expansion during the last two decades is regarded as enviable by many people and even as a miracle by some. While the four countries are often grouped together as the Asian ADCs (Advanced Developing Countries), there are significant differences among them. Nevertheless, the merits of export-oriented growth strategy in terms of growth rates of GNP, employment, and real wages have been well demonstrated in all of them, but there are serious problems, both internal and external, still to be overcome.

For instance, their ability to control domestic inflation, to reach and maintain high levels of investment, to sustain balance-of-payments equilibrium, and to adjust industrial structures as comparative advantage is lost in unskilled, labor-intensive manufactures to other less developed countries may be inadequate to sustain rapid growth. Also their success in improving the distribution of income may not be sufficient to forestall serious social unrest. Externally it may become more difficult for these countries to acquire the raw materials and fuel essential for their domestic and export industries and, most importantly, the developed countries might greatly increase protective import barriers against their exports.

The purpose of this conference was to analyze the growth and trade of these advanced developing countries including the differences among them, examining the problems these countries face, and search for ways to overcome such problems through changes in domestic economic policies and also through improved economic cooperation in the Pacific Basin Area.

The conference was organized by the Korea Development Institute and directed by a committee comprising Mahn Je Kim, Wontack Hong, and Chong Hyun Nam. It was assisted by advice from the international steering committee of the conference series, comprising Kiyoshi Kojima (chairman) and Saburo Okita in Japan, Lawrence B. Krause and Hugh Patrick in the United States, Narongchai Akrasanee in Thailand, Romeo Bautista in the Philippines, H. Edward English in Canada and Sir John Crawford and Peter Drysdale in Australia.

The conference was made possible by financial support from the Korea Development Institute and the Ford Foundation. Support was also obtained from the Asian Development Bank. The manuscript was prepared with the assistance of Kirk W. Kimmell of the Brookings Institution and the detailed editing was performed by Anne Evans, Young Hak Jeon, and Richard B. Samuelson.

Wontack Hong
Seoul University

Lawrence B. Krause
The Brookings Institution

PARTICIPANTS

Kym Anderson, *Australian National University, Australia*
Narongchai Akrasanee, *UN ESCAP, Thailand*
Mohamed Ariff, *University of Malaya, Malaysia*
Robert E. Baldwin, *University of Wisconsin, U.S.A.*
Romeo M. Bautista, *National Economic and Development Authority, Philippines*
Colin I. Bradford, *Yale University, U.S.A.*
K. Y. Chen, *University of Hong Kong, Hong Kong*
W. Max Corden, *Australian National University, Australia*
Dono Iskandar Djojosubroto, *Ministry of Finance, Indonesia*
Peter Drysdale, *Australian National University, Australia*
H. Edward English, *Carleton University, Canada*
Fernando Fajnzylber, *UNIDO/NAFINSA, Mexico*
Ronald Findlay, *Columbia University, U.S.A.*
Seung J. Han, *Korea University, Korea*
Gerald K. Helleiner, *University of Toronto, Canada*
Wontack Hong, *Seoul University, Korea*
Kiyoshi Ikemoto, *Kobe University, Japan*
Hisao Kanamori, *Japan Economic Research Center, Japan*
Robert Keohane, *Stanford University, U.S.A.*
Byung J. Kim, *Sogang University, Korea*
Mahn Je Kim, *Korea Development Institute, Korea*
Kwang Suk Kim, *Korea Development Institute, Korea*
Soo Y. Kim, *Korea International Economic Institute, Korea*
Kiyoshi Kojima, *Hitotsubashi University, Japan*
Lawrence B. Krause, *The Brookings Institution, U.S.A.*
Bon Ho Koo, *Han Yang University, Korea*

xi

Anne O. Krueger, *University of Minnesota, U.S.A.*
Hoe Sung Lee, *Korean Institute of Energy and Resource, Korea*
Ching-ing Hou Liang, *National Chengchi University, Taiwan*
Kuo-Shu Liang, *National Taiwan University, Taiwan*
Tzong Biau Lin, *Chinese University of Hong Kong, Hong Kong*
Chong Hyun Nam, *Korea University, Korea*
Yung Chul Park, *Korea University, Korea*
Hugh Patrick, *Yale University, U.S.A.*
Michael G. Porter, *Monash University, Australia*
Bruce Ross, *Canterbury University, New Zealand*
A. E. Safarian, *University of Toronto, Canada*
Ben Smith, *Australian National University, Australia*
Ernesto Tironi, *CEPAL, Chile*
Toshio Watanabe, *University of Tsukuba, Japan*
Kum Poh Wong, *National University of Singapore, Singapore*
Ippei Yamazawa, *Hitotsubashi University, Japan*
Yasukichi Yasuba, *Kyoto University, Japan*
David Yoffie, *Stanford University, U.S.A.*

PART I

EXPORT ORIENTED GROWTH

EXPORT-LED INDUSTRIAL GROWTH RECONSIDERED

*Anne O. Krueger**

I. Introduction

By the early 1970s, it was apparent to all observers that the rates of growth achieved by the export-promotion or outer-oriented developing countries were vastly superior to those achieved by countries adhering to restrictive trade policies, and encouraging the growth of their industrial sectors through import substitution. Numerous studies, including those of the P.E.C.D. analyzed in Little, Scitovsky and Scott (1970), and those of the National Bureau of Economic Research, synthesized in Bhagwati (1978) and in Krueger (1978), all attested to the many difficulties inherent in import-substitution strategies, and the better performance associated with export promotion.

At first glance, the superiority of the export-promotion strategy appeared to vindicate the view of trade theorists, who had advocated free trade and who saw export promotion as coming closer to a free trade regime than did import substitution. Proponents of import-substitution policies have appealed to "dynamic" considerations and infant industry arguments as the basis for their departures from free trade, static first-best policies. With the evident superiority of the export-promotion policies, it was natural to conclude, as did Bhagwati and Srinivasan, that "it would appear that the pattern of incentives, and hence of export promotion, is less skewed in practice

* Professor of Economics, University of Minnesota, U.S.A. The author is indebted to T.N. Srinivasan for helpful comments.

than the chaotic pattern of import-substituting incentives under the restrictive trade regimes,'' and that the greater neutrality of incentives appeared to be a factor accounting for superior performance (1979, p. 17).

Closer examination of experience with export-led growth, however, has raised an important set of questions. On one hand, the classical free-trade arguments, while indicating the superiority of free trade, do not provide any hint as to why that superiority should be demonstrated in a more rapid rate of growth (as contrasted with a higher level of income, after sustaining once-and-for-all losses associated with protection).[1] On the other hand, even if the losses from departures from first-best optimality were several times as great as traditional theory would suggest, the difference in growth rates seem to be greater than can conceivably be accounted for by the exporting sector of the economy.[2] Even if one assumes a simple Keynesian multiplier mechanism on export growth, which is entirely too naive, overall economic performance seems in general to exceed what could conceivably be associated with the direct and multiplier-induced effects of export growth.

The questions therefore center upon why performance under export promotion has been so much better than under import substitution. There are a number of plausible hypotheses, but evidence and research to date have not yielded definitive results to permit distinguishing among them. It is likely that a wide variety of factors have contributed to the general overall success of export-promotion strategies, and further, that the relative contribution of various components has differed between countries depending on their initial circumstances including, for example, size, geographic location and natural resource endowment, and at different points in time.

In this paper the underlying theory is reviewed, and the possible reasons for the superior performance under export promotion are discussed. No attempt is made to assign relative weights to the various strands of the analysis, nor is available empirical evidence systemati-

---

[1] It is possible, in a Harrod-Domar world, for a reduced incremental capital-output ratio, and an increased savings rate out of higher income, to alter the rate of growth. In the neo-classical model, however, the steady-state growth rate is unaffected (but the level of real income is).

[2] Most observers of the international economy are astonished to learn that exports constitute only about 15 percent of Japanese GNP, and that the share has been relatively constant since the early 1960s.

cally assembled, although some possibly significant items are cited.

What emerges is a set of questions which call for a great deal of research. It is not enough to know that export promotion out-performs import substitution. It is equally important to understand why. This is essential in light of the fact that other countries are beginning to adopt export-promotion policies; those policies assume a variety of forms and utilize a wide variety of instruments. Depending on which mechanisms yield better performance under export promotion, the efforts to emulate the successful exporters will succeed or fail as the instruments chosen capture or miss those key elements responsible for the success of export promotion.

Section II outlines the neoclassical theory and the infant industry framework for analysis. Section III then reviews the experience under import substitution, and the unsatisfactory aspects of growth under that strategy. Each hypothesis regarding export promotion and its superiority focusses upon a key difference between the export-oriented strategy and import substitution in one or more essential characteristics. The three basic hypotheses—better policy, technology, and economic behavior—are covered in Section IV. A final section then summarizes and suggests some of the kinds of information that would be helpful in reaching a verdict.

II. Neoclassical Theory and the Infant Industry Argument

The classical argument for free trade is simple and appealing: international trade represents an alternative "technology" to domestic production. The slope of the transformation curve between any pair of commodities represents the domestic marginal rate of transformation between those commodities in production, while the slope of the price line (in the absence of monopoly power in trade) represents the marginal rate of transformation between the commodities in trade. For any commodity whose marginal rate of transformation in domestic production is less than in trade, real income, real consumption, and community welfare could be increased by reducing production of that commodity, increasing production of the other, and trading internationally to obtain the commodity in question. Such reallocation should proceed between all pairs of commodities until the marginal rate of transformation between each pair in domestic production equals the marginal rate of transformation between each pair in trade. When a country possesses no monopoly power in trade, the marginal rate of transformation in trade can be taken as equal to the inverse of the price ratio between any pair of commodities. It is readily shown that a static welfare optimum can be achieved for any allocation of resources to the tradable goods sector of the economy, when the marginal rate of transformation in domestic production equals the inverse of the international price ratio.[3]

In the two-commodity case, a country's comparative advantage lies in producing whichever commodity is domestically cheaper at autarky. Whether there will be complete or incomplete specialization depends upon whether there is a sufficiently rapidly diminishing marginal rate of transformation between commodities so that the IMRT = DMRT condition is not met before complete specialization is reached. Gains from trade are readily demonstrated: they lie in the greater consumption possibility set associated with free trade than with autarky.

For present purposes, the main point is that the static optimality of free trade (when there is no monopoly power in trade and when domestic factor and commodity markets are competitive) does not provide any insights into the likely path of economic growth under autarky, under restricted trade, or under free trade. Indeed, the simple 2 × 2 comparative advantage model would seem to suggest that growth rates will be the same under autarky and under free trade, once the once-and-for-all losses associated with accepting a non-optimal trade policy are absorbed. Thus, there are no theorems from standard trade theory with regard to the effects on the growth rate of departures from optimal trade policy.[4]

By contrast, the infant industry case for departures from free trade is based squarely on a presumed dynamic effect, that an industry or industries which presently have domestic marginal rates of transformation exceeding the terms on which the goods can be imported will,

---

[3] There are, of course, optimality conditions necessary to insure that production takes place on the production possibility frontier, and that the domestic price ratio equals the inverse of the domestic marginal rate of transformation. Those considerations do not alter the basic argument being made here.

[4] One could, of course, build in assumptions (such as higher savings out of returns to capital and the capital-intensive industry being the import substitute) that would generate such a result. The point is that the free trade case is made in terms of static optimality, not in terms of growth.

over time, experience sufficient cost reductions to permit them to compete. To be sure, proponents of infant industry protection have recognized that, even if the conditions for promoting an infant industry are present, protection is second-best to a production subsidy because of the excess consumption cost incurred via the latter. Baldwin (1969) has demonstrated that, under most circumstances that might generate gains in output per unit of input, appropriate policy will in general be to subsidize the source of the gain, as in workers learning their trade, and in importing the technology.

Nonetheless, nothing in theory has ever contradicted the proposition that there might be dynamic factors which resulted in lower costs over time, where the benefits accruing from the industry included externalities not profiting the initial investors. If there were such an industry or industries, it seems clear that policies inducing their growth, at an appropriate rate, taking into account that their costs would have to fall sufficiently to earn a return adequate to cover the present losses owing to their high costs, could result in a superior growth preformance compared with that which would occur under free trade.

In terms of assessing import-substitution policies as a strategy with which to confer inducements to infant industries, it is important to note that the theory of infant industry itself is ambiguous in indicating what the source of the dynamic factor might be: on one hand, if such dynamic factors are specific to particular industries such as glass-blowing or electronics, then the number of industries which should receive infant industry protection at any given time should be relatively small. If, on the other hand, externalities and dynamic cost reductions are a function of the size of the entire industrial sector, then inducements to produce should be fairly uniform across industrial activities, as the same dynamic benefits would accrue regardless of the precise industries which were growing rapidly.

Attention will return to the possibility that infant industries deserve encouragement. For present purposes, it is important to note that, if the appropriate mix of infant industries was encouraged at the optimal rate, superior growth performance would emerge as a result. To be sure, both the classical defense of free trade and the infant industry argument presume that domestic factor and product markets are fairly competitive, a phenomenon not always observed in developing countries.

III. Experience under Import Substitution

1. Definition of Export Promotion and Import Substitution

If, in theory, incentives should be such that resources are allocated to equate earnings and savings of foreign exchange per unit of domestic resources, it makes sense to ask why export promotion and import substitution cannot coexist. Indeed, it would appear logical to define an export-promotion policy as anything which gave greater incentive to produce an item to be exported than would occur under a free trade situation, while an import-substitution inducement would be one providing greater incentives to produce rather than import the item than would exist in a free trade situation.[5] In principle, both sorts of policies could coexist, with industries receiving neither sort of incentive being discriminated against.[6]

In practice, there are several reasons to distinguish regimes of export promotion from those of import substitution even though there are always some "export-promotion" measures within import-substitution regimes and some import-substitution activities within export-oriented regimes. A first reason lies in the fact that many so-called "export-promotion" measures undertaken within import-substitution regimes are really nothing more than offsets to the dis-incentives otherwise created for exporting or else they tie the profit to be made in selling in the home market to a precondition that the firm also export some fraction of its output.[7] A second reason is that import-substitution regimes tend to rely on protection, often in the form of import prohibitions, against imports of goods that would compete with domestic production; by contrast, a genuine export-

---

[5] With equalized incentives, one would expect to observe the development of some industries to sizes that would produce both for the domestic market and for export, while others would develop only enough to meet domestic demand (in part or in entirety). When tariff or quota protection is used to induce domestic production, many export industries would be observed to be "import-competing" industries.

[6] Import-substitution regimes inherently discriminate by place of sale for the same commodity. Some export-promotion regimes provide a greater incentive to sell the same item abroad than on the home market, but that is not a necessary feature of such regimes.

[7] See the interesting analysis of Carvalho and Haddad of the changing composition of Brazil's exports when its trade strategy is altered.

promotion orientation requires that individual exporters have free and ready access to international markets for their raw materials, intermediate goods, and spare parts, in order to compete successfully in foreign markets. An import-substitution regime, in that regard, generally discourages exporting. Thirdly, the very fact that import-substitution regimes tend to discourage exports also means, as will be further discussed, "foreign exchange shortage" that tends to be a chronic problem; exchange control measures are usually evoked as a partial response. Such measures generally entail quantitative restrictions and an overvalued exchange rate, neither of which are conducive to encouraging exports. Finally in terms of production activities, discrimination in favor of some activities can successfully pull resources into those lines only if there is simultaneous discrimination against other activities. The notion that one can protect some industries without "deprotecting" others is faulty.[8]

Thus, an import-substitution regime can be defined as one where the overall bias of incentives favors production for sale in the home market, replacing imports. Although it is not necessarily the intent of the authorities to discriminate in favor of sales in the home market, the very fact that tariffs are applicable only for imports entering a country is sufficient to insure that import substitution discriminates by the trade status of the commodity: potential exportable goods, even if they are the same goods as import-substitution goods, are eligible for favored treatment only for sale at home.

Formally, bias is defined as the divergence between the domestic price ratio of importables and exportables to the foreign price ratio. An import-substitution regime is biased in favor of import-competing production and domestic sale, and is reflected in a higher domestic price for import-competing goods relative to exportables domestically than prevails internationally.[9]

Bias is distinct from openness of an economy. Openness refers to the extent to which domestic prices are linked to international prices. When import substitution is encouraged through nonprohibitive tariffs, for example, the trade regime is biased toward import sub-

---

[8] If resources are not fully employed, the appropriate policy instrument would be macroeconomic.

[9] Let P_x and P_m represent the international prices of exportables and importables, and q_x and q_m be the corresponding domestic prices. Then, $B = \dfrac{q_m/q_x}{P_m/P_x}$. If $B > 1$ the regime is biased toward import substitution.

stitution, but open export-oriented regimes are, of necessity, open.

An export-promotion regime, by contrast, is biased in favor of the foreign market. That is, the domestic price received for export sales relative to sales of goods produced for the home market exceeds the same price ratio internationally. There are two ways in which this can be accomplished: on the one hand, one could have no duties on imports, while maintaining implicit or explicit subsidies for export sales. Alternatively, there could be some positive level of protection in the home market, but even higher incentives and subsidies for sales abroad. There are thus two relative prices of some importance: on the one hand there is the relative price of the same commodity depending on its point of sale; and there is the relative price of different commodities depending on the nature of the incentive structure in place within a given country. An export-promotion regime will typically provide more incentives for selling an item abroad than at home, whereas an import-substitution regime provides the opposite.[10]

Under either an import-substitution or an export-promotion regime, therefore, there are several policy choices to be made: there is, first, the matter of determining the range of industries or activities to be subject to incentives; second, there is the variance in incentives across activities according to industry; and finally, there is the variance in incentives for the same activity depending upon the product's destination.

2. Experience under Import Substitution

The purpose here is to describe some of the sorts of difficulties that seem to arise fairly systematically under import substitution. To be sure, there have been important differences between countries, due in part to their domestic structure and in part to their particular mix of policy instruments. Nonetheless, there are a number of similarities in patterns which emerge, and which are worth mentioning as a prelude to consideration of possible reasons for differences in performance.

In this section, no attempt is made to trace possible causal mechanisms for the various phenomena discussed, nor are the inter-relationships between them analyzed. Analysis of possible causal

---

[10] It is noteworthy that, in Korea, only those who exported were eligible to be importers. This assured that whatever profits there were to be had on import rights accrued to exporters.

mechanisms is left to the next section, although it should be stressed that there is considerable scope for debate over a number of issues, including the most important question of whether the difficulties that have been experienced were inherently the fault of import-substitution strategy, or whether they occurred because the policies were not optimal. According to the latter reasoning, an alternative set of policies inducing import substitution might have achieved substantially better performance, the fault being in the choice of policy instruments rather than in the strategy. That question is not addressed here, although it does seem that the similarity of experience across import-substitution countries is so great that there is a presumption that it is the strategy, and not the particular policy instruments, that is at the root of the differences.

Without attempting to be exhaustive, there are seven main features which appear to have characterized the experience of virtually all the countries which have sustained import-substitution policies for any extended period of time. These include the slowing down in the rate of growth as further import substitution became harder and harder; the universal tendency for the demand for imports to grow at least as quickly, if not more quickly, than GNP; the general tendency for export earnings to grow more slowly than GNP, if at all; the felt necessity to resort to increasing controls over foreign exchange transactions, and over imports in particular, as foreign exchange shortage increasingly has come to be perceived as a major barrier to growth; the emergence of an industrial structure characterized by monopolistic or oligopolistic market structures in individual industries, excess capacity, high-cost inefficient firms, and low-quality output; the failure of industrial employment to grow at a rate even approaching the rate of industrial output; and, finally, the emergence of an atmosphere of increasing suspicion and distrust between the government and business sectors of the economy.

The fact that sustained growth has become increasingly difficult over time under import-substitution regimes requires little discussion. It is widely recognized that countries will encourage the "easy" industries first, and that it becomes increasingly difficult to find new industries that can contribute to growth. The differences in incremental capital-output ratios are striking: for the 1960-73 period, incremental capital-output ratios ranged between 1.7 to 2.5 for Korea, Singapore and Taiwan, while the corresponding figures for Chile and India, two import-substitution countries, were 5.5 and 5.7.[11] For Brazil, with her

switch in trade strategy, the incremental capital-output ratio fell from
3.8 in 1960-66 to 2.1 in 1966-73. Although high and rising incremental
capital-output ratios cannot, without further evidence, be taken as a
necessary product of an import-substitution strategy, decelerating
growth rates have been a major reason for attempting to alter trade
strategies.[12]

That import substitution was "import intensive" came as a surprise
to everyone. As Diaz-Alejandro (1965) has documented, import-
substitution policies were generally accompanied by a rapidly rising
demand for imports despite the substitution in domestic production
that was occurring. The almost universal experience was that policy
makers underestimated the increase in import demand likely to
accompany any given rate of growth of output.

Indeed, one of the many paradoxical features of import substitution was that as a policy, it was initially undertaken in part because
countries wanted to rid themselves of their dependence on trade.
Ironically, rather than eliminating it, import substitution appears to
have increased it. On the one hand, the establishment of domestic
factories producing final consumer goods generally entailed a growing
demand for imported parts, components, intermediate goods, and
raw materials necessary for the factory's operation. Thus, "dependence" on imports for consumption did not cease, but rather was
intensified as dependence extended to employment as well. In like
vein, planners were naturally reluctant to induce high-cost domestic
production of capital goods and other items deemed "essential" for
the development process. The consequence was a tariff and quota
structure that encouraged the domestic production of "luxuries" and
"non-essentials," while leaving the import bill consisting only of
"bare necessities." Rather than reducing dependence on imports,
import-substitution policies often had the effect of increasing the
rigidity of the country's economy, as there were few "inessential"
imports that could be reduced in the event of foreign exchange shortfalls. As the policy continued and import substitution "progressed"
further, the costs mounted rapidly.

The failure of exports to grow as rapidly as GNP was, as already
noted, largely a function of import-substitution policies themselves.
Exchange rate overvaluation, the fact that incentives strongly pulled

[11] See Balassa (1978)
[12] See Prebisch (1964, p. 21 ff.)

resources toward import-competing activities, and constraints upon purchases of foreign-source inputs all served to impede the growth of foreign exchange earnings. Interestingly enough, lagging behavior of export earnings was particularly pronounced in the natural-resource-based activities, as authorities tended to compensate, at least somewhat, for exchange rate overvaluation with respect to nontraditional exports. Thus, evidence from the N.B.E.R. project suggested a relatively larger supply response to devaluation from primary commodities than from nontraditional exports (Krueger, 1978, Ch. 9).

The conjunction of import-intensive import-substitution activities, requiring relatively rapid increases in imports to sustain output and permit additional investment, and lagging foreign exchange earnings served universally to lead to "foreign exchange shortage." To be sure, some countries altered their exchange rate policies and restrictive monetary and fiscal policies sooner than others did, but in almost all cases, a major policy was to impose quantitative restrictions upon international transactions. These quantitative restrictions, imposed for balance-of-payments motives rather than for purposes of further encouraging import substitution, nonetheless further served to bias the regime in favor of import substitution. The restrictiveness of the regime itself would, in any event, have imposed costs on the economy, but in many cases these costs were heightened by the apparently inexorable tendency of controls (and surcharges and other taxes) to proliferate as the implicit premium on import licenses increased. In part, this proliferation seems to have arisen because of the inevitable bureaucratic mandate to be "fair," which in turn entails the formulation of rules and criteria for allocation. Such rules in and of themselves often create incentives for wasteful use of resources, as firms invest in additional capacity, or hire additional workers, or otherwise attempt to alter their eligibility for imports under the criteria by which import licences are allocated. Additionally, of course, paperwork and delays themselves have sizeable costs under import-substitution regimes, even prior to periods when non-availability of foreign exchange resulted in long delays or stoppages in granting foreign exchange.

One characteristic of import-substitution regimes which resulted from this and which emerged as a major prototype in the N. B. E. R. project was the periodic swings in economic policy that resulted: countries would find their controls over imports becoming increasingly complex, with surcharges on imports, prior deposit requirements, export subsidies, and a host of partial-pricing measures, pro-liferating over time. Eventually, a decision would be taken to attempt to reform the regime, and a period of simplification, devaluation, and usually monetary and fiscal restriction ensued. Exports would in-crease, at least for a while, while import demand would drop, or fail to rise, as a consequence of both the devaluation and the restrictive monetary and fiscal stance. In some instances, of course, success under these policies was followed by further liberalization and an export-oriented regime (as in Korea in 1960, after the earlier liberali-zation effort of 1957, and in Brazil in 1967); more frequently, however, foreign exchange shortage would again set in as political pressures or other factors led to a resumption of GNP growth. These "Phase III" episodes, as they were characterized in the National Bureau project, themselves had costs: the stop-go macroeconomic policies that accompanied them undoubtedly affected firms' invest-ment and production plans. Diaz-Alejandro (1976) believes that the escape from the stop-go consequences of foreign exchange shortage was especially important in Colombia's higher rate of economic growth following the switch to more export-oriented trade policies.

Yet another almost universal characteristic of import-substitution regimes, clearly related to the exchange control and licensing proce-dures that were employed, has been the indiscriminate and generally high-variance pattern of protection that resulted. In and of itself, this pattern, which was often the consequences of automatic import prohibitions which resulted when domestic production capabilities had been established, violated the optimality conditions discussed in Section II, and the high costs associated with the very high levels of protection afforded to some industries undoubtedly contributed directly to poor overall industrial performance. Hypotheses relating to these aspects of differences in growth performance are evaluated in Section III.

Here, the point is slightly different. Under the blanket protective policies of the import-subststution regimes, a structure of industry emerged which had several distinct characteristics. First and foremost, after the "easy" import-substitution phase (and, for smaller countries, perhaps even then), the size of the market for individual goods was generally small enough so that plants were of uneconomi-cally small size or there were only one or two producers of each commodity, or both. A monopolistic domestic industrial structure consequently resulted. Moreover, the fact that there were only one or two suppliers of many industrial goods itself often caused other difficulties. On the one hand, a single strike or production stoppage could quite rapidly affect a major industrial sector of the economy.[13] On the other hand, a generally poor quality industrial product became the hallmark in these import-substitution regimes, whether this was attributable to the industrial structure or to other aspects of the regimes. While low-quality clothing and footwear primarily cause consumer inconvenience, failure to adhere to measurement and technical standards in the case of most industrial goods is itself a source of high costs to firms using their outputs. Moreover, in cases of potential exporters, it was not only higher domestic prices paid for intermediate goods and raw materials that served as a factor in impeding their competitive position, it was also the quality of domestically produced inputs.

The fact that industrial employment in most import-substitution countries grew relatively slowly, if at all, is well known. In general, elasticities of employment with respect to output were less than one, and often were not noticeably greater than .2. In part, this was a consequence of overvalued exchange rates and the authorities' understandable reluctance to impose surcharges on imports of capital goods; for those fortunate to obtain licenses to import capital equipment, the result was often a very distorted relative price of employing labor and capital.[14]

The seventh and final general characteristic of experience under import substitution related to the relationship between the government and the producing sector of the economy. In almost all import-substitution regimes, the control mechanisms employed for containing the excess demand for imports have led to significant divergences between private incentives and the behavior desired by government officials. Individual businesses had every incentive to overstate their desired level of imports, and bureaucrats had every reason to suspect license applications. Quite aside from the growth of black markets, smuggling, and illegal transactions, much of the time and energy of the country's scarcest resource—its managers and educated workers—

---

[13] Appropriate inventory policy could presumably offset part of this effect, but would itself entail additional costs relative to a more open trade policy.

[14] For Pakistan, Guisinger (1981) estimates that firms eligible for "investment incentives" were confronted with a cost of employing capital goods about one-fourth of that which would have prevailed under an optimal pricing policy.

became involved in frustrating other managers and educated workers. This factor, of the conflict between government objectives and the objectives of the business community, is potentially one of considerable importance in evaluating differences in policy making under alternative regimes.

IV. Possible Reasons for Performance Differentials

Experience under export promotion has avoided, to a greater or lesser extent, most of the difficulties described above regarding import substitution. As already indicated, vastly higher rates of economic growth have been the result. A key question is why this is so.

There are three sets of factors which have contributed undoubtedly to the differential in performance: the policy set used under each regime; the technological factors which affect output per unit of input; and the underlying selection mechanism for increases in output under alternative regimes. Each set of factors has certainly played a role in influencing differences in overall performance. It is not enough, however, to believe each is of importance: crucial questions center around their relative contribution. It is possible, and perhaps even likely, that the relative importance has varied between countries and possibly also time periods within the same country.

It should also be remembered that there are two interpretations of the difference in experience, regardless of the reasons for them. The neoclassical view could be taken, and the argument made that export promotion has come noticeably closer to a free trade first-best optimum than has import substitution. However, many of the phenomena outlined below are consistent with an "infant industry" notion of industrial development. It is possible that the "infant industry" proponents are correct in their basic argument that there is a period of learning and of relatively high costs, and that an export-promotion strategy is a far more efficient way of developing an efficient, low-cost industrial structure. In terms of policy prescription for an efficient export-promotion strategy, the distinction is crucial, and considerable research is called for concerning patterns of growth of output per unit of input in different industries in the successful export-oriented countries.

1. Better Policy

There are several strands to the argument that policy is "better" under export promotion than under import substitution. The case could be made that the deviations from a first-best optimal policy of equalized incentives for all industries are smaller under export promotion than under import substitution. Alternatively, there are also several important reasons for believing that policies adopted under export promotion are simply "more realistic," and provide more feedback as to mistakes than do policies under import substitution. As with other considerations, these alternatives are not entirely independent of each other.

The first argument that deviations from a first best optimum are smaller under export promotion can be couched in several ways. First, quantitative restrictions over imports or over exports are clearly incompatible with an export-promotion orientation. Moving away from import substitution probably entails a gain simply in eliminating some of the excess costs associated with quantitative restrictions. This can be so either because quantitative restrictions themselves have costs, or because import-substitution policies also lead to detailed controls of a type that are simply incompatible with export promotion.

Second, casual observation of effective rates of protection of several hundred percentage points or more under import substitution is sufficient to convince most observers that export-oriented governments are surely going to be unwilling to grant subsidies and incentives to exporting industries of commensurate size. In this regard, it can be pointed out that the costs of encouraging different industries are simply more readily apparent to policy makers under regimes where incentives, rather than controls, are used.[15]

This consideration, in turn, has two interpretations. On the one hand, it can be argued that export-oriented policy makers will in general tend to encourage the development of *any* line of industrial activity that can generate exports: generally incentives will be set contingent only upon export performance. That provides a market test for potential recipients of incentives, and simultaneously provides not-

---

[15] Not only is the height of an export subsidy more apparent than the implicit protection conveyed by a quota, but also a subsidy requires financing which may add to resistance.

too-equal treatment to all industries.[16] Export incentives are usually applicable in large part to all exporters, at least of nontraditional or industrial commodities. As such, greater uniformity of incentives automatically prevails under export promotion.

On the other hand, the fact that mistakes may be more readily evident is also consistent with "infant industry" ideas. It may be that some industries were well suited to rapid increases in output per unit of input while others are high cost and poor candidates for development. Further, it may be that development should be relatively selective. If both those considerations have validity, then export promotion would have the double advantage over import substitution that it is generally considerably more selective and also that the high cost of incentives necessary to induce a particular industry will serve as a signal to policy makers that they should perhaps reconsider the desirability of developing that particular industry. It is at least plausible that it has been the very high-cost industries, which were not suitable infants, which have been chiefly responsible for poor overall performance under import substitution, and that elimination of some of the worst mistakes would significantly have improved achievements under import substitution. Finally, it can be argued that the flow of information between the government and the production sector of the economy is more reliable under an incentive system than it is under a control system, and that this phenomenon in itself permits better decision-making on the part of both parties. Government officials have, so the reasoning would go, an objective test of performance: a firm's ability to export.[17] Given that test, they can devote their efforts to facilitating production activities, assured that firms will not simply cheat without performing the desired functions. The fact that government and the business sector appear to be cooperating and working toward common goals in export-oriented economies, and in conflict in import-substitution economies, perhaps reflects this fundamental difference. How important it is as a factor in affecting productivity and growth is difficult to determine.[18]

---

[16] Treatment is not equal because credit subsidies implicitly are of greater value to more capital-intensive industries; the same rate of export subsidy provides a greater rate of effective incentive to industry with a lower domestic value added content.

[17] Under regimes of export subsidies there is an incentive for firms to overinvoice. Requiring the sale of foreign exchange to the government is a partial solution, but maintenance of a fairly realistic exchange rate keeps the size of export subsidies relatively small and thus reduces incentives for overworking.

2. Technological Hypotheses

Here, the major arguments have to do with the degree to which an efficient pattern of production for a developing country is likely to be specialized and with the size distribution of optimal-size industries relative to the size of domestic markets in developing countries.

The first question really concerns the degree to which there are large differences in factor proportions or productivity between industries. If some industries have relatively constant marginal costs and generate ten and twenty times as much international value added per unit of domestic resource as other industries then the consequences of failing to specialize in those industries will be substantial. Similarly, there may be large differences in labor-capital ratios between industries. If a country's capital stock is the binding constraint upon the rate of expansion of the industrial sector, there may be very large gains to concentrating resources in industries closest to the country's comparative advantage, and costs of diverging from optimal specialization will be high.[19] This would also be the case if the "infant industry" argument was valid, but the choice of infants should be highly selective.

This consideration leads directly to the second technological hypothesis. Suppose that the minimum efficient size of output in most industrial activities is fairly large, and in particular, larger than domestic consumption of most industrial commodities in most developing countries. If further, the costs of producing on an inefficiently small scale are very high, an import-substitution policy which generates industries of suboptimal size will entail relatively high costs on technological grounds.[20] Engineers often use the "seven-

---

[18] A striking instance of information difficulties arising under import substitution currently is Turkey. It is difficult, if not impossible, for domestic policy makers or foreign observers to assess the impact of more or less foreign assistance in the current balance of payments crisis, because many imports entered the country illegally over the past several years. Policy makers do not know what the volume of those imports was relative to officially recorded imports or the extent to which the illegal flows continue. No one knows the proportionate difference a loan of any particular size will make to Turkey's ability to import.

[19] Note that even this argument is open to either the free trade or the infant-industry interpretation.

[20] The argument mixes with the economic behavior considerations discussed below, insofar as policymakers are confronted with a choice under import substitution between more very small firms (with some degree of competition among them) and fewer somewhat larger firms, with a more monopolistic industry structure.

tenths'' rule, asserting that costs increase about 70 percent when output doubles. It is estimated that the minimum efficient size of an auto assembly plant is one producing at least 200,000 cars per year. In India, the largest auto factory produces less than 30,000 cars per year. If the seven-tenths rule is correct, and otherwise the Indian industry is operating on the same cost curve as its foreign counterparts, this would imply that Indian costs would be approximately three times as high as they would be at the 200,000 rate. If, in addition, the seven-tenths rule applies to inputs to automobiles, it is readily seen that the cost difference may be quite sizeable simply because of inappropriately small scale, when production runs are destined almost exclusively for the domestic market.

Depending on the nature of the industrial process and the magnitude of indivisibilities and other factors, such as length of production run, which influence minimum efficient size, the very fact that import-substitution policies skew incentives toward the home market may lead to high-cost industries. By contrast, export promotion is clearly more conducive to plants operating at efficient scale, which in itself is potentially a source of increased efficiency in the use of inputs.

It may be that the above considerations are really only a way of characterizing the fact that import-substitution policies get progressively more difficult once "easy" import-substitution industries are established. If in fact modern industrial methods, whether labor- or capital-intensive, do entail fairly large batches of output in order to minimize inputs per unit of output, the very small sizes of the market for industrial goods in most developing countries could be an important factor in explaining relatively poor performance under import substitution.

3. Economic Behavior

Three strands of analysis are involved with this set of considerations. There is a hypothesis that economic behavior simply may be different when individuals are confronted with incentives than when they are confronted with controls. Related to that, but not the same thing, is the proposition that competition, in the form of the international market place, may make firms more X-efficient than does a sheltered domestic market. Finally, there are interesting questions about the relationship of growth rates of firms and industries under alternative strategies.

The first strand simply questions the efficiency of controls, as contrasted with incentives, for inducing desired economic behavior. By its nature, an export-oriented policy cannot rely on controls, and must employ incentives. "Domestic content requirements," mandates that inputs should be purchased from the small-scale sector, and similar quantitative regulations, even if their objectives conform with a social optimum, seem, so the argument goes, to generate less favorable responses than do policies awarding positive rewards to those undertaking the desired policies. To state the argument otherwise: whenever direct controls are imposed that mandate behavior different from that which would be profitable in their absence, some efforts and resources will be directed to avoiding the controls, rather than achieving the objective.

The second hypothesis focusses upon the monopolistic or oligopolistic market structures encountered in most import-substitution countries. Whether these structures arise from the conflicts already discussed between optimal-size plants and the small size of the domestic market, or whether instead they arise because of import licensing mechanisms and other phenomena which tend to restrict the scope for altering market shares, the phenomenon of relative rigidity of market shares and consequent monopolistic or quasi-monopolistic behavior is a pervasive feature of import-substitution regimes. The X-efficiency argument centers upon the proposition that firms with sheltered markets and assured market shares, generally operating in sellers' markets, have fewer incentives for efficiency than would the same firms under more competitive conditions. Managers of firms with monopoly positions may choose to take out part of their monopoly rent in the form of the "quiet life," or in the form of inattention to costs. Indeed, in countries where price controls are in vogue, or where high profit rates are suspect, the path of wisdom may lie in failing to reduce costs. In these circumstances, many firms may have higher cost structures than would be observed under alternative incentive structures.

The third hypothesis focusses again upon market structure, but a different aspect of it. Here, the basic proposition is that, under competitive conditions, low-cost firms and industries will expand relatively rapidly, while high-cost activities will either expand more slowly or in fact contract. If there are only inefficient firms in an industry, new entrants will appear. Thus, the overall rate of growth of output is not simply the average rate of growth of individual firms; nor is the rate of growth of output per unit of input a weighted average of the rate at which output per unit of input increases in individual firms. On the contrary, there are new entrants and rapidly growing firms are increasing their market shares, so that the average rate of growth of all firms lies below the industry's growth rate. Likewise, efficiency gains arise from firms' increasing outputs per unit of inputs, because resources accrue to firms which have below-average outputs per unit of input, and because new firms enter the industry.

Thus, under an export-promotion strategy, an efficient firm can expand more rapidly than the rate of growth of demand for the industry's product, perhaps not only by increasing its share of the small domestic market, but also by expanding its export activity. By contrast, efficient firms under import-substitution regimes have constraints placed on their rate of growth both by their share of import licences and other bureaucratic rules which dictate "fairness" and by the fact that the incentives are so skewed to sale in the home market that only in exceptional cases will it be profitable to engage in export activity.

Taking this view, the world market provides the competition against which domestic firms can compete and grow at rates commensurate with their inherent competitive position. This, it should be noted, is quite independent of any propositions concerning optimal-size plants or which industries have competitive advantage. It may well be that there are efficient and inefficient firms in every industry, and that the exporting requires both the right entrepreneur and the right product, for optimal growth. Under this view, it might be that the right product and the right entrepreneur was more likely in, say, labor-intensive industries than in more capital-intensive ones, but the focus is squarely on differences in individual entrepreneurial abilities and products.

V. Implications for Policy and for Further Research

As the preceding discussion makes clear, knowledge that export-promotion policies of some type can generate growth performance superior to that of import-substitution policies is not enough. Research yielding that result has raised as many questions as it has answered.

First, there are a number of important questions that pertain to the microeconomic aspects of growth of the industrial sector. On the one hand, there are a variety of interesting questions, about which there is almost no suggestion of an answer based on existing evidence, concerning the history of rates of increase of output per unit of input in different exporting industries in the export-promoting countries. The extent to which there were highly successful firms, which started at high cost, and which experienced rapid productivity growth is unknown. It is not known whether such firms, if they existed, were randomly scattered over a wide range of industries, or were concentrated in certain sectors with key technological or other characteristics. What their characteristics were, why and how they achieved rapid growth as exporting endeavors, and the measures that encouraged them are all questions that deserve attention.

Second, the policies that were adopted in pursuit of export promotion are not fully understood, nor are the interactions between choice of policies and other key economic and political variables. Korean effective exchange rates and credit subsidies are known; how decisions were taken as to which industries to subsidize and which not to is not known. While the available evidence would tend to suggest that Korean economic policies in the late 1960s were relatively close to optimal (Frank, Kim, and Westphal, 1975, Chapter 9), there is a basis for believing that the divergence from optimality, in the form of increasingly large implicit credit subsidies, widened substantially in the 1970s (Hong, 1981).

In that regard, a careful analysis of the decisions to promote particular export industries, including any decisions that were later reversed, and evidence with regard to mistakes as well as successes, in the export-promoting countries, and the specific instruments of promotion employed, would be very useful.

Even more troublesome is that the political-economic interactions in policy making are little understood. Many of the hypotheses discussed above centered upon links between types of controls adopted and economic performance. But the decision to undertake import-substitution policies is obviously not completely independent of the underlying economic and political situation. There are clearly dynamic interactions between the economic problems confronting the policymakers and the types of instruments they employ to achieve their objectives. Whether policymakers choose import substitution because they have different objectives from the ones adopting export promotion, whether they are constrained politically to adopt import-substitution policies despite the fact that they know better, or whether import-substitution policies of the sort described above have been adopted out of a lack of understanding of the economic process is an important question. Yet, to date, economists have tended to treat the choice of industrialization and trade strategy as being exogenous to the economic growth process itself.

Finally, there are questions concerning policies themselves. First and foremost, an important and unanswered set of questions concerns the degree to which export-promotion policies can depart uniformity of incentive and still induce the kind of high growth performance that has been associated with Korea, Taiwan, and Brazil. Clearly, the measures used in all countries to provide a bias toward exporting have also led to some static distortions within those economies. Equally clearly, the cost of those distortions has not, at least within the short run, been sufficient to offset the dynamic benefits of the strategy. Whether those costs were necessary to realize the benefits, or whether instead benefits could have been even greater in the absence of distortions, is an open question.

The second major set of policy questions focusses on the changing nature of optimal policy over time. It is possible, if not likely, that the cost of distortions increases over time while the gains from distorted bias toward export promotion diminish. If, for example, distortions in the form of credit subsidies start by applying to a very small and previously-discriminated-against set of industries, it may be that the positive effect of encouraging the rapid development of those industries outweighs the initial costs of, for instance, the use of disproportionately capital-intensive techniques. Over time, however, the relative size of the sector eligible for credit subsidies grows, while the degree to which further expansion, at a rate more rapid than the rest of the economy, is desirable, diminishes. Thus the costs of the departure from optimality grow as the size of the subsidy increases, while the gains diminish. Clearly, there may be some point at which the policies which are beneficial at an early stage of development become detrimental. There is at least some superficial evidence that this may have been true in the case of Israel, where credit subsidies probably encouraged healthy industrial growth in the 1960s, but have perhaps had the opposite effect in the 1970s.

A third set of questions with important policy implications pertains to which set of arguments are most effective in explaining the gains derived from an export-oriented strategy; that set encompassing factor proportions and division of labor or that encompassing economies of scale and competition. If factor proportions differences provide a major source of gain from trade for export-oriented developing countries, regional trading arrangements among developing countries with roughly similar factor proportions are likely to be able to contribute little to the development process, and may even be detrimental to growth objectives. Even if considerations of market size and the minimum efficient size of plants were major ones, it is clear that customs unions among developing countries must, in most cases, be second-best to worldwide free trade from their viewpoint, but there are then substantial potential gains contrasted with inward-looking policies adopted in isolation.

Finally, if factor proportions are an important source of the gains from an outer-oriented trade strategy, then the prospect for success of additional developing countries adopting export promotion strategies increases. If there really are "stages" in the development of different industries as factor endowments shift with capital accumulation in the industrial sector, the rest of the world will more easily be able to accommodate new entrants into labor-intensive industries as the advanced developing countries themselves shift their industrial structure toward the production of more skill- and capital-intensive production activities. Indeed, it may be that the crucial phenomenon for the prospects of the non-advanced developing countries will not be the protectionist pressures in developed countries, but rather the extent to which the advanced developing countries can adjust their own industrial structures and shift their output mix successfully. As Korea, Brazil, Taiwan and other successful exporters increase their real wages and accumulate skills and capital, they themselves should become additional markets for the unskilled labor-intensive products of other developing countries emulating their policies.

REFERENCES

Balassa, Bela, "Export Incentives and Export Performance in Developing Countries: A Comparative Analysis," *Weltwirtschaftliches Archiv* 1: 24-61, 1978.

Baldwin, Robert, "The Case Against Infant Industry Protection," *Journal of Political Economy,* Vol. 77, No. 3, May/June 1969, pp. 295-305.

Bhagwati, Jagdish, *Foreign Trade Regimes and Economic Development: Anatomy and Consequences of Exchange Control Regimes,* Ballinger Press, Cambridge, Mass., 1978.

_____ and T. N. Srinivasan, "Trade Policy and Development," Rudiger Dornbusch and Jacob A. Frenkel (eds.), *International Economic Policy: Theory and Evidence,* Johns Hopkins Press, Baltimore, 1979.

Carvalho, José and Cláudio Haddad, "Foreign Trade Strategies and Employment in Brazil," Anne O. Krueger, Hal B. Lary, Terry Monson and Narongchai Akrasanee (eds.), *Trade and Employment in Developing Countries, 1: Individual Studies,* University of Chicago Press, Chicago, 1981.

Diaz Alejandro, Carlos, *Foreign Trade Regimes and Economic Development: Colombia,* Columbia University Press, New York, 1976.

_____, "On the Import Intensity of Import Substitution," *Kyklos,* Vol. 18, Fasc. 3, 1965, pp. 495-509.

Frank, Charles R., Jr., Kwang Suk Kim, and Larry E. Westphal, *Foreign Trade Regimes and Economic Development: South Korea,* Columbia University Press, New York, 1975.

Guisinger, Stephen, "Trade Policies and Employment: The Case of Pakistan," Anne O. Krueger, Hal B. Lary, Terry Monson and Narongchai Akrasanee (eds.), *Trade and Employment in Developing Countries, 1: Individual Studies,* University of Chicago Press, Chicago, 1981.

Hong, Wontack, "Export Promotion and Employment Growth in South Korea," Anne O. Krueger, Hal B. Lary, Terry Monson and Narongchai Akrasanee (eds.), *Trade and Employment in Developing Countries, 1: Individual Studies,* University of Chicago Press, Chicago, 1981.

Krueger, Anne O., *Foreign Trade Regimes and Economic Development: Liberalization Attempts and Consequences,* Ballinger Press, Cambridge, Mass., 1978.

Krueger, Anne O., Hal B. Lary, Terry Monson and Narongchai Akrasanee (eds.), *Trade and Employment in Developing Countries, 1: Individual Studies,* University of Chicago Press, Chicago, 1981.

Little, Ian, Tibor Scitovsky, and Maurice Scott, *Industry and Trade in Some Developing Countries,* Oxford University Press, London, 1970.
Prebisch, Raul, *Towards a New Trade Policy for Development,* United Nations, 1964.

• COMMENT

Kwang Suk Kim, *Korea Development Institute*

This paper makes one wonder why only a very limited number of developing countries have adopted an export-led industrialization strategy if that strategy can really bring about superior growth performance in all countries. The paper lists only four countries— Korea, Taiwan, Brazil and Israel—that have so far attained some success using export-led growth. Singapore and Hong Kong may have been excluded because of their small size. In any case, one may question why only four or six developing countries have adopted an export-oriented industrialization strategy.

In trying to answer this question, it will be discovered that an export-oriented policy cannot really be successfully adopted in all countries. The successful adoption of an export-promotion policy itself requires some initial preconditions. The author included size of each country, geographic location and natural resource endowment as the factors contributing to the general success of export-promotion strategies. In addition to these factors, it seems that the initial conditions of a country reflecting the general level of education, the stage of development or industrialization and the cultural heritage, will prove to be very important for the successful adoption of export-oriented strategies.

If these initial conditions are really important determinants of successful export-promotion strategies, it will be difficult to say that export-oriented strategies can be adopted and that if adopted will produce better economic performance in developing countries. Thus, it is insufficient to simply explain why the export-oriented strategy outperforms import substitution. It will be important to extend the analysis to examine what preconditions are required for the successful adoption of an export-oriented strategy.

The second point is related to the import substitution required for continued export expansion and economic growth over an extended period of time. Even if a country follows an export-oriented industrialization strategy, it will need to invest in import-substitution industries to achieve a sustained export and GNP growth over any extended period of time. This indicates that even a country following an export-oriented policy has to continuously promote import substitution on a selective basis. In this case it will be difficult to apply the one-sided observations concerning export promotion or import substitution, supplied in this paper.

Third, the paper suggests that the tariff and quota structure that encourages the domestic production of luxuries and non-essentials results from government reluctance to induce high-cost domestic production of capital goods and other essential items. The causation is the other way around. The government usually levies a high tariff and places a quota on luxuries and non-essential goods to discourage the import of such items for domestic consumption. This industrial protection structure then brings about increased domestic production of such luxury goods.

Fourth, it may be true that an import-substitution policy has the effect of increasing the rigidity of the country's economy. However, the rigidity is related to the stage of industrialization in many countries. Because industrial production in a country normally begins with less sophisticated consumer goods and then moves on to more sophisticated intermediate and capital goods, the imports of a country at some middle or later stages of industrialization may not include many finished consumer goods, but include mainly intermediate and capital goods. This is what has been experienced in Korea.

Finally, it is stated that in Korea the divergence from optimality, in the form of increasingly large implicit credit subsidies, widened substantially in the 1970s. Certainly the implicit subsidies could have increased in the 1970s. But, it should be pointed out that the increase has been caused by the government support of import-substitution industries; that is, the promotion of major heavy and chemical industries. So the increased divergence from optimality was not directly related to the continued enforcement of an export-promotion strategy in Korea, but was related mainly to the promotion of import substitution.

Ronald Findlay, *Columbia University*

The remarkable performance of the so-called "gang of four"—
Korea, Taiwan, Hong Kong and Singapore—during the last two
decades in the achievement of very high GNP growth rates with
manufactured exports as the spearhead is one of the most striking
features of modern economic history. All previous experience,
whether of the pioneers of the Industrial Revolution in Western
Europe or the "latecomers" such as Russia and Japan, seems modest
in comparison, at least statistically. The question naturally arises as to
what set of factors can account for success on such a scale.

One hypothesis would involve discounting Hong Kong and Singapore on the ground that they are mere city-states. The argument one
sometimes hears from Indian civil servants and economists holding
official positions, for example, is that of course Bombay or Calcutta
could have comparable success with Hong Kong or Singapore if only
they could operate as independent enclaves within the Indian
economy. The development strategy for India as a whole would have
to be different since one could not imagine what would happen to
world markets if India's manufactured exports per capita were to be
at Hong Kong and Singapore levels. In reply it may be pointed out
that the absolute level of Indian exports is now below that of both
Hong Kong and Singapore, so perhaps Bombay and Calcutta should
be turned loose if comparable results can be expected. Something
more than just the phenomenon of the "small base" seems to be
involved.

The performance of Korea, Taiwan, Hong Kong and Singapore
raises the question as to why exports as such should be particularly conducive to growth. In competitive markets with no distortions, a dollar's worth of exports at world prices should be no more or
no less valuable to the economy than a dollar's worth of consumption
or investment or government expenditure or import substitution, if all
of these are also measured at world prices. One possible meaning of
export promotion or export-led growth strategy is therefore that it is
simply a laissez faire or free trade strategy, in which the speed and
pattern of development is that which would come about by the free
play of external and internal market forces, with no intervention by
the state in any direction beyond the traditional Smithian "duties of

the sovereign.'' With respect to the "gang of four" it would seem that it is only Hong Kong that may be said to approximate to this norm, with Korea at the other end of the spectrum with a wide variety of measures that intervene directly in the markets for agricultural and industrial goods and in the crucially important capital markets.

Krueger's opinion is that the substantial gross state intervention discernable in Korea more or less cancels itself out insofar as the foreign exchange and trade regime is concerned so that there is not much net intervention as compared with the free trade position. This view is difficult to accept. The papers by Nam and Hong for this conference do not seem to provide evidence in its favor though they are not necessarily inconsistent with it. The Korean economy, for its size and level of development, seems more "open" than it would be in a free trade regime. In other words, there is a positive export bias in the overall balance of state intervention in terms of effective incentives to producers.

In terms of the standard theory of trade and welfare a bias in favor of exports is no better in principle than a bias against them. In Figure 1 the level of welfare for a small open economy with fixed terms of trade as a function of the volume of exports equal to the value of imports under balanced trade is plotted. Starting from the autarky level at the origin the curve rises to a maximum at the free trade point and declines thereafter. In comparison with the optimal free trade level a "right wing deviation" in trade policy that discriminates in favor of exports is no better than the equivalent "left wing deviation" that discriminates in favor of import substitution. It is therefore hard to see why an export-promotion strategy should produce such successful results, since both types of bias are equally to be condemned from the standpoint of static allocative efficiency.

It is clear that an answer must be sought outside the conventional bounds of the standard model, in the murky but relevant waters of such concepts as X-efficiency and "learning by doing." Krueger suggests that there is a crucial performance test that export industries must pass, unlike import-substitution projects that have captive markets, namely they have to compete against foreign products in the world market. Elastic world demand curves permit rapid expansion by successful firms, while failure to make headway becomes quickly apparent and resources can be re-allocated. Krueger rightly stresses that even if exports as a whole are subsidized these beneficial effects

Figure 1.

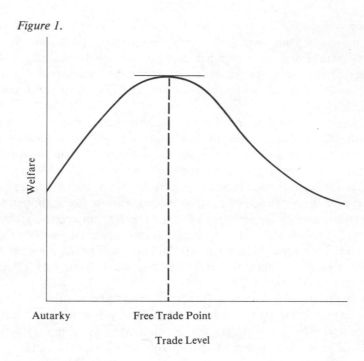

can occur so long as there is no discrimination in favor of some particular export lines at the expense of others. The idea that the true application of the "infant industry" argument might be to export promotion rather than import substitution, with competition in the world market providing the incentive to keep managers alert and adaptive is intriguing and provocative. As with X-efficiency, there seems to be a somewhat mysterious "Omega Factor" at work in connection with manufactured exports that leads to rapid productivity growth through technology transfer as a result of competitive pressures and receptivity to new ideas stimulated by an open environment. Hence the so-called "dynamic gains" which have been so often sought but not found in connection with import substitution may exist, but on the other side of the free trade optimum.

All this, however, is only speculation, requiring much more research before any confident pronouncements can be made. What does seem evident is that the more advanced LDCs seem to be marked by relatively low wages in relation to the quality of the labor force, access to world technology and capital markets through links with multinational corporations and high profit rates resulting from the combination of the above two factors, which permits rapid growth of the domestically owned capital stock by re-investment of profits. The rapid productivity growth arising from technology transfer permits wages to rise after an initial "dualistic" phase without reducing the rate of profit that is the driving force of capital accumulation, both foreign and domestic. The rising wage leads to qualitative transformation in the composition of manufacturing production and exports, with more capital-intensive and technologically sophisticated goods progressively replacing the initial labor-intensive products such as textiles and footwear.

The vigorous chastisement that Krueger administers, on this as on previous occasion, to import substitution should be softened. It should not be forgotten that many great manufacturing export industries, from cotton textiles in Lancashire to Japanese steel and automobiles, started with import substitution. Also, it is not only import-substitution strategies that result in current account deficits. Korea's spectacular export drive has also been accompanied by growing trade deficits. This merely reflects the fact that investment opportunities outrun domestic saving in rapidly growing economies, requiring import of capital from more developed countries, where the reverse is the case.

GENERAL DISCUSSION

Import substitution is limited by the growth of domestic market size. With a large domestic market, a country may pursue an import-substitution strategy for a long period of time. However, with a small domestic market, the static losses in productivity, saving and profit rate increase rapidly as the rate of protection increases. Export promotion enables access to a much larger market, and hence a country can take advantage of factor endowment without being subject to demand constraint for specialization.

Perhaps the higher growth rates associated with export-oriented growth strategy may be explained in terms of higher savings rate and higher human and physical capital formation that temporarily raise the rates of capital accumulation and growth. That is, the higher growth rates may be explained by a conventional factor, that is, capital.

If export-oriented growth strategy is really optimal, it is very difficult to understand why so many underdeveloped countries do not adopt such a strategy. There might be a positive relationship between export promotion and high growth rate in general. Perhaps there are some other factors which are conducive to both export expansion and high growth. There may be some preconditions, such as political pressures to act, perhaps caused by poor natural resource endowment. Resource-rich countries may keep exporting natural resources with rising per capita income if prices of natural resources rise rapidly. The world market condition may be important for timing of the promotion of manufactured exports. Perhaps the diminishing returns to export promotion may be amplified in the long run just as in the case of import-substitution strategy. With proper timing, import-substitution strategy may be as efficient. A country may specialize in any kind of industry which generates scale economies and learning economies. Perhaps there is no reason to go beyond the neutrality of incentives.

One may argue that import-substitution strategy can be successful, taking the Japanese efforts on import substitution of automobiles and steel in the 1950s and 1960s, and possibly also of computers in the 1970s, as examples. However, one may also argue that Japanese promotion of import substitution of automobiles and steel was carried out with export in mind in the long run. Therefore, it was ultimately in line with export-promotion strategy. An optimum mix of import-substitution and export-promotion policies should be taken under consideration.

Preconditions for successful export-oriented growth strategy may be listed as entrepreneurship, infrastructure, an efficient bureaucracy, and political stability.

Korea may have to slow down its growth rate in order to accumulate technical knowledge and skill to produce and export more sophisticated manufactures.

THE INDUSTRIAL DYNAMIC
IN ADVANCED DEVELOPING COUNTRIES

Fernando Fajnzylber*

I. Introduction

Concern for the subject of the Advanced Developing Countries (ADCs), and their impact on production and trade of manufactures began to become evident in the early 1970s when, in the advanced economies, the unprecedented dynamism of the years following World War II began showing clear signs of erosion. At the same time, in some developing countries where, as part of their industrial strategy, manufactured exports to international markets played an important and in some instances decisive role, there was a growing awareness of the fact that recession in the developed countries, accompanied by protectionist trends, cast doubts upon an industrial strategy that had been formerly associated with high growth rates.

This paper supports the hypothesis that in order to advance in the analysis of the strategic options open to the ADCs, it is necessary to overcome the limited scope of trade relations between these countries and the advanced economies, and to further move towards placing this whole subject within the more general and undoubtedly more complex framework of the structure and dynamics of the industrial systems of advanced countries.

As a framework for the contents of this paper, the following is a schematic characterization of the unprecedented industrial growth of advanced economies in the years after World War II. Among the

* UNIDO/NAFINSA, Mexico

factors explaining this rapid growth are the availability of a large store of technological knowledge built up during the 1930s and World War II, and the importance, influence and attraction exerted by the consumption pattern and industrial organization of the United States on other advanced countries. Also significant was the availability of skilled labor combined with entrepreneurial capacity which maintained its strength especially in Japan and Germany, in spite of the partial destruction of their industrial installations. Also influential was the widespread consumption of durable goods and the substitution of natural products by synthetics, the effect this had on industry as a whole and the response of the capital goods sector in incorporating, multiplying and spreading technical progress. There was ready access to energy sources, the prices of which even dropped during that period. The modernization of the agricultural sector and its integration into the network of inter-industrial relations proceeded as well as the linkage between leading enterprises and the State, which was expressed in a concentrated and selective development effort within strategic sectors. Later the "cumulative virtuous circle" of growth, technical progress, international trade and growth began to gain mometum with its particular relationship to the capital goods sector as an embodiment of the growth-productivity phase of the cycle.

The later loss of dynamism at the end of the 1960s should be able to be explained in terms of a weakening of the factors which caused that growth, and the rise of obstacles or barriers generated by that growth itself. An attempt to identify such factors is the goal of the following section.

One of the consequences of increased dynamism was that during the 1960s, the relative availability of labor began to decline; this found expression in a strengthening of labor unions whose national unity was furthered by international detente and by the fact that the growth of wages began to outpace growth of productivity. This phenomenon was present, to different degrees, in all of the advanced countries.

The imitative spread of consumption of durable goods and automobiles began to show inevitable symptoms of saturation. Forecasts of the future consumption of automobiles as well as forecasts of the process of substituting synthetics for natural products were substantially more modest than those of the 1950s and the early 1960s. At this time, profitability began to be seriously undermined by heavy wage increases, increases in the relative burden of taxes associated with public sector expansion during the growth period, and the saturation of demand in the sectors which had been stimulating the rest of industry. This undermining tendency was intensified by the nature of technical progress and the resulting changes in industrial structure, which produced a drop in the ratio of increased capacity to investment.

It could be assumed that this situation does not have the same effect on the leading enterprises in the advanced countries which are the internationalized firms, as it does on the rest of the production system of those countries. It is possible that for the leading firms and sectors, differences in productivity and wages are non-existent and their sectorial diversification and international expansion have enabled them to neutralize the tax burden and evolution of exchange terms better than the others.

On the other hand, it is possible that in the internationalized sector, dominated by oligopolistic structures composed of industries having a high internal and external financial capacity through debts, there is a greater drop in the use of installed capacity than may be seen in the competitive sector.

In the latter, the loss of dynamism results simply in the elimination of marginal firms. Nevertheless, wage pressures on profits would be stronger in the competitive sector. For this reason, along with a lack of necessary empirical evidence, it is very difficult to formulate a hypothesis related to systematic differences in the profit rates of the internationalized sector versus the competitive sector, at least within the borders of their countries of origin. What can be definitely stated is that the ways in which each group strives to neutralize the forces exerting a downward pressure on profit rates are completely different.

It is possible that this gap between the leading strong, internationalized sectors and the rest of the advanced economies provides the main explanation for the different way in which each group views international economic relations: the former, apparently influential at the highest government levels of the advanced countries, cry out for an intensification of international liberalization; the latter, more powerful in legislative circles and regional and local bodies, push towards the introduction and strengthening of protectionist pressures.

From the moment that dynamism began to falter, the "virtuous circle" reversed its direction, and productivity began to drop. This trend was found in several of the advanced countries, in varying degrees, from 1969 on. Together with the well-known fact that sectorial variations in productivity are greater than variations in wages, this situation reinforced a tendency for wages to increase more than global productivity and undoubtedly became a source of pressure in the inflationary process.

The lower growth rate, drop in productivity and increase in the margins of unused installed capacity slowed down the innovation process and thus further consolidated the overall trend toward deterioration. All of this, combined with precarious growth prospects, stimulated a rise of protectionist pressures, thus reducing the dynamic effects of international trade and creating further negative effects on growth. The rapid industrial growth of the previous period was accompanied by a rapid increase in debts at the family, business and government levels.

The overall situation of growing indebtedness tends to motivate and to favor the rapid internationalization process initiated in the late 1960s by private banking, led first by U.S. institutions and later by the Europeans and Japanese. At this time, the market for Euro-dollars was created, beyond any governmental control, and is estimated to have reached $860 billion in 1978. Apart from the obvious implications this has for the degree of autonomy and effectiveness of the monetary and fiscal policies of the different governments, this enormous mass of resources was instrumental in stimulating speculative movements, such as were seen in raw materials between 1971 and 1973 and which later on were to be accentuated with the intensification of inflation.

All of the foregoing shows that the fourfold rise in oil prices in 1973, which had a tremendous impact, really only reinforced and intensified pressures that already existed, according to the analysis presented here. The effect on exchange terms in developed countries and the ensuing pressure on rate of return and, thus, growth, appear to be undeniable.

Nevertheless, it is interesting to point out the rapidity with which some developed countries have more than compensated for rising petroleum import costs through a substantial rise in their manufacturing sector surplus. The most significant case is Japan whose oil imports rose by $17 billion between 1973 and 1977 while its surplus in manufacture trade reached $40 billion during the same period, creating a net surplus of $22 billion. Germany shows a similar although less spectacular situation. These facts reaffirm the power, in terms of trade, created by a high level of competitiveness in the capital goods sector which is the major source of the trade surplus in these two countries.

The ability of the oil-producing countries to significantly raise their prices in 1973 can be explained not only by the sustained increase in demand during the two previous decades and the drop in relative price, but also almost certainly by the emergence of a marked bipolarity in international and, especially, military spheres.

The increase in international liquidity associated with the enormous expansion of the U.S. balance of payments deficit and with global debt, part of which is due to changes taking place in the real economy and part to the speculative process resulting from the recession, is probably another factor in the intensification of the inflationary process.

According to all of the above considerations, the decline in the industrial pattern of the advanced countries played an important part in the recession and inflation felt today. It could be theorized that this is the threshold of a transitional period, perhaps a long one, in which the market economies may start to put together the elements needed for creating a new pattern of industrial development.

If that is the case, it would be pertinent to pose the question as to what extent the decline in the industrial pattern experienced by the advanced countries would be reproduced in the semi-industrialized countries of Latin America. Questions to be considered should include whether a recession coupled with inflation in the advanced countries will affect the industrial development of Latin American countries, and what the foreseeable effects of the new developments taking place in the advanced countries during this transition period will be on the future industrial options of Latin America. Also to be considered are what options are opening up for the industrialization of the semi-industrialized countries of Latin America, taking into account the complex panorama of internal elements within the industrial model of Latin America and the external elements provoked by the recession plus inflation of advanced countries and possible future changes in those countries.

Section II provides an analysis of some aspects of the industrial system of the ADCs, particularly in Latin America, and identifies the similarities which mark their inclusion in the technological pattern of advanced countries, as well as the omissions and distortions that differentiate them and modify their industrial dynamic.

Section III deals with some considerations regarding the opportuni-

ties for strategic options open for ADCs, particularly in Latin
America. In particular, it contrasts the prospects implied by a
"passive inclusion" in the international market with the proposal for
reinforcing an "internal nucleus of technological dynamization"
(INTED), as a necessary step to develop a strategy towards reaching
international competitive levels that may allow an ever-growing
penetration. At the same time, it is intended to analyze the obstacles
to the creation of the Internal Nucleus of Technological Dynamization, taking the capital goods sector as an example. In summary, it is
intended to show the importance of establishing the INTED but, at
the same time, to demonstrate that this is not a small task.

II. Expansion of the Industrial System in Latin American ADCs

1. Asian and Latin American ADCs: A Schematic Contrast

This section will be concerned with contrasting the industrialization
pattern of the Asian ADCs with that of the Latin American ADCs.

During the period of rapid growth in 1950-70, the industrialization
of developing countries coincided with an increasing interest shown
by developed countries, to the extent that it presented possibilities for
expanding international trade and direct investment. The prospects
changed in the early 1970s when there was a decline in dynamism and
a rise in unemployment accompanied by inflation. Those developing
countries which had achieved significant increases in their exports to
developed countries during the previous period were soon seen as
competitors. Various academic studies were initiated by national and
international organizations and the subject aroused increasing attention even in the international press.[1]

The following paragraphs will point out some of the differences
which distinguish the industrial strategy of the Latin American ADCs
from that of the Asian ADCs; later the Latin American ADCs will be
compared with other countries of the region and finally attention will
be concentrated on the analysis of the specific nature of the Latin

---

[1] See Chenery (1979), Keesing (1979), Baldwin (1976), Lydell (1975), and UNIDO/
ICIS (1978).

American ADCs which, according to the definition given by the OECD (1979), would be Brazil and Mexico. The four Asian countries defined as being in this category are Hong Kong, Singapore, Korea and Taiwan. Four European countries, Greece, Portugal, Spain and Yugoslavia also fit into the category on the basis of growth rate of industrial production and volume of exports. As a group, these countries increased their participation in world industrial production from 5.4 percent to 9.3 percent between 1963 and 1977. (See OECD, 1979, Table 1.)

It is interesting to note that the increase in the participation of these ten countries is closely comparable with the growth observed in Japan during the same periods. The rise of Japan and the ADCs taken together, and the deterioration of the relative position of the United States and England during that period, are the most significant changes undergone by the manufacturing export and production structure. The rest of the developed and developing countries maintained or only slightly modified their relative positions.

This fact might present a partial explanation of a recurring concern for discouraging the ADCs from trying to follow in Japan's footsteps.[2] Japan itself is currently recommending the liberalization of the ADC economies.[3]

The group of ADCs share the common characteristics of rapid industrial growth and increasing export of manufactures to developed

---

[2] "The postwar history of Japan reveals the risks which are posed for an open world economy by a country which views itself as poor and dependent long after it has become a major force in world trade, and fails to take into account the repercussions on its own most vital interests of waiting too long to assume truly reciprocal obligations —such as opening its own markets to imports and eliminating export aids which are no longer needed. It is our strong hope that today's ADCs will not repeat this serious mistake." F. Bersten, Adjunct Secretary of the Treasury for External Affairs. Presentation delivered before the Association of American Chambers of Commerce in Latin America, Rio de Janeiro, November 7, 1978. Department of Treasury News.

[3] "We should welcome the development of the advanced developing countries which are succeeding in achieving industrialization because it will contribute to the expansion of the world economy... with the aim of achieving both expansion and equilibrium in world trade, we must adopt the following basic position: that we will accept an expanded inflow of manufactured goods from these countries, and that, in accordance with their stage of development, will request them to liberalize their market . . . In order to adjust our economies to the situation brought about by the development of these countries, we must work for increased rationalization and sophistication in our own industries." Nobuhijo Ushiba, Minister for External Economic Affairs of Japan, published in the *OECD Observer*, July 1978.

countries. Nevertheless, in terms of dynamism, the Asian ADCs show substantially greater economic growth. In the period from 1963 to 1973, the growth of GNP of Asian ADCs came close to 10 percent annually, while for the rest of the European and Latin American ADCs it was approximately 7 percent. (See OECD, 1979, Table 23.) If the relative importance of industrial exports is contrasted with production, which indicates strength of foreign objectives within the industrial strategy of a country, an even more marked difference is observed; while the ratio of exports to industrial product fluctuated from 28 percent to 78 percent in the Asian countries, it varied between 6 percent and 20 percent in the European nations and in the case of Mexico and Brazil did not even reach 10 percent. (See OECD, 1979, Table 26.)

Mexico and Brazil's industrial strategy is predominantly oriented toward their internal markets, although it receives some support from manufactures exports, whereas the industrial strategy of the Asian countries is concerned with their penetration of the international market and this tends to define their sectorial policies as well. Import substitution played an important role in the Asian ADCs but mainly in reinforcing the dynamism of international competitivity.

A comparison of the absolute export volume of manufactures also reveals significant differences: in 1976 Hong Kong, Taiwan, and Korea generated export volumes of manufactures of over $6 billion, while Mexico and Brazil each showed volume levels of approximately $2 billion. The contrast is even more striking if the figures are presented in terms of exports per capita: Korea had the lowest level of exports per capita of the Asian ADCs, with $188 in 1976, but Brazil reached only $21 and Mexico $38 per capita. Hong Kong, Taiwan and Korea showed 80 percent of manufactures within their total exports, whereas the proportion in Brazil and Mexico was 27 percent and 52 percent, respectively (Chenery, 1979:22).

It would also be useful to compare the role of transnational enterprises in Mexico and Brazil and in Korea. Available information suggests that in Korea, industrial leadership has mainly come from groups that are closely linked with the government. In Brazil and Mexico, on the other hand, such leadership came from foreign enterprises, both on a sectoral level and in participation in production.

It is estimated that in 1970 foreign investment in Korea represented approximately 5 percent of total capital invested in industry whereas in Brazil it reached 49 percent and in Mexico 36 percent. It should also be added that in the most dynamic industries of Mexico and Brazil, there is strong foreign participation (Westphal, 1978 and UN, 1978).

One important indication of the difference between the industrial strategies of Latin American ADCs and the Asian ADCs, apart from the Asian ADCs greater emphasis on international competitiveness, is the relative weight of their foreign debt, its service cost and its relative importance vis-a-vis exports. While the service cost of the Asian countries' foreign debt in 1977 came to less than 9 percent, in Brazil and Mexico it represented more than 40 percent (OECD, 1979, Table 29).

The above considerations indicate that while the ADCs have in common an increasing penetration of their respective markets, they have pursued very different industrial strategies in regard to sectoral selectivity and inclusion in the international market.

2. *Latin American ADCs and Other Latin American Countries*

In 1973, Brazilian and Mexican industry generated 62 percent of the total industrial production of Latin America, a rise from 42 percent in 1950. While the industrial growth of Latin America between 1950 and 1978 was 6.5 percent, Brazil's expansion reached an average annual rate of 8 percent, and Mexico 8.3 percent. During the same period, Argentina's industrial growth was only 4.1 percent. In 1950, industrial production in Argentina represented 31 percent of the region's total, but by 1973 it had dropped to 15 percent.

In considering Argentina, Brazil and Mexico, it can be seen that their industrial structure differs greatly from that of the medium and small Latin American countries. In 1975 the former's non-durable consumer goods represented 35 percent of industrial production and durable consumer goods and capital goods represented 28 percent. In the case of the medium-sized countries, these proportions were 48 percent and 17 percent respectively, and in the small markets, 65 percent and 9 percent. In terms of their degree of industrialization, the large countries showed a proportion of 29 percent, the medium countries 20 percent and the small countries 18 percent. Between 1950 and 1975, the three large countries were responsible for 80 percent of the increase in industrial production of the region and 87 percent of the production growth of durable consumer and capital goods; the medium countries covered 13 percent and 10 percent, and the small countries 13 percent and 7 percent respectively. In short, the two Latin American countries included in the OECD definition of ADCs do represent the most dynamic segment of Latin American industry and the part having the highest absolute value. In terms of its level of industrialization, Argentina is on a comparable plane, with a higher per capita industrial product than Mexico and Brazil. However, in regard to industrial dynamism, Argentina has clearly fallen behind.

3. *The Latin American ADCs and the Pattern of the Advanced Countries*

When the industrial development of Mexico and Brazil is compared with that of advanced countries, some important similarities can be noted, one of the first being their postwar industrial growth.

A comparison of the sectoral industrial structure of developing countries and advanced countries[4] shows that in Brazil, Mexico and Argentina the branches that have taken the lead in industrial growth, the chemical and engineering sectors, are the same as for the advanced countries.

It is evident that at least in the areas of industrial growth and structure and of sectoral leadership, the industrialization of the Latin American ADCs has followed a pattern comparable to that of the advanced countries. In the advanced countries, a "cumulative virtuous circle" of growth and technical progress leading to international competitiveness was clearly perceptible and the capital goods sector played a strategic role. In this sense, it is useful to continue with the series of comparisons being made, giving special attention to the situation of the capital goods sector.

4. *The Lag of the Capital Goods Sector in Latin American ADCs*

A comparison of the capital goods sectors of Mexico and Brazil with those of the developed countries reveals that the engineering sector, including metallic products, non-electrical machinery, electri-

---

[4] The comparison is made through a coefficient of similarity which contrasts the relative weight of each industrial branch within the manufacturing industry as a whole in each country. The maximum value possible in this index is 1, and Brazil, Mexico and Argentina reach levels of 0.95, 0.87 and 0.95, respectively. See "World Industry Since 1960: Progress and Perspectives," Table III. 4, p. 72, UNIDO, 1977.

cal machinery and transport equipment, had relatively less importance in Mexico and Brazil than in the developed countries.

Within the engineering branch, the electrical and non-electrical machinery branches have relatively greater importance in the advanced countries, while, significantly, the metallic products branch, which is less technically complex is more important in the Latin American countries. In Mexico, in 1974, this latter branch represented 30 percent of total engineering production, while in the advanced countries it represented 17 percent. In the transport equipment branch, automobiles represented one-third of production in the advanced countries whereas in Latin America their proportion was almost two-thirds. In electrical equipment, durable consumer goods represented 20 percent in the advanced countries: and in Latin America, close to 50 percent. Thus, it can be seen that the portion of durable consumer goods in the engineering production of Latin America is significantly greater than in that of the advanced countries.[5]

The capital goods that are produced in Latin America incorporate a much lower degree of technological complexity than the capital goods that are imported; they generally belong to smaller sizes of the respective product families and, at least in the case of Mexico, have a very low degree of integration. Even in Brazil, where the capital goods industry has made the most advances in terms of the range, size and complexity of products, the technological content of the capital goods produced is very limited and the national component of such technology is, at the moment, very small.[6]

An additional consideration is that a majority of capital goods production is carried out in the subsidiary plants of enterprises from

---

[5] "Industrie et Biens de Capital," UNIDO/ICIS 70. "Documento Introductorio al Seminario sobre la Estrategia e Instrumentacion para Promover las Industrias de Bienes de Capital en los Paises en Desarrollo," Algeria, 7-11, December 1979, UNIDO, Tables 5-6. "Estrategia para Desarrollar una Industria de Bienes de Capital," *op. cit.*

[6] For Brazil, see "The Capital Goods Sector in Brazil, Development, Problems and Perspectives," R. Bonnelli, L.O. Facanha, presented in the Working Group on Capital Goods Sector, Vienna, October 1977. "Sustitucion de Importacion de Bienes de Capital: Posibilidades y Limitaxions," Flavio P. Castelo, Branco, Pesquisa Y Planejamento Economico, April 1977. "Absorcao e Criacao de Technologia na Industria de Bens de Capital," F.S. Erber, J.T. Araujo, Jr., S.F. Alvcs, L.G. Reis, and L.M. Eredinger, FINEP, Serie pesquisas, No. 2, "A Industria de Maquinas-Ferramenta no Brazil" IPEA (1974), Serie Estudios para o Planejamento, No. 8. For Mexico, See "Estrategia-para Desarrollar una Industria de Bienes de Capital," *op. cit.* and Sectoral Monographs.

advanced countries, which perform the simultaneous functions of producers and importers with the obvious implications for national technological development and arbitration decisions dealing with local production and importation.

The lag in the capital goods industry in Latin America can be traced to the pattern of industrialization followed by the region during the last decades. A central element in industrialization policy was the quantitative stimulation of investment, especially private investment, and to accomplish this it was necessary to create conditions under which investments would have the lowest possible cost. This was achieved to a great extent by encouraging the importation of capital goods. Stimulus was provided for the production of non-durable consumer goods, and, later, for durable and intermediate goods, but the local production of machinery and equipment, whose initial phase would have raised the cost of investment, was neglected. The protection level granted to the capital goods industry is significantly lower than that enjoyed by other industrial activities.[7] It is useful to distinguish between users in terms of public enterprises, transnational affiliates and private national enterprises. For public enterprises the main restriction in purchasing capital goods has been financial. Decentralized public enterprises in Latin America characteristically have a deficit in the capital account because they price their products at less than cost to subsidize their acquisition. The deficit is neutralized by access to international financing which is associated with the importation of capital goods. As a result, there is a structural and financial element in the functioning of public enterprises which impedes their dynamic participation in promoting locally-produced capital goods. There is a marked difference between this situation and the role that public enterprises have played in the development of the capital goods industry in developed countries. There, a close collaboration between public enterprises and national producers has been stimulated in both commerce and technology, at times in response to questions of national interest. This has been the case in the energy, communications, transport and armament sectors, among others. As a result, a good part of the development of these industries has revolved around the central role played by this close

---

[7] "Condiciones de Acceaso de los Bienes de Capital al Mercado de los paises Miembros del ALALC", Estudio Conjunto NAFINSA/CEPAL. El Mercado de Valores, Suplemento 37, 1975.

connection between public enterprise demand and the larger national private firms of those countries.

The importation of capital goods is the form in which direct investment to the country is expressed. It is not in the form of liquid financial resources but rather embodied in machinery and equipment. Also the division of work established by the affiliates policies means that for some products in the final phase of the "product cycle" certain production activities are transferred and, along with them, there is a transference of the necessary equipment and machinery from installations in developed countries to affiliates in developing countries. Due to these circumstances, even though the demand for capital goods corresponding to the transnational affiliates is a substantial portion of total demand, it does not really represent much support for local production.

In the case of private national enterprises, mostly medium and small-sized firms, the problem of financing conditions offered in the purchase of capital goods is a decisive factor and the conditions offered by local producers are notably less attractive than those found on the international market.

In considering capital goods suppliers, a differentiation must also be made between national and foreign producers. Originally foreign producers had an open market for exporting goods from their country of origin. As long as this option was open, their motivation for coming to developing countries to install local production centers was very low due to the lack of technical infrastructure and the idea that local markets were small.

Later, however, certain markets began to close because of rising protection levels or, in some cases, because some began to take advantage of their maintenance and repair installations to install local production units. Similar enterprises sought to establish themselves locally, but without causing any substantial alteration of the stable export currents. This was accomplished by restricting their local production to the simplest sizes and kinds of equipment and by keeping the degree of local integration relatively low. For the foreign producer, the option of local production only became interesting at the moment in which there was a risk of losing the market.

For national producers, the capital goods sector was just one of many investment opportunities and, for reasons mentioned above, was considered a less attractive option from the point of view of profitability and its greater exposure to international competition where buyers were technically more demanding and more inclined to satisfy their demand abroad. These considerations along with the apparently greater technological complexity of the capital goods sector, tended to turn national private capital toward other sectors, making capital goods production a relatively marginal component of enterprises whose main activities were concerned with other industries.

In keeping with the hypothesis that technological development is incorporated into the capital goods industry, it can be assumed that the weakness observed in the technological sphere in Latin America is associated with the lag in the capital goods sector. To overcome this problem it will not be enough to simply create specific norms directed toward stimulating research and development activities at the enterprise level and to regulate foreign technology transfer, as long as all of the factors making up the "ind· strialization style" of Latin American countries remain unchanged. The solution to this problem is a challenge to introduce well planned, coordinated modifications in an industrialization pattern which up to now has tended to reject the expansion of this sector.

5. The Leadership of Affiliate Firms

A second specific feature of the industrialization pattern in Latin America, particularly in Mexico and Brazil, is the strong influence exerted by the affiliates of foreign firms on the expansion of the most dynamic industrial sectors. The fact that industrial leadership is provided by the affiliates of foreign firms suggests that production transformations are linked, at least partially, with a process that is developing on an international level. In the case of the advanced countries, there is an important connection between the state and the foremost industrial enterprises in strategic sectors. Internal technological innovation and increased productivity accompany the investment process and have an effect, as does the expansion of manufactures for international trade on growth and technical innovation. There is a dynamic linkage between industrial and agricultural growth and that has repercussions on trade and price stability.

In the case of Latin America, these links do not have the same dynamism. In fact, in Brazil and Mexico, the situation is the exact opposite of what occurs in the countries of origin. Moreover, the contribution of the affiliates in terms of local technological innovations is limited almost exclusively to the transfer of products, processes and manufacturing techniques developed in the country of origin and suitable for existing conditions there, but not necessarily suitable for an adequate utilization of local resources. This last aspect is especially important in view of the abundance of natural resources and labor available in Latin American countries.

It is important to note that the very specific nature of the industrialization pattern resulting from this situation in which leadership has come from firms whose local strategy is part of a global strategy found within the overall dynamics of the advanced countries. This fact is particularly important and much more obvious during the 1970's in which the advanced countries began to lose their dynamism.

6. Protectionism and National Objectives

A third specific feature of the industrialization pattern of Latin America comes from the high degree of protection that has sheltered industrial growth. Paradoxically, this very feature is shared by the country that has achieved the most significant results in terms of its industrialization process, Japan. It is obvious that since protection for the internal market was a common feature of both strategies, it could hardly be considered in itself to be a decisive factor in defining the results produced by industrialization in each case. In spite of their common high level of protection, these two strategies have substantial differences in terms of the content of industrialization, the agents which led the development process in each case and the selectivity and timing characteristic of each.

In Japan there was a virtual absence of foreign companies, in Latin America their presence has been decisive. Obviously, Japan's postwar internal market of 100 million people was highly attractive for foreign enterprises but there they found themselves faced with the opposition of a national entrepreneurial sector closely aligned with a government whose long-range plans implied reserving the internal market for the expansion and development of an industry that aspired to reach a sufficient degree of excellence to penetrate and consolidate its position in international markets.

Growing dissatisfaction with the results of industrialization in Latin America has given rise to the idea that protection has been heavily responsible for industrial inefficiency. The evidence found in Japan's case indicates that such an idea needs to be qualified. In Latin America the high and indiscriminate level of protection as well as the massive presence of the transnational enterprises (TE) are more an expression of the weakness of the national entrepreneurial sector than the cause of the evident inefficiency in industry. Therefore it is not enough to eliminate protection to get rid of inefficiency. Simple elimination of protection would mean returning to a situation in which national enterprises carry out activities that are not exposed to international trade such as commerce, finance, civil construction and exporting natural resources. This has been the path taken by the small Centroamerican countries and the results are not very encouraging.

The fact that in Latin America, responsibility for the deficiencies of industrialization is often attributed to the TE implies a refusal to accept the responsibility corresponding to the public and private national entrepreneurial sector and, consequently, postpones the search for truly viable options toward achieving efficient regional industrialization.

Thus, the specific nature of industrialization in Latin America does not lie only in the imitation of a consumption pattern spread by the TE but in the rather more important inability of the national entrepreneurial sector to formulate and carry out an industrial strategy based on the deficiencies and potentialities in terms of natural resources, of the region's countries. This situation became even more apparent and more serious in the 1970s, when the dynamism of the industrial pattern of the advanced countries began to show unmistakable signs of stagnation.

III. Reflections on Industrialization Options

1. Passive Inclusion in International Markets

There is general agreement as to the deficiencies of the industrialization process in Latin America. An inefficient productive structure has resulted in a serious manufacturing trade balance deficit. The industrial pattern of advanced countries has not been adapted to suit local conditions and the lack of adequate linkage between the industrial and agricultural sectors has increased inflationary pressures and adversely affected the trade balance.

Interpretations of why this has happened differ. One view is that high protection and heavy public intervention are the causes, and that elimination of protection and a reduced role for public action will effect a remedy.

From this point of view, concern for the specific matter of industrialization is reduced, since it is assumed that the country ought to produce those goods with which it can effectively compete on an international level, whether they are agricultural, industrial or mining products. This thesis does not recognize any special attributes in the industrial sector in terms of its potential for technological stimulation and transformation of the production structure. If it is estimated that the country is not in a position to compete in the industrial sphere but has abundant natural resources, the export of those resources would be the basis for productive activity, along with other activities which do not enter into the international market such as construction, trade, financial services and tourism. The financial sector would take a leading role in implementing this concept because it can transfer resources between sectors and can link the national with the international market. In the short term this policy will result in a decrease in internal demand and the relative cost of labor and encourage a flow of exports. However, this implies a passive inclusion in the international market.

2. An Alternative Solution

The interpretation which is supported in this paper maintains that the weakness of national industrial entrepreneurial circles is to a large extent responsible for high protection levels and part of the public intervention in support of industrial development. According to this interpretation and to an analysis of the experiences of countries which have successfully passed through "late industrialization,". it can be concluded that in order to attack this problem, it is necessary to focus on the internal factors, and especially on the nucleus of internal agents that must assume responsibility for the conception and instrumentation of the strategic development project. In view of the fact that for transnational enterprises, local activites are a marginal element in their global strategy, it is naive to suppose that they could be expected to make an effort to seek innovations for adapting their operations to local deficiencies and potentials. Therefore other remedies must be sought.

3. "INTED" as an Alternative

A central element of the option which is considered worthy of
further exploration is the creation or substantial reinforcement of a
nucleus made up of internal public and private agents, production
enterprises, engineering firms and basic and applied research
organizations, all linked around certain specialized sectoral pivots
which should be identified, in terms of industrial prospects at the
international level and of existing potentialities, as having the capacity
for negotiating with external agents in regard to the technical conception of projects, a phase that defines an important part of the
characteristics of the future productive structure. The existence of an
"internal nucleus for technological dynamization" (INTED) opens up
the possibility for advancing the exploitation of potentialities in
natural or human resources, and for adapting the "cosmic"
consumption pattern to specific local conditions. It was the
importance of this INTED that allowed Japan to create a productive
structure capable of achieving a surplus in the trade balance of
technology-intensive products, in comparison to the United States,
the very country which was Japan's major source of technological
inspiration, as evidenced by the substantial Japanese deficit in
technology payments to the U.S.

Through the INTED it is possible to make an internationally-
acquired technological reserve compatible with specific local
conditions. Because of the existence of an INTED it is feasible to
build strategic projects that take into account prospective technological trends and, on that basis, to take a rational stand on links with
the TE.

These are the considerations that have inspired the governments of
the developed countries to support and subsidize programs aimed at
technological development in the fields of electronics, telecommunica-
tions, computing, nuclear energy, non-conventional energy and others
that have a future strategic function. Such acts of "national will" and
"state intervention" are what determine the "comparative advantages" of countries.

In the absence of the INTED, options are effectively reduced to
passive inclusion in the international market with specializations
based on static comparative advantages which, in the majority of
countries, mean a return to export of natural resources or an
extrapolation of the known model, which would lead to more acute

versions of the deficiencies that have been mentioned.

The efficiency criterion of the proposal to be explored is that industry reaches a level of efficiency when it can generate the foreign exchange necessary for acquiring abroad those goods and services required by the country in order to achieve a growth level that allows full utilization of resources, with an "adequate" degree of income distribution. On a microeconomic level, efficiency is important as long as it does not interfere with growth objectives, the rise of productivity and employment and a "reasonable" distribution of income.

4. *The Complexity of the Task: An Illustration Provided by the Capital Goods Industry in Mexico*

To implement an industrial strategy based on INTED, there needs to be a political commitment to such a long-term national project as well as technological challenges. Demanding changes in the industrial pattern is bound to affect established interest.

As well as the important political dimension, there must be a consideration of the thematic areas through which the relative importance of the INTED is expressed: development of an efficient capital goods industry, industry-agriculture interconnections and linkage between big business and the small and medium firms.

Mexico is currently endeavoring to develop a capital goods industry. However, simple expansion of this sector does not guarantee adequate economic growth. The capital goods sector is used as an example of the nature and complexity of the decisions necessary to activate an industrial strategy linked around an INTED. Other factors, including modernizing agriculture and creating a dynamic link between it and industry may be more significant. However, considering the problems to be overcome in the capital goods sector it serves to illustrate the complexity involved in determining long range national strategy.

The capital goods sector has certain specific characteristics that not only distinguish it from other industrial sectors, but make it essential that the content of a Development Program aimed at contributing to efficient production expansion go beyond the simple listing of independent projects. An indication of what some of those specific characteristics are and how they form the basis for the sequence and content of a capital goods development program follows.

a. Capital Goods Demand: Linkage with the Productive Sectors

Capital goods requirements are determined by the expansion of productive capacity in different sectors, including the capital goods sector itself. Since the time periods needed for the establishment of industrial plants and the construction of equipment are relatively long, it is necessary to have access to long and medium range views as to the expansion of economic activity in terms of individual sectors.

In order to produce heavy equipment it is necessary to have installations that can carry out the basic processes of casting, forging, platework, machining and heat treatment. To estimate the demand for these activities requires a knowledge of the investment programs of the major strategic sectors in the economy, the specific projects that make up such investment programs, the main equipment involved in those projects and the components, materials and manufacturing processes that enter into the production of each kind of equipment.

In the case of multi-use equipment used in a wide range of industrial plants such as motors, pumps and valves which are produced in standard size within a certain range, the technical differences in user's projects are less relevant and coefficients based on historical tendencies, and global future projections may be used to provide relatively satisfactory figures for estimating future demand.

If the production of capital goods were carried out in industrial plants defined along the lines of single products and manufacturing processes, using technologies that had reached a high level of maturity and stability, the specific character of the capital goods sector would be limited to the aspects that have been thus far indicated. In the following paragraphs, consideration will be given to the aspects pertaining to the multiproductive, multiprocess, technologically dynamic character of the design, manufacture and, in some sectors, utilization of capital goods.

b. Capital Goods Supply: Internal Linkage versus Foreign Integration

From the point of view of government policy, there are two clearly differentiated options: to stimulate the kind of plant concept that corresponds to the preferences of foreign investors, who are the technology suppliers and whose proliferation usually results in supply fractionalization and low national content. This option represents the "path of least resistence," conforming to the will of the foreign supplier. The other option is one which seeks to shape a productive structure that is adequate for the internal expansion of capital goods manufacturing but at the same time attempts to raise efficiency through horizontalization of production. The technological element of each of these options can be a decisive factor in the long range results obtained from the development of the capital goods industry.

In the specific case of heavy equipment manufacture in Mexico, a systematic comparison of these two alternative concepts of productive structure was made, including economic factors such as investment, employment, foreign exchange and strictly technological factors. It was concluded that the option implying a group of independent plants with higher in-plant integration and lower national integration required less investment than the "horizontalized" and specialized production structure with its lower degree of in-plant integration and higher proportion of national integration. Nevertheless, it was found that the difference in the amount of investment could be recovered in two years through savings in imports generated by the possibility of "internal interrelation." Significant technological advantages can also be obtained in terms of potential for developing design capacity, improved efficiency in the utilization of installations and an enhanced degree of specialization in production processes. All of this logically would result in lower costs and a greater capacity for competing on the international level.

c. The Capital Goods Sector: An Embodiment of Technological Progress

One of the specific characteristics of this sector is that within the development of the industry an important objective is the strengthening of the country's reserves of technological data. Its expansion implies a greater probability of participating in the process of technological innovation on an international scale. This is, however, by no means a self-evident implication. It cannot be assumed that national technological capacity can be strengthened by the development of any capital goods industry regardless of the conditions of its development. Likewise, not just any methodology used in developing the capital goods industry will automatically result in the achievement of the goal of local technological development. On the other hand, it is quite evident that the absence of the capital goods sector would make it very unlikely that the technological level of the country could be strengthened. The development of the capital goods industry seems to be a necessary but by no means sufficient condition for the strengthening of national technology.

Within the selected subsectors, there are some lines of production that are in a semi-experimental phase: these will probably show a rapid increase in technological innovation in the future but at the same time are not devoid of certain risks of failure.

There is another group of lines of production that are in a phase of technological refinement with a relatively rapid process of technical innovation in production growth and diversification. These are categories that face intense competition, whose appeal lies precisely in their high degree of dynamism. A third group of products consists of those in which technology has reached a stable and terminal stage in the technological cycle, where the rhythm of innovation has subsided and where international competition has probably increased due to free access to established technologies and excess use of installed capacity. In this category, the risk of future substitution by new products being developed must always be taken into consideration.

The selection of products suitable and desirable for local production becomes a complex process of considering all of the elements described previously, together with technological trends within the different subsectors.

These technological trends provide a basic frame of reference which must be kept in mind when it comes to selecting the products most suitable for development, and also for negotiations with technology suppliers.

Most recommendations concerning technology transfer place emphasis on the "conditions" of the transfer and the need for developing countries to avoid restrictive clauses and excessive costs. However, it is equally or even more important to consider the "content" or "quality" of the information that is being acquired and this is determined by the extent to which the user makes an effort to study and compare his technical requirements and the available technologies on the international level, before entering into negotiations with a specific supplier.

It is often the case in Latin America that negotiations are begun without having invested the time and resources necessary to formulate such a preliminary conception. Under such conditions, the technology supplier, interested in consolidating his position and avoiding competition, often takes the lead in proposing the technical conception of the project that will later result in a contract for technology transfer. And it is precisely this phase of technical realization that determines to a large extent the nature of the technological contribution, in terms of design, process and manufacturing engineering, that the project will make to the country. This phase, along with the definition of training programs, will ultimately define the "content and quality" of the technology transfer.

One of the factors determining the possibility for channeling capital goods demand toward national suppliers is the degree of technological development attained by the large user enterprises in the public and private sectors particularly in the fields of basic and detailed engineering. Thus, development of the technological level of the major user enterprises is a decisive factor in the potential development of the national capital goods sector.

The above considerations tend to confirm that the development of the capital goods industry must be approached on the basis of an integrated program of actions that can influence the complex decision-making system made up of national and foreign producers, public and private users, engineering firms, financial and commercial intermediaries and the whole of the supporting technological infrastructure.

IV. Final Considerations

The comments on the capital goods sector are intended to illustrate the nature of the decisions which must be made in order to achieve much-needed changes in the industrialization pattern. The formation of an "internal nucleus of technological dynamization" is far more important than the development of this sector in itself. And the obstacles faced in the agricultural and energy sectors will require acts of political will and technical and organizational competence compared to which the development plans for the capital goods sector could represent a minor problem.

There is evidence that in the public and private sectors of Latin American countries, at the level of labor, enterprise and basic and applied research, certain nuclei exist which, in spite of the general conditions described previously, have shown the readiness, organizational ability and technical competence needed to reach levels of relative excellence in their respective fields. These nuclei, however, in spite of their importance, have lacked the necessary strength to dominate and direct industrial development. Nevertheless, they do represent an indication that this path is a feasible one. The essence of these considerations lies precisely in their emphasis on the importance of identifying, linking and strengthening such nuclei so that they may assume a growing responsibility in the orientation of future industrial development.

One of the primary political requirements posed by the existence of a strategy shaped around an INTED, is that the center of gravity of social movements should lie in sectors which have a decisive committment to the development of national potentialities and the solution of internal deficiencies. Such central agents would vary with different countries and circumstances; however, one necessary condition that can positively be stated is that they must possess a good measure of will.

The other proposal, that is, passive inclusion in international markets, involves less complex problems and, being strictly functional with regard to the requirements of the internationalized sector of the advanced countries, has met with hearty acceptance in some international circles.

History has shown, however, that the solidity of advances achieved through national will and efforts is much greater than the progress circumstantially obtained in exchange for a loss in autonomy.

REFERENCES

Baldwin, Robert E., "Trade and Employment Effects in the U.S. Multilateral Tariff Reductions," *American Economic Review,* May 1976.

Chenery, Hollis B., "The Changing Composition of Developing Countries' Exports," World Bank Staff Working Paper, No. 314, January 1979.

Keesing, Donald B., "Structural Trends and Developing Countries' Exports," World Bank Staff Working Paper, No. 316, January 1979.

Lydell, H. F., *Trade and Employment: A Study of the Effects of Trade Expansion on Employment in Developing and Developed Countries,* Geneva: ILO, 1975.

OECD, *The Impact of the Newly Industrialized Countries,* 1979.

UNIDO/ICIS, *The Impact of Trade with Developing Countries on Employment in Developed Countries,* No. 85, 1978.

United Nations, *Transnational Corporations and World Development,* 1978.

Westphal, Larry E., *Korea's Experience with Export-Led Industrial Development,* World Bank Reprint Series, No. 54, 1978.

• COMMENT _____

Kiyoshi Ikemoto,   *Kobe University*

Recognizing both the weakness of entrepreneurship and the slower progress of production technologies, Fajnzylber points out the critical importance of cooperation among various agents, for which he coined the new terminology of "INTED," that is, internal nucleus for technological dynamization. According to Fajnzylber, it was the importance of this INTED that allowed Japan to create a production structure capable of reaching a surplus in the trade balance of technology-intensive products and it is the INTED that has made it possible for a country like South Korea to achieve high levels of penetration in the U.S. market.

The concept of "INTED" is not clear. It may be interpreted as an expansion of inter-industry relationship, or as the localization of imported production technologies and the formation of economic planning with collaboration among various agents. Those countries which are quoted by him, such as Japan, Korea, Northern European countries and Eastern European countries, have, as Fajnzylber points out, their own distinguishable INTED. Although the purpose of INTED is shown as the localization of imported technologies, other features should be clearly stated. These include the field into which INTED is directed, how INTED should be organized and how the responsibility of INTED is divided between government and private agents.

Sources of funding for INTED must be found and personnel educated and trained and criteria for judging the performance of INTED would have to be established. It is necessary to make clearer the formation and function of the framework of INTED for each type of country or country group. Fajnzylber points out the necessity of a close connection between demand for and internal supply of capital goods. Stronger nationalism seems necessary in this case.

Brazil has FINEP (Agency for the Financing of Studies and Projects), STI (Secretariat of Industrial Technology), BNDE

(National Economic Development Bank), CEBRAE (Brazilian Center of Management Assistance to Small and Medium Firms) and IRT (Institute of Technological Research). The relationship of these Brazilian organizations to INTED is not explained. It is desirable to show the functioning of organizations such as CONACYT (Consejo National de Ciencia y Technologia) in Mexico.

The second comment refers to the capital goods sector which is emphasized by Fajnzylber. He asserts that higher economic growth in developed countries after World War II has been due to rapid development in the capital goods industry, and that Latin American ADCs have lagged in development of this industry. He also mentions that the capital goods industry is labor-intensive and that it is seen as an outstanding training mechanism for the rest of the industrial complex. However, it is better to characterize the capital goods industry described by Fajnzylber as a technology-intensive industry. This aspect of the capital goods industry makes it clear that the lag in Latin American ADCs is essentially caused by a technology gap between them and developed countries, along with gaps in economic scale and in demand pattern. Therefore, it is difficult for Latin American ADCs to follow directly the example of developed countries at their present stage of economic development without relevant production technologies. On the other hand, the industrial dynamism in developing countries, especially in ADCs, may appear even in light industry such as textiles and apparel as has been seen in Hong Kong, Korea and Taiwan. This type of industrial dynamism generated by light industry will lead to the next higher stage of economic development through a learning effect. The point to be emphasized is that the viable development of a capital-goods industry is feasible if economic development proceeds to a higher stage. Although Fajnzylber emphasizes the critical significance of the capital goods industry, he declares that this industry seems to be a necessary but by no means sufficient condition for the strengthening of national technology. If INTED is a necessary and sufficient condition, he must clarify his description of the importance of the capital goods industry.

Fajnzylber compares Latin American ADCs with Asian ADCs. But there are two groups among Asian ADCs: Hong Kong and Singapore on the one hand, and Korea and Taiwan on the other. The former show a higher dependence on direct foreign investment. It is not clear whether this means that Hong Kong and Singapore have INTED. Furthermore, the comparison of both Latin American and Asian

ADCs is too superficial. It is better to present the differences in factors as well as mechanisms of economic development between them. In comparing Latin American ADCs with other Latin American countries, it is desirable to explain the reasons why the latter countries are not dynamic. It should also be mentioned that exports of manufactures from Latin American ADCs have been supported by other Latin American countries, especially through LAFTA.

A. E. Safarian, *University of Toronto*

For Latin America in particular, the author questions whether the lack of more adequate development can be related clearly to heavy protection and government regulation, as some claim. Instead, he believes these are themselves a response to inadequate development of national entrepreneurial capacities. In turn he relates this to the slower development of the capital goods sector by both public and private national firms and multinational firms, though for different reasons. He contrasts two models of development. One involves what he calls a passive response to the demands of the international market, particularly as implemented through multinational firms, and involving a relatively low level of development of the capital goods sector in particular. The other model depends heavily on the creation or reinforcement of what he calls the "internal nucleus for technological dynamization" (INTED). This involves the development of strong linkages between public and private agents at various stages of research, production and marketing, within selected sectors deemed to have strong international market and supply potentials. The emphasis again is on capital goods which he regards as having many advantages including strong growth rates and labor training. Despite some stated reservations about the costs of protection and the need for other policies, the model's major policy emphasis is clearly protectionist, emphasizing public buying to guarantee markets and the use of other non-tariff controls on trade and foreign direct investment.

There are a number of useful emphases in this paper. The process by which advanced developing countries pass to stronger emphasis on the production and exports of capital goods, and the consequences for the developed countries' near monopoly of such exports, is one such emphasis. The conditions for the development of national entrepreneurial groups is another useful emphasis, not least in economies where the entrepreneur disappears for decades at a time. However, there are four points which need clarification.

First, Fajnzylber has not offered a convincing rationale for his emphasis on the composition of production. Rapid growth of real GNP and of industrial production is clearly possible without comparable growth of the capital goods sector, as he demonstrates for a number of advanced developing countries. However, he continues to emphasize achievement of roughly comparable growth in capital goods. One possible explanation is the lower growth of developed countries which he predicts, but this would slow their demand for imports of capital goods also, among other things. Another possible explanation according to this paper is the view, frequently stated, that technological dynamism rests in certain manufacturing industries and related service sectors. It is never really clear from the paper why the natural resource sector is incapable of technological dynamism and entrepreneurial development, given the same kinds of public attention as he suggests needs to be focussed on manufacturing. There is certainly little emphasis on the problems of developing the latter where a country has significant advantages in the former. (See the paper by Kym Anderson and Ben Smith for this conference.) It would have been preferable to see more emphasis on types of primary resources and related primary manufacturing, as against types of other manufacturing, in terms of developmental opportunities and effects. There seems to be far too much emphasis on some sort of normal development path in terms of the composition of output for countries with similar per capita incomes, despite the very different resource, market and societal characteristics of the advanced developing countries at any given time. It would have been useful, for example, if the author had pursued, for his sample of countries, the ramifications of the pattern of capital goods production which he outlines for the now-developed countries. More than half of the exports of capital goods in the advanced industrial countries are from three countries, and there is increasing specialization in such products among the developed countries.

It might be noted that the author never really addresses the question as to how increased protection through the government purchasing preferences and the like can be reconciled with the need for large external markets in many countries whose national markets cannot supply efficient scale for many capital goods. Moreover, fuller comment on some of the other determinants of the differences in the experience of the Latin American and other newly industrialized countries would have been useful in his study. There is only passing mention of such things as investment in human capital, political stability, and social rigidities, any of which could strongly affect the development of the capital goods sector among other things. Indeed, it is not clear finally just how critical Fajnzylber considers this sector to be, because, contrary to the emphasis of much of the paper, towards the end he downgrades its potential importance substantially.

It may well be that the emphasis on a particular sector is designed to reduce reliance on the multinational firm. Autonomy of decision-making is given a high priority as one of the objectives of the link between government and national enterprises as well as the development of a capacity to deal with multinationals more effectively. That being the case, one might have expected more than a footnote reference to the literature for, while the complaints about multi-nationals are legion, the evidence is quite uneven. In particular, one would have been interested to know how effective, in terms of growth objectives, the alternatives to such firms have proven to be, parti-cularly in certain high-technology capital goods sectors where they tend to predominate. Infant industry subsidies to national entrepreneurship in these particular sectors are proving costly and difficult to develop, as even some highly industrialized countries have found. The evidence on these and related matters needs much more development. The author notes a study on Mexico, for example, which suggests that plants with a higher degree of national integration required more investment, but this was compensated for within two years by import savings. Other technical effects are all described as positive from a national viewpoint. That is a strong set of conclu-sions, and it is a pity that neither the source nor much description of the study is given.

Finally, it seems that Fajnzylber spends too much time comparing the costs of the "passive" international model, with the benefits of the "INTED" model. To redress the balance somewhat, attention should be drawn to the decisions necessary in implementing the second model. One complex decision is to choose the sectors and the national agents who will receive the various kinds of special treatment proposed, and to hold the rest at bay. When speaking of capital goods with long planning periods and important linkages throughout industry and education, a high degree of consistent general planning is required over time. In the process it is likely that income and power will be skewed strongly towards particular groups. At some point these special privileges must be scaled down, not only for reasons of income distribution, but also because the rest of the economy is not expected to bear such costs indefinitely and because the ultimate removal of the privileges is a strong incentive to efficiency. There may be states where long-term planning exercises of that kind can be effectively carried out but it is likely the societies which are capable of it are infrequent. Others may prefer to develop more decentralized and more uniform, that is, more directly market-oriented planning processes especially since, in the end, the outcomes are supposed to be competitive without subsidy on world markets, or in terms of opportunity costs in that market. All of this assumes the developed countries' markets will be open to such capital-goods exports, despite a substantial increase in supply in response to national protection.

Finally, the author's argument that the question of entrepreneurial development be placed at center stage is valid despite reservations on how he approaches it. There is a wide range of ideas in economics which relate to this and to associated aspects of the dynamics of change. For example, there is Schumpeterian innovation, X-efficiency, learning by doing, and minimization of organization costs, among a variety of ideas drawn from economics and other fields. What is lacking is systematic analysis and general testing of these and related ideas. One would be more confident of the advice economists give in these areas if such analysis and testing were more advanced.

GENERAL DISCUSSION

The case for the government program advocated by Fajnzylber depends on whether the economy is performing well enough without it. That judgment depends on the size of the country and its level of per capita income; that is, one should not expect to find the same kind of sophisticated economy, including capital goods industry, in a small country with a low level of income that exists in a large industrially advanced country. If there are distortions and biases against sophisticated industries, these should be removed first before positive actions are taken. The Fajnzylber program of selection of desirable firms and industries seems similar to the industrial policies being designed in OECD countries. However, in reality there is no substance to the OECD industrial policies and what Fajnzylber advocates is closer to the central planning of Eastern Europe which has generally failed. The rationale for the Fajnzylber program may be found in external economies and the desire to change the distribution of income rather than the arguments in the paper. In any case, the paper conveys a sentiment that seems to be distinctly Latin American and somewhat alien to many people in Asian ADCs.

PART II

TRADE STRATEGY AND INDUSTRIALIZATION

EXPORT-ORIENTED GROWTH AND INDUSTRIAL DIVERSIFICATION IN HONG KONG

*Tzong Biau Lin &
Yin Ping Ho**

I. Introduction

Hong Kong is perhaps the most trade-dependent and export-oriented economy in the world. As a small, densely populated city-state with virtually no natural resources,[1] Hong Kong has relied heavily on trade for its existence. Approximately 90 percent of its manufactured goods are exported, and the overwhelming bulk of industrial raw materials, intermediate inputs, and producer durables for its industry are imported, not to mention its basic foodstuffs and consumer goods. Increased export is a prerequisite for virtually any increase in the domestic activities of production, consumption or investment. Obviously, manufacture for export is Hong Kong's "engine" of economic growth. Through its direct and indirect influence on effective demands, the state of Hong Kong's export trade determines the level of its domestic output, income and employment.[2] Thus, Hong Kong can be characterized as an extreme case of an export demand-generated economy.[3] Its growth and prosperity rest on

---

*Professors of Economics, Chinese University of Hong Kong.

[1] The total present land area in Hong Kong is about 1,052 square kilometers, or 406 square miles. Of this about 13.6 percent is built up, and less than 12 percent is arable. Most of its 5 million people are crammed in an area of about 129 square kilometers of the built-up land.

[2] A detailed analysis of the contribution of exports to Hong Kong's growth and employment is given in Lin, Mok and Ho (1980).

[3] For a full discussion of export demand-generated growth, see Lim (1969).

its ability to manufacture for export.

Hong Kong differs from the majority of developing countries (LDCs) in that its export performance has been remarkably successful. By the early 1960s, it had become the largest supplier of manufactures among the LDCs and was one of the 20 leading exporting countries in the world. In terms of exports per capita it has been among the top ten since the late 1960s.[4] Exports per capita in 1978 stood at HK$11,694 (US$2,493), over 50 percent higher than the British, about three times the Japanese and roughly quadruple the United States' average.[5] Its manufactured exports[6] per head of working population is one of the highest in the world.

The rise of Hong Kong as one of the leading manufacturing centers in the world has been frequently acclaimed as an economic miracle. Hong Kong was lucky in that it started its export-oriented industrialization about a decade earlier than its closest competitiors, South Korea and Taiwan, which were heavily preoccupied with political and military exigencies in the late forties and early fifties. It has also benefited greatly from the continuous income growth in the advanced economies since World War II and the general trend towards trade liberalization particularly in the 1960s and early 1970s under the Dillon and Kennedy Rounds. As an early starter, it rapidly gained access to the vast markets of the industrially advanced countries. However, since the latter half of the 1970s, Hong Kong has been beset by problems relating to its trade prospects. On the one hand, an increasing number of LDCs, notably South Korea, Taiwan and Singapore, have successfully industrialized and become serious contenders in the international markets of light manufactures which Hong Kong used to dominate. In addition, the rising tide of protectionism in Hong Kong's export markets was intensified by the increasingly harsh terms of the textile and garment restraint agreements which the European Economic Community (EEC) and the United States imposed on Hong Kong in recent years.[7] This came as

---

[4] Excluding Organization of Petroleum Exporting Countries (OPEC).

[5] As computed from the recent December issue of *International Financial Statistics*, the corresponding figures in the same year for the following selected countries are: the United Kingdom, US$1,285; Japan, US$856; the United States, US$657; Taiwan, US$753; South Korea, US$343; and India, US$10.

[6] Unless otherwise stated, the definition of "manufactured exports" used in this study covers all commodities from SITC (Standard International Trade Classification) 512 to SITC 899.

[7] For a fuller analysis of the development of tariff and nontariff trade barriers on

a great shock because of the predominant role of the textile and clothing industries in Hong Kong's industrial structure. In 1979, these two industries still accounted for over 43 percent of the total domestic export receipts and of total workforce in manufacturing. There was wide recognition of the danger of such high concentration and the need to reduce Hong Kong's heavy dependence on a narrow range of industries. A sense of urgency was reflected in the Government's decision to appoint an Advisory Committee on Diversification in late 1977 to look into the whole issue of diversification.[8]

The purpose of this study is to draw on Hong Kong's past experience in order to shed some light on how the economy may further develop in the future. Section II provides a general discussion of Hong Kong's postwar growth performance. Some salient features that characterize its export trade will be discussed in Section III. Section IV reviews the widening of its economic base that has been going on during the past two or three decades. Section V identifies the constraints upon growth of the economy and suggests what can be done in order to further diversify and broaden Hong Kong's economic base. The concluding section provides some general remarks on export-oriented growth and diversification in broad economic perspective.

II. An Overview of Postwar Industrial Development

Hong Kong was originally a trading center, earning its income from entrepot activities, particularly with China. Hong Kong's industrial development did not really begin until the early 1950s when two major external events occurred which affected the course of its economy. First, there was the change of government in China which led to a drastic diminution in its trade with Hong Kong. Second, there was the outbreak of the Korean War with the subsequent United States embargo on the import of all goods of Chinese origin and the United Nations embargo on the export of essential materials and

---

manufactures imported into the developed countries and their effect on Hong Kong's export trade, see Lin and Mok (1980), Chapters 3 and 4.

[8] A report of the Committee was published in late 1979. Its major recommendations will be discussed in Section V of this paper.

strategic goods to China. On the one hand, Hong Kong's inhabitants found themselves substantially deprived of their traditional means of livelihood. On the other, it had to face the problem of providing food and shelter for a population increase of almost 50 percent in a few years, due to the influx of immigrants from mainland China. Severe unemployment resulted from these two adverse events.[9] For its economic survival, Hong Kong had to establish a new economic frontier: that is, "export industrialism". What is surprising is the speed, extent and success of the transformation of the economy from a relatively obscure entrepot into a thriving manufacturing and financial center.[10]

1. Growth Performance

Table 1 presents an overall view of Hong Kong's postwar growth record. It shows the rapid growth in national income, employment, public finance, bank loans and deposits, money supply, and the slower growth of population and price indices. In general, the period covered is 1959-79, which is further split for intertemporal comparison into two subperiods, 1959-69 and 1969-79.

The most logical place to begin an examination of Hong Kong's economic performance is with the gross domestic product (GDP). Over the period 1961-79,[11] its total GDP at current market prices has grown at an average compound annual rate of 16.0 percent and in constant prices at about 10.0 percent. On a per capita basis, the corresponding growth rates exceeded not only the average for all other LDCs but also the average for the developed countries (DCs) during the period. By 1979, its per capita GDP had reached a level of HK$17,825 (US$3,561), placing it, in Asia, behind only Japan and probably Singapore.

The performance of the manufacturing sector is especially remarkable. In the period 1959-79, Hong Kong's domestically produced

---

[9] According to Hong Kong Labor Department's estimate, the total unemployed labor in 1951-52 was about 15 percent of the estimated labor force; an unofficial estimate put the figure at the time as high as 34 percent. See Hambro (1955), p. 47.

[10] A lucid analysis of Hong Kong's postwar industrialization is to be found in Riedel (1974).

[11] No official GDP estimates were available for Hong Kong until 1973. Since then, the estimates have been published annually, with additions for each year; and in 1975, the estimates were extended backward to 1961.

Table 1. *Major Indicators of Growth of Economic Activity in Hong Kong*

(in percent per annum)

Indicators	Nominal Growth Rates			Real Growth Rates			1979 Level
	1959-69	1969-79	1959-79	1959-69	1969-79	1959-79	
Population (mid-year)	—	—	—	2.66	2.41	2.53	4.90 mn.
GDP (at market prices)							
Total GDP	13.17*	18.30	15.99*	10.69*	9.02	9.76*	$87,345mn.
Per Capita	10.39*	15.52	13.21*	7.98	6.46	7.13*	$17,825
International Trade							
Total Exports	14.95	19.12	17.02	12.77	9.24	10.99	$75,934mn.
(Per Capita)	11.97	16.31	14.14	9.85	6.67	8.25	$15,497
Domestic Exports	16.51	18.18	17.34	14.31	8.38	11.30	$55,912mn.
Re-exports	10.41	22.28	16.19	8.32	12.14	10.21	$20,022mn.
Imports	11.65	19.14	15.33	9.91	10.06	9.99	$85,837mn.
Manufacturing							
Employment	—	—	—	11.46	5.20	8.28	870,898
Establishments	—	—	—	11.98	11.62	11.80	42,282
Wages (workers)	8.35	11.87	10.10	6.49	6.21	6.35	$48/day
Money and Banking							
Bank Deposits	19.59	21.75	20.67	17.62	13.98	15.79	$88,014mn.
Bank loans	19.10	28.19	23.56	17.14	20.00	18.56	$94,468mn.
Money Supply, M1	10.84	17.27	14.02	9.02	9.78	9.40	$27,761mn.
Money Supply, M2	17.38	20.95	19.15	15.45	13.23	14.33	$95,303mn.
Public Finance							
Revenue	14.07	20.90	17.44	12.20	13.18	12.69	$16,550mn.
Expenditure	11.09	21.49	16.17	9.26	13.73	11.47	$14,232mn.

Sources: For GDP data; Census and Statistics Department, *Estimates of Gross Domestic Product*, Hong Kong; Government Printer, various years. For trade and their price deflators; Census and Statistics Department, *Hong Kong Trade Statistics*, and *Hong Kong Review of Overseas Trade*, Hong Kong; Government Printer, various years. For employment and wage data; Commissioner of Labour, *Annual Departmental Report*, Hong Kong; Government Printer, various years. Other underlying data; Census and Statistics Department, *Hong Kong Statistics, 1947-1967*, Hong Kong; Government Printer, 1969, and *Hong Kong Monthly Digest of Statistics*, Hong Kong; Government Printer, selected issues.

Notes: All growth rates in this table are compound rates, and money values are in Hong Kong dollars. A dash (—) in this table indicates that the item is not applicable. Due to the lack of official GDP data, the initial year of the covered period for the starred (*) figures is 1961 instead of 1959. Manufacturing employment before 1974 relates only to establishments registered with or recorded by the Labour Department. Statistics on money and banking excluded those concerned with merchant banks and finance companies. Revenue and expenditure are in financial year, *i.e.*, March-end, figures.

exports grew at an average compound rate of 17.3 percent per annum in nominal terms and 11.3 percent in real terms, roughly twice the growth rate of the world trade. In the meantime, exports per head of population expanded more than fourteen-fold; their value rose from HK$1,104 in 1959 to HK$15,497 in 1979. Hong Kong's manufacturing industries, which sell predominately in the markets of advanced countries, have been the prime movers of its economic activity. Export trade is the most important contributory factor to employment creation in Hong Kong. In most LDCs, manufacturing employment has a minority status, seldom encompassing as much as 20 percent of the total workforce. Hong Kong is exceptional in this regard.[12] According to its 1971 Population and Housing Census, manufacturing employment accounted for about 43 percent of Hong Kong's total industrial labor force, and the latest By-Census shows that the ratio stood at approximately 45 percent in 1976. The rapid export-generated employment growth can be appreciated if it is noted that in 1959, there were only 4,541 registered factories employing 177,271 people. By the end of 1979, the number of manufacturing establishments had increased to 42,282 employing 870,898 people. The growth of manufacturing industries, together with the development of other economic activities, brought about an increased demand for labor, large enough to absorb the increase in supply. Since the early sixties, there has been something approaching full employment.[13] There has been a substantial increase in real wages. For manufacturing as a whole, nominal average daily wages have increased at a compound rate of over 10 percent since 1959. On the other hand, inflation, as reflected by the consumer price indices, has been relatively low, at only about 4 percent per annum. As a result, manufacturing wages in real terms have increased about 6 percent compounded annually over the period. Unlike the situation in most industrialized countries, institutional factors play only a marginal role in wage determination in Hong Kong. Since the prevailing

---

[12] According to a survey article on employment implications of industrialization, Hong Kong tops 100 countries, both developed and underdeveloped, in the percentage figure of manufacturing employment to total labor force. For details, see Morawetz (1974).

[13] As recorded in the 1961 Census, open unemployment including first-job seekers was 1.7 percent; excluding those job seekers, it was only 1.3 percent. These figures reflect the fact that labor absorption through export-oriented industrialization during the latter half of the 1950s was immensely rapid.

economic creed is laissez-faire, the government imposes no minimum wage regulation upon employers. Moreover, trade union activity is extremely limited.[14] The wage level in Hong Kong is essentially the result of an interplay of market forces of supply and demand.

As for growth in money and finance, the annual compound rate of increase in nominal money stock during 1959-79 was 14.0 percent for narrow money M1 and 19.2 for broad money M2. This rapid growth in money supply is an obvious indicator not only of booming economic activities, but also of Hong Kong's financial deepening.[15] Bank deposits, a positive yardstick of earning and saving capacity, have risen at a phenomenal rate. During the period total deposits grew at annual compound rates of 20.7 percent in nominal terms and 15.8 percent in real terms. On the other hand, bank loans increased about sixty-nine times in nominal terms and about thirty-fold in real terms, or at annual compound rates of 23.6 percent and 18.6 percent, respectively. Bank credits expanded at considerably higher rates than deposits indicating the role of the banking system as an intermediary through which savings were injected into the economy was clearly an active one. The ratio of bank loans to total deposits averaged 66.0 percent and 87.0 percent respectively during the decades 1959-69 and 1969-79, indicating an increasingly high degree of utilization of bank resources for the financing of economic activity in Hong Kong.[16]

2. Factors Accounting for Growth

A number of factors have contributed to Hong Kong's impressive record of economic development.

a. Historically Inherited Infrastructure

Hong Kong's hundred years of entrepot activities provided it with

---

[14] For an account of the reasons leading to the slow development of trade unionism, see, for instance, Joe England and John Rear (1975), Chapter 5.

[15] In 1961, the ratio of broad money M2 to GDP, a rough indicator of financial deepening, was 70.2 percent, which rose to 109.1 percent in 1979. For a quantitative study of the relationship between money supply, foreign trade and national income in Hong Kong, see Lin (1971).

[16] A detailed analysis of sectoral allocation of bank loans in Hong Kong is presented in Jao (1974), Chapter 8.

much physical and commercial infrastructure, such as warehousing and port facilities, valuable commercial ties and vast marketing experience, which, together with its efficient banking, insurance and shipping system, have created an economic structure highly conducive to developing an export trade in the light manufactures which form the mainstay of its present growth.

b. Influx of Factor Inputs

Hong Kong's export industrialism was first stimulated by a massive influx of manpower, capital and entrepreneurs from China during the late forties and early fifties. A group of industrialists came from Shanghai, and their entrepreneurial flair and capital led to the immediate expansion of the textile industry which spearheaded the first stage of Hong Kong's postwar industrialization. The great influx of immigrants from China, mostly young, industrious and dexterous, provided an almost unlimited supply of labor relative to the then existing level of economic activities. If political boundaries are ignored, Hong Kong is simply an urban center of South China, and even though many people came for political reasons, the process of immigration can be likened to the absorption of rural unemployed by the industrial sector as described by Arthur Lewis.[17]

c. Positive Non-Interventionism

As is well documented, Hong Kong is an economy with little government intervention. The city-state has often been described as one of the world's last bastions of the nineteenth century free-trading laissez-faire economy.[18] Its economic success in the past quarter of the century owes much to a prudent public finance system and liberal government policy towards the private sector.[19] Despite some upward adjustments during the postwar period, Hong Kong has the lowest standard rate of tax on earnings and profits of any industrial state.[20]

---

[17] C.F. Lewis (1954), pp. 139 *et seq.*

[18] A succinct and vivid account of the political economy of Hong Kong is given in Rabushka (1979).

[19] For some detailed discussion of Hong Kong's public finance system and the role of government in its economic development, see, *inter alia*, Ho (1979), Rabushka (1973, 1976), and Glassburner and Riedel (1972).

[20] Earnings and profits tax in Hong Kong is charged at a standard rate. The standard rate of tax was raised to 15 percent from April 1966 having stood at 12.5 percent for the previous 15 years and at 10 percent before then. In the fiscal year 1975/76 the tax

The light tax burden has made possible the reinvestment of a high proportion of business earnings and contributed to the quick turnover of capital which is a feature of investment in Hong Kong. From its inception, the Hong Kong government has maintained a hands-off policy towards private economic activity. It does not try to set up priorities on development, nor to provide protection or subsidies for its industries. It intervenes in the factor or the product market only in response to overriding social pressure or economic needs. This non-interventionist attitude has allowed Hong Kong to make best use of the factor most important to its economic development, entrepreneurship. Dependence on external trade means that it would be generally unwise for the government to interfere, since decisions on which industries to develop and which markets to sell in would be better taken by businessmen with their direct and intimate knowledge of them. However, the Hong Kong government does not adhere dogmatically to a hands-off approach to all of its public economic activities. The government is the ground landlord in Hong Kong and spends about 20 percent of the national income, providing different types of physical infrastructure for fostering overall industrial growth, compulsory primary education, extensive medical and health services, subventions for numerous social welfare agencies, and public low-cost housing for about 45 percent of the population. In order to help promote foreign trade and enhance external competitiveness for its industries, a number of important statutory institutions have been established during the postwar period.[21]

d. Financial and Free Trading Haven

Given its political stability and consistent government policies as well as its well-established foreign-exchange banking network, Hong

---

on profits from incorporated businesses was raised to 16.5 percent and again to 17 percent in 1976/77.

[21] For instance, recognizing the need for Hong Kong to foster the growth and development of its manufacturing industries, the government sponsored the establishment by statue in 1960 of the Federation of Hong Kong Industries; the Hong Kong Trade Development Council, established by statue in 1966, promotes foreign trade and overseas investments in Hong Kong; to help raise productivity in local industry, especially medium and small scale industries, the Hong Kong Productivity Council was set up in 1967; and realizing the importance of providing protection against those risks in overseas trading which are not normally insurable commercially, the government also sponsored the formation of Hong Kong Export Credit Insurance Corporation in 1968.

Kong has long been an important center for the receipt and transfer of funds for mainland and overseas Chinese business and commercial interests. Hong Kong also continues to attract a considerable amount of capital from Southeast Asian nations suffering from political and economic instability. This continuous inflow of funds, besides benefiting Hong Kong as an offset to the chronic balance of merchandise trade deficit has greatly contributed to the direct capital formation and credit base for trade and industrial financing. Much direct investment has been attracted to Hong Kong by its liberal trading environment and it has been chosen as an offshore base for labor-intensive and foot-loose manufacturing industries. These inflows of overseas capital and technology, particularly from the United States, Japan and West Germany, have made substantial contributions to Hong Kong's industrial growth, employment generation, product diversification and sophistication. In the 1970s, factories with overseas interest accounted for about 10 percent both of total capital investment and of the employment of Hong Kong's labor force engaged in manufacturing. However, this overseas investment represents some of the most advanced sectors of Hong Kong's industry. It has brought with it technology, standards, marketing and management techniques whose spin-off contribution to Hong Kong's industrial diversification is substantial.

III. Some Salient Features of Hong Kong's Export Trade

Hong Kong had been a trade-dependent and export-oriented economy long before its manufacturing industries came into prominence. An overall view of the changing pattern of Hong Kong's export trade and its growth over the period 1959-79 is shown in Appendix Table A-1 (hereafter Table A-1). The degree of Hong Kong's reliance on trade and its success in its export drive can be seen from its import/GDP and export/GDP ratios. The import ratio averaged about 90 percent over the period. Exports as a percentage of GDP rose steadily from about 65 percent in 1959 to about 87 percent in 1979, indicating the increasingly heavy reliance of the Hong Kong economy on exports. In 1979, the total value of Hong Kong's two-way trade was about 1.8 times GDP. This proportion is perhaps the highest in the world. The chronic merchandise trade deficits throughout the postwar years have been amply compensated for by net invisible export receipts such as the tourist trade, shipping and financial services, and net capital inflow. The stability of the exchange rate between the Hong Kong dollar and the currencies of its major trading partners is a hallmark of Hong Kong's overall favorable balance of payments situation. It is interesting to observe from Table A-1 that the magnitude of the trade deficit relative to total trade has shrunk drastically over time. In the early sixties, the excess of imports over exports was about 50 percent of total exports; the difference narrowed down to around 10 percent in the latter half of the seventies.

1. Re-Exports: Ups and Downs

In the earlier postwar era, exports from Hong Kong were primarily re-exports of goods produced elsewhere. In 1951, at the height of the Korean War, Hong Kong's total exports were greater in value than 10 years later, but 88 percent of the total were re-exports. Total exports fell after 1951 mainly because of the Korean War embargo on trade with China, but domestic exports began to gather momentum.[22] By the late fifties the entrepot trade accounted for less than one-third of total export receipts. The proportion further declined during the sixties, and its share in total exports dropped to less than one-fifth at the end of the decade. Hong Kong did not go through import-substitution before turning to export-orientation. It has always been an outward-looking economy. Industrialization has only changed its position from an obscure entrepot to a lucrative manufacturing center.

Entering the 1970s, owing to China's entry into the United Nations and the subsequent lifting of the ban on imports from China, the traditional entrepot trade started to re-emerge. More recently, thanks to China's ambitious modernization programs and its active trade rapprochement with the West, the volume of entrepot trade has expanded by leaps and bounds in the past few years. Its share rose to over one-fourth of the total exports in 1979. However, its significance

---

[22] Hong Kong's exports to China, consisting overwhelmingly of re-exports, fell from HK$1,604 million in 1951 to HK$519 million in 1952. In terms of percentage share, at its height China took about 40 percent of Hong Kong's total exports in 1950; this share fell to about 4 percent in 1956 and to less than 1 percent in 1966.

is still very much overshadowed by the phenomenal expansion of domestic exports. It is unlikely that it will regain its predominant role since entrepot activity per se cannot provide sufficient employment opportunities. However, in a period when increasing trade protectionism and the need for industrial diversification have become more apparent, the re-emergence of entrepot trade will certainly be of great help to the growth of the overall economy.[23]

2. *Manufactured Exports: Continual Expansion*

The principal factor leading to Hong Kong's postwar economic progress, as can easily be seen from Table A-1, is the remarkably high rate of continual expansion in its export trade of domestic origin. One of the major distinctive features which characterizes the pattern of Hong Kong's domestic export trade is its increasing concentration on light manufactures. At the outset of the sixties, manufactured exports already accounted for 90 percent of Hong Kong's total domestic exports. This proportion rose to 96 percent throughout the seventies. Income, in the sense of value-added, derived from these export receipts, is equivalent to about one-third of GDP.[24] Thus, the domestic economy of Hong Kong is inextricably linked to the performance of its manufactured exports and changes in manufactured exports would have significant employment implications for the manufacturing industries and other sectors.

3. *High Commodity Concentration*

Hong Kong manufactured exportables are very limited in their range. In terms of the SITC 3-digit commodity group classification, textiles proper (651-657), clothing (841), electrical and electronic products (722-729), sundry metal products (691-698), precision instruments (861-864: mainly watches and clocks), handbags (831), footwear (851), and miscellaneous manufactured articles n.e.s. (891-899:

---

[23] For some further discussion, see "Hong Kong's Position as an Entrepot: A Reappraisal," *Hang Seng Economic Quarterly*, January 1979.

[24] In 1973 the manufacturing sector contributed about 37 percent of the GDP at factor cost. The proportion slipped to about 33 percent and 31 percent in 1976 and 1977 respectively. The decline has resulted from a relatively higher expansion of the financial sector in recent years (Computed from 1973 Census of Industrial Production and sample surveys of industrial sectors conducted during these two years).

principally plastic flowers, toys and dolls, and wigs in the late 1960s and early 1970s), comprised between 70 and 80 percent of Hong Kong's gross domestic export receipts throughout the past two decades. Averaging out year-to-year fluctuations, an upward concentration trend is obviously discernible.

Appendix Table A-2 shows that the export basket is heavily weighted towards clothing and textile products which, except for a number of years during the late 1960s and early 1970s,[25] constituted well over 50 percent of total export receipts between 1959 and 1976. Undoubtedly, their gradual decline below the 50 percent mark since 1977 was largely due to the increasingly harsh quotas and voluntary restraints imposed on Hong Kong by the Western European countries and the United States in recent years. In spite of the relative decline in the face of growing protectionism, the present concentration of these two traditional product groups is still high, accounting for 43.3 percent of total domestic export earnings in 1979. While the five major commodity groups in 1959 accounted for about two-thirds of gross export receipts, by 1979 they accounted for three-quarters, implying that a 13 percent increase in concentration occurred during the period. The familiar Hirschman-Gini concentration coefficients[26] shown in Table 2 generally agree with this development. It is defined as the square root of the sum of squares of the percentage shares of individual commodity receipts.[27] If exports involved just one com-

---

[25] The slight relative decline during the period resulted from a relatively higher expansion in wigs manufacture. At its height in 1970, its export earnings accounted for some 8 percent of total export receipts. Due to changes in market demand and consumer tastes as well as the low-cost competition from other LDCs, notably South Korea and Taiwan, the wigs industry in Hong Kong boomed and declined within a short number of years.

[26] This index was developed and employed by Albert Hirschman in his analysis of the extent to which one country could exploit another through the latter's dependence. See Hirschman (1945). When the index is used for measuring industrial concentration, the second principal area of its application, it is more commonly referred to as the Herfindahl index, which is similarly defined but without taking the square root of the sum of squares thus obtained.

[27] Its algebraic formula and mathematical limits are:

$$100 \, (n^{-1/2}) \; \leq \; C_t = 100 \, [\; \sum \, (x_{it}/X_t)^2]^{1/2} \; \leq \; 100$$

where x_{it} is the export value of commodity i in year t, while X_t is the total export receipts in the same year. For convenience, the index is usually expressed in percentage form. One of the advantages of this index is that, in addition to accounting for the proportion which each individual commodity represents within the series, it takes

Table 2.   *Hirschman-Gini Coefficients of Commodity Concentration of Hong
           Kong's Domestic Exports Based on SITC 3-Digit Commodity
           Groups, 1964-78*

| | | | | | | | (in percent) | |
Year	1964	1966	1968	1970	1972	1974	1976	1978
Index	40.5	39.7	40.0	40.1	43.2	40.9	45.5	41.4

Source: Computed from Census and Statistics Department, *Hong Kong Trade Statistics: Exports and Re-Exports,* Hong Kong: Government Printer, various December issues.

Note: Although the SITC 6-Digit commodity item classification was available through the entire postwar period, trade statistics in Hong Kong revealed the classified SITC 3-digit commodity group only from 1964 onwards.

modity, the index would be 100; if exports were divided equally among n commodities, the index would be 100 $(n^{-1/2})$. Thus, the lower the index, the less the concentration. It is observable from the table that, after smoothing out inter-year variations, there is a slight upward trend over time. The index averaged about 40 percent and 43 percent for the subperiods 1964-70 and 1972-78, respectively. Intriguingly, this situation concurred with a long period of continual export expansion despite protests for quite a number of years.

4. High Market Concentration

Another feature of Hong Kong's export trade is its direction, which is primarily directed towards the DCs, particularly the mass consumer markets of North America and Western Europe. The distribution of domestic exports according to major trading countries and areas is shown in Appendix Table A-3. The share of Hong Kong's domestic exports going to DCs[28] in 1950 was less than one-fifth, but in the early 1960s about two-thirds of total exports went to these countries. The share went up to more than four-fifths by the late 1960s. Throughout the decade of the 1970s, the DCs' share shows no significant decline.

---

account of the number of commodities within the series itself. Thus, unlike the traditional Gini measure, which is sensitive only to inequality of distribution, this index is a function of both unequal distribution and fewness.

[28] In this study, by developed countries we only covered the United States, Western Europe, Canada, Japan and Australia. All the rest are treated as developing.

Three countries, the United States, the United Kingdom and West Germany, have constituted Hong Kong's leading markets over the period although their relative shares have changed quite considerably. The market concentration in these leading importing countries is the same as the commodity concentration on the three major product groups, clothing, textiles and electronics. In terms of Hirschman-Gini coefficients set out in Table 3, the market concentration ratio has also shown no discernible decline over time.

Table 3. *Hirschman-Gini Coefficients of Market Concentration of Hong Kong's Domestic Exports, 1964-78*

(in percent)

Year	1964	1966	1968	1970	1972	1974	1976	1978
Index	36.4	40.6	45.3	45.1	44.4	37.5	39.1	41.0

Source: Computed from Census and Statistics Department, *Hong Kong Trade Statistics: Country by Commodity — Exports and Re-Exports*, Hong Kong: Government Printer, various December issues.

Note: The coefficient of market concentration is defined in exactly the same manner as that of commodity concentration.

The danger of such concentration on a limited number of markets is beyond question. It is clear that Hong Kong's export development is tied closely to economic conditions and commercial policies in its main overseas markets.

5. Labor-Intensive Manufactures

Within the export basket of manufactures, an overwhelming proportion is accounted for by the products of labour-intensive industries. One could not fail to see that the pattern of Hong Kong's exports has conformed to the Heckscher-Ohlin factor proportions theory. Given the availability of the innovative entrepreneurial resource, exports serve to overcome the narrowness of the domestic market. As an early starter and with few competitors on international markets, Hong Kong rapidly moved into the DCs' market and established itself as the leader par excellence in the export of light manufactures. Regarding Hong Kong's international status in export

performance, it is not surprising that, in a study of exports of manufactures of LDCs to eleven major DCs[29] over the period from 1960 to
1970, Mahfuzur Rahman found that Hong Kong took the lead in 14
out of 26 groups of major labor-intensive commodities.[30] The
commodities in which Hong Kong did not perform well were mainly
natural resource-based ones. In a more recent study of the employment implications of trade expansion in manufactures and semi-
manufactures, Lydall also found Hong Kong took the lead in 7 out of
10 groups of major labor-intensive manufactures.[31] In fact, according
to an earlier study, Hong Kong supplied 28 percent of DC imports of
light manufactures from all LDCs in 1965.[32] The record is even more
spectacular if it is noted that Hong Kong alone supplied half of the
DC imports of manufactures other than food and industrial raw
materials.[33] In short, Hong Kong's outstanding performance in
exports has built upon its labor-intensive manufactures for markets in
the economically advanced economies.

6. High Fluctuation

Another distinctive feature of Hong Kong's manufacturing sector is
fluctuation, especially at the individual commodity or industry level.[34]
Hong Kong's unusually high export-output ratio, coupled with its
correspondingly high ratio of manufacturing employment to total

---

[29] The "developing economies," as defined by Mahfuzur Rahman, included all
countries under the United Nations classification Economic Class II, while the eleven
major DCs covered in the study were: the U.S., the U.K., Canada, West Germany,
France, Italy, the Netherlands, Belgium-Luxembourg, Sweden, Australia and Japan.
See Mahfuzur Rahman (1973), p. 107.

[30] The 14 leading commodity groups are: clothing (841), cotton fabrics (652), toys
and sports goods (894), footwear (851), miscellaneous textiles (656), radio receivers
(724.2), miscellaneous electrical machinery (729), plastic products (893), travel goods,
handbags etc. (831), jewellery (897), furniture (821), base metal household equipment
(697), cutlery (696), and watches and clocks (864). For further details, see Mahfuzur
Rahman (1973), pp. 114-129.

[31] Our ranking is based on the exclusion of commodity groups not falling within SITC
sections 5 to 8. The 7 leading commodity groups were: knitwear (841.1 plus 653.7),
footwear (851), clothing (841 minus 841.4), made-up textiles (656), sundry metal
products (69), electrical goods (724 plus 729 plus 891.1), and precision instruments
(861). For further details, see Lydall (1975), pp. 49 et seq., Table 11.

[32] See Lary (1968), p. 102.

[33] Ibid.

[34] See Lin and Ho (1979).

labor force, implies that the demand for manufactured exports, and hence the derived demand for labor in the manufacturing sector, originates predominately in its overseas markets. The problem for the Hong Kong economy is that when overseas demand slackens, its production and employment will inevitably decline. Since the early 1970s, many favorable conditions which Hong Kong possessed have begun to fade. In spite of so much deliberation on the establishment of a New International Economic Order (NIEO) since the sixth special session of the United Nations General Assembly in 1974, developments in this regard have been disappointing. The recent world recession and slow recovery have accentuated the rapidly gathering protectionism. During the latter half of the 1970s, Hong Kong concluded a long series of bilateral voluntary export restraint (VER) agreements with the major importing countries.[35] In these trade pacts, the imprint of rising protectionist pressure is visible in various degrees. Because of its relatively more advanced status and sizable volume of manufactured exports, Hong Kong has been discriminated against in some major restriction schemes.

In view of the dominant role of textiles and clothing in Hong Kong's industrial structure, the long-term effects of such trade pacts will no doubt blunt the growth momentum of the economy which is highly dependent on export trade. An increasing number of LDCs have successfully jumped on to the export industrialism bandwagon and undermined Hong Kong's competitive supremacy in traditional labor-intensive light manufactures. Since Hong Kong has little, if any, bargaining power, and there is no room for retreat, it must continue to rely on its proven ability to produce and sell. Therefore, subject to squeezes at both ends, how to trade up and broaden its industrial base in order to enhance its external competitiveness and minimize its vulnerability to external shocks and changes is of vital concern to the Hong Kong economy.

[35] A detailed account of the past and recent developments in textile and clothing trade pacts is furnished in a recent research report by the Hong Kong and Shanghai Banking Corporation (1978).

IV. The Past Record of Diversification Effort

The rapid and continual economic growth in the past two or three decades has lifted the Hong Kong economy out of the developing world into the ranks of the advanced developing countries. But this new status has also left it more vulnerable to the vagaries and vicissitudes of a rapidly changing external environment including Western recession, rising protectionist practices, and growing challenges from other advanced developing countries, notably South Korea, Taiwan, and Singapore. Hong Kong has, since the later 1970s, been undergoing a fretful stage of survival adjustment. It is against this general background that the government set up a 16-man Advisory Committee on Diversification (hereafter ACD) under the chairmanship of the Financial Secretary, Sir Philip Haddon-Cave, a supporter of laissez-fairism, in October 1977, to study the prospect for diversification of the Hong Kong economy.[36] The main findings and recommendations[37] of the ACD are presented in a 336-page report plus 88 pages of annexes, published in late 1979. The report was not well received by many businessmen and economic analysts. It was criticized for suggesting little more than what has already been publicly debated. Many critics object to the recommendations of increasing government

---

[36] As specified in its terms of reference, the ACD was required to consider: (i) the principal factors which have contributed to Hong Kong's economic growth over the past 15 years; (ii) the past, present and likely future course of the regulation of international trade in textiles and the implications for the growth of the economy; (iii) the factors which have been influential in attracting or deterring the establishment of new activities in the manufacturing and other sectors of the economy in recent years, including: (a) financial facilities, (b) fiscal policies, (c) land policies and procedures, (d) policies relating to education and industrial training, and (e) comparative practices in comparable economies which have successfully encouraged the establishment of new industries; and to advise: whether the process of diversification of the economy, with particular reference to the manufacturing sector, can be facilitated by the modification of existing policies or the introduction of new policies. For further details, see Government Secretariat, *Report of the Advisory Committee on Diversification 1979*, Hong Kong: Government Printer, November 1979 (hereafter referred to as *ACD Report*).

[37] Taken together, there are 47 specific recommendations imparted in the *ACD Report*, embracing 4 items on Hong Kong's economic relationship with China, 8 items on land utilization and development policies, 5 items on financial and related facilities, 17 items on education and manpower training, 4 items on industrial precision development, 5 items on trade and industrial investment promotion, 2 items on the conduct of external commercial relations, and 2 miscellaneous issues.

intrusion and assistance on the grounds of efficient allocation of resources under the free enterprise system.[38] However, it is almost impossible for a trade-dependent island to maintain the free market mechanism. Moreover, the market itself has inherent defects, one of which is a lack of long-range vision. So, with changing circumstances, some government intervention in the economy seems inevitable. Perhaps the *ACD Report* can best be viewed as a watershed in the history of economic development of Hong Kong for the government to take up the paternal role of an active overseer of the economy.

The drive for diversification has become a commonplace development strategy in most LDCs, export-oriented or otherwise. A priori, it seems reasonable to expect that concentration on a limited range of exportables or markets would give rise to instability.[39] Obviously, in the case of an export-led economy like Hong Kong's, the problem is greatly compounded. Diversification, on the other hand, has the advantage of obtaining compensation elsewhere when adverse conditions are encountered in certain products or markets.

1. Concept of Diversification

The idea of diversification has been aired in Hong Kong for a number of years. However, it is disturbing to note that it is sometimes seen as a panacea for all Hong Kong's economic maladies. There is also a tendency to talk about diversification exclusively in terms of the creation and development of new industries, the implication being that old and traditional industries can be neglected or even abandoned. This is not only misleading, but can also be dangerous. As the word has been used in different senses, it would be appropriate to spend a few lines on the meaning and objectives of diversification.

In the words of Robinson, diversification is "the lateral expansion of firms neither in the direction of their existing main products, as with horizontal integration, nor in the direction of supplies and outlets, as with vertical integration, but in the direction of other different, but often broadly similar, activities."[40] In a similar manner Gort defines diversification in terms of "heterogeneity of output from

---

[38] See Ho (December 1979), pp. 34 *et seq.*

[39] Cf., for instance, Massell (1970), and Erb and Schiavo-Campo (1969).

[40] See E.A.G. Robinson, *The Structure of Competitive Industry*, London: Cambridge University Press, 1958, p. 114. Cited in Utton (1979), p. 3.

the point of view of the number of markets served by the output."[41]
Quite a number of subsequent writers have taken largely the same
view.[42] These definitions delineate, at best, only one specific form of
diversification, lateral diversification. In the *ACD Report*, diversification is defined as: "A process whereby resources are continually re-
deployed in response to shifting market conditions, to changes in the
availability and relative costs of factors of production, and the
technological innovations."[43] This laconic statement rightly charts out
the future course not only of Hong Kong's industrial development,
but also of any market economy. As a definition, however, it should
not be accepted uncritically. It can be envisaged that the end result of
such continual reallocation of resources and profit maximization
exertion in response to changing market conditions may result in a
higher degree of industrial specialization rather than diversification.

Basically, the conceptual definition of diversification has something
to do with the minimization of risk. In simple words, the loss in one
investment is likely to be offset by gain in another, so that the overall
risk is reduced. This basic concept applies equally well to national
economies.

Two types of diversification can be distinguished: product and
market diversification. Product diversification can be further differentiated into vertical and horizontal diversification.

As regards market diversification, two common forms can also be
differentiated: domestic and foreign market diversification. From the
standpoint of a national economy which is export-propelled with a
small domestic base, such as Hong Kong, foreign market diversification is much more important and relevant. Diversification must
take a long time to achieve, and this is especially so with a national
economy. Moreover, even when it is achieved, all diversification can
do is to reduce overall risk, or in the case of a national economy,
reduce its vulnerability to external shocks, cyclical fluctuations and

---

[41] Cited in Utton (1979), p. 3.

[42] The focal point of such a traditional view was on the lateral diversification of individual firms rather than on the industrial diversification of the economy as a whole.
Of course, one may argue that the diversification of overall industrial structure should
be an aggregate result of the individual drive. But this end result is only an ex post
summary indication and thus may not be the socially desired one. For some further
definitional discussion of diversification, interested readers may refer to Utton (1979),
pp. 3 *et seq.*

[43] See *ACD Report*, p. 7.

capricious consumer tastes in world markets.

2. Past Record of Diversification

Hong Kong has come a long way from the days when it was still a relatively obscure entrepot, and produced mainly cheap, "bazaar" type of goods. Despite the fact that the export concentration ratios, as shown in Tables 2 and 3 above, have experienced very few variations throughout the postwar years, much has been done to trade up and diversify, both productwise and marketwise, and the increasingly harsh trade restraints and growing competition have no doubt precipitated efforts in these directions. This seemingly contradictory phenomenon of diversification within concentration should be seen in proper perspective. The concentration measures in economic literature, however defined, are only an ex post summary indicator of the overall industrial performance at large. For one thing, they cannot reflect the development of trading-up along an existing line of prduction, and of interindustry and intraindustry adjustments to events in the past.

a. Interindustrial and Intraindustrial Diversification

Undoubtedly, over the past two or three decades, a great deal of diversification, both interindustrially and intraindustrially, has taken place in response to changing political and market conditions in Hong Kong. Interindustrially, in the postwar years, many new industries have emerged and grown. In the manufacturing sector, the most prominent are of course plastics and electronics, which started in the early fifties and late fifties respectively. There are other new secondary industries such as watches and clocks, travel goods, precision instruments, and genuine and imitation jewelleries. There are also quite a number of transient fads and low-wage industries, such as wigs, enamelware and rattanware, which, in the course of economic development, have boomed and declined.

Intraindustrially, textiles is a notable case in point. The industry began with only a few rope-making, weaving and knitting cottage establishments. It was not until the late 1940s that cotton spinning mills were set up in Hong Kong when several textile industrialists from Shanghai moved their newly ordered machinery here. Thanks to the system of Commonwealth Preference which gave Hong Kong considerable tariff concessions, the industry expanded rapidly in the

1950s. Since then the industry has been diversifying both vertically and horizontally; vertically from cotton spinning and weaving to bleaching and dyeing, stencilling and printing, and horizontally from cotton to wool, silk and man-made fibers, from low-count spinning to high-count spinning, from grey goods to carpets and rugs, from common printed fabrics to high-quality printed fabrics.

From a modest start in the early 1950s, the clothing industry has diversified horizontally from basic items like knitted underwear, sweat shirts, children attire and gloves to model leisure wear, well-tailored outer garments, and high fashion dresses. The quality and value-added content of all these items have been improving. Since the late 1950s the industry has been the largest export earner and employer in Hong Kong. It has replaced Italy as the world's leading exporter of clothing since 1975. The development and maturing of the industry was in part the natural result of growth, and in part a response to Western trade restrictions on Hong Kong's clothing exports. Quota restrictions are set in terms of quantity rather than value, and so the obvious way to increase sales receipts was to laterally diversify and manufacture up. However, unlike textiles proper, which has become relatively capital-intensive in the course of development, the manufacturing of clothing still involves relatively labor-intensive processes. Also, unlike the textiles industry, which supplies a large proportion of its output to the clothing manufactures, the growth performance of clothing can be assessed almost entirely by reference to exports.[44]

The two other leading industries, electronics and plastics, follow much the same pattern of product sophistication and diversification. The electronics industry began only in 1959 with a couple of factories engaged in the assembly of transistor radios from almost wholly imported parts. The industry is increasingly manufacturing component parts both for its own use and for exports. It replaced the textiles industry as the second largest export earner in the mid-1970s. It is also interesting to note that, as distinct from other manufacturing industries, the electronics industry has relied very heavily on direct foreign capital participation since its inception.

The plastics industry had its humble origins in the early fifties producing mainly artificial flowers and simple domestic wares. Now, the industry has not only diversified into a variety of decorative articles,

---

[44] See *ACD Report*, p. 45, note 69.

household utensils, and fiber-glass reinforced plastic furniture, but has also become the world's largest supplier of toys since 1972. Apart from both vertically and laterally moving up-market there is an increasingly upward trend in the use of high-quality plastics in place of conventional materials, such as rubber and leather, in the manufacture of footwear, garments, handbags, as well as shells and frames for consumer electronics.

The growth of the manufacturing of watches and clocks exemplifies the diversification resilience of Hong Kong. The industry has developed from making watch and clock accessories to become one of the world's leading watch exporters. The industry has witnessed a dynamic one thousand-fold increase over the past one and a half decades. By 1978, Hong Kong had replaced Switzerland as the world's largest exporter of watches by quantity and in terms of value was the third largest after Switzerland and Japan.[45] Virtually unknown before the 1970s, electronic digital watches presently account for well over half of Hong Kong's exports of complete watches. Digital watches have already been replaced by liquid crystal display (LCD) timepieces, as a quick response to changing consumer tastes. Electronic quartz analogues, actively promoted by the world's other leading watch suppliers such as Japan and Switzerland in recent years, are also being rapidly caught up by Hong Kong's watch manufacturers. It is interesting to note that Hong Kong was initially, and still is, an important supplier of watch parts, especially cases and bracelets, for Switzerland, which are accepted by the trade as fully up-to-grade merchandise.[46]

It is clear that product diversification of all forms has been going on in Hong Kong, though not without fitful moments of agony and irritation. Moreover, raising the value-added content of its exportables, the linkage effect, both forward and backward, has also been greatly enhanced. For instance, the early textiles industry developed forward linkage from the traditional weaving and spinning to clothing manufacturing. The electronics industry developed backward linkage from the assembling of electronic components to the manufacture of the components. These processes of linkage formation have permitted Hong Kong to, in Hirschman's words, "bite off as large pieces of value added at a time as the underdeveloped country can possibly

---

[45] See Hong Kong Trade Development Council (1979), p. 1.
[46] *Ibid*, p. 15.

digest."[47]

b. Market Diversification

Diversification in the market sense has also been taking place concomitantly with the rise of new industries and products. In its earlier stage of industrialization, the United Kingdom and other British Commonwealth countries accounted for the predominant share of Hong Kong's exports, mainly because of the Imperial Preference system. In 1955, the United Kingdom alone took around 20 percent of Hong Kong's total exports while the other Commonwealth countries took another 20 percent. The United States, in contrast, accounted for a meager two percent of its global exports while the share of other industrial nations, like West Germany and Japan, were negligible. After the institution of the "certificate of origin" system, however, the United States market has expanded by leaps and bounds to become Hong Kong's largest export market. In the meantime, other rich industrial countries have also increased in their relative importance. Some of these developments were quite gradual, as with the Dutch, Swedish, Swiss and Japanese markets, while others were more pronounced, such as the rapid rise of the West German market. West Germany has overtaken the United Kingdom as Hong Kong's second largest export outlet since the mid-1970s. On the other hand, the market shares of the United Kingdom and other Commonwealth countries have evidenced a relative decline, especially as a result of the termination of the Imperial Preference system.[48] In recent years, Hong Kong has also diversified into new markets in East Europe, the Middle East, Latin America and even Africa with some success.

c. Tourism Expansion

The same trend can be seen at work in the non-manufacturing sectors, notably tourism. The industry began on a very modest scale, with only a few hotels relying mainly on Hong Kong's reputation as a shopping paradise.[49] It did not become an organized industry until the

---

[47] See Hirschman (1958), p. 119.

[48] A detailed analysis of the effects of the rise and fall of the Imperial Preference system on Hong Kong's export performance with respect to the Commonwealth countries is given in Lin and Mok (1980), pp. 26-31.

[49] According to Hong Kong Tourist Association's estimates, tourist shopping, on the average, accounted for well over 60 percent of total tourists' expenditures in Hong Kong during the period 1961-79.

establishment of the Hong Kong Tourist Association in 1957, but now has become one of the major pillars of the Hong Kong economy. In recent years, Hong Kong has become the venue for a growing number of international meetings by business groups and professional organizations.[50] More recently, owing to the changing political and economic relationship between China and the West, a new dimension affecting Hong Kong's tourism industry is the high priority being accorded to China tourism. Many of the rapidly increasing numbers of visitors to China enter and leave via Hong Kong, and an excellent relationship has been established between the Hong Kong Tourist Association and the tourism authorities in China. The tourism industry has triggered off a rapid growth of related businesses such as hotels, airlines, travel agencies, tourist shops, tailoring and catering establishments, that contribute significantly to Hong Kong's aggregate employment and income.[51]

d. Financial Diversification

Whereas even as recently as a decade ago Hong Kong had only one type of bank, the licensed commercial bank engaged mainly in the retail banking business, there was little, if any, functional specialization and institutional diversification.[52] It was not until 1970 that merchant banks appeared. Since then a host of similar institutions ranging from joint ventures or subsidiaries of multinational concerns to small local finance companies have proliferated. In 1976 they were given a collective title of "deposit-taking companies" (DTCs) by the regulatory authorities.[53] Generally speaking, the multinational DTCs tend to specialize in loan syndications, foreign exchange and money market dealings, underwriting, corporate and project finance, portfolio management, and financial consultancy services. The smaller

---

[50] In 1979 Hong Kong attracted 143 international conferences and meetings with an overseas attendance of more than 29,500, an increase of more than 100 percent over the attendance figure in the previous year.

[51] A fuller discussion of the role of tourism in Hong Kong's economic development is given in Lin and Wong (1979).

[52] Cf. Jao (1974), p. 69.

[53] One common characteristic that distinguishes the DTCs from the licensed commercial banks is their exclusion from the retail end of banking business—under the 1976 Deposit-taking Companies Ordinance they are not allowed to maintain checking accounts and to accept time deposits of less than HK$50,000. They are also not allowed to use the word "bank" in their title. Apart from these limitations, however, they are given a free rein to transact every conceivable wholesale banking business.

local DTCs, on the other hand, lacking capital resources, professional expertise and international connections, tend to specialize in the local stock market, consumer mortgage and personal loans. The aggressive actions of these newly emergent financial intermediaries, especially those multinational giants, have no doubt sharpened competition and tended to undermine the entrenched positions of the established commercial banks, particularly in the area of wholesale banking.[54]

Hong Kong possesses nearly all the elements of a viable financial center. The city-state is centrally located in the Asian Pacific region, supported by a natural harbor and an excellent transport and tele-communication network. Its time-zone position and flexible working hours enable it to engage in arbitrage operations between the Atlantic and Pacific seaboard centers. Being a gateway to China, it is a magnet for both multinational banks and non-bank financial intermediaries anxious to establish or strengthen business ties with China. Financially, as was mentioned earlier, Hong Kong is blessed with a free foreign exchange market, a prudent fiscal system with simple tax structure and low tax rates, and a relatively stable currency. It is therefore not surprising that Hong Kong today is the center of hundreds of international banking and near-banking institutions transacting the whole gamut of retail and wholesale banking business.[55] It is estimated that, of the top 100 commercial banks of the world, over 80 are now operating in Hong Kong in one form or another.[56] Furthermore, both banking operations and money market activities have become increasingly internationally oriented,[57] and in recent years, Hong Kong has also witnessed an influx of international money brokers, exchange

---

[54] By offering competitive interest rates in the market, DTCs are able to absorb an increasingly high volume of deposits from the public at the expense of the licensed banks in Hong Kong. At the end of 1979, deposit liabilities of the 269 DTCs in Hong Kong reached HK$24,495 million, equivalent to 36 percent of aggregate bank deposits. This reflected the rapid financial penetration of DTCs in Hong Kong when compared with the corresponding share of 17.4 percent in December 1978. (Balance-sheet statistics of DTCs are available only from the end of 1978.)

[55] Aside from the 269 DTCs, at the end of 1979, there were 115 licensed banks with 1,011 banking offices and 114 representative offices of foreign banks in Hong Kong.

[56] Cf. Beazer (1978), p. 97.

[57] For instance, a notable balance-sheet item that highlights the growing internationalization of banking operation in Hong Kong is the phenomenal growth of "loans and advances abroad" from HK$204 million in December 1969 to HK$45,556 million in December 1979. The relative share of such offshore loans in total bank credit rose in the same ten-year period from only 2.6 to 37.5 percent.

dealers, and securities houses. Together with Singapore, Hong Kong is now one of the twin Asian dollar centers in the region. In the past, Singapore has acted largely as a funding center for offshore loans emanating from Hong Kong's banking offices. This was to a large extent due to the relatively favorable tax situation in Hong Kong, but recent changes in this respect have tilted the balance more in Singapore's favor.[58]

Another significant dimension of financial diversification is the establishment of a free gold market in 1974 and a commodity market in 1977. Trading in silver, suspended in 1935 when Hong Kong followed China in abandoning the silver standard, was also reactivated in June 1978.[59] Hong Kong's rise as a leading financial center in the Asian-Pacific region is itself an unmistakable sign of the maturity and diversification of the economy.[60]

e. Infrastructural Improvements

The internal infrastructure of Hong Kong has also been undergoing a rapid process of diversification and growth in adapting itself to the changing structure of the economy. It has been very quick to start the containerization of its port, now one of the four largest terminals in the world. Besides serving its own needs, the terminal has also attracted considerable feeder traffic from neighboring countries which lack such facilities. Hong Kong is the world's seventh largest port in terms of tonnages of shipping using its facilities and sea cargo handled. Its air cargo industry is also among the top ten in the world.[61] A cross-harbor tunnel has been in operation for eight years, and with the recent opening of the initial stage of the mass transit

---

[58] Prior to the fiscal year 1978/79, Hong Kong was an absolute tax haven for offshore banking operation profits. However, as from April 1978, the government imposed a standard profits tax rate of 17 percent on net interest income from offshore loans and related transactions arranged by banks and other financial institutions in Hong Kong.

[59] Cf. Hislop (1977), p. 25.

[60] For some further expository discussion of the factors responsible for Hong Kong's rise as a financial center as well as the growth and structural changes that have taken place in Hong Kong's banking system and other financial sectors over the past decade, interested readers may refer to Jao (1979) and Li (1979).

[61] It is reckoned that the volume of freight forwarded by air carriers accounted for more than 20 percent of Hong Kong's domestic exports in terms of value, and about one-third of the re-export trade (see *Hong Kong 1980,* Hong Kong Government Printer, 1980, pp. 159-160).

railway Hong Kong has entered an era of high-speed commuting.

An equally important aspect of widening the economic base is the social and educational infrastructure. Barely two decades ago, Hong Kong had only one university and one technical college with a combined enrollment of about 1,500. Today, it has two universities with a total full-time enrollment of nearly 11,000, one polytechnic with a full-time enrollment of about 7,100 and part-time enrollment of over 18,000. In addition, there are four technical institutes with a combined enrollment of another 24,500. The diversification into, and expansion of, technical and vocational education is of pivotal importance to the Hong Kong economy, if opportunities for diversification are to be well exploited.

Hong Kong has come a long way since the early postwar years when it was still a relatively obscure trading port. The economic base has been widened so that Hong Kong today is an internationally renowned manufacturing and financial center. Concomitant with this buoyant diversification record, the living standard of its population has also improved markedly. Its industrial wages are now the highest in Asia after Japan and its professional salaries are among the highest in the world. Despite its success, it is still far from achieving the goal of a truly diversified economy. What makes diversification most urgent today is Hong Kong's need to sustain its economic growth and to provide employment opportunities for a population of more than five million when the industrialized world has lost faith in expanding global trade in the interests of all. In view of this rising tide of protectionism along with the increasingly government-induced competition from other newly industrialized countries, notably South Korea, Taiwan and Singapore, some moderate step away from the cherished policy of "positive non-interventionism" seems inevitable.

V. Constraints upon Growth and the Future Course of Diversification

1. Demand-side Considerations

As regards the demand side, the ACD points out that in an economy as responsive to changes in world trading environment as Hong Kong, the major determinants of and constraints on growth are the expansion in world trade volume, the shifts in commodity composition of world demand and the changes in the disposition of other economies, particularly those major industrialized countries, to permit their demands to be supplied from external sources.[62]

Conceivably, an export-led economy such as Hong Kong gravitates to external development, especially those emanating from the demand side. Worst of all, as a dependent British enclave, Hong Kong has virtually no bargaining power in international trade councils. Thus in all its past conduct of external commercial relations, Hong Kong has relied heavily on the letter and spirit of international trade instruments, particularly those under the auspices of the General Agreement on Tariffs and Trade (GATT), and on the skill of its negotiators. So far, Hong Kong has been able to maintain its quotas largely in the form of VER under bilateral agreements. The VER system has enabled Hong Kong to maximize the utilization of the limited quantities available in response to overseas demand. Since Hong Kong undertakes voluntary restraint, it enjoys the right to allocate its quota internally.[63]

The implementation of import quotas goes through a process of increasing severity. In recent years, quite a number of importing countries have introduced a unilateral global quota system in lieu of the VER agreements. The possible proliferation of this practice is a real threat to the future growth of Hong Kong's textiles and clothing industries. At a time when nearly all the industrialized countries are

---

[62] In an analysis of the determinants of Hong Kong's export expansion, it is found that the increase was mainly attributable to the world trade expansion and shifts in commodity composition of world demand. See Lin, Mok and Ho (1980), pp. 122-125.

[63] This is undoubtedly better than when export control is exercised at the importing country. It can retain all the economic rent by pushing up prices as high as the market can competitively bear. The internal distribution of the "quota rent" is a different matter. As regards the internal allocation of quotas, there is much public controversy about the right of quota-holders to sell their quotas to other manufacturers and exporters who have either no or insufficient quotas. When overseas demand is strong and there are not enough quotas to meet with, the premium for quota transfer can reach an outrageous level. In some circumstances a holder may find it even more profitable to sell his quotas rather than to produce and fulfill the quotas himself. Although the then Department of Commerce and Industry, following a major review in 1976, devised a set of measures to curb profiteering by "quota farmer," loopholes still remained. Furthermore, it is widely felt that the present allocation system favors the large and well-established firms, whose market strength is entrenched by the difficulties of new entrants in obtaining sufficient quotas.

coming under increasing pressure from within their economies to protect their domestic industries, it may no longer be sufficient to rest on those GATT instruments and on the tact of mono-negotiation to preserve Hong Kong's right of access to overseas markets. Where institutional arrangements so permit, as pointed out by the Advisory Committee, Hong Kong should unite with other LDCs in contesting protectionist measures and policies in the industrialized world. In order to enhance the effectiveness of its future bilateral negotiations, the Committee also suggests that information-gathering and representational activities of the existing overseas offices of the Trade, Industry and Customs Department should be further strengthened.[64]

Because of the extreme dependence of the Hong Kong economy on overseas markets, its ability to diversify must ultimately depend on whether its products will have access to such markets. So far textiles and garments are the main products that suffer most from import controls abroad. An obvious corollary is that Hong Kong should diversify into or give more priority to those industries that are not affected by quota restrictions. But if the present tide of protectionist sentiment is not going to be checked, it will very likely spread to other products. Then the desired effects of broadening the manufacturing base will be discounted greatly. That is why the recent rise of protectionism in industrialized countries is so disturbing. Another immediate logical development is market diversification. This has the advantage that it is principally concerned with export promotion, and does not involve direct structural change. But, for a number of reasons, the scope for this kind of maneuver is quite limited. In spite of the fact that in recent years Hong Kong has diversified into new markets such as East Europe, the Middle East, Latin America and Africa, it is rather doubtful whether these markets can grow to absorb a significant portion of Hong Kong's global exports. The average consumer in East Europe has much less freedom of consumption choice than his counterpart in the West, while in the oil-rich countries of the Middle East, the relatively small size of their population along with high income disparity tends greatly to impair their capacity to import merchandise from Hong Kong. Penetration into such markets is

---

[64] Many a time when Hong Kong had become observant of its negotiating partners' intention to seek more restrictive schemes, that intention had already become firm policy. This experience indicates that Hong Kong should try to collect reliable on-the-spot information and try to influence attitudes as quickly and effectively as possible.

hampered, furthermore, by government controls on trade, exchange regulations and political obstacles.

Protectionism is no doubt the greatest growth constraint for an open economy such as Hong Kong. But one should not adopt an overly pessimistic attitude. There is still much room for product sophistication even within the existing range of manufactures, for the essence of the various restraint agreements has been to specify a maximum growth rate in quantity, but not in value. A feasible way to beat such quantitative restrictions is to shift towards higher value-added manufactures. Higher value-added exports entail continuous upgrading of products, particularly those under restraint agreements of one form or another. This is the direction in which Hong Kong's local manufacturers should move in the future. But the success of such a move is dependent on supply-side factors.

2. Supply-side Considerations

a. Deficiency in Manpower Training

If Hong Kong's industries are to move further up-market technologically, there will be a much greater demand for trained manpower and skilled technicians, currently in short supply. Although Hong Kong's hardworking and adaptable labor force has contributed to the growth momentum of the economy, one frequent criticism of Hong Kong's laborers is that their average technical and general education attainments are comparatively low. On the basis of all industries surveyed in the early 1970s, operatives and general workers account for 75 percent of total employment; craftsmen and technicians only account for 19 percent and less than 6 percent respectively.[65] The 1976 By-Census reveals that 96 percent of the employed population in the manufacturing sector have not acquired technical and vocational training, while the corresponding figure for the tertiary sector was estimated to be 89 percent.[66] It was also found that at that time about 59 percent of the labor force had received no secondary education. By 1978, the comparable statistic was about 56 percent.[67] In an effort to improve the technical skills of the labor force, the government had developed, since the setting up of the Hong Kong

---

[65] For detailed figures, see Hetherington and others (1971), Appendix F.

[66] See *ACD Report,* p. 223, note 279.

[67] *Ibid.,* p. 29, note 49.

Training Council in 1973, a network of industry training boards designed to meet the requirements of specific industries. But the scope of industrial training initiated by the Hong Kong Training Council is obviously inadequate to produce the skilled manpower required by industry and commerce. This has stemmed from the fact that only two out of the eight training schemes so far prepared by the Training Council are being properly implemented. The ACD points out that the failure of the remaining schemes to get off the ground is attributed principally to government's existing policy that industry should pay for its own training through individual levies.[68]

The persistent insufficiency of trained manpower which has hampered the progress of trading-up in Hong Kong is a classic instance of the doctrine of externalities. In the early stage of Hong Kong's industrial development, only relatively unskilled labor and simple technology were needed. These were in abundant supply because of external inflows. Under these conditions, the free market performed well. But what worked well in the past may not work tomorrow. There can be no doubt that, with changing circumstances, the government has found it difficult to maintain its non-interventionist attitude.

Amongst other general education recommendations, the ACD also recommends that Hong Kong should in the future subsidize all industrial training from the general revenue in lieu of the existing levies. To implement the proposed subsidization schemes the ACD also suggests that the existing non-statutory Hong Kong Training Council should be reorganized into a statutory Industrial Training Authority which would forecast manpower needs, plan training programs and coordinate their implementation with other existing technical institutes and the Hong Kong Polytechnic.

Apart from industry-specific training, an overall manpower policy embodying wider-scope training and longer-term plans should be emphasized. Training should not be only for existing industries but also with the purpose of promoting new industries and training of skills which are common to industry at large. Furthermore, one should guard against the simplistic notion that the training of specific skills is all that is needed. It is conceivable that a man with a good general education can adapt quickly to changes in the labor market, while a man trained for only a specific skill may have difficulty in

---

[68] *Ibid.*, p. 248.

doing so. This suggests that both general and technical education should develop side by side. They are by no means competitive but rather complementary.

b. Poor Technical Infrastructure

One of the factors inhibiting Hong Kong's efforts to move up-market is that most individual manufacturing industries include few large firms which are surrounded by a large number of small-scale establishments whose activities are largely responsive to subcontracting orders.[69] Many of these small firms lack both the capability to absorb new and advanced technologies and the resources to invest in plant and equipment incorporating such technologies. In addition, Hong Kong's efforts to encourage product and process improvements may also be hindered by the lack of technical back-up services, such as product testing, quality certification, calibration and measurement facilities, for manufacturing industries as a whole. Their significance is evidenced by the fact that as manufacturers move up-market, they are increasingly subject to a requirement by overseas importers that their products meet standards of quality and assurances of consumer safety.

Hong Kong's manufacturing industries have reached the stage where they need a more comprehensive range of industrial support facilities and technical back-up services, but there is little incentive or ability to invest in such technical infrastructure. The need for an adequate range of these facilities and services is further underlined by the fact that Hong Kong's neighboring Asian competitors have already provided, to a greater or lesser degree, such arrangements for their domestic industries.[70]

To redress Hong Kong's technological deficiencies, the ACD recommends that the Hong Kong Productivity Centre undergo some

---

[69] The average size of Hong Kong's industrial enterprise is small by any international standard. Two decades ago, the average number of workers per factory was about 39; by 1979, the average number dwindled to only 20.

[70] For instance, South Korea has an Institute of Science and Technology, Fine Instruments Center, Industrial Advancement Administration, and a Scientific and Technological Information Center. Taiwan boasts an Industrial Technology Research Institute and National Science Council, National Bureau of Standards, Metal Industries Development Center, and a Machine Tool Development Center. Singapore also has an Institute of Standards and Industrial Research, which provides a wide range of technical back-up services.

drastic expansion so as to undertake the coordination of research and development activities, technology transfers and technical information services. The existing testing and standards centers of the Hong Kong Federation of Industries and Chinese Manufacturers's Association should be upgraded and amalgamated into one independent, far-ranging quality certification, calibration and industrial standards center. To cater to existing needs, industrially-oriented research should also be emphasized. Finally, the Advisory Committee suggests that an Industrial Development Board be established to plan, monitor, advise and coordinate programs for industrial diversification.

The recommendations just mentioned can largely be adopted, but the Advisory Committee has said too little on how research and development (R & D) can be assimilated, on how foreign technology can be scrutinized and attuned, and on how technical information can be diffused. Above all, nothing has been mentioned on the financial implications of their implementations. Aside from such deficiences, an active policy for both product and process innovation should be encouraged, and not a policy just to purvey industry-specific needs. Basic research common to industries at large should also be emboldened. This may be undertaken by the concerted effort of government, industry and academic institutions. Furthermore, instead of being confined to the coordination of industrial promotion matters, the scope of the proposed Industrial Development Board may be broadened to a coordinating body for all factors of production.

c. Shortage of Industrial Land

Of all the factors of production, land has been and will continue to be the scarcest factor in Hong Kong. An interesting economic feature in Hong Kong is its land tenure policy. Title to all land in Hong Kong is held by the British Crown, which in turn leases land to the private developers.[71] The so-called "land owners" in Hong Kong are in reality tenants of the Crown who hold land subject to the terms of

---

[71] In the early days, Crown leases when first granted ran for periods of 75 or 99 years, with a few for 999 years. They have now been made uniform in the urban areas of Hong Kong island and Kowloon to a term of 75 years, usually renewable for a further 75 years at a reassessed Crown rent. In the New Territories and New Kowloon new leases will terminate three days prior to the expiration of the lease with China on July 1, 1997.

their Crown lease and also to resumption for various public purposes. This is a far cry from free enterprise in land. The leases are generally sold at public auctions. The terrain at auctions simply goes to the highest bidder, which presumably assures that land is allocated to those able to use it most efficiently and that the government gets the greatest possible revenue from the transaction for the community. The underlying principle is that the community creates the development potential in land[72] and, therefore, if a developer wishes to purchase land for development, or to redevelop land held under an existing lease, he must pay the market price to the community for this valuable right. Implicit in this principle is the belief that if land were not sold at its market value to a developer, the community would be the loser and developers would make even larger profits.[73]

The perennial shortage of land has resulted in exorbitantly high prices for land in general and for industrial land in particular. During the period 1959-79, the average industrial land price from government auctions rose from HK$105 per square meter in 1959 to HK$13,876 per square meter in 1979, a compound growth rate of about 28 percent per annum.[74] The high industrial land prices have encouraged a concentration on those light industries which can operate in multi-storey factory buildings and have discouraged the development of capital- and land-intensive industries.

The effect of high land prices will permeate every sector of the economy. Whether high land prices mean to each exporting firm either a cut in profit or an increase in the price of the final products,

---

[72] The demand for land, like any other factor of production, is a derived demand. That is to say, the value of land, as reflected by its price, is simply derived from the value of its final products rather than vice versa.

[73] This is the theory; in practice the shortage of land and accommodation results in the price paid by the developer at a public auction being passed on to the final user in addition to the profit element.

[74] An analysis of government land auction data shows the following average land prices by industrial and non-industrial uses (excluding New Territories):

Year/Period	Industrial	Commercial	Residential
HK$/Square Meter			
1959	104.85	1,668.44	164.59
1969	877.20	17,285.88	439.24
1979	13,876.10	70,967.74	14,327.89

* For other yearly figures, see "A Study of Land Values in Hong Kong," *Hang Seng Economic Quarterly*, April 1980, p. 7, Table 1.

it will always be to the detriment of Hong Kong's export competitiveness in world markets. Moreover, when capital gains from property speculation are astronomic, an increasing amount of the economy's savings would be channelled to such speculation which is not only inflationary but also nonproductive. The real estate boom in recent years has clearly exerted considerable strain on the manufacturing industries, not the least of which is a substantial rise in rentals and land prices. The boom has also generated a diversion of resources into real estate speculation, some of which may become a permanent loss to the manufacturing sector. This is particularly true when manufacturers shift their industrial land and premises to property development and the capital proceeds obtained are not re-injected into the manufacturing sector.

In view of the fact that the government is the ultima de jure landlord and by far the largest producer of land in Hong Kong, it has been both widely felt and publicly discussed that the provision of land for industry is one area in which the government alone can make a major contribution to the broadening of the economy's base in particular via the establishment of new industries by leasing land to them at preferential terms. In hindsight, the government land production policy during the 1950s and early 1960s was based on an incremental approach without any overall plan; land was provided only after the need became apparent. The provision of industrial sites on a planned basis became a priority consideration in the early 1970s, but the criterion for granting land at preferential prices to new industries employing high-technology manufacturing processes was mainly based on the creation of employment opportunities in areas where new housing projects were contemplated.[75] In other words it was not based on the likely demand for land by industrialists. It was not until very recently that the government decided to establish specific industrial estates, with a view to widening the industrial base and facilitating the establishment of new firms that complement the existing industrial structure. Subsequently, the Hong Kong Industrial Estates Corporation was established by statute in 1977 to implement this new policy.[76] However, even at concessionary prices the available

---

[75] This approach was facilitated by the Hong Kong Outline Plan in 1970 (the plan was inaugurated in the mid-1960s), which laid down spatial, environmental and other standards to be followed in reserving land for various types of development, including industrial development.

[76] After taking over the responsibilities of the former Hong Kong Industrial Estate

sites are considerably more expensive than those available in neighboring competing economies,[77] so that the cost of industrial land and premises is likely to remain a major deterrent to diversified growth. The government's decision to modify its industrial land policy and to build industrial estates is no doubt a positive step in the right direction. However, although efforts to attract more industrial investment with a higher technological basis are of vital importance to diversification, one should not neglect the importance of the small industrial units which do not qualify for the industrial estates. Such enterprises are still the backbone of Hong Kong's industrial structure,[78] and therefore both the private and public sectors should continue their construction programs of flatted factory buildings to cater to their needs.

d. Financial Lacunae and Deficiencies

Unlike other factors of production, the supply of capital has not constituted an impediment to Hong Kong's diversified growth. It is generally held that the financial sector, particularly those licensed commercial banks, played an active part in the rapid emergence of Hong Kong as a manufacturing center. Commercially viable firms do not seem to have encountered difficulty in raising capital funds from the local financial markets. In addition, business savings have also provided a ready source of capital finance. Aside from providing

---

Provisional Authority in March 1977, the Corporation was immediately charged with the task of developing a 45-hectare industrial estate at Taipo. A year later a further 72-hectare at Yuen Long was added.

[77] For instance in 1978, the first plot of industrial land at Taipo was sold at a concessionary price of HK$484 per square meter (or about HK$45 per square foot) under a 15-year lease to those industrial developers meeting the stringent selection criteria of the Hong Kong Industrial Estates Corporation, as compared with an average price of about HK$12,000 per square meter for other industrial land being sold by public auction. Whereas in South Korea, the cost of land in an industrial estate ranged form about HK$0.50 in Changwon to some HK$60 per square meter in Seoul; and in the Jurong industrial district in Singapore, rentals were between HK$0.48 to HK$0.78 per square foot per year over a period of lease of 30 to 90 years depending on the types of industries concerned. For further details, see Chan (1978).

[78] The available statistics show that the number of those small enterprises employing fewer than 50 workers out of the total establishments prolifcrated from about 80 percent in 1961 to 87 percent in 1971 and then to 92 percent in 1977. Most run on low levels of capital and virtually all of them operate from rented premises. For a detailed account of the contributory role of the small-scale industries in Hong Kong's industrial development, see Sit, Wong and Kiang (1979).

supporting financial services to domestic industries in recent years the
financial sector has also been emerging as a foreign exchange earner
in its own right by directly exporting services to overseas business
and institutions. However, such gratifying developments will by no
means sustain themselves. In fact, there are quite a number of
lacunae and deficiencies in the financial sector.

First, the gradual replacement of labor-intensive industries by those
with a higher capital intensity may give rise to a greater requirement
for long-term financing. Up to now, Hong Kong's business firms
have relied heavily on credits supplied by the commercial banks which
tend to adhere to short-term, self-liquidating loans. Moreover, the
present distribution of bank credit leaves much to be desired. Many
critics point out that only the large and well-established firms have
access to adequate facilities at favorable terms; the smaller firms,
which constitute the overwhelming majority of Hong Kong's business
enterprises do not have easy lines of credit and oftentimes have to rely
on small money lenders for support.[79] While acknowledging that the
problem of long-term finance may become more acute in the future,
the ACD was content to say: "This problem [should] be reviewed
from time to time, and such reviews should take into account
the possible need for an industrial development bank that would
ensure the availability of long-term finance."[80] Hong Kong's
economy has at present reached a stage of development when long-
term finance is more than ever necessary for maintaining its growth
momentum in the face of increasingly stiffer competition in world
markets, and the issue of the establishment of a specialist institution
like an industrial development bank that concentrates on long-term
financing of industrial and infrastructural development should receive
priority consideration.[81]

Second, because of the lack of short-dated government and com-

---

[79] See, for instance, Jao (1968), pp. 55 *et seq.*

[80] *ACD Report,* p. 210

[81] In fact, the government had looked into the idea of an industrial development
bank some two decades ago. An Industrial Bank Committee under the chairmanship of
Sir John J. Cowperthwaite was appointed by the government in 1959 "to advise
whether there was a need for an industrial bank for the financing of industry in Hong
Kong and, if so, whether government would take steps to set up such an institution."
The proposal was turned down by the said Committee as unnecessary. However, it did
not "exclude the possibility that an industrial bank may become necessary, or at least
desirable, at a future stage of development." See *Far Eastern Economic Review,*
XXIX, August 4, 1960, pp. 226-231.

mercial papers, virtually all of the short-term and medium-term financial transactions in the Hong Kong dollar money market are in the form of inter-bank deposits, the use of certificates of deposit (CDs) and bankers acceptances (BAs) being still at an infancy stage.[82] The negotiability of these instruments is still uncertain because of the lack of depth of the secondary market. As the financial sector continues to expand, a broadening of the money market instruments such as CDs and BAs will not only improve its efficiency and flexibility in attracting deposits and funding, but also ultimately benefit the depositor and investor. Seen in this connection, the ACD also urges the government to take an early step to include those local CDs and similar instruments in the formal liquidity ratio calculations for banks and DTCs so as to encourage their proliferation, and assist the development of a secondary market for such instruments in Hong Kong.

The Advisory Committee also urges the government to reform the existing interest withholding tax which yields relatively little revenue and discourages the issue of debt instruments in Hong Kong.[83] It is generally held that a good deal of money goes offshore from Hong Kong into such instruments as US-dollar CDs issued in Singapore, which no longer has a withholding tax on interest, or London and into short-term bank deposits in the London-based Eurodollar or the Singapore-based Asia dollar market. Hong Kong gets no benefit in terms of financial-service earnings from these flows.[84]

---

[82] CDs were introduced unsuccessfully in Hong Kong in 1973 by Slater Walker Securities, but Wardley successfully reactivated this instrument in 1977. By the end of 1979, a total of 16 CDs, amounting to some HK$1 billion, about 1 percent of total deposits in Hong Kong, had been successfully issued. BAs were first launched in mid-1979 by Citibank. However, secondary trading in these instruments is virtually inactive. For further details, see Chen (April 1980).

[83] Interest withholding tax applies to interest arising in or derived from Hong Kong. Tax receipt from such interest earnings in the fiscal year 1978-79 amounted to HK$118 million, representing less than 1 percent of total general government revenue.

[84] However, based on a newly-found tax-avoiding formula, a US-dollar CD issue of US$20 million was introduced in Hong Kong in May 1980 by the local branch of European Asian Bank. Subsequently, the local branch of the Bank of Tokyo also issued a similar US$10 million worth of negotiable, and the local Fuji Bank came in with another US$20 million during the same month. The Hong Kong Government seems to have been convinced that these new US-dollar CDs should be immune from withholding tax under its adopted territorial concept of liability. The implication of this development is that Hong Kong, long a leader on the loan syndication side of the Asian

Finally, as for the need for improved communications between government and the financial sector as well as cooperation amongst the latter's subsectors, the ACD points out that the present arrangements for formal and informal contacts are inadequate. Recently the Financial Secretary, Sir Philip Haddon-Cave, had lamented the apparent unwillingness of the Exchange Bank's Association (EBA)[85] to raise interest rates at a time when inflation was high and the Hong Kong dollar was weakening.[86] More recently many foreign banks here have been mourning that the prime rate is not determined by the market forces of supply and demand, but by the inter-bank rate, which in turn is heavily influenced by certain large, locally incorporated banks. However, the ACD has not commented on the dangers of Hong Kong's financial markets outgrowing their regulatory framework.

With the proliferation of financial institutions in Hong Kong and an increasingly complex international environment, the need for local interest rates and exchange rates to be able to adjust quickly to world economic forces is obvious. The frequent and regular consultations between government and EBA, particularly on monetary matters, is no doubt instrumental in determining such things as the level of interest rates, but the recent proposal to incorporate by statute the informal EBA, needs some careful reconsideration. For an extremely open and trade-dependent economy like Hong Kong, any measure to be introduced should be aimed at regulating the market concerned so as to provide a robust and dependable framework within which market forces could operate, not at directing and controlling the market itself. Obviously, further progress of Hong Kong's financial standing and diversification will depend a great deal on how these lacunae and deficiencies can be remedied.

---

dollar market, has now begun to challenge Singapore's traditional supremacy on the funding side. For further details, see Rowley (1980), pp. 73-74.

[85] EBA is an informal body with voluntary membership. It sets deposit rates under the Interest Rate Ageement reached in July 1964. The said Agreement specifies the maximum interest rates payable by all banks which are divided into five categories, according to their background and size of deposits. The rate differential between each category is 0.25 percent.

[86] For a succinct discussion of the main factors contributing to the recent weakening of the Hong Kong dollar and possible remedial measures, interested readers may refer to Hsing (1979).

3. The China Connection

An analysis of Hong Kong's future economic prospects and course of diversification would not be complete without an examination of its relationship with China. Clearly, the recent, rapid opening of China has given a new dimension to diversification. China's newly-launched modernization programs and active rapprochement with the West will provide ample trade opportunities for Hong Kong. On the one hand, it is clear that China's emphasis on economic construction and increase of exports to earn foreign exchange will reactivate Hong Kong's traditional role as an entrepot for the China trade. In the face of increasing trade protectionism and in a period when manufactured goods are evolving from early stages to more sophisticated and diversified ones, the revival of entrepot trade brought about by China's development programs will be a timely contribution to Hong Kong's overall economic growth. On the other, the opening up of four special economic zones of Shantou, Zhuhai, Shenzhen and Shekou in China, especially the latter two industrial zones, has given Hong Kong a good opportunity to shift such traditional industries as textiles and other relatively labor-intensive industries to the other side of the border. They would otherwise lose their competitive edge in overseas markets as local factory rents and wage levels continue to soar. Meanwhile, Hong Kong will be able to concentrate on developing those relatively capital-intensive and high-technology industries.

On buttressing Hong Kong's role vis-a-vis China's modernization and opening up, the ACD has made the following specific recommendations. First, Hong Kong should improve and augment its transportation infrastructure, particularly those links with neighboring Guangdong,[87] so as to facilitate its re-emerging role as entrepot. Secondly, in order to reap the maximum benefits from China's intensive oil exploration in the South China Sea and Pearl River Estuary, the Committee urged the government to plan actively for the provision of a logistics support base site.[88] Thirdly, in order to take further advantage of China's oil development and facilitate the diversification

---

[87] As regards Hong Kong-Guangdong links, a Chinese team has recently been investigating the feasibility of a six-lane highway to Shenzhen and a railway from Guangdong to the Kwai Chung Container Terminal in Kowloon.

[88] As of December 1979, six international oil companies have already been granted permission to conduct drilling surveys in the coastal line of the South China Sea from Fujian Province to Hainan Island.

of industries, the feasibility of setting up an oil refinery in Hong Kong should be reconsidered. Finally, the Committee advocates the creation of a special office within the Government Secretariat to better coordinate relations between the authorities in China and the local and international community and to identify those opportunities for co-operative efforts.

The long-term relationship between Hong Kong and China is a political question whose "solution" is largely dependent on the maintenance of a balance of tripod interests between China, Britain and the local people. Over the past thirty years, China has been able to supply Hong Kong with ample basic food-stuffs, consumer goods and raw materials at competitive prices, and in turn Hong Kong has been China's most important single source of foreign exchange earnings.[89] This state of mutual reliance has never been hindered by any political events in China. Now, at a time when China is clearly set upon the path of economic growth requiring international cooperation of every sort, the role to be played by Hong Kong is multiple. Hong Kong's great wealth of business expertise, production know-how, plus its role as a financial center and as a focal point of international communications will operate as a "training center" for China across a wide spectrum of manufacturing, trading and banking activities. To Hong Kong, the greatest benefit which it enjoys arising from an industrially modernizing China will be a rapid business expansion and diversified industrial expansion, leading to a peaceful atmosphere of political stability.

VI. Concluding Remarks

Alfred Marshall has said, "the causes which determine the economic progress of nations belong to the study of international trade"[90] and "the field of employment which any place offers for labor and capital depends, firstly, on its natural resources; secondly, on the power of turning them to good account, derived from its

---

[89] Leaving aside personal remittances, remitted profits and earnings from tourism, it is estimated that China derives approximately one-third of its gross convertible foreign exchange earnings (approximately US$3 billion in 1979) from its visible trade with Hong Kong. See *ACD Report*, p. 155.

[90] See Marshall (1920), p. 225.

progress of knowledge and of social and industrial organization; and thirdly, on the access that it has to markets in which it can sell those things of which it has a superfluity.''[91] As an extremely small and natural resource-poor economy, Hong Kong's economic growth has to be export-led. Being an utterly export-oriented economy, it simply has to go where the markets are.

At a time when there is much talk about industrial diversification, particularly diversification away from textiles and clothing, it is germane to point out that diversification does not imply the abandonment or even neglect of existing industries. The principal objective of diversification is a change in the relative share of individual industries in the overall industrial structure, whether measured in terms of export value or of employment so that a more evenly distributed pattern of industrial activity can be achieved. In the quest for a more balanced and diversified economic base, it is perfectly possible for the traditional mainstays like textiles and clothing to continue to grow in absolute terms but to decline gradually in their relative weights in the overall industrial structure.

There are industries which in the course of economic development will decline in both the absolute and relative sense or even eventually perish. In Hong Kong, industries such as enamelware, rattanware and wigs come readily to mind. But their decline has been largely due to changes in market demand and consumer tastes, and not to any artificial protectionist restrictions. As long as this is the case, there is nothing one can do about it. Hong Kong has always been a free port, and there have never been any protective means or subsidies to support inefficient and dying industries. But the textile and clothing industries are certainly not inefficient and dying ones. Another important fact is that the demand for wearing apparel is highly income-elastic. Therefore, as long as world population is growing and the general standard of living is improving, Hong Kong's textile and clothing industries still have a great future before them, and should be allowed to grow in an absolute sense. Indeed, if there had not been protectionist measures of one kind or another, they would have expanded even faster in response to market needs.

The increasing trade barriers, especially the import quotas imposed on textiles and garments by the industrially advanced countries, have made it imperative for Hong Kong to broaden its industrial structure.

---

[91] *Ibid.*, p. 556.

However, one should realize that there are certain limits to diversification, given the resources endowment of Hong Kong. Simon Kuznets has rightly pointed out that since small economies are deemed to have a smaller variety of natural resources than their larger counterparts, they may be able to export only a relatively smaller number of exportables.[92] Implicit in this statement is the notion that, in a small economy, according to the principle of economies of scale, excessive diversification is incompatible with competitive exports. On this point, a recent United Nations study also remarks that excessive diversification in many LDCs may well lead to a scattering of resources, higher costs and a less established selling position.[93] This implies that when attempting to form policy judgments for diversification, the gains achievable and the costs arising from reduced specialization need careful consideration. One may say that the dangers of a purely technocratic approach are greater in diversification than in almost any other sphere of development. Naturally, different countries should make different specialization-diversification choices at different stages of development with reference to their size and physical endowment.

Furthermore, one should always bear in mind that diversification is a long and arduous process. Miracles of transforming an economy from its heavy dependence on textiles and clothing to a well-diversified industrial base capable of weathering the storms of protectionism and coping with a slow world trade growth cannot be performed in a few simple strokes. Inevitably, a long gestation period is required for diversifying into new and unexplored fields. Apart from the entrepreneurial expertise which is required for raising capital and organizing other factor inputs for new industries, product testing and market research are time-consuming. It is therefore unrealistic to expect new industries or new products to emerge overnight simply because we have decided to embark on a program of diversification.

Admittedly, a country's pattern of trade is dictated by the basic principle of comparative advantages and its change over time when the problem of economic development is involved. In the early postwar years, Hong Kong had been especially successful in the labor-intensive manufacturing industries where the amounts of land and capital, and the level of technology required, were generally not high. However, labor-intensive manufacturing is easy to imitate, and from

---

[92] See Kuznets (1964), p. 55.
[93] See United Nations (1974), p. 11.

the late fifties onwards, South Korea, Taiwan and Singapore have all followed the same path of export-oriented industrialization.[94] The present position is that exports of the former two have grown so rapidly that they are increasingly threatening Hong Kong's market shares.[95] In view of its rising costs in rentals and wage levels, Hong Kong can no longer compete with them on cost consideration alone, and only its lead in technology and product quality enables it to preserve its external competitiveness.

There can be little doubt that Hong Kong has at present arrived at the stage of developing new industries which are relatively intensive in capital and technology. But, at the same time, over-generalization must be guarded against. For instance, given its size, natural resource scarcity and factor endowment skewness, Hong Kong cannot hope to follow the footsteps of Japan and develop large-scale heavy industries such as chemicals and automobile industries. These highly land- and capital-intensive industries are also labor-saving ones, and are thus inappropriate from the viewpoint of employment generation. Moreover, the high fixed-capital intensity of such industries would also tend to impair the usual flexibility and resilience of Hong Kong's industrial structure. Thus, a sensible development strategy would be to develop relatively skill- and technology-intensive industries which may not easily be imitated by its rival competitors. But this is not all. What is attainable by Hong Kong today will also become technologically feasible by other LDCs tomorrow. One has to realize that, due to rapid technology progress and diffusion, the average product-life-cycle is becoming shorter, so that a new product may easily become mature and standardized in a few years' time, which will make it possible for the low-cost LDCs to enjoy full comparative advantages in its production and export. Therefore, in order to preserve its competitiveness, Hong Kong has to move fast to produce those new products in the early phase of the product-cycle when both their prices and market acceptances are still on the upswing.

So far the deliberation on the problem of diversification has been confined to the manufacturing industries. In view of the export-oriented nature of the Hong Kong economy, this emphasis seems

---

[94] For a recent comparative study of rapid growth in these countries, see Chen (1979).

[95] Hong Kong's overall domestic exports were more than double of their combined total at the early 1960s. And by the late 1960s, it was still approximately equal to their total. But both South Korea and Taiwan have outstripped Hong Kong since the mid-1970s.

both understandable and justifiable, and it seems likely that, for a very long time to come, Hong Kong's prosperity will continue to depend heavily on exports of manufactured goods. But one should not neglect the non-manufacturing sectors, especially the financial service industries. It is a common development feature in most industrialized and industrializing countries that as they become more affluent, the service industries will gain in relative importance vis-a-vis the manufacturing industries. There are ample signs that Hong Kong has steadily entered this phase of economic development since the mid-1970s. Such a trend is fully consonant with its aim to achieve a more diversified and balanced economic structure.

As Professor Kindleberger has conceived it, the world of international trade is one of change; and a country's capacity to transform, that is, to experience economic growth and development is its capacity to react to change, regardless of its source, by adapting to economic structure.[96] Hong Kong has thrived in the past because of its very high flexibility and resilience. Its institutional framework, characterized by minimum government interference, low taxation, a free exchange market, and good industrial relations, provides all the necessary conditions for such flexibility and resilience. This framework must be preserved if Hong Kong's economic growth is to be sustained over time. Any policies and practices which, however suitable elsewhere, may increase rigidity and reduce flextibility here, should be denounced.

Although the implementation of the various recommendations made by the Diversification Committee will require the government to intervene in the market to an increasing degree, its prima facie objective is to provide a favorable framework within which the process of the resources reallocation in response to changing market conditions can be facilitated. In this sense one can say that by adopting the ACD report the Hong Kong government has no intention whatsoever of giving up its cherished policy of minimum interventionism. Certainly the government is bound to play a more active role in the working of the economy in the future, but it is still a far cry from a planned economy. Within the framework which is to be created by the government according to the recommendations a successful diversification of the industrial structure depends mainly on the hard work of its labor force on the one hand and the innovative entrepreneurship of its industrialists on the other.

---

[96] See Kindleberger (1962), pp. 99-100.

Appendix Table A-1.   The Changing Pattern of Hong Kong's Export Trade, 1959-79

Year	1959	1961	1963	1965	1967	1969	1971	1973	1975	1977	1979
Value: in Current HK$ Million											
Total Exports (X)	3,227	3,930	4,991	6,530	8,781	13,197	17,164	25,999	29,832	44,833	75,934
Re-exports (RX)	995	991	1,160	1,530	2,081	2,679	3,414	6,525	6,973	9,829	20,022
Domestic Exports (DX)	2,282	2,939	3,831	5,027	6,700	10,518	13,750	19,474	22,859	35,004	55,912
Manufactured Exports (MX)	2,019	2,635	3,506	4,694	6,366	10,071	13,252	18,822	22,168	33,874	53,779
Total Imports (M)	4,949	5,970	7,412	8,965	10,449	14,893	20,256	29,005	33,472	48,701	85,837
Total Trade (X + M)	8,227	9,900	12,403	15,494	19,230	28,090	37,420	55,004	63,304	93,534	161,771
Trade Balance (X − M)	−1,672	−2,040	−2,421	−2,435	−1,668	−1,696	−3,092	−3,006	−3,640	−3,868	−9,903
Proportion: in Percentages											
RX / X	30.36	25.22	23.24	23.02	23.70	20.30	19.89	25.10	23.37	21.92	26.37
DX / X	69.64	74.78	76.76	76.98	76.30	79.70	80.11	74.90	76.63	78.08	73.63
MX / DX	88.48	89.66	91.52	93.38	95.01	95.75	96.38	96.65	96.98	96.77	96.19
(X − M) / X	−51.02	−51.91	−48.51	−37.29	−19.00	−12.85	−18.01	−11.56	−12.20	−8.63	−13.04
X / GDP	—	64.96	62.43	62.10	69.74	81.09	78.47	76.55	73.52	75.44	86.94
M / GDP	—	98.68	92.72	85.25	82.99	91.51	92.61	85.40	82.50	81.95	98.27
(X + M) / GDP	—	163.64	155.15	147.34	152.73	172.60	171.08	161.95	156.02	157.38	185.21

Sources: For trade data: Census and Statistics Department, *Hong Kong Trade Statistics*, Hong Kong: Government Printer, various December issues. For GDP data: Census and Statistics Department, *Estimates of Gross Domestic Product*, Hong Kong: Government Printer, various years.

Note: "Manufactured Exports" refers to all commodities which fall into the SITC (United Nations' Commodity Indexes for the Standard International Trade Classification) 512 to SITC 899.

Appendix Table A-2. Export Composition of Hong Kong's Domestically Manufactured Products, 1959-79

(in percent)

Product Group	1959	1961	1963	1965	1967	1969	1971	1973	1975	1977	1979
Textiles	18.14	22.76	16.91	16.59	13.97	10.71	10.17	12.08	9.38	7.70	7.27
Clothing	34.75	29.33	36.10	35.27	34.58	36.39	39.74	38.28	44.63	39.73	36.00
Electricals/Electronics	1.53	2.48	3.97	5.83	8.81	10.06	11.21	13.46	13.97	15.52	15.66
(Electronics)	—	(0.44)	(1.77)	(2.55)	(3.13)	(6.96)	(8.89)	(9.94)	(9.79)	(10.53)	(9.87)
Precision Instruments	0.61	0.68	0.76	0.78	1.34	1.74	1.99	2.48	3.91	6.59	9.35
(Watches and Clocks)	(0.22)	(0.14)	(0.13)	(0.16)	(0.64)	(1.03)	(1.27)	(1.50)	(2.82)	(4.84)	(7.79)
Toys and Dolls	3.90	4.56	5.48	7.50	8.30	8.43	8.61	7.72	6.54	7.96	7.47
Plastic Products	3.59	6.77	6.60	5.85	4.90	3.99	3.38	3.53	1.77	2.09	1.91
Sundry Metal Products	5.26	4.12	3.68	3.12	2.99	2.78	2.51	2.68	2.65	2.84	2.75
Handbags	0.70	0.65	0.76	0.92	1.19	1.36	1.66	2.08	1.99	2.03	2.19
Footwear	4.78	3.54	3.81	3.04	3.27	2.80	2.55	1.37	1.12	1.04	0.93
All Other Manufactures	26.74	25.11	21.93	21.10	20.65	21.74	18.18	16.32	14.04	14.50	16.47
Textiles and Clothing	52.89	52.09	53.01	51.86	48.55	47.10	49.91	50.36	54.01	47.43	43.27
Top Three of the Year	58.15	58.86	59.61	59.36	57.36	57.16	61.12	63.82	67.98	63.21	61.01
Top Five of the Year	66.83	67.54	69.06	71.04	70.56	69.58	73.11	75.07	78.43	77.50	75.75

Sources: Computed from Census and Statistics Department, *Hong Kong Trade Statistics*, and *Hong Kong Review of Overseas Trade*, Hong Kong: Government Printer, various years.

Notes: All figures are percentages of total domestic exports. Product description in terms of the SITC code:—Textiles: 651-657; Clothing: 841-842; Electricals and Electronics: 722-729; Precision Instruments: 861-864; Toys and Dolls: 894.210-894.239; Plastic Products: 893 and 899.931-899.939; Sundry Metal Products: 691-698; Handbags: 831; and Footwear: 851.

Appendix Table A-3. Distribution of Hong Kong's Domestic Exports by Principal Markets, 1959-79

(in percent)

Region/Country	1959	1961	1963	1965	1967	1969	1971	1973	1975	1977	1979
By Region											
North America	27.34	25.31	27.64	36.88	40.67	45.46	45.03	37.68	35.47	42.06	36.55
Western Europe	26.38	28.62	34.95	32.54	30.08	29.62	30.66	34.56	36.41	31.04	34.87
Rest of the World	46.28	46.07	37.41	30.58	29.25	24.92	24.31	27.76	28.12	26.90	28.58
By Country											
United States	24.72	23.10	25.42	34.20	37.37	42.10	41.51	35.05	32.08	38.72	33.62
United Kingdom	19.24	20.04	22.55	17.13	17.12	13.93	14.15	14.45	12.15	8.67	10.68
West Germany	3.16	3.61	5.66	7.38	5.54	7.27	8.20	9.77	12.51	10.48	11.35
Japan	4.12	3.64	3.16	2.65	2.82	3.38	3.52	5.47	4.18	3.96	4.75
Australia	2.63	2.08	2.19	2.67	2.97	2.72	2.92	3.96	4.52	3.56	3.20
Rest of the World	46.13	47.53	41.02	35.97	34.18	30.60	29.70	31.30	34.56	34.61	36.40
The Three Western DCs	47.11	46.75	53.64	58.71	60.03	63.30	63.86	59.27	56.74	57.87	55.65
The Five DCs Above	53.87	52.47	58.98	64.03	65.82	69.40	70.30	68.70	65.44	65.39	63.60

Sources: Same as Appendix Table A-2.

Notes: All figures are percentages of total domestic exports. "The Three Western DCs" refer to the United States, the United Kingdom and West Germany.

REFERENCES

Beazer, William F., *The Commercial Future of Hong Kong*, New York: Praeger Publishers, 1978.

Becker, Gary S., "Investment in Human Capital: A Theoretical Analysis," *Journal of Political Economy*, LXX, Supplement, October 1962, pp. 9-49.

Caves, Richard E., "'Vent for Surplus' Model of Trade and Growth," J. Theberge (ed.), *Economics of Trade and Development*, New York: John Wiley and Sons, 1968, pp. 211-228.

Chan, Cecil S.O., "While the Philosophy is Logically Sound, to What Extent can Diversification be Feasible?" (a speech presented at a Symposium on Diversification of the Electrical and Electronics Industries in Hong Kong held on April 28, 1978), reprinted in Hong Kong Industrial News, May 17, 1978, pp. 4-5.

Chen, Edward K.Y., *Hyper-Growth in Asian Economies: A Comparative Study of Hong Kong, Japan, Korea, Singapore and Taiwan*, London: Macmillan Press Ltd., 1979.

————, "Industrial Diversification in Hong Kong" (a speech given in the Rotary Club Lunch Meeting on January 7, 1980).

Chen, Michael S.T., "Building Up the New Wall Street of Asia," *Far Eastern Economic Review*, CVIII (April 4, 1980), pp. 65-67.

Corden, W. Max, *The Theory of Protection*, Oxford: Clarendon Press, 1971.

Eckaus, R.S., "Investment in Human Capital: A Comment," *Journal of Political Economy*, LXXI, October 1963, pp. 501-504.

England, Joe, "Industrial Relations in Hong Kong," Keith Hopkins (ed.), *Hong Kong: The Industrial Colony — A Political, Social and Economic Survey*, Hong Kong: Oxford University Press, 1971, pp. 207-259.

England, Joe, and John Rear, *Chinese Labour under British Rule: A Critical Study of Labour Relations and Law in Hong Kong*, Hong Kong: Oxford University Press, 1975.

Erb, Guy F., and Salvatore Schiavo-Campo, "Export Instability, Level of Development, and Economic Size of Less Developed Countries," *Bulletin of the Oxford University Institute of Economics & Statistics*, XXXI, November 1969, pp. 263-283.

Glassburner, Bruce, and James Riedel, "Government in the Economy of Hong Kong," *Economic Record*, XLVIII, March 1972, pp. 58-75.

Hambro, Edvard, *The Problem of Chinese Refugees in Hong Kong*, Leyden: A.W. Sijthoff, 1955.

Hang Seng Bank, Research Department, "Hong Kong's Position as an Entrepot — A Re-appraisal," *Hang Seng Economic Quarterly*, January 1979, pp. 10-17.

————, "A Study of Land Values in Hong Kong," *Hang Seng Economic Quarterly*, April 1980, pp. 6-11.

Hirschman, Albert O., *National Power and the Structure of Foreign Trade*, Berkeley: University of California Press, 1945.

————, *The Strategy of Economic Development*, New Haven: Yale University Press, 1958.

Hislop, Ian, "Gold Movements Make Hong Kong a Leading Market," *Banking, Finance and Investment Review*, Hong Kong: South China Morning Post, July 1977, pp. 25-26.

Ho, Henry C.Y., *The Fiscal System of Hong Kong*, London: Croom Helm Ltd., 1979.

Ho, Kwon Ping, "A Hesitant Boost for Planning," *Far Eastern Economic Review*, CVI, December 28, 1979, pp. 34-35.

Hong Kong and Shanghai Banking Corporation, Corporation Secretary's Department, *Hong Kong Textile and Garment Export Restrictions*, June 1978.

Hong Kong Tourist Association, Survey & Statistics Department, *A Statistical Review of Tourism*, various issues.

Hong Kong Trade Development Council, Research Department, *The Watches and Clocks Market in Switzerland*, January 1979.

Hsing, Mo-huan, "How to Cope with Dollar Dilemma," *South China Morning Post*, April 19, 1979.

Hufbauer, Gary, *Synthetic Materials and the Theory of International Trade*, Cambridge: Harvard University Press, 1966.

Jao, Y.C., "A Commission on Money and Finance for Hong Kong," *Hong Kong Economic Papers*, No. 4, November 1968, pp. 50-56.

————, *Banking and Currency in Hong Kong: A Study of Postwar Financial Development*, London: Macmillan Press Ltd., 1974.

————, "Hong Kong as a Regional Financial Centre: Evolution and Prospects" (a paper presented at a Conference on "Hong Kong: Dilemmas of Growth" conducted at the Australian National University in Canberra between December 10-14, 1979).

_____, "Financial Structure and Monetary Policy in Hong Kong," 1979 (mimeo.)

Johnson, Harry G., *Comparative Cost and Commercial Policy: Theory for a Developing World Economy*, Wicksell Lectures, Stockholm: Almqvist & Wiksell, 1972.

_____, *Technology and Economic Interdependence*, London: Macmillan Press Ltd., for the Trade Policy Research Centre, 1975.

Kindleberger, Charles P., *Foreign Trade and National Economy*, New Haven: Yale University Press, 1962.

Kravis, Irving, "Availability and Other Influences on the Commodity Composition of Trade," *Journal of Political Economy*, LXIV, April 1956, pp. 143-155.

Krueger, Anne O., "The Political Economy of the Rent-Seeking Society," *American Economic Review*, LXIV, June 1974, pp. 291-303.

Kuznets, Simon, "Quantitative Aspects of Economic Growth of Nations: IX. Level and Structure of Foreign Trade: Comparisons for Recent Years," *Economic Development and Cultural Change*, XIII, October 1964, Part II.

Lary, Hal B., *Imports of Manufactures from Less Developed Countries*, New York: Columbia University Press, 1968.

Lewis, Arthur W., "Economic Development with Unlimited Supplies of Labour," *Manchester School of Economic and Social Studies*, XXII, May 1954, pp. 139-192.

Li, David K.P., "Hong Kong as a Financial Centre" (a speech given in a seminar organized by the Stanford Research Institute in February 1979), reprinted in *Hong Kong Manager*, July 1979, pp. 8-20.

Lim, Edwin Roca, *A General Equilibrium Model of an Export-Dependent Economy*, unpublished Ph.D. thesis, Harvard University, 1969.

Lin, Tzong-biau, *Monetary Behaviour under the Sterling Exchange Standard: Hong Kong as a Case Study*, Hong Kong Series — Economic Research Centre Occasional Paper 1, Hong Kong: Chinese University of Hong Kong, 1971.

Lin, Tzong-biau, and Yin-ping Ho, "Export Instabilities and Employment Fluctuations in Hong Kong's Manufacturing Industries," *Developing Economies*, XVII, June 1979, pp. 182-202.

Lin, Tzong-biau, and Kar-yiu Wong, *The Economic Impact of the Tourism in Hong Kong* (a paper presented at a Conference on "Hong Kong: Dilemmas of Growth" conducted at the Australian National University in Canberra between December 10-14, 1979).

Lin, Tzong-biau, Victor Mok and Yin-ping Ho, *Manufactured Exports and Employment in Hong Kong*, Hong Kong: Chinese University Press, 1980.

Lin, Tzong-biau, and Victor Mok, *Trade Barriers and the Promotion of Hong Kong Exports*, Hong Kong: Chinese Universty Press, 1980.

Lin, Tzong-biau, Rance P.L. LEE and Udo-Ernst Simonis (eds.), *Hong Kong — Economic, Social and Political Studies in Development*, New York: M.E. Sharpe, Inc., 1979.

Linder, Staffan B., *An Essay on Trade and Transformation*, New York: John Wiley and Sons, 1961.

Lydall, H.F., *Trade and Development: A Study of the Effects of Trade Expansion on Employment in Developing and Developed Countries,* Geneva: International Labour Office Publication, 1975.

Mahfuzur Rahman, A.H.M., *Exports of Manufactures from Developing Countries: A Study of Comparative Advantage*, Netherlands: Rotterdam University Press, 1973.

Marshall, Alfred, *Principles of Economics*, 8th Edition, London: Macmillan Press Ltd., 1920.

Massell, Benton F., "Export Instability and Economic Structure," *American Economic Review*, LX, September 1970, pp. 618-630.

Morawetz, David, "Employment Implications of Industrialization in Developing Countries: A Survey," *Economic Journal*, LXXXIV September 1974, pp. 491-542.

Morkre, Morris E., "Rent-Seeking and Hong Kong's Textile Quota System," *Developing Economies*, XVII, March 1979, pp. 101-118.

Myint, Hla, "The 'Classical' Theory of International Trade and the Underdeveloped Countries," *Economic Journal*, LXVIII, June 1958, pp. 317-337.

"No Industrial Bank for Hong Kong?," *Far Eastern Economic Review*, XXIX, August 4, 1960, pp. 226-231.

Owen, Nicholas, "Manpower Deficiencies and Industrial Training," *Hong Kong Economic Papers*, No. 7, September 1972, pp. 45-59.

Posner, Michael, "International Trade and Technical Change," *Oxford Economic Papers*, XIII, October 1961, pp. 323-341.

Rabushka, Alvin, *The Changing Face of Hong Kong: New Departures in Public Policy,* Washington, D.C./Stanford: American Enterprise Institute for Public Policy Research/Hoover Institution on War, Revolution and Peace, 1973.

_____, *Value for Money: The Hong Kong Budgetary Process,* Stanford: Hoover Institution Press, 1976.

_____, *Hong Kong: A Study in Economic Freedom,* Chicago: University of Chicago Press, 1979.

Riedel, James, *The Industrialization of Hong Kong*, Kieler Studien 124, Tubingen: J.C.B. Mohr, 1974.

Rowley, Anthony, "Breaking of a Monopoly," *Far Eastern Economic Review*, CVIII, May 30, 1980, pp. 73-74.

Sit, Victor Fung-shuen, Siu-lun Wong and Tsin-sing Kian, *Small Scale Industry in a Laissez-Faire Economy: A Hong Kong Case Study*, Hong Kong: Centre of Asian Studies, 1979.

Tyler, William G., "Manufactured Exports and Employment Creation in Developing Countries: Some Empirical Evidence," *Economic Development and Cultural Change*, XXIV, January 1976, pp. 355-373.

United Nations, Department of Economic and Social Affairs, *Industrialization for New Development Needs*, New York: United Nations Publication, 1974.

Utton, M.A., *Diversification and Competition*, London: Cambridge University Press, 1979.

Vernon, Raymond, "International Investment and International Trade in the Product Cycle," *Quarterly Journal of Economics,* LXXX, May 1966, pp. 190-207.

World Bank, Sector Working Paper, *Tourism*, Washington, D.C., June 1972.

Hong Kong Government Publications:

Census and Statistics Department, *Hong Kong Statistics, 1947-1967,* 1969.

Census and Statistics Department, *Monthly Digest of Statistics*, selected issues.

Census and Statistics Department, *Estimates of Gross Domestic*

Product, various years.

Census and Statistics Department, *Hong Kong Trade Statistics*, various December issues.

Census and Statistics Department, *Hong Kong Review of Overseas Trade*, various years.

Census and Statistics Department, *Hong Kong Population and Housing Census: 1971 Main Report*, 1973.

Census and Statistics Department, *Hong Kong By-Census 1976: Main Report*, 1979.

Census and Statistics Department, *1973 Census of Industrial Production: Volume I — Report and Summary Statistics*, 1977.

Census and Statistics Department, *1976 Census of Industry*, 1979. (mimeo.)

Commissioner of Labour, *Annual Departmental Report*, various years.

Government Secretariat, *Report of the Advisory Committee on Diversification*, 1979.

Government Secretariat, *Hong Kong Annual Report*, selected years.

Government Secretariat, *The 1980-81 Budget: Speech by the Financial Secretary, moving the Second Reading of the Appropriation Bill*, 1980.

Hetherington, R.M., and others, *The Final Report of the Industrial Training Committee*, 1971.

• COMMENT _____

H. Edward English,   *Carleton University*

It is interesting to speculate on the economic consequences for Hong Kong of this curious form of colonialism. Lin and Ho note that, as a colony, Hong Kong loses much in international bargaining power. But perhaps it is precisely because it is a colony of this unique sort in this unique location that it has become so impressive an export performer. Any other form of regime might long ago have begun to intervene more directly or extensively in Hong Kong's economic development. But Britain apparently chose the free market route, not out of nostalgia for a commitment to laissez-faire it has long since abandoned, but rather out of assurances that it would be awkward and inappropriate to attempt an interventionist strategy in the face of the strength of local culture and of challenges of various kinds from its near neighbor. In short, apart from land rents and some port income, Britain left the garden alone.

For those familiar with all the previous literature, this paper has the advantage of bringing one up to date and projecting the future of the private sector and of government policy. Yet when all is said, one concludes that Hong Kong will find its own way into the economic future, and that the only real challenge to its continuity is what it has always been, China. There is no fundamental problem of multi-cultural cohesion or rural-urban tension, or federalism in any form. There is certainly no problem of intractable institutional barriers to the development of whatever skills and potentials are needed. There is only China, the source of Hong Kong's opportunities and of its challenges; China which has supplied its labor force, but also its excessive and sometimes unpredictable growth of population; China which has given Hong Kong its fundamental role as an entrepot, but also created great uncertainty about the future of that role; China which can be a major market for Hong Kong's goods and services while being a partner in a massive new investment in export potential, yet which can seriously frustrate or undermine that partnership through the maze of its marvelous bureaucracy and the political pitfalls that may handicap its modernization strategy.

This paper provides no convincing evidence that Hong Kong will fail to find a way around the problems of the policies of Western industrialized states which adversely affect its export growth. Perhaps it will be done by a kind of diversification that is not primarily the result of explicit actions of its government but, rather, is consequence of the facts of life. These facts include the market diversification that is the consequence of the high economic growth rate throughout East and Southeast Asia, and the product diversification that occurs as a consequence of private experience and new private initiatives, experience with a product line that develops backward and forward product and process research and development endeavors, and appropriate response to a changing regional pattern of goods and services demands. With a per capita income in the neighborhood of $3,500 and land values that reflect its uniquely crowded conditions, it will have to move into labor-upgrading and land-economizing activity. Its efforts to do the former will give it new export strengths in the markets of the developed world to replace those that were achieved when it was the leader among users of low-cost labor to supply acceptable labor-intensive products. This, as the authors suggest, will include some of the more capital-intensive stages in the textile chain, but perhaps particularly the same skill-, style- and marketing-intensive products from the textile sector. But it could and probably will also involve supply of some skill-intensive intermediate products to East and Southeast Asian markets. On the other hand, Hong Kong's comparative advantage in the supply of commercial, financial and managerial services is likely to provide a foundation for the relative growth of services exports, particularly if the PRC partnership thrives. In these circumstances the Hong Kong dollar will appreciate in response to a strength outside manufacturing and the export of such products will have to adjust accordingly just as resource-rich countries cannot expect to compete as easily in markets for manufactured products that are not resource-intensive.

Lin and Ho feel that Hong Kong may not be able to rely quite so much on a non-interventionist strategy in the future. On some matters they seem confident that the upgrading of skills is required, and that this will be supportive of the diversification process. It is surprising to learn that the level of skills is not higher, and it seems acceptable that adjustment may involve externalities that will require a government levy and subsidy system favoring those firms that make more effort to train their workers.[1] The skills that may need particular support are those required by the newer industries but it is difficult to be confident that the government could identify specific winners, almost as difficult as crediting government with being able to pick winners in a system of R & D subsidies. Skills that are applicable to a variety of industrial situations are a somewhat better bet for government intervention.

Incidentally, one of the more controversial elements in Singapore's record of government intervention is its educational policy, which some say has placed too much emphasis upon science and engineering and not enough on technical and managerial skills. The argument that there is the need for government involvement in the improvement of what the authors call "technical infrastructure" which includes product testing, quality certification, and measurement facilities for "drastic expansion" of the Hong Kong Productivity Centre to coordinate research and development activity, transfer of technology and technical information services is not overwhelmingly convincing. Much of this is accomplished by the sophisticated buyers of textile and other products Hong Kong supplies and by multinational enterprises. It is not self-evident that there are externalities in these sectors, or that if there are, they are not covered by intra-industry efforts to exchange technical information, and pursue complementarity or in some cases joint research.

Some of the policies Lin and Ho suggest to fill financial "lacunae" warrant comment. For example, they see the need for larger supplies of capital as Hong Kong turns to more capital-intensive activity, particularly debt capital. They report the demand for an Industrial Development Bank. Since they note that the average size of manufacturing enterprises is small, and even declining, the case seems plausible. But the private financial institutions available to Hong Kong should be capable of supplying the financial requirements and even of developing new long-term financing institutions. On a survivor-theory basis, indeed, it looks as though smaller operations have grown in relative importance. As for the larger capital-intensive enterprises, the multinationals do not appear to be an unwelcome source.

There also seems to be concern about the reluctance of the Ex-

---

[1] The 1976 Census reveals that 96% of employed population in the manufacturing sector have acquired technical or vocational training.

change Bank's Association, Hong Kong's monetary authority to raise interest rates in times of inflationary pressure. This may well be a point on which the government is too much influenced by the short-term interest of large private banks. However, there is a question as to whether a more independent monetary authority is an impossibility in the Hong Kong setting.

Basically, Singapore is leading where Hong Kong is likely to go, if one can make two assumptions about the future. One is that China will be an important economic partner and will continue to consider Hong Kong as a vital source of services in the development of its export enclaves; and the other is that Hong Kong stabilizes its own population, and no longer has to admit substantial numbers of unskilled refugees.

If the former happens, Singapore and Hong Kong will both become increasingly important as providers of both capital-intensive intermediate products and commercial, financial and management services to their neighbors with large development potential and lower-wage labor.

If the latter happens Hong Kong will gradually decline in relative importance as a supplier of the traditional labor-intensive manufactures and follow more closely Singapore's example in switching to other more technologically-intensive products. For some time to come, Hong Kong will probably retain a relatively wider variety of manufactures, though it may also move more slowly into the newer types, partly because government will not place as much pressure in this direction as it does in Singapore.

Some criticism has to be made of statements such as the following: "For a country like India to attain a similar manufactured-export/population ratio, it would require that its manufactured exports be greater than total world trade in manufactures." The familiar notion that, ceteris paribus, the relative importance of trade is inversely related to the size of a national market and directly related to per capita income should not be forgotten.

In discussing diversification, the authors state that the conceptual definition of diversification has something to do with the minimization of risk. This notion of risk and the related one of vulnerability has been overworked in the trade literature. Perhaps a true one-crop economy is something to worry about if the crop is subject to supply fluctuation due to weather or is especially vulnerable to synthetic substitute development. But when non-resource-based manufactures and especially consumer goods other than the major durables are being discussed, the whole notion of risk-reduction through diversification seems less compelling. When the authors go on to show how much diversification has already occurred within sectors, they make the above mentioned case that much stronger.

GENERAL DISCUSSION

The Hirschman-Gini coefficient estimated on the basis of SITC 3-digit classification gives a misleading impression of the extent of export diversification in Hong Kong because most export diversification was achieved within the 3-digit classification. In terms of market diversification, more emphasis must be given to other less developed countries that can provide very rapidly growing markets for the type of products into which Hong Kong intends to diversify.

One can argue that the protectionist policies of advanced countries helped Hong Kong to initiate its effort towards diversification at an early stage. On the other hand, perhaps the efficient allocation of quotas within Hong Kong may be more important than quota restrictions by advanced countries themselves.

Improvement in education and labor skills, and creating human capital in general may be very crucial to achieve industrial diversification. In the future, unlike in the past, government may have to intervene actively in human capital creation if Hong Kong wants to promote skill-intensive, capital-intensive and technology-intensive industries.

By actively participating in the modernization effort of mainland China, especially in the industrialization of Southern China, Hong Kong may be able to maintain the high growth rates it has achieved until now. Furthermore, through Hong Kong, Korea, Taiwan, Singapore, Japan, and others may enhance their access to Chinese markets and participation in the Chinese modernization effort.

There is also an important institutional problem to consider. With only 17 years remaining of the current status of Hong Kong, industrial decisions may tend to be biased towards short-run optimization, and hence hinder Hong Kong's movement to capital- and technology-intensive industries.

THE FINANCING OF TRADE
AND DEVELOPMENT IN THE ADCs:
THE EXPERIENCE OF SINGAPORE

*Kum Poh Wong**

I. Introduction

Singapore has chalked up a creditable record of economic growth over the last two decades. This record is also characterized by relative price stability. Industrialization is the linchpin of Singapore's economic policy. The success of industrialization is evidenced by the increased share of manufacturing industries in the real GDP. External trade and other sectors have also kept pace with the general economic advance.

Singapore is a small city-state, lacking natural resources of any significance. Before embarking on the industrialization program, it was essentially an entrepot, a collecting and distributing center of goods for the neighboring countries. Its success in setting up modern industries and expanding trade raises a host of questions regarding how the wherewithal was obtained to finance the growth, how modern technology was transferred, how the infrastructure was developed to support the growth, and how and where the domestic products were marketed. In this paper an attempt is made to sketch an answer to the question of how the economic growth was financed, and how the growth of industries and trade was financed. Since relative price stability is an important feature of the growth process, some attention will be paid to the issue of non-inflationary development financing.

* National University of Singapore

The paper is divided into five sections. In Section I a broad picture is presented of the development of the Singapore economy, showing the flows of national saving and foreign capital and their role in financing capital formation. Section II deals with the financing of public-sector expenditure. The non-inflationary aspects of government budgetary operations will be highlighted. Section III is devoted to the industrial sector, with due emphasis placed on the role of foreign capital. Section IV takes up the problem of trade financing and includes a brief discussion of the Asian Dollar Market. In the last section the findings are summarized and some conclusions are drawn.

II. Growth, Saving and Capital Inflow

The economic performance of Singapore for the period 1960 to 1979 and for subperiods thereof is summarized in Table 1. It can be seen that GDP in real terms grew at an average rate of 8.7 percent per annum during the first decade, 1960-69. The sixties may be considered a period in which the foundations of modern industrial Singapore were laid. Industrial estates were established, port and wharf facilities improved or expanded, the provision of utilities upgraded and public housing programs implemented. There can be no doubt that manufacturing was the leading sector which provided the main impetus to growth. The high rate of growth of construction activity reflected the vigorous expansion in physical infrastructure, including public housing.

With the groundwork well laid, and given the initial success of industrialization, the economy was poised for accelerated growth in the following period 1969-73. It grew at an average double-digit rate of almost 13 percent. Manufacturing again played the leading role. Industries which forged ahead were electronics, transport equipment and petroleum. This period also witnessed a diversification of the economy. As air, sea and telecommunication services expanded, the transport and communication sector registered a high growth rate of almost 18 percent. Consequent upon the strategy of developing Singapore into a regional financial center, the financial and business services sector gathered momentum, growing at an average rate of 16 percent. With the promotion of tourism and the associated buoyancy of the hotel and restaurant business, the trade sector pushed ahead at

Table 1.   *Average Annual Growth in Real GDP, 1960-79*

(in percent)

	1960-69	1969-79	1969-73	1973-75	1975-79
Total	8.7	9.4	12.6	5.4	8.2
Agriculture and Fishing	4.0	2.2	3.6	-2.6	3.3
Manufacturing	12.8	12.1	18.5	0.9	11.7
Utilities	10.1	10.1	11.9	5.5	10.6
Construction	15.1	7.0	10.4	10.7	2.0
Trade	7.9	7.6	10.1	5.4	6.2
Transport and Communication	6.3	14.7	17.5	9.0	14.9
Financial and Business Services	11.6	11.2	16.1	7.7	8.2
Other Services[a]	6.6	6.9	8.5	7.5	5.1

Source: Ministry of Finance, Singapore, *Economic Survey of Singapore, 1979.*

Note: [a] Includes Public Administration and Defense, Social and Community Services, Personal and Household Services and Ownership of Dwellings.

10 percent per annum. The growth rate would have been higher but for the fact that entrepot trade had slowed down.

The oil crisis and worldwide recession brought the growth rate of the economy down to an average of 5.4 percent from 1973 to 1975. Manufacturing industries, particularly textiles, electronics and transport equipment, proved to be sensitive to external developments and recorded barely a 1 percent growth. Construction and transport and communication continued to expand at creditable rates, reflecting the government's anti-recessionary policy of stepping up infrastructural construction activities.

After its worst post-war recession, the Singapore economy showed signs of re-gaining its previous momentum. The average growth rate of 8 percent during 1975-79 is nevertheless modest by the 1969-73 standards. One reason for the relatively modest performance is the high base from which the growth rate is computed. Another reason is the uncertainty which still plagued the industrial world and resulted in a hesitant pace of investment.

Table 2 shows the structural changes that had taken place during the period 1960-79. The share of manufacturing had grown steadily and the picture revealed is unaffected by the choice of years in the

Table 2.   Gross Domestic Product by Industry

(at 1968 factor cost, %)

	1960	1973	1979
Agriculture, Fishing and Quarrying	4.5	2.3	1.7
Manufacturing	13.2	22.6	23.6
Construction	3.7	5.8	4.8
Trade	33.6	28.6	25.0
Others	45.0	40.7	44.9
Total	100.0	100.0	100.0

Source: Ministry of Finance, Singapore, *Economic Survey of Singapore,* various issues.

table. Within the manufacturing sector, too, there had been significant structural changes. In the earlier years low-skill labor-intensive industries predominated, examples being textiles and garments, and soldering and assembling operations in electronics. The 1970s saw the shift to relatively high-skill and technology-intensive industries like precision engineering, ship and oil-rig building and computer-software manufacturing.

Lately, a conscious and deliberate policy has been pursued to phase out low-skill labor-intensive industries in order to release labor for high-skill and high-technology industries. The reason is two-fold. First, two decades of sustained growth has created a tight labor market and labor shortage has become a bottleneck to further growth, which, in the context of the Singapore economy, can only be brought about by a technological upgrading. Second, protectionist policies pursued by the industrial countries are directed mainly against traditional manufactured products exported from the developing countries. To keep up the export drive to these countries, Singapore finds it necessary to turn to the production of less sensitive products, which is at the time consistent with its long-term development objectives—those of upgrading skills and technology.

As was mentioned at the outset, Singapore's economic growth had been achieved with relative price stability. This subject merits some further discussion. Prices had been stable from 1960 to 1972, the rate of increase in the Consumer Price Index (CPI) averaging less than one percent per annum. In 1973 and 1974, the CPI rose by 20 percent and

22 percent respectively as a consequence of food shortages and oil price increases. Since 1975 inflation has been brought down and averaged 3 percent per annum. (See Choi, 1979.) Special circumstances excepted, four major factors are responsible for the maintenance of price stability in Singapore. First, under the free-trade policy producers and consumers have few import duties to bear and may turn to cheaper sources of foreign supply. Second, the provision of low-cost public housing keeps down the cost of living for the majority of the population. Third, the floating of the Singapore dollar and its upward movement offer an offset to the increase of import prices in foreign currency. Fourth, prudent government budgetary policy, coupled with forced savings in the form of contributions to the Central Provident Fund, removes the dangers of spending beyond one's means and reduces the possibility of a demand-pull inflation emerging. This last factor will be examined in some detail in the next section.

Having outlined the course of economic development of Singapore over the last two decades, it would be instructive to examine the way in which the development process was financed. There are, of course, two sources of finance: internal and external. National saving is the internal source, and capital inflow in one form or another the external source. Table 3 provides information on the absolute and relative magnitudes of these two sources of finance. While national saving and capital inflow increased in value over time, their relative shares displayed a fair amount of variation. Foreign capital contributed approximately one-fifth to one-third of the wherewithal for domestic capital formation.

Table 4 throws additional light on the role played by foreign capital and personnel in the development process of Singapore. It can be seen that resident foreigners and companies accounted for one-fifth of the country's GNP in 1979. Their share shows a clear tendency to increase over time. It would seem fair to say that foreign capital, with the technologies, expertise and international markets it brings with it, was a very important catalyst of economic growth. Without the participation of foreign capital, Singapore's economic performance might have been much less creditable. In this sense, the figures in both Tables 3 and 4 tend to underestimate the importance of foreign capital in Singapore's economic growth.

Table 3.   Saving, Capital Formation and Capital Inflow

(million Singapore dollars)

Year	Gross Domestic Capital Formation (GDCF)	Gross National Saving		Net Borrowing from Abroad	
		Amount	% of GDCF	Amount	% of GDCF
1968	1,075.2	865.3	80.5	209.9	19.5
1973	4,000.0	2,595.1	64.9	1,404.9	35.1
1979	7,580.8	5,019.2	66.2	2,561.6	33.8

Source: Department of Statistics, Singapore, *Yearbook of Statistics,* various issues.

Table 4.   Foreign Share of Income

(million Singapore dollars)

Year	Gross Domestic Product (GDP)	Share of Resident Foreigners and Resident Foreign Companies	
		Amount	as % of GDP
1968	4,315	624	14.5
1973	10,205	2,090	20.5
1979	19,590	4,965	25.3

Source: Department of Statistics, Singapore, *Yearbook of Statistics,* various issues.

III. Financing of Public-Sector Expenditure

In Singapore the government plays a key role in economic development. The government does not only identify problem areas, formulate appropriate policies and provide the requisite incentives for investment accordingly, but also actually participates in a wide range of economic activities. Many agencies, referred to as statutory boards, have been set up to discharge functions in specialized areas, such as the Port of Singapore Authority in charge of ports and wharves, the Housing and Development Board in charge of public housing, and the Jurong Town Corporation in charge of Jurong Town, which has evolved from an industrial estate set up in the early sixties. To examine the revenue and expenditure of the government, a broader view should be taken of the public sector which includes the statutory boards. A broader view will be taken where appropriate published data exist.

In contrast with many other governments, particularly those in the advanced industrial countries, which indulge in budgetary profligacy, the Singapore government may be said to have practiced budgetary parsimony. It has geared its current expenditure strictly according to the needs of the economy. Government current expenditure has increased over the years closely in step with the growth of the economy, consistently forming about 10 percent of GDP. Even during the 1973-75 recession, the Minister of Finance insisted on trimming current expenditure and refused to use it as an anti-recessionary policy instrument. Current revenue always exceeds current expenditure to give rise to a surplus, which is then used to finance development expenditure, that is to say, expenditure on capital projects. The government relies, to a limited extent, on development expenditure as a tool of stabilization policy. Thus, development expenditure was increased in 1975 to counter the recessionary conditions which were fully felt in Singapore in that year.

The public sector makes a very significant contribution to capital formation. It accounts for one-quarter to one-third of total gross domestic capital formation. Public-sector capital formation mainly takes the form of buildings and construction, which includes public housing, land reclamation, expansion of ports and installation of telecommunication facilities, such as satellite antennas.

Table 5 shows the consolidated accounts of the government and six major statutory boards. Several features may be noted. First, there is always a surplus on current operations. Second, this surplus is used to finance development expenditure. Third, for those years in which an overall deficit is incurred, it is relatively small, reaching a maximum of 6 to 7 percent of total current revenue. The fourth feature is that net borrowings are positive in every year and far exceed the overall deficit in those years in which such a deficit is incurred. Lastly, the bulk of net borrowings is obtained domestically through the issue of government securities. For example, in 1978 out of the total net borrowings of $1,657 million, $1,400 million were domestic debt.

Being the single most important holder of government securities, the Central Provident Fund (CPF) is a chief source of funds for the government. The CPF has been established to collect contributions from both employers and employees with a view to returning these

Table 5. Public Sector's Consolidated Accounts

(million Singapore dollars)

Item	1972/73	1973/74	1974/75	1975/76	1976/77	1977/78	1978-79ᴾ
Current revenue	2,605	3,260	3,636	4,361	4,884	5,343	5,641
Current expenditure	1,516	1,839	2,259	2,862	3,230	3,591	3,699
Current surplus	1,089	1,421	1,377	1,499	1,655	1,751	1,943
Development expenditure	904	1,337	1,440	1,793	1,843	2,094	2,059
Overall surplus/deficit (−)	185	84	−49	−294	−188	−343	−117
Net borrowings	634	536	942	1,032	1,893	1,657	1,874
Use/accumulation (−) of cash balances	−819	−620	−893	−738	−1,705	−1,314	−1,757

Source: The Monetary Authority of Singapore, *Annual Report*, various issues.

ᴾ =preliminary

Note: Public sector comprises the government and the major statutory authorities, namely, the Housing and Development Board, Jurong Town Corporation, Port of Singapore Authority, Public Utilities Board, Telecommunication Authority of Singapore and Urban Redevelopment Authority of Singapore.

monies plus interest to the employees on their retirement at age 55. Contributions are compulsory and effectively amount to forced savings. Over time the rate of contribution has been raised by steps to reach the present level of 38.5 percent of the employee's wage or salary. In the earlier years, when the contribution rates were low, the scheme played a negligible role in mobilizing savings. Even as late as 1968, CPF savings accounted only for about 7 percent of total national savings. But as the contribution rates have been raised, the scheme is fast becoming a major source of saving. In 1978-79, for example, it contributed as much as 22 percent of total national saving.

As budgetary parsimony is practiced and insofar as an overall deficit occurs, it is entirely financed by domestic borrowings, government expenditure, or, rather, public-sector expenditure is non-inflationary. Furthermore, public-debt policy, coupled with the CPF forced savings, is such that a great deal of the consumers' purchasing power is siphoned off to impart a deflationary bias to the economy.

IV. Financing Industrial Development

The participation of foreign capital in Singapore's economic development is most visible in the industrial sector. Foreign investors may choose to establish wholly-owned companies or to cooperate with local investors to set up joint ventures. Wholly-owned foreign companies have been variously estimated to constitute about 34 percent to 38 percent of total manufacturing companies. Surveys of major industrial establishments carried out by the Economic Development Board indicate that wholly foreign and joint ventures make up 80 percent to 90 percent of the number of establishments covered, and account for 87 percent to 90 percent of total paid capital, and 91 percent to 94 percent of total gross fixed assets.[1]

The magnitudes of foreign investment in Singapore's manufacturing sector by region of origin for various years are shown in Table 6. It may be added the United States contributes the bulk of foreign industrial capital from North America, Japan contributes about half of the same from Asia, and the United Kingdom, the Netherlands and

---

[1] *Report on the Annual Survey of Manufacturing Activity,* various issues.

Table 6. Foreign Investment in Singapore's Manufacturing Industries by Region (Gross Fixed Assets as at End of 1965, 1970, 1975-78)

(million Singapore dollars)

	1965	1970	1975	1976	1977	1978
North America	23	347	1,127	1,244	1,378	1,613
Europe	85	423	1,170	1,306	1,407	2,005
Asia	49	225	1,083	1,189	1,360	1,624
Total	157	995	3,380	3,739	4,145	5,242

Source: Economic Development Board, Singapore, *Annual Report for 1978/79.*

West Germany together contribute the bulk of the same from the EEC.

The distribution of foreign capital by industry is shown in Table 7. It can be seen that there is a high degree of concentration in petroleum and petroleum products, electrical machinery apparatus, appliances and supplies, and non-electrical machinery, all of which are characterized by capital intensity, advanced technology and export orientation. A notable feature of foreign enterprises is that they are highly export-oriented. The limitations of a narrow domestic market in Singapore being too obvious to escape recognition, the establishment of foreign plants here must be motivated by what the city-state can offer as a logistic base within their global or regional marketing network. The surveys referred to above reveal that foreign firms export a much higher proportion of their output than local firms. For example, in 1978 wholly foreign and joint ventures exported 77 percent of their output, as compared with 31 percent for the wholly local manufacturing firms.

The Economic Development Board (EDB), a government agency, has offered various forms of financial assistance to industries from time to time. Currently, two schemes are available. First, the Capital Assistance Scheme has a budget of $100 million and provides financial assistance to companies with specialized projects of unique economic and technological benefit to Singapore. Under this scheme an industrial investor can obtain equity or loan capital. The EDB may provide up to 50 percent of the equity capital required and is prepared to sell back its equity shares at a later stage. Second, under the Small Industries Finance Scheme, funds are lent to small industries to

Table 7. *Foreign Investment in Manufacturing Industry by Industry Group (Gross Fixed Assets as at End of 1965, 1970, 1975-78)*

				(million Singapore dollars)		
	1965	1970	1975	1976	1977	1978
Food, Beverages & Tobacco	9	31	123	130	143	176
Textiles			154	141	152	150
Wearing Apparel, Made-up Textile & Footwear	7	45	81	89	103	106
Leather & Rubber, Processing of Natural Gums Except Rubber Processing	8	26	30	35	38	46
Wood & Cork Products		17	160	153	162	163
Paper & Paper Products	3	18	41	42	47	59
Industrial Chemicals			90	100	63	73
Other Chemical Products Except Plastic	5	61	81	102	113	115
Petroleum & Petroleum Products	99	555	1,426	1,520	1,617	2,304
Plastic Products	3	8	41	46	64	75
Non-Metallic Mineral Products	3	31	57	71	83	82
Basic Metal Industries		19	39	42	54	75
Fabricated Metal Products Except Machinery & Equipment	19*	34	77	99	124	130
Machinery Except Electrical			250	336	385	487
Electrical Machinery, Apparatus, Appliances & Supplies	1	82	354	412	505	620
Transport Equipment	—	51	209	247	287	326
Precision Equipment & Photographic & Optical Goods		17	142	150	172	212
Other Manufacturing Industries	—		25	24	33	43
Total	157	995	3,380	3,739	4,145	5,242

Source: Economic Development Board, Singapore, *Annual Report for 1978/79.*

Note: Data from 1975 are not comparable with that of previous years on account of reclassification of companies according to the Singapore Industrial Classification, 1969.

*Includes Basic Metal Industries, Fabricated Metal Products, Machinery Except Electrical, and Transport Equipment.

encourage their further development and technical upgrading of operations.[2]

V. Financing of Trade

The financing of trade is interwoven with the financing of industrial development. Imports of capital and intermediate goods, for example, are a chief way of effecting a capital transfer. However, for analytical and expositional convenience, the issue will be dealt with separately.

As Singapore is a small open economy which ultimately imports most of its requirements for consumers and industries, and exports a substantial proportion of its industrial products, and as entrepot trade is still sizable, total external trade is more than twice the GDP in value. On merchandise account, the value of imports invariably exceeds that of exports. Net earnings from services are, however, positive on account of growing receipts from tourism and transport services. These provide about 70 percent to 80 percent of the finances required to meet the deficit in merchandise trade. Capital inflows have been of such magnitudes that they more than cover the residual deficit in merchandise trade to result in a steady increase in Singapore's foreign exchange reserves. (See Table 8.)

The non-monetary private sector is the main channel through which foreign capital flows in. Such private capital inflows include foreign direct investment, inter-company financing and trade credits. Unfortunately there are no published data showing the breakdown into these various components. In view of the dominant position of giant multinational corporations in Singapore, inter-company financing is believed to be sizable. Thus, in 1979, "larger credits were obtained by the petroleum refining companies from their parent companies to finance the stocks of crude oil, as their import bill was inflated by higher oil prices."[3] Official capital inflows, chiefly loans raised abroad through the issue of foreign-currency bonds, are negligible in amount. It may be noted that short-term capital inflows which cannot be clearly traced and identified are captured in the "balancing items."

---

[2] For a detailed review of various forms of incentives and financial assistance for the period up to 1971, see S.H. Huang (1971).

[3] Ministry of Finance, Singapore, *Economic Survey of Singapore, 1979*, pp. 28-29.

Table 8.   Balance of Payments

		(million dollars)	
	1970	1976	1979ᵖ
A. Goods and Services (net)	− 1,727.2	− 1,623.8	− 2,487.5
Exports of Goods & Services	6,132.3	22,475.8	38,141.7
Merchandise incl. non- monetary gold	4,428.3	15,288.3	29,013.8
Freight & insurance	34.5	404.8	868.6
Travel	279.9	891.2	1,359.7
Investment income	203.4	514.1	967.7
Government n.i.e.	416.6	95.7	104.8
Other transportation & services n.i.e.	769.6	5,281.7	5,827.1
Imports of Goods & Services	7,859.5	24,099.6	40,629.2
Merchandise incl. non- monetary gold	7,047.7	20,756.0	35,583.5
Freight & insurance	466.3	1,319.7	1,828.3
Travel	31.9	141.7	263.5
Investment income	89.4	860.9	1,122.8
Government n.i.e.	11.9	18.3	26.2
Other transportation & services n.i.e.	212.3	1,003.0	1,804.9
Trade Balance	− 2,619.4	− 5,467.7	− 6,569.7
Balance of Services	892.2	3,843.9	4,082.2
B. Transfer Payments (net)	− 23.6	− 121.1	−74.1
Private	− 63.5	− 113.0	− 66.3
Government	39.9	− 8.1	− 7.8
Current Account Balance	− 1,750.8	− 1,744.9	− 2,561.6
C. Capital (net)	532.6	2,097.7	2,082.3
Nonmonetary Sector (net)	429.1	1,892.0	2,481.4
Private	349.9	1,791.3	2,516.7
Official	79.2	100.7	− 35.3
Monetary Sector (net)	103.5	205.7	− 399.1
Commercial banks:			
foreign assets	− 13.8	− 855.2	− 2,118.2
foreign liabilities	117.3	1,060.9	1,719.1
D. Allocation of Special Drawing Rights	—	—	14.3
E. Balancing Item	1,783.0	384.6	1,602.1
F. Overall Balance (A + B + C + D + E)	564.8	737.4	1,137.1
G. Official Reserves (net)	− 564.8	− 737.4	− 1,137.1
Special Drawing Rights	—	—	− 34.4
Reserve Position in the Fund	—	—	− 23.5
Foreign Exchange Assets	− 564.8	− 737.4	− 1,079.2

Source: Ministry of Finance, Singapore, *Economics of Singapore, 1979.*

Finally, a fair amount of capital inflow is typically channelled through the monetary sector, that is to say, through the banks. Interbank flows, quite often via the Asian Dollar Market, account for the bulk. The year 1979 appears to be exceptional in that the monetary sector recorded a net overflow of funds. Interest differentials in favor of external rates and a more stable U.S. dollar were factors contributing to the outflow.[4]

In connection with the above discussion, it may be useful to say a few words about the Asian Dollar Market, which was established in 1968 and has assumed growing importance as a financial intermediary which moves funds across national borders, serving the needs not only of Singapore but also of the region at large. Table 9 shows the assets and liabilities of the Asian Currency Units (ACUs), which are separate entities licensed to operate in the Asian Dollar Market. As can be seen, the size of the Market, as measured in terms of the total assets/liabilities of ACUs, increased from US$31 million at the end of 1968 to US$38,000 million at the end of 1979. It can also be seen that interbank funds form the bulk on both the assets and liabilities sides. The data do not show how much of these interbank funds were ultimately channelled to finance trade and industry. Direct loans to nonbank customers, though a relatively small item in the ACUs' portfolios, had increased at an impressive rate.

As no data are published showing the breakdown of ACUs' loans by country and industry, a useful glimpse may be obtained from the following quotation. Reporting on the year 1979, the Monetary Authority of Singapore stated that "as in 1978, nonbank financial institutions and the manufacturing sector absorbed more than 56 percent of total nonbank loans. Among the main industries were the chemical and chemical products industries including petroleum refining, the metals industry and textiles and clothing. Financing trade and general commerce was also significant. In addition, some of the loans were used for the financing of balance of payments needs of countries adversely affected by the higher oil prices during the year."[5]

---

[4] The Monetary Authority of Singapore, *Annual Report 1979/80*, p. 15.
[5] *Ibid.*, p. 49.

Table 9. Assets and Liabilities of ACUs

	(million U.S. dollars)		
	End of Period		
	1968	1974	1979
Assets			
Loans to nonbank customers	1.4	2,697.7	8,484.0
Interbank funds	29.0	7,459.7	28,093.7
In Singapore	—	223.0	1,100.4
Inter-ACU	—	2,144.7	5,999.3
Outside Singapore	—	5,092.0	20,994.0
Other assets	0.1	199.9	1,585.0
Total	30.5	10,357.3	38,162.7
Liabilities			
Deposits of nonbank customers	17.8	1,614.2	5,771.4
Interbank funds	12.6	8,531.4	29,424.9
In Singapore	—	675.6	1,881.8
Inter-ACU	—	2,144.7	5,999.5
Outside Singapore	—	5,711.1	21,543.6
Other Liabilities	0.1	211.7	2,966.4
Total	30.5	10,357.3	38,162.7

Source: The Monetary Authority of Singapore, *Quarterly Bulletin,* various issues.

VI. Summary and Conclusion

The Singapore economy has grown at a relatively high and sustained rate. This has been made possible by the continual inflow of foreign capital. National saving, though substantial in size, is inadequate to finance the rate of capital formation which averages about one-third of the GDP. While industrialization is the linchpin of development policy, external trade has also grown at a commensurate pace. Foreign direct investment, trade credits and inter-company transfers provide the finances to meet the recurring deficit in merchandise trade.

From a policy viewpoint, two factors appear to be critical to Singapore's success in financing trade and development without running into inflationary bottlenecks. The first factor is prudent budgetary and financial policy. The government has consistently generated a surplus on current operations and used it to finance development expenditure. Any shortfall that may still arise from time to time is met by domestic borrowings. The amount of domestic borrowings is always in excess of the financial requirements of the government and tends to exert a deflationary influence on economy. A large captive market for government debt is provided by the CPF funds which are essentially a form of forced savings. The government's insistence on the principle of productiveness for its infrastructural investment and on commerical viability for its economic enterprises precludes wastage of resources and forestalls any draining of finances that will occur with the subsidization of white elephants and sick industries.

The second factor is the open policy adopted with respect to foreign capital. Incentives are provided to attract foreign investment. Free repatriation of capital as well as profits is guaranteed by the government. Modern technology as embodied in foreign capital has helped upgrade industries and management and labor skills. The influx of funds has contributed critically to a higher rate of economic growth than would have been sustainable by national saving alone. Improvement in and expansion of financial institutions, particularly the establishment of the Asian Dollar Market, have meant better and easier access to international funds and further encouraged both long-term and short-term capital inflows.

REFERENCES

Choi, Shiok Chin, "Consumer Prices in Singapore, 1935-1978," Department of Economics and Statistics, University of Singapore, 1979/80.

Huang, S.H., "Measures to Promote Industrialization," You Poh Seng and Lim Chong Yah (eds.), *The Singapore Economy*, Singapore: Eastern University Press, 1971.

• COMMENT _____

Hisao Kanamori, *Japan Economic Research Center*

Professor Wong explains how Singapore has succeeded in non-inflationary development financing.

Success is attributed to these facts. First, the government has exercised budgetary parsimony, and the current operations have always been surplus. Second, the government has allocated the surplus in the current account to development expenditure. Third, government securities have been bought by the Central Provident Fund. Finally, as the government has adopted an open policy toward foreign capital, the inflow of foreign capital has been smooth.

One question which arises is whether it is possible for the Central Provident Fund to maintain forever sufficient net surplus to purchase government securities. When the retirement from office of government employees increases in number in the future, will it still be possible for the Fund to maintain a surplus?

A. E. Safarian, *University of Toronto*

Wong has outlined the major elements in the financing of the rapid economic growth of Singapore, with some emphasis on the issue of non-inflationary development financing. The following remarks are directed to some aspects of foreign financing of that growth. Net borrowing and direct investment from abroad amounted to one-fifth of annual capital formation in 1968 and one-third in each of 1973 and 1979.[1] The share of resident foreigners and foreign-owned companies

_____

[1] Presumably the data on net capital inflow in Table 3 include retained earnings. If not, the proportions noted above would be significantly higher.

in gross domestic product rose from 15 percent to 25 percent over the same period. Among the major industrial establishments, wholly foreign-owned companies and joint ventures make up 80 to 90 percent of the number of establishments. These are striking figures. The interpretation placed on them in the context of the author's conclusions raises some interesting points.

Consider, first, the conclusion that national saving, though large, was inadequate to finance the high rate of capital formation, hence the reliance on a major inflow of foreign capital. In an ex post sense that was obviously the case. But it should be related to the author's other conclusion about budgetary financial policy. The consolidated accounts of the government and six statutory boards show a consistent current surplus in the seventies, which is used to finance development expenditure. In addition, the government has made very substantial net borrowings, largely in the domestic market. It is not clear from the tables in the paper just how these net borrowings have been utilized, but, on the basis of the partial data presented, one may ask if they have gone to a considerable degree into an increase in foreign exchange reserves. It is not clear what the precise justification for this was, although Wong regards the domestic borrowing side as one aspect of the avoidance of inflationary problems. One wonders if it may also have pushed the private sector into financing abroad, and whether the simultaneous increase in both foreign exchange assets and foreign financing of industry left Singapore, on balance, better off.

To go a step further, one of the remarkable aspects of public financing is the role of the retirement fund, the Central Provident Fund, which is the largest holder of government securities. Compulsory contributions by employers and employees now amount to 38.5 percent of the employees wage or salary. These funds are heavily invested in housing, which accounts for 20 percent of gross national product; about 70 percent of the population now lives in homes provided by government agencies.[2] Once again there may be perfectly good reasons why this was the preferred pattern of investment allocation. One can point in particular to the desire for social stability in the particular situation of Singapore, as well as the specialization of functions between domestic and foreign capital and technology owners. But one should note that the degree and even distribution of foreign financing would have looked quite different over time if such

---

[2] Singapore: a Survey, *The Economist,* 29 December 1979, pp. 6 and 24.

a large portion of domestic saving had not been allocated by government to public housing investment.

The second and related point is the statement that Singapore's high and sustained rate of growth was made possible by the foreign capital inflow. The magnitudes quoted earlier would certainly seem to suggest this, but it would have been interesting to have more information on the degree to which direct investment contributed to the high and sustained growth rate. Like many other countries, Singapore has made important tax and other concessions to attract such direct investment. How do the output gains associated with increased capital and technical inputs look when tax concessions are omitted? Most of the literature suggests that the various improvements associated with direct investment can be captured by the multinational firm, with the state gaining the tax share of increased output, or it can spill over into the rest of the economy. How far the latter has occurred in terms of labor training, improvements in supplying firms and the like is not answered here. Singapore's experience with export-oriented direct investment, almost half in petroleum and products, and one-fifth in electrical and non-electrical machinery, confirm or deny a number of studies which suggest such spill-overs may be small. Whatever the answer, today in Singapore an attempt is being made to further upgrade product lines for world markets. That in turn will provide an interesting test both of the adaptability of multinational firms to new and changed opportunities and pressures in the more advanced developing countries, and also of the increased adjustment problems in their home countries.

GENERAL DISCUSSION

In Singapore, government has a very important role in deciding what to promote. In 1968, it decided to switch to export-oriented growth strategy by introducing various promotional legislations. In the beginning the government subsidy schemes emphasized labor-intensive industries such as textiles and plastic products, but in later stages it has begun to promote high-technology-intensive and more capital-intensive industries for export expansion in order to become less vulnerable to competition from other developing countries.

As a form of forced household saving, each employee contributes up to 18.5 percent of his wage earnings to the Central Provident Fund. The employer has to match by contributing an amount equivalent to 20 percent of wage payment every month. These contributions can be taken out at retirement which is at age 55. CPF is used mostly to buy government securities and to finance government development expenditures on infrastructure building such as housing. CPF also finances loans to various statutory bodies. These loans have been increasing very rapidly. In Singapore, government expenditure is heavily concentrated on housing, education, health and defense, but the government spends very little on other general welfare expenditure. Under the given demographic structure, CPF is expected to generate a surplus for a long period of time.

The location of a fairly large international capital market in Singapore has provided the Singapore economy with a ready access to an enormous flow of capital funds, especially after the oil crisis. One may then question how the government maintains price stability. A huge inflow of foreign capital and consequent accumulation of foreign exchange reserves may cause inflation if there is no adequate sterilization policy. Taiwan has a similar problem, and it has been restricting the foreign capital inflow which is to be used just as working capital. Perhaps government budget surplus and forced household saving in the form of CPF might have helped offset inflationary pressure.

The price level in Singapore has been very stable. The government has never controlled prices directly except in the case of rent control on housing. There is little protection of domestic industries. Many assembling plants have closed down because of the absence of protection and rising wage rates. Because of the labor shortage, government does not try to take actions to prevent such close-downs.

Singapore does not emphasize pure R & D activities. Instead, it emphasizes imitation by promoting education of scientists and engineers. One might argue that what Singapore needs more is skilled labor, and not the scientists and engineers, to promote a new generation of non-labor-intensive industries.

Singapore encourages multinational corporations to benefit from the technology spill-over effect. Foreign investment, especially the Japanese investments, finance petroleum refining, petrochemicals and electronics. Downstream processing of petro-chemical products is fairly labor-intensive, and therefore a petroleum processing base located in Singapore might have a significant spill-over effect on other ASEAN countries. However, what the local spill-over effect would be is debatable. Perhaps Singapore is moving into capital-intensive industries too rapidly.

TRADE STRATEGY AND THE EXCHANGE RATE POLICIES IN TAIWAN

Kuo-Shu Liang &
Ching-ing Hou Liang*

I. Introduction

The incentive policies in Taiwan before 1958 were those typically associated with an import-substitution strategy. The diversification and expansion of industrial production placed primary emphasis on the domestic market. It was agriculture together with U.S. economic aid which financed industrialization in the early stage of postwar economic development. The government adopted a multiple exchange rate system and strict import controls during this period.

The simple and relatively easy phase of import substitution reached its limit, however, in a relatively short period of time in the protected narrow domestic market. It was recognized that only an outward-looking or export-oriented industrialization strategy could sustain a high rate of economic growth in such a small island economy as Taiwan, and accordingly, a series of policy reforms were undertaken during 1958-61. Overvalued currency was devalued, and the complicated exchange rate structure was simplified and finally unified in June 1961. Laws and regulations governing investment and imports were liberalized. The emphasis of trade strategy shifted from strict import controls to export promotion.

The unified and stable exchange rate not only simplified the administration of foreign exchange, but also assured the exporters

---
* Professors of Economics, National Taiwan University and National Chengchi University, Taiwan.

reasonable earnings free from exchange uncertainties, provided that the internal price level is relatively stable. The 1978 revaluation was accompanied by the decision to float the currency and abandon the long-standing fixed exchange rate system which exposed the country to inflationary pressure from abroad. This study examines the shift in emphasis in trade strategy and the exchange rate policies in Taiwan in roughly chronological order.

II. Trade Strategy and the Exchange Rate Policies During the Period of Inward-Oriented Growth

With the Communist insurgence on the mainland and the loss of major outlets in Japan, ready markets for such primary products as sugar, rice, bananas, canned pineapple, and tea were no longer available. As a result, Taiwan suffered from severe foreign exchange shortages and rapid inflation during the late 1940s. Despite these adverse factors, the reconstruction of the Taiwan economy began in earnest in 1949, a year which witnessed the relocation of the mainland government to the island. The major government measures consisted of land reform, currency reform, and inward-oriented trade policies.

A broad base for economic development was laid by land reform which was carried out during 1949-1953 (Tang and Lian, 1973:116-117). The positive role played by the agricultural sector in Taiwan offers a sharp contrast to the experiences of many other less developed countries, where lack of agricultural development acted as a drag on industrial and general economic development.

The prewar production level was by and large restored during the years 1948-51, and U.S. economic aid was resumed in June 1950 after the outbreak of the Korean war. Taiwan was the beneficiary of a substantial U.S. aid program. A total of $1,444 million was appropriated over the period 1951-65, amounting to $10 per capita a year. Aid played an important role in helping to control inflation in the early 1950s. In addition, were it not for U.S. aid, Taiwan's trade gap would have become a serious factor limiting its economic development until the early 1960s. U.S. aid broke this bottleneck by augmenting foreign exchange resources and sustaining the import of necessary inputs that complemented domestic labor and other investment components. The share of U.S. aid imports in total imports

remained above 30 percent until 1961, but declined rapidly afterwards (Liang and Lee, 1974: 296-299).

As noted earlier, Taiwan suffered from severe foreign exchange
shortages and rapid inflation during the late 1940s. The government
introduced a currency reform in June 1949 which consisted of issuing
the new currency, called the New Taiwan Dollar (NT$) with one
hundred percent reserves which were made up of gold, silver, foreign
exchange and export commodities, and the exchange rate was pegged
at five NT dollars to one U.S. dollar. In addition, the maximum
amount of currency issue was limited to NT 200 million and the old
currency was allowed to be converted to NT dollars at the rate of
40,000 to one.

Due to the government budget deficits and the easy credit granted
to public enterprises, the currency issue, however, exceeded the
prescribed limit of NT$200 million by early 1950, and continued to
increase thereafter. The resulting inflation forced the government to
devalue the exchange rate repeatedly. At the same time, the exchange
rate system moved from a single rate to multiple rates in an effort to
deal with recurrent balance of payments difficulties. Foreign exchange
rates varied depending upon the types of imports and the sources of
foreign exchange, with applications for an import license being discouraged by requiring importers to deposit in advance of importation
100 percent of the domestic currency equivalent of foreign exchange.

Exports of sugar and rice generally received a relatively unfavorable
exchange rate that formed part of the government's system of taxing
farmers. With the exception of U.S. aid imports of basic raw materials
and industrial products, and imports by government enterprises
whose prices were controlled, a tax in the form of a higher exchange
rate was applied to other imports. In addition to this, high tariffs
were levied on many finished goods and luxury items, and imports
were severely restricted by licenses.

Foreign exchange rates on May 1, 1955 are shown in Table 1.
Measures such as the multiple exchange rate system and tariff and
non-tariff protection increased the profitability of import substitution,
and were partly responsible for the doubling of manufacturing
production during the period 1950 to 1958. However, the import
substitution strategy had its adverse effects (Scott, 1979: 315-316).

The implementation of a complicated system of multiple exchange
rates required considerable administrative cost. Foreign exchange
allocation became selective and discriminatory among various cate-

Table 1.   *Foreign Exchange Rates on May 1, 1955*

(NT dollars per U.S. dollar)

Buying Rates	
Rates for Exports	
Exports by Government Enterprises	
Sugar, Rice, Petroleum, Aluminum, and Salt	$15.55[a]
Others	20.35[b]
Exports by Private Enterprises	
Bananas	18.60[c]
Others	20.43[d]
Rates for Inward Remittances	
Government Agencies	15.55
Private	
Paid in NT Dollars for Whole Amount	21.55[e]
Paid in NT Dollars and Certificate	21.65[f]
Selling Rates	
Rates for Imports	
Imports by Government and Government Enterprises	
Whose prices are Controlled	18.78[g]
Other Imports by Government Enterprises	24.78[h]
U.S. Aid Imports	
Basic Raw Materials and Industrial Project	18.78
Ordinary Imports under Commercial Procurements	24.78
Imports by private Enterprises	
Raw Materials and Equipment for End-users	24.78
Others	24.88[i]
Rates for Outward Remittances	
Government Agencies' Ordinary Remittances	14.78
Private Ordinary Remittances	24.78

Source: Economic Research Department, The Central Bank of China, *The Republic of China: Taiwan Financial Statistics,* March 1972, pp. 81-82, Table 28.

Notes: [a] Official buying basic exchange rate

[b] $15.55 (basic exchange rate) + 80% × $6.00 (official price of certificate)

[c] $15.55 + 50% × $6.10 (market price of certificate)

[d] $15.55 + 80% × $6.10

[e] $15.55 + $6.00

[f] $15.55 + $6.10

[g] $15.65 (official selling basic exchange rate) + $3.13 (defense tax)

[h] $15.65 + $6.00 + $3.13

[i] $15.65 + $6.10 + $3.13

gories of commodities without any economic rationale. Under the strict foreign-exchange and import controls, the premiums over duty-inclusive import costs of many industrial materials and consumer goods were substantial. For instance, wheat flour commanded a premium of 48 percent, soybeans 141 percent, cotton yarn 33 percent, cotton piece goods and poplin 152-163 percent, woolen wear 350 percent, soda ash 275 percent, ammonium sulfate 102 percent, and steel plate 35 percent in 1953 (Lin, 1973: 50-51). The control system induced entrepreneurs to compete for licenses rather than encouraging low-cost production and provided an inducement for corruption. Moreover, preferential allocation of undervalued foreign exchange for imported raw materials and capital equipment created incentives to expand capacity even when there was underutilization of existing capacity. The squeeze, applied through both direct and hidden methods on agriculture, also resulted in depressed incomes and consumption for farmers (Tang and Liang, 1973: 138).

As shown in Table 3, the industrial survey for 1959 indicates that many plants producing simple manufactures, such as rubber canvas shoes, electric fans, soap, insulated wire, plywood, synthetic fabrics, woolen yarn, sewing machines, iron rods and bars, and paper, were operating at only 23 to 67 percent capacity. Import substitution was a self-limiting process, and the growth rate of GNP decelerated during the period 1956-60, as shown in Table 2.

The government promulgated the Regulations for Rebate of Taxes on Export Products in July 1955, providing for the rebate of import duty, defense surtax, and commodity tax so as to encourage processing of imported materials for export. This did not prove sufficient, however, and as the government began to recognize that only export-oriented industrialization could sustain a high rate of economic growth in such a small island economy as Taiwan, a series of major policy reforms were undertaken during 1958-60.

Table 2.   Major Economic Indicators: 1952-79

	1952	1955	1960	1965	1970	1975	1979
A. Computation of Per Capita Income							
GNP (NT$ million at 1976 prices)	89,864	116,349	160,978	252,909	403,210	613,414	940,561
Population (thousand persons)	8,128	9,078	10,792	12,628	14,676	16,150	17,479
GNP per capita (NT$1,000 at 1976 prices)	11.0	12.8	14.9	20.0	27.5	38.0	53.8
B. Percentage Shares in GDP (at current prices) at Factor Cost by Industrial Origin							
Primary Production	37.13	33.72	33.87	28.30	19.81	15.76	10.56
Manufacturing	9.82	14.40	17.44	20.01	27.31	30.54	42.12
Social overhead[a]	9.61	10.47	11.08	12.26	13.74	15.56	14.96
Services	42.83	42.86	39.39	40.15	42.03	40.66	34.58
C. Percentage Shares in GNP							
Government revenue	23.56	24.59	23.75	20.06	22.68	23.35	26.70
Government savings	5.47	5.08	3.99	2.06	3.46	7.04	8.38
Total domestic savings	15.38	14.63	17.84	20.47	25.71	26.96	32.70
Gross capital formation	15.40	13.74	20.26	23.23	25.69	30.81	32.85
Exports	8.07	8.28	11.32	18.59	29.72	39.50	54.42
Imports	14.21	12.62	18.87	21.89	29.77	42.82	53.83
D. Percentage Share of Manufactured Exports in Total Exports							
Manufactured Exports (NT$ billion)[b]		0.14	1.69	7.78	43.60	163.53	505.83
Manufactured Exports/Total Exports		7.6	28.2	42.6	76.7	81.3	87.3

Table 2. (Continued)

	1952-55	1955-60	1960-65	1965-70	1970-75	1975-79	1952-79
E. Compound Annual Growth Rates							
GNP (at 1976 prices)	9.0	6.7	9.5	9.8	8.8	11.3	9.1
GNP per capita (at 1976 prices)	5.1	3.1	6.1	6.6	6.7	9.1	6.1
Index of manufacturing output	16.7	10.9	13.8	20.6	13.5	17.8	15.3
Total exports (at 1976 prices)	4.5	11.7	21.1	22.2	15.4	18.4	16.1
Employment							
Total	1.2	2.1	2.3	4.3	3.8	3.9	2.9
Manufacturing	4.8	4.8	5.3	8.3	9.9	8.5	7.8
Agriculture	0.4	0.6	0.5	-0.7	-0.3	-4.4	-1.0
Real Wages							
Manufacturing	5.7	-0.1	5.5	6.5	7.9	10.7	5.8
Prices							
GNP deflator	10.3	8.5	2.8	4.8	11.1	6.9	7.2
Wholesale price index	8.3	9.0	2.0	1.9	11.4	5.6	6.2

Sources: Directorate-General of Budget, Accounting and Statistics, *National Income of the Republic of China*; Economic Planning Council, *Taiwan Statistical Data Book*; Department of Statistics, Ministry of Finance, *Monthly Statistics of Exports and Imports, The Republic of China*; Research, Development, and Evaluation Commission, *Commodity Trade Statistics of the Republic of China (SITC Revised), 1954-74*, Aug., 1976; Overall Planning Department, Economic Planning Council, *Research Report* No. (66) 120. 119, July 1977.

Notes: [a] Includes construction; electricity, gas and water; transport, storage and communication.
[b] Includes SITC categories 5 through 8.

III. Trade Strategy and the Exchange Rate Policies During the Period of Outward-Oriented Growth

The timely promulgation of the Program for Improvement of Foreign Exchange and Trade Control in April 1958 was epoch-making. Several major steps were subsequently carried into effect.

The government devalued the overvalued currency, and a dual rate, namely the basic official exchange rate and the exchange certificate rate, replaced the multiple rate structure. Export proceeds and inward remittances were given the exchange certificates which were transferrable and represented full import rights. Market demand and supply determined the exchange certificate rate, and the rate was stabilized at NT$40 to U.S. $1 by August 1958. The basic official exchange rate and the exchange certificate rate were finally merged at this level in June 1961, giving rise to a single unitary exchange rate. This unified and stable exchange rate not only simplified the administration of foreign exchange, but also assured the exporters of making a sound economic calculation and realizing reasonable earnings free from exchange uncertainties.

Table 4 shows purchasing-power-parity effective exchange rates on exports. The purchasing-power-parity effective exchange rate on exports is defined as the official exchange rate of NT dollars per U.S.

Table 3. *Rates of Capacity Utilization of Selected Manufactures: 1959 and 1970*

	1959	1970
Rubber Canvas Shoes	23.3	70.9
Electric Fans	38.1	65.3
Soap	39.2	82.1
Insulated Wire	40.0	64.6
Plywood	46.9	86.2
Synthetic Fabrics	49.7	85.4
Woollen Yarn	52.6	100.0
Sewing Machines	64.3	51.2
Iron Rods and Bars	65.4	98.7
Paper	67.4	90.2

Source: Ministry of Economic Affairs and Council for International Economic Cooperation and Development, Executive Yuan, *Industry Surveys in Taiwan*, various years.

Table 4. Purchasing-Power-Parity Effective Exchange Rates on Exports: 1956-78

	1956	1957	1958	1959	1960	1961	1962	1963	1964	1965	1966
A. Official Exchange Rate for Exports[a] (NT$ per U.S. dollar)	24.71	25.53	34.14	39.38	39.73	38.83	39.83	39.87	40.00	40.00	40.00
B. Incentives NT$ per U.S. dollar of Exports											
Interest Subsidy[b]		0.005	0.017	0.021	0.031	0.038	0.086	0.086	0.06	0.073	0.083
Customs Duties Rebate[c]	0.21	0.22	0.50	1.22	1.69	1.87	2.23	2.48	2.69	2.97	3.24
Indirect Tax Rebate[d]	0.01	0.06	0.15	0.36	0.68	0.97	1.00	0.77	0.92	1.07	1.07
Sub-total	0.22	0.285	0.667	1.601	2.401	2.878	3.316	3.336	3.67	4.113	4.393
C. Nominal Effective Exchange Rate (A + B)	24.93	25.82	34.81	40.98	42.13	42.71	43.15	43.21	43.67	44.11	44.39
D. Taiwan's Wholesale Price Index (1960=100)	73.13	78.33	79.38	87.71	100.00	103.33	106.46	113.33	116.04	110.63	112.29
E. Average Wholesale Price Index of Major Trade Partners[e]	98.69	101.86	97.76	98.73	100.00	101.14	100.94	103.89	103.49	104.85	109.25
F. Exchange Rate Index[f]	101.77	102.36	101.92	101.38	100.00	97.57	97.56	95.60	97.74	97.51	95.64
G. Purchasing-Power-Parity Effective Exchange Rate on Exports (C×E/D×F)	34.24	34.37	43.69	46.77	42.13	40.79	39.91	37.87	38.07	40.76	41.31

Sources: DGBAS, Commodity-Price Statistics Monthly, Taiwan District, The Republic of China; IMF, International Financial Statistics; Economic Research Department, The Central Bank of China, The Republic of China, Taiwan Financial Statistics Monthly; Department of Statistics, Ministry of Finance, Yearbook of Financial Statistics of the Republic of China; Census and Statistics Department, Hong Kong, Consumer price Index Report.

Notes: [a] Where the rates fluctuated over a period, the mean of the range was taken. The rate up to April 14, 1958 was that applicable to exports by private enterprises. Therefore, until September 30, 1963, it was the rate applicable to all exports other than a few commodities (e.g. sugar, rice, salt, banana) for which lower rates applied. The same rate applied to all exports after September 30, 1963 (See Scott 1979, p. 326).

[b] The difference in the interest on export loans and that on unsecured loans is treated as an export subsidy.

[c] Includes defense surtax and harbor dues.

[d] Includes commodity tax, salt tax, and flood rehabilitation surtax.

[e] An average of wholesale price indexes in Australia, Canada, West Germany, Hong Kong, Japan, Korea, Netherlands, Singapore, United Kingdom, and the United States, weighted by Taiwan's annual export value with the respective countries. In case wholesale price index is not available, consumer price index is used.

[f] An average of exchange rate index weighted by Taiwan's annual export value with the respective major trade partners. The exchange rate is expressed in terms of U.S. dollars per unit of the currencies of Taiwan's trading partners.

Table 4. (Continued)

	1967	1968	1969	1970	1971	1972	1973	1974	1975	1976	1977	1978
A. Official Exchange Rate for Exports[a] (NT$ per U.S. dollar)	40.00	40.00	40.00	40.00	40.00	40.00	38.16	37.90	37.95	37.95	37.95	35.95
B. Incentives NT$ per U.S. dollar of Exports												
Interest Subsidy[b]	0.077	0.096	0.1	0.093	0.1	0.095	0.074	0.083	0.083	0.076	0.057	0.05
Customs Duties Rebate[c]	3.49	3.37	3.48	4.06	4.27	3.68	2.82	2.47	2.70	2.14	2.11	1.65
Indirect Tax Rebate[d]	1.19	1.23	1.27	1.36	1.34	1.24	0.98	0.87	1.12	0.89	0.89	0.77
Sub-total	4.757	4.696	4.85	5.513	5.71	5.015	3.874	3.423	3.903	3.106	3.057	2.49
C. Nominal Effective Exchange Rate (A+B)	44.76	44.70	44.85	45.51	45.71	45.02	42.03	41.32	41.85	41.06	41.01	38.44
D. Taiwan's Wholesale Price Index (1960 = 100)	115.21	118.54	118.33	121.45	121.67	127.08	156.04	219.38	208.33	214.17	220.00	227.71
E. Average Wholesale price Index of Major Trade Partners[e]	112.50	112.79	116.93	121.74	125.67	130.16	146.34	180.76	193.95	198.59	211.85	223.25
F. Exchange Rate Index[f]	93.45	95.63	95.36	96.03	96.92	101.45	109.33	103.63	104.65	106.89	106.95	113.30
G. Purchasing-Power-Parity Effective Exchange Rate on Exports (C×E/D×F)	40.84	40.67	42.26	43.80	45.76	46.78	43.09	35.28	40.77	40.70	42.24	42.69

dollar of exports, adjusted for changes in export incentives, in whole-sale prices in Taiwan and abroad, and in the exchange rates of Taiwan's major trade partners. Since the estimates of export incentives only include interest subsidy and rebates on customs duties and indirect taxes, it is an imperfect estimate of export incentives. These export incentives reduce costs of production for exports to below those for the domestic market. The resulting estimates clearly show that the repeated devaluations and simplification during the late 1950s, following the policy reform, together with the export incentives provided and the relative domestic price stability, maintained the purchasing-power-parity effective exchange rate as a fairly stable one over the period 1958-73. It was particularly favorable for exports during the periods 1958-60 and 1969-73. The fairly stable purchasing-power-parity effective exchange rate helped induce producers to prefer export over domestic markets and accelerated export expansion despite a continually expanding base.

The reform initiated in April 1958 was also aimed at reducing the strict controls on foreign exchange allocation. The government gradually liberalized and finally abolished the commodity import quota system. The restrictions on imports of materials and equipment to be used for exports were substantially eased from 1958 onwards. Devaluation, accompanied by import liberalization, was not necessarily inflationary (Scott, 1979: 328).

Table 5 shows the ratio of customs revenues to imports. Column (1) lists the ratio of net customs revenues, including import duty, defense surtax, and harbor dues, to total imports while Column (2) lists the ratio of gross customs revenues which are the sum total of net customs revenues and those rebated to exporters, to total imports. The gross ratio is probably a better measure of the average degree of protection since it is not affected by the increasing importance of processed exports and assembly operations based on imported inputs which were exempt from tax (Scott, 1979: 334-335). Both net and gross ratios show an obvious declining trend in the average level of protection during the period under review. The higher ratio on gross revenues than that on net revenues suggests that tariffs on inter-mediate products were often fairly high. Unless these taxes were rebated, the manufacturers could not possibly export. Power has been given to vary the tariff rates up or down by half without reference to the Legislative Yuan in recent years, and to enable expedient reduction to be made whenever necessary.

Table 5. Ratios of Customs Revenues to Imports: 1955-78

(in percent)

Fiscal Year	Net Revenues[a] (1)	Gross Revenues[a] (2)
1955	66.94 (42.28)[b]	68.06 (42.98)[b]
1960	28.21	31.72
1965	22.01	31.81
1970	18.00	26.13
1975	11.82	17.97
1978	13.42	18.60

Source: Department of Statistics, Ministry of Finance, *Monthly Statistics of Exports and Imports, The Republic of China* and Department of Statistics, Ministry of Finance, *Yearbook of Financial Statistics of the Republic of China.*

Notes: [a] Net customs revenues include import duty, defense surtax, and harbor dues. Gross customs revenues are sum total of net customs revenues and those rebated to exporters.

[b] For fiscal year 1955 the average exchange rate used by Customs to convert imports from U.S. dollars to NT dollars was NT$15.65 per U.S. dollar, whereas the exchange rate applicable to the bulk of imports was probably NT$24.78. The figures in parentheses show the ratios with appropriate corrections.

The ratio of customs revenues to imports is a crude measure of the average degree of protection since it is affected by the changing composition of imports. Import liberalization, which allowed an increase in such imports as consumer durables and cars at higher customs duties, appeared to have resulted in the higher average ratios of customs revenues to imports in 1978 as compared with those in 1975.

Table 6 groups manufactured commodities in various categories which were classified as permissible, controlled, or prohibited. Imports are controlled mainly for protective purposes. Control means that import licenses are given only if comparable goods are not produced domestically. Permissible imports mean that import licenses are in general granted automatically, although there may be restrictions on particular sources of origin or the status of the applicants. The principle that domestic availability justifies import control is an important part of the protective system in Taiwan as in many other developing countries. Manufactures were protected in many cases by tariff as well as nontariff restrictions. However, there has been some liberalization since the early 1960s as the criteria used to justify the

Table 6. Changes in the Classification of Various Categories of Manufactured Importables: 1953-78

		Categories of Importables								
		Permissible		Controlled		Prohibited		Others[a]		Total	
		No. of Items	%	No. of Items	%	No. of Items	%	No. of Items	%	No. of Items	%
1953		280	55.23	185	36.49	28	5.52	14	2.76	507	100.00
1956		252	48.10	241	45.99	25	4.77	6	1.14	524	100.00
1960		506	53.72	381	40.45	33	3.50	22	2.33	942	100.00
1966		493	52.34	395	41.93	36	3.82	18	1.91	942	100.00
1968	(Dec.)	5,451	57.92	3,770	40.05	191	2.03	—	—	9,412	100.00
1970	(July)	5,612	57.08	4,030	40.99	190	1.93	—	—	9,832	100.00
1972	(July)	10,860	82.09	2,365	17.87	5	0.04	—	—	13,230	100.00
1974	(Feb.)	12,645	97.71	293	2.26	4	0.03	—	—	12,942	100.00
1975	(Jan.)	12,688	97.52	318	2.44	4	0.03	—	—	13,010	100.00
1976	(June)	12,846	97.16	362	2.74	13	0.10	—	—	13,221	100.00
1978	(July)	15,773	97.57	375	2.32	17	0.11	—	—	16,165	100.00

Source: The Foreign Exchange and Trade Commission, Classification of Imports and Export Commodities of the Republic of China, various editions, and Hsing (1971), p. 208.

Note: [a] Imports partly permissible, controlled, or prohibited.

control of imports of a commodity have been progressively tightened. Domestic manufacturers seeking protection have to show that the quantity and quality of their products are adequate to satisfy domestic demand, and that the cost of imported raw materials required for the manufacture of the product does not exceed 70 percent of the total production cost. The ex-factory price of the controlled commodity was not allowed to exceed the prices of comparable imports (inclusive of all duties) by more than 25 percent in 1960. In 1964 this was reduced to 15 percent, in 1968 to 10 percent, and in 1973 to 5 percent. Although these rules were not applied strictly, they helped entrepreneurial attention be devoted more closely to production efficiency rather than to the maintenance of a quasimonopoly position. Although changes in the number of items falling into the different categories provide only a crude indication of the extent of import control, it appears that the degree of import control intensified during the period 1953-56, with a significant increase in the number of items as classified controlled imports. However, there has been a general tendency towards trade liberalization as was shown by the relative increase in the number of permissible imports since 1960.

Furthermore, the margin deposits on import application was removed in September 1963. The margin deposit required to be paid on ordinary imports on the date of L/C being opened was reduced from 100 percent to 50 percent in May 1967. It has been further reduced to between 10 and 15 percent since August.[1] The interest burden of importers was thus substantially reduced.

There was much more competition between manufactures in the 1960s than there was in the 1950s. The prevailing market situation in most of the newly developed industries is oligopolistic or monopolistic competition rather than monopoly. Even goods on the controlled list have been permitted to be imported, provided they are for the use of export processing. When import controls are relaxed, resources that would otherwise be absorbed in import-competing industries are released to export industries, thus lowering the costs exporters have to pay and enabling them to expand exports more efficiently than otherwise would be the case. The increased competition from imports has also helped improve the quality of domestic manufacturing.

The emphasis of trade policy has gradually shifted from strict

---

[1] The government changed the minimum margin requirements from time to time as an instrument of selective credit controls.

import controls to export promotion, following the 1958 reform. Export incentives in Taiwan consist of rebates on customs duties, including a defense surtax and harbor dues, and a commodity tax on imported raw materials,[2] exemption from business and related stamp taxes, deduction of two percent of annual total export earnings from taxable income and a 10 percent tax reduction allowed for manufacturing, mining, or handicrafts corporations that can meet the criterion of having more than 50 percent of their output exported.[3] Retention of foreign exchange earnings was allowed for the import of raw materials and machinery without having to go through the procedures for the application for foreign exchange, together with the privilege of selling such import rights to other firms.[4] Special low-interest loans to help finance pre-shipment production and the importation of raw materials were offered, along with export insurance by a government agency. The government also encouraged the formation of trading organizations by manufactures as in the cases of textiles, canned mushrooms, canned asparagus spears, and citronella oil to control production and export by means of export quotas and unified quotation of export prices. Direct subsidy for exports was devised by a few industries, such as cotton spinning, steel and iron, rubber products, monosodium glutamate, woolens and fabrics, and paper and paper products, financed through the manufacturers' associations concerned. These schemes amounted to private levies on domestic sales, or on materials used to manufacture for domestic sales, with corresponding bounties on exports.[5] There are many other export promotion measures .undertaken by government and semi-government agencies. Exports have been assisted by these agencies for export inspection, managerial, technical, and trade consultation services, market research, and participation in international trade fairs. The China External Trade Development Council was founded in July 1970 to promote exports and do market research. The Council has been entitled to levy 0.0625 percent on exporters'

---

[2] Furthermore, 'bonded warehouses can be established to avoid the cumbersome problem of assessing and refunding taxes.

[3] The government abolished income tax reductions for exports in December 1970.

[4] A margin ranging from one to four NT dollars per U.S. dollar was generally paid by the transferee. Such a practice was not in conformity with a unitary exchange rate system. Negotiation of retained or registered foreign exchange was terminated on July 30, 1970.

[5] These schemes to subsidize exports do not exist any longer. For instance, the cotton spinning scheme ended in 1972. (See Lee, Liang, Schieve and Yeh, 1975.)

revenue as United Funds for Promotion and Extension of Exports.[6] Moreover, exports have been assisted by the creation of tax- and duty-free export processing zones since 1965. The zones have been erected to encourage investment in the processing and assembling of such exportables as electronic products, garments, and plastic products. The Export Processing Zone Administration representing all the relevant administrative offices of the government is responsible for management of the zones, and has greatly simplified procedures for registration, import and export licensing and foreign exchange transactions. Exports from all three zones in 1975 amounted to U.S.$453 million and imports were U.S.$256 million, 8.5 percent and 4.3 percent respectively of total exports and imports. Imports from the domestic customs territories amounted to 9.5 percent of the exports from all three zones. Perhaps the most important benefit from the zones was increased employment at higher wages. Employment in the zones amounted to 66,115 persons, 4.4 percent of total employment in manufacturing.[7]

In addition to changes more directly related to foreign exchange and trade policies, there were several key reforms aimed at improving the investment climate. Laws and regulations governing investment were liberalized. A new industrial establishment eligible under the Statute for the Encouragement of Investment was given a five-year holiday from the starting date of its operation and exemption from import duties on machinery and equipment.

Table 7 provides some key indicators of Taiwan's success in financial deepening. Financial deepening means an accumulation of financial assets at a pace faster than accumulation of nonfinancial wealth (Show, 1973: vii).[8] Of the measures aimed at financial growth, the most important was to offer savers a positive real rate of return. Financial deepening advanced progressively when stability in the wholesale prices was achieved in the 1960s. The M_2/GDP ratio increased from 27.9 percent in 1961-65 to 34 percent in 1966-70. M_2

---

[6] The rate was reduced to 0.04 percent during the period July 1974 to August 1975 as the economy was affected by the serious global trade decline.

[7] Export Processing Zone Administration, *Export Processing Zones Essential Statistics,* December 1975.

[8] Table 7 provides some indicators of Taiwan's progress in financial deepening by computing changes in the ratios of financial instruments outstanding as percentage of GDP. GDP is used as the denominator due to the unavailability of national wealth statistics. In a steady state, capital stock must grow at the same rate as output.

Table 7.   Key Indicators of Financial Deepening: 1961-79

	1961-1965	1966-1970	1971-1975	1976-1979
1. Ratio of M_1 to GDP (%)	13.1	13.5	15.3	18.8
2. Ratio of M_2 to GDP (%)	27.9	34.0	44.1	58.9
3. Percentage change in wholesale price index (annual)	2.11	1.89	12.57	5.73
4. Interest rate on one-year deposits (%)	12.91	9.83	10.91	10.56
5. Real return on holding one-year deposits (%)	10.80	7.94	−1.66	4.83
6. M_2 at 1976 constant prices (NT$billion)	52.5	106.9	238.2	500.5
7. Ratio of net private national saving to national income (%)	10.2	13.9	19.7	19.6
8. Government bonds outstanding as percentage of GDP	1.8	4.2	2.4	1.3
9. Corporate bonds outstanding as percentage of GDP	0.2	0.3	0.3	1.2
10. Market value of stocks outstanding as percentage of GDP	20.0[a]	8.3	12.1	14.9

Sources: DGBAS, *Commodity Price Statistics Monthly,* Taiwan District, *The Republic of China;* Economic Research Department, The Central Bank of China, *Financial Statistics Monthly,* Taiwan District, *The Republic of China;* DGBAS, *National Income of the Republic of China*; Taiwan Stock Exchange.

Notes: [a] 1962-65.

The stock market was established in 1962.

M_1 = Net currency issued + demand deposits adjusted.

M_2 = M_1 + quasi-money.

M_2 at 1976 constant prices is deflated by the wholesale price index.

deflated by the wholesale price index, which represents the real lending capacity of the organized banking sector, doubled during the period (McKinnon, 1973: 114). The strengthened liquidity position provided an important base from which credit expansion of the commercial banks could proceed. The increase in the credit availability and the relative price stability in turn had the effect of reducing interest rates to some extent.

Since corporate bonds and market value of stocks outstanding as a percentage of GDP have not revealed a clearly increasing trend during the period under review, the contribution of the banking system to

economic growth has been considerable. One of the principal characteristics of corporate finance in Taiwan is a low proportion of bond
financing and a correspondingly heavy dependence on bank credit.

The dampening of inflationary expectations contributed not only to
the financial growth observed, but also to the rise in the measured net
private saving ratio. Relative price stability and financial deepening
invariably aided economic development.

With a favorable investment climate and a high profitability in
exporting created by outward-oriented government policies, industry
underwent radical changes, aided also by an abundant and efficient
labor force. Manufactured exports expanded rapidly, especially after
1963.[9] By the mid-1960s, the somewhat pessimistic views of the late
1950s had been replaced by a popular sense of confidence and
prosperity. It can be seen from Table 3 that, with the exception of
sewing machines, the rates of capacity utilization of simple manufactures had improved significantly in 1970 as compared with those in
1959. The economic indicators of the economy shown in Table 2 also
clearly reveal the fact that economic performances in the 1960s and
the early 1970s improved greatly as compared with those in the 1950s.
The average annual rate of growth of manufactured output accelerated
from 11 percent in 1955-60 to 14 percent in 1960-65 and again to 21
percent in 1965-70. Underlying the acceleration of manufacturing
output growth, the share of manufactured products in total exports
rose from 28 percent in 1960 to 77 percent in 1970.

With the rapid development of labor-intensive export industries,
economic growth became more labor-absorptive than before. Manufacturing employment rose 8.3 percent a year in 1965-70, while
real wages increased at a rate of 6.5 percent.

Outward orientation has been a highly successful strategy in
Taiwan. The expansion of manufactured exports has contributed to
efficient industrialization by permitting specialization according to
comparative advantage and stimulating technological improvement. It
has also improved income distribution through the creation of
productive employment and rapid increases in wages (Liang and
Liang, 1978).

After 1973, however, disturbances emanating from abroad and
disequilibrium manifested in the form of raw material and fuel shortages, not to mention the quadrupling of petroleum prices, disrupted

---

[9] An exceptionally high export price of sugar in 1963 and 1964 helped build up
exchange reserves and stabilize the exchange rate.

Table 8. *Rates of Increase in Money Supply and Price Level*

	Growth Rate of M_1 (1)	Trend Value of the Growth Rate of GNP (10-year moving) (2)	Ratio of Excess Supply of M_1 (3) = (1) – (2)	Rate of Change in GNP Deflator (4)
1962	6.9	7.5	– 0.6	2.2
1963	20.9	7.5	13.4	3.4
1964	25.5	7.8	17.7	4.2
1965	6.4	8.1	– 1.7	– 0.7
1966	9.7	8.4	1.3	2.8
1967	30.1	8.8	21.3	4.5
1968	9.6	9.0	0.6	6.8
1969	11.1	9.2	1.9	6.4
1970	11.3	9.6	1.7	3.5
1971	24.8	10.2	14.6	3.1
1972	37.9	10.8	27.1	5.8
1973	49.3	11.1	38.2	15.0
1974	7.0	10.0	– 3.0	32.1
1975	26.9	9.3	17.6	2.3
1976	23.1	9.8	13.3	5.6
1977	29.1	9.7	19.4	6.2
1978	34.1	10.2	23.9	4.7
1979	7.0	10.1	– 3.1	11.3

Sources: Economic Research Department, The Central Bank of China, *The Republic of China, Taiwan Financial Statistics Monthly*; DGBAS *National Income of the Republic of China.*

the economy and contributed to inflation. In addition, the high rates of money expansion in 1972-73 increased "home-made" pressure and resulted in high rates of inflation in 1973-74. In Table 8, an attempt is made to estimate the trend values of GNP growth rate by employing ten-year moving averages. The ratios of excess supply of M_1 are then computed from the trend values of GNP growth rate and the measured growth rate of M_1. Generally speaking, whenever, the ratio of excess supply of M_1 exceeds the rate of inflation, as measured by the rate of change in GNP deflator, with a wide margin in a certain year, there is a tendency for the rate of inflation to accelerate in the following year.

To cope with the situation, the government introduced an economic stabilization program on January 27, 1974 which entailed tight credit through a large-scale across-the-board upward adjustment of bank rates as well as once-and-for-all substantial price increases on such government-controlled goods and services as petroleum products, electricity, transportation services, and alcoholic beverages and tobacco.

These measures produced the desired effect. After a period of sharp increases in late 1973 and early 1974, the price level stabilized. The upward adjustment of bank rates not only forced enterprises to reduce their inventories but also curtailed consumers' demand and encouraged savings. The subsequent decline in the price of raw material and food imports, the shift of the trade balance from surplus to deficit, and a growing government budget surplus were also helpful to economic stabilization.

As inflation in Taiwan proceeded more rapidly than abroad, and the exchange rate appreciated 5 percent in February 1973, the purchasing-power-parity effective exchange rate as shown in Table 4 deteriorated notably in 1974. Although the estimation of export incentives only include interest subsidy and rebates on customs duties and indirect taxes, Table 4 also clearly shows that the government has reduced export incentives since 1973. A previous program under which exporters could borrow for working capital against a credit line based on the previous year's trade performance was discontinued in January 1974. Pre-shipment preferential export credit to finance working capital needs is currently available only with L/C backing. More strict rules were applied to rebates on customs duties.

The deterioration in purchasing-power-parity effective exchange rates adversely affected the profitability of exports and aggravated the trade and economic slowdown created by the world recession. The recession bottomed out in mid-1975. Although recovery was slow and erratic, the commodity trade balance swung from deficits of U.S. $1,327 million and U.S.$643 million in 1974 and 1975 respectively to a surplus of U.S.$567 million in 1976. The purchasing-power-parity effective exchange rate exporters received had begun to increase again, which in turn was mainly attributable to the success in containing domestic inflation.

It should be recognized that Taiwan and other countries following outward-oriented policies were able to weather the recession much better than countries which followed inward-oriented policies (Balassa,

1978). Broadly speaking, inward orientation tends to set in motion many forces which can have adverse impacts on efficiency and growth over the longer term, namely price distortion, social tension, financial shallowing, and discouragement of foreign private investment caused by strict controls on imports and payments. Conversely, price stability and placing greater importance on export competitiveness are indicative of outward orientation. With a quicker payoff in terms of productivity, export earning, and financial deepening, outward orientation would be the more desirable strategy (de Vries, 1967: 11-14, 46-47 and 55-56).

IV. Managed Exchange-Rate Flexibility

From the fourth quarter of 1977 onward, the economy of Taiwan showed an extensive recovery. Helped by the appreciation of the Japanese yen, a rapid expansion in exports accelerated the pace of industrial production and boosted real GNP growth by 13.9 percent in 1978. Exports expanded by 36 percent and manufacturing by 27 percent from a year earlier. These impressive increases over the preceding year's comparable levels suggest an economic boom, despite concern for protectionist sentiments abroad and slower-than-expected recovery in major industrialized countries.

Mainly as a result of a large merchandise-trade surplus and the continuous inflow of long-term foreign capital, the growth rate of the money supply remained at an excessively high level. Money supply increased at an average annual rate of 34 percent, net foreign assets of all commercial banks at 51 percent, and loans and investment of these banks at 27 percent in 1978. The rapid expansion of the money supply and higher prices for imports from Japan and Western Europe, all have contributed to an acceleration of inflation. The rates of inflation were 8.4 percent for wholesale prices, and 7.7 percent for consumer prices in 1978. It is noteworthy that the foreign exchange surplus, which was welcome in the earlier stage of economic development as a contributor to the accumulation of an appropriate stock of currency reserves, has become a potential source of inflation in the late 1970s.

External equilibrium can be achieved by adjustment through domestic inflation or by appreciation of the NT dollar against the

U.S. dollar. As a matter of fact, the two adjustment paths reflect alternative choices with a short-run trade-off between income growth and price stability. In this context, the revaluation in July 1978 highlights the government's stability orientation. It was accompanied by the decision to abandon the long-standing fixed exchange rate system which exposed the country to inflationary pressure from abroad. In order to help importers and exporters adapt to the new exchange rate system and reduce the ·exchange risk, the Central Bank began to provide the forward cover facility of U.S. dollars on August 11, 1978, and revised the related regulations subsequently to further meet the requirements of importers and exporters.

The government unpegged the N.T. dollar from the U.S. dollar and adopted a managed floating exchange rate system. Unpegging the N.T. dollar from the U.S. dollar meant severing officially the direct and rigid link between the two countries. In the past, the N.T. dollar was pegged to the U.S. dollar mainly due to the fact that the United States was the most important trading partner and most of the foreign trade transactions were conducted in U.S. dollars. As a result, the pegging not only was institutionally the simplest, but also helped reduce the uncertainties in economic calculation and encouraged trade expansion. Such a system, however, has a least two shortcomings (Crockett and Nsouli, 1975: 11-12). First, the movements of the pegged exchange rate of the N.T. dollar do not reflect actual developments in its balance of payments; rather, they reflect actual development in the U.S. balance of payments. The factors affecting the equilibrium of the exchange rates of the two countries were not closely related. Second, fluctuations of the exchange rate interfere with the pursuit of internal policy objectives, since the fluctuations were exogenous and independent of government policy. The domestic economy was therefore subject to undesired and largely unpredictable inflationary and deflationary impulses transmitted through the foreign sector.

The exchange rate of the two major trading partners, the United States and Japan, has undergone drastic fluctuation in recent years. As a result, the U.S. dollar pegging system became incompatible with internal policy objectives. The main prupose of floating the N.T. dollar against the U.S. dollar was to avoid harmful effects from large-scale fluctuations of the US$/Yen exchange rate. The choice of an appropriate exchange rate policy is of great importance to a country as it will have important implications for the conduct of its domestic

Figure 1.   The Foreign Exchange Arrangements before the Foreign Exchange Reform

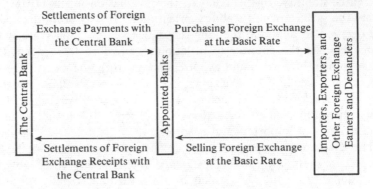

and international economic policies.

Under the fixed exchange rate system of the U.S. dollar pegging, the exchange rate was adjusted at one stroke by the government, with disruptive effects, whereas under the floating exchange rate system, it is expected that the exchange rate will change continuously and moderately, avoiding drastic variations over the short run. A floating exchange rate would tend to remain stable so long as underlying internal and international economic conditions remain unchanged. If the underlying economic conditions change drastically, necessary adjustments under a fixed rate system are brought about belatedly and abruptly through devaluation and appreciation by the government.

The main difference between the foreign exchange arrangements before the foreign exchange reform and the establishment of a foreign exchange market can be shown in the following diagrams. Under the foreign exchange arrangements operating prior to the foreign exchange reform, those who earned foreign exchange were required to sell it to the Central Bank at the basic rate, as shown in Figure 1. Those who wanted foreign exchange had to purchase it from the Central Bank. Appointed banks were allowed to handle foreign exchange transactions on behalf of the Central Bank.

Under the provisions of the revised foreign exchange regulations, foreign exchange earners may hold foreign exchange in the form of special deposit accounts. There are two types of foreign exchange deposits, namely, passbook deposits and time deposits. Appropriate interest is paid on time deposits to encourage foreign exchange earners to hold foreign exchange. The depositors can withdraw the foreign exchange deposits for their own use in accordance with the related provisions, or sell foreign exchange deposits through appointed banks in the foreign exchange market to those buyers with import permits or other approved certificates for foreign exchange settlement. Foreign exchange is no longer wholly bought by or sold to the Central Bank. The supply and demand fluctuations in the foreign exchange transactions form the base of a foreign exchange market, but the variation in exchange rates is moderate since domestic economic considerations and international competitiveness of export industries is duly taken into account in the daily fixing of exchange rates.

As is shown in Figure 2, the foreign exchange market is divided into two submarkets, namely, the bank-customer market and the inter-bank market. The bank-customer market handles transactions with bank customers at the market exchange rate. The representatives of five major appointed foreign exchange banks, namely, the Bank of Taiwan, the International Commercial Bank of China, First Commercial Bank. Hwa-Nan Commercial Bank, and Chang Hwa Commercial Bank, meet at the foreign exchange center before 9:00 a.m. to fix the daily rates for buying and selling. The limit of permissible daily fluctuation is one percent of the mean of the buying and selling rates on the previous business day. The inter-bank market handles transactions among the appointed banks. Each bank transacts for each other through the foreign exchange center in order to maintain its position at the desired level. The overnight and cumulative position limits of the appointed banks are set by the Foreign Exchange Department of the Central Bank. The appointed banks maintain the maximum permissible inventories of foreign exchange necessary to serve ther clients. This facilitates smooth daily transactions as well as finances buyers' usance credit and customers' importation of raw materials.

The Central Bank acts as a banker of last resort, maintaining the spot price within the stated daily limit through its intervention whenever necessary. It is the function of the Central Bank to maintain an orderly exchange market so as to avoid large and sudden fluctuations in exchange rates and to maintain a desirable exchange rate compatible with the domestic and international policy objectives. Foreign ex-

Figure 2.   The Framework of Transactions in the Foreign Exchange Market

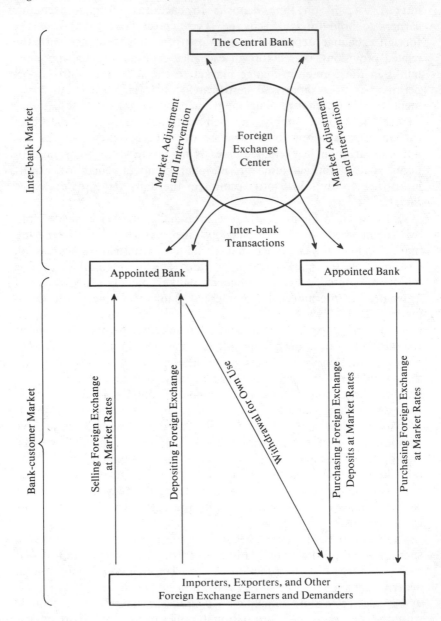

Table 9. *Average Annual Percentage Changes in Wages, Labor Productivity, and Unit Labor Costs in Manufacturing, 1952-79*

	1952-55	1955-60	1960-65	1965-70	1970-75	1975-79	1952-79
Money wages	16.11	9.42	8.04	11.19	21.01	17.56	13.48
Consumer prices	9.90	9.52	2.39	4.36	12.20	6.23	7.24
Real wages[a]	5.65	−0.07	5.52	6.54	7.85	10.66	5.82
Labor productivity	12.78	5.07	8.04	11.34	3.63	11.12	8.22
Unit labor costs[b]	3.33	4.35	0	−0.15	17.38	6.44	5.26

Sources: Council for Economic Planning and Economic Development, *Taiwan Statistical Data Book; The Adjusted Statistics of Manufacturing in Taiwan Area* (1st Quarter 1952-4th Quarter 1976); *The Adjustment of Labor Force, Unemployment and Employment by Sectors in Taiwan Area (1952-77);* Ministry of Economic Affairs, *Taiwan Industrial Production Statistics Monthly;* DGBAS, *Commodity-price Statistics Monthly; Monthly Bulletin of Labor Statistics.*

Notes: [a] Money wages divided by the index of urban consumer prices.
[b] Difference between rate of change of money wage and rate of change of labor productivity. Labor productivity is calculated by dividing output index by employment index.

change transactions for purely financial reasons are prohibited so as to prevent speculation.

The Taiwan economy has had to adjust to endogenous changes of a long-term nature. The interesting feature of the figures in Table 9 is the lack of continuity of past trends in the changes in real wages and labor productivity. The rise of labor productivity accelerated and unit labor costs remained unchanged or even declined in the 1960s. This undoubtedly strengthened the competitive position of Taiwan's labor-intensive manufactures in the world market. However, the absolute size of the agricultural labor force began to decline in 1969 as the outflow rate accelerated in the late 1960s. The economy reached a turning point, and the era of relatively stable real wage rates and unit labor costs ended. Taiwan should be able to continue to grow quickly provided its policies remain well adapted to the changing internal and external economic conditions. Special emphasis needs to be given to such skilled-labor intensive exports as machinery. Machinery is skill-intensive at relatively low capital and domestic resource costs, and could be next in line for the achievement of a high rate of export expansion as the growth of experience and capacity in manufacturing permits the economy to move beyond simple labor-intensive types of production. Increased export incentives can take the form of extending the scope of export credits, especially extending medium- and long-term credit to foreign buyers of machinery and equipment, reforming export insurance and guarantee systems, and initiating additional export promotion programs.

Both the domestic and international environments of the economy have been changing at an accelerated pace in recent years. Inadequate and out-of-date institutional arrangements should be changed as rapidly as possible to adapt to the new environments. It is expected that the establishment of the foreign exchange market will allow the exchange rate to find its own level so as to promote easier balance-of-payments adjustment, and allow greater independence from external disturbances which will render the operation of monetary policy more effective. Even so, the exchange market still remains controlled and the exchange rate has been adjusted from time to time only in very small steps, the principal purpose of steps taken towards liberalization being to substitute market forces for government regulations.

Needless to say, changes in exchange rates by themselves are no panacea, although they do work if they are accompanied by appropriate supporting measures (Emminger, 1980: 17). As pointed out earlier, whenever the ratio of excess supply of M_1 exceeds the rate of inflation by a wide margin in a certain year, there is a tendency for the rate of inflation to accelerate in the following year. The central bank has to adopt timely measures to discourage drastic short-term fluctuations in monetary aggregates so as to avoid "home-made" inflation being combined with imported inflation. Nevertheless, the stabilization effect of monetary and exchange rate policies will be greatly limited if the price of imported oil continues to increase. Accordingly, the government should adopt appropriate policies to conserve energy.

It has to be stressed that the strategy of liberalization should reach beyond the financial sector and be linked with such complementary measures as trade liberalization. It is desirable to carry out the liberalization of import restrictions and the reform of the tariff structure on the basis of a program made public in advance. This will permit firms to make preparations. Trade liberalization will lower the cost of exports through reduced prices of imported machinery and raw materials, provide a spur for improvements in productivity, trigger accelerated adjustment among the industries that have to compete with imports, and may even obtain better treatment for exports in foreign markets through bilateral negotiations to obtain mutual concessions.

V. Conclusion

Taiwan provides an example of an economy following its comparative advantage and reaping the gains from trade illustrated by the traditional theory of international trade. The expansion of manufactured exports has contributed not only to efficient industrialization by permitting specialization according to comparative advantage and stimulating technological improvement, but also to higher living standards, as well as improved income distribution through the creation of new productive employment.

REFERENCES

Balassa, B., "Export Incentives and Export Performance in Developing Countries, A Comparative Analysis," *Weltwirtschaftliches Archiv*, March 1978.

Crokett, A.D. and S.M. Nsouli, "Exchange Rate Policies for Developing Countries," *Document of International Monetary Fund*, DM/75/68, August 1, 1975.

de Vries, B.A., *Export Experiences of Developing Countries*, Baltimore: Johns Hopkins, 1967.

Emminger, O., "The Exchange Rate as an Instrument of Policy," *Economic Impact*, No. 30, 1980/2.

Hsing, Mo-Huan, *Taiwan: Industrialization and Trade Policies*, London: Oxford, 1971.

Lee, T.H., Huo-shu Liang, Shive, Chi, and Yeh, Ryh-song, "The Structure of Effective Protection and Subsidy in Taiwan," *Economic Essays*, November 1975.

Liang, Huo-shu and Teng-hui Lee, "Process and Pattern of Economic Development in Taiwan," S. Ichimura (ed.), *The Economic Development of East and Southeast Asia,* Honolulu: University of Hawaii Press, 1974.

Liang, K.S., and C. Liang, "Export Expansion and Economic Development in Taiwan," mimeographed paper presented at the Conference of the Asian Studies on the Pacific Coast, Anaheim, California on June 9, 1978.

Lin, Ching-yuan, *Industrialization in Taiwan, 1946-72: Trade and Import-Substitution Policies for Developing Countries*, New York: Praeger, 1973.

McKinnon, R.I., *Money and Capital in Economic Development*, Washington, D.C.: The Brookings Institution, 1973.

Scott, Maurice, "Foreign Trade," W. Galenson (ed.), *Economic Growth and Structural Change in Taiwan: The Postwar Experience of the Republic of China,* Ithaca: Cornell University Press, 1979.

Shaw, E.S., *Financial Deepening in Economic Development*, New York: Oxford, 1973.

Tang, Anthony M. and Kuo-shu Liang, "Agricultural Trade in the Economic Development of Taiwan," G.S. Tolley and P.A. Zadrozny (eds.), *Trade, Agriculture and Development*, Cambridge, Massachusetts: Ballinger, 1973.

• COMMENT

Soo Yong Kim,   *Korea International Economic Institute*

Taiwan switched from import substitution to an outward-oriented trade strategy in the late fifties, followed by similar policy shifts in several other developing countries during the sixties. In most cases, including Taiwan and Korea, the policy of promoting exports and liberalizing imports has worked toward accelerating industrialization and growth of the economies. The question is whether the economic conditions in either Taiwan or Korea in the early sixties were such that the shifts in trade strategy were inevitable, or were the policy shifts mainly initiated by policy authorities. Liang and Liang imply that the limit of import substitution became apparent from the low capacity utilization of manufactures. But over time the excess capacities would have been reduced even under import substitution as resources moved to new industries and market demand increased. Many developing countries have chosen to continue their import-substitution policy under similar circumstances. From this it appears that economic policy-makers in Taiwan as well as in Korea were the decisive factor for transforming these countries into the advanced developing countries they are today.

Looking at Table 2, one can see that the purchasing-power-parity effective exchange rate on exports has been fairly stable over time. But a stable rate in itself is not sufficient to induce exports to expand rapidly. For the comparison of the relative profitability of exporting versus sales to the domestic market, the same effective exchange rate on imports should have been included in the paper. Judging from the ratios of customs revenue to imports in Table 3, the effective exchange rate on imports would seem to have been very high, supplying strong incentives for producing for the domestic market.

Taiwan has been a model case of a developing country that achieved rapid economic growth without a high rate of inflation. The authors state that whenever the ratio of excess supply of M_1 exceeds the rate of inflation by a wide margin in a certain year there is a tendency for the rate of inflation to accelerate in the following year. The figures in

Table 6 seem to support this generalization. However, it would be useful to know how it is possible to have such erratic changes in the growth rate of money supply as were observed in 1965, 1967, 1974 and 1979, and at the same time very stable annual growth rates in real GNP, except for 1974-75, not to speak of stable prices.

Concerning the revaluation of Taiwanese currency in July 1978, the authors explain that it was a measure taken to restore external equilibrium to the balance of payments surplus situation. Policy authorities chose adjustment through appreciation instead of domestic inflation. The question could be asked as to whether at that time policy authorities seriously considered reducing export incentives and tariff rates concurrently so as to achieve freer international trade and, if they did, why they opted for revaluation instead.

In the last part of the paper, the authors say that the Taiwanese economy reached a turning point and thereafter the era of relatively stable real wages and unit labor cost ended. It is true that the increases in money wages as well as real wages accelerated in the seventies but the growth of real wages always lagged behind the growth of labor productivity except for the period of 1970-75. Because of the rapid increases in labor productivity, unit labor cost increases slowed down during 1975-79. From these figures it is very difficult to tell when the economy reached the turning point.

Although the policy emphasis on skilled labor-intensive exports in recent years is justified and is the correct policy direction for Taiwan as well as several other advanced developing countries, it is a policy which is more difficult to achieve than that of exploiting a given comparative advantage in unskilled labor-intensive exports, as in the past. Here lies the real test for policy makers' ingenuity — to adapt to changing economic conditions.

Hugh Patrick,   *Yale University*

This paper is somewhat broader than the title might imply since the focus is primarily upon trade strategy, with somewhat less emphasis upon exchange rate policy. This is desirable since for most of the period the exchange rate was pegged to the U.S. dollar.

An important point, well documented in this paper, is that in switching from import substitution to an export orientation, a country does not immediately drop all import controls. Indeed, it tends first to engage in a variety of export-promoting subsidies, in large part to offset the existing structure of disincentives to export activities. In this sense export promotion is an attempt to move from the left toward the optimal free trade point, in Findlay's diagrammatic terminology. It is necessary to distinguish in the terminology among export promotion which implies direct incentives to export activities, trade liberalization which indicates reduction of barriers on imports and exports, and hence openness and free trade.

As the paper shows, the success of Taiwan's export promotion policies has enabled Taiwan to reduce import barriers over time, and also to reduce the number and degree of export-promoting subsidies. Table 2 documents the ongoing export subsidies in the form of tax and custom duty rebates and low-interest rate export credits. On the whole they have been relatively modest, reaching a peak of about 15 percent of the nominal exchange rate in 1971, and declining thereafter to about 7 percent in 1978. The text suggests that direct subsidies for certain export products, tax benefits, and sale of import rights were probably more important forms of export promotion. Their removal in the early 1970s indicates the process by which Taiwan moved from a narrow form of export promotion to a more general system of trade liberalization, that is, to greater openness as a trading nation. Similar liberalizing steps were taken over time for imports.

Thus, over time Taiwan has moved considerably closer to the free trade point, though it still remains to Findlay's left — at least in his purely technical terminology. Two points concerning the current situation on the degree of trade liberalization are raised in the paper. First, on the import side, even though import quotas are only 2 percent of the total number of manufactured imports, how significant are they as kinds of commodities? The discipline of using import prices to control the domestic prices of these items is good; now that the premium has declined to 5 percent, could not these quotas simply be eliminated? Related to this, the data suggest fairly high remaining tariff barriers. However, nothing is mentioned concerning consideration of their reduction and eventual elimination.

Second, on the export side it now appears that export subsidies are a minor element in Taiwan's export success. The correctness of this can be queried, as can the extent to which export subsidies are acceptable. It seems to be the case that as Taiwan and other ADCs become increasingly large and visible, their export-promotion programs which have used unacceptable forms of subsidy will be subject to counter-vailing duty and anti-dumping legal actions in the United States. It is wise for ADCs to move away from such vulnerable forms of export promotion; it appears that Taiwan has already done so.

On the whole Taiwan has contained potential inflationary pressures well. Money supply and M_2 have grown rapidly, reflecting an effective policy of positive and relatively high real interest rates, which has encouraged financial deepening. The private domestic saving rate is impressively high, and the dependence on foreign capital inflows appears low — certainly relative to Korea, Hong Kong, and Singapore. It would be useful to have more information on the role of foreign portfolio and direct investment capital. Nonetheless, at times domestic money supply has grown very rapidly. The authors of the paper relate the growth of M_1 relative to average GNP growth to indicate inflation potential with a one-year time lag, in Table 6. This is a somewhat rough form of estimation; indeed, there seems to be a close relationship in 1971-73 and again in 1978-79. This analysis could beneficially be developed and refined.

The analysis of Taiwan's exchange rate policies is somewhat limited, but as the rate was pegged to the U.S. dollar for most of the period perhaps that is appropriate. As the authors show, Taiwan moved from a multiple, discriminatory, overvalued exchange rate system in the 1950s to a unitary rate by 1961. The pegged rate was appreciated slightly in 1973 and 1974, and again in 1978. Table 2 is very useful in providing annual data on the nominal rate for exports, the nominal effective rate, and the purchasing-power-parity (inflation-adjusted) effective exchange rate. The sharp appreciation in the effective rate in 1974, which is termed a "deterioration" in the paper in terms of Taiwan's ability to price-compete, is appropriately criticized as wrong at a time of domestic recession; the effective rate rather quickly adjusted in 1975 as Taiwan was able to reduce its wholesale price index while those of its major trading partners continued to rise.

In February 1979 Taiwan switched to a managed float system, which seems closely controlled. This was in response to the side fluc-tuations in the exchange rates of its two main trading partners, Japan and the United States. It is not clear exactly what is going on, though the authors indicate that the market remains tightly controlled by the central bank, with short-term capital flows also being controlled. This raises questions as to what criteria the central bank uses in managing the float and to what extent it is actually pegging to a trade-weighted average of the yen and the US dollar. It would be useful to know how the rate has moved during the past 18 months of management.

There are two final points raised by the paper. First, given the publicity Taiwan's export processing zones received, it was surprising to see the relatively modest role they apparently played as of the mid-1970s, providing only 8.5 percent of total export in 1975. It was unclear whether this has generally been the situation, or whether their role had been more important earlier.

Second, much of the discussion regarding Taiwan and the other advanced developing countries has focussed on their export success. Also it should be stressed that successful export performance has enabled far larger imports. Indeed the ADCs continue to be even larger markets for imports than suppliers of exports. Their growth as import markets is a factor which should not be forgotten by policy-makers in the economically advanced countries — the industrial nations — of the Pacific.

GENERAL DISCUSSION

Taiwan seems to have maintained a less distorted market mechanism compared to other developing countries such as Korea. However, distortions apparently occurred for both export promotion and import substitution. It is not clear whether those distortions offset each other, leading to a balanced free trade position.

Taiwan seems to have been more successful in achieving equity in income distribution than other East Asian countries. This may be partly attributed to the absence of high inflation.

Taiwan might have achieved higher growth rates, if it had started export promotion in the early 1950s without going through the import-substitution stage.

Taiwan's shift to a flexible exchange rate system in 1979 was due to the dollar-yen fluctuation. Taiwan has a substantial current account surplus with respect to the U.S. that is offset by the similar amount of deficit with respect to Japan. Under this situation, if the yen appreciates there occurs a serious imported inflation. Taiwan's exchange rate with the yen has to be made more flexible, and yet the government does not seem to know what to do. Perhaps a small developing country does not really have any policy option to offset major currency disturbances. It may be the responsibility of the U.S. and Japan to eliminate excessive fluctuations in their exchange rates which tend to overshoot. The benefit of reduced fluctuation may not be limited to better resource allocation in the U.S. and Japan, but will be extended to a host of other countries such as Taiwan. The terms of trade effect of realignment in the exchange rates among major currencies does not seem to be significant.

Even after Taiwan shifted to a flexible exchange rate system, the rates seem to have been fairly stable. Perhaps Taiwan has only short-term fluctuation problems caused by, for example, fluctuations in the oil import bill. It is not clear whether short-term instability had any serious adverse impact on export growth. The effective exchange rate has been very stable in the late 1970s.

One may question whether Taiwan's current system is truly a flexible exchange rate system. Actual operation of the system seems to be similar to the original pegged exchange rate system, with perhaps a little bit more flexibility. The central bank still intervenes very heavily. Little real change occurred in Taiwan's exchange rate policy.

PART III

EFFECTIVE PROTECTION, BALANCE OF PAYMENTS AND INCOME DISTRIBUTION

TRADE AND INDUSTRIAL POLICIES, AND THE STRUCTURE OF PROTECTION IN KOREA

*Chong Hyun Nam**

I. Introduction

During the past four Five-Year Economic Plans (1962-1981), the Korean government has relied on a variety of incentive measures to accomplish its economic goals. Consequently, the system of industrial incentives in Korea has become extremely complex. For example, despite the import liberalization attempts since the early 1960s, most of the import-substitution industries are still highly protected by various import controls, and export industries receive special treatment such as preferential loans and tax credits.[1] Furthermore, since the early 1970s when the government began to emphasize heavy and chemical industries, a multitude of package assistance programs have been available for industries designated as so-called strategic industries, through special industrial promotion laws.

Economic theory suggests that special government intervention may be called for when external benefits or costs arise in the process of industrial development. These externalities spring mainly from such activities as the training of labor, developing overseas markets, spending on research and development, and promoting the balanced growth of associated industries.[2] It is well known that the optimal

---

* Korea University.

[1] For excellent studies on Korea's trade and industrial policies since the end of the Second World War, see Frank, Kim and Westphal (1975), Hong (1979), and Krueger (1979).

[2] For a careful analysis of externalities and optimal policies, see Bhagwati (1968).

governmental intervention policies should be directed to compensate for those externalities. However, the instruments of trade policy which include tariffs, quotas, and export incentives have been widely used by developing countries to accelerate industrialization or to protect infant industries.[3] It is unclear how important such trade policies have been in bringing about the desired changes in these areas. It is clear that alternative policy instruments are generally available that could have attained the same goals with a lower economic cost.[4] Therefore, it is important to carefully evaluate the causes and consequences of each incentive policy as well as the combined effect of all applicable incentives. What is relevant to an industry or a firm is the cumulative effect of the various incentives applied at any time.

It is the purpose of this study to examine the importance of major industrial incentive policies adopted in Korea, particularly those pertaining to import substitution and export promotion, and to quantify the effects of incentive measures at the individual industry level. This paper reports on findings with regard to the inter-industry structure of protection by estimating nominal and effective rates of protection as well as effective rates of subsidies given to export production in 1978.

The paper is organized to present, in Section II, a brief history of the trade and industrial policies undertaken during the 1954-1978 period. This section also presents estimates of real effective exchange rates for exports and imports for the period 1966-1978. Section III persents estimates of various incentive rates in 1978, discussing the

---

[3] In general, trade policies are not optimal because they not only fail to reflect externalities correctly but also tend to discriminate among import substitution, export, and non-traded goods sectors even while protecting infant industries. For a fuller assessment of industrialization policies for a number of developing countries, see Little, Scitovsky and Scott (1971), Bhagwati (1978), Krueger (1978) and Balassa (ed.) (1971 and forthcoming).

[4] See Corden (1971, 1975) and Magee (1972) for a careful analysis and measurement of economic costs of protection involved with trade policies. It should be noted, however, that there are economists who argue that the effects of trade policies should be evaluated in terms of contributions to overall economic development rather than static allocative efficieny alone, because in many countries the static inefficiency is much less important than the ability to bring about structural changes that are necessary to secure economic growth. They further indicate that in most developing countries policy instruments have to be chosen among second-bests. See Chenery and Carter (1973).

results in comparison with estimates made for 1968. Conclusions are presented in the final section.

II. Trade and Industrial Policies and Real Effective Exchange Rates

1. Trade and Industrial Policies: 1954-1978

South Korea's average annual real GNP growth rate was more than 10 percent during the 1964-1978 period and has attracted worldwide attention. This contrasts with an annual growth rate of 4.2 percent during the preceding decade (1954-1963). Prior to 1960, there was little economic policy relating to development goals in South Korea, except that emphasis was placed on import substitution through tariffs and quantitative restrictions on imports. The 1960s, however, saw numerous reforms and economic plans. The Five-Year Economic Plans were formulated, the first one for the period 1962-66. The development of key industries, the modernization of industrial structure and the creation of an adequate supply of social overhead capital were stressed in each plan. The major policy shift, however, began with the financial and payments-regime reforms during 1964-65.[5] Other important policies introduced together with or immediately after these reforms were the introduction of a comprehensive export-promotion scheme; gradual attempts to liberalize import controls; and the encouragement of the inflow of foreign loans to fill the domestic savings gap.

The result of this outward-looking development strategy that began in the early 1960s was rather impressive. The unusually rapid expansion of exports was achieved on the basis of the rapid growth of labor-intensive industries in which Korea was believed to have a comparative advantage. As can be seen in Table 1, the amount of exports, both goods and services, was very small in the period 1960-1964, ranging from 2.7 to 4.4 percent of the GNP. Thereafter, exports rose rapidly to 41.8 percent of the GNP by 1978. Moreover, manufactures

---

[5] The Korean currency was devalued from 130 won to the dollar to 255 won to the dollar in May 1964 and the interest rate on ordinary loans of banking institutions was raised from 16 percent to 26 percent per annum in September 1965.

Table 1. Major Economic Indicators: 1954 to 1978

(in 1975 prices)

	1954	1960	1964	1968	1972	1976	1978
1. GNP (billion won)	2,318.5	2,845.6	3,671.5	5,195.6	7,365.6	11,275.5	13,877.1
2. Population (million persons)	20.8	25.0	28.0	30.8	33.5	35.9	37.0[a]
3. GNP per Capita (thousand won)	111.4	114.1	131.2	168.5	219.8	314.4	374.9
4. Share of Value Added in GNP (%)							
Primary Production	50.2	44.3	45.9	34.2	27.8	24.0	19.1
Manufacturing	5.3	8.4	9.7	15.0	20.9	28.2	31.6
Social Overhead	44.5	47.3	44.4	50.8	51.3	47.8	49.3
5. Ratio of Exports to GNP (%)	1.3	2.7	4.4	11.2	21.3	34.9	41.8
6. Ratio of Imports to GNP (%)	10.2	12.3	11.1	25.9	30.6	40.6	52.8
7. Average Annual Growth Rate (%)		1954-63	1964-78	1966-73	1974-78	1954-78	
GNP		4.2	10.0	10.2	10.4	7.7	
GNP per Capita		1.1	7.8	7.9	8.7	5.2	
Manufacturing Value Added		11.3	19.6	21.2	17.2	16.1	
Real Wages in Manufacturing		0.2[b]	13.5	17.5	12.9	—	
GNP Deflator		16.8	16.5	14.5	21.8	18.3	
Wholesale Price Index		21.2	14.4	7.8	20.3	15.4	
Exports		13.0	29.1	35.4	19.9	24.6	
Imports		7.3	22.9	28.1	19.3	15.4	

Sources: Bank of Korea, *National Income in Korea*, 1971, and 1979; Bank of Korea, *Economic Statistics Yearbook*, 1975, and 1979; Economic Planning Board, *Major Statistics of Korean Economy*, 1979.

Notes: [a] Estimate

[b] Average annual growth rate only for the 1958-1963 Period.

have been the dominant element in the growth of exports since the early 1960s. Manufactured exports comprised 18.1 percent of total exports in 1960 but by 1978 accounted for 87.9 percent of the total.

In the early 1970s, however, especially in the preparation of the Fourth Five-Year Plan (1977-81), the government began to emphasize the development of both the heavy and chemical industries. Development in those areas was promoted in the expectation of rising domestic wage-rental ratios, as a result of the rapid accumulation of capital relative to labor which, in turn, would lead to the loss of comparative advantage in the relatively unskilled labor-intensive manufactures. Rising protectionism abroad against imports of light industrial products was also seen as limiting the possibility of continued export expansion essential to finance the growing imports required for sustained economic growth throughout the 1980s. It was during the Second Five-Year Plan (1967-1971) period that the government first introduced a series of laws to promote heavy and chemical industries. In 1973, the Heavy and Chemical Industry Development Committee was established to provide government support for the successful completion of the largely government-sponsored investment project.

The success of the industrial shift towards heavy and chemical industries would, however, depend on a number of factors such as the extent of competition and protectionism abroad, and the uncertainty involved in exporting. Should these newly developed industries fail to perform successfully in terms of international competitiveness, Korea may be forced to retreat from an outward-looking development policy. It is, therefore, important to make rational industrial policy, particularly concerning the problem of shifts in industrial structure.

2. The Structure of Incentives and Real Effective Exchange Rates

Beginning in the early sixties a new set of export incentives were introduced in Korea in order to reinforce those already in existence. At the same time, traditional import controls were gradually relaxed, though only to a limited degree. It is not entirely clear whether exports have been relatively favored over import substitution as a result of this incentive system. In this section, the system of incentives introduced since the early 1960s is described, and a quantitative assessment of the overall impact of the incentive measures is attempted by estimating real effective exchange rates for exports and imports over the period 1966-1978.

a. Export Incentives

Important export incentives introduced during the 1960s include tariff exemptions on direct and indirect imported intermediate goods and on capital equipment for export production and exemptions from indirect taxes on intermediate inputs and export sales. There was a reduction of direct taxes on income earned in export activities and reserve funds were created from taxable income to create new foreign markets and defray export losses. An accelerated depreciation allowance for fixed capital used directly in export production was offered. Access was provided to subsidized short- and long-term credit for export proceeds, for the purchase of inputs and for the financing of fixed investment. Generous wastage allowances were granted on imported duty-free raw materials, over and above the requirements of actual export production. An export-import linkage system permitting access to otherwise prohibited imports was in operation and preferential rates on several overhead inputs such as electricity and railroad transportation were made available.

Commencing in 1965, these export incentives were extended to producers of intermediate goods used in export production. Some of the incentive measures discussed above, however, should not be regarded as genuine subsidies. For example, exemption of intermediate inputs and export sales from indirect taxes, and exemption from import duties on imported inputs allowed exporters to operate under a virtual free trade regime. They were allowed to buy their inputs and sell their outputs at world market prices. However, the rest of the incentives, including reductions in direct taxes, subsidized loans, wastage allowances, the export-import linkage system, and preferential rates on electricity and railroad transport, can be regarded as genuine subsidies.

The system of export incentives remained virtually unchanged through the early seventies. Beginning in 1973, however, the government tried to reduce the scope of export incentives. The 50 percent reduction in profit taxes on export earnings was abolished in 1973, although tax exemptions on reserve funds for developing export markets and for export losses remained intact. In July 1975, the system of prior tariffs exemptions on imported inputs used in export production was changed to a drawback system. The discount on electricity was abolished in 1976, and wastage allowances have been repeatedly reduced, bringing them closer to the real rate during the 1970s. However, the government continued to introduce various measures to promote export expansion. The Export Insurance Law was promulgated in December 1968 in order to reduce exporters' risks. The Korea Export-Import Bank was established in July 1976 to support exports on a medium- and long-term credit basis. Furthermore, the government has steadily increased preferential loans to export industries, including short- and long-term credits of various types. For instance, outstanding short-term loans to export industries increased from 4.8 billion won in 1966 to 883.5 billion won in 1978, and the outstanding long-term loans to export industries increased from 1.2 billion won to 776.2 billion won for the same period. As a result, the share of preferential credits to export industries in the total domestic credits increased from 5.1 percent in 1966 to 20.5 percent in 1978.[6]

Table 2 represents the quantitative evaluation of subsidies generated by various export incentives. The nominal effective exchange rate for exports has been obtained by adding all subsidies per dollar of export to the official exchange rate. Next, the real effective exchange rate for exports has been calculated by adjusting for changes in purchasing power parity. (See note in Table 2.) A few remarks must be made, however, with regard to the estimation of subsidies. First, the accelerated depreciation allowance, reserve funds for developing export markets and for export losses, subsidies provided by wastage allowances, the export-import linkage system, and preferential rates on overhead inputs have not been included in the quantification of total subsidy, because of both the lack of time-series data and the relative insignificance in magnitude. Second, the interest subsidy in the table has been measured as the difference between interest paid by exporters on outstanding preferential loans and the interest payable at non-preferential bank lending rates. The non-preferential bank lending rate has been under complete government control, however, and has often been set at unrealistically low rates, rates much lower than those obtainable under free market

---

[6] The weighted average interest on all outstanding preferential loans to export industries was 7.7 percent in 1966 and 10.6 percent in 1978, whereas the non-preferential commercial bank lending rate on ordinary loans was 26.4 percent in 1966 and 19.0 percent in 1978. The data on loans and interest rates were obtained from the Bank of Korea.

Table 2.   Nominal and Real Effective Exchange Rates for Exports, 1966 to 1978

	1966	1967	1968	1969	1970	1971	1972	1973	1974	1975	1976	1977	1978
A. Official Exchange Rate (won per U.S. dollar)	270.3	268.3	276.3	288.4	310.4	350.1	394.0	398.5	406.0	484.0	484.0	484.0	484.0
B. Subsidies on Exports (won per dollar export)													
1. Interest Subsidy	4.1	7.8	13.8	14.1	16.6	18.9	12.6	8.6	7.2	10.1	12.3	9.4	11.0
2. Direct Tax Reduction	2.3	5.2	3.2	3.9	3.6	5.1	2.0	1.4	—	—	—	—	—
3. Indirect Tax Exemption	17.8	18.9	21.2	29.0	28.5	34.1	27.2	21.3	22.8	33.3	36.1	65.9	42.7
4. Tariff Exemption	21.3	25.7	42.3	36.2	42.6	50.9	68.5	65.4	55.8	33.8	35.9	30.6	30.0
C. Nominal Effective Exchange Rate													
1. Gross $(A+B_1+B_2+B_3+B_4)$ (won)	315.8	325.9	356.9	371.7	401.8	459.1	504.3	495.1	491.9	561.2	568.4	589.9	567.6
2. Net $(A+B_1+B_2)$ (won)	276.7	281.3	293.3	306.4	330.7	374.1	408.6	408.5	413.2	494.1	496.3	493.4	495.0
D. Wholesale Price Index & Parity Index (1975 = 100)													
1. Korea	31.3	33.4	36.2	38.5	42.0	45.7	52.0	55.6	79.0	100.0	112.1	122.2	136.5
2. Major Countries[a]	53.6	54.1	56.0	57.9	59.2	68.2	72.4	81.6	95.1	100.0	105.5	114.9	131.4
3. Purchasing Power Parity Index[b]	171.4	162.1	154.6	150.3	140.9	149.3	139.2	146.8	120.4	100.0	94.1	94.0	96.3
E. Real Exchange Rate $(A \times D_3)$ (won)	463.3	434.9	427.2	433.5	437.4	522.7	584.4	585.0	488.8	484.0	455.4	455.0	466.1
F. Real Effective Exchange Rates Adjusted for Purchasing Power Parity Index (won)													
1. Gross $(C_1 \times D_3)$	541.3	528.3	551.8	558.7	566.1	685.4	702.0	726.8	592.2	561.2	534.9	554.5	546.6
2. Net $(C_2 \times D_3)$	474.3	456.0	453.4	460.5	466.0	558.5	568.8	599.7	497.5	491.1	467.0	463.8	476.7

Source: Bank of Korea; Ministry of Finance.
Notes: [a] The average wholesale price index of U.S.A. and Japan, weighted by the annual trade volume with Korea, where Japan's price index is adjusted by the exchange rate of Yen per U.S. dollar.
[b] (Wholesale Price Index in Major Countries) ÷ (Wholesale Price Index in Korea)

situations.[7] Thus, there is a strong possibility that the interest subsidy measured here represents a substantial underestimate, perhaps on the order of 100 percent. Finally, as already mentioned, exemptions from indirect taxes and duties on inputs used in export production do not represent genuine subsidies, although they tend to lower production costs for exports vis-a-vis production for domestic markets. Thus, two measures of the effective exchange rate have been calculated on the basis of gross and net subsidies, where gross subsidy includes indirect tax and tariff exemptions, and the net subsidy does not include them.

The estimates show fluctuations in the net real effective exchange rates for exports from 474 won per dollar in 1966, hitting a peak of 600 in 1973 with subsequent declines, to a low point of 477 in 1978.

The large depreciation of the real effective exchange rate of the won between 1966 and 1973 with subsequent appreciations between 1974 and 1978 seems roughly comparable with the average annual growth rates of exports, 35.4 percent between 1966 and 1973, but only 19.9 percent between 1974 and 1978, in 1975 constant prices. However, it is difficult to separate the effects of the changing export competitiveness due to appreciation of the real effective exchange rate from the effects of the world recession following the first "oil shock" in 1973, when explaining the sluggish growth of exports since 1973.

b. Incentives to Import Substitution

Changes in competitiveness of Korean exports over time have been examined. Further information on incentives extended to import substitution is needed, however, to compare incentives provided to exports and to import substitution.

Legal tariffs are to a large extent inoperative in Korea. Many imports are exempt from duties and a number of commodities are subject to virtually prohibitive tariffs. Table 3 presents the data on tariffs actually collected and exempted, and the data on commodity imports. According to the data, the legal tariff rates for all commodity imports far exceeded the actual tariff rates during the period of 1966-1978: on average, the legal tariff rate was 20.4 percent

---

[7] The non-preferential bank lending rate was 19 percent in 1978. However, the active curb market interest rate was estimated at 42 percent in 1978, and the average nominal rate of return on capital in the manufacturing sector was estimated at 43.2 percent for the period 1972-75. See D. Cole and Y. C. Park (1979), p. 161, and Hong (1979), p. 176-205.

for the 1966-1978 period. It is also interesting to observe that despite substantial reductions in legal tariff rates since 1974, the actual tariff rates showed a rising trend through 1978, suggesting that reductions in legal tariff rates had little relationship with the extent of import liberalization.

Table 3 also provides nominal as well as real effective exchange rates for imports, estimated by adding the actual tariff proceeds per dollar to the official exchange rates. The resulting real effective exchange rates for imports appreciated from 493 won per dollar in 1966 to 446 in 1969, and then depreciated to 613 in 1973 with a subsequent appreciation to 543 in 1978. These figures, however, should by no means be taken as equivalent to or comparable with the real effective exchange rates made for exports. This is because quantitative import restrictions have been far more important than tariffs as measures protecting import-substitution industries in Korea.

Together with the import liberalization attempts undertaken in 1967, the so-called positive list system was changed to a "negative" list system, where all commodities not listed were automatically approved for imports (AA items). Twice a year the government announced the number of import-restricted items in each commodity group. Generally the items and their number to be restricted were determined on the basis of import needs, the balance-of-payments situation, and the protection requirements of domestic industries. Thus, the quantitative restrictions were mostly applied to import-competing items and imports of nonessential or luxury goods, whereas imports of raw materials and non-competitive intermediate goods were normally approved automatically.

In the second half of 1967 when the negative system was adopted, more than 60 percent of the 1,312 basic import items (SITC 4-digit) became AA commodities, 118 were prohibited import items, and 402 items were subject to various restrictions such as quotas and recommendations from the Ministry of Commerce and Industry or other appropriate ministry. The number of prohibited items, however, decreased steadily from 118 in 1967 to zero in 1978, whereas the number of restricted items increased continuously from 402 in 1967 to 602 in 1975, but declined again to 424 in 1978. As a result, in 1978 about 40 percent of the 1,097 basic items still remained as import-restricted items. (See Table 4.)

There was another form of import restriction which had tariff-equivalent effects. Since 1961, advance deposits were required for

Table 3. Nominal and Real Exchange Rates for Imports, 1966 to 1978

	1966	1967	1968	1969	1970	1971	1972	1973	1974	1975	1976	1977	1978
A. Official Exchange Rate (won per U.S. dollar)	270.3	268.3	276.3	288.4	310.4	350.1	394.0	398.5	406.0	484.0	484.0	484.0	484.0
B. Tariff Collected & Exempted (billion won)													
1. Tariff Collected	18.0	25.4	37.9	44.7	50.9	52.2	59.1	82.4	126.7	181.0	275.5	385.9	642.2
2. Tariff Exempted	20.3	32.3	66.4	86.2	107.1	143.6	214.5	319.6	302.8	222.7	329.8	413.2	554.2
3. Total Legal Tariffs $(B_1 + B_2)$	38.3	57.7	104.3	130.9	158.0	195.8	273.6	402.0	329.5	403.7	605.3	799.1	1,196.4
4. Total Import (c.i.f.) (million dollars)	716.4	996.2	1,462.9	1,823.6	1,984.0	2,394.3	2,522.0	4,240.3	6,581.8	7,274.4	8,773.6	10,810.5	14,971.9
5. Total Import (billion won)[a]	193.6	267.3	404.2	471.2	615.8	838.2	993.7	1,689.8	2,781.8	3,520.8	4,246.4	5,232.3	7,246.4
C. Actual & Legal Tariff per Dollar Import													
1. Actual Tariff $(B_1 \div B_4)$ (won)	25.1	25.5	25.9	24.5	25.7	21.8	23.4	19.4	18.5	24.9	31.4	35.7	42.9
2. Legal Tariff $(B_3 \div B_4)$ (won)	53.5	58.0	71.0	71.8	79.6	81.5	108.5	94.8	62.7	55.5	69.0	73.9	79.9
D. Nominal Effective Exchange Rate $(A + C_1)$	295.4	293.8	302.2	312.9	336.1	371.9	417.4	417.9	424.5	508.9	515.4	519.7	526.9
E. Tariff Rate (%)													
1. Actual Tariff Rate $(C_1 \div B_5)$	9.3	9.5	9.4	8.5	8.3	6.2	5.9	4.9	4.6	5.1	6.5	7.4	8.9
2. Legal Tariff Rate $(C_2 \div B_5)$	19.8	21.6	25.8	24.9	25.7	23.3	27.5	23.8	15.4	11.5	14.3	15.3	16.5
F. Wholesale Price Index and Parity Index (1975=100)													
1. Korea	31.3	33.4	36.2	38.5	42.0	45.7	52.0	55.6	79.0	100.0	112.1	122.2	136.5
2. Major Countries[a]	52.3	52.5	53.4	54.9	57.0	62.9	68.4	81.6	96.0	100.0	105.9	116.1	138.4
3. Purchasing Power Parity Index[c]	167.0	157.1	147.6	142.6	135.7	137.6	131.5	146.7	121.5	100.0	94.5	95.0	101.4
G. Real Exchange Rate $(A \times F_1)$	451.4	421.5	407.8	411.3	421.2	481.7	518.1	584.6	493.3	484.0	457.4	459.8	490.8
H. Real Effective Exchange Rate for Imports $(D \times F_1)$	493.3	461.6	446.0	446.2	456.1	511.7	548.9	613.1	515.8	508.9	487.1	493.7	543.3

Sources: Bank of Korea; Office of Taxation
Notes: [a] This estimate is the import value multiplied by the official exchange rate.
[b] The average wholesale price index of U.S.A. and Japan, weighted by the annual trade volume with Korea, where Japan's price index is adjusted by the exchange rate of Yen per U.S. dollar.
[c] (Wholesale price Index in Major Countries) ÷ (Wholesale price Index in Korea)

Chong Hyun Nam

Table 4. *Non-tariff Import Restrictions in Korea: 1967 to 1978*

	Prohibited	Restricted	Automatic Approval (A)	Total[a] (B)	Rate of Import Liberalization (= A/B) (%)
1967 II	118	402	792	1,312	60.4
1968 I	116	386	810	1,312	61.7
II	71	479	756	1,312	57.6
1969 I	71	508	728	1,312	55.5
II	75	514	723	1,312	55.1
1970 I	74	530	708	1,312	54.0
II	73	526	713	1,312	54.3
1971 I	73	524	715	1,312	54.5
II	73	518	721	1,312	55.0
1972 I	73	570	669	1,312	51.0
II	73	571	668	1,312	50.9
1973 I	73	569	670	1,312	51.1
II	73	556	683	1,312	52.1
1974 I	73	570	669	1,312	51.0
II	73	574	665	1,312	50.7
1975 I	71	592	649	1,312	49.5
II	66	602	644	1,312	49.1
1976 I	66	584	662	1,312	50.5
II	64	579	669	1,312	51.0
1977 I	63	580	669	1,312	51.0
II	61	560	691	1,312	52.7
1978 I	50	456	591	1,097	53.9
May	—	431	666	1,097	60.7
1978 II	—	424	673	1,097	61.3
Sep.	—	385	712	1,097	64.9

Source: Ministry of Commerce and Industry.

Note: [a] The classification of import items was based on the 4-digit SITC codes through 1977, but since then it was based on the 4-digit BTN (CCCN) codes.

general imports with varying deposit rates set by the government depending upon the need for import controls. For example, in 1968 the advance deposit rates were 150 percent for nonessential and luxury items, 100 percent for general items, and 30 percent for raw materials imported for export production. The system of advance deposits, however, was removed in 1978, except for a 40 percent deposit requirement for luxury items.

In conclusion, non-tariff restrictions of varying intensities seem to have played an important role in the protection of Korea's import-substitution industries. Therefore, to measure the extent of protection with any degree of accuracy, one would have to rely on information on tariffs and other import controls, and on price comparisons between domestic and international markets. This subject is discussed in the next section.

III. The Structure of Protection

It has been noted in the preceding section that Korea's system of industrial incentives is complex. Some incentives directly affect the prices of outputs and inputs, while others take the form of direct and indirect subsidies. It is, therefore, necessary to consider all these incentives in order to quantify the total impact of government incentive policies on economic activity. In this section an attempt is made to measure various rates of incentives, and, in particular, a quantitative comparison is made with regard to relative incentives granted to domestic versus export sales.

1. Estimates of Nominal and Effective Protection Rates

The nominal rate of protection is the price difference between the domestic and world markets, expressed as a percentage of the latter. It is, thus, an estimate of the degree to which incentive policies affect the domestic producer prices relative to those that would exist under a free trade regime. The nominal rate of protection, however, is not a good measure of the degree of protection afforded to domestic producers when trade is allowed for intermediate products, because the protection of certain production activities are affected not only by the nominal protection on the product itself, but also by nominal rates on traded inputs. The effective rate of protection is designed to capture the degree of protection afforded to value-adding processes, and is expressed as the percentage of excess domestic-producer-price value added over world price value added.

It was noted earlier that legal tariffs have never been a good index of nominal protection in Korea. Therefore, a price survey has been undertaken to make direct price comparisons between the domestic and world markets for a total of 539 comparable commodities in 1978. In making price comparisons, the ex-factory has been used as the relevant domestic price, and it has been compared with the c.i.f. import price or f.o.b. export price depending on whether commodities were classified as potentially import-competing or for export.[8] The implicit tariff rate has been taken as the percentage excess of the domestic price over the world price.

Next, the appropriate nominal rate of protection has been selected among legal, actual, and implicit tariff rates on the basis of such supplementary information as the relative importance of imports or exports of the commodity, the presence of price controls in the domestic market, and the type of import controls imposed on the commodity. The estimates of nominal rates of protection for 539 commodities have been aggregated into 318 commodity groups in order to match those of the Bank of Korea's 1975 input-output table. Using these estimates of nominal protection and production levels for 1978, and input-output coefficients at world prices derived from the 1975 input-output table, effective rates of protection have been calculated for the 318 sectors. However, summary statistics aggregated into 11 major industry groups are presented and discussed herein.[9] Aggregations were made using the value of domestic sales at world prices as weights in the averaging of nominal protective rates, and the value added as weights in the averaging of effective protective rates.

Table 5 gives estimates of nominal and effective rates of protection by industry group for 1978, and a comparison with those estimated for 1968. Estimates of effective rates of protection were obtained by both the Balassa and Corden methods.[10]

---

[8] For the purpose of this study, a commodity was classified as potentially import-competing if its import value exceeded its export value, and/or its imports grew faster than its exports, and classified as export when the reverse was demonstrated.

[9] Estimates of nominal and effective rates for the 318 sectors will be available on request from the author.

[10] The Corden method includes the value added of non-traded intermediate inputs with the value added of the industry in question assuming that non-traded inputs are protected to the same degree as the industry in question. The Balassa method, however, assumes that non-traded goods are supplied at constant costs and their prices vary only by the amount of changes in the cost of intermediate inputs used in their production. Thus, the Balassa method is preferable when one wants to measure incentives provided to particular industries, while the Corden method is useful when the effective rate of protection is estimated to measure the cost of protection to the economy. See Balassa (1971) and Corden (1971).

Table 5. *Nominal and Effective Rates of Protection: Industry Groups*

(in percent)

| Industry Group | Nominal Protection | | | | Effective Protection for Domestic Sales | | | | | |
| | Legal Tariff | | Nominal Protection | | Balassa | | Corden | | | |
	1968[a]	1978	1968[a]	1978	1968[a]	1978	1968[a]	1978		
I. Agriculture, Forestry, & Fishing	36.5	26.7	17.0	55.2	18.5	77.1	17.9	73.4
IV. Mining & Energy	12.2	6.3	8.9	−19.8	4.0	−25.7	3.5	−23.8
Primary Production, Total	35.1	24.2	16.5	45.8	17.8	61.9	17.1	58.7
II. Processed Food	61.5	41.1	2.9	39.8	−18.2	−29.4	−14.2	−16.0
III. Beverage & Tobacco	140.7	133.2	2.2	20.2	−19.3	28.0	−15.5	22.8
V. Construction Materials	32.2	29.5	3.9	−7.2	−11.5	−15.0	−8.8	−11.9
VI-A. Intermediate Products I	36.6	23.2	2.8	−2.4	−25.5	−37.9	−18.8	−27.4
VI-B. Intermediate Products II	58.7	34.7	21.0	1.3	26.1	7.9	17.4	5.3
VII. Nondurable Consumer Goods	92.3	49.3	11.7	14.9	−10.5	31.5	−8.0	21.9
VIII. Consumer Durables	98.3	44.3	38.5	40.2	64.4	131.2	39.8	81.0
IX. Machinery	52.6	27.5	29.9	17.8	44.2	47.4	29.5	33.2
X. Transport Equipment	62.4	57.0	54.9	30.9	163.5	135.4	83.2	73.8
Manufacturing, Total	67.6	41.4	12.2	10.0	−1.4	5.3	−1.1	3.7
All Industries	54.3	37.7	14.0	17.8	10.5	30.6	9.0	24.1
Primary Production Plus Processed Food	40.7	28.5	13.6	44.2	13.8	55.5	13.0	50.0
Manufacturing, Excl. Bev. & Tob.	60.6	34.1	13.2	9.1	0.5	2.7	0.3	1.9
Manufacturing, Excl. Bev. & Tob. and Processed Food	60.4	33.3	15.9	5.5	5.9	5.1	4.1	3.1
All Industries, Excl. Bev. & Tob.	49.6	31.8	14.6	17.7	11.7	30.8	10.0	24.2

Source: [a] Westphal and Kim, *Industrial Policy and Development*, 1977, Table 2.A and 2.B.

A number of interesting features can be observed from Table 5. First, there seems to have been little if any overall import liberalization during the 1968-78 period. The weighted average of nominal rates of protection for all industries rose from 14 percent to 18 percent for the 1968-78 period despite the fact that the weighted average of legal tariffs declined from 54 percent to 8 percent for the same period, suggesting that legal tariffs have been to a large extent misleading in Korea. At any rate, both legal and nominal rates of protection seem to have been relatively low in Korea when compared with those in other developing countries. (See Balassa, 1971, and forthcoming.)

Second, the pattern of protection in Korea seems to be unique among developing countries in that it is biased in favor of the primary sector and against the manufacturing sector. Furthermore, the extent of discrimination between the two sectors has become substantially greater during the 1968-78 period. For instance, in 1968, nominal protective rates were about 17 percent for the primary sector and 12 percent for the manufacturing sector, showing little difference between the two sectors. This changed to 46 and 10 percent, respectively, in 1978. Greater divergence in the effective rate of protection between the two sectors also resulted during the same period.

Third, estimates of both nominal and effective rates of protection show much greater variation among industry groups in 1978 than in 1968, indicating that incentives provided to individual industries have become much more discriminatory. For example, the nominal rate of protection for the agricultural, forestry, and fishing industries rose from 17 percent in 1968 to 55 percent in 1978, whereas that for the mining and energy industries fell from 9 percent to −20 percent during the same period. During the same 1968-78 period nominal rates of protection fell for capital goods such as machinery and transport equipment, and even fell to almost zero or negative values for intermediate goods such as construction materials and intermediate goods I and II, but rose for consumer goods including processed food, beverages and tobacco, and durable and nondurable consumer goods. As a consequence, one can observe a roughly escalating trend in the level of protection from lower to higher fabrication for nonfood manufacturing products. Nominal and effective protective rates tend to be the lowest on intermediate goods, and the highest on capital and consumer goods. The escalation in the structure of protection also explains why effective rates exceed nominal rates in 1978 for non-food manufacturing industries, except the "Construction Materials" and "Intermediate Products I" industries.

Finally, perhaps the most notable feature is that in 1978, nominal rates of protection were negative for three industries, mining and energy, construction materials, and intermediate products I, in striking contrast to 1968 when no industry was subject to negative nominal protection. Two reasons may explain the unusual phenomena observed in 1978. First, the survey of price comparisons showed domestic ex-factory prices below world prices for a number of commodities, yielding negative implicit tariffs. In general, one is tempted to take zero nominal protective rates for such cases, assuming that such a result could only be ascribed to quality differences between domestic and foreign products. It should be noted, however, that price controls have been widely applied to a number of commodities in Korea with varying intensities over time. In particular, in 1978 the economy as a whole was under great inflationary pressure and prices were strictly controlled for commodities that were subject to government price stabilization and fair trade laws or other special laws. In fact, about one third of the 539 commodities for which price comparisons were made belonged to the price-controlled group in 1978. The second reason is that it is well known that all or a substantial portion of such key industries as coal, iron and steel, fertilizer, and oil refining are under government ownership in Korea, and prices of those industrial products are often set artificially low or increase more slowly than costs of production.[11] The official prices set by the government at lower than world prices, however, tend to generate

---

[11] The following table may provide some insight into the importance of price control in determining negative nominal rates of protection for three manufacturing industries in 1978.

Industry Group	Values of Domestic Sales in Million Won, 1978 (in World Price)	Share (%)	Nominal Rate of Protection, 1978 (%)
IV. Mining & Energy	597,660		−19.8
Anthracite	357,654	59.8	−40.0
V. Construction Materials	600,342		−7.2
Cement	285,450	47.6	−20.0
VI-A. Intermediate Products I	5,105,379		−2.4
Petroleum Products	1,574,139	30.8	−3.0

implicit premiums in the actual markets. Thus, to the extent that such premiums were important in 1978, implicit tariffs estimated in the study may have been underestimated by unknown degrees.

2. Relative Incentives to Export and Domestic Sales: 1978

To gain a better understanding of Korean incentive policies, it is necessary to make a quantitative comparison of incentives granted to stimulate domestic sales versus those geared toward export sales.

As discussed in Section II, in 1978 exporters benefited from a number of incentives including exemptions from tariffs and indirect taxes on their inputs and export sales, reduction of direct taxes, subsidized credits, and a wastage allowance system. However, in contrast to a free trade situation, export sales received genuine subsidies from the direct tax and credit preferences and the wastage allowance system. Implicit subsidies afforded to export production are estimated here only on the basis of direct tax and credit preferences, assuming that the impact of the wastage allowance system is negligible.

Interest subsidies accruing to individual industries from preferential export loans were calculated by multiplying the outstanding export loans to individual industries and the interest rate differential between export loans and non-preferential bank loans. Since the actual amount of export loans allocated to individual industries was not available, it was approximated by reapportioning the total outstanding export loans in 1978 to individual industries on the basis of each industry's share in the value of total exports.[12]

Implicit tax subsidies given to individual industries were estimated from the following three sources of tax preferences: accelerated depreciation allowance for fixed capital used in export production;[13]

---

[12] In general, short-term loans were granted to exporters almost in proportion to the value of exports, without discrimination among industries. However, two types of export loans were designed for specific industries: a fund for exports of agricultural and fishing products, and a fund to finance exports of machinery and transport equipment on credit. These loans were reapportioned to the corresponding industries on the basis of the industry's export shares. For detailed information on export financing, see Hong (1979), pp. 54-55.

[13] The additional depreciation allowance was equivalent to 30 percent of the normal depreciation allowance when the ratio of revenue from exports to total revenue exceeded 50 percent, and when the ratio was less than 50 percent the additional allowance was calculated by the following formula: additional allowance = normal allowance × 0.3 × (export revenue × 2/total revenue).

a reserve fund created from taxable income to develop new foreign markets;[14] and a reserve fund created from taxable income to defray export losses.[15]

Estimates of the effective subsidy rates afforded to export production from all export incentives were then obtained by taking the ratio of the total interest and tax subsidies to an industry to the value added generated by the industry's export production at world prices. The resulting estimates of the effective subsidy rates on export sales are presented in Table 6, comparing them with estimates of effective protection rates for domestic sales. Table 6 also gives estimates of the overall effective incentive rates afforded to individual industries in 1978, where the effective incentive rates were derived from the weighted averages of effective subsidy rates for export sales and the effective protection rates for domestic sales.

Several features of Table 6 are noteworthy. First, the relative incentives provided by the effective rates of protection seem to favor domestic sales over export sales in the aggregate of all industries, with a rate of about 24 percent effective protection for domestic sales versus about 14 percent for export sales. It should be noted, however, that this result stems mainly from the exceptionally high protection given to the domestic markets of the agricultural sector. In contrast, the relative incentives accorded to the manufacturing sector, which accounted for nearly 90 percent of exports in 1978, reveal that export sales, on average, receive greater incentives than domestic sales, with 16 percent of effective incentives for export sales versus 4 percent protection for domestic sales. Second, within the manufacturing sector, export sales are favored more than domestic sales in the processed food, intermediate products I and II and construction materials industries, whereas domestic sales are more favored than export sales in the beverage and tobacco, nondurable and durable consumer goods, and machinery and transport equipment industries. Finally, the effective subsidy rate on export sales shows relatively little dis-

---

[14] The tax subsidy due to the allowance for developing new export markets was estimated to be one percent of total export revenue, assuming that all firms received benefits up to the legal limit of the allowance.

[15] The tax subsidy due to the allowance for export loss was estimated to be equivalent to the imputed interest subsidy generated from one percent of export revenue that firms may legally set aside. If no actual export loss occurs, the firm must repay in three subsequent years the portion of the allowance owed to the government for any given year. It is assumed here that no firm experienced an actual export loss.

Table 6.   Relative Incentive Rates on Export and Domestic Sales in 1978

(in percent)

	Effective Subsidy Rate for Export Sales		Effective Protection Rate for Domestic Sales		Effective Incentive Rate for Total Sales	
	Balassa	Corden	Balassa	Corden	Balassa	Corden
I. Agriculture, Forestry & Fishing	15.9	15.1	77.1	73.4	72.6	69.1
IV. Mining & Energy	11.4	10.6	-25.7	-23.8	-23.6	-21.8
Primary Production, Total	15.3	14.5	61.9	58.7	58.6	55.5
II. Processed Food	31.7	16.7	-29.4	-16.0	-23.0	-12.6
III. Beverage & Tobacco	13.2	10.8	28.0	22.8	27.8	22.6
V. Construction Materials	19.1	15.1	-15.0	-11.9	-10.5	-8.4
VI-A. Intermediate Products I	23.6	17.1	-37.9	-27.4	-31.4	-22.7
VI-B. Intermediate Products II	26.3	17.6	7.9	5.3	12.0	8.1
VII. Nondurable Consumer Goods	17.3	12.1	31.5	21.9	24.0	16.7
VIII. Consumer Durables	38.0	23.1	131.2	81.0	83.2	51.2
IX. Machinery	24.4	16.9	47.4	33.2	43.2	30.3
X. Transport Equipment	26.1	16.9	135.4	73.8	87.2	48.7
Manufacturing, Total	22.8	15.8	5.3	3.7	9.7	6.7
All Industries	17.9	13.9	30.6	24.1	27.8	21.9
Primary Production Plus Processed Food	15.6	14.0	55.5	50.0	52.3	47.1
Manufacturing, Excl. Bev. & Tob.	23.6	16.2	2.7	1.9	8.2	5.6
Manufacturing, Excl. Bev. & Tob. and Processed Food	22.9	15.9	5.1	3.5	10.0	7.0
All Industries, Excl. Bev. & Tob.	18.1	14.0	30.8	24.2	27.9	21.9

persion across industries compared with that of the effective protection rate, ranging from about 11 percent for the mining and energy industry to about 23 percent for the consumer durables industry when measured under the Corden convention.[16] Consequently, the ranking of industries according to their effective protection rates is not altered by adding the effective subsidies for export sales to the effective protection for domestic sales to obtain the effective incentive rates on total sales.

Since the manufacturing sector represents the most important aspect of Korea's trade structure, Table 7 presents estimates of the various incentive measures averaged by trade category of the manufacturing sector.

Among manufacturing sectors classified by trade category, the sectors receiving the highest legal tariff protection in 1978 were the export and non-import-competing sectors, with 47 and 51 percent respectively. The pattern of nominal protection shows, however, just the opposite: the export and non-import-competing sectors received the least nominal protection, 4 and 5 percent respectively, with import-competing and export and import-competing sectors receiving the highest, 21 and 15 percent, respectively.[17] The pattern of effective protection also indictates that the export and non-import-competing sectors receive the least protection for their domestic sales, −1 and −13 percent respectively, while domestic markets are highly protected for the import-competing and export and import-competing sectors, 35 and 26 percent respectively, far exceeding the effective subsidy rates on their export sales. In fact, the ranking of effective protection among the four sectors classified by trade category remains unchanged when effective subsidy rates on export sales are compared. Hence, when effective incentive rates on total sales are compared, the import-competing sector followed by the export and import-competing sector receive the highest effective incentives, and the non-import-competing sector followed by the export sector receive the lowest effective incentives.

Thus, if the relative levels of effective incentive rates are indicative of comparative advantage in the Ricardian sense, it appears that on

---

[16] In fact, the value of implicit export subsidies is nearly proportional to the gross value of exports, and thus the rate of export subsidy across industries varies inversely with the ratio of value added to export sales.

[17] This result reconfirms that the legal tariff is very misleading, particularly for manufactured exports and non-import-competing goods.

Table 7.   Average Incentive Rates by Trade Category in 1978

					(in percent)
	X^a	IC^a	NIC^a	XIC^a	Total
Manufacturing Sector					
Legal Tariff Rate	47.4	25.4	50.8	33.1	41.4
Nominal Protection Rate	3.6	20.8	5.4	15.0	10.0
Effective Protection Rate for Domestic Sales	−0.5	35.2	−12.8	26.2	3.7
Effective Export Subsidy Rate for Export Sales	15.4	24.9	13.7	17.9	15.8
Effective Incentive Rate for Total Sales	6.2	34.8	−12.4	22.4	6.7

Note: [a] The definitions for assigning industries to trade categories employed here follow the convention used in Westphal and Kim (1977): exporting (X) if more than 10 percent of output is exported; import competing (IC) if more than 10 percent of domestic supply is imported; non-import competing (NIC) if neither the export nor the import share exceed 10 percent; and export-and-import competing (XIC) if both shares exceed 10 percent.

average Korea's non-import-competing goods followed by exports are the most efficiently produced, whereas import-competing goods followed by export and import-competing goods are produced most inefficiently.

Finally, it should be noted that the measurements of incentives estimated in the study are gross estimates in the sense that no adjustment has been made for the overvaluation of the Korean currency. Thus, to the extent that the Korean won has been overvalued due to various policy measures, the estimates of effective incentives presented in the study tend to overstate the true effective incentive rates.

IV. Summary and Conclusions

Since the early 1960s, the Korean government has relied on a variety of industrial incentive policies to bring about the desired economic transformation. While in the past such incentive policies may have been conducive to the rapid growth of GNP, exports, and

manufacturing output, it seems that the incentive system as a whole
has become extremely complex, and is often too cumbersome to
secure the efficient allocation of scarce resources.

The purpose of this paper has been to review the system of
incentives that has been used in Korea during the past two decades,
and to quantify the effects of incentive measures, in particular those
pertaining to import substitution and export promotion. The paper
goes on to report the resulting estimates of nominal and effective
protection rates on domestic sales as well as effective subsidy rates on
exports at industry levels in 1978, discussing the results in comparison
with estimates made for 1968. The following is a summary of the
major findings of the study.

There appears to have been little overall import liberalization
during the 1968-78 period. Despite the fact that both the average legal
tariff rates and the number of restricted import items for all industries decreased over the 1968-78 period, the average nominal rate of
protection rose slightly during the same period. It is interesting to
note that nominal protection rates were negative for three industries,
mining and energy, construction materials, and intermediate products
I in 1978, whereas no industry was subject to negative nominal
protection in 1968. However, the negative nominal protection rate is
largely the result of government price control strictly applied to
certain manufacturing output in 1978. Thus, this should not be taken
as an indication that domestic production technologies are superior to
those of foreign countries.

The system of protection in Korea may differ from other developing countries in that it is biased in favor of the primary sector and
against the manufacturing sector. Furthermore, the extent of discrimination between the two sectors has become greater during the 1968-78
period. This result stems mainly from the exceptionally high protection given to the domestic markets of the agricultural sector in 1978.
Within the manufacturing sector, estimates of nominal and effective
rates of protection for domestic sales also show much greater variations among industries in 1978 than in 1968, suggesting that the relative efficiency of resource allocation has become worse during the
1968-78 period. The estimates of nominal and effective protection are
also characterized by an escalating trend from lower to higher fabrication: the rates tend to be lower on raw materials and intermediate
goods and higher on finished products. In contrast, estimates of the
effective subsidy rate on export sales show little dispersion across indus-

tries. Thus, the ranking of industries according to their effective protection rates is not altered by adding the effective subsidies on export sales to the effective protection to obtain the effective incentive rates on total sales.

The third finding was that under the incentive system prevailing in Korea in 1978, it appears that domestic sales are favored over export sales in the aggregate of all industries. The relative incentives accorded to the manufacturing sector, which accounted for nearly 90 percent of Korea's exports in 1978, however, reveal that export sales, on average, receive greater incentives than domestic sales, with 16 percent effective protection for export sales versus 4 percent for domestic sales.

Finally, the pattern of effective protection among the four manufacturing sectors classified by trade category indicates that the export and non-import-competing sectors receive the least protection for their domestic sales, -1 and -13 percent respectively, while domestic markets are highly protected for the import-competing and export and import-competing sectors, 35 and 26 percent respectively. A similar pattern is obtained for estimates of effective subsidy rates on exports, and hence for the effective incentive rates on total sales. If the relative levels of effective incentive rates are indicative of comparative advantage in the Ricardian sense, it appears that on the average Korea's non-import-competing goods are the most efficiently produced, followed by exports, whereas import-competing goods, followed by export and import-competing goods, are produced most inefficiently.

REFERENCES

Balassa, B. (ed.), *The Structure of Protection in Developing Countries,* Baltimore: The Johns Hopkins Press, 1971.

_____, *Development Strategies in Semi-Industrial Countries,* World Bank, forthcoming.

Bhagwati, J., *Foreign Trade Regimes and Economic Development: Anatomy and Consequences of Exchange Control Regimes,* National Bureau of Economic Research, Cambridge: Ballinger, 1978.

_____, *The Theory and Practice of Commercial Policy: Departure from Unified Exchange Rates,* Princeton University Press, 1968.

Chenery, H.B. and N.G. Carter, "Foreign Assistance and Development Performance, 1960-1970," *American Economic Review,* 63 (May 1973), pp. 459-468.

Cole, D. and Y.C. Park, *"Financial Development in Korea, 1945-78,"* Working Paper 7904, Korea Development Institute, 1979.

Corden, W.M., *The Theory of Protection,* Oxford: Clarendon Press, 1971.

_____, "The Costs and Consequences of Protection," P.B. Kenen (ed.), *International Trade and Finance,* Cambridge: Cambridge University Press, 1975, pp. 51-92.

Frank, Charles R., K.S. Kim and L.E. Westphal, *Foreign Trade Regimes and Economic Development: South Korea,* New York: National Bureau of Economic Research, 1975.

Hong, Wontack, *Trade, Distortions and Employment Growth in Korea,* Korea Development Institute, 1979.

Krueger, Anne O., *Foreign Trade Regimes and Economic Development: Liberalization Attempts and Consequences,* National Bureau of Economic Research, Cambridge: Ballinger Press, 1978.

_____, *The Developmental Role of the Foreign Sector and Aid,* Studies in the Modernization of the Republic of Korea: 1945-1975, Cambridge: Havard University Press, 1979.

Little I., T. Scitovsky, and M. Scott, *Industry and Trade in Some Developing Countries,* London: Oxford University Press, 1970.

Magee, Stephen P., "The Welfare Effects of Restrictions on U.S. Trade," *Brookings Papers on Economic Activity,* 3 (1972), pp. 645-707.

Westphal, Larry E. and Kwang Suk Kim, "Industrial Policy and Development in Korea," World Bank Staff Working Paper No. 263, Washington D.C.: International Bank for Reconstruction and Development, August 1977.

• COMMENT

W. Max Corden,   *Australian National University*

The feature of protective structure which is special to Korea is the extensive protection for exports of manufactures provided through the ready availability of credit at below-market interest rates. Thus the calculation of implicit export subsidies provided through this method is crucial to the study.

The calculations show that effective subsidies for exports of manufactures are quite even, averaging about 16 percent. This figure seems surprisingly low. There is the possibility of a considerable understatement, for reasons given by Nam. It would not be surprising if an alternative calculation yielded a figure of perhaps 30 percent. However, this might still be regarded as quite low, considering Korea's impressive export performance.

Protection of manufacturing for the home market is very variable, with some high positive rates and some negative ones. The high protection for consumer durables, machinery and motor cars is noticeable. The average of 5 percent is low but this is not the main feature. The dispersion of protection, resulting primarily from quantitative restrictions, is crucial. This characteristic of dispersion, as well as the high protection in particular fields, is similar to that which can be found in many other developing countries, though it is unusual to have a large element of negative effective protection in the manufacturing sector.

Protection for agriculture is very high, averaging more than 70 percent, and has greatly increased since 1968. This alone is sufficient reason not to describe Korea as a "free trade" country, given both the lower average protection for manufacturing as well as the dispersion there. With respect to agricultural protection Korea is similar to Japan and the European Economic Community rather than other developing countries.

Since 1968 effective protection of manufactures for the home market seems to have become more dispersed, suggesting a worsening of the resource allocation effects of the protection structure.

There are some questions raised in the course of studying this paper. While export subsidies provided through cheap credit are the principal special feature of the Korean protective structure, and the boom in exports of manufactures is the principal feature of the dramatic Korean growth experience, it is rather surprising that the implicit rate of protection provided was so low. This would be true even if one doubled Nam's average figure. This raises the question of the relative importance of the implicit subsidy in producing the boom. Possibly there were other factors that were important, or even crucial. Perhaps the main feature was the absence of restrictions on the availability of credit. Finance for export production could be obtained without difficulty. Given the underlying conditions favorable to Korean growth, the official non-market encouragement of exports, and moderate protection for the home market, the unrestricted provision of credit at something near the world real rate of interest would still have permitted the same growth in exports of manufactures. However, it is difficult to see how one would set up research to resolve this question.

With regard to protection of manufactures for the home market one needs to know how significant the high protection cases are, how important are they at a point in time in terms of value added and employment, and what role have they played in the growth process. Furthermore, it would be interesting for example to have an explanation for the reasons for the particular pattern of dispersion with regard to the roles, of sectional pressures, of assessment of future world market prospects, and of particular philosophies of development.

The motives for the strong protection of agriculture were not clarified. One possible reason for this atypical action would be to ensure security of food supplies. Also there may have been income distribution considerations.

In characterizing Korea's economy, one cannot call it free trade. Furthermore, in view of the variability of protection, the various protective rates are not offsetting in such a way as to lead to the same resource allocation result as free trade would have achieved. But perhaps the departures from the net free trade result may not be very significant. Perhaps the net difference between the actual outcome and the hypothetical free trade outcome is only that agricultural employment has declined at a somewhat slower rate than it would

have otherwise, and that a limited number of manufacturing industries with high home-market protection have been kept going or are
bigger than they would have been otherwise.

Anne O. Krueger, *University of Minnesota*

In this analysis of the Korean structure of protection and its relationship to trade and industrial policies, Nam has not only given us
estimates for 1978 based on careful price comparisons, but in addition he has taken care to insure that his estimates would be comparable with those of Westphal and Kim for the mid-1960s. This makes
them all the more valuable, especially in light of the great interest
which attaches to the Korean experience. His analysis and results
confirm much of what has been suspected: the Korean structure of
protection has become increasingly complex over time, and the
pattern of incentives more differentiated.

It would be useful to examine the extent to which Nam's finding
and those of Westphal and Kim before him can be used to conclude
that the Korean regime was not biased toward export promotion.
First, as Nam indicates, the rates of effective protection and subsidy
given to various Korean industries have been low by comparison with
most developing countries. Intermediate Products I and mining and
energy products in fact have been subject to negative effective protection. For the manufacturing sector, excluding beverages, tobacco and
processed food, the effective subsidy rate for export sales was 15.9
percent; and that for domestic sales was 3.5 percent. Despite considerable variation for individual manufacturing sectors, these rates are
comparable to OECD country figures.

But, while these figures indicate that the average rate of subsidy
and protection was low, they also indicate that, on average, there was
slightly more incentive to sell abroad than to sell in the domestic
market. In addition to these numbers, there are other considerations that lead to the conclusion that there was a bias, probably
somewhat greater than the averages suggest, toward the export
market for some of the following reasons. First, in many industries,
the right to sell in the domestic market at the higher effective protec-

tive rates indicated in the third and fourth columns of Nam's Table 6 was generally reserved to those firms that were exporting. That is, protection in the home market was contingent upon being an exporter. Second, the fact that exporters were entitled to import with no payment of duty subject only to their re-exporting within a one-year period has limited the extent to which protection accorded to domestic producers has really insulated the domestic market from imports. In an economy geared to exporting, the protection an import-substitution firm receives is undermined if all exporters can import the competitive product. Third, the effective subsidy measures include the explicit value of low interest rates to exporters, but in fact, as Hong's work has indicated, all loans through official channels in the 1970s were extended at negative real rates of interest and allocated through credit rationing. The implicit value of these loans far exceeded the interest rate subsidy. Because exporters received highly preferential treatment in the allocation of those loans, they received a far larger effective subsidy than use of the official interest subsidy figures would suggest. Fourth, it is impossible for any researcher to estimate the value, which must have been considerable, of the informal incentives which the government provided to exporters. The degree to which the machinery of government was geared to facilitating exports is well known. This included the attention of the highest officials to exporters' difficulties; the somewhat more lenient perusal of tax returns than happened to other businesses; the more rapid expedition of paperwork and government formalities; and the greater assurance that future production would be profitable if it was geared to the export market. No one has yet devised a means of estimating the importance of these types of considerations, but it cannot be doubted that they affected the relative profitability of exporting contrasted with production for the domestic market.

Based on these factors, it is clear that the Korean regime in 1978 retained its bias toward exporting contrasted with import substitution, but it is evident also that, as Nam contends, the incentive structure had become more complex and more differentiated than had earlier been the case. It will be Nam's results with respect to the relationship between the shift in incentives between 1968 and 1978 and the changing Korean industrial structure.

Finally, Nam's Table 1 very usefully provides a number of indicators of the structure of the Korean economy and its growth. He includes the ratio of exports to GNP as one variable, and shows it rising to 41.8 percent in 1978 from 11.2 percent ten years earlier. A rise of that magnitude is truly remarkable. One question, however, is the fraction of value added in exports to GNP. It is well known that Korean exporters import a sizable fraction of their intermediate goods and raw materials; insofar as there is a considerable import content in exports, the use of value added in exporting relative to GNP would provide a more reliable indicator of the importance of exports to the Korean economy.

GENERAL DISCUSSION

To a certain extent many protective measures adopted in Korea simply compensated for the overvalued exchange rate. Hence the question was raised as to whether all effective protection measures cancelled out each other and led to a free trade situation, or led to over-expansion of exports, and whether one can have any idea of what would be the trade volume in a perfectly free trade regime. To some people, the trade volume/GNP ratio in Korea seems too high. On the other hand, as far as foreigners are concerned, import restrictions may be condemned as a deviation from the free trade principle, but export promotion, which may result in resource misallocation in the promoting country, cannot be condemned by foreigners because they are getting goods at cheaper prices.

Most advanced countries tend to protect domestic agricultural production regardless of the comparative advantage position. Perhaps Korea entered this stage of agricultural protection relatively early in her growth process.

Nam's estimate of effective subsidy rates on exports shows little dispersion across industries. This may be due to the fact that Nam approximated export loans allocated to individual industries by re-apportioning the total outstanding short-term export loans to individual industries on the basis of each industry's share in the value of total exports. Had long-term loans for export expansion been included in the estimation, the result might have been different. Furthermore, all bank loans in Korea have been distributed giving the most preferential treatment to promotion of export industries. The non-short-term bank loans may well have been fairly unevenly distributed among industries.

One has to examine short-run and long-run responses of industries to export incentives and to shifts in incentive structures. The dynamic resource-pull effect of shifts in effective protection structure over time also has to be examined.

EXPORT GROWTH AND THE BALANCE OF PAYMENTS IN KOREA, 1960-78

*Yung Chul Park**

I. Introduction

A growing number of studies on Korean development have in recent years shown that the export-oriented development strategy and policy measures adopted to implement it have contributed to the rapid growth of output and employment, have resulted in increased factor utilization and allocative efficiency, and have improved distributive equity.[1]

In has also been argued that the rapid growth of exports has contributed to a gradual improvement in the balance of payments in the current account.[2] This argument seems to reflect the view that when a country's high rate of growth is based on its success in expanding its export market, growth tends to improve the balance of goods and services, henceforth referred to as trade balance. However, except in some of the rigid-priced Keynesian models, the effect of the expansion of exports on the trade balance is not unambiguous. If indeed the growth of exports could lead to an improvement in the trade balance over time, it appears that the process through which

* Korea University. The author is grateful to Professor W. Max Corden for his helpful comments on an earlier draft of this paper.
[1] For a growing literature on Korea's experience with export-led industrialization, see Kim and Roemer (1979), Hasan and Rao (1979), Krueger (1979), Hong (1976 and 1979), Kim and Westphal (1977), Hasan (1976), Frank, Kim, and Westphal (1975), Westphal (1975 and 1978), and Frank (1974).

[2] See Hasan and Rao (1979), pp. 3-4, and Korea Development Institute (1980), p. 80.

this improvement could be brought about is not well expounded in the literature.

The purpose of this paper is to analyze the channels through which the growth of exports has influenced the balance of trade in Korea during 1960-78. Section II discusses some of the characteristic features of Korea's balance of payments and on the basis of this discussion develops a framework of analysis which introduces three goods: exportables, importables, and non-tradables. Section III analyzes the effect of export expansion on the relative prices and outputs of the three goods. Under a certain set of assumptions it is shown that an increase in exports produces an income or output effect and a substitution effect and that the former effect helps reduce trade deficit. Section IV turns to the causal nexus between exports and domestic absorption. It is argued that the growth of exports exerted a positive effect on domestic saving and hence moderated the growth of domestic absorption in Korea.

II. Characteristics of Korea's Balance of Payments: A Framework of Analysis

1. Characteristics of the Balance of Payments

The growth of exports in Korea during 1960-78 was impressive by any international standards. In 1961, commodity exports amounted to $32.8 million and consisted largely of such primary products as metallic ores, crude animal and vegetable materials, fish, and raw silk. Since then exports rose to nearly $13 billion in 1978, 90 percent of which was manufactured products, increasing the share of exports in GNP from 4 percent in 1960 to 38 percent in 1978. The average real growth of exports during the period was over 30 percent a year.

Although Korea suffered from a chronic current account deficit throughout the period (see Table 1), its balance of trade as a proportion of total exports including invisibles declined gradually over time. The deficit in the balance of goods and services was more than twice the size of the value of exports of goods and services in 1962-63. Within a decade after launching an export promotion strategy in the middle of the 1960s, the trade deficit fell to about 16 percent of total exports in 1972-73. After the oil crisis period, the proportion fell

Table 1. Balance of Payments (Summary Table)

(in million dollars)

	60	61	62	63	64	65	66	67	68	69
Current balance	13.4	33.1	-55.5	-143.3	-26.1	9.1	-103.4	-191.9	-440.3	-548.6
Trade balance	-272.6	-242.2	-335.3	-410.2	-245.8	-240.8	-429.6	-574.2	-835.8	-991.7
Exports	32.8	40.9	54.8	86.8	119.1	175.1	250.3	334.7	486.2	658.3
(change, %)		24.7	34.0	58.4	37.2	47.0	42.9	33.7	45.3	35.4
Imports	365.4	283.1	390.1	497.0	364.9	415.9	679.9	908.9	1,322.0	1,650.0
(change, %)		-7.3	37.8	27.4	-26.6	14.0	63.5	33.7	45.5	24.8
Invisible trade balance	10.2	43.8	43.3	7.4	23.9	46.1	106.5	157.1	169.3	197.3
Unrequited transfers (Net)	275.7	231.5	236.5	259.5	194.9	203.3	219.6	225.2	226.1	245.8
Long-term capital	7.9	16.4	7.8	69.5	29.0	37.3	211.8	201.2	433.8	576.2
Basic balance	21.3	49.5	-47.7	-73.8	2.9	46.4	108.4	9.3	-6.5	27.6
Short-term capital	0.6	-2.0	-6.7	18.4	-4.4	-23.1	6.4	85.9	13.2	56.5
Errors and Omissions	-2.1	-1.6	-2.1	-0.4	-1.2	-7.1	4.4	23.0	-20.2	-7.6
Overall balance	19.8	45.9	-56.5	-55.8	-2.7	16.2	119.2	118.2	-13.5	76.5

Source: The Bank of Korea, Economic Statistics Yearbook, various issues.

Table 1. *(Continued)*

	70	71	72	73	74	75	76	77	78	79ᵖ
Current balance	-622.5	-847.5	-371.2	-308.8	-2,022.7	-1,886.9	-313.6	12.3	-1,085.2	-4,238.9
Trade balance	-922.0	-1,040.6	-574.5	-566.0	-1,936.8	-1,671.4	-590.5	-476.6	-1,780.8	-4,565.0
Exports	882.2	1,132.2	1,675.9	3,271.3	4,515.1	5,003.0	7,814.6	10,046.51	12,710.6	14,701.8
(change, %)	34.0	28.3	48.0	95.2	38.0	10.8	56.2	28.6	26.5	15.7
Imports	1,804.2	2,178.2	2,250.4	3,837.3	6,451.9	6,674.4	8,405.1	10,523.1	14,491.4	19,266.8
(change, %)	9.3	20.7	3.3	70.5	68.1	3.4	25.9	25.2	37.7	30.0
Invisible trade balance	119.3	27.8	32.9	67.1	-308.3	-442.2	-71.8	266.0	224.0	-112.8
Unrequited transfers (Net)	180.2	170.6	169.8	190.1	222.4	226.7	348.7	222.9	471.6	438.9
Long-term capital	448.8	527.8	505.1	666.3	946.4	1,178.3	1,371.2	1,312.7	2,166.3	2,485.9
Basic balance	-173.7	-319.7	133.9	357.5	-1,376.3	-708.6	1,057.6	1,325.0	1,081.1	-1,753.0
Short-term capital	122.4	134.6	-16.3	84.0	-45.4	679.5	356.5	21.4	-1,171.0	843.6
Errors and Omissions	-5.2	13.1	30.1	18.8	27.9	-121.5	-240.5	-31.7	-312.0	-63.9
Overall balance	-56.5	-172.0	147.7	460.3	-1,093.8	-150.6	1,173.6	1,314.7	-401.9	-973.3

Table 2. Balance on Goods and Services, 1960-78

(in million dollars)

	1960-61	62-63	64-65	66-67	68-69	70-71	72-73	74-75	76-78
Balance on goods and services (A)	− 360.8	− 694.8	− 416.6	− 740.2	− 1,460.9	− 1,815.5	− 1,040.5	− 4,358.7	− 2,429.9
Exports of goods and services (B)	262.4	338.7	499.4	1,097.5	2,024.1	2,995.0	6,346.0	11,237.0	39,692.2
A/B×100	137.5	205.1	83.4	67.4	72.2	60.6	16.4	38.8	6.1

Source: The Bank of Korea, *Economic Statistics Yearbook*, various issues.

further to 6 percent in 1976-78. (See Table 2.) Although it turned out to be premature, a recent study went so far as to predict that Korea could eliminate its current account deficit in the late 1970s.[3]

From the early 1950s, after the Korean War, to the middle of the 1960s, the deficit in the trade account including invisibles was by and large supported by foreign aid and grants. During the period, capital flows, whether short- or long-term, were negligible. From 1966 onward, however, long-term capital inflows rose markedly, replacing foreign aid and grants as the major source of foreign exchange resources. Massive long-term capital inflows during 1966-1969 were partly induced by policies to attract foreign capital, but largely by the monetary reform in 1965 which raised the real interest rate on time and saving deposits to over 10 percent per annum for the next five years, introduced a system of governmental guarantees on foreign loans, supported trade liberalization, and maintained a realistic exchange rate.

Long-term capital inflows reached their peak in 1969, and with the rapid growth of exports thereafter the relative importance of long-term capital inflows as a source of foreign exchange declined. During the oil crisis, Korea experienced considerable difficulties in securing an adequate amount of long-term capital and had to resort to short-term borrowing.

Long-term capital inflows consist, in order of importance, of public and commercial loans, trade credits with a maturity longer than a year, direct and portfolio investments, and other miscellaneous items. As presented in Table 3, long-term loans and trade credit accounted for over 90 percent of the total long-term capital inflows throughout the period. Portfolio capital movements were non-existent until 1974 when a state-owned bank issued and sold for the first time bonds denominated in foreign currencies in international capital markets. From 1974 to 1978, the cumulative total of portfolio capital inflows amounted to $205.2 million which was less than 2 percent of the total long-term capital inflows during the same period. Direct investment was a relatively smaller source of foreign exchange in the 1960s. It rose rapidly during the first half of the 1970s; since then its share of total long-term capital has fallen below 5 percent.

Commercial loans, which are tied to the imports of capital goods, and long-term trade credits require a prior approval by the govern-

---

[3] See Hasan and Rao (1979), p. 4.

Table 3. Long- and Short-term Capital Movements

(in million dollars)

	1960-63				1964-65				1966-67				1968-69			
	Credit		Debit		Credit		Debit		Credit		Debit		Credit		Debit	
	Amount	%	Amount	%	Amount	%	Amount	%	Amount	%	Amount	%	Amount	%	Amount	%
Long-term Capital, Net	101.6				66.3				413.0				1010.0			
Public and Commercial Loans	68.6	64.8	2.7	62.8	74.5	83.1	12.0	51.5	421.4	91.0	36.5	72.7	963.0	80.2	116.2	60.9
Direct Investment	5.4	5.1	—	—	6.3	7.0	1.5	6.4	21.0	4.5	—	—	35.1	2.9	0.3	0.2
Trade Credits	31.0	29.3	0.4	9.3	8.6	9.6	9.5	40.8	20.3	4.4	7.5	14.9	191.9	16.0	39.6	20.7
Portfolio Investment	—		—		—		—		—		—		—		—	
Others[a]	0.9	0.8	1.2	27.9	0.2	0.2	0.3	1.3	0.5	0.1	6.2	12.4	10.9	0.9	34.8	18.2
Total	105.9	100.0	4.3	100.0	89.6	100.0	23.3	100.0	463.2	100.0	50.2	100.0	1200.9	100.0	190.9	100.0
Short-term Capital, Net	10.3				−27.5				92.3				69.7			
Trade Credit	27.0	100.0	—		1.3	100.0	17.6	61.1	93.7	97.1	—		474.4	90.1	418.4	91.6
Advance Payments on Exports	—		—		—		—		—		—		33.9	6.4	6.6	1.4
Export on Credit	—		—		—		—		—		—		18.1	3.4	31.7	6.9
Others[b]	—		8.7	100.0	—		11.2	38.9	2.8	2.9	4.2	100.0	—		—	
Total	27.0	100.0	8.7	100.0	1.3	100.0	28.8	100.0	96.5	100.0	4.2	100.0	526.4	100.0	456.7	100.0

Source: The Bank of Korea

Notes: [a] Includes Cooley loans and repayments, subscriptions to international organizations, fund transactions between headquarters and foreign branch offices of deposit money banks, and advanced payments for imports.
[b] Includes advance payments for imports from 1960 to 1967.

Table 3. *(Continued)*

(in million dollars)

	1970-71 Credit Amount	%	Debit Amount	%	1972-73 Credit Amount	%	Debit Amount	%	1974-75 Credit Amount	%	Debit Amount	%	1976-78 Credit Amount	%	Debit Amount	%
Long-term Capital, Net	976.5				1171.4				2124.7				4850.3			
Public and Commercial Loans	1224.4	83.7	241.4	49.7	1363.8	75.2	463.8	72.3	2234.6	70.6	622.5	59.9	6630.4	74.4	1935.8	48.0
Direct Investment	109.0	7.5	3.5	0.7	222.1	12.3	10.9	1.7	185.7	5.9	28.1	2.7	290.4	3.3	82.5	2.0
Trade Credits	102.4	7.0	205.0	42.2	214.6	11.8	115.0	17.9	645.0	20.4	349.4	33.6	1541.7	17.4	1657.7	41.1
Portfolio Investment	—	—	—	—	—	—	—	—	19.0	0.6	—	—	186.2	2.1	—	—
Others	26.5	1.8	35.9	7.4	12.1	0.7	51.5	8.0	80.0	2.5	39.6	3.8	230.8	2.6	353.2	8.8
Total	1462.4	100.0	485.8	100.0	1812.6	100.0	641.2	100.0	3164.3	100.0	1039.6	100.0	8879.5	100.0	4029.2	100.0
Short-term Capital, Net	257.0				67.7				634.1				-793.5			
Trade Credit	893.0	75.8	727.8	79.0	1304.4	73.9	1192.1	70.2	3476.0	81.3	2930.9	80.5	10434.6	74.4	10402.8	70.2
Advance Payments on Exports	175.4	14.9	64.8	7.0	145.4	8.2	154.7	9.1	291.2	6.8	135.2	3.7	1078.5	7.7	1281.4	8.6
Export on Credit	110.2	9.3	129.0	14.0	315.0	17.8	350.3	20.6	508.3	11.9	575.3	15.8	2491.5	17.8	3134.8	21.2
Others	—	—	—	—	—	—	—	—	—	—	—	—	20.9	0.2	—	—
Total	1178.6	100.0	921.6	100.0	1764.8	100.0	1697.1	100.0	4275.5	100.0	3641.4	100.0	14025.5	100.0	14819.0	100.0

ment. The repayments of interest and principal on loans are then guaranteed by the banks owned or strictly controlled by the government or by the government itself. In the early 1960s these governmental guarantees even required formal approval by the National Assembly.

Short-term capital inflows consist mostly of trade credits, advance payments on exports, and exports on credit, and they are all trade-related. Until 1967, trade credits were virtually the only form of short-term capital movements. Since then, advance payments on exports and exports on credit increased rapidly, but still trade credits accounted for well over 70 percent on average of the total short-term capital inflows. As in the case of long-term loans and credits, short-term borrowing requires formal approval by the government, and repayment of these loans is guaranteed by the banks or the government itself.

The preceding discussion of the characteristics of capital movements suggests that the capital account has basically financed the current account deficit. It also implies that all foreign borrowing is in fact done by the government. This is because, insofar as the government has the final responsibility for repayment, there is no point in distinguishing private borrowing from government indebtedness. Therefore, it is not altogether unreasonable to treat capital movements as being exogenous in Korea.

2. A Framework of Analysis

In developing a framework of analysis for the balance of payments, one could in general rely on one of the following four approaches to the balance of payments: the absorption, elasticities-absorption, monetary, and portfolio balance approaches. The question of which approach is more appropriate for a country like Korea is a difficult one, but the choice of one framework over another would to a large extent be dictated by the question of which balance-of-payments transaction should be viewed as autonomous and which should be thought of as accommodating. If capital account transactions are accommodating and only current account transactions are endogenous, then one could focus on the current account of the balance of payments and utilize an absorption or an elasticities-absorption model. On the other hand, if asset transactions are also autonomous, then one should concentrate on the overall balance and rely on either a monetary or portfolio balance approach as a framework of analysis.

The discussion in Section I makes it clear that capital transactions have been accommodating and hence a proper model for a balance-of-payments analysis for Korea would be the one that places emphasis on current account transactions. However, we will explain some of the reasons why both the monetary and portfolio approaches are not applicable to Korea.

The advocates of the monetary approach to the balance of payments view it as a monetary phenomenon and as such should be analyzed by models that explicitly specify monetary behavior and integrate it with the real economy (Johnson, 1977, p. 217). According to this approach, balance of payments disequilibria reflect either an excess-flow supply of or demand for money and require analysis of stock adjustment processes in the money market. If this view is accepted, then the prime focus of analysis should be the overall, not the trade or current account balance.

The monetary approach to the balance of payments has been criticized on a number of theoretical grounds,[4] but the major difficulty in applying this approach to the Korean economy is that the balance of payments adjustment process implied by the approach has not been in operation in Korea mainly because of the passive and accommodating features of the capital account. As discussed before, practically all capital movements have been trade-related and served to supplement movements of goods and services.

Trade deficits in Korea may initially have been the consequences of excessive domestic credit creation and of real changes accompanied by policies involving either the running down of international reserves or borrowing. However, if the government authorities borrow continuously as they have done in Korea to support the trade deficit, then the automatic adjustment mechanism inherent in the monetary approach may not function; that is, changes in the overall balance of payments may not be determined in and by the money market. It is true that in the face of a continuing trade deficit, the government may not be able to borrow indefinitely. This is beside the point, however, because such deficit financing was possible for Korea during the period under discussion. In fact, some studies suggest that the availability of private foreign capital has been in response to Korea's impressive

---

[4] See Whitman (1975), Tsiang (1977), and Corden (1977, Chapter 3).

export performance and the consequent improvement in its trade balance.[5]

During 1970-78, the annual rate of increase of the supply of domestic credit in Korea was close to 35 percent on average per annum and in the sixties the rate of increase was much higher. Despite the rapid expansion of domestic credit, the trade balance displayed a sustained improvement over the period. The manner in which the government authorities controlled the supply of domestic credit as well as money also indicates the limited applicability of the monetary approach to Korea.

For a given deficit in the current account, the government authorities in the first instance attempted to maintain an equilibrium in the overall balance by imposing or relaxing a ceiling on foreign borrowing (both short- and long-term) or prohibiting certain categories of foreign loans and credits. When they failed to neutralize the effects of changes in the overall balance of the supply of money, which was often the case, they then adjusted the supply of domestic credit to attain a predetermined rate of growth of money supply. In short, changes in the supply of domestic credit have been in response to, rather than a cause of, reserve gains or losses.

The portfolio or asset-market approach to the balance of payments places emphasis on the behavior of the asset-markets in determining the balance of payments in a fixed exchange rate system. In this framework, capital movements are endogenous and treated as episodes in the process of portfolio optimization.[6] The portfolio models are often integrated with the markets for goods and services and factors of productions thereby making them general equilibrium Keynesian models. While this approach is more general than the monetary approach and may be useful for analyzing the balance of payments in the advanced countries, its applicability is again seriously limited in an economy where capital movements have very little to do with portfolio optimization.

In view of the preceding discussion, it would be reasonable to focus on the current account balance as the proper concept of the balance of payments in Korea. Since examining the causal nexus between export growth and the trade balance and the effect of relative price

---

[5] See Hasan and Rao (1979), p. 7 and Westphal (1978).

[6] See Dornbusch (1975) and Allen and Kenen (1979) for the structure of the portfolio model of an open economy.

changes on the trade balance is of primary interest, a good place to start would be an elasticities-absorption model.

In this study, a modified version of an absorption model developed by Corden (1977, pp. 7-34) will be relied on, one which introduces three types of goods: exportables, importables, and non-tradables (pp. 7-21). Exportables include actual exports and their close substitutes that are sold domestically. Importables consist of actual imports and import-competing goods. Non-tradables are those tradables that are not in fact traded because of transportation costs, quotas, or prohibitive tariffs.

The domestic demand for the three commodities is a function of relative prices (the prices of exportables and importables in terms of the price of non-tradables) and real spending. The domestic prices of tradables are in the long run determined by the exchange rate, transportation costs, tariffs, and export subsidies. The price of non-tradables is determined by the domestic demand for and supply of these goods.[7]

Domestic absorption of these goods and services is generated by expenditure on consumption and investment. When the market for non-tradables is in equilibrium, trade deficit is equal to the excess of domestic absorption (spending) over income.[8]

Throughout the analysis it is assumed that the exchange rate is fixed and that the monetary authorities offset changes in the supply of money arising from flows of reserves as well as changes in the demand for money arising from changes in income through open market operations. Unilateral transfers are assumed to be exogenous so that the balance of trade including invisibles is equivalent to the current account balance.

Production of tradables and non-tradables require labor and capital, which includes imported capital goods as inputs. Moreover, it is governed by a fixed-proportions production function. This assumption is made to emphasize the fact that capital is the scarce factor. It will be assumed that there exists in this economy a surplus of labor, which keeps the money wage rate at a constant level. However, capital is fully employed and mobile between the sectors. In produc-

---

[7] In a small open economy facing given terms of trade, exportables and importables may be combined into a single commodity.

[8] For a structural linkage between domestic expenditure and the goods markets, readers are referred to Allen and Kenen (1979, pp. 25-37). In our framework, the goods markets are linked with domestic absorption through income and the income identity.

tion, the exportables sector is more labor-intensive than the others. For simplicity, the factor intensities of importables and non-tradables are assumed to be the same.[9]

III. Export Growth and the Balance of Trade: The Gains from Trade and Substitution Effect

In order to analyze the effect of export expansion on the trade balance it should be assumed that there occurs an exogenous increase in the international price of exportables in terms of both importables and non-tradables.[10] It is also assumed that the market for non-tradables is initially in equilibrium and that the economy is experiencing a trade deficit which is equal to the domestic excess demand for tradables or the excess of real spending over real income. The increase in the relative price of exportables produces a substitution effect and an income effect. The substitution effect reverses the initial improvement in the trade balance associated with the relative price change whereas the income effect brings about a permanent improvement.

The improvement in the terms of trade would, other things being equal, induce the economy to produce and sell abroad more exportables than before. On the demand side, the rise in the relative price of exportables will shift the demand for exportables towards importables and non-tradables. As will be discussed below, the increase in the relative price of exportables implies a terms-of-trade gain and therefore a rise in real income and spending, which will in turn lead to increased domestic demand for all three goods. On the supply side, capital will be induced over time to move out of produc-

---

[9] In a fully employed economy, fixed-proportions production functions may lead to specialization in the production of those commodities in which the economy in question has comparative advantage and termination of the production of importables. This special case does not arise in this model, however, because of the assumptions that the production functions exhibit diminishing returns and that there exists unemployed labor. The transformation schedule of the economy would be convex to the origin.

[10] An increase in the foreign demand for exportables would, other things being equal, entail a real appreciation or an improvement in the terms of trade so that the effect of export expansion on the trade balance could be analyzed in terms of an exogenous increase in the price of exportables.

tion of importables and non-tradables into the production of exportables as the profit rate in the exportables sector rises. These demand and supply adjustments will make more goods available for exports and initially reduce the trade deficit.

However, at constant absolute prices of importables and non-tradeables, there will be excess demand for these goods as consumers substitute toward them, while at the same time capital has been induced to move out to these sectors. As a result, given the exchange rate, the price of non-tradables will rise until the excess demand for them is eliminated. This price rise in the non-tradable sector would then negate the initial improvement in the trade balance. In the market for importables, the excess demand could, assuming no import restrictions, be satisfied by additional imports without increasing the domestic absolute price of importables; equilibrium in this market could be restored entirely through a quantity adjustment. But the additional imports would offset the initial reduction in the trade deficit. Thus, the subsequent price and quantity adjustments in the three markets set in motion by an increase in the relative price of exportables will in the end reverse the original improvement in the trade balance. This is the substitution effect.

The improvement in the terms of trade induces an income effect which results in a permanent reduction in the trade deficit and which stems from three sources. One source is the gains from trade that could be translated into a rise in real income, which raises the level of domestic absorption or spending as it increases the demand for all three goods. However, real spending on domestic goods will rise less than income because part of the increased real income is saved or spent on imports. The income effect will improve the balance of trade.

Another source of the income effect is related to the use of imported intermediate and capital goods in the domestic production of the three goods. Suppose that actual imports consist of not only consumer's but also intermediate and capital goods. As the international price of exportables increases while the absolute prices of importables and non-tradables remain unchanged, a unit of exportables can now be exchanged for a larger quantity of imports than before. To the extent that imported capital and intermediate goods are extensively used in domestic production as they are in the case of Korea, the improvement in the terms of trade is equivalent to an implicit production subsidy on the use of these imported goods.

The subsidy would tend to reduce the costs of domestic production of the three goods, thereby making exports more competitive in foreign markets and augmenting the supply of both tradables and non-tradables. As a result, the production subsidy generates an income effect and, more importantly, moderates the increase in the excess demand for both importables and non-tradables that export expansion initially generates. This in turn restrains the rise in the domestic prices of non-tradables and exportables, and hence induces in the end a permanent shift of capital from the production of non-tradables and importables to that of exportables. Although capital is fully employed, the favorable terms of trade make relatively more exportables available to foreigners than otherwise would be the case. In this model, imported intermediate goods have no place, but to the extent that the domestic capital stock consists in part of imported capital goods, and domestic and foreign capital goods are perfect substitutes in production, the result will be the same.

A third source of the income effect is associated with the capacity augmenting effect of export growth. If the bulk of imports consists of capital and intermediate goods, and foreign and domestic capital goods are a perfect substitute in production, the growth of exports increases the rate of growth of domestic capital, thereby expanding the productive capacity of the economy.[11] Exports provide a means of trading a surplus factor, in this case labor, for a scarce factor which is capital.

A rigorous analysis of the capacity augmenting effect of export growth may require the two-tiered production structure developed by Corden (1971), but such an analysis is beyond the scope of this study. In this model, this effect could at best be represented by an outward shift of the economy's transformation schedule.

For a given improvement in the terms of trade, the lower the capital intensity of exportables and the larger the share of imported intermediate and capital goods in production, the greater is the income effect. When exportables are relatively less capital-intensive, an export increase will bring about relatively smaller domestic excess demand for importables and non-tradables and, consequently a smaller increase in the domestic absolute price of these goods. This will in turn maintain the international competitiveness of exports. In a labor-surplus economy therefore, the expansion of labor-intensive exports tends to be

---

[11] For an analysis on growth and trade in consumer and capital goods, see Bardhan (1970, Chapters 3 and 4).

less inflationary than otherwise. The presence of a strong income effect appears to be one of the reasons why export growth could lead to an improvement in the trade balance, in a country like Korea.

While the income effect could be sizable when the exports of labor-intensive products grow rapidly as they did during 1960-78 in Korea, the growth of exports by itself may not eliminate a given trade deficit. It may have to be accompanied by disabsorption policy. What the analysis implies is that when exportables are labor-intensive in production, the dosage of disabsorption required is likely to be less than when importables and non-tradables are relatively more labor-intensive. Likewise, labor-intensive exports, other things being equal, will strengthen the effectiveness of a switching policy such as devaluation in a labor-surplus economy.

Another implication of the analysis is that the level of employment would definitely rise as capital is shifted towards production of labor-intensive exportables as a result of export growth, but the real wage rate will fall because of the rise in the average price. Therefore, it is conceivable that, despite the increase in employment, the share of labor in national income will fall, altering the intra-sectoral distribution of income. As will be discussed in Section IV, this change in the distribution of income helps improve the trade balance as it raises the propensity to save of the economy as a whole.

A third implication is that an export-oriented development strategy may be superior to an import-substitution strategy in restoring an adverse trade imbalance, even if the two different strategies could result in an identical rate of growth. This is because, given a high capital-labor ratio in the importables sector, an import-substitution strategy is likely to generate a smaller income effect and greater inflationary pressures than an export-promotion strategy would.

The result of this model concerning the favorable effect of export growth on the trade balance is sensitive to the assumptions that non-tradables and importables are relatively more capital-intensive than exportables and that capital is the scarce factor. These assumptions appear to be borne out by the available data in Korea.

Given the resource-poor endowment and the surplus of labor, it would not be unreasonable to assume that capital was the constraining factor of production throughout the period under discussion in Korea. The direct factor estimates by Westphal and Kim (1977) show that between 1960-68 manufactured exports were substantially more labor-intensive over time. Their findings also show that whereas

Table 4.   Sectoral Capital-Labor Ratios[a]

	1960	1963	1966	1968	1970	1973	1975
Total Exports[b]	0.59	0.71	1.00	1.15	1.48	2.13	3.13
Total Imports[b]	0.54	0.94	1.58	1.46	1.55	2.60	2.75
Primary sector	0.11	0.12	0.16	0.21	0.22	0.28	0.37
Manufacturing sector	1.62	1.53	1.27	1.63	2.00	2.62	3.00
Exports	1.13	0.97	1.13	1.14	1.50	2.17	3.79
SOC and Services sector	1.51	1.50	1.46	1.65	2.07	2.63	2.96
Whole Industry	0.58	0.62	0.70	0.84	1.06	1.28	1.48

Source: Hong (1979), Tables 2.7 and 2.11 on pp. 22-23 and pp. 32-33.
Notes: [a] Capital stock in million 1970 dollars devided by labor in thousand persons.
[b] Aggregated capital-labor ratios; include indirectly employed capital and labor.

manufactured exports were less labor-intensive than average manufacturing in 1960, they were more labor-intensive by 1968 (p. 4-49). A
recent study by Hong (1979) confirms these results (pp. 18-
35). As presented in Table 4, Korea's exports were more labor-
intensive than its imports which consisted mostly of raw materials and
capital goods until 1973. From this one may infer that importables,
which includes import-competing goods, were employing more capital
than exportables in general. Non-tradables consist mainly of services.
Table 4 shows that the capital-labor ratio of the social overhead (SOC)
and service sector, which may be classified as the major non-tradable
sector, was consistently higher than that of exports during 1960-73.

In this model, export expansion is induced by a rise in the relative
price of exportables in terms of both importables and non-tradables.
As shown in Table 5, the international exchange ratio improved
continuously during 1961-68 in Korea. A marked improvement in the
ratio took place in 1966 when it rose almost 16 percent. For the next
seven years, the unit value index of exports was 40 percent higher
than that of imports; this was also the period of rapid growth in
exports. After a sharp deterioration during the 1974-75 oil crisis, the
terms of trade once again improved substantially.[12]

---

[12] As for the major sources of the improvement in and favorable trend of the terms
of trade, one influence was that import prices of raw materials including mineral fuels
that account for the bulk of Korea's imports remained relatively stable at a level below
that of international prices of manufactured exports until the mid-1970s. Another
source may be that Korean exporters have gradually relied for their export marketing
less on subcontracting, contractual relationships with large foreign buyers and

The improvement in the terms of trade has increased the purchasing power of Korea's exports and increased her capacity to import. Translated into real income, Korea gained about 1.7 percent of real GNP a year from improved terms of trade between 1966-70 and close to 4 percent (see Table 6) in the years thereafter.

Although the terms of trade gains have been conducive to the expansion of exports, it should be emphasized that the gains were not the only, and certainly not the most important, factor responsible for the growth of exports in Korea. As the experience of many developing countries show, it is not altogether clear whether the favorable terms of trade would be sufficient to sustain rapid growth of exports. Korea was presented with an opportunity to exploit, export promotion represented a means for doing so, and unlike other developing countries, Korea was able to export her labor-intensive products. What the analysis implies is that export growth in Korea might not have been sustained and reduced the trade deficit had it not been accompanied by a gradual improvement in the terms of trade which generated a strong income effect.

IV. Export Growth and Domestic Absorption[13]

1. Overview

In the preceding section, it was indicated that an expansion of exports increases the level of domestic absorption through an income or Keynesian multiplier effect. However, the different influences the export increase may exert on different components of domestic absorption were ignored, namely, consumption and investment expenditures. In this section, it will be shown that the growth of exports in

---

Japanese trading houses as they succeeded in developing their own marketing network. A third and most important source has been the shift in the composition of Korea's exports to high-quality products requiring skilled labor. In a variety of products, including clothing, footwear, and electronics, Korea has moved from low- to high-price lines over time. On the other hand, the increasing share of some other skill- and capital-intensive exports has not helped to improve the terms of trade, largely because in the absence of any strong demand for these exports Korean exporters have had to undercut their prices below the international level.

[13] This section draws heavily on Park (1980, Section III).

Table 5.   Terms of Trade (1975 = 100)

	Unit Value Index of Exports (I)	Unit Value Index of Imports (II)	Net Barter Terms of Trade (III = I/II)	Export Deflator (IV)	Import Deflator (V)	Ratio of Export to Import Deflator (VI = IV/V)
1961	52.6	44.4	118.5	14.71	13.85	1.06
1962	53.2	44.4	120.0	14.85	13.94	1.07
1963	53.9	44.4	121.4	18.00	14.77	1.22
1964	55.1	44.9	123.7	25.81	23.67	1.09
1965	57.2	45.7	125.2	30.98	27.84	1.11
1966	63.0	45.3	139.4	33.88	28.98	1.17
1967	65.9	45.7	144.5	34.57	29.80	1.16
1968	67.9	45.3	150.2	35.87	30.96	1.16
1969	64.5	44.6	144.7	36.23	31.79	1.14
1970	67.4	46.2	145.7	40.19	34.93	1.15
1971	66.5	46.0	144.5	45.20	38.87	1.16
1972	67.3	46.8	143.7	52.32	44.99	1.16
1973	85.2	62.5	136.4	64.86	56.34	1.15
1974	107.9	97.2	111.0	87.87	80.91	1.09
1975	100.0	100.0	100.0	100.00	100.00	1.00
1976	111.7	98.0	114.0	110.86	100.27	1.11
1977	122.3	100.2	122.0	120.74	105.18	1.15
1978	135.4	105.8	128.0	132.89	114.04	1.17

Source: The Bank of Korea, *Economic Statistics Yearbook*, various issues.

Table 6. GNP and Gains from Trade

(billion won)

	GNP in 1975 prices (I)	Gains from Trade[a] (II)	Gains as % of GNP (III) = II/I (%)	GNP adjusted for terms of trade (IV)
1953	2,205.19	18.78	0.85	2,223.97
1954	2,318.53	5.55	0.24	2,324.08
1955	2,422.61	17.03	0.70	2,439.64
1956	2,389.81	6.10	0.26	2,395.91
1957	2,570.45	10.36	0.40	2,580.81
1958	2,711.05	16.69	0.62	2,727.74
1959	2,814.92	16.33	0.58	2,831.25
1960	2,845.64	15.17	0.53	2,860.81
1961	3,004.58	6.69	0.22	3,011.27
1962	3,071.14	7.97	0.26	3,079.11
1963	3,350.65	28.93	0.86	3,379.58
1964	3,671.50	14.73	0.40	3,686.23
1965	3,884.99	25.02	0.64	3,910.01
1966	4,378.48	53.33	1.22	4,431.81
1967	4,669.39	67.00	1.43	4,736.39
1968	5,195.61	92.58	1.78	5,288.19
1969	5,911.39	111.11	1.88	6,022.50
1970	6,347.70	143.19	2.26	6,490.89
1971	6,908.74	186.33	2.70	7,095.07
1972	7,305.01	255.27	3.49	7,560.28
1973	8,377.08	368.02	4.39	8,745.10
1974	9,009.39	202.89	2.25	9,212.28
1975	9,644.24			9,644.24
1976	11,016.39	415.27	3.77	11,431.66
1977	12,175.23	731.05	6.00	12,906.28
1978	13,693.26	907.11	6.62	14,600.37

Source: The Bank of Korea, *National Income in Korea*, 1978.
Note: [a] Nominal exports deflated by import deflator minus export in 1975 prices.

Korea during the period under discussion generated positive effects on domestic savings by bringing about an inter- as well as intra-sectoral distribution of income and by providing incentives to save and invest. As a result, the expansion of domestic absorption caused by the export growth was smaller than otherwise would have been the case.

Strong prospects for export expansion encourage heavy investment since such prospects make large expansion of capacity profitable. Without corresponding decreases in domestic absorption, consumption or government spending, export and investment expansion will be thwarted by the inflationary pressures that they generate. It has been shown in the model that an increase in the prices of importables and non-tradables caused by the export expansion negates some of the initial improvement in the trade balance. In Korea, it appears that export growth was less inflationary than otherwise because of its positive effects on domestic savings.

A casual examination of the raw data shows that the variability of exports has been rather closely associated with domestic savings in Korea. As shown in Figure 1, the ratio of domestic savings to GNP has, except for a few years, moved in the same direction as the ratio of exports to GNP over the 1960-78 period. While this association does not prove any causality between the two variables, there are a number of factors which suggest that domestic savings have indeed been dependent on export earnings.

It is generally accepted in the economics literature that, for a given level of disposable income, profit-earners or "capitalists" save more than wage earners. Several empirical studies have found that the marginal propensity to save in the urban sector is higher than in the rural sector in developing countries (Mikesell and Zinser, 1973, p. 7). These disparities between the sectoral propensities to save have been confirmed by two recent studies on the saving behavior in Korea. A comparison of the savings behavior between rural and urban households shows that urban dwellers save more out of their disposable incomes than do rural farmers (Kim, 1977, pp. 216-218). Song (1980) finds that the marginal propensity to consume of urban income (0.78) was much lower than that (0.93) of rural income. He also shows that the marginal propensity to consume of salary and wage income (0.91) is significantly higher than that (0.57) of property income which includes profits. As a dual economy develops and as urbanization continues, Song argues, the level of saving continues to increase.

These differences in the sectoral propensities to save imply that two forms of redistribution of income within the private sector would tend to raise the overall propensity to save: an intra-sectoral redistribution from the household to the business sector and an inter-sectoral redistribution from the rural to urban sector. In the following section, it will be shown that export growth has in a large measure been

Figure 1. Domestic Savings and Exports as Percentage of GNP
(at current market prices)

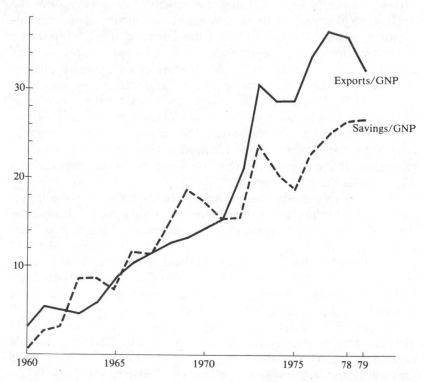

Source: The Bank of Korea, *Economic Statistics Yearbook,* various issues.

responsible for these two forms of redistribution, and hence has been favorable to saving and the balance of trade.[14]

---

[14] The positive effect of export growth on savings operating through the inter-sectoral redistribution may be described as the structural change effect in that it is associated with the declining share of rural incomes. This effect should be distinguished from the intra-sectoral redistribution effect operating through a shift in factor shares. This is because the structural change effect would have taken place under any industrialization strategy whereas the intra-sectoral effect might not. As far as the structural change effect is concerned, one could argue that the net contribution of exports in the context of Korea's industrialization would be the extent to which it raised the rate of industrial growth over what it might otherwise have been.

2. Export Growth and Intra-Sectoral Redistribution of Income

It was shown in Section II that the growth of exports expands the level of employment as it induces capital to move out of capital-intensive sectors and move into labor-intensive ones. Despite the increase in employment, however, it was pointed out that the share of labor in national income could fall if there is a surplus of labor in the economy which keeps money wages from rising. As shown by several studies,[15] exports contributed to a remarkable growth of employment and to increased labor productivity in Korea. This was more significant in the manufacturing sector. Despite the rapid growth of employment, there occurred a noticeable decline in the labor share in the manufacturing sector as well as in the economy as a whole during the 1960-75 period.[16]

According to the estimates made by Hong (1980) with the input-output data for the 1960-75 period, there was a significant drop in the share of employee compensation in gross value added in manufacturing (from 38 to 32 percent) and the SOC sector (from 51 to 37 percent), whereas there was no significant change in the labor share in GNP due to erratic fluctuations in the labor share in the other sectors during the period. When imputed wages to unpaid workers are included, the labor share in GNP fell from 57 percent in 1970 to 49 percent in 1975 (Hong, pp. 52-94). On the basis of the Bank of Korea's sectoral value-added data and Economic Planning Board's manufacturing census data, Hong also shows an increase or a slight decrease in the late 1960s, a significant decrease in the early 1970s, and a substantial rise of the labor share in manufacturing thereafter (Hong, p. 96).

Although the level of employment grew rapidly and labor productivity rose sharply, real wages in the manufacturing sector remained stable until the late 1960s when they began a sharp rise. Between 1960 and 1968, real wages increased at a compound rate of 2.7 percent whereas labor productivity rose by more than 4.5 percent a year during 1963-69. (See Table 7.)

---

[15] See footnote 1.

[16] In a neoclassical world where labor is fully employed and wages are completely flexible, an increase in exports shifts income distribution towards factor intensive in the production of exports. If exports are labor-intensive, then the overall propensity to save will fall (Corden, 1971, p. 131). In a Lewis model with unlimited supply of labor, however, the opposite result follows.

Table 7. Real Wages and Value Added per Worker (Labor Productivity in Manufacturing)

	Real Wages (Won)[a]		Value Added Per Worker[b]
	I	II	
1960	17,923	17,388	
1961	17,635	17,400	
1962	17,267	17,055	
1963	16,392	14,722	531.0
1964	14,809	13,197	559.0
1965	15,972	14,420	555.8
1966	17,261	15,530	604.0
1967	19,880	18,043	599.5
1968	23,204	21,538	662.0
1969	29,273	27,690	768.7
1970	33,690	32,159	884.4
1971	37,963	37,310	1,010.0
1972	38,662	38,886	1,064.5
1973	40,162	39,773	1,092.3
1974	38,239	36,795	1,143.7
1975	38,378	38,378	1,174.8
1976	46,106	47,072	1,186.2
1977	56,602	59,290	1,298.6
1978	68,064	75,167	1,442.3
Rate of increase			
1960-68	2.9%	2.7%	4.5% (1963-68)
1969-78	8.8%	11.7%	7.2%

Source: The Bank of Korea, *Economic Statistics Yearbook,* various issues; The Bank of Korea, *National Income in Korea,* 1978.

Notes: [a] Monthly earnings per employee devided by the wholesale price index (I) and consumer price index (II).

[b] Value Added in 1975 prices (million won) divided by thousand persons employed.

The stable real wages during the period could in part be attributed to the absence of labor strife, but was mostly due to surplus labor. The urban industrial sectors were therefore able to draw on additional labor from large reserves of unemployed or underemployed workers without raising real wages, and were thus able to increase their profits. The tendency for real wage rates to remain stable throughout most of the sixties helped keep profits high and stimulated business saving.[17]

The relative stability of real wages was not the only factor responsible for the redistribution of income in favor of profit earners. Another equally important factor was the gains in real income from the favorable terms of trade, as shown in Table 6. An improvement in the terms of trade raises real income. In a fully employed economy, therefore, real wages must rise if equilibrium is to be restored. When there exists a large pool of unemployed workers as was the case in Korea in the sixties, the improvement does not necessarily raise real wages and hence tends to distribute much of the increase in real income to profit-earners.

This profit-augmenting effect was reinforced by the high import content of Korea's exports and liberal policy towards the importation of raw materials for use in export production and importation of capital goods in general. The share of domestic value added in Korea's manufactured exports was roughly 50 percent between 1965-78.[18] Exporters have had literally unlimited access to imported inputs and have paid neither tariffs nor indirect taxes on them.[19]

On the other hand, imports of consumer durables and luxury con-

---

[17] Since the late 1960s, however, real wages in the manufacturing sector have risen rapidly due to a steady decline in the overall unemployment rate and the rising capital intensity of the economy, particularly in the export sector. The growing volume of exports of construction services to the Middle East since the mid-1970s has further tightened the labor market conditions and has put added pressure on wages. Unlike in the 1960s, therefore, exporters have not been able to employ additional labor without paying higher real wages and as such, have experienced a considerable squeeze on their profits. This squeeze in turn appears to have had a depressing effect on business saving.

[18] The continued high import content of exports is not a consequence of the export incentive system; it has resulted from Korea's export specialization in labor-intensive commodities.

When the domestic market is protected and currency is overvalued, such an import policy could lead to a bias in favor of using imported inputs. Westphal argues that the bias has not been serious because protection and overvaluation have been low in Korea, and moreover, the system of using domestic letter of credit which gives the full range of export incentives to producers of intermediate goods supplied to exporters has favored only those backward linkages that have permitted efficient production (Westphal, 1978, p. 351).

[19] Since 1961, imported materials for export production, strategic industries, and foreign investment have been exempted from tariffs. The tariff law has allowed the duty-free import of basic plant facilities and equipment for the so-called key industries since 1949. This law had been applied to imports of machinery and other capital goods for export production from 1964 until 1974, when the system was changed to a deferred payment scheme based on an installment system.

sumption goods have been subject to high tariffs or prohibited. Imports of food grains and other consumption goods including consumer durables were less than 15 percent of Korea's total imports between 1966-78. Given this composition of imports, the gains from trade in the first instance would be shifted to exporters and business firms in general, who are also favored importers, in the form of profits. Over time, some of the gains may have been shifted to consumers as the imports tend to lower the prices of domestically produced goods. However, protection and imperfect competition in the domestic market is likely to have limited such a diffusion of the gains throughout the economy. The rising real wage rate in the 1970s may have depressed profits, but the adverse effect appears to have been substantially offset by the profit-augmenting effect of the favorable terms of trade.[20]

3. Export Growth and Inter-Sectoral Redistribution of Income

Export growth has in a large measure been responsible for an inter-sectoral redistribution of income from the rural agricultural to urban industrial sector. This redistribution was unmistakable during the 1960s, but less so in the 1970s. Given a relatively high propensity to save in the urban sector, this redistribution is likely to have raised the overall propensity to save.

The relative decline in agricultural income since the mid-1960s has been dramatic. Between 1960-64, the share of agriculture in national income in current market prices was close to 37 percent, on average. During the next five years, the average share fell by more than 12 percentage points to 25 percent. Since then the share has been relatively stable at about 22 percent.[21]

The substantial decline in relative farm income in the latter part of the 1960s may have been caused by several developments, but the most important one was no doubt a substantial reduction in both farm population and labor which, in turn, was the result of the rapid industrialization fueled by export growth. With the expansion of exports that began in the early 1960s, there has been not only a relative, but also an absolute decline in farm population. (See Table 8.)

---

[20] Another factor responsible for the intra-sectoral redistribution was the incentive system for exports. See Hong (1979, Chapters 4, 5, 6) for the system in Korea.

[21] These figures are from The Bank of Korea, *National Income in Korea,* 1978.

Table 8. *Population, Employment, and Terms of Trade in Agriculture*

(thousand person)

| | Population | | | Employment | | Agriculture parity ratio[b] | Relative income position of farmers[c] |
	Farm Population (%)	Non-Farm population (%)	Total	Agri., Forestry & Fishery (%)[a]	Mining and Manufacturing (%)[a]		
1960	14,559 (58.3)	10,430 (41.7)	24,989				
1961	14,509 (56.3)	11,257 (43.7)	25,766			75.8	
1962	15,097 (57.6)	11,416 (42.4)	26,513			75.9	70.3
1963	15,266 (56.6)	11,996 (43.4)	27,262	4,837 (63.1)	667 (8.7)	100.0	116.2
1964	15,553 (56.2)	12,431 (43.8)	27,984	4,825 (61.9)	690 (8.8)	99.5	129.2
1965	15,812 (55.1)	12,893 (44.9)	28,705	4,810 (58.6)	849 (10.4)	78.5	99.7
1966	15,781 (54.1)	13,655 (45.9)	29,436	4,876 (57.9)	913 (10.8)	75.8	80.6
1967	16,078 (53.4)	14,053 (46.6)	30,131	4,811 (55.2)	1,115 (12.8)	79.2	60.1
1968	15,908 (51.6)	14,930 (48.4)	30,838	4,801 (52.4)	1,282 (14.0)	81.4	62.6
1969	15,589 (49.4)	15,955 (50.6)	31,544	4,825 (51.3)	1,346 (14.3)	80.4	65.3
1970	14,422 (45.9)	17,819 (54.1)	32,241	4,916 (50.4)	1,395 (14.4)	89.6	67.1
1971	14,712 (44.7)	18,171 (55.3)	32,883	4,876 (48.4)	1,428 (14.2)	91.8	78.9
1972	14,677 (43.8)	15,828 (56.2)	30,505	5,346 (50.6)	1,499 (14.2)	98.4	83.0
1973	14,645 (42.9)	19,458 (57.1)	34,103	5,569 (50.0)	1,821 (16.3)	101.0	87.4
1974	13,459 (38.8)	21,233 (61.2)	34,692	5,584 (48.2)	2,062 (17.8)	100.5	104.6
1975	13,244 (38.2)	22,037 (61.8)	35,281	5,425 (45.9)	2,265 (19.1)	100.0	101.6
1976	12,785 (35.7)	23,075 (64.3)	35,860	5,601 (44.6)	2,743 (21.9)	99.3	100.4
1977	12,309 (33.8)	24,127 (66.2)	36,436	5,405 (41.8)	2,901 (22.4)	98.9	102.0
1978	11,528 (31.1)	25,491 (68.9)	37,019	5,181 (38.4)	3,123 (23.2)	99.2	98.3

Source: Economic Planning Board (EPB), *Major Statistics of the Korean Economy*, 1979
Notes: [a] Percent of total employed population.
[b] Ratio of prices received to prices paid in agriculture.
[c] Ratio of real income of farm household to real income of urban salary and wage earners (per household).

Table 9. *Relative Prices of Investment Goods (1975 = 100)*

		I Aggregate			II Manufacturing	
	GNP deflator (a)	Investment goods price deflator (b)	Ratio (b/a) (%) (c)	Value added deflator (a)	Investment goods price deflator (b)	Ratio (b/a) (%) (c)
1953	2.2	2.5	113.6	4.1	2.8	68.3
1954	2.9	3.1	106.9	6.3	4.3	68.3
1955	4.7	5.5	117.0	8.8	5.3	60.2
1956	6.3	7.0	111.1	10.1	6.3	62.4
1957	7.7	8.1	105.2	11.9	6.4	53.8
1958	7.6	8.4	110.6	12.8	7.5	58.6
1959	7.7	10.6	137.7	13.7	9.5	69.4
1960	8.6	11.3	131.4	14.0	8.8	62.9
1961	9.8	13.1	133.7	15.9	12.4	78.0
1962	11.6	15.5	133.6	18.2	13.7	75.3
1963	15.0	15.3	102.0	22.6	15.6	69.0
1964	19.5	22.2	113.8	31.2	21.4	68.6
1965	20.7	25.6	123.7	33.5	24.1	71.9
1966	23.7	27.2	114.8	37.8	26.7	70.6
1967	27.4	29.8	108.8	39.3	29.5	75.1
1968	31.8	33.4	105.0	42.1	30.9	73.4
1969	36.5	34.2	93.7	45.7	31.4	68.7
1970	42.1	40.3	95.7	49.2	35.2	71.6
1971	47.4	42.6	89.9	51.3	37.1	72.3
1972	54.8	49.1	89.6	58.3	42.0	72.1
1973	62.1	58.8	94.7	65.4	55.6	85.0
1974	80.8	81.1	100.4	83.0	79.1	95.3
1975	100.0	100.0	100.0	100.0	100.0	100.0
1976	118.5	108.6	91.7	115.3	104.8	90.9
1977	136.8	120.4	88.0	126.4	118.1	93.4
1978	162.5	134.3	82.7	136.7	124.9	91.4

Source: The Bank of Korea, *National Income in Korea, 1978.*

The relative decline in farm employment in the latter part of the 1960s was equally impressive. In the early 1960s, the agricultural sector accounted for more than 60 percent of total employment. By 1970, the proportion of agricultural employment fell below 50 percent. (See

Table 9.) Much of the labor released by agriculture was in turn absorbed into the urban industrial sector, which possesses a relatively higher propensity to save, thereby increasing the propensity to save of the private sector.[22]

In the 1970s, exports have continued to grow at a rapid rate despite a growing base and an appreciable slowdown in the expansion of world trade. As can be seen in Table 8, the growth of exports has contributed to a continuous transfer of labor from the farm sector to the manufacturing sector in the 1970s. Unlike during the 1960s, however, the shift in labor has not brought about any significant drop in the agricultural share of national income. The share declined from 24 percent in 1970 to about 20 percent in 1978, whereas farm employment share fell from 50 to 38 percent during the same period.[23]

4. Export Growth and Incentives to Invest and Save

The growth of exports and foreign capital inflows, which have been in response to Korea's impressive export performance, have greatly

[22] The shift in employment was undoubtedly the major cause of the sharp decline in the share of agriculture in national income during 1965-69. But the decline was also induced by the low grain price policy pursued until about 1968, mainly to promote price stabilization. As a result of the low grain price policy, the farm sector parity ratio, i.e., the ratio of prices received to prices paid, deteriorated by 25 percent between 1963 and 1969. This deterioration also led to a marked relative decrease in per farm household real income. From 1964 to 1969, the ratio of rural real income to urban real income per household declined by more than 30 percent. (See Table 8.)

[23] There are several reasons for the moderate decline in the share of agriculture in the national income in the 1970s. The shift of labor to the industrial sector has raised the real wage rate in the farm sector. Within the manufacturing sector capital intensity has been rising, thereby reducing its labor absorptive capacity. Finally, in 1969, the government shifted its policy of low grain prices to a policy of high rice prices and began to increase agricultural investment. Due mainly to this shift in policy, the farm household parity ratio began to improve substantially since 1969. Reflecting this improvement, farm incomes also gained on urban incomes until the middle of 1970s when the farmers' relative position was restored to their 1965 position of near equality.

As a result of these developments, the positive effects of export growth on household savings through the inter-sectoral redistribution of income has been weakened in the 1970s, and the available evidence partly supports this.

Household savings as a proportion of GNP registered no significant increase in 1970-72 compared to the preceding four years. In fact, the ratio of household savings net of agricultural inventories to GNP fell to 2.2 percent in 1970-72 from 3.7 percent in 1966-69. The household saving ratio shot up to 9.1 percent in 1973 when exports grew by more than 80 percent, and has remained at a level of 8.5 percent, excluding 1975, for the past six years.

augmented its capacity to import. Korea, as is to be expected of a country with a poor resource endowment, has imported mostly raw materials and capital goods. Imports of most of the capital goods have neither been subjected to high tariffs nor restricted. Thus the growing volume of capital goods imported at world market prices (which have been lower than those in the home market) has tended to moderate the increase in domestic prices of capital goods relative to those of consumer goods and, in so doing, to reduce the cost of investing.[24]

During the fifties and the early sixties, prices of investment goods rose at a faster pace than those of consumer goods, reflecting the relative scarcity of capital. From 1966 onward, however, the rate of increase of the prices of capital goods as measured by the investment deflator slowed down considerably compared to other deflators. Between 1968-73, the price of investment goods was 5 percent lower on average than the GNP deflator and 8 percent less than the consumer goods deflator. From 1965 to 1973, the ratio of investment deflator to GNP deflator declined by more than 3 percent a year. After a sharp rise in 1974-75 which was caused by the oil crisis, the ratio has been falling again for the past three years during which the investment deflator was 13 percent lower than the GNP deflator. (See Table 9.)

The decline in the relative price of capital goods, given the cost of borrowing and depreciation allowances, would tend to lower the costs of fixed investment. This reduction would in turn stimulate business investment and at the same time include a higher rate of business saving. The reasons for this are related to imperfect capital markets and an underdeveloped financial system in general.

Corporate savings, which consist of undistributed profits and depreciation allowances, are the major sources of firms' internal funds and represent a decision to retain earnings for financing their current and future investments. If capital markets are competitive and hence firms can borrow fully to meet the financing needs of a planned level of investment at a given market rate of interest, business saving may be regarded as a deliberate decision and hence may not be related to their desired amount of investment. However, in Korea, capital markets have been moribund, bank loans have been strictly rationed,

---

[24] Trade expansion lowers the domestic prices of importables relative to the prices of exportables. If investment goods are importables-intensive, the price of investment goods relative to the price of consumption goods will fall. See Corden (1971), p. 127.

and only a limited number of large firms have had access to foreign financing. A majority of business firms were closed corporations owned by a single individual, a family, or a group of individuals (or families) until the middle of the 1970s when the government began to promote actively the opening-up of these closed corporations.

Therefore, these owners of closed corporations were making investment as well as savings decisions at the same time. Under these circumstances, improved investment opportunities, given the limited availability of outside financing, are likely to induce firms to save more. Thus, the growth of exports has helped stimulate business investment and savings by facilitating the import of relatively inexpensive foreign capital goods.

The successful promotion of exports has not only tended to reduce the costs of capital investment, but has also raised the rate of return to capital by bringing about improved factor utilization and an efficient resource allocation. It would be reasonable to assume that given its capital-scarce factor endowment, Korea's comparative advantage during the 1960s was in labor-intensive as opposed to capital-intensive activities. Thus, the trade structure characterized by labor-intensive exports and capital-intensive imports would, as a first approximation, indicate that resource allocation was generally efficient. Reflecting the efficient allocation of resources, the rate of return to capital, measured by the ratios of gross incremental value added to investment, more than doubled during the rapid growth of labor-intensive manufactured exports from 12 percent in 1954-61 to 26 percent in 1967-71. With the marked rise of the capital intensity of exports, however, the rate of return to capital has remained at about 27 percent since 1972 (Hong, 1979, pp. 176-196). The capital-output ratio in the manufacturing sector, another crude measure of the rate of return on capital, has declined continuously since the mid-1960s. Over a decade, from 1966-76, the ratio fell by 75 percent. Thus, the marked increase in the rate of return on capital in the sixties, especially in manufacturing, was conducive to business investment and saving.

V. Concluding Remarks

The purpose of this paper has been to analyze the effects of the growth of exports on the balance of payments in the current account of Korea during 1960-78. The proper concept of the balance of payments for a country like Korea is a difficult issue. Although Korea is a very open economy, its money and capital markets have been isolated from the international financial markets. Capital movements have been tightly controlled and have mainly served to finance the deficit in the current account. All borrowing has in fact been done by the government. These considerations have led observers to ignore capital movements and to concentrate on the trade balance.

Utilizing an absorption model with three goods, the paper has shown that the growth of labor-intensive exports in which Korea possessed a comparative advantage contributed to a gradual improvement in the trade balance. In the supply of goods and services, the growth of labor-intensive exports until the early 1970s brought about sizable gains from trade and at the same time augmented the productive capacity of the economy. These two effects moderated the rise in domestic price of exportables and non-tradables that the export expansion would have caused, thereby making more exportables available for foreign demand. As a result, export growth was less inflationary than it would otherwise have been. On the absorption side, the rapid growth of exports exerted a positive effect on domestic saving by causing a redistribution of income from sectors with a low propensity to save to those with a higher one, by reducing the cost of investment, and by improving the rate of return on capital. Perhaps these arguments are not new and not well understood; an attempt has been made to present them in a systematic, not necessarily rigorous manner with supporting evidence.

While the focus on trade balance for analysis may be justifiable to the extent that capital flows are exogenous, the study is nevertheless deficient in that it cannot analyze the effects of changes in the supply of money arising from reserve flows on exports and imports. A more general model with a financial sector is required for such an analysis.

Over the past two years, Korea has experienced a sharp deterioration in its balance of trade. Although the oil crisis and worldwide recession are the prime causes, the analysis indicates that the rising capital-intensity of exports, which partly resulted from an excessive promotion of heavy and chemical exports, and tightening of the labor market have also made the deficit problem more serious and the future prospects for improvement less promising.

REFERENCES

Allen, P.R. and P.B. Kenen, "The Balance of Payments, Exchange Rates, and Economic Policy," Reprints in International Finance No. 19, April, 1979, International Finance Section, Princeton University.

Bardhan, P.K., *Economic Growth, Development, and Foreign Trade*, Wiley-Interscience, 1970.

Corden, W.M., *Inflation, Exchange Rates and the World Economy*, The University of Chicago Press, 1977.

_____, "The Effects of Trade on the Rate of Growth," J. Bhagwati (eds.), *Trade, Balance of Payments, and Growth*, Amsterdam: North-Holland Publishing Co., 1971.

Dornbusch, R., "A Portfolio Balance Model of the Open Economy," *Journal of Monetary Economics*, January 1975, pp. 3-10.

Frank, C.R., "Foreign Trade Regimes and Economic Development: Republic of Korea," *Trade Strategies for Economic Development: The Asian Experience*, Asian Development Bank and NBER, New York, 1974.

Frank, C.R., Jr. and K.S. Kim, and L. Westphal, *Foreign Trade Regimes and Economic Development: South Korea*, National Bureau of Economic Research, New York, 1975.

Hasan, P., *Korea: Problems and Issues in a Rapidly Growing Economy*, The Johns Hopkins University Press, 1976.

Hasan, P. and D.C. Rao, *Korea: Policy Issues for Long-Term Development, The Johns Hopkins University Press, 1979.*

Hong, Wontack, *Factor Supply and Factor Intensity of Trade in Korea,* Seoul: KDI Press, 1976.

_____, *Trade, Distortions and Employment Growth in Korea,* Seoul: KDI Press, 1979.

_____, *Trade Policy and Income Distribution in Korea,* KDI Working Paper 8004, May 1980.

Johnson, H.G., "The Monetary Approach to Balance of Payments

Theory and Policy: Explanation and Policy Implications,'' *Economica*, August 1977, pp. 217-229.

Kim, K.S., "Household Savings Behavior," C.K. Kim (ed.), *Planning Models and Macroeconomic Policy Issues*, KDI Press, 1977.

Kim, K.S. and M. Roemer, *Growth and Structural Transformation*, Studies in the Modernization of the Republic of Korea, 1945-75, Harvard University Press, 1979.

Korea Development Institute, "Development Strategy and Policy Priorities for the Fifth Five-Year Development Plan," KDI Working Paper 8003, April 1980, Seoul, Korea.

Krueger, A.O., *The Developmental Role of the Foreign Sector and Aid*, Studies in the Modernization of the Republic of Korea, '1945-75, Harvard University Press, 1979.

Mikesell, R.F. and J.E. Zinser, "The Nature of the Savings Function in Developing Countries: A Survey of the Theoretical and Empirical Literature," *Journal of Economic Literature,* March 1973.

Park, Y.C., "*Export-Led Development: The Korean Experience, 1960-78,*" Asian Employment Programme Working Paper, WP II-6 ARTEP-ILO, June 1980.

Song, B.N., "Empirical Research on Consumption Behavior: Evidence from Rich and Poor LDC's," *Economic Development and Cultural Change*, forthcoming, 1980.

Tsiang, S.C., "The Monetary Theoretic Foundation of the Modern Monetary Approach to the Balance of Payments," *Oxford Economic Papers*, (New Series), November 1977, pp. 319-338.

• COMMENT _____

Dono Iskandar Djojosubroto,   *Ministry of Finance, Indonesia*

Park stated that his paper was intended to analyze the effects of the growth of exports on the balance of payments from 1960 to 1978. He pointed out that Korea, with a relatively open economy, controlled the capital flows in order to finance the deficit in the current account.

On the basis of the data presented in Park's paper, it is not very clear whether there was a close relationship between long-term capital inflows regulated by the government and the deficit in the current account. For example, from 1964 to 1965 there was an improvement in the current account but it was accompanied by an increase in the long-term capital inflow. From 1973 to 1974 the current account deteriorated considerably but the long-term capital inflow increased only slightly. From 1975 to 1976 there was great improvement in the current account but again it was accompanied by an increase in the long-term capital inflow.

Moreover, it seems impractical to use long-term capital to balance the current account not only because long-term capital is usually project-oriented, but because there is a considerable lag between the commitment and the imports.

On the contrary, the data showed a closer relationship between exports and long-term capital flows. It is, therefore, much more possible that the government has used long-term capital in promoting exports either through government borrowings or export incentives.

It is likely that at the beginning of the period observed, export promotion succeeded in increasing the exports and improved the current balance but exerted inflationary pressures on the economy afterwards. Inflation caused the domestic currency to appreciate and might have wiped out the export incentives. In a fixed exchange rate regime, one possible short-term solution is devaluation. It can be seen from the data that Korea has experienced high inflation which was counteracted by acts of devaluation.

The export incentives given by the Korean government to the

industrial sector were accompanied by massive imports financed by foreign borrowing. A question may arise from the fact that inflation rates were quite high despite the imports. This could be answered by referring to the fact that the imports were actually directed to support industry and not to provide consumer goods.

W. Max Corden, *Australian National University*

This paper raises an interesting question concerning the means by which an increase in exports can affect the current account of the balance of payments. To answer the question a simple analytical framework will be set out, the basic methodology used being that of the absorption approach to balance of payments analyses.

It is assumed that there is an exogenous rise in exports, resulting either from an improvement in the terms of trade or an improvement in factor productivity. The question is how this affects the excess or shortfall of investment over saving, that is, net hoarding. If hoarding increases, the balance of payments on current account improves; if hoarding falls and investment rises more than savings, the balance of payments worsens. Net hoarding means that Korea as a whole accumulates financial assets, whether in the form of foreign exchange reserves or private capital outflow. If the country is not hoarding, the reserves are going down, the government is borrowing abroad, or the private sector is doing the borrowing, or some combination of these.

In considering savings, the rise in exports represents a rise in real income. If the marginal propensity to save is positive, savings will increase on that account. At this stage income distribution effects were disregarded. It can be supposed that the marginal propensity to save is the same for all the main sectors of the community. The increase in savings may be temporary; it may represent a process of adjustment during which the ratio of wealth to income is restored, but this adjustment period could be quite long.

Next, income distribution effects have to be introduced. If the marginal propensity to save out of profits is greater than that out of wages, a shift in income distribution towards profits will then raise the national or average savings propensity, while a shift towards wages would have the opposite effect. Supposing that the shift were towards wages it is then possible that total savings could fall even though total national income had risen. The rise in exports could affect income distribution in various ways. It is at this point that Hong's paper relates to the present paper. One aspect is that a rise in the relative price of exportables to importables will shift income distribution towards factors intensive in exportables.

The effect on the size of the non-tradable sector is complex. This sector will tend to expand because of the income effect, since more total spending will lead to more spending on non-tradables, hence raising their prices and moving resources into the non-tradable sector. On the other hand, with exportables being more profitable, there may also be some tendency for resources to move out of non-tradables, this being the substitution effect. These resource movements in a three-product model have been much discussed in trade theory, mainly with respect to the effect of the imposition of a tariff. Such resource movements will be associated with income distribution effects.

In turning to investment it seems likely that the higher profitability of export industries would increase investment at a given interest rate in these industries. This could conceivably be offset by the adverse effect on investment of lower profitability in import-competing industries. But if the income effect offsets the substitution effect, investment will increase.

To summarize, focusing on overall income effects, the main points can be put very simply. Greater exports make Koreans better off, and hence they are likely to save more. For that reason at least, holding investment constant for the moment, the extra export income will not be matched by an equal rise in imports. On the other hand, higher exports will raise profit expectations, and so raise investment, hence increasing the pressure on resources and raising imports. On balance, taking both effects into account, in the long run the rise in exports could have led to an even greater rise in imports.

Park makes the important point that in Korea foreign borrowing is wholly government-determined even when the borrowing is by the private sector. Total borrowing will depend on many considerations. A crucial factor is the willingness of foreigners to lend at reasonable rates of interest, and this is presumably much influenced by the expected profitability of Korea's industries. If total borrowing is determined by government policy, and this is within the limits where loans are readily available from abroad, this means that government policy determines the excess of investment over savings.

One could now take savings as given by private behavioral reactions and make investment the residual. Exports increase, savings increase, and the government decides on a borrowing level. Investment must then be adjusted appropriately. The process of adjustment can be through the provision of credit at domestic interest rates which are quite separate from world market interest rates, as in Korea. If the borrowing level is held constant by policy, that is, if the government decides that the current account balance shall stay unchanged, the increase in exports will lead to a rise in investment equal to the rise in savings. This approach seems to be quite a good stylized description of the Korean situation.

There are two alternatives. One is to make foreign borrowing the residual; this was implicit in the initial presentation, which involved an independent analysis of the effects of export growth on savings and on investment. Of course the availability of foreign funds, as expressed by the interest rate (margin above LIBOR) that Korea has to pay, could still affect the story. The more being borrowed the higher an interest rate Korea has to pay to foreigners, and this could filter through to the domestic interest rate structure, a higher domestic interest rate discouraging investment. The second alternative to treating investment as the residual is to make savings the residual. This brings one close to the "two-gap" approach once popular in development economics. This time an investment target is given, determined perhaps by a desired rate of capital accumulation, or by a desired growth rate and given capital-output ratio. In addition, foreign borrowing is given. In the first instance, private savings may be determined in the way described earlier, rising on account of the real income effect of the export increase, and also influenced by income distribution changes. A savings gap, whether positive or negative, then emerges. If the investment target is unaffected by the rise in exports, if foreign borrowing is also held constant, and if private savings rise as a result of the export increase, a savings gap then emerges in the form of excess savings, provided public savings are unchanged. Equilibrium, that is, desired borrowing and target investment, is restored by a reduction in public savings, brought about by an increase in public expenditure or a decline in tax rates. Presumably there would be elements of such an adjustment mechanism in Korea, though it hardly seems realistic to regard either investment or foreign borrowing as being unaffected by an export increase.

Park's view that the monetary approach to balance of payments analysis is less useful than the absorption approach for analyzing the question under discussion is sound. The monetary approach is of course still relevant for considering domestic monetary effects of external disturbances. The special characteristic of the monetary approach is that it focuses on the official settlements balance rather than on the current account. It seeks to explain changes in the former, and lumps private trade in goods and in bonds together, making foreign exchange reserve over investments the residual. But when the government directly or indirectly controls all foreign borrowings, the official settlements balance is not an interesting figure.

GENERAL DISCUSSION

The gains in terms of trade observed by Park may not be to the advantage of Korea with respect to other countries. The gains may be those of manufactured goods in relation to crude oil instead of those vis-a-vis other industrial countries. Furthermore, a shift in base year may significantly change the estimates for the gains in terms of trade.

The assumption of exogenously determined export growth rate may not be reasonable in the case of Korea. There may be also a substantial time lag between export promotion of, for example, heavy and chemical production and improvements in the current account of the balance of payments.

The existence of tariffs themselves may not change the endogeneity of imports. However, if there are severe quantitative restrictions of imports, such as the restriction of the import volume according to a desired level of foreign borrowing, imports may have to be treated as an exogenous variable. In any case, the impact of tariffs and that of quantitative restrictions have to be differentiated.

A capital account surplus may be taken as an exogenous variable determined by the government, which may worry about the growth of external debt even though the rest of the world is willing to lend capital to Korea. In such a case, the current account deficit is determined by a government decision and hence we can go back to the elasticity approach in terms of determining relative prices, and determining the current account deficit so that it is consistent with the permitted capital account surplus. An elasticity approach may not be ruled out if the initiation of the export-oriented growth was based on changes in the foreign currency price of exports. On the other hand, there is nothing inherently desirable in achieving balance in current account and eliminating capital account surplus. There can be many different balance of payments approaches which are, depending on the local situation examined, equally valid.

One also has to take account of the fact that these days almost all countries have, in effect, a flexible exchange rate system.

TRADE, GROWTH AND INCOME DISTRIBUTION: THE KOREAN EXPERIENCE

Wontack Hong*

I. Basic Issues

Since the early 1960s, Korea has pursued an export-oriented growth strategy and achieved rapid growth in manufactures exports and GNP as well as in the standard of living of the so-called subsistence sector. However, by 1976, the relative share of labor in national income had not increased compared to its share in the early 1960s, nor had there been an improvement in personal income distribution.[1] Indeed, rapid growth in exports and GNP led to rapid growth in both employment and real wages in Korea. To this extent, the export-oriented growth strategy helped to improve income distribution. However, some important policy measures adopted by the Korean government to promote industrialization and export expansion seem to have worked against improving the overall income distribution. For instance, credit subsidy financed by seigniorage and inflation tax was one of the most important policy measures adopted in Korea to pursue its export-

* Seoul University, Korea. The author would like to thank Robert E. Baldwin, W. Max Corden and Hans W. Singer for helpful comments.

[1] The decreasing share of labor in national income in spite of the rapid accumulation of capital per worker may simply be explained in terms of the Lewis model, with constant subsistence real wages, or in terms of the aggregate version of marginal productivity theory, i.e., in terms of greater than unitary aggregate elasticity of substitution between capital and labor, taking the rate of return to non-labor as the rate of profit and, in turn, regarding this as being identical to the shadow rate of interest and the actual rental price for capital service. However, one might well feel extremely dissatisfied with such simple explanations.

oriented growth strategy, and this policy might have been conducive to worsening the distribution of income.

This paper aims to examine the income distribution effect of Korea's export-oriented growth policies, especially the credit subsidy policy. The purpose is to gain insights into why the distribution of income in Korea became more unequal during 1970-76. Section II examines the shifts in income distribution statistics associated with trade and industrial growth in Korea during the period 1960-76. Section III sets up a conceptual framework to understand such shifts. Sections IV and V examine the credit subsidy policy and preferential tax system in Korea. Section VI makes some inferences concerning the impact of trade policy on the distribution of income, and Section VII examines Korea's full-employment period of 1976-78, future prospects and policy implications.

II. Growth and Income Distribution in Korea

Korea achieved one of the highest growth rates in the world during the period 1962 to 1979. During that period, per capita GNP, in 1979 dollars, rose from about $475 to $1,625, yielding an average annual growth rate of nearly 8 percent. Korea's annual commodity exports, which amounted to less than $0.1 billion before 1962, increased at an average annual rate of about 40 percent (30 percent in constant prices), amounting to about $15 billion in 1979; the ratio of commodity and service exports to GNP increased from about 5 percent to about 30 percent. By 1979, about 27 percent of GNP originated in manufacturing compared to 14 percent in 1962. Manufactured products, which had never exceeded the 20 percent level during the period 1953 to 1961, comprised more than 90 percent of total commodity exports.

In manufacturing, employment increased by about 1.8 million during 1960-75. About 40 percent of this additional employment resulted from export expansion. Nearly 25 percent of the total 4.8 million additional jobs created during the period 1960-75 resulted from export expansion. Since 1973, about 30 percent of all workers in manufacturing were employed for export production, and about 10 percent of the total number of employed persons in Korea worked in export activities (Hong, 1979: 22).

According to the BOK's (Bank of Korea) national income statistics, the share of compensation of employees in total national income hovered around 34 percent throughout the period 1953-66. However, this share increased to about 40 percent during 1967-76, presumably reflecting the shifts in the industrial structure and the rising wage rate. The share of property income and corporate gross savings amounted to less than 15 percent of total national income during 1953-64. This share also increased to more than 20 percent in 1973-76, presumably due to the rapid capital accumulation and business expansion since 1966.

On the other hand, the share of the income of non-agricultural unincorporated enterprises did not change greatly while the share of the agricultural sector decreased substantially from more than 40 percent of total national income in 1953-64 to around 20 percent in 1973-76. Much of the income from unincorporated agricultural and non-agricultural enterprises is really an implicit return to unpaid family workers and proprietors, income which should have been imputed as labor income.[2] Therefore, although the share of compensation of employees in total national income increased significantly during 1953-76, the drastic fall in the share of agricultural income during this period implies that the actual changes in the share of labor cannot be clearly discerned on the basis of the BOK's national income statistics alone. For instance, if the view of classifying the entire income from agriculture as pure labor income is the one taken, the share of employee compensation in total national income has decreased from approximately 71 percent in 1957-61 to about 63 percent in 1972-76.

According to the BOK's input-output table data, the share of employee compensation in total gross value added has been falling in the manufacturing and the SOC sectors during the period 1960-75. Furthermore, in most of the manufacturing sectors that experienced a sharp rise in export-output ratios, one could observe a declining share of wages to value added. Due to erratic fluctuations in the labor share in the primary and the service sectors, however, the labor share in GNP has fluctuated at around 30 percent without showing any

---

[2] Due to the land reforms enforced in the late 1940s, the rent element in agriculture seems to be much less important in Korea than in other countries. In the Lewis model, if one subtracts subsistence wages from agricultural value added, there should be, by definition, nothing left to be counted as rent in the landlordless economy.

definite upward or downward trend.

The employee compensation presented in the input-output table did not include imputed wages for family workers and proprietors, which are abundant in the agricultural sector and in the service sectors such as the wholesale and retail trade. When imputed wages were included by applying the sectoral average wage rates to unpaid workers, the share of labor became 57 percent of total national income in 1970, and fell to 49 percent in 1975. This declining trend in the share of labor was evident in every sector in Korea after 1970.

Empirical studies by Adelman (1973), Oshima (1977) and the IBRD-Sussex team (Chenery, 1974), among others, indicate that the personal distribution of income in Korea was among the best in the developing world by 1964 and remained so in 1970. According to Adelman, the proper preconditions, including land reforms, the Korean War and mass education, had occurred in Korea by the early sixties, the government followed appropriate growth strategies in the sixties, and as a result the U-shaped upturn took place between 1964 and 1970 marking the last phase of the development process (Chenery, 1974: 280-285).

On the basis of the estimated distributive measures for selected benchmark years of 1965, 1970 and 1976, Choo (1978) concludes that personal income distribution in Korea improved a little during 1965-70 but there was a rapid deterioration after 1970. The distribution of income in the farm sector was more equal than that in the non-farm sector throughout the period 1965-76, and there was a substantial increase in labor productivity in the agricultural sector, enough to produce a significant reduction in the gap between urban-rural earnings.[3] However, the relative importance of agriculture in GNP as well as in total employment declined rapidly. Furthermore, the reduced gap between urban and rural household income also implies that the impact of the rapid sectoral transfer of population on overall income distribution became less significant in the seventies. According

---

[3] During the period 1966-76, the per worker income in rural farm households increased at about 7.5 percent per annum. The per worker income in urban wage earners' households, on the other hand, increased at about 4.3 percent on average. Since 1974, the average rural household income has become larger than the average urban household income. Therefore, not only were there significant shifts in the labor force from the low-productivity agricultural sector to the high-productivity industrial sector, there was also a substantial reduction of absolute poverty in the agricultural sector.

to Choo, the primary cause of income disparity in Korea was inequality in the non-farm sectors. The main cause of inequality within employee households in the sixties was prevailing urban unemployment. Hence the rapid growth of labor-intensive manufactures exports and the consequent decline in urban unemployment must have improved the distribution of income among employee households. In the seventies, however, a substantial worsening of income distribution took place among the employee households primarily because of the increasing wage differential between highly educated and skilled labor on the one hand and less educated and unskilled labor on the other.[4] In addition to this worsening distribution of income among employee households, there occurred a very pronounced polarization of income distribution among employer households which Choo regards as the factor most responsible for income inequality in 1976. As a result, all the measures of inequality show that income distribution deteriorated from 1970 to 1976 falling to a level even worse than that of 1965. Therefore, Choo concludes that, after more than a decade and a half of rapid economic growth, the relative equity in income distribution that existed in the fifties and continued in the sixties began to break down at the beginning of the seventies.

III. Conceptual Framework

1. Growth and Functional Distribution of Income

Initially, this section analyzes the behavior of relative factor shares under three different growth conditions. That is, the economy moves from the initial phase of an unlimited supply of labor and a price-inelastic supply of foreign capital, to a phase of limited but price-elastic supply of labor and foreign capital, and then to a phase of unlimited supply of foreign capital but price-inelastic supply of labor. Credit subsidies will then be introduced and their impact on

---

[4] The average wage rate for a college graduate was 3.3 times larger than that for a primary school graduate in 1971, but the former became 4.1 times larger than the latter in 1977. The average wage for labor in managerial occupations was 2.7 times larger than the average wage in 1971, but the former became 3.3 times larger than the latter in 1977 (data from the Office of Labor Affairs).

the functional distribution of income will be examined. The linkage between functional and personal distribution of income will also be examined.

Suppose that the advanced sector is able to draw on a reservoir of labor in the non-profit-maximizing traditional sector at an institutionally determined minimum wage rate. Assuming a given set of international commodity prices and constant returns to scale, the profit-maximizing entrepreneurs in the advanced sector will completely specialize in the production of a commodity or a bundle of commodities with identical factor intensities.[5] Labor will be employed up to the point (L^*) where the marginal productivity of labor at the given capital stock that is fully employed in the advanced sector (K) equals the minimum institutional wage rate (w).

Suppose that the entire physical capital in the advanced sector is owned by entrepreneurs (including government enterprises) but the entire monetary financial capital is owned by the government-owned bank in the form of loanable funds and is lent to entrepreneurs at an interest rate (i^*) which is identical to the marginal productivity of capital, *i.e.*, the rate of return on capital (r^*). Although the entrepreneurs employ the entire physical capital stock, the owner of monetary wealth, in this case the government, may be regarded as having "indirect" (mortgage) claims on the portion of total physical capital stock that is equivalent to the amount of total loanable fund. For a given w, the capital intensity of production in the advanced sector is determined by K/L^*. Any variation in interest rate (i) will only change the rate of profit ($e = r^* - i$) which reflects the magnitude of incentives for static entrepreneurial activities. That is, variation of interest rate has only an income distribution effect and no efficiency effect on production techniques.[6]

---

[5] Although a small open economy and hence a given set of international commodity prices are assumed, identical production technology is not assumed all over the world even in equilibria. Neither are identical production techniques assumed among every firm within a country in disequilibria. A multi-commodity complete specialization trade model is being postulated in which the Heckscher-Ohlin effect (factor endowment difference) dominates the Ricardian effect (technology difference). Cf. Krueger (1977).

[6] However, if the interest rate is set too low, the excessive provision of incentives for static entrepreneurial activities will lead either to credit rationing, including the deadweight loss associated with rent-seeking competition, or to government restrictions on entry into entrepreneurial activity, resulting in an unequal windfall distribution of income for those lucky enough to secure credit. (See Krueger, 1974.)

Although the assumption begun with was that the entire monetary financial capital in the advanced sector is owned by government-owned banks, an entrepreneur will in due course have to own monetary assets. Then he will receive imputed interest payments as a capitalist lending to himself. In a static framework of fully-employed capital stock, the entrepreneurial group may be seen as a rentier class in the sense that they receive the residual income after payments of institutional wages to workers employed in the advanced sector.

If the wage rate remains constant at the given minimum level both in the advanced sector and in the traditional sector as the advanced sector expands, the share of entrepreneurs' surplus in the national income will increase. Furthermore, if the only source of saving is non-labor income, savings and capital formation will also increase as a proportion of the national income.[7] Capital accumulation will keep increasing output in the advanced sector without altering the capital intensity of production technique. This stage may be regarded as a pure Lewis world. However, if one applies this pure Lewis model to Korea, the rapid rise in real wages throughout the period 1962-76 can not be explained.

However, even before reaching full employment of labor available in the country, a rise in the average product of labor in the traditional sector resulting from the reduction of workers, or from capital deepening and agricultural technical progress in the sector, may simply cause an increase in the minimum institutional wage rate in the same proportion. Such a rise in the minimum wage floor in the advanced sector may not only force adjustment in production techniques and in output pattern towards more capital-intensive direction, but also can reduce the non-labor share in GNP even with surplus labor.[8] Of course, this is a departure from the pure Lewis

---

[7] If the savings propensity of the government and that of entrepreneurs were identical, and if the aforementioned propensities were uninfluenced by the rates of return on savings, or if all the capitalists act as entrepreneurs, then the variation in interest rate will not affect the growth rate of the economy. However, if workers also save, and if their savings are influenced by the rate of return on saving, a low-interest regime will reduce the growth rate of the economy by reducing workers' savings.

[8] In such a case, the government may decide to siphon off the surplus output of the traditional sector generated by the withdrawal of workers from this sector in order to provide subsidies to entrepreneurs and to equate the effective wage rate to the optimal shadow wage rate. In the absence of such policies, and in the face of an ever-increasing minimum wage floor, the advanced sector can expand only by adopting more capital-

world. One may regard it as a modified Lewis model. Korea seems to have started this stage in the early 1960s and terminated it by the late 1970s.

Over a given period, the economy may reach full employment. After complete absorption of the excess labor supply, one may expect the wage rate to rise much more rapidly, as was observed in Korea during 1976-78, and also expect the entrepreneurs' share of the national income to keep decreasing.

Once full employment is postulated, one may also postulate that labor and capital are paid according to the marginal productivity theory with zero residual profits. In what Schumpeter described as the "circular flow of economic life," the effects of capital formation on the share of wages may be analyzed using the concept of elasticity of substitution. That is, it may be simply postulated that factor shares depend on the relative growth rates of factors of production and their elasticity of substitution. In a two-factor, constant returns to scale model, if capital accumulates more rapidly than labor, the non-labor share increases only if, by definition, the elasticity of substitution exceeds unity.[9] If the elasticity of substitution is less than one, the results are favorable to the employment and equity objectives, though output grows less rapidly. However, if rent, quasi-rents, Schumpeterian profits and monopoly profits are introduced, the above elasticity argument holds only for the subset of income consisting of wages and interests.[10]

Since the two-factor aggregate version of the neo-classical theory does not seem to provide an adequate conceptual framework to

intensive techniques of production or by producing more capital-intensive commodities. This implies less employment of labor with the given capital stock and a slower rate of employment growth with a given rate of capital accumulation. More labor is supplied to the advanced sector only at a higher wage rate even with surplus labor in the traditional sector.

[9] The fall in the rate of return on capital (now being regarded identical to the interest rate) will lead to continuous shifts in the pattern of specialization towards the more capital-intensive commodities. However, if only capitalists save at a constant saving propensity, the associated fall in saving reduces the rate of capital accumulation and hence may lead to a steady state first.

[10] Since the entrepreneurs will choose the technique which gives the lowest cost of production of a given commodity at a given set of international prices, only wages and interest, and not the rate of net profits (*i.e.*, non-labor residual income excluding interest payments), directly affect the capital-labor ratio chosen to produce the commodity.

understand a developing economy like Korea, the framework of
analysis will be extended to allow for the prevalence of rents and entrepreneurial profits. When the actual income distribution data of Korea
is examined, it will be noted that the Schumpeterian profits and the
Marshallian quasi-rents which arise in disequilibria and short-period
equilibria, as well as Ricardian rents, are added onto the neo-classical
steady state zero profit functional income distribution.

As the country continues to grow, at some point it may become
sufficiently integrated with world capital markets so that it faces an
unlimited supply of capital at a fixed interest rate; then the country may take on characteristics symmetrical to those of the pure
Lewis model.[11] One may postulate a minimum rate of interest (r) that
should be paid for capital use, for example, the prevailing interest
rate in the international financial market, a rate necessary to prevent
the outflow of domestic capital under perfect international capital
mobility.[12]

2. Income Distribution Effect of Credit Subsidies

It is now necessary to investigate the income distribution effect of
credit subsidies under the different growth conditions described
above. It is possible that loanable funds are lent through banks
to entrepreneurs at a subsidized interest rate (i^{**}) on the condition
that the entrepreneurs must undertake more capital-intensive production as specified by the government. The benefit of a lower

---

[11] That is, the supply of relevant entrepreneurial talents has vastly increased,
domestic absorptive capacity of foreign capital became infinite, and hence one does not
have to assume either a falling marginal rate of return on foreign capital or a rising
marginal cost of foreign borrowing.

[12] If the supply of capital is unlimited at r, for a given constant number of workers
L, capital will be hired up to the point where its marginal productivity is equal to r.
There may be an outflow, inflow, or no flow of capital to attain such an equilibrium
point. The country will specialize completely according to the criterion of maximizing
the rate of return on labor. We may postulate that the labor force employed is constant
at any specific point in time and supplies labor independently of the real wage. We may
further postulate that labor grows at a given constant rate over time. Then, the labor
class becomes a rentier class. In the absence of Schumpeterian innovation, the only
remaining source of (static) entrepreneurial profit will be the sharing of wage income
that now constitutes the residual income, $GNP - rK$. The relative shares may depend on
the relative bargaining strength of workers and employers. This may set the stage for
the classical Marxian class struggle between labor and entrepreneurs.

interest rate will be either totally or partly offset by the lower rate of return on capital that is implied by the higher capital intensity of a specified project.[13] If the subsidized loans were allocated without specified obligations, the entrepreneurs would maximize the windfall gain, that is to say, the income transfer from the government, simply by maintaining their old labor-intensive project. However, if the only available alternative is either to refuse the subsidized loans or to undertake more capital-intensive production, the entrepreneurs may gain positive profits by accepting such loans.

In the Lewis model, since the selected project is more capital-intensive than that which would be undertaken in the absence of credit subsidies, the marginal productivity of labor will, for the given capital stock (K), equal the minimum institutional wage rate (w) at a lower employment rate $(L **)$.[14] On the other hand, under the postulation of full employment, the interest-rate-subsidized loans will never have any employment effect on the country as a whole; they will have only an efficiency effect and an income redistribution effect.

Suppose that the economy has initially specialized entirely in the production of a single commodity or a set of commodities with identical capital intensity under conditions of full employment, and then interest-subsidized loans are provided to selected entrepreneurs in order to promote export expansion. Suppose also that credit subsidies are financed by seigniorage and inflation tax. Due to the existence of such subsidized loans, the unsubsidized ones will have to pay higher interest rates than before, and consequently, will have to either adopt a more labor-intensive technique or produce a more labor-intensive commodity, reducing marginal productivity of labor in their production, and ultimately resulting in a lower equilibrium wage rate in the country. A Pareto-efficient commodity production is replaced by a combination of excessively capital-intensive and excessively labor-intensive production.[15]

---

[13] Clearly, the lower the interest rate (compared to the rate of return on capital), the higher will be the income of this entrepreneurial group. However, this is a redistribution of capitalist income from the government to the private sector and not a change in the share of non-labor income in GNP.

[14] If the subsidized interest rate is identical to the new lower rate of return on capital in more capital-intensive production, the association between the shift in wage-interest ratio (from $w/i*$ to $w/i**$) and the shift in capital-labor ratio (from $K/L*$ to $K/L**$) may be related to the concept of elasticity of substitution.

[15] However, in a more realistic and complicated framework of analysis, one may well regard export promotion as a means to eliminate the constraint of insufficient

For the country as a whole, the credit subsidies rationed to selected entrepreneurs will imply less employment in the Lewis model, and a smaller labor share of national income, as well as a smaller GNP evaluated at the given international price set under the postulation of both surplus labor and full employment. This is a possible static loss which is an undesirable by-product of subsidization in the form of credit rationing.

The interest income accruing to government-owned capital may be regarded as distortion-free revenue that can be used to finance government subsidy activities. In the Lewis model, if this fund were allocated to individual entrepreneurs on the condition that they had to expand output using more labor-intensive techniques, there would have been larger employment and output in the advanced sector.[16] Perhaps even Pareto-efficiency could have been achieved for the country as a whole. However, even in the absence of any kind of dynamic external economies associated with more capital-intensive production activities, if the expansion of capital-intensive production were conducive to an increase in export earnings, such an expansion might in the long-run induce larger foreign capital inflows by enhancing the creditworthiness of the country in the international financial market. This in turn might increase the growth rate of the economy. In a dynamic context, if interest subsidy is allocated on the basis of a correctly applied infant industry doctrine, the gain in future income stream would more than offset the static efficiency loss.[17]

---

effective demand; a successful export promotion policy implying an elimination of Keynesian underemployment. Various tax-subsidy measures adopted to promote export-oriented growth may extend market potential on a global scale, make entrepreneurs more optimistic, and consequently encourage investment activities to achieve full employment. Increased demand for exports can lead to extra output from existing resources, and further induce increased saving and investment by raising expected rates of return.

[16] The non-labor share will decrease, and benefits will accrue to workers as a whole. However, if extra benefits are completely taxed away from workers, it will more than offset the initial subsidy given to the entrepreneurs for output expansion. (See Corden, 1974: 228-290.)

[17] Deducing the direct employment effects of trade and subsidy policies cannot provide an adequate basis to judge the overall efficiency of such policies in the presence of dynamic external economies. For instance, without subsidized credits, the shift towards more capital-intensive techniques of production and more capital-intensive outputs may proceed more slowly. Then perhaps the exports may not grow rapidly. Slower growth in export earnings might result in a slower growth of GNP and overall employment.

However, if subsidized loans are allocated at a uniform rate to all export activites, there may be an immediate income-transfer effect to the exporters of labor-intensive goods, while in the case of exporters of capital-intensive goods, the interest subsidy may just offset the static efficiency loss. Therefore, subsidized credits can become an important means of redistributing financial wealth from the government or from the general public to selected entrepreneurs.[18]

3. Revenue for Interest Subsidy

In addition to the regular tax revenue and interest income accruing to government-owned monetary financial capital, two other, possibly more important, sources from which the government may obtain the revenue to finance its subsidy activities can be considered. One is the monopsonistic profits of the government that arise from its foreign borrowing and the other is the revenue from seigniorage-cum-inflation-tax.

Seigniorage encourages the government to adopt inflationary financial policies, and inflation itself benefits entrepreneurs through expanding allocation of low-interest bank loans, and diminishing the real value of their past debts. If the government persistently maintains fixed nominal interest rates on bank deposits and loans, even the correctly anticipated inflation will not reduce or eliminate the wealth

---

[18] For the sake of simplicity in our exposition, we have ignored possible distortions arising from import restrictions. However, in order to encourage savings, the import of consumption goods, as well as investment in import-competing consumer industries may be discouraged by the government. This may generate substantial monopoly profits for a limited number of entrepreneurs. Import restrictions on consumption goods may result in a shift in output pattern and hence reduce the real national income evaluated at the given fixed international prices. Higher prices of consumption goods will reduce the real income of every household unit and may reduce the real income of workers who may consume most of their income to a far greater extent proportionately than capitalist-entrepreneurs. If wages were set at a minimum subsistence level which cannot be reduced any further, then regardless of the types of import restrictions or export subsidies enforced by the government, the final result would be a lower rate of return on capital due to static efficiency losses. However, the wage rate may have been rising as the economy grows, and its growth rate may be reduced without annihilating the labor force. If there is only an income-redistribution effect and no resource-allocation effect, the growth rate of real wages will fall while the growth rates of capital accumulation and GNP will increase. If, however, there is a significant shift in choice of technique or output pattern towards more capital intensity, the efficiency losses may more than offset the positive effect of a relative decrease in consumption on growth.

transfer from net monetary creditors to net monetary debtors. Through inflationary financing of development expenditures, control over substantial amounts of real resources is transferred from the general public to the government and ultimately to a limited number of entrepreneurs.[19]

On the other hand, if the country has been pursuing an export-oriented growth strategy, and as a result has become a fairly open economy with regard to trade and capital financing, it may be possible to draw on substantial foreign capital. At a given period of time, however, there may be significantly diminishing returns on foreign capital due to limited absorptive entrepreneurial capacities, and the international financial market may not supply larger amounts of capital without raising the risk premium. This carries the implication that an increasingly unfavorable assessment of the absorptive capacity of the country may result in a higher risk premium. One can then postulate a monopsony situation, that is, a given constant rate of return on capital in the country and a rising marginal cost of foreign borrowing.[20] If the government acts as "a monopsonistic agent" in importing foreign capital and allocating it among domestic entrepreneurs, the difference between the average rate of return on investment and the average interest rate on foreign borrowing will accrue to the government as monopsonistic profits which in turn may be used as subsidy funds.[21] From the viewpoint of a small economy, the monopsonistic solution represents a Pareto optimality. Differential endowment of absorptive entrepreneurial capacities can account for differences in the observed rate of return on capital among countries.

---

[19] Since most of the low-income wage earners' households would not be able to find suitable alternative forms of saving except that in monetary form because of ignorance, transaction costs, minimum transaction amount, and the inconveniences involved in seeking available alternatives, the low interest rate ceilings on bank deposits can be viewed as a systematic means of transferring income from lower income savers to upper income entrepreneurs. The rich tend to have the bulk of their assets in the form of variable price non-monetary financial assets such as common stocks and non-financial assets such as real estate; hence the rich tend to be the biggest gainers from inflation.

[20] Of course, one may not only postulate an upward sloping supply curve of foreign capital, but also postulate a downward sloping demand curve for foreign capital, directly reflecting the falling marginal rate of return on foreign capital. In any case, marginal rate differs from average rate.

[21] Monopsonistic profits can arise also with a horizontal supply curve of foreign capital and a downward sloping demand curve for foreign capital if the government, as a monopsonistic agent, restricts foreign capital inflow below the equilibrium level.

Suppose that the more foreign capital is forthcoming to this country, the higher the rate of interest paid for capital. Suppose that the initial distortion free equilibrium in the capital market is destroyed and capital use is subsidized across the board by taxing workers. Then, either more capital-intensive commodities will be produced or more capital-intensive techniques of production will be adopted. The cost of capital to entrepreneurs, as well as the equilibrium rate of return on capital, falls while the pre-tax real wages rise. The supply price of capital excluding the interest subsidy rises. The after-tax real income of workers would be smaller than before, representing a net efficiency loss caused by capital market distortion. Since there is a net extra foreign capital inflow, GNP might be larger than before, but because of the postulation of optimality of pre-distortion equilibrium, the net increase in GNP would always be smaller than the net increase in actual interest payments to foreign capitalists. The higher GNP growth rate is achieved at the expense of the real income of workers.[22] (See Corden 1974: 297-301.)

Credit subsidies to selected entrepreneurs financed by seigniorage-cum-inflation-tax on workers and unprivileged entrepreneurs shift real income from the latter to the former group. However, when the credit subsidy is financed neither by workers nor by the unprivileged entrepreneurs in the country but comes from outside the system in the form of monopsonistic profits of the government arising from its foreign borrowing, there would be a net positive income effect that would raise the demand for labor and the real wage compared with the situation without any foreign capital inflow at all. That is, no one in the country may experience any absolute decrease in real income, and there occurs only shifts in "relative" income distribution away from labor and unprivileged entrepreneurs to the selected group of privileged entrepreneurs.

4. Personal Distribution of Income

The linkage between functional and personal income distribution has become much weaker in modern society. Each labor unit owns varying amounts of physical and human capital. In general, however,

---

[22] When labor is taxed to finance credit subsidy, labor price to entrepreneurs for any given labor supply rises. Subsidizing the use of capital unnecessarily increases the capital intensity of production.

it is still true that non-labor income is of greater importance at the top of the income scale. In this sense, changes in the share of wage and property income still have a significant effect on the share of the different income groups. Therefore, one can statistically identify social classes according to the relative share of each group of property owners. In a growing economy and in the long run, this method is equivalent to identifying social classes in terms of differences in saving behavior. However, the causes of such differentiation and stratification in property ownership and saving behavior have yet to be investigated. Furthermore, profits to entrepreneurship and interest payments on capital have to be differentiated.

With an export-oriented growth strategy, the newly generated wealth from the growth process will most likely be concentrated in the hands of people with personal characteristics, skills, and entrepreneurial abilities that contribute to successful export expansion. That is, people who are especially talented in expanding export activities will ultimately gain, both relatively and absolutely. To take account, formally, of this efficiency rent is not difficult; one need only postulate decreasing returns to scale production technology for the model.[23]

On the other hand, the policy of maintaining extremely low rates of return on the savings of workers and government may be conducive to expanding investment activities of selected entrepreneurs by enhancing their residual income, thereby increasing further the wealth accumulation of privileged entrepreneurs. Credit subsidies based on seigniorage and inflation tax encourage the investment activities of privileged entrepreneurs without discouraging their saving propensity. The income of capitalist-entrepreneurs consists of gross profit on their capital, which is the sum of imputed interest payments on their capital and net residual profits, and the difference between the interest payments on worker's or government's capital lent to them and the gross rate of profit on this capital. The non-labor income arising from entrepreneurs' own capital is not influenced by the contractual rate of interest. On the other hand, the low-interest rate regime discourages saving by workers who have to lend their

---

[23] With decreasing returns to scale in a two-factor (capital and labor) model, which may partly be ascribed to the law of diminishing returns caused by the limited availability of qualified entrepreneurs, payments remitted according to the marginal productivities of capital and labor generate a residual income, a rent whose legitimate title may be claimed by entrepreneurs. With commodity prices held constant, increase in employment and capital accumulation will amplify the returns to this specific factor.

savings to entrepreneurs in exchange for an interest rate which is lower than the rate of gross profit entrepreneurs can obtain. If workers somehow habitually save a large proportion of their current income in spite of negligible rates of return on their savings, there will be a continuous and substantial income redistribution in favor of the class that employs capital.

Governmental efforts to fully exploit scale economies in production activities, up to the point of reaching constant or decreasing returns to scale, necessarily result in a concentration of wealth among a few selected entrepreneurs, and the government preferential tax system is conducive to keeping such accumulated wealth in their hands permanently. The postulation of non-increasing returns to scale technology hinges on the assumption that the government is successful in such efforts.

IV. Credit Subsidies

During 1967-75, about 40 percent of gross fixed capital formation was in the form of machinery and transport equipment. According to the BOK's input-output tables, the import content in the machinery component was as high as 73 percent in 1963, and 71 percent in 1973. During 1966-74, the absolute value of tariff exemptions on capital goods imports was equivalent to approximately 5 percent of the value of annual gross fixed capital formation in Korea.[24] On the other hand, the scope of the accelerated depreciation allowance has tremendously expanded since the early seventies in terms of degree and industry coverage. This shift seems to have had a very biased impact on investment towards capital-intensive sectors and techniques. During 1962-71, about 40 percent of annual gross fixed capital formation in the manufacturing sector consisted of the legal allowance for the consumption of fixed capital. This ratio jumped to nearly 70 percent in 1972-78.

Pursuing an export-oriented growth strategy, the Korean government has introduced widespread restrictions on economic activity throughout the country. These restrictions have produced a variety of rents. However, the credit subsidies based on seigniorage and infla-

---

[24] Statistical data for this section are from Hong (1979, Chapter 7).

tion tax seem to have been the largest source of rent in Korea.

DMB (Deposit Money Banks) loans constituted from 40 to 50 percent of total loans (year-end balance) in Korea during 1964-76. The share of KDB (Korea Development Bank) loans amounted to between 20 and 30 percent of total loans during 1964-66, but the share was reduced to around 10 percent thereafter. The share of foreign loans was negligible until 1962, but this share has rapidly increased to about 30 to 40 percent of total outstanding loans in Korea since 1966. The share of curb loans, admittedly underestimated, amounted to around 11 percent of total loans during 1964-71, and to around 7 percent during 1972-76.

The weighted average real interest rate on DMB loans reached a peak of 13 to 15 percent in 1966-69, but fluctuated from negligibly low rates to substantially negative rates in other years. The rate on KDB loans was always negative, except in 1966-71 and 1973. Taking into account the devaluation effect, the real interest rate on private foreign borrowing, mostly in the form of supplier credits for imported capital goods, was estimated to have been about 8 percent during 1962-66, 3 percent during 1967-71, and -6 percent in 1972-76. The real interest rate on government foreign borrowings was estimated to have been about 5 percent during 1962-66, about 0 percent during 1962-71, and about -9 percent during 1972-76, on average.

The estimated average real rate of return on capital, that is to say, the rate of return on all factors but labor, in manufacturing was about 12 percent in 1954-61, about 17 percent during 1962-66, 26 percent during 1967-71, and 27 percent during 1972-76.

The ratio of the total interest subsidy associated with domestic and foreign loans in the manufacturing sector to gross fixed capital formation in manufacturing increased from 40 percent during 1962-66 to around 75 percent during 1966-71, and to more than 100 percent after 1972. The most remarkable fact is that although the absolute amount of interest subsidies associated with foreign loans was negligible prior to 1966, it was equivalent to more than half of the total interest subsidies associated with KDB and DMB loans together after 1966.

Since 1967, there has been rapid capital accumulation and capital deepening in Korea accompanied by a quickly rising wage/rental ratio (Hong 1979: 18-27). It is only natural to expect the rising capital intensity of Korean industries to follow the increase in per capita capital stock and the associated rise in wage rates. However, the prevalence of interest subsidies makes one speculate that there must have been excessive capital deepening in many Korean industries above the level that can be justified by a shift in the basic comparative advantage position or by the dynamic infant industry arguments.[25]

V. Preferential Tax System

Government tax revenue has always been dominated by income from indirect taxes. The ratio of indirect taxes to GNP increased from about 5 percent in 1962-66 to about 9 percent during 1975-77, while direct taxes increased from about 1.5 percent to about 3.5 percent of GNP. About one-third of the revenue from direct taxes consisted of corporate taxes.[26] The preferential corporate tax treatment was concentrated on those industries which the government intended to promote.

Since the income of most wage earners fell below the minimum tax exemption level, the average direct tax rate on wage income was around 3 to 4 percent throughout the period 1962-77. If one computes the effective tax rate by dividing the amount of tax actually collected (as presented in the Statistical Yearbook of National Tax published by the Office of National Tax Administration) by the factor income (as presented in the National Income in Korea published by the

---

[25] The most notable phenomenon has been associated with the change in the growth rate of labor productivity in the manufacturing sector. This is manifested by the rapid rise of labor productivity in the late sixties, and then the significantly declining rate of increase in labor productivity in the seventies in spite of growing capital intensity in all industries. This phenomenon may be attributed to the decline in efficiency brought by the subsidized financing which became extremely conspicuous and arbitrary in the seventies. In manufacturing, the decrease in the growth rate of labor productivity was most drastic in the chemicals and basic metal sectors.

[26] Until the early 1960s, foreign aid financed a large proportion of the government budget. The ratio of government revenue to GNP amounted to around 15 percent while the ratio of tax revenue to GNP amounted to about 9 percent during 1962-67. Since the late sixties, the share of tax income in the total government revenue has steadily increased and the difference has been financed more by foreign borrowing than by foreign grant-in-aid. The ratio of government revenue to GNP amounted to around 17 percent, while tax revenue (including local tax and defense surtax) amounted to around 15 percent of GNP during 1967-77.

BOK), the average effective tax rate on interest, dividend, and rent income amounted to only about 1 percent before 1967. Since the late sixties, this rate has been raised to about 3 to 4 percent. On the other hand, the rate on non-agricultural unincorporated business income amounted to about 3 percent in the early sixties and was raised to about 5 to 8 percent thereafter.

Since the BOK's national income statistics include a large amount of imputed interest, dividend and rent which cannot be subject to income tax, the effective tax rates computed above unduly underestimate the rates actually applied to individual household income. If the average tax rate for the top 100 taxpayers in 1977 whose taxable income exceeded 206 million won per person is computed, the average effective global income tax rate was about 33 percent. The income of these taxpayers consisted mostly of interest and dividend receipts. Although the highest nominal global tax rate reached 90 percent, various tax exemption schemes substantially reduced the effective rates. Until the early seventies, the majority of capital gains were exempt from taxes. On the other hand, revenues from inheritance and gift taxes have always been negligible.

Since in the seventies approximately 25 percent of total government expenditure was spent on general administration, 30 percent on defense expenditure, 25 percent on investment activities for economic growth, and the remainder on social development expenses, primarily for elementary education, it can be said that the Korean government has never attempted to improve distribution or to expand public welfare activities on the basis of the government tax-expenditure mechanism. That is, if economic factors, such as a rising share of profit income, have accentuated the deteriorating trend in the distribution of income in the seventies, the government tax-expenditure system has never initiated any new efforts to reverse the trend.[27]

[27] In 1975, for example, government expenditures on fertilizer subsidies and grain price support amounted to about 2 percent of GNP, and those on education (mostly on elementary education) about 3 percent of GNP. These expenditures must have had a beneficial effect on personal income distribution. However, farm households with smaller land holdings tend to consume a greater proportion of their grain production and to derive a smaller proportion of their income from the output that is marketed (Rao, 1978). We should furthermore note the fact that higher education, which has become very expensive, has mostly been financed by individual households. Since there have been increasing disparities in employee household income according to the level of skill and education, non-equitable opportunities for higher education must have contributed to the worsening of income distribution among employee households in Korea.

VI. Impact of Export-Oriented Growth Policies on Income Distribution

The fact that export activities have been heavily subsidized implies that there must have been static efficiency losses arising from a departure from the Pareto efficient pattern of specialization. Furthermore, the fact that the most important means of promoting export expansion was through the supply of low-priced capital, particularly in the form of credit subsidies and accelerated depreciation allowances, implies that there must have been additional static efficiency losses arising from the adoption of excessively capital-intensive methods of production. At the same time, the fact that the trade regime has been distorted in order to maintain relatively low prices for imported capital goods implies that there must also have been static efficiency losses caused by discouraging domestic production of capital goods.

On the other hand, the simple fact that Korea could maintain nearly a 10 percent average annual growth rate of GNP during the period 1962-79 suggests that the positive effect of dynamic external economies associated with infant export industries must have been considerably larger than all the static efficiency losses caused by the export-oriented policies. Therefore, the object of this paper is not to argue about the growth-promoting effect of Korea's export-oriented strategy, but rather to examine its effect on income distribution. However, the fact that the average real wage rate in manufacturing establishments operating with more than ten workers has been increasing at around 10 percent per annum on average during the period 1962-79 implies that the working class as a whole must have benefitted substantially in "absolute" terms, even though some groups of workers, particularly the highly educated and skilled, must proportionately have benefitted much more. This is the reason why this paper has focussed on such questions as why there was no substantial increase in the "relative" share of workers and why there was no substantial improvement in personal income distribution in spite of the rapid expansion of exports, employment and GNP in Korea.

On the basis of the conceptual framework delineated in Section III and observations made in the following sections, it is perhaps possible to make the following inferences. First, the fact that export activities have been heavily subsidized implies that substantial rents must have been created for those people with special entrepreneurial talent and skills for export expansion. Second, the prevalence of generous export subsidies implies the prevalence of possible windfall income transfers caused by the allocation of excessive subsidies exceeding the true infant industry costs.[28]

Planning in Korea implied setting up physical targets and marshalling various tax-subsidy measures to achieve these objectives. However, it was the individual entrepreneurs who acted as the ultimate agents to carry out the actual task of investment and production. The entrepreneurial rule of the game was largely based on "folklore capitalism." High growth rates in exports, productivity, and GNP should benefit from economies of scale and time. Being in an early phase of capitalism, the ownership of capital and entrepreneurship tend to merge together in Korea. Therefore, government efforts to fully exploit scale economies in production, up to the point where constant or decreasing returns to scale prevail, have led to concentrated wealth. Government efforts to take advantage of the internal economies of time or experience have resulted in institutional arrangements designed to preserve such concentrated wealth in the hands of the original owners. For instance, the fact that the government has restricted subsidy allocations to a limited number of entrepreneurs in order to take advantage of scale economies implies a concentration of wealth, while the preferential tax system to encourage entrepreneurs to retain and reinvest their profits without fear of a large amount of inheritance taxes being collected implies perpetuation of such concentrated wealth. On the other hand, trade distortions to reduce the relative prices of capital goods must have caused losses of consumer surplus; low-interest rate regimes must have reduced the returns from whatever capital the workers possessed and discouraged them from saving; credit subsidies financed by seigniorage and inflation tax must have imposed a proportionately heavier burden on workers and unprivileged entrepreneurs; and the preferential tax system must in general have been fairly regressive.[29]

Therefore, one can argue that these kinds of possible side-effects, while substantially raising the growth rate of GNP, in fact contributed

---

[28] Imperfections in private information and in the capital market, as well as external economies in creation of various forms of human capital, might have often been exaggerated, resulting in windfall income transfers (and deadweight efficiency losses). Even when government subsidies have induced the ignorant entrepreneurs to generate dynamic "internal" economies, the internalized benefits may seldom have been taxed away later from those enlightened entrepreneurs.

[29] In Korea, the ratio of government saving to GNP rose from about 3 percent in

more to undermining the positive effect of employment expansion and to the overall deterioration of income distribution.

VII. Future Prospects and Policy Implications

Korea achieved a record growth rate of 14.7 percent in 1973. Total employment for the whole industry increased by 5.5 percent, while manufacturing employment increased by as much as 22.8 percent in 1973. Yet, the real wage rate increased by only 6.2 percent if deflated by the consumer price index, and declined by 3.2 percent if deflated by the GNP deflator for the whole industry. Although GNP and employment grew at an average annual rate of 8.5 percent and 3.9 percent respectively during 1970-75, the real wage rate increased by only 1.9 percent per annum if deflated by the GNP deflator and by 5.0 percent per annum if deflated by the consumer price index during 1971-75.

Korea achieved another record growth rate, 14.2 percent, in 1976, followed by growth rates of 10.5 percent in 1977 and 12.5 percent in 1978. Total employment increased by 4.5 percent per annum during 1976-78. This time, however, the real wage rate increased by 13.6 percent per annum if deflated by the GNP deflator and by 17.9 percent per annum if deflated by the consumer price index. The unemployment rate of the non-farm household sector declined from 7.4 percent in 1970 to 6.6 percent in 1975, and declined further to 5.0 percent in 1978. The unemployment rate for the whole country declined from 4.5 percent in 1970 to 3.2 percent in 1978 (EPB, 1978).

The period 1971-75 included an oil crisis and extremely high inflation. The period 1976-78 was characterized by Korea's recovery from the adverse impact of a worldwide recession and the unusual experience of a fairly severe labor shortage. One may argue that the latter half of the seventies represents for the Korean economy the

1962-71 to about 5 percent in 1972-78 on average, while that of corporate saving rose from 6 percent to 10 percent and that of household saving from about 3 percent to about 7 percent. The ratio of foreign saving to GNP fell from about 9 percent on average during 1962-71 to about 5 percent in 1972-78. The government's saving propensity rose from about 20 percent to about 29 percent, while that of the household sector rose from about 4 percent to about 9 percent. The rate of increase in saving propensity of the average Korean household is still much lower than that of Taiwan or Japan in the seventies (data from BOK's *National Income Statistics*).

complete termination of its surplus labor phase, as characterized by Lewis, and the beginning of a phase of full-employment, though perhaps with a fairly price-elastic supply of labor due to 39 percent employment in the primary sector as of 1978.[30]

With full employment, the real wage rate began to increase much more rapidly than the growth rate of labor productivity in the late seventies. If this trend continues, one can only expect substantial increases in the share of labor in GNP, despite extensive subsidized capital financing and the preferential tax system. This will help to reduce inequality in personal income distribution.

However, the continuance of vigorous promotion of investment in, and export of, heavy industrial products based on an exaggerated infant industry doctrine will accentuate the pattern of ever-increasing capital-intensive industrial production and the tendency for capital returns to fall. If profit margins are squeezed further by rapidly rising real wages, one can only expect a relative decrease in entrepreneurial savings for capital formation. Unless an offsetting increase in wage-earners' saving occurs, which is unlikely in a negative interest regime of subsidized capital financing, one may have to expect a lower rate of GNP growth in the 1980s because of lower domestic saving propensity.

On the other hand, the existing power balance may not allow a sustained increase in the relative share of wage income in GNP such as that observed during 1976-78. The pessimistic view may rather expect more extensive foreign borrowing, a further inflationary policy to reduce the growth rate of real wages in the non-unionized and non-indexed labor market, and a more regressive taxation of labor income to offset the fall in saving caused by diminishing profit margins and the absence of any incentive for wage earners to increase their saving propensity. These factors will work against wealth accumulation on the part of wage earners and equitable income distribution, even though relatively high growth rates in GNP may be maintained.

Another factor that has to be stressed in addition to credit subsidies as a source of the unfavorable shift in income distribution in the 1970s is a widening gap between high and low paid workers. In the 1960s when Korea was competing in the international market for the

---

[30] One may argue that there still exists some underemployment in agriculture in the sense that the number of employed in agriculture can decline without substantial losses of output, provided some means are found to cope with the very sharp seasonal peaks in labor demand (Rao, 1978).

expansion of simple labor-intensive manufactures, the level of elementary education in Korea could be ranked as highest among the developing countries with comparable per capita income. By the late 1970s, however, when Korea began to compete on the international market for the expansion of more skilled labor-intensive and somewhat more capital-intensive manufactures, the level of Korean higher education did not measure up to that of the countries with which Korea now had to compete. As production activities and export marketing became more sophisticated in the seventies, the demand for highly educated and trained labor rapidly expanded. Since the government has more or less ignored the need to effect essential improvements in the quality and standards of higher education, the rent accruing to the small group among the labor force that happened to possess the required aptitude and qualifications began to increase rapidly. This seems to have become the major cause for the deterioration in income distribution among employee households.

With suitable institutional improvements and reasonable incentive systems, the savings of wage-earners' households might easily expand substantially in the form of human capital formation. Savings transformed into invisible human capital are less likely to be exploited than if transformed into monetary financial capital that can readily be exploited through a low-interest rate regime, Human capital may foster economic growth as much as physical capital, and furthermore, the benefits are more likely to remain in the hands of individual workers.

Korea may have no choice but to continue its export-oriented growth strategy. Nevertheless, a more desirable set of policy measures to adopt in pursuance of this strategy might be to reduce excessive income transfers and efficiency losses arising from credit subsidies, to enforce a more equitable tax-expenditure system, to avoid forced saving in the form of inflationary financing, and to increase the savings and wealth accumulation of wage earners.[31] That is, by

---

[31] Non-inflationary development financing implies that the government restricts the magnitude of subsidies within the limit of seigniorage arising from non-inflationary increases in demand for currency associated with economic growth, plus government net revenue surplus which includes income flow from past government investments. The fact that the allocation of low-interest-rate foreign loans can also be controlled by the government implies that the scope of government subsidy activities can be extended without necessarily causing inflation. By renouncing inflationary financing, a significant amount of forced saving might disappear, but in the absence of inflation increased voluntary savings may more than offset such a loss, resulting in a higher aggregate saving ratio to GNP.

reducing the scope of government subsidy activities, undesirable distributional side-effects may be substantially reduced, while efficiency and growth, on the other hand, may show no substantial decline and may even increase by eliminating excessive interferences in the market mechanism.

REFERENCES

Adelman, I., *Redistribution with Growth: the Case of Korea,* December 1973. (mimeographed)

Bank of Korea, *Economic Statistics Yearbook.*

Chenery, H.B., et. al. (eds.) *Redistribution with Growth,* London: Oxford University Press, 1974.

Choo, H.C., *Economic Growth and Income Distribution in Korea,* Korea Development Institute, 1978. (mimeographed)

Corden, W.M., *Trade Policy and Economic Welfare,* London: Oxford University Press, 1974.

Economic Planning Board, *Annual Report on the Economically Active Population Survey.*

Hong, W., *Trade, Distortions and Employment Growth in Korea,* Seoul: KDI Press, 1979.

Krueger, A.O., "The Political Economy of the Rent-Seeking Society," *American Economic Review,* June 1974.

_____, *Growth, Distortions, and Patterns of Trade Among Many Countries,* International Finance Section, Princeton University, February 1977.

Oshima, H.T., "Income Inequality and Economic Growth: the Post-War Experience of Asian Countries," *Malayan Economic Review,* October 1970.

Rao, D.C., "Economic Growth and Equity in the Republic of Korea," *World Development,* Volume 6, Number 3, 1978.

Table 1. Major Indexes for Trade, Growth and Income Distribution in Korea

Average Annual Growth Rate	Commodity Exports (Nominal)	Commodity Exports (Real)	GNP (In 1975 Price)	Employment (Whole Industry)	Employment (Manufacturing)	Real Wage (Consumer Price Index)	Real Wage (Deflated by GNP Deflator)
1953-62	12.4%		3.8%	—	—	—	—
1963-71	39.6%	34.0%	9.5%	3.5%	10.5%	8.7%	12.1%
1972-78	45.0%	29.8%	10.3%	4.1%	12.4%	11.1%	10.9%

Percentage Share	Employment for Export (In Manufacturing)	Employment for Export (In Whole Industry)	Compensation of Employees in GNP	Labor Income in GNP[a]	I-O Data Labor Share (Manufacturing)	I-O Data Labor Share (Whole Industry)	Entrepreneurial Income Share[b]
1963	6%	2%	31%	85%	38%	26%	6.4%
1970	25%	6%	40%	81%	36% (39%)[c]	31% (57%)[c]	8.4%
1975	30%	11%	39%	78%	32% (33%)[c]	29% (49%)[c]	10.9%

	Gini Coefficients	Income Share of Lowest 20 Percent[d]	Theil Index	Foreign Saving	Government Saving	Corporate Saving	Household Saving
				Sources of Saving (% of GNP)			
1965	0.34%	38.5%	0.23%	6.4%	1.7%	5.5%	3.4%[e]
1970	0.33%	47.6%	0.21%	9.3%	6.5%	6.3%	4.5%
1976	0.38%	35.7%	0.25%	2.4%	6.2%	10.2%	6.7%

Source: The Bank of Korea; Hong (1979) and Choo (1978).

Notes: [a] Sum of compensation of employees and income from unincorporated agricultural and non-agricultural enterprises.
[b] Sum of dividends, corporate savings and others (corporate transfer payments, direct taxes on corporations and government income from property and entrepreneurship) divided by national income. The shares of rent and interest income were about 5% during 1964-77 and about 6% during 1966-77 respectively.
[c] Adjusted for unpaid family workers and proprietors.
[d] Ratio to income received by the highest 5 percent (in percentage).
[e]1963 figure was presented in order to show the actual trend.

• COMMENT _____

Yasukichi Yasuba,   *Osaka and Kyoto University*

Hong, while recognizing the workings of dynamic development forces, is generally critical of the subsidized capital financing and the preferential tax system in Korea's export-oriented growth.

Hong relied a bit too heavily on empirical evidence from the rather special period between 1970 and 1975. It is true that the oil crisis affected Korea's growth relatively little, but without question there was some retardation. Moreover, the deterioration in the terms of trade between 1972-75 was as much as 43 percent, one of the worst of any country. Korea's relatively high dependence on exports as a proportion of GNP, on the order of 30 percent after 1973, made the damage unusually severe, lowering real national purchasing power by approximately 13 percent of GNP during 1972-75. In all, Korea probably lost nearly 20 percent of GNP in this period because of the oil crisis.

Most of the preferences to export industries were introduced in the 1960s, well before Hong's observation period. In particular, the major changes of interest rates took place in 1965. The interest rates on deposits and on ordinary loans were raised, while the interest rates on export loans were further reduced, widening the preference margin to more than 25 percentage points. However, at the beginning of the 1970s, the preference margin was reduced to about 10 percentage points. Under those circumstances, it appears to be difficult to explain the improvement in equity during the latter part of the 1960s and the deterioration between 1970 and 1975 in Hong's terms.

It may be more persuasively argued that the unfavorable effect on labor income and income distribution was caused by the oil crisis and the flexibility of Korean wages. According to this interpretation, as the terms of trade improved by about 30 percent between 1975 and 1978, and as growth continued at an accelerated pace, Korea resumed the trend of improving income distribution which was already apparent in the latter half of the 1960s.

Compared with many other developing countries, Korea should be credited with introducing a number of reforms at relatively early stages of development. De facto indexation of financial assets and liabilities was introduced in 1965, as mentioned before, with the real rate of interest on bank deposits becoming significantly negative only in the crisis years of 1974 and 1975. The exchange rate was adjusted by the early part of the 1960s, terminating the overvaluation of the won. Import liberalization was pushed forward from the middle of the decade, reducing the number of restricted items and lowering tariff rates on a wide variety of imports.

Even the much-criticized promotion of exports, when this is done indiscriminately, may be favorably compared with the policy of import substitution, since the former tends to encourage labor-intensive industries almost by definition, while the latter tends to favor capital-intensive industries. Hong's judgment is sound concerning the damage done to the Korean economy by the selective promotion of capital-intensive export industries and the channelling of low-interest funds into a limited number of special interest groups. To the extent that these were important factors between 1970 and 1975, they may explain a part of the deterioration in equity in that period.

As for the future, Hong seems unduly pessimistic. While the most labor-intensive types of industries will have to be phased out, the Korean economy can move toward intermediate industries such as light machinery, shipbuilding, electronics, electric appliances, and perhaps iron and steel. If exports of these commodities become internationally competitive, the market for them will be almost unlimited, as Korean products will merely replace the exports of somebody else in the markets of the third countries.

Hong seems to worry about higher education and savings. Japan faced a similar situation, perhaps 15 years ago, with inadequate research and teaching at universities. Imported technology, via licensing agreements and direct investment, domestic research and development, and on-the-job training at firms largely solved the problem. Korea may have to worry about research and teaching at universities in the future, but it is only after its economy reaches the forefront among world economies.

With regard to savings, the real interest rate on one-year deposits in Japan was negative (-1.1%) on the average during the last twenty years. Yet the propensity to save among workers, particularly those with lower incomes, has continued to rise until the average propensity to save exceeded 20 percent, with that for the lowest quintile reaching a level only slightly lower than 20 percent. On an average, the real rate of interest on deposit in Korea appears to have been only slightly lower than that in Japan. If the hypothesis to the effect that the Koreans, the Chinese, and the Japanese tend to behave more or less similarly is true, it is expected that the propensity of worker-households in Korea to save will increase as real wages increase further. Hence, the shortage of savings is unlikely to become a limiting factor on growth in the future.

The inequitable tax system may be a real problem just as in Japan, but even in this field there appears to be some signs of improvement in the 1970s, particularly in taxes on dividend and rent, on non-agricultural unincorporated enterprises, and on capital gains. The expenditures on social programs such as education and rural development appear to be increasing.

Hong is correct in saying that taxation in Korea has been inequitable, but it is not at all clear whether it is more inequitable than in other developing countries with similar per capita incomes. It is always extremely difficult to impose progressive income tax, tax on property and tax on capital gains in developing countries. While economists should not stop criticizing the government for unfair practices, the performance of tax collection can be evaluated only after consideration of what is feasible. It would be useful for Hong to elucidate further on these points.

Finally, Hong says, that low-interest capital financing will not lead to a higher capital intensity, unless a higher capital intensity is required as a condition of receiving the favored loans. This is not totally convincing. Otherwise the only thing that is certain is that the margin between a higher opportunity cost and lower special interest rate will accrue to the hands of the preferred borrowers. They may simply determine capital intensity based on the opportunity cost of capital and pocket the differential in interest rates. Probably, much of the subsidized capital financing is made on the condition that borrowers should adopt technology embodying high capital-intensity. Or, alternatively, borrowers are people who are more interested in prestige than in profit, and will choose capital-intensive technology anyway. It would be interesting to know more of this problem in Korea.

Robert E. Baldwin, *University of Wisconsin*

Hong begins by considering development within the Lewis model, a stage that he states was not completely terminated until the latter half of the 1970s. It is when one applies the Lewis model that the question arises as to how the favorable income distribution of the 1960s can be explained. As the author points out, when capital accumulation takes place in this model, the share of national income going to capitalists increases. Yet apparently this did not happen in Korea. The explanation that he suggests is that as the labor supply is reduced in the traditional sector the minimum institutional wage may rise so much that the non-labor share in GNP declines. But, of course, this is a departure from the Lewis model. Another possibility that is more consistent with the Lewis framework is to assume that the minimum wage that must be paid to workers in the advanced sector is considerably higher than the minimum wage in the traditional sector, a point that Lewis has made. Then, although each wage rate remains fixed as accumulation occurs, labor's share in GNP may not decline.

Hong then investigates an interest-subsidy policy in the Lewis model but it is not entirely clear what conclusions should be drawn from this analysis. He assumes that the capital stock is initially owned by the government and lent to private entrepreneurs at an interest rate less than the marginal productivity of capital. Clearly, the lower this interest rate the higher will be the income of this entrepreneurial group. However, it would be best to regard this policy as simply a redistribution of capitalist income from the government to the private sector and not a change in the share of non-labor income in GNP.

In the model where labor and capital are fully employed, Hong first points out that under distortion-free conditions the behavior of factor shares simply depends on the relative growth rates of capital and labor and their elasticity of substitution. He then introduces interest subsidies to selected entrepreneurs that distort production and lower real GNP as well as the wage rate. It would be very helpful if he analyzed this situation in a more formal manner so that one could see more clearly its possible implications for income distribution. He considers two sources from which the interest-subsidy revenue may be obtained. One is the monopsonistic profits of the government that arise from its foreign borrowing and the other is the seigniorage

stemming from inflationary government financial policies. Under
both conditions it seems fairly clear that interest-subsidies financed in
these ways could shift the distribution of income away from labor.
But, demonstrating how this could arise in a formal way would
improve the paper.

A factor that he stresses in addition to interest-subsidies as a source
of the unfavorable shift in income distribution is a widening of the
gap between high and low income workers. The emphasis by the
government on more capital-intensive, higher-technology production
created a strong demand for more skilled, better-educated workers,
and their wages consequently rose relative to those of unskilled
employees. These income shifts as well as the relative rise in the
income of capitalists could, he notes, have been offset, at least in
part, by appropriate tax policies. However, he points out that the tax
system gave preferential treatment to income earned in the sectors
being subsidized by the government and that personal income and
inheritance taxes did little to mitigate the income inequalities brought
about by the government's export-oriented policies. Another way
these shifts might have been slowed is by greater government efforts
to increase the supply of skilled and highly educated workers.
However, little was done along these lines according to the author.
Consequently, the result was that in the 1970s high growth rates were
achieved but at the expense of a more unequal distribution of income.

The author appreciates that this growing inequality may have been
a necessary price for high growth rates but he clearly does not accept
this as self-evident. He is particularly concerned with the social and
political implications of a continuation of this income-distribution
trend. He argues for a reduction in the use of subsidized loans, the
implementation of a more equitable tax-expenditure system, and the
avoidance of inflationary financing techniques. These policies will, he
claims, not only improve the pattern of income distribution but may
actually increase growth rates.

These recommendations appear to be appealing. The growth rate in
Korea will slow down for one of the reasons that slowed expansion
under the import-substitution approach, a shortage of factors needed
for the type of growth being emphasized. The government has
decided to stress capital-intensive, higher-technology production and
this production requires labor skills that are not abundant in the
country. The reason for this policy shift appears to be a fear that the
markets for labor-intensive products will either be limited by

protectionist policies or taken over by less-developed countries. In other words, government officials became concerned about a lack of demand. But, perhaps, they have simply exchanged a fear on the demand side for the reality of supply side shortages. If their demand fears are valid, then, as Hong argues, they must give more attention to improving the quality of the labor force. Continuing to subsidize capital-intensive industries may prove to be highly distorting and ineffective because of the shortage of skilled labor. Now may be the time to shift government policy toward more infrastructure activity, especially an expansion of education expenditure, at the same time leaving production decisions to free-market forces to a greater degree.

GENERAL DISCUSSION

There may be statistical problems in comparing the Gini coefficient estimated for 1965 and that for 1976. The observed changes in distributional statistics may not reflect any real significant changes in income distribution.

If the distributional statistics for Korea are taken as they are, the declining share of the lower 20 percent income bracket in the 1970s may be attributed to the high effective protection accorded to agricultural products which take a relatively larger portion of the budget of the lower income class. On the other hand, the worsening distribution of income among employee households may be simply reflecting a short-run market phenomenon related to shortage of skilled labor in the transitional phase of shifting from labor-intensive production to capital- and skill-intensive industries. During 1976-78, there was full employment and severe shortages of unskilled labor in Korea which must have improved the income distribution among employee households.

More study may be needed to determine who has been paying for the credit subsidies in Korea. For instance, most of the credit subsidies might have been financed by foreign lenders in the form of low-interest rate foreign loans. Even in cases when Korean deposit money holders have been financing most of the credit subsidies, the increase in the rate of return on bank deposits may not improve the distribution of income, unless, as in Japan, the majority of bank deposit holders are small, low-income families. In Korea, perhaps the major deposit money holders are rich families. However, one may argue that rich families have more access to savings in the form of variable price assets such as real estate, common stocks and self-financing of their own investment activities, while poor families have very limited access to alternative forms of saving which can evade inflation tax.

The similarity between the pattern of Korea and Israel was indicated by the way in which, in both countries, credit subsidy and credit rationing helped in transforming an import-substitution-oriented economy to an export-oriented one, the positive resource pulling effect outweighing the negative income distribution effect. However, as the credit subsidies were continuously provided and expanded in absolute magnitude, the positive effect became smaller. In the later stages, negative effects more than offset the positive effects, not only in terms of income distribution but also in terms of macro effect, as indicated by the high rate of inflation.

PART IV

TRADE WITH RESOURCE-RICH COUNTRIES

CHANGING ECONOMIC RELATIONS BETWEEN THE ASIAN ADCs AND RESOURCE-EXPORTING ADVANCED COUNTRIES OF THE PACIFIC BASIN

Kym Anderson &
Ben Smith*

I. Introduction

Korea, Taiwan, Hong Kong and Singapore are presently among the fastest growing, most rapidly industrializing and most open developing economies in the world (OECD, 1979). These advanced developing countries (ADCs) all have very low natural resource endowments, in terms of agricultural land and minerals, per capita. Of significant interest is the impact of rapid growth in these resource-poor economies on resource-rich countries, particularly those within the Pacific region, and the role that trade in natural resource-based (NRB) goods has in promoting that growth. This paper is concerned specifically with the interdependent economic relationship between these resource-poor ADCs (hereafter Group A) and the resource-exporting developed countries of the Pacific Basin, namely Australia, Canada and New Zealand (Group B).

The first section of the paper extends the presently received theory of changing comparative advantage to include more systematically the roles of primary products and services as well as manufactured goods. It discusses the theory of trade resistances, relating it to various categories of primary and manufactured goods, and examines the role of foreign investment in the process of economic development. The

* Australian National University.

implications of the theory for Group A and Group B countries in particular are stressed throughout.

The second section examines the relative factor endowments and economic growth rates of non-Latin American Pacific rim countries. These data, in conjunction with the theory of Section One, provide expectations about the changing economic relationships between Group A and Group B countries. Available trade statistics for both groups of countries are then examined to see how closely these expectations are fulfilled. Since Japan is a former Group A country and the United States in some senses a former Group B country, these two countries are included as reference cases. The statistics provide strong empirical support for the theory, given the two groups' relative factor endowments and economic growth rates.

Section Three takes a close look at factors affecting comparative advantage in, and the location of, minerals processing. Particular emphasis is given to changing comparative advantage in processing minerals following recent energy price rises, and to institutional arrangements to reduce risk for both buyers and sellers of minerals and metals. Finally, Section Four briefly considers likely future developments in economic relations between these two groups of economies. Their bilateral trade and investment prospects are, of course, dependent on the types of policy initiatives taken by the various governments. The paper concludes with a discussion of the implications of alternative policy options for both the resource-poor developing economies and the resource-rich countries.

II. Changing Comparative Advantage in Growth Context: The Theory

1. A Three-Factor Model with Natural Resources

Following the apparent failure of the simplest version of the Heckscher-Ohlin trade model to explain satisfactorily the pattern of trade specialization,[1] numerous attempts have been made to modify the theory or to provide alternative explanations. Johnson (1968) has synthesized the bulk of this work in a reinterpretation of the two-

---

[1] A survey of the relevant empirical literature is provided by Stern (1975).

sector Heckscher-Ohlin model, in which capital is defined broadly to include not only physical capital equipment but also human skills, social capital, technological and organizational knowledge and natural resources, while labor is defined in the narrow sense of human labor time availability. The relative capital intensity of different activities is reflected in flow terms by relative value added per unit of labor time input. Although this model has considerable explanatory power, particularly with respect to trade patterns in manufactures, the treatment of natural resources as part of the total capital stock limits its usefulness. Unlike other forms of capital, natural resources take predetermined forms and are more or less specific to particular types of primary production. Thus, the pattern of comparative advantage as between primary products and manufactures cannot be explained adequately by a model which assumes a single, homogeneous capital stock.

Krueger (1977) and Garnaut and Anderson (1980) have suggested that the explanatory power of the model is improved if natural resources are treated as a third factor of production. Following Jones (1971), their model includes two sets of products, manufactures and primary products, and three sets of factors; natural resources, which are specific to the primary sector; capital which is specific to manufacturing; and labor, which is used in both sectors, is intersectorally mobile and exhibits diminishing marginal product in each sector. In this model, at a given set of international commodity prices, the wage rate is determined by the overall per worker endowment of capital and natural resources, as in the Johnson synthesis, while the pattern of comparative advantage as between manufactures and primary products is determined by the relative endowments of capital and natural resources.

An underdeveloped country with little capital will have a wage rate determined predominantly by its per worker natural resource endowment, and will export primary products in exchange for manufactures. As incomes grow and capital is accumulated, labor will be attracted to the manufacturing sector which will expand relative to the primary sector. For any given rate of capital accumulation per worker, the speed of the reallocation of labor towards manufacturing will be greater the lower is the initial wage rate; that is, the smaller the natural resource endowment is per worker. This is because the low wage will give the resource-poor country an international comparative advantage in initially labor-intensive, standard-technology manufactures. Hence, it will switch from being predominantly a primary producer to being an exporter of manufactured goods at a low level of capital per worker. Over time, as the per worker endowment of capital increases, the comparative advantage within the manufacturing sector will shift towards more capital-intensive activities. By contrast, a resource-rich country with a relatively high initial wage rate will switch much more slowly towards specialization in manufacturing, absorbing its accumulation of capital in the development of a more limited range of relatively capital-intensive manufactures.[2]

2. Extension of the Three-Factor Model[3]

While the three-factor model outlined above provides a better explanation of the pattern of trade in primary products than the Johnson synthesis, a fuller explanation requires an allowance for the international mobility of some forms of capital; the use of capital in primary production; the fact that services are also produced, many of which are tradable; and the influence of demand and comparative growth factors on trade specialization.[4]

a. International Capital Mobility

If there were free and costless movement of all forms of capital and some barriers to commodity trade, the incentive for trade in commodities would tend to be eliminated (Mundell, 1957). In the absence of complete specialization this would be true even if there were differences in immobile natural resource endowments across countries (Caves, 1971).[5] In reality, though, there are substantial barriers to

---

[2] Within the developing world, the extreme examples of this latter case are found among the oil-producing countries of the Middle East.

[3] The following discussion draws in part on Anderson (1979) and Garnaut and Anderson (forthcoming, Chapter 2).

[4] Because it involves a number of special factors, the important issue of what determines the pattern of comparative advantage in minerals processing is addressed separately in the third section of the paper. Some of the issues relating to agricultural, timber and fish processing, which are not dealt with in detail in this paper, are addressed by Martin (1980) and Byron (1980).

[5] Within the three-factor model in which capital is specific to manufacturing, complete specialization could only occur where a country had a natural resource endowment which was, by itself, capable of generating a real wage level higher than could be earned in manufacturing in any other country. Capital flows from such a country to natural resource-poor countries would then increase rather than reduce the degree of trade specialization.

international capital movements which vary across types of capital and bilateral economic relationships. Capital that is embodied in human skills and social organization is generally much less mobile than that embodied in physical assets which can be installed relatively easily with the transfer of financial capital. Indeed, the latter form of capital would only be attracted to a developing country once minimal infrastructural and organizational capital is in place. All forms of capital tend to move more readily between countries that share similar cultural and political traditions, have colonial or aid ties, are geographically proximate and participate in relatively intense bilateral trade. The lower the resistances to foreign capital inflow into a country, the more rapidly that country can proceed along the development path and change its comparative advantage.

b. Capital in Primary Production

The fact that capital is required in addition to natural resources and labor in primary production strengthens the likelihood that resource-rich countries will begin manufacturing at a later stage of capital accumulation per worker and will specialize less in it than will resource-poor countries. It also means that resource-rich developed countries may retain a comparative advantage in primary production, vis-a-vis resource-rich developing countries, for longer than would otherwise be the case. There are a number of reasons for this. In the case of agriculture, there is a high degree of substitutability between capital and both labor and land (Binswanger, Ruttan and others, 1978; Naya, 1967). Hence the productivity of labor and land in agriculture can be raised by combining them with more and more capital. The greater the per worker agricultural land endowment of a country, adjusted for quality differences across countries, the more likely it is that capital can be employed more profitably in agriculture than in manufacturing at a given level of capital per worker. In addition, insofar as agricultural capital, including new production technology, tends to be less transferable internationally than mining or manufacturing capital, the capital-scarce, land-abundant developing countries may be unable to attract sufficient capital to their agricultural sector to match the cost reductions achieved by substituting capital for other factors in resource-rich developed countries' agriculture.

Similarly with mining, the greater a country's endowment of minerals per worker (again adjusted for quality differences across countries), the more likely it is that capital can be employed more profitably in mining than in manufacturing, or in agriculture for that matter, as is discussed in Part (d) below. Unlike in agriculture, however, the degree of substitutability between labor and capital in mining is so low that, at all observed wage/rental ratios, mining operations are very capital-intensive. Although foreign investment via large mining corporations reduces the major capital constraint of developing countries' mining sectors, the cost advantage due to the low wage rates in these countries is not very significant in such a highly capital-intensive activity. At the same time, the effect of general capital scarcity on the supply of infrastructure investments and, often, the existence of political uncertainties create a cost disadvantage for investments in developing countries (Garnaut and Clunies-Ross, 1975; Krause and Patrick, 1978). Hence there is a tendency for mineral products to be produced more cheaply from natural resources of a given physical quality in countries with relatively high capital/labor ratios, despite their higher wage costs (Kravis, 1956; Vanek, 1963).

Certainly in the case of agriculture at least, it is possible for a country to offset its factor scarcity by investing in the production of new technologies which save most its scarcest factor. The development of technological changes that are land-saving in Japan and Europe and labor-saving in North America and Australia are cases in point (Binswanger, Ruttan and others, 1978). It is then possible for these new technologies to be transferred to and adapted by poorer but similarly land-scarce or land-abundant countries, as these countries accumulate sufficient capital to make such technologies profitable for farmers to adopt. This has in fact happened in North Africa and the Near East (from Australia) and in Korea and Taiwan (from Japan — see Hayami and Ruttan, 1971). It is conceivable that land-scarce developing countries could have a sufficiently greater rate of farm technological advance than land-abundant countries, especially developed countries, to enable them not to lose comparative advantage in agriculture, but it is rather unlikely for a number of reasons. First, the rates of return from agricultural research are going to be greater, the larger the domestic industry to which the results will be most relevant, especially because there are economies of scale in agricultural research (Evenson, 1971). Hence countries with large areas of agricultural land are likely to have the fastest rates of farm technological advance. This will be reinforced by the fact that since land-saving technologies, both biological and technical, needed in resource-poor countries have more public goods characteristics than labor-saving mechanical technologies appropriate for resource-rich developed countries, the former tend not to be produced by the private sector; and for politico-economic reasons discussed elsewhere (Anderson, forthcoming), governments tend to underinvest grossly in public agricultural research. Second, the usually more favorable prices facing agriculture in developed as compared with developing countries which are likely to induce relatively more research as well as production in the former (Peterson, 1979), together with the fact that agricultural research is capital-intensive, especially in terms of human capital, will help to ensure further that land-abundant developed countries retain a glôbal comparative advantage in those agricultural products able to be produced in their physical environments.[6]

c. The Services Sector

Finally on the supply side, the existence of tradable services should not be ignored. These activities generally require few natural resources, are relatively intensive in the use of labor time, but often offer considerable scope for substituting capital, especially human capital, for labor. Consequently, resource-poor countries are likely to have a comparative advantage in supplying tradable services at various stages of their development, wherever natural and other barriers to such trade are sufficiently low. If, for example, either construction laborers or managers, or both, are prepared to travel internationally, an advanced developing country may well be able to export construction services to labor-scarce developing countries and to make use of expertise recently developed for providing such services domestically. Further examples of tradable services likely to be profitable in appropriate circumstances are retailing and associated tourist services and stevedoring. While the incentive for low-wage, labor-abundant countries to provide labor-intensive retailing services and associated tourist services to international travellers at international prices is largely the result of trade barriers to manufactures in most other countries, there is also an element of genuine comparative advantage while wage rates and distribution costs remain low. The capacity to provide stevedoring services depends both on relative labor abundance and geographic location. Given the economies of scale in providing

---

[6] These points are discussed in more detail in Anderson (1980b).

port and communication facilities, Singapore is ideally situated to provide a regional base for ships to and from the major trading countries of Europe and North America, breaking the bulk of goods from those countries for re-export in smaller quantities to neighboring Southeast Asian Countries and doing the opposite for the primary exports of its neighbors. Hong Kong is similarly placed with respect to mainland China. One would expect re-exports to represent a high proportion of imports for these countries, and imports of raw materials to be largely from neighboring countries. Finally, as human capital accumulation proceeds, the resource-poor developing countries may have a comparative advantage in providing a range of commercial and financial services, at least on a regional basis. Such a development would be most likely in the case of the city-states, given their location, and would be a natural extension of the entrepot role.

.In general, one might expect that capital accumulation in densely populated city-states would be directed towards skill-intensive manufacturing and tradable services, rather than towards those physical capital-intensive heavy industries that are also intensive in their use of urban land and in their generation of pollutants. Processing of raw materials, in particular, would be restricted to limited processing of materials passing through the entrepot where transport cost considerations make such processing worthwhile before re-export over long distances, and where the smaller capital constraint and the ability to take advantage of economies of scale give a country like Singapore a cost advantage over the countries of origin of the raw materials.

Throughout, the fact has been ignored that many goods and services are nontradable internationally because of prohibitively high transport costs. While the addition of a nontradable sector to the model does not change its conclusions about comparative advantage as between different tradable industries, it does of course modify the conclusions about the structure of an economy. This has particular significance for resource-rich developed economies, because the simple model without nontradables implies that most labor and capital resources will be employed in the primary sector. In practice, of course, the majority of non-natural resources are employed in nontradable service industries in developed countries. The lack of understanding of this point often leads to fears that without manufacturing protection, resource-rich developed countries would be made up of capital-intensive farms, mines and quarries, and with not enough jobs for the workforce.

d. Demand and Comparative Growth Factors

Trade specialization depends not only on supply factors but also on factors affecting demand. The demand for foodstuffs increases with population and per capita income while the demand for industrial raw materials increases with manufacturing production. Thus a country's export specialization in food products will tend to be related negatively to its GNP per agricultural hectare, while its export specialization in minerals will tend to be related positively to its mineral resources per dollar of manufacturing output.

While domestic economic growth, capital accumulation and industrialization in a developing country will tend to weaken specialization in primary products, with the qualifications outlined above, economic growth and industrialization abroad may initially have the opposite effect if it results in increased foreign demand for food and industrial raw materials and a consequent terms-of-trade improvement. However, rapid economic growth in the developed world as a whole will not only result in an improvement in the terms of trade for primary products, the extent of which will in any case be modified by supply responses from resource-rich developed countries and innovations in their production and use (Magee and Robins, 1978); it will also generate an improvement in the terms of trade for labor-intensive manufactures due to the increasing relative scarcity of labor, particularly unskilled labor, in developed countries. Thus, although developed country growth may strengthen export specialization in primary products for resource-rich developing countries, it may have the opposite effect for resource-poor developing countries, at least after some lagged adjustments have taken place.[7]

So far as the impact of growth in resource-poor developing countries on the pattern of their import demands is concerned, the share of food in total imports should be expected to drop over time due to the low income elasticity of food demand, with the pattern of food

---

[7] The adjustment lags may be considerable, given both the nature of the transformation required and the likely resistance to industrial restructuring in developed countries until pressures become irresistible. It is possible to interpret the recent rapid growth of the ADCs as a response to past growth rates in the developed world, with adjustments occurring after developed country growth has slowed down. These particular countries, rather than other labor-abundant developing countries, may have been the ones to take advantage of the opportunity most successfully because of their relatively more open trade and investment policies.

imports shifting towards the relative luxuries of red meat and dairy products. Also, raw materials for labor-intensive processing industries, such as cotton, wool and hides, would first increase their share of imports as industrialization begins, and then fall as the derived demand for imports of raw materials or processed materials for more capital-intensive manufacturing expands.

For resource-rich developed countries, this would mean a relatively greater growth in demand for their minerals and metals, as compared with their agricultural exports, by the resource-poor industrializing countries. This impact is likely to be strengthened by the desire of those countries to restrict imports of food in order to protect domestic agriculture. (See below.) If, at the same time, there is resistance in the resource-rich developed countries to allowing adjustment to the weakened competitive position of domestic labor-intensive manufacturing, minerals export growth will generate exchange rate/inflationary pressures which will weaken the terms of trade for agriculture, in domestic currency terms, despite growth in demand for agricultural exports (Gregory, 1976; Snape, 1977; Smith, 1978a; Stoeckel, 1979; Vincent, et al., 1979).

3. The Causes and Effects of Trade and Investment Resistances

The theory outlined is incomplete in its ability to explain changing trade and investment patterns of countries, particularly Group A and Group B countries, in that it does not explain the magnitude of changes in relative resource endowments, nor does it explain the pattern of political, geographic and informational resistances which influence trade and investment flows. No explanation of comparative growth rates is attempted here,[8] but some comments on the various types of barriers affecting trade specialization are perhaps worth making.

a. Political Barriers

Trade and investment barriers are raised by governments presumably because it is in the interests of a country's politicians to raise them,

---

[8] For an interesting politico-economic theory of comparative growth rates, see Olson (1978). An important element in such a theory is an explanation of relative resistances to adjustment to a changing economic environment, since the ability and willingness of people in a country to adjust can be a major determinant of economic growth (Kindleberger, 1962, pp. 99-100; Schultz, 1975).

given the factors affecting the demand for and supply of such barriers including non-economic community. preferences. As a country's per capita income rises, it can more readily afford to assist industries facing employment declines. In resource-poor ADCs, agriculture will be under pressure to decline rapidly whereas in resource-rich developed countries it is the labor-intensive sections of manufacturing which are losing comparative advantage fastest. This, together with the desire for a more 'balanced,' less specialized economy, and perhaps partly for risk-aversion reasons, may lead one to expect policies protecting the import-competing primary sectors of resource-poor industrializing countries, most notably agriculture, and the import-competing labor-intensive manufacturing sectors of resource-rich developed countries.[9] Hence the share of foodstuffs in total imports of resource-poor ADCs would drop faster over time than would be the case in the absence of distortions, while these countries' exports of labor-intensive manufactures to developed countries, especially the resource-rich, would grow more slowly than without such barriers. The agricultural exports of resource-rich developed countries, particularly foodgrains as well as fibers for labor-intensive export manufacturing, would be lowered by these protectionist policies both because of the reduced import demand overseas and because of the earlier-mentioned reduced intersectoral competitiveness of agriculture domestically as a result of improving terms of trade for mining and protection for manufacturing.

---

[9] For other explanations of these protectionist policies, drawn from the neoclassical economic theory of politics, see Anderson (1980 and forthcoming) and Garnaut and Anderson (forthcoming). There is strong empirical support for the casual observation that food-deficit countries tend to assist their agricultural sector more than food-surplus countries, especially as their per capita incomes rise. This evidence, presented in Anderson (1979, p. 6), makes use of an index of real domestic farm prices during 1968-70 for each of 49 non-communist countries, as compiled by Peterson (1979). When this price index (P) is regressed on per capita GNP in 1969 (Y) and the average share of domestic grain production exported during 1967-71 (E), one obtains

$$P = 19.7 + 9.07Y - 187E, \quad R^2 = .482$$
$$\quad (6.52) \quad (2.25)$$

The signs of the coefficients and their significance (indicated by the t-values in parentheses) suggest that a country's domestic farm prices tend to be lower, the smaller its GNP per capita and the larger its export surplus. Also, P is positively associated with the share of domestic grain consumption imported. The increasing agricultural protection of food-deficit Japan and Korea in particular is now well-documented (Hayami, 1975; Nam, 1980).

b. Geographic and Information Cost Barriers

Resistances to international tràde in the form of transport costs are certainly not insignificant (Finger and Yeats, 1976), and they may be becoming more important with rising fuel prices. Hence, greater distances between trading partners' ports affect adversely the bilateral trade volume. Factor endowments of nearby economies tend therefore to be more important in determining a country's comparative advantage than the factor endowments of more distant economies. It follows that a country's export specialization will tend to strengthen in commodities in which import specialization is strong in rapidly expanding economies nearby. Strong growth in nearby economies with complementary resource endowments will tend to raise a country's terms of trade more than strong growth in more distant economies with similarly complementary resource endowments (Drysdale, 1969).

Finally, costs of acquiring information on trading and investment opportunities in a foreign country are clearly less, the greater one's familiarity with that country's language, culture, governmental procedures and business practices. The degree of familiarity is often greater, the closer that country or the more colonial, political or aid ties there have been between the two countries (Drysdale, 1969; Garnaut, 1972). The British connection with Singapore and Hong Kong, for example, undoubtedly facilitated the development of the latters' entrepot trade (Seow, 1979).

4. Recapitulation

In summary, the theory discussed above has the following to say concerning the changing international trade and investment patterns of rapidly growing, resource-poor developing countries (Group A) and resource-rich developed countries (Group B), particularly as it affects their bilateral economic relationships.

Group A countries will switch from export dependence on primary products to exporting mainly manufactures at a relatively early stage of development, whereas Group B countries will tend to retain a comparative advantage in primary production despite high levels of capital accumulation and competition from resource-rich developing countries. In general, for supply reasons a country's comparative advantage in primary products relative to manufactures will tend to be related negatively to its ratios of labor and capital stocks to natural resource endowments, compared with the rest of the world, though the important role of capital in many areas of primary production and capital's international mobility make the natural resource endowment per worker the more critical ratio. When demand factors are also taken into account one would expect a country's export specialization in food products and minerals to be related negatively to its income per hectare of agricultural land and its manufacturing output per unit of mineral resources, respectively.

Growth of Group A countries will result in increased import demands for raw or processed primary products, so that when these countries are growing more rapidly than Group B countries, the primary product export specialization of the latter group will strengthen. The share of food in Group A countries' imports may expand at first but then will decline gradually as these countries grow. The share of imports of agricultural raw materials for labor-intensive manufacturing activities will also grow strongly at first but eventually will fall as those for capital intensive activities expand.

For the extremely natural-resource-poor city-states, economic growth is likely to be directed more towards human capital-intensive industries including services than towards physical capital-intensive heavy industries, so that their imports of primary products from Group B countries will be predominantly foodstuffs rather than minerals and metals.

All of the developments suggested above will be lessened by resistances to trade and investment in bilateral relations between Group A and Group B countries. Policy-induced resistances are less likely to apply to trade and investment flows relating to mineral raw materials, and perhaps also to metals, than to food imports into Group A countries, and may be more severe against labor-intensive manufactured exports from Group A to Group B countries than against the export of more sophisticated goods. Resistances due to geographic and informational barriers are likely to be smaller, the closer are the trade partners and the greater their political, cultural or aid ties.

III. Changing Comparative Advantage: Empirical Evidence

   This section first presents data on relative factor endowments and economic growth rates of non-Latin American Pacific rim countries. These data, together with the above theory, provide expectations concerning changing trade relations between Group A and Group B countries. International trade statistics relating to the past 15 years or so are then examined. They are seen to provide strong empirical support for the theory, which suggests insights into likely future developments in these bilateral economic relationships.

   Tables 1 and 2 provide a number of indicators of relative factor endowments and economic growth rates for the major non-Latin American Pacific rim countries. It is clear from columns (6) and (9) of Table 1 that Australia, Canada, New Zealand and, to a lesser extent, the United States are extremely well endowed with various types of land per capita. By contrast, the four ADCs and Japan have extremely low per capita endowments of land and minerals. To the extent that these per capita endowments are useful proxies for the ratios of agricultural, forest and mineral resources to labor, one would expect the four ADCs and Japan to have a strong comparative disadvantage in the production of goods based on these resources.[10] Group B countries, on the other hand, would be expected to have a strong comparative advantage in producing NRB goods. The supply reasons for these expectations are reinforced by NRB import demand factors since, as Column 5 of Table 1 and the numbers in parentheses in Table 2 suggest, Group A countries have extremely high and Group B countries have very low incomes per unit of agricultural land and manufacturing outputs per unit of mineral resources. The rapid rates of GNP and export growth and of industrialization in Group A countries (Columns 10 to 14) would also lead one to expect their

   _____

   [10] Since fishing in international waters has not been constrained greatly to date, it is an activity not heavily dependent on national fishing resource endowments. Comparative advantage in fish products, as with manufactures, would depend mainly on value added per worker in that industry, although strong domestic demand for fish may enable comparative advantage in its production to strengthen through the effects of this assured demand on large-scale investments to capture possible economies of scale. As with agriculture, though, there is a wide range of capital intensity of production technologies available in the fishing industry, so that comparative advantage may not even depend too much on a country's capital endowment per worker.

Table 1. *Relative Factor Endowments and Economic Growth Rates, Selected Pacific Rim Countries, 1977*

	Population (millions)	Area (million hectares)	GNP ($US billions)	GNP per capita ($US)	GNP per thousand agricultural hectares ($US)	Land endowment per capita (hectares) Total	Arable	Permanent pasture	Forest or woods	Real GDP growth rate (% p.a.) 1960-70	1970-77	Real industrial growth (% p.a.) 1970-77	Share of GDP exported (%) 1960	1977
	(1)	(2)	(3)	(4)	(5)	(6)	(7)	(8)	(9)	(10)	(11)	(12)	(13)	(14)
Resource-Poor ADCs (Group A)														
Korea	36.0	9.8	29.5	820	13.0	.27	.06	.00	.18	8.5	10.4	17.0	3	40
Taiwan	16.3	3.6	19.7	1,170	10.4	.21	.05	.00	.13	9.2	7.7	12.2	11	54
Hong Kong	4.5	.1	11.7	2,590	1,300.0	.02	.00	.00	.00	10.0	8.2	6.8	79	98
Singapore	2.3	.1	6.6	2,380	825.0	.04	.00	.00	.00	8.8	8.6	8.6	163	160
Resource-Rich DCs (Group B)														
Australia	14.1	769	103.5	7,340	.21	54.54	3.17	31.96	7.59	4.1	3.8	3.9	15	16
Canada	23.3	998	197.1	8,460	2.95	42.83	1.87	1.00	14.00	5.6	4.7	3.8	18	24
New Zealand	3.1	27	13.5	4,380	.99	8.68	.13	4.42	2.16	3.9	2.0	—	23	28
Other DCs														
United States	220.0	936	1,874.0	8,520	4.39	4.25	.84	1.09	1.32	4.3	2.8	2.3	5	8
Japan	113.2	37	641.8	5,670	116.00	.33	.04	.00	.22	10.5	5.3	5.7	11	14
Other West Pacific LDCs														
Indonesia	133.3	190	40.1	300	.73	1.42	.11	.09	.92	3.5	7.7	12.9	13	22
Malaysia	13.0	33	12.1	930	1.86	2.54	.24	.00	1.67	6.5	7.8	9.3	54	50
Philippines	44.5	30	20.0	450	2.21	.67	.12	.02	.29	5.1	6.4	8.7	11	19
Thailand	43.8	51	18.4	420	1.02	1.16	.36	.01	4.82	8.2	7.1	10.3	17	22
Papua New Guinea	2.9	46	1.4	490	3.03	15.86	.01	.03	12.56	6.5	5.0	—	17	45
Mainland China	885.6	960	345.4	390	1.09	1.08	.12	.24	.14	6.6	5.8	9	1	2

Sources: World Bank, *World Development Indicators,* Washington, D.C., 1979; Food and Agricultural Organization, *Production Yearbook 1978,* Rome, 1973; Central Intelligence Agency, *China: Economic Indicators,* Washington, D.C., 1978.

Table 2. *Mineral Reserves Per Capita (and Per Thousand US Dollars of Manufacturing Output), Selected Pacific Rim Countries*

(thousand tonnes in 1976 except as noted)

	Copper	Lead	Zinc	Tin	Nickel	Cobalt	Bauxite	Iron Ore[a]	Coal[b]	Uranium[c]	Oil[d]	Natural Gas[e]
Resource-Poor ADCs (Group A)												
Taiwan	..	..	..	..	..	..	..	..	..	..	0.7 (2)	1.2 (3)
Resource Rich DCs (Group B)												
Australia	560 (400)	1,190 (850)	860 (610)	25 (18)	..	3.6 (2.6)	298,000 (213,600)	780 (560)	14,500 (10,400)	21 (15)	150 (110)	65 (45)
Canada	1,350 (890)	510 (330)	1,450 (950)	..	380 (250)	1.3 (0.9)	..	470 (310)	4,700 (3,100)	7 (5)	260 (170)	55 (45)
New Zealand	..	..	..	..	..	..	..	..	..	..	35 (35)	55 (55)
Other DCs												
United States	390 (190)	250 (120)	130 (65)	..	1	..	170 (85)	17 (8)	16,700 (8,200)	2.4 (1.2)	140 (70)	30 (15)
Japan	..	..	..	..	..	..	..	..	..	..	0.6 (0.4)	0.1
Other West Pacific LDCs												
Indonesia	..	..	..	20 (740)	..	..	..	..	..	..	75 (2,800)	5 (185)
Malaysia	..	..	..	65 (390)	..	..	..	..	..	..	200 (1,200)	40 (240)
Philippines	390 (3,470)	..	..	..	..	..	..	..	..	..	2 (18)	..
Thailand	..	..	..	30 (360)	..	..	..	..	..	..	..	..
Papua New Guinea	3,140 (71,000)	..	..	..	..	..	..	..	..	..	..	..
Mainland China	..	..	..	2 (50)	..	..	..	3 (75)	..	..	24 (600)	0.9 (25)
Total World	110 (55)	35 (18)	40 (20)	2.5 (1.2)	14 (7)	0.4 (0.2)	5,400 (2,700)	23 (12)	2,800 (1,400)	n.a. (n.a.)	160 (80)	18 (9)

Sources: Compiled by Drysdale (forthcoming) from U.S. Bureau of Mines, *Commodity Data Summaries, 1977* and OECD Nuclear Energy and International Atomic Energy Agency, *Uranium: Resources, Production and Demand*, December 1977.

Notes: a Recoverable iron, million tonnes.
b Bituminous coal and lignite, million tonnes.
c As at January 1977, recoverable in the cost range to $US 80/kg U.
d As at January 1978, recoverable at current technology and prices, million barrels.
e As at January 1978, recoverable at current technology and prices, billion cubic metres.

imports from Group B countries of raw materials for capital-intensive industries such as metals and minerals, as a share of total and NRB imports, to be expanding at the expense of import shares of food-stuffs and raw-materials for labor-intensive industries such as wool and hides. In the city-states of Hong Kong and Singapore, the extreme population densities and relatively high per capita incomes, which are an index of human and organizational capital abundance per worker, and hence comparative advantage in skill-intensive industries such as tradable services, may lead one to expect their import demand for NRB goods to be concentrated in foodstuffs rather than industrial raw materials.

Among Group B countries and the United States, Column 7 of Table 1 suggests Australia and North America are likely to be large suppliers of temperate crops; Column 8 suggests Australia, New Zealand and to a much lesser extent North America are likely to have large grazing industries, although the possibility of grain-fed livestock production reduces the natural advantage associated with extensive grazing land; Column 9 suggests Canada and New Zealand would be substantial forest products producers, the Australian woodlands on the whole having relatively little commercial timber value; and Table 2 suggests Australia, Canada and the United States would be the substantial minerals and energy producers of the region. The extent to which these production tendencies translate into export specialization depends on domestic demand for these NRB goods. The much higher rate of GNP to agricultural land in North America compared with Australia (Column 5) suggests that the latter are more likely to specialize in agricultural exports than the former. Also, because the output of manufactures is so very much greater in the United States that in Canada or Australia, the U.S. endowment of mineral resources per dollar of manufacturing output is, on average, consideraly lower than in Canada or Australia. (See numbers in parentheses in Table 2.) Hence the latter two countries are more likely to be exporters of mineral-based products than the U.S. or New Zealand.[11]

Perhaps the only readily available proxy for the endowment per worker of broadly defined capital, excluding natural resources, is GNP per capita.[12] Crude though this proxy is, it probably provides a

---

[11] Table 2 also shows the relatively large reserves of certain minerals in Southeast Asia per dollar of their manufactures, and hence their ability to be significant exporters of those minerals.

not-too-unreliable index of a country's capital/labor ratio and hence of the likely capital intensity of its exports of manufactures. From the data in Column 4 of Table 1, one would expect the ADCs' exports of manufactures to be made up mostly of labor-intensive goods and those of Group B countries as well as of Japan and the United States to be mostly capital-intensive, and conversely for each group's imports.

Columns 10 to 12 of Table 1 show that Group A has been growing in aggregate at two or three times the pace of the Group B economies. Moreover, the industrial output of Korea and Taiwan in particular has been growing at three to five times the Group B pace in recent years. Their much more rapid growth, together with that of Japan, would lead one to expect Group B's comparative advantage in NRB goods and its comparative disadvantage in manufactures, especially those which are labor-intensive, to be strengthening.

In summary, the crude proxies for relative factor endowments and NRB goods demands and the data on comparative growth rates presented above, in conjunction with the theory of the previous section, provide the following two sets of expectations concerning changing comparative advantage for the total trade of Group A and Group B countries and for bilateral trade between Group A and Group B countries, each of which is strongly supported empirically.

In considering the total trade of Groups A and B, the share of NRB goods in Group B's exports should be high and not declining as rapidly as the NRB goods share in the exports of Group A. Group A's exports of manufactures should have a large, but soon declining, proportion of labor-intensive goods, while Group B's exports of labor-intensive manufactures, as a share of all manufactured exports, should be very small and declining.[13]

Evidence bearing on this set of expectations is presented in Table 3 which shows that the shares of NRB goods (defined as SITC sections 0 to 4) plus item 51365 (alumina) and division 68 (nonferrous metals)

---

[12] The use of this proxy assumes not only that countries do not differ in their per capita contributions of labor time but also that the NRB sectors produce the same value-added per worker as the rest of their economies, or at least that the bias introduced by any difference in sectoral value-added per worker is uniform across countries.

[13] The empirical discussion will concentrate more on exports than imports or exports net of imports, because imports are typically distorted much more severely by trade policies than are exports.

in total exports for Group A countries and Japan have declined dramatically since the early 1960s.[14] By contrast, the NRB shares for Group B countries and the United States have declined much more slowly and are still at relatively high levels for developed countries, particularly in the case of Australia.

Secondly, Table 3 shows that the shares of labor-intensive manufactures such as textiles, clothing and footwear are very high in the low-wage Group A countries of Korea and Taiwan, are lower and declining in the higher wage countries of Hong Kong and Singapore, as well as Japan, but are extremely low and declining in the Group B countries of Australia, Canada and the United States. The only reason New Zealand's share of exports of these goods is rising is that it has been given highly favorable access to the Australian market via import quotas.

Regarding bilateral trade between Groups A and B, Group A's exports to Group B should be more heavily dominated by labor-intensive manufactures than its exports to the world as a whole, while its imports from Group B should be growing rapidly and be relatively strongly concentrated in NRB goods. The shares of agricultural goods in both total and NRB imports by Group A from Group B should be declining gradually as mineral and metal imports for capital-intensive industries expand. Group B's share of NRB goods in its exports to Group A countries should be growing rapidly and be greater than the NRB goods share of its exports to the world as a whole, except perhaps for exports to the city-states where only the food component of the NRB goods share should be comparatively high. The shares of NRB goods in Group B's imports from Group A should be small and declining, their shares of labor-intensive manufactures from Group A should be high but declining, and their shares of other manufactures should be rising.

Table 4 shows that Group A's exports to Group B in 1976 were more heavily dominated by labor-intensive manufactures than its exports to the world as a whole, while its imports from Group B were strongly concentrated in NRB goods both absolutely and relative to its imports from all countries. Similarly, Table 5 shows that Group

---

[14] The declining shares for Singapore are more obvious if petroleum refining is considered a manufacturing activity, as the numbers in parentheses in Table 3 indicate. The sawing of timber and the processing of crude rubber (the raw materials for which are imported from nearby Malaysia and Indonesia) make up the bulk of the remaining share of Singapore's NRB exports.

Table 3. Shares of NRB and Certain Labor-Intensive Manufactured Goods in Total Exports, Selected Pacific Rim Countries, 1964 to 1977[a]

		(in percent)			
		1964-66	1969-71	1974-76	1977
Resource-Poor ADCs (Group A)					
Korea	– Agricultural Goods	28	9	5	4
	– Other NRB Goods	15	12	11	11
	– Textiles, Clothing, Footwear	33	33	40	36
Taiwan	– Agricultural Goods	52	20	14	13
	– Other NRB Goods	9	5	6	3
	– Textiles, Clothing, Footwear	14	30	34	31
Hong Kong	– Agricultural Goods	7	4	3	3
	– Other NRB Goods	0	0	0	0
	– Textiles, Clothing, Footwear	12	10	10	7
Singapore[b]	– Agricultural Goods	42	39	9	10
	– Other NRB Goods	28(8)	32(8)	48(17)	46(16)
	– Textiles, Clothing, Footwear	6	6	5	5
Resource-Rich DCs (Group B)					
Australia	– Agricultural Goods	77	34	45	45
	– Other NRB Goods	8	46	38	39
	– Textiles, Clothing, Footwear	0.8	0.8	0.4	0.4
Canada	– Agricultural Goods	23	11	12	10
	– Other NRB Goods	39	36	41	39
	– Textiles, Clothing, Footwear	0.9	1.0	0.8	0.4
New Zealand	– Agricultural Goods	95	77	75	67
	– Other NRB Goods	0	13	8	.14
	– Textiles, Clothing, Footwear	0.0	1.2	2.0	2.9
Other DCs					
United States	– Agricultural Goods	24	17	22	21
	– Other NRB Goods	9	11	9	9
	– Textiles, Clothing, Footwear	3	2	2	2

Table 3.   (Continued)

		1964-66	1969-77	1974-76	1977
Japan	– Agricultural Goods	5	2	1	0
	– Other NRB Goods	5	6	5	4
	– Textiles, Clothing, Footwear	14	9	5	4

Other West Pacific LDCs

		1964-66	1969-77	1974-76	1977
Indonesia	– Agricultural Goods	(98)	40	13	17
	– Other NRB Goods		59	86	81
	– Textiles, Clothing, Footwear	0	0	0	0
Malaysia	– Agricultural Goods	50	46	44	42
	Other NRB Goods	44	47	41	38
	– Textiles, Clothing, Footwear	1	1	2	2
Philippines	– Agricultural Goods	60	44	59	52
	– Other NRB Goods	34	49	26	23
	– Textiles, Clothing, Footwear	3	1	3	5
Thailand	– Agricultural Goods	82	69	65	63
	– Other NRB Goods	16	25	16	17
	– Textiles, Clothing, Footwear	1	2	7	8
PNG	– Agricultural Goods	95	69	28	57
	– Other NRB Goods	0	17	63	43
	– Textiles, Clothing, Footwear	0	0	0	0

Sources: United Nations, *Yearbook of International Trade Statistics,* various issues; Statistical Department, Inspectorate General of Customs, *Trade of China (Taiwan District),* various issues; Food and Agricultural Organization, *Trade Yearbook,* various issues.

Notes: [a] Natural resource-based (NRB) goods are defined as SITC sections 0 to 4 plus item 51365 (alumina) and division 68 (nonferrous metals); the agricultural goods component is food and agricultural products as categorized by FAO. Textiles, clothing and footwear include SITC items 65, 841 and 851.

[b] Figures in parentheses for Singapore are the shares when refined petroleum is included in manufacturing rather than resource-based commodities.

Table 4.   *Japan's and Asian ADCs' Exports to (Imports from) Group B Countries and the World, by Commodity Category, 1976[a]*

(in percent)

Commodity Category	Korea Group B	Korea World	Hong Kong Group B	Hong Kong World	Singapore Group B	Singapore World	Japan Group B	Japan World
Agriculture[b]	1.4	4.7	2.0	1.0	11.9	20.8	1.3	1.6
	(49.7)	(15.6)	(44.7)	(22.6)	(44.2)	(16.8)	(33.8)	(18.2)
Forestry[c]	0.0	0.5	0.0	0.2	1.4	1.9	0.1	0.1
	(2.5)	(6.2)	(0.1)	(0.4)	(0.1)	(1.2)	(5.5)	(6.2)
Fishery[d]	0.7	4.1	1.1	1.1	0.6	0.6	1.4	0.9
	(1.5)	(0.2)	(2.7)	(2.0)	(1.0)	(0.6)	(1.9)	(2.7)
Petroleum[e]	1.9	1.7	0.0	0.0	51.4	29.7	0.1	0.1
	(0.0)	(18.8)	(2.2)	(6.0)	(5.1)	(27.3)	(0.7)	(36.3)
Other Fuel Minerals[f]	0.0	0.2	0.0	0.0	0.0	0.2	0.0	0.1
	(15.8)	(1.0)	(0.1)	(0.2)	(0.0)	(0.0)	(25.7)	(7.8)
Nonfuel Minerals & Nonferrous Metals[g]	0.0	1.1	0.1	0.6	0.0	1.4	3.4	1.1
	(16.8)	(5.1)	(12.3)	(2.0)	(6.3)	(1.3)	(27.1)	(10.3)
Total NRB Goods	4.0	12.3	3.2	2.9	65.3	54.6	6.3	3.9
	(86.3)	(46.9)	(62.1)	(33.2)	(56.7)	(47.2)	(94.7)	(81.5)
Manufactures, Group 1[h]	47.2	32.6	54.3	52.0	2.5	4.2	3.4	1.8
	(0.0)	(0.6)	(0.7)	(6.4)	(0.8)	(2.8)	(0.0)	(1.7)
Manufactures, Group 2[h]	26.9	23.9	17.1	13.9	8.7	9.5	9.6	18.8
	(1.0)	(11.4)	(3.5)	(16.1)	(2.8)	(9.8)	(1.5)	(3.6)
Manufactures, Group 3[h]	16.9	18.9	21.8	27.6	20.3	24.1	61.9	52.0
	(4.6)	(24.2)	(10.5)	(26.3)	(16.2)	(27.6)	(0.5)	(6.0)
Manufactures, Group 4[h]	5.0	11.8	3.5	3.4	3.1	7.4	18.6	23.2
	(8.1)	(16.1)	(22.5)	(17.4)	(23.4)	(12.3)	(3.4)	(6.8)
Total Manufactures	96.0	87.2	96.7	96.9	34.6	45.2	92.6	95.8
	(13.7)	(52.3)	(37.2)	(66.2)	(43.2)	(52.5)	(5.4)	(18.1)
All Goods	100.0	100.0	100.0	100.0	100.0	100.0	100.0	100.0
	(100.0)	(100.0)	(100.0)	(100.0)	(100.0)	(100.0)	(100.0)	(100.0)
[Value, $US Million]	[472]	[7,691]	[620]	[6,637]	[384]	[6,522]	[4,487]	[66,471]
	[(344)]	[(8,821)]	[(284)]	[(8,896)]	[(297)]	[(6,084)]	[(8,490)]	[(64,222)]
Share of Country's Total Trade	6.1	100.0	9.3	100.0	5.8	100.0	6.8	100.0
	(3.9)	(100.0)	(3.2)	(100.0)	(3.3)	(100.0)	(13.2)	(100.0)

Source: United Nations, *Yearbook of International Trade Statistics,* 1977.

Notes: [a] Group B countries are Australia, Canada and New Zealand. The export shares are actually based on Group B's import data rather than each country's export data. Import shares are shown in parentheses. Data for Taiwan were not available. Percentage shares may not add to 100 because of rounding.

[b] SITC 001 to 431 n.c.c.

[c] SITC 241 to 251

[d] SITC 031, 032

[e] SITC 331, 332

[f] SITC 321, 341, 351

[g] SITC 271, 273, 274, 275, 276, 281, 283, 285, 286, 681 to 689; 513. 65 including in Manufactures Group 4.

[h] SITC 5 to 8 have been categorized by Garnaut and Anderson (1980, Appendix) into four groups, Group 1 consisting of the most labor-intensive manufactures through to Group 4 consisting of the most capital-intensive items.

Table 5. *Australia, Canada, New Zealand and United States Exports to (Imports from) Group A Countries (excluding Taiwan) and the World, by Commodity Category, 1976[a]*

(in percent)

Commodity Category	Australia Group A	World	Canada Group A	World	New Zealand Group A	World	United States Group A	World
Agriculture[b]	50.9	47.0	23.6	11.7	64.3	71.0	30.4	21.8
	(1.5)	(5.9)	(7.8)	(8.9)	(2.7)	(7.3)	(1.8)	(10.1)
Forestry[c]	0.1	0.1	0.4	10.5	8.4	3.8	2.7	2.3
	(0.6)	(2.2)	(0.2)	(0.8)	(0.1)	(0.4)	(0.0)	(2.2)
Fishery[d]	1.1	1.0	3.1	1.6	2.6	1.3	0.3	0.3
	(0.7)	(1.0)	(1.2)	(0.5)	(0.2)	(0.3)	(1.3)	(1.6)
Petroleum[e]	3.4	1.8	0.0	6.7	0.0	1.2	0.4	0.9
	(23.9)	(9.7)	(0.0)	(9.4)	(27.8)	(14.8)	(1.5)	(26.6)
Other Fuel Minerals[f]	6.3	10.9	7.3	6.8	0.3	0.0	0.5	2.9
	(0.0)	(0.0)	(0.0)	(1.6)	(0.0)	(0.0)	(0.0)	(1.8)
Nonfuel Minerals & Nonferrous Metals[g]	11.1	20.1	18.1	13.8	5.7	3.9	4.2	3.0
	(0.1)	(1.6)	(0.0)	(2.9)	(0.0)	(4.7)	(0.2)	(5.2)
Total NRB Goods	72.9	80.9	52.5	51.1	81.3	81.2	38.5	31.2
	(26.8)	(20.4)	(9.2)	(24.1)	(30.8)	(27.5)	(4.8)	(47.5)
Manufactures, Group 1[h]	0.6	0.2	0.1	0.3	0.4	1.0	0.9	1.2
	(29.7)	(6.5)	(25.4)	(3.6)	(21.0)	(2.9)	(41.6)	(5.5)
Manufactures, Group 2[h]	2.0	1.7	2.8	2.2	3.7	4.1	4.9	5.2
	(23.4)	(9.1)	(10.9)	(6.3)	(23.9)	(13.3)	(13.9)	(4.2)
Manufactures, Group 3[h]	8.6	5.2	17.6	28.8	4.4	6.2	38.9	39.0
	(16.5)	(43.1)	(22.4)	(50.1)	(23.2)	(33.5)	(32.6)	(27.4)
Manufactures, Group 4[h]	15.5	11.9	26.8	16.7	10.3	7.4	16.1	22.3
	(3.5)	(20.2)	(5.1)	(15.4)	(1.1)	(21.9)	(6.8)	(14.2)
Total Manufactures	26.7	19.0	47.3	48.0	18.8	18.7	60.8	67.7
	(73.1)	(78.9)	(90.8)	(75.4)	(69.2)	(71.6)	(94.9)	(51.3)
All Goods	100.0	100.0	100.0	100.0	100.0	100.0	100.0	100.0
	(100.0)	(100.0)	(100.0)	(100.0)	(100.0)	(100.0)	(100.0)	(100.0)
[Value, $US Millions]	[627]	[12,629]	[201]	[38,010]	[96]	[2,797]	[4,271]	[112,209]
	[(672)]	[(10,946)]	[(639)]	[(37,269)]	[(164)]	[(3,754)]	[(5,287)]	[(119,257)]
Share of Country's Total Trade	4.9	100.0	.5	100.0	3.4	100.0	3.8	100.0
	(6.1)	(100.0)	(1.7)	(100.0)	(5.0)	(100.0)	(4.4)	(100.0)

Source: United Nations, *Yearbook of International Trade Statistics,* 1977.

Notes: [a] Group A countries included are Korea, Hong Kong and Singapore; Taiwanese data were not available. The export shares are based on Group A's import data rather than each country's export data. Import shares are shown in parentheses. Percentage shares may not add to 100 because of rounding.

[b] to [h] See notes on Table 4.

B's exports to Group A in 1976 had a strong concentration of NRB goods. However, their exports to the world as a whole were equally strongly concentrated, more so in Australia's case; this is because in the absence of Taiwanese data Singapore and Hong Kong dominate in the table, and they are only minor minerals and metals importers. As expected, agricultural exports are relatively more important for Australia than for North America, forest products exports are more important for Canada and New Zealand, and mineral and metal exports are more important for Australia and Canada.

To see how the mix of one Group B country's exports to and imports from Group A have changed over time, consider Tables 6 and 7 which refer to Australia. Table 6 shows that NRB goods have accounted for a consistently greater share of Australian exports to Korea, Taiwan and Japan than to the world as a whole; typically more than 90 percent compared with less than 80 percent. As expected, industrial raw materials account for a much smaller proportion of the exports to the city-states of Hong Kong and Singapore. Also as expected, the shares of foodstuffs in exports to group A countries (except Hong Kong) are declining faster over time than the share of these goods in Australia's total exports. The shares due to wool, hides and skins have also declined over the period shown in the table, both absolutely and relative to their shares in Australia's exports to all countries.

Table 7 details the commodity composition of Australia's imports from these five resource-poor countries. It is evident that the ADCs are rapidly increasing their shares of Australian imports, albeit from a small base. The data confirm that the relatively small shares of NRB imports from these countries have been declining slightly (less than 10 percent of Australia's total imports from them, compared with 20 percent of Australia's imports from all countries). The very high import shares of labor-intensive manufactures such as textiles, clothing and footwear have also been declining over time as these countries develop, with the share of these goods from Japan now being less than the share of these goods from the world as a whole. Finally, and again as expected, the shares of other manufactured goods in these countries' imports into Australia are rising rapidly. Indeed, the share has already exceeded 50 percent even for Korea, the lowest-income country in this group.

The share of Australia's total exports going to Group A countries and Japan has, to date, been much greater than the shares of Canada's

Table 6. Shares of NRB Goods in Australian Total Exports and Exports to Asian Countries, 1966/7 to 1978/9

	1966-67 to 1968-69	1974-75	1975-76	1976-77	1977-78	(in percent) 1978-79
Total Exports						
Foodstuffs, Oils, Fats (SITC 0, 1, 4)	34	35	33	31	31	30
Wool, Hides, Skins (SITC 21, 26)	27	10	10	15	12	13
Nonfuel Minerals (SITC 27, 28)	8	14	15	14	14	18
Coal (SITC 32)	3	8	11	11	12	11
Nonferrous Metals (SITC 68)	5	6	5	5	5	6
Total NRB Goods (SITC 0-4, 68)	79	75	76	79	77	81
(Value of Exports, A$m)	(3,148)	(8,726)	(9,640)	(11,646)	(12,245)	(14,247)
Exports to Korea						
Foodstuffs, Oils, Fats	5	58	37	27	35	34
Wool, Hides, Skins	84	14	27	29	23	21
Nonfuel Minerals	2	9	10	15	14	14
Coal	—	12	18	21	19	16
Nonferrous Metals	3	0.2	0.5	2	1	4
Total NRB Goods	94	93	93	94	91	90
(Value of Exports, A$m)	(10)	(123)	(120)	(189)	(266)	(449)
(% of Aust. Exports)	(0.3)	(1.4)	(1.2)	(1.6)	(2.2)	(3.2)
Exports to Taiwan						
Foodstuffs, Oil, Fats	25	59	56	39	31	29
Wool, Hides, Skins	36	13	19	23	16	19
Nonfuel Minerals	2	3	4	6	14	12
Coal	4	5	2	5	18	17
Nonferrous Metals	7	7	9	15	14	9
Total NRB Goods	74	87	90	88	90	86
(Value of Exports, A$m)	(22)	(81)	(114)	(134)	(182)	(299)
(% of Aust. Exports)	(0.7)	(0.9)	(1.2)	(1.2)	(1.5)	(2.1)

Table 6.   (Continued)

	1966-67 to 1968-69	1974-75	1975-76	1976-77	1977-78	1978-79
Exports to Hong Kong						
Foodstuffs, Oils, Fats	22	25	27	29	29 .	25
Wool, Hides, Skins	13	7	8	8	7	4
Nonfuel Minerals	0.2	0.6	0.4	0.5	0.2	0.3
Coal	0.1	—	—	—	—	—
Nonferrous Metals	5	6	5	5	5	5
Total NRB Goods	41	39	41	46	41	35
(Value of Exports, A$m)	(65)	(105)	(147)	(189)	(215)	(321)
(% of Aust. Exports)	(2.1)	(1.2)	(1.5)	(1.6)	(1.8)	(2.3)
Exports to Singapore						
Foodstuffs, Oils, Fats	49	34	35	42	33	33
Wool, Hides, Skins	0.8	0.2	0.7	0.5	0.1	—
Nonfuel Minerals	0.3	1	1	1	0.4	2
Coal	—	—	—	—	—	—
Nonferrous Metals	1	3	3	4	3	6
Total NRB Goods	61	43	48	54	48	47
(Value of Exports, A$m)	(59)	(206)	(185)	(184)	(238)	(264)
(% of Aust. Exports)	(1.9)	(2.4)	(1.9)	(1.6)	(1.9)	(1.9)
Exports to Japan						
Foodstuffs, Oils, Fats	17	23	24	24	22	24
Wool, Hides, Skins	38	10	12	12	10	12
Nonfuel Minerals	21	32	27	26	27	26
Coal	13	23	28	27	28	26
Nonferrous Metals	3	3	2	2	2	2
Total NRB Goods	92	91	92	91	89	97
(Value of Exports, A$m)	(704)	(2,456)	(3,192)	(3,956)	(3,877)	(4,111)
(% of Aust. Exports)	(22.4)	(28.1)	(33.1)	(34.0)	(31.7)	(28.9)

Source: Australian Bureau of Statistics, *Australian Exports, Country by Commodity* various issues.

Table 7. Shares of NRB and Manufactured Goods in Australian Total Imports and Imports from Asian Countries 1966/7 to 1978/9

(in percent)

	1966-67 to 1968-69	1974-75	1975-76	1976-77	1977-78	1978-79
Total Imports						
NRB Goods	20	20	20	20	21	18
Textiles, Clothing, Footwear	9	8	10	9	9	9
Other Manufactured Goods	70	70	70	65	69	73
(Value of Imports, A$m)	(3,259)	(8,080)	(8,241)	(10,411)	(11,167)	(13,752)
Imports from Korea						
NRB Goods	19	10	11	11	7	5
Textiles, Clothing, Footwear	44	46	47	39	41	41
Other Manufactured Goods	31	44	41	49	52	54
(Value of Imports, A$m)	(2)	(48)	(71)	(96)	(120)	(136)
(% of Aust. Imports)	(0.1)	(0.6)	(0.9)	(0.9)	(1.1)	(1.0)
Imports from Taiwan						
NRB Goods	8	7	5	4	5	4
Textiles, Clothing, Footwear	59	45	38	40	42	43
Other Manufactured Goods	32	48	57	55	53	53
(Value of Imports, A$m)	(8)	(113)	(134)	(213)	(247)	(338)
(% of Aust. Imports)	(0.2)	(1.4)	(1.6)	(2.0)	(2.2)	(2.5)
Imports from Hong Kong						
NRB Goods	4	1	2	2	2	2
Textiles, Clothing, Footwear	56	59	59	51	47	45
Other Manufactured Goods	40	40	39	47	50	53
(Value of Imports, A$m)	(37)	(172)	(217)	(254)	(265)	(332)
(% of Aust. Imports)	(1.1)	(2.1)	(2.6)	(2.4)	(2.4)	(2.4)
Imports from Singapore[a]						
NRB Goods	92[39]	79[5]	78[5]	77[6]	72[5]	68[8]
Textiles, Clothing, Footwear	0.1	5	5	4	4	4
Other Manufactured Goods	7[56]	15[89]	18[90]	19[90]	25[9]	28[88]
(Value of Imports, A$m)	(10)	(127)	(160)	(196)	(265)	(278)
(% of Aust. Imports)	(0.3)	(1.6)	(1.9)	(1.9)	(2.4)	(2.0)
Imports from Japan						
NRB Goods	12	4	3	3	3	2
Textiles, Clothing, Footwear	22	8	9	7	7	7
Other Manufactures Goods	66	88	88	90	90	91
(Value of Imports, A$m)	(351)	(1,418)	(1,610)	(2,150)	(2,112)	(2,426)
(% of Aust. Imports)	(10.8)	(17.5)	(19.5)	(20.7)	(18.9)	(17.6)

Source: Australian Bureau of Statistics, *Australian Imports, Country by Commodity,* various issues.
Note: [a] Figures in square parentheses are the shares when refined petroleum is included in manufacturing rather than resource-based commodities.

or New Zealand's exports going to these countries. While New Zealand is rapidly increasing the share of its export trade with Group A, as it adjusts to the reality of poor growth prospects in its traditional European markets, the continued small share of Canada's exports to Group A reflects the high transport cost resistances to trade across the Pacific as compared to trade with the United States and Europe. For the reverse direction of trade, the share of Group A exports going to Australia has increased much more markedly than those to the other developed countries. More detailed data (not presented in the Tables) reveal that the increased intensity in trade between Australia and Group A is, in both directions, due principally to a reduction in resistances to trade flows between the trade partners, rather than to a closer matching of their commodity compositions of exports and imports.

Overall, the data in Tables 3 to 7 provide strong empirical support for the theory outlines in Section II, given the relative factor endowments, comparative growth rates and trade resistances in the region. This prompts an attempt in the final section to discuss the likely future developments in the economic relationships between Group A and Group B countries and the policy responses necessary to facilitate those developments. But before doing so, the important issue of changing comparative advantage in and location of minerals processing needs to be considered in some detail.

IV. Changing Comparative Advantage in Minerals Processing

1. Theory and Empirical Evidence

Like mining, the processing of minerals is highly capital-intensive (Vanek, 1963; Smith, 1978b; Roemer, 1979), but capital associated with this activity is mobile within essentially the same group of large companies as is mining capital. Thus, although relative capital abundance influences to some extent the optimal location of processing facilities, it tends to be less important than other factors, particularly transport costs, energy availability, pollution control costs, size of market to which processing facilities have access, the long-term, large-scale nature of mining operations and comparative political stability. Because of the highly capital-intensive nature of the processing activity, availability of low-wage labor is not a crucially important factor.

Given the high share of mineral raw materials costs in the value of most metals, and the relatively high cost of transporting minerals compared with metals, there are significant advantages, other things being equal, in locating processing facilities close to the source of the raw materials. However, where more than one major raw material input is involved, as with steel, and where the sources of the materials are geographically separate, the transport cost advantage of locating processing facilities near one of the sources rather than in a third location may be only slight.

Minerals processing is, characteristically, intensive in the use of energy inputs. While oil provided a cheap, readily available source of energy which could be transported internationally across long distances at relatively low cost, the relative abundance of indigenous energy resources was not a major factor in determining the optimal location of processing facilities. However, the alternative, and now relatively cheaper, energy raw materials, principally coal, are more expensive to transport internationally. To some extent the difference in transport costs is presently exaggerated by the fact that trade in steaming coal is not fully developed, so that port facilities and vessel sizes do not permit the full exploitation of economies of scale. Nevertheless, it remains true that transport costs per unit of energy will be greater for coal, or for liquefied natural gas, than for oil, and that there has been a permanent shift in comparative advantage in energy-intensive production processes in favor of those countries with relatively abundant, indigenous, non-oil energy resources.

Both because of the need to dispose of large volumes of waste materials in the process of refining basic minerals, and because the heavy consumption of fuels required to provide energy inputs generates substantial waste gas emissions, minerals processing activities are highly pollution-intensive. A movement towards coal as the primary energy source exacerbates the problems because of the need to dispose of large quantities of ash. The adverse effect of pollution control costs on competitiveness in metals production may be expected to increase with population density, the density of industrial activity, and per capita income.[15]

---

[15] For a detailed discussion of the effects of pollution control costs on the location of minerals processing in the Asian/Pacific region, see Smith and Ulph (1979).

Economies of scale are important in the production of basic metals, so that size of market is a significant factor in determining optimal location. Since transport cost resistances are relatively small for trade in metals, under free trade conditions market size would not provide a major constraint. However, effective rates of protection for processing activities tend to be high in most industrial countries, so that export market access is often difficult to obtain.

Some important implications follow from the fact that there are three peculiar characteristics of the major minerals and metals markets: profitability of investments in mining and processing depends on prices expected to prevail over a long period of time; the investments in both areas need to be very large to capture economies of scale; and processing facilities tend to be tied by technological considerations to particular sources of supply. These characteristics mean that overall investment risks can be reduced by common ownership of the extraction and processing stages or by long-term contracts between arm's length buyers and sellers (Caves, 1971, 1978; Smith and Drysdale, 1979; Stuckey, 1979). They have also led to a high degree of concentration of the mining/processing industry. The technological and organizational capacities of the large companies involved provide them with a substantial advantage in undertaking new mining projects, even where the vertical integration motive is not present. Any new entrant to the processing industry would face significant additional costs and uncertainties in finding and developing its own sources of raw materials, and would need to rely for security of supply on long-term contract arrangements. While these may be negotiated relatively easily with existing mines, taking up marginal tonnages while the new processor has only a low level of demand, problems may be encountered as demand increases but remains too small to underwrite the development of efficient large-scale new mining operations.

None of the above suggests that relatively small, densely populated, resource-poor developing countries are likely to have a comparative advantage in minerals processing activities in general despite•the existence of low wages. Transport cost and energy cost factors create a permanent disadvantage, while relative capital scarcity and the small size of the domestic market are likely to be important constraints in the early stages of industrialization, and pollution control costs and problems of securing adequate supplies of mineral raw materials are likely to become more severe as industrialization proceeds.

How does this a priori reasoning compare with actual metals production and trade in Pacific rim countries, particularly between Australia, Japan, Korea and Taiwan? Japan has traditionally imported minerals in raw or lightly processed forms, with Australia being the major supplier, and has produced metals to meet virtually all its domestic needs as well as for export (Drysdale, 1970). The large-scale trade in mineral raw materials between Australia and Japan has been developed under arm's length, long-term contracts (Smith 1978b, 1978c; Kojima, 1978). More recently, Japan's industrial development has swung away from physical capital-intensive, heavy processing industries towards skill-intensive, high-technology industries. At the same time, the rapid increase in the price of oil has stimulated interest in alternative energy resources. Thus, the focus of Australia-Japan trade is shifting away from mineral raw materials towards energy goods such as steaming coal, uranium and liquefied natural gas and, though much more cautiously, towards more highly processed mineral products. As is clear from Tables 8 and 9, however, Australia's mineral exports to Japan remain heavily dominated by mineral raw materials.[16] The focus on un-processed minerals in Japan's imports from Australia is only marginally greater than in Japan's imports from the rest of the world (Table 9), but Australia's exports to Japan and, to a lesser extent, to Korea and Taiwan, are substantially more heavily dominated by unprocessed minerals than are its exports to the rest of the world (Table 8).

For Hong Kong and Singapore, the extent of comparative dis-advantage in minerals processing and heavy industry generally is such that their imports of minerals are at a relatively high level of processing or fabrication, while their import demand for energy goods is limited by the absence of energy-intensive processing activities. This is borne out clearly by the data presented in Table 9, which also show that Japan is the dominant supplier of processed minerals to these countries.

The rapid growth in government-stimulated metals production in Korea and Taiwan in recent years might suggest that these countries

---

[16] It should be noted that the large trade in black coal between Australia and Japan shown in Tables 8 and 9 is predominantly of coking coal for use in steel making. While there are substantial prospects for rapid expansion of the steaming coal trade, this is at present still relatively small.

Table 8. Australia's Minerals and Metals Exports to Northeast Asia and Elswhere, 1978-1979[a]
(\$A million and percent of total minerals and metals listed for each country)

SITC Item	Japan		Korea		Taiwan		Hong Kong		Singapore		Rest of World	
	Value	(%)	Value	(%)	Value	(%)	Value	(%)	Value	(%)	Value	(%)
Ores and Concentrates												
Black Coal (322.2)	1082	(54)	73	(44)	24	(29)	—	—	—	—	339	(21)
Iron Ore (281.5, .6)	701	(35)	33	(20)	25	(29)	—	—	—	—	208	(13)
Lead (287.4)	3	(0)	—	—	—	—	—	—	—	—	32	(2)
Zinc (287.5)	31	(2)	5	(3)	—	—	—	—	—	—	21	(1)
Sub-Total	1924	(95)	115	(69)	49	(58)	—	—	—	—	614	(38)
Lightly Processed Metals												
Basic Iron and Steel (671,672)	29	(1)	33	(20)	9	(11)	26	(54)	2	(8)	175	(11)
Copper, unwrought (682.1)	6	(0)	9	(5)	—	—	—	—	—	—	88	(6)
Aluminium, unwrought (684.1)	48	(2)	2	(1)	—	—	2	(4)	1	(4)	29	(2)
Lead, unwrought (685.1)	7	(0)	—	—	5	(6)	—	—	2	(8)	246	(15)
Zinc, unwrought (686.1)	—	—	1	(0)	18	(21)	9	(19)	3	(12)	80	(5)
Tin, unwrought (687.1)	—	—	—	—	—	—	—	—	—	—	16	(1)
Sub-Total	90	(4)	45	(27)	32	(38)	37	(77)	8	(30)	634	(40)
Highly Processed Metals												
Other Iron and Steel (673-679)	1	(0)	1	(0)	4	(5)	8	(17)	13	(50)	280	(18)
Copper, wrought (682.2)	1	(0)	5	(3)	—	—	2	(4)	4	(15)	40	(3)
Aluminium, wrought (684.2)	—	—	1	(0)	—	—	1	(2)	1	(4)	14	(1)
Lead, wrought (685.2)	—	—	—	—	—	—	—	—	—	—	2	(0)
Zinc, wrought (686.2)	—	—	—	—	—	—	—	—	—	—	9	(1)
Tin, wrought (687.2)	—	—	—	—	—	—	—	—	—	—	2	(0)
Sub-Total	2	(0)	7	(4)	4	(5)	11	(23)	18	(69)	347	(22)
Total	2016	(100)	167	(100)	85	(100)	48	(100)	26	(100)	1595	(100)

Source: Australian Exports, 1978-79 (Preliminary), Canberra, 1980.
Notes: [a] A number of mineral and metal items are not shown due to unavailability of country breakdown of exports.

Table 9. *East Asian Imports of Minerals and Metals from Australia, Japan and Elsewhere, 1977.*

(*$US millions and percent of mineral and metal imports listed for each country*)

SITC Item	Japan Australia Value (%)	Japan R.O.W. Value (%)	Korea Australia Value (%)	Korea Japan Value (%)	Korea R.O.W. Value (%)	Hong Kong Australia Value (%)	Hong Kong Japan Value (%)	Hong Kong R.O.W. Value (%)	Singapore Australia Value (%)	Singapore Japan Value (%)	Singapore R.O.W. Value (%)
Ores and Concentrates											
Black coal (322.2)	1382 (42)	2091 (13)	51 (54)	2 (0)	54 (11)	—	—	—	—	—	—
LPG (341.3)	170 (5)	1627 (10)	—	—	—	—	—	—	—	—	—
Iron Ore (281.5, .6)	1152 (35)	1402 (19)	28 (29)	—	22 (4)	—	—	—	—	—	—
Copper (287.1)	39 (1)	8798 (54)	—	1 (0)	35 (7)	—	—	—	—	—	—
Nickel (287.2)	96 (3)	179 (1)	—	—	—	—	—	—	—	—	—
Bauxite & Alumina (287.3)	171 (5)	44 (0)	—	6 (1)	6 (1)	—	—	—	—	—	—
Lead (287.4)	6 (0)	50 (0)	—	—	—	—	—	—	—	—	—
Zinc (287.5)	40 (1)	145 (1)	—	—	—	—	—	—	—	—	—
Tin (287.6)	—	—	—	—	4 (1)	—	—	—	—	—	1 (1)
Manganese (287.7)	34 (1)	108 (1)	3 (3)	—	4 (1)	—	—	—	—	—	9 (7)
Other Nonferrous (287.9)	25 (1)	273 (2)	1 (1)	—	3 (1)	—	—	—	—	—	3 (2)
Sub-Total	3115 (96)	14717 (91)	83 (87)	9 (1)	128 (26)	0 (0)	0 (0)	0 (0)	0 (0)	0 (0)	13 (10)
Lightly Processed Metals											
Basic Iron & Steel (671,672)	33 (1)	168 (1)	10 (10)	245 (35)	14 (3)	17 (55)	1 (0)	7 (5)	2 (9)	5 (2)	2 (1)
Copper, unwrought (682.1)	24 (1)	347 (2)	—	10 (1)	5 (1)	—	—	—	—	1 (0)	1 (1)
Nickel, unwrought (683.1)	16 (0)	35 (0)	1 (1)	—	2 (0)	1 (3)	3 (2)	4 (3)	—	1 (0)	—
Aluminium, unwrought (684.12)	62 (2)	460 (3)	—	43 (6)	26 (5)	—	—	24 (16)	1 (4)	—	3 (2)
Lead, unwrought (685.1)	4 (0)	19 (0)	—	4 (1)	4 (1)	—	—	1 (1)	2 (9)	2 (1)	8 (6)
Zinc, unwrought (686.1)	—	19 (0)	1 (1)	8 (1)	2 (0)	6 (19)	—	6 (4)	1 (4)	—	6 (4)
Tin, unwrought (687.1)	—	294 (2)	—	1 (0)	10 (2)	—	—	9 (6)	—	—	—
Sub-Total	139 (4)	1342 (8)	12 (13)	311 (45)	63 (13)	24 (77)	4 (2)	55 (37)	6 (26)	8 (3)	23 (17)
Highly Processed Metals											
Other Iron & Steel (673-679)	—	87 (1)	—	324 (47)	300 (60)	6 (19)	191 (77)	72 (49)	13 (57)	276 (95)	66 (49)
Copper, wrought (682.2)	—	9 (0)	—	22 (3)	2 (0)	1 (3)	42 (17)	8 (5)	3 (13)	18 (6)	11 (8)
Nickel, wrought (683.2)	—	18 (0)	—	2 (0)	—	—	—	1 (1)	—	—	2 (1)
Aluminium, wrought (684.2)	—	40 (0)	—	21 (3)	6 (1)	—	10 (4)	9 (6)	1 (4)	9 (3)	17 (13)
Lead, wrought (685.2)	—	—	—	1 (0)	1 (0)	—	—	—	—	—	1 (1)
Zinc, wrought (686.2)	—	—	—	—	—	—	1 (0)	1 (1)	—	—	—
Tin, wrought (687.2)	—	—	—	1 (0)	1 (0)	—	—	1 (1)	—	—	2 (1)
Sub-Total	0 (0)	154 (1)	0 (0)	371 (54)	310 (62)	7 (23)	244 (98)	92 (63)	17 (74)	303 (97)	99 (73)
Total	3254 (100)	16213 (100)	95 (100)	691 (100)	501 (100)	31 (100)	248 (100)	147 (100)	23 (100)	311 (100)	135 (100)

Source: United Nations, *Commodity Trade Statistics*, Series D, New York, 1977.

intend following the Japanese route. Already they are significant exporters of iron and steel products, produced principally from Australian iron ore and coking coal. As of 1977, however, they were still heavily dependent on imports for most nonferrous metals with these coming predominantly from Japan (Table 9). Korea, for example, relied on imports to meet around one third of its requirements of copper and zinc, 60 percent of its requirements of lead, and 83 percent of its requirements of aluminum in 1976. A presently important question in the development strategies of Korea and Taiwan is whether they should seek to achieve effective self-sufficiency in metals production, or whether they should largely bypass this area of industrialization and focus on securing import supplies of metals for their growing fabricating and user industries.

2. The Relevance of Japan's Experience for Korea and Taiwan

The situation of Japan is important for two major reasons in considering the appropriate strategies for securing supplies of basic metals by Korea and Taiwan. First, Japan's apparent success in pursuing a development path involving a heavy emphasis on domestic metals production and the large-scale importing of mineral raw materials is likely to suggest that similarly endowed developing countries should follow the same route. Second, a continuing high level of dependence of Japan as a source of imported metals, to be used in activities whose growth involves strong competition with older Japanese industries, is likely to be perceived as undesirable both for monopoly bargaining and supply security reasons. Under these circumstances, it is worthwhile to consider some aspects of the Japanese industries' initial position with regard to competitiveness and in what ways this has changed.

Japan's embarkation on large-scale processing took place before the dramatic shift in relative energy prices was envisaged and when there was little interest in, or concern about, pollution control problems. Recent developments have had a substantial adverse impact on Japanese processing activities, and this is compounded in the short- to medium-term by the fact that the existing capital stock and infrastructure cannot readily be adapted to meet changing circumstances.

Even without the recent adverse cost movements, it is doubtful whether Japan would have had other than a relatively short-lived comparative advantage in metals production. In the absence of any immediate potential for rapid expansion of nonferrous metals production elsewhere in the region, the Japanese industries developed under a certain amount of natural protection provided by distance from alternative sources of supply and by the high level of vertical integration characterizing much of Japanese industry. The competitive positions of the industries were enhanced by their ability to take advantage of most recent technology and to reap economies of scale (both in processing itself and in the securing of raw materials supplies) in catering for a rapidly growing and large domestic market, as well as by import restrictions on processed products. In general, Japanese nonferrous metals production has been little more than marginally competitive and aluminum smelting, in particular, has been submarginal. In the case of iron and steel, the competitiveness of the Japanese industry has depended on efficiency in securing supplies of relatively low-cost iron ore and coking coal and on the use of first-best technology in blending and production processes. The successful development of the Korean and Taiwanese steel industries has been based on the same factors, with the disadvantages of small scale in securing supplies of raw materials having largely been avoided to date by purchasing from sources principally developed to meet Japanese needs.

While Japan's already fragile competitive position in basic metals production has been seriously eroded by changing market forces, those same changes provide an impetus to the establishment of higher levels of processing in the resource-supplying country, Australia. Relatively abundant indigenous energy resources, generally lower pollution control costs and waste disposal problems, experience gained from the limited development of processing facilities to date and the demonstration of reasonable stability as a supplier of mineral products all add to the basic transport cost advantage of locating processing facilities close to the mine site, while that advantage has itself been increased by rapidly rising liquid fuel costs. New Zealand's competitive position as a producer of highly energy-intensive processed products has also improved, as a result of its relative abundance of low-cost hydro-resources and natural gas.[17]

---

[17] New Zealand already has significant aluminum exports based on Australian alumina supplies. Most of Hong Kong's aluminum imports from the "Rest of the World" in Table 9 come from New Zealand, while a significant proportion of Japan's supplies from the "Rest of the World" come from that country.

The broad thrust of the above arguments is that efficient production of metals in the Western Pacific region will involve a shift in the location of processing facilities away from Japan. Although the newly industrializing countries of Korea and Taiwan have a competitive advantage over Japan in that wages and pollution control costs are presently lower and that technologies appropriate to current relative prices can be adopted, the pollution control cost advantage in particular may be relatively short-lived, given the population densities of these countries and the prospect of continued rapid income growth. Also, Korea and Taiwan have a smaller domestic market than Japan had and, in any case, it is doubtful whether it would be sensible to follow the Japanese 'example' independently of the changes in economic conditions which have occurred since the 1960s. However, of substantially greater importance than any shift in competitive advantage between resource-poor developed and resource-poor developing countries is the large movement of comparative advantage in favor of the minerals- and energy-rich countries, particularly Australia.

Clearly, the circumstances are not precisely the same for all processing activities. At one extreme, aluminum smelting, with its very high energy requirements, is an activity in which Australia and, to a more limited absolute extent, New Zealand has an obvious and considerable competitive advantage over Japan, Korea and Taiwan. Standard technology steel-making may be considered to lie at the other extreme, but even there the comeptitiveness of the Japanese and, more recently, the Korean and Taiwanese industries may be relatively short-lived. In the longer term it is likely that the ·comparative advantage in large-scale, basic steel production will lie with resource-rich countries such as Australia and Brazil, rather than with resource-poor industrial countries. Increasingly, the steel industries of the latter group will focus on higher levels of processing and on the production of steels required for specific local uses.

In summary, while it can be expected that metals production in Korea and Taiwan will continue to expand as those economies grow, requiring efforts to be made to secure supplies of mineral raw materials, it seems sensible to argue that industrialization strategies should not be predicated upon self-sufficiency across the range of basic metals production. In most cases, it will be more rational to regard large-scale domestic processing as a secondary option, to be exercised in cases where it does not prove possible to obtain secure and adequate supplies of metals, at competitive prices, from overseas.

3. *Prospects for Expanded Minerals Processing in Australia*[18]

Development in the bilateral trade in mineral-based products between Australia and Group A countries will involve a substantially greater focus on the possibilities of processing in Australia than did the earlier development of the minerals trade with Japan, and the issues and appropriate trade and investment arrangements will be somewhat different.

In order for Korea and Taiwan to be able to remain substantially dependent on imports of processed mineral products, adequate guarantees of supply security will be required, while the development of large-scale, export-oriented processing facilities in Australia will require similar guarantees of long-term market access. Although these problems have been handled relatively satisfactorily in the historical trade in mineral raw materials by the negotiation of arm's length long-term contracts, reliance on such arrangements may be less acceptable for the trade in processed products. An important characteristic of the mineral raw materials trade is that technological and transport cost factors create substantial resistances to short-term switching of trade patterns (Smith and Drysdale, 1979), so that contractual arrangements are strengthened by these constraints. In the case of basic metals, however, the products involved are considerably more homogeneous, transport costs are relatively less important, and the possibility exists for competing production, possibly protected by import barriers, to commence in the purchasing country. For these reasons, security in the bilateral trade in processed minerals is more likely to require equity ties than has been the case in the mineral raw materials trade.

One possible model is provided by the establishment of a joint venture alumina refinery at Gladstone in Queensland, involving an Australian bauxite producer and a number of overseas consumers of alumina. Each participant's share of the output is equal to its equity share, and it is responsible for disposing of that output. Operating costs of the plant are borne in proportion to equity shares, while

---

[18] Since Canada's minerals exports go predominantly to the U.S. and Europe and New Zealand is not a major minerals exporter, this section focuses on Australia's trade with Group A countries.

bauxite is purchased by each participant under separately negotiated long-term contracts. Similar arrangements appear to be involved in the establishment of joint venture aluminum smelters currently planned to take advantage of low-cost electricity generated from N.S.W. and Queensland steaming coal.

One possible pattern for the development of processing facilities in Australia, then, is through direct foreign investment by overseas consumers of the processed product in joint-venture operations initiated, and possibly managed, by Australian suppliers of raw materials or intermediate products. The latter companies may generally be expected to take only small equity shares in the joint venture unless they are themselves foreign-owned companies requiring supplies of the processed product for their own overseas-based operation.

Within this structure, there is likely to be little trade in processed minerals under arm's length conditions, and the bulk of the exports would be transfers within corporate enterprises. The effective point of transfer of Australian mineral resources to overseas purchasers would continue to be the sale of mineral raw materials under arm's length, long-term contracts, and it is in these transactions that the principal ongoing issues of security and bargaining would continue to arise. In general, the issues are no different from those encountered under long-term contract arrangements for the export of mineral raw materials and these have been extensively analyzed elsewhere (Smith, 1978b; Kojima, 1978; Smith and Drysdale, 1979).

Aside from advantages associated with the generally lower costs of processing in Australia than in consuming countries, the establishment of joint-venture processing facilities allows relatively small consumers to benefit from economies of scale in processing and provides a channel for coordinated purchases of raw materials by otherwise disparate, and competing, consumer interests. The latter point is of substantial importance. Coordinated raw materials purchasing strategies by Japanese minerals processors were crucial to the development of large Australian mineral deposits during the 1960s, because the contracts negotiated were able to provide a guaranteed market for the bulk of mine production. With future slower growth, or decline, of Japanese metals production, and until Korean and Taiwanese metals requirements have grown substantially, extension of minerals mining in Australia will to a much greater extent depend on demands by wider groups of smaller consumers.

Difficulties in coordinating the mineral raw materials purchasing strategies of individually small and geographically dispersed processors would be likely to result in individual contracts being serviced by extensions of existing mines, at possibly higher costs of production than could be achieved by the opening of a large new mine. The establishment of joint-venture processing operations in Australia, attractive to the individual consumers because of cost savings in energy, pollution control, scale of operation, and transport, can provide an important means of securing a market for large-scale mining developments.

While the approach described above for providing secure market ties have emphasized the role of direct foreign investments in processing by overseas consumers, in principle there is no reason why the investment links should always be in that direction. Alternatively, Australian mining/processing companies could take equity shares in overseas fabricating operations and establish secure market access through forward vertical integration. Indeed, in a situation where the consuming country is relatively capital-scarce and has not established channels for coordinating overseas investment and purchasing strategies for metals, equity participation in fabricating operations by Australian processors may be a significantly more efficient means of achieving the required investment links. It should be noted that joint-venture processing operations in Australia have, to date, involved Japanese consumers and U.S. and European multinationals, for all of whom capital is relatively cheap and easily mobilized. It is not clear, for example, that Korean aluminum consumers will be as easily able to organize participation in joint-venture smelters in Australia. Investment in aluminum fabricating in Korea, by Australian companies with ready access to capital and established expertise in the area, may be both more efficient and easier to organize. Alongside supplies of aluminum to the vertically integrated fabricating operations, it would be relatively easy to arrange arm's length, long-term contract sales to non-fabricator users of aluminum in Korea.

The sorts of possible developments outlined in this section will require a higher level of cooperation between countries than has been required for the trade in unprocessed minerals if the resource-poor ADCs and China are to be able confidently to avoid pressures for inefficient self-sufficiency in metals production. Direct foreign investment links will be more important in providing market security but the appropriate direction of vertical integration will depend on the circumstances of particular cases. Attitudes towards inflows and outflows of foreign investment in both Australia and the developing countries will be critical variables, as will the preparedness of competing consumers in the developing countries to accept dependence on the same sources of supply for their metal inputs. Finally, the scale and range of competitive processing in Australia will, at least in the short term, depend heavily on what approaches are adopted by Japanese consumers of metals. The greater the extent to which they are willing, or able, to depend on imports, the easier it will be to establish joint-venture processing facilities in which the resource-poor developing countries are also able to participate, or from which they are able to obtain supplies.

V. Future Trade Growth Prospects and Policy Issues

It is clear from the above that trade growth prospects are likely to continue to strengthen over time between Group A and Group B countries, particularly between Australia and both Korea and Taiwan. For Canada, the Western Pacific is likely to remain less important as a market for its raw materials, as compared with Australia, while resistances to its exports to the United States and Europe remain relatively low. For New Zealand, on the other hand, Group A and other East and Southeast Asian countries potentially offer a very important set of export markets, particularly if there continues to be slow growth in New Zealand's traditional European markets for its agricultural exports and if it expands substantially the exploitation of its potential energy resources. The manufacturing sector in all three developed countries will face ever stronger competition over a rapidly expanding range of manufactures exported from Group A countries. That pressure on their import-competing manufacturing sectors may be compounded by a strengthening in the exchange rates of their currencies following strong primary export demand growth. Hence these resource-rich developed economies will tend to see more of an employment growth in nontradables at the expense of import-competing manufactures over time. Prospects for minerals and particularly energy-intensive metals export growth from Group B to Korea and Taiwan in particular are likely in the long run to be especially bright.

The extent to which these likely developments will take place depends heavily on the policy and investment responses in both groups of countries. The high and rising protection provided to labor-intensive manufacturing in Group B and other developed countries and the similarly high and rising protection provided to agriculture in Korea and Taiwan, as well as Japan and elsewhere, in an attempt to prevent what is felt would be an excessive rate of decline in those respective import-competing sectors, is clearly going to inhibit bilateral trade growth in the products of these sectors. This is especially so with respect to agriculture because, insofar as agricultural trade barriers are designed also to reduce domestic instability in agricultural markets, the resulting volatility of markets will make them less attractive than otherwise to exporters. Assistance to metals production in Korea and Taiwan, as in Japan, has less effect on reducing trade than agricultural or other manufacturing protection because these resource-poor countries still have to buy minerals from Group B or other resource-exporting countries.

The inevitability of growing comparative disadvantage in labor-intensive manufacturing in Group B countries, and in agriculture in Group A countries, suggests that policies to assist structural adjustment out of these declining industries may be desirable. Protection policies will be incapable of preventing these declines unless ever increasing rates of protection are applied, at ever increasing cost to the protecting country's consumers-cum-taxpayers. It is particularly important for Korea and Taiwan to recognize this now, before they become too entrenched in supporting a high cost agricultural sector, as has happened in Japan (Bale and Greenshields, 1978). Since, for Australia, the early 1980s is likely to be a period of strengthening balance of payments because of the increasing demand for non-oil energy resources, this is a time when protection cuts for items such as textiles, clothing and footwear would be a particularly sensible alternative to letting the exchange rate revalue from an efficiency viewpoint. Recent protectionist decisions suggest, however, that it is may not be politically feasible to thrust the burden of adjustment to the mining boom on an already pressured group rather than spreading it to all tradable industries.

The future location of minerals processing is going to depend crucially on protection policies not only in Group A and Group B countries but also in Japan. It will also depend heavily on the foreign investment policies of Groups A and B and the extent to which energy prices continue to rise. Potentially, Australia probably offers the most economically efficient location in the Western Pacific for many of the mineral processing activities. But it is unlikely to become the actual location unless Japan reduces its import barriers to these processed minerals and unless buyers in Japan, Korea and Taiwan and sellers in Australia are able to each provide the other with market security. Joint-venture minerals processing is probably an efficient way to achieve that security, although it might be even more efficient in some cases for Australian metal producers to establish equity holdings in fabricating operations in Northeast Asia.

Clearly, there is rapidly increasing scope for more cooperation and greater economic integration between Group A and Group B countries. But the extent to which it is realized will depend heavily on the extent to which each country's xenophobia is reflected in its trade and investment policies.

REFERENCES

Anderson, K., "Australia's Trade with Resource-Poor Developing Economies of Asia, with Emphasis on Korea," Research Paper No. 63, Australia-Japan Economic Relations Research Project, ANU, Canberra, 1979.

_____, "The Political Market for Government Assistance to Australian Manufacturing Industries," *Economic Record,* 56 (153), June 1980 (a).

_____, "Changing Agricultural Comparative Advantage in the Pacific Basin," K. Anderson and A. George (eds.), *Australian Agriculture and Newly Industrializing Asia: Issues for Research,* Canberra: Australia-Japan Economic Relations Research Center, ANU, 1980 (b), Chapter 2.

_____, "Politico-Economic Factors Affecting Public Agricultural Research Investment in Developing Countries," International Association of Agricultural Economists' Occasional Papers (forthcoming).

Bale, M.D. and B.L. Greenshields, "Japanese Agricultural Distortions and their Welfare Value," *American Journal of Agricultural Economics*, 60 (1): 59-64, February 1978.

Binswanger, H.P., V.W. Ruttan, et al., *Induced Innovation: Tech-*

nology, Institutions and Development, Baltimore: John Hopkins University Press, 1978.

Byron, N., "Recent Developments in Forest Products Trade in Newly Industrializing Asia," K. Anderson and A. George (eds.), *op. cit.,* 1980, Chapter 10.

Caves, R.E., "Policies Towards Australia's Resource-Based Industries," J.G. Crawford and S. Okita (eds.), *Raw Materials and Pacific Economic Integration,* London: Croom Helm, 1978.

Drysdale, P., *The Economics of International Pluralism: Economic Policy and the Pacific Community* (forthcoming).

Drysdale, P. and R. Garnaut, "Trade Intensities and the Analysis of Bilateral Trade Flows in a Many-Country World," mimeo, Australian National University, April 1979.

Evenson, R.E., "Economic Aspects of the Organization of Agricultural Research," W. Fishel (ed.), *Resource Allocation in Agricultural Research,* Minneapolis: University of Minnesota Press, 1971, pp. 163-182.

Finger, J.M. and A.J. Yeats, "Effective Protection by Transportation Costs and Tariffs: A Comparison of Magnitudes," *Quarterly Journal of Economics,* 90: 169-76, February 1976.

Garnaut, R., *Australia's Trade with Southeast Asia: A Study of Resistances to Bilateral Trade Flows,* unpublished Ph.D. thesis, Australian National University, Canberra, 1972.

————, "Australia as a Recipient and Source of Pacific Instability," L.B. Krause and S. Sekiguchi (eds.), *Economic Interaction in the Pacific Basin,* Washington, D.C.: The Brookings Institution, 1979, Chapter 4.

Garnaut, R. and A. Clunies-Ross, "Uncertainty, Risk Aversion and the Taxing of Natural Resource Projects," *Economic Journal,* 85: 272-87, June 1975.

Garnaut, R. and K. Anderson, *Industrial Country Protection and the Developing Countries: Australia,* World Bank research monograph (forthcoming).

Gregory, R.G., "Some Implications of the Growth of the Mining Sector," *Australian Journal of Agricultural Economics,* 20 (2): 71-91, August 1976.

Hayami, Y., "Japan's Rice Policy in Historical Perspective," *Food Research Institute Studies,* 14(4): 359-380, 1975.

Hayami, Y. and V.W. Ruttan, *Agricultural Development: An International Perspective*, Baltimore: John Hopkins University

Press, 1971.

Johnson, H.G., *Comparative Cost and Commercial Policy: Theory for a Developing World Economy,* Stockholm: Alqvist and Wiksell, 1968.

Jones, R.W., "A Three-Factor Model in Theory, Trade and History," J. Bhagwati, et al. (eds.), *Trade, Balance of Payments and Growth,* Amsterdam: North Holland, 1971, Chapter 1.

Kindleberger, C., *Foreign Trade and the National Economy,* New Haven: Yale University Press, 1962.

Kojima, K., "Japan's Resource Scarcity and Foreign Investment in the Pacific: A Case Study of Bilateral Devices between Advanced Countries," L.B. Krause and H. Patrick (eds.), *Mineral Resources in the Pacific Area,* San Francisco: Federal Reserve Bank of San Francisco, 1978, Chapter 11.

Krainer, R.E., "Resource Endowments and the Structure of Foreign Investment," *Journal of Finance,* 22: 49-57, 1967.

Krause, L.B. and H. Patrick (eds.), *Mineral Resources in the Pacific Area,* Proceedings of the Ninth Pacific Trade and Development Conference, San Francisco: Federal Reserve Bank of San Francisco, 1978.

Kravis, I.B., "Availability and Other Influences on the Commodity Composition of Trade," *Journal of Political Economy,* 64(2): 143-55, April 1956.

Krueger, A., *Growth, Distortions and Patterns of Trade Among Many Countries,* Princeton, N.J.: International Finance Section, 1977.

Martin, L., "Some Factors Influencing Australian Exports of Processed Agricultural Products to Newly Industrializing Asia," K. Anderson and A. George (eds), *op. cit.,* 1980, Chapter 13.

Mundell, R.A., "International Trade and Factor Mobility," *American Economic Review,* 48(3): 321-35, June 1957.

Nam, C.H., "Trade and Industrial Policies and the Structure of Protection in Korea," this Volume, 1981.

Naya, S., "Natural Resources, Factor Mix and Factor Reversal in International Trade," *American Economic Review,* 57(2): 561-70, May 1967.

OECD, *The Impact of the Newly Industrializing Countries on Production and Trade in Manufactures,* Paris: OECD, June 1979.

Olson, M., "The Political Economy of Comparative Growth Rates," mimeo, University of Maryland, 1978.

Peterson, W.L., "International Farm Prices and the Social Cost of Cheap Food Policies," *American Journal of Agricultural Economics,* 61(1): 312-21, February 1979.

Roemer, M., "Resource-Based Industrialization in the Developing Countries," *Journal of Development Economics,* 6: 163-202, 1979.

Schultz, T.W., "The Value of the Ability to Deal with Disequilibria," *Journal of Economic Literature,* 13(3): 827-846, September 1975.

Seow, G., *The Service Sector of the Singapore Economy,* unpublished M.Ec. thesis, Australian National University, Canberra, 1979.

Smith, B., "Australian Minerals Development, Future Prospects of the Mining Industry, and Effects on the Australian Economy," W. Kasper and T.G. Parry (eds), *Growth, Trade and Structural Change in an Open Australian Economy,* Sydney: Centre for Applied Economic Research, University of New South Wales, 1978 (a), Chapter 6.

_____ , "Long-Term Contracts for the Supply of Raw Materials," J.G. Crawford and S. Okita (eds.), *Raw Materials and Pacific Economic Integration,* London: Croom Helm, 1978 (b), Chapter 12.

_____ , "Australia's Minerals Production and Trade: Case Study of a Resource-Rich Country," L.B. Krause and H. Patrick (eds.), *Mineral Resources in the Pacific,* San Francisco: Federal Reserve Bank of San Francisco, 1978 (c), Chapter 6.

Smith, B. and P. Drysdale, "Stabilization and the Reduction of Uncertainty in Bilateral Minerals Trade Arrangements," Research Paper No. 65, Australia-Japan Economic Relations Research Project, ANU, Canberra, 1979.

Smith, B. and A. Ulph, "The Impact of Environmental Policy in Developed Countries on the Trade of Developing Countries in the ESCAP Region," paper prepared for an ESCAP/UNEP Seminar on Environment and Development, Bangkok, 14-18 August 1979.

Snape, R.H., "Effects of Mineral Development on the Economy," *Australian Journal of Agricultural Economics,* 21(3): 147-56, December 1977.

Stoeckel, A., "Some General Equilibrium Effects of Mining Growth on the Economy," *Australian Journal of Agricultural Economics,* 23(1): 1-22, August 1979.

Stuckey, J., "Joint Ventures in the Aluminium Industry," Research Paper No. 67, Australia-Japan Economic Relations Research Project, ANU, Canberra, 1979.

Stern, R., "Testing Trade Theories," P.B. Kenen (ed.), *International Trade and Finance,* Cambridge: Cambridge University Press, 1975, Chapter 1.

Vanek, J., *The Natural Resource Content of United States Foreign Trade, 1870-1955,* Cambridge: Harvard University Press, 1963.

Vincent, D.P., P.B. Dixon, B.R. Parmenter and D.C. Sams, "Implications of World Energy Price Increases on the Rural and Other Sectors of the Australian Economy," IMPACT General Paper No. G-23, Industries Assistance Commission, Melbourne, August 1979.

• COMMENT _____

Hoe Sung Lee, *Korean Institute of Energy and Resource*

In this paper the theory of changing comparative advantage was extended to treat more formally the role of natural resource-based goods. The extended model explains the existing trade patterns of resource-poor developing countries and resource-rich developed countries. The implication is, therefore, that the current trade patterns will continue into the future. The analysis was also extended to evaluate the future location of mineral processing.

The authors seem to assume that natural resources, though given an explicit role, are in essence not different from the other factors of production. What is ignored is that some natural resources are exhaustible. This may not alter the configuration of comparative advantages. However, the constraint of exhaustion may change the behavior of natural resource producers due to the user cost accruing to the depletion of natural resources. Since the evaluation of the future is different among resource owners and the user cost is subject to uncertainty, the existence of large reserves may not necessarily mean high rates of production and specialization. Reserve is an economic concept. The fact that the quality of resource deposits is not uniform and that the distribution of depletion technologies is also not uniform among countries implies that the possession of reserves carries with it a great deal of qualification.

Furthermore, mineral production generally involves a high degree of pollution of the natural environment. When the meaning of natural resources is expanded to include natural environment, as in the works of economists at the *Resource for the Future,* the evaluation of relative specialization may become complicated. Since many mineral reserves are located on the public road especially in the United States, the collective decision-making under the pressure of growing public awareness about the environment may result in production patterns different from private decision-making.

As for the recommendation that industrialization strategies should not be predicated upon the goal of self-sufficiency in basic metal production and that large-scale domestic processings should be viewed as a secondary option to imports of processed metal, it is difficult to object to them. It is fair to say that very often investment decisions were not made on the basis of prior economic calculation. Given the heavy energy and resource requirements for metal production, the preference of imports over domestic processing is quite appropriate. The security of supply and the stability of price are the major concerns that hinder this preference from materializing.

The suggestion that equity ties between producer and consumer will be preferable to a long-term contract for processed minerals need further investigation. Such preference is said to be generated by the market environment where processed minerals are more homogeneous than mineral raw materials. Secondly, transport costs are relatively less important, and thirdly, the possibility exists for competing production to begin in the consuming country. If these are the reasons for preferring equity ties, one wonders if equity involvement is to protect producers. To a certain extent, this was true in the case of international petroleum refining operations. During the relative abundance of crude oil supplies, major oil companies' foreign affiliates were generally denied price discounts which were allowed to third-party contract buyers. During the extreme shortage, both foreign affiliates and third-party contract buyers suffered. It may very well be that market organization of minerals is different from petroleum. At any rate, a fuller examination of appropriate market relations between minerals producer and consumer may be desired.

Bruce J. Ross, *Canterbury University*

As far as the theory propounded in the paper is concerned, it is clear that the inclusion of natural resources as part of factor endowment does much to help to explain comparative advantage and the direction of trade. There is a problem in that it is impossible to quantify relative natural resource endowments precisely, but the direction and trends in trade are certainly all in conformity with the hypotheses put forward. Restrictions of various sorts certainly modify the trade flows, but it is reassuring to see that truth, or at least economic logic, will out in the end.

With regard to changes in comparative advantage, the authors make a strong case for the theory that the direction of investment, as growth proceeds, will be to a large extent determined by relative national resource endownment. The New Zealand case fits the model. When the amount of capital per worker in the New Zealand agricultural and manufacturing sectors was last estimated, some 2-3 years ago, it appeared that the average worker in the agricultural sector was associated with 2-3 times as much capital as the average worker in manufacturing. This is in spite of forty years of policies which have discriminated in favor of manufacturing, though to be fair it is true that the partially offsetting policies of recent years have been aimed at getting more capital, rather than more men, onto New Zealand farms.

Thus it is easy to accept the Anderson-Smith ideas as far as they go, but they do not go far enough. The changing capital intensity associated with economic growth will certainly change relative factor endowments, and therefore comparative advantage, but changes in technology are likely to be as important. Technological change is mentioned by the authors, but it should be given a great deal more emphasis.

It is technology which will determine to a large extent, just what is, and what is not, a resource. Uranium was not a worthwhile resource before there were ways of using it to produce energy. Technology may be about to convert tar sands and oil shale deposits, which until now have been interesting curiosities, into valuable sources of petroleum.

The New Zealand experience of the last century provides a striking example of the way in which technology can change comparative advantage, and patterns of trade and hence industrial development.

By the end of the 1870s in New Zealand, the gold rushes had petered out, and there were insufficient jobs available on the extensive sheep farms to provide employment for the total available labor force. The scene was thus set for the development of a manufacturing sector, and industrial development got underway with the establishment of woolen mills, clothing factories and other activities typical of the early stages of industrial growth. In 1881, however, the first shipment of frozen meat was carried successfully to the United Kingdom, and a new era began. The development of refrigerated shipping meant that the New Zealand land resource, which could previously only be used for the production of wool or grain for export, suddenly had a strong comparative advantage in the production of meat and dairy products for the U.K. The whole direction of development in New Zealand changed rapidly. Over the succeeding years the big farms were cut into smaller, one family, farms running sheep or dairy cattle, and the density of rural settlement was greatly increased. Manufacturing activities were largely concentrated in the processing of meat and dairy products.

The Liangs made the following statement: "Taiwan provides an example of an economy following its comparative advantage and reaping the gains from trade illustrated by the traditional theory of international trade." New Zealand also provided an example of this phenomenon, and whilst it adhered to those activities in which it had, and still has, a comparative advantage, it reached the position of being in the top 3 or 4 nations of the world for income per capital. In the last forty years, however, policymakers have been trying to force industrialization on the country. It may be, as has been suggested in other cases, that the methods, rather than the strategy, were wrong and the existence of many industries with effective rates of protection of several hundred percent certainly indicates that methods were poor. Nevertheless, it is possible that a large part of the decline in New Zealand's relative per capita income position has resulted from policies which have ignored comparative advantage.

The New Zealand experience also indicates that high incomes can result from the proper exploitation of a national resource. Industrialization in the usual sense is not necessary, and this calls into question the assertions that take-off requires openness and industrialization. A more general statement would be that take-off and growth is associated with the exploitation of a country's comparative advantage.

In discussing comparative advantages, it is notable that once again agriculture has been treated as something special and different from the rest of the economy. Yamazawa was able to justify protection of the silk industry in Japan as being protection for silkworm growers, and nobody challenged him. Korea's economic performance in the seventies is blemished by the fact that income distribution has worsened and the increased effective rate of protection for agriculture has a regressive effect on the standard of living of the urban poor, which makes their position even worse than the figures would indicate. It is hard to understand the justification for this when there are other mechanisms by which farm incomes can be supported, and in some cases the Korean policy has even resulted in a net foreign exchange cost. At one stage, the cost of imported feed grain was greater than the cost of the equivalent amount of milk powder. Kojima pointed out that the liberalization of imports is of benefit to the importing country, whether or not partner countries respond. It is to be hoped that he will remind the Japanese Ministry of Agriculture of this fundamental truth on his return home.

This paper is a reminder that changes in comparative advantage over time, for whatever reasons, mean that even countries with similar relative resource endowments to Japan should not necessarily take Japan for a model. What was correct for Japan in 1960 may not be so for Korea in 1980.

The theory of comparative advantage as expounded in the paper gives a good idea of the way in which development will proceed in an economy once growth gets underway; the deficiency in the theory is that it does not indicate when growth will begin. That ubiquitous omega factor is still not within reach.

A criticism of the paper relates to the statement that "the agricultural exports of resource-rich developed countries, particularly feed grains as well as wool and hides for labor-intensive export manufacturing" would be lowered by protectionist policies. The agricultural commodities most affected by protection are the final consumer items of meat and dairy products. Grains are imported by farmers in resource-poor countries, in order to feed local livestock. In the absence of any protection the imports of grain might fall, to be replaced by meat, butter, cheese and milk powder. The actual final effect on grains would depend on whether the lowering of trade barriers was offset to any extent by assistance to local farmers.

It may be of interest to mention a recent study in New Zealand which takes account of the energy content of both the production and transport of agricultural exports from New Zealand. The conclusion was that the total energy input per kilogram of beef delivered to New York was much lower for New Zealand than for most production systems in the United States. Thus, in at least some cases, energy advantages in production may offset the transport disadvantages associated with higher energy costs. In other words, the net change in comparative advantage resulting from an increase in energy cost depends on relative energy use in production, as much as on the effect on transport costs.

GENERAL DISCUSSION

Extension of the simple two-factor Heckscher-Ohlin model to include a natural resource factor enhances the explanatory power of traditional trade theory. Trade and growth theories can be merged very naturally into such a framework also. Ricardo's interest in abolishing the Corn Law was based on the expectation that such an abolition would stimulate the growth rate of manufacturing by transferring income from the agricultural sector to thrifty industrialists.

It may be desirable to expand the model further by separating human and physical capital and by separating skilled and unskilled labor. Such an expanded model may be very difficult to formalize, but even in informal form it may be much more illuminating in analyzing the trade and growth of not only advanced developing countries and resource-rich advanced countries but also those of resource-rich less developed countries such as the ASEAN countries. Such a model can amplify the interplay between natural resource endowment and the prospect of comparative advantage in manufacturing.

Since transportation costs rose sharply after the oil crisis, one may have to reexamine the old-fashioned location theory. On the basis of transportation cost alone one may, for instance, suggest that Japan give up cattle breeding, metal smelting and paper and pulp industries. Perhaps one must differentiate further the various stages of metal processing because even when the primary stage of processing may not be efficient, the later-stage processing may be efficient. For instance, a disintegrated steel mill using imported iron scrap may be economic while a giant integrated steel mill may not be competitively operated.

One may not underestimate the advantage in production technology. For example, Japan may not have a comparative advantage in nonferrous metal processing, but may have a comparative advantage in steel production because of technology superiority. Hence, a joint investment in steel production between Japan and

Australia might be suggested instead of Australia undertaking steel production by itself, ignoring its handicap in production technology. For such an analysis, manufacturing has to be clearly separated into two groups: primary processing of natural resources and secondary manufacturing. The size of countries may also make differences.

TRADE RELATIONS BETWEEN LATIN AMERICAN AND THE ASIAN ADCs

Ernesto Tironi*

I. Introduction

The purpose of this paper is to examine trade relations between the Asian and Latin American Advanced Developing Countries (ADCs) and the extent to which those trade flows could be expanded in the future. The Asian ADCs include Hong Kong, Korea, Singapore, and Taiwan. Most South American countries might be defined as "advanced," but in this paper five nations with relatively higher per capita income will be concentrated on, namely, Argentina, Brazil, Chile, Mexico, and Venezuela. These countries account for over 70 percent of the region's population and for about 60 percent of the region's exports.

There are several reasons why the analysis of trade relations between Latin American and Asian ADCs is interesting. First, in endeavoring to establish a new International Economic Order, the expansion of trade and cooperation among developing countries is extremely important. In this respect, the importance of the Latin American and Asian ADCs is very substantial, although it has been almost ignored until now. In fact, this very small group of countries, that is to say 9 ADCs, accounts for well over a third of the total exports, other than oil, from developing countries (World Bank, 1979, Table 12).

A second reason why it is important to look at trade relations

* CEPAL, Chile.

between these two sets of countries is that Asian and Latin American ADCs have been growing very rapidly in the last decades. On the average, from 1965 to 1977 the former's GNP grew by more than 8 percent per annum, and exports, in constant prices, increased more than 12 percent per year. These high rates of growth are very likely to continue in the future so that, according to the World Bank's projections, by 1990 the Asian ADCs alone will account for about 27 percent of all LDCs (less developed countries') exports, as compared to about 12 percent in 1976. The Latin American ADCs are also expected to grow faster than other developing and industrialized countries. Therefore, the aggregate share of the ADCs in the developing countries' exports will increase from about 35 percent in 1976 to over 45 percent in 1990.

In the third place, as this paper will show, there is scope for large increases in trade flows between Asian and Latin American ADCs. The main reasons, aside from their rapid income growth, is that on the one hand, the Asian ADCs are relatively poor in natural resources, while Latin American ADCs are rich in them, having a large availability of many of the raw materials that the Asian ADCs will need for their continued industrialization. On the other hand, Latin America's trend towards opening to free trade will imply an expansion of exports of primary products and an increase in the demand for imports of low-cost consumer goods produced by the Asian ADCs.

Finally, it may be interesting to look at Latin American-Asian trade relations, because there is a growing interest in Latin America concerning the Asian development experience. Several countries in this region are implementing very strong policies of outward-oriented growth. A key aspect in this respect, is whether the Asian example could be replicated in Latin America.

Unfortunately, however, there is very little knowledge about Asia in Latin America, and vice-versa. There are very few studies about their trade relations and their prospects. For that reason, this paper attempts to provide only a general introduction to the basic characteristics of the recent trade flows between the Asian and Latin American ADCs, rather than a full and comprehensive analysis of the topic. In particular, there is no attempt to provide an explanation for the level nor the nature of trade flows between the two regions. Some dissaggregation is made by countries, however, because—even though this is somewhat tedious—it is more realistic and useful for policy purposes than referring to abstract conglomerates of countries which seldom behave as one economic unit.

This paper is organized in four sections. The first one provides a broad picture of the main macroeconomic similarities and differences between the Asian and Latin American ADCs, as well as a comparative analysis of their trade structures and their positions in the world economy. The following section examines trade flows between the two groups of ADCs, as they have evolved during recent years. (Unfortunately, the lack of data precludes a very dissaggregated analysis of trade by commodities and countries.) The composition and evolution of Latin American exports of primary products, and the extent to which they can form the basis of deeper trade relations is then examined. Finally, there is a brief section concerning the prospects of future trade between the Asian and Latin American ADCs and some suggestions for further research.

II. The Asian and Latin American ADCs

Before analyzing the trade relations between Latin America and the Asian ADCs, it may be useful to give a general view of the main characteristics of these economies.

1. Macroeconomic Similarities and Differences

Table 1 gives some basic comparative indicators of population, GDP and structures of demand and supply in the Asian and Latin American ADCs circa 1977. First, it can be noted that on the average, the Latin ADCs are larger than Asian ADCs in terms of population. The total population of the former group is almost four times that of the latter group. Internally, the two sets of countries have a similar degree of heterogeneity in population size. The Latin American ADCs, however, are relatively more homogeneous in terms of urbanization and the urban population is between 60 to 80 percent of total population in Latin American ADCs, while in Asian ADCs it ranges between 49 and 100 percent.

In the second place, it is worth noting that the difference between the average GDP of the Latin American and Asian ADCs is bigger than between populations. The main reason is that in Latin America

Table 1. Asian and Latin American ADCs: Basic Economic Indicators, 1977

	Popu-lation (million)	Urban[a] (percen-tage)	GDP (billion US$)	GDP per Capita Value 1977 (US$)	GDP per Capita Growth 1960-77 (percen-tage)	Structure of Demand Public Con-sump-tion	Structure of Demand Gross Invest-ment (percen-tage of GDP)	Structure of Demand Exports[b]	Structure of Supply Agri-culture (of GDP)	Structure of Supply Industry (percen-tage of GDP)	Structure of Supply Service	Income Distribution[c] Share of lower 40% (percen-tage)	Income Distribution[c] Share of Top 10%
Asian ADCs	59.6		67.3	1,431	7.0								
Taiwan	16.8	51	19.6	1,170	6.2	17	27	54	12	46	42	22	25
Hong Kong	4.5	90	11.6	2,590	6.5	7	25	98	2	31	67	—	—
Korea	36.0	49	29.5	820	7.4	13	26	40	27	35	38	17	28
Singapore	2.3	100	6.6	2,880	7.5	10	34	160	2	35	63	—	—
LA ADCs	229.5		322.1	1,403	3.7								
Argentina	26.0	81	45.0	1,730	2.7	9[d]	19	13	13	45	42	14	35
Brazil	116.1	61	158.0	1,360	4.9	12[d]	22	8	12	37	51	7	51
Chile	10.6	79	12.3	1,160	1.0	12	9	17	10	29	61	13	35
Mexico	63.3	63	70.9	1,120	2.8	12	20	10	10	36	54	10	37
Venezuela	13.5	80	35.9	2,660	2.7	15	32	37	6	17	77	10	36

Source: World Bank, *World Development Report, 1979*, Annex, Washington, D.C.

Notes: [a] Refers to 1975

[b] Exports of goods and services not attributable to factors.

[c] Most data refers to the period 1970-1972, except Chile's (1968), Korea's (1976) and Mexico's (1977).

[d] For 1960.

the countries with large populations have relatively higher GDPs per capita, while the opposite occurs in Asia.

Thirdly, the average GDP per capita of the Latin American ADCs is almost the same as that of the Asian ADCs. However, differences among countries are smaller within Latin America; the ratio between the highest and lowest income countries, Venezuela and Mexico, is 2.4 to 1 in this region, while it is 3.5 to 1 in Asia, between Singapore and Korea.

To complete the comparative picture at an aggregate level, it is worth stressing again that the Asian ADCs have been growing much faster than the Latin ADCs. The rate of growth of GDP per capita has been, on the average, almost 90 percent higher in Asia than in Latin America between 1960 and 1977. What is more interesting, is that growth performance has been more consistent and homogeneous in Asia also. All the Asian countries showed an income growth rate above 6 percent. The Latin American ADCs, however, with the exception of Brazil, all showed a growth rate below 3 percent.

Relatively less is known about differences and similarities in demand and supply structures. The comparison in this respect is restricted almost exclusively to the degree of "openness" of the economies to foreign trade. The Asian ADCs are much more open economies: excluding the special cases of the city-states, Hong Kong and Singapore, the ratios of exports to GDP range between 40 and 54 percent in these countries. In Latin America, by comparison, those ratios go from only 8 percent, Brazil, to 17 percent, Chile, when one leaves aside the special case of the region's main oil-exporting country, Venezuela, whose export ratio is 37 percent, a ratio still lower than that of any Asian ADC.

There are other differences and similarities between the two groups of countries about which there is little awareness. Firstly, the significance of public consumption differs from what most experts believe, at least in Latin America. The prevailing view in Latin America is that the Asian countries have almost completely free market economies with little state intervention. The truth is, however, that public consumption as a proportion of GDP in most Asian ADCs is much higher than in Latin America.

Secondly, gross investment as a proportion of GDP is also significantly higher in Asian ADCs. The investment ratio is about 27 percent there, as compared to only about 20 percent in Latin America. This fact is important because it implies that the Asian

ADCs' success in terms of growth cannot be attributed exclusively, or even mainly, to foreign policy, but is also a result of higher invest-ment ratios.

In terms of aggregate supply structures it is interesting to note that the two sets of countries show a very similar degree of industrializa-tion, and that agriculture is slightly more important in Asian ADCs than in Latin American ADCs while the service sector is more im-portant in the latter, with the exceptions of Argentina in Latin America and the city-states in Asia. No Latin American ADC has more than 13 percent of GDP generated by agriculture, while Korea has almost twice the ratio of GDP generated by the agricultural sector.

Finally, income distribution is much less unequal in the Asian ADCs than in Latin America, although data about this is incomplete. In Korea and Taiwan, the share of income going to the poorer 40 percent of the population is almost twice that going to the same group in the Latin American ADCs, except Argentina and Chile. Income is also much less concentrated in the hands of the more wealthy groups of the population; the richest tenth of the population takes only between one-half and three-fourths of the fraction of income earned by the same groups in the Latin American ADCs.

2. Comparative Trade Structures

The total value of exports of all Asian ADCs is about 10 percent higher than that of the Latin American ADCs, although the aggregate GDP of the former group is less than a fourth of the latter's. (See Table 2.) The value of exports is very similar in each Asian ADC; between 8 and 10 billion dollars in 1977. The amount of exports in the Latin American ADCs range from $2.2 billion in Chile, to as much as $12 billion in the case of Brazil. In this respect, Latin America is considerably more heterogeneous.

Export growth has been significantly higher in the Aisan ADCs during the last two decades. During the 1960s, the annual rate of growth of exports from Asian ADCs as a group was about 15 percent, almost four times higher than in Latin America. During the seventies, the growth of exports accelerated more in Latin America than in Asia, but still the annual growth rate of the Asian ADCs was over three times that of Latin America.

Export growth has been extremely rapid in Taiwan and Korea,

Table 2. Foreign Trade Indicators of Asian and Latin American ADCs, 1977

	Value of Exports (billion US$)	Export Growth (percentage per annum)		Structure of Exports[a]				Structure of Imports[a]				Destination of Exports (percentage)		
		1960-70	1970-77	Fuel and Minerals	Other Primary Goods (percentage)	Manufacturers Textile and Cloth	Others	Food	Fuel	Other Primary Goods (percentage)	Manufactures	DCs	LDCs	Others[b]
Asian ADCs	37.3	14.7	16.4											
Taiwan	9.4	3.7	16.7	2	13	30	55	11	17	14	58	70	26	4
Hong Kong	9.6	12.7	6.5	1	2	44	53	18	6	9	67	70	26	4
Korea	10.1	35.2	30.7	3	9	36	52	9	20	19	52	73	17	10
Singapore	8.2	4.2	9.8	31	23	6	40	10	27	10	53	47	48	7
LA ADCs	33.7	3.6	4.8											
Argentina	5.7	3.3	5.5	1	74	2	23	5	18	12	65	46	45	9
Brazil	12.1	5.0	6.5	8	62	4	21	8	32	6	54	61	30	9
Chile	2.2	0.6	7.7	83	12	0	5	15	19	14	54	65	33	2
Mexico	4.1	3.3	1.9	26	43	5	26	8	6	7	79	79	20	1
Venezuela[c]	9.6	2.0	10.5	74	26	0	0	18	1	10	71	61	39	0

Notes: [a] 1976.

[b] Mainly socialist countries.

[c] Data on trade structure refers to 1960.

while in Singapore it was much closer to the average of Latin American ADCs during the sixties. However, during that decade the Asian ADC with lower export growth still showed a better performance than all Latin American countries except Brazil. This pattern became less pronounced in the seventies. The performance of Latin America with respect to export expansion has been more heterogeneous.

The structure of exports is very different in both sets of countries. The share of manufactures in total commodity exports is approximately four times bigger in Asia than in Latin America. This factor obviously explains at least partially the differences in export performance of both continents. Except in the case of Singapore, manufactures represented over 85 percent of the total exports in the Asian ADCs in 1976. In Latin America that share was at most 30 percent in the case of Mexico. Textiles and clothing represented at most one sixth of total exports in the Latin ADCs, while they represented at least a third of them in Taiwan, Hong Kong, and Korea.

Primary products are much more significant in Latin America, reflecting the differences in natural resource availability. Exports of crude oil are not the main explanation of that result, except in the cases of Singapore and Venezuela. Minerals are relatively more important in Brazil with iron, and Chile with copper. Agricultural commodity exports are significant in Singapore with rubber, Argentina with cereals and beef, Brazil with coffee, and Mexico with coffee and cotton.

There are considerably less differences in aggregate import structures between the Asian and Latin American ADCs. In both continents manufactures consistently account for well over half of total imports. Dependence on manufactures imports appears to be higher than the average in Mexico and Venezuela.

The main difference in this respect arises in food imports. Asia has to rely more on imported food, especially in case of Hong Kong. The need for fuel imports is very heterogeneous in both regions, with no clear over all pattern. Finally, the need to import other primary products is similar in Latin American and Asian ADCs.

To conclude this general comparative picture, it is worth looking at the geographical destination of exports by both sets of countries. The Asian ADCs sell a slightly higher fraction of their exports to developed countries. But the difference is not significant; no country sells over half of their exports to other LDCs. The ones that come closest are Singapore (48 percent), Argentina (45 percent) and

Venezuela (39 percent). All the rest sell less than a third of their goods to other LDCs, and a few, including Korea and Mexico, less than a fifth.

3. *The ADCs in the World Economy*

It is interesting to analyze briefly the position of the Asian and Latin American ADCs in the world economy today and their development prospects in this coming decade.

The World Bank's *Development Report* has data on those two issues, although statistics are more aggregated than might be wished. The available information shows that the "Intermediate Income Countries" of East Asia and the Pacific and of Latin America will increase their share of the world's GDP and trade markedly. According to the data the two sets of countries should increase their joint share in the world's GDP from about 6 percent in 1976 to 9 percent in 1990. Their share in total world exports should grow from 10 percent to 12 percent during the same period.

The fastest growth will come from the Asian ADCs: their share in the developing countries' GDP will grow from 9 percent in 1976 to 13 percent in 1990, and from 19 percent to 27 percent in the LDC's exports. Latin America, however, will maintain its share in the developing countries GDP of 33 percent and exports of 25 percent.

GDP is most likely to grow at 7.6 percent per annum in Asia during the 1980s and at 5.7 percent in Latin America. As a result of this performance, income per capita in Asia should increase from $580 in 1975 to $1,400 in 1990, while in Latin America it should rise from $1,100 to $1,630 (all measured in dollars of 1975, equivalent to approximately $1.33 of 1979; *ibid.,* Table 17).

The expected trends in trade imply that the tendency towards a fall in the share of the non-oil exporting developing countries in world trade will be reversed in the 1980s. That share had fallen from 24 percent in 1960 to 21 percent in 1976, but now it will increase slightly to 22 percent in 1990. Aside from the fast growth in manufactured exports of 11 percent which will sustain that trend, it is interesting to note that the growth of primary exports in LDCs is not likely to continue to be as slow as in the past, compared to the advanced countries. The share of non-ferrous mineral and non-food agricultural products in total LDC's exports will increase significantly, from 33 percent to 38 percent and from 30 percent to 34 percent, respectively.

Since Latin America is a continent which is relatively rich in natural resources, and East Asia is not, the trends described above open interesting trade opportunities for both, at least in principle.

III. Trade between Asian and Latin American ADCs

Looking at the broad picture provided in the previous section, it seems that the Asian ADCs have comparative advantages mainly in manufactures, while Latin America has them in primary products. Therefore, relatively important trade flows could be expected between these two regions.

1. Trade from the Asian Perspective

Table 3 sets out some information on the issue of trade. Contrary to what would be expected in theory, the share of Asian ADCs exports to Latin America is very small, amounting to about 2.4 percent in 1978. It has been increasing rapidly, however, since it amounted to 1.7 percent at the end of the nineteen sixties and to 2.1 percent in 1974. In current dollars, the Asian ADCs' exports to Latin America have increased from about $94 million in 1969 to $1,111 million in 1978.[1] Although that fraction seems to be very small, it amounts to almost two fifths of the Asian ADCs' exports to other developing countries, excluding the oil exporters and their Asian neighbors.

Taiwan is the Asian ADC that sells the largest fraction of the region's exports to Latin America, 37 percent in 1978. The remaining Asian ADCs sell a similar proportion of the region's total (about 20 percent). Excluding exports to Panama, the biggest Asian ADC exporters to Latin America are Hong Kong and Singapore and the least important exporter in 1978 was Korea.

If one excludes Panama and other smaller Latin American countries, the Asian ADCs' exports to Latin America have been growing at a rate somewhat higher than that to the rest of the world. Therefore, in Latin America the Asian ADCs' share has increased slightly. That result is not the consequence of homogeneous behavior among all exporters and importers. Hong Kong and Singapore showed a

---

[1] See Table A.1 in the Appendix.

Table 3. Asian ADCs; Trends of Export Growth to Different Regions and Their Shares: 1969-78

	Export Growth			Share by Region		
	(rate per annum in current value)			(percentage)		
	1969-78	1969-74	1974-78	1969	1974	1978
Latin America	31.6	36.8	25.2	1.7	2.1	2.4
(LA ADCs)	(29.7)	(35.2)	(23.1)	(0.7)	(0.8)	(0.9)
Argentina	17.3	27.0	6.2	0.2	0.15	0.1
Brazil	38.0	67.5	8.4	0.1	0.3	0.2
Chile	62.5	43.1	90.5	..[a]	..[a]	0.2
Mexico	21.9	23.3	20.1	0.2	0.2	0.2
Venezuela	31.2	28.8	34.3	0.2	0.2	0.2
Others	25.0	31.6	17.2	0.7	0.7	0.6
Panama	44.2	50.8	36.3	0.3	0.5	0.9
DCs	28.3	34.8	20.6	60.3	66.6	65.1
Asian LDCs	22.8	26.3	18.5	25.3	20.2	18.3
Oil exporters	41.6	43.0	39.8	3.0	4.5	8.0
Other LDCs	21.1	22.5	19.3	9.7	6.6	6.2
Total	27.2	32.2	21.3	100.0	100.0	100.0

Source: Table A.1 in the Appendix, from IMF, *Direction of World Trade 1969-75,* 1978.
Note: [a] Less than 0.05.

relatively sluggish performance as exporters, and Argentina, Brazil and Mexico as importers, especially between 1974 and 1978 in the case of the former. Brazilian imports from Hong Kong and Taiwan even fell between 1974 and 1978.

Those reductions have been compensated for by significant increases in the importance of Korea and Taiwan as exporters (see Table 4) and of Chile and Venezuela as export markets for the Asian ADCs. Chile has increased its imports from this region, especially during the second half of the 1970s at an astonishing rate of over 90 percent per year between 1974 and 1978. This trade has developed with all Asian ADCs, but it has grown particularly fast with Taiwan, increasing from about $0.1 million in 1969 to $38 million in 1978, and with Korea from the same value in 1969 to $22 million in 1978.

Table 4 shows the significance of Latin America from the point of

(in percent)

Table 4. Asian ADCs; Share of LA in Total Country Exports and Main Partners: 1969-78

	1969[a]	1978	Rate of Growth 1969-78	Main LA Importing Countries in 1978
Taiwan	0.6 (.6)	2.4 (1.4)	59.1 (50.2)	Panama (41); Venezuela (14); Chile (9)
Hong Kong	2.3 (1.8)	2.1 (1.4)	18.9 (16.9)	Panama (32); Venezuela (17); Mexico (6)
Korea	0.8 (.5)	1.8 (1.1)	52.1 (51.9)	Panama (38); Chile (10); Venezuela (10)
Singapore	2.1 (1.0)	2.5 (1.7)	24.5 (20.8)	Panama (31); Brazil (29); Mexico (11)
All Asian ADCs	1.7 (1.5)	2.2 (1.4)	31.4 (27.5)	Panama (36); Venezuela (11); Brazil (9) and Chile (7)

Source: Table A.1 in the Appendix.
Note: [a] Figure in parenthesis is the share in each country's exports to Latin America excluding Panama.

view of each individual Asian ADC as an exporter. The Latin
American market is most important for Singapore, although it still
accounts for only a small share of total exports, 2.5 percent, and even
less for Korea at 1.8 percent. However, the trend during the last
decade shows that Latin American's preponderance has been growing
quite fast for Taiwan, increasing four fold in 9 years, and Korea,
increasing two and a half times in the same period.

Panama is the principal partner for most individual Asian ADCs. It
is interesting to note that the largest Latin American country, Brazil,
is not among the three major importers from any of the largest Asian
ADCs. Apparently it imports only raw materials from Singapore. On
the other hand, one of the smaller Latin American countries, Chile, is
a relatively important partner of Korea and Taiwan.

To complete this overview of trade from the Asian perspective it is
necessary to look at the import side. In particular, aggregate "trade
symmetry" between countries is of interest; that is to say, the extent to
which a partner is similarly important as a source for imports as it is
as an export market. This gives a first indication of whether trade is
carried out by relatively equal as opposed to "unequal" partners.

Table 5 offers some evidence on that issue at an aggregate level.
For the Asian ADCs as a group, Latin America is relatively more
important as a market for exports than as a source of imports. The
preponderance of Latin American as an import source has been
falling while it has been rising as an export market.

The main explanation of that result is the behavior of Hong Kong,
Singapore and Taiwan, which have been buying considerably less
from Latin America in relative terms. The increased purchases by Korea
have not been sufficient to disturb that trend. By 1978, the latter
represented only about one fourth of all the Asian ADCs imports
from Latin America, while Taiwan accounted for over one third,
Singapore for one fifth and Hong Kong for about 16 percent.

Brazil, the largest Latin American country, has been the main
source of imports for most Asian ADCs, especially for Singapore.
Argentina is also a prominent source for that country and for Hong
Kong.

Trade among individual countries did not show notable asymmetries
as of 1978 except in the cases of Singapore and Hong Kong. For these
two countries Latin America was the least prominent source of
imports among all Asian ADCs (0.8 percent), while it accounted for
2.5 percent and 2.1 percent of each country's total exports. (See Table 4.)

Table 5.   Asian ADCs; Share of Imports from Latin American ADCs in Total Imports by Country: 1969-78

	1969	1978	Main LA Exporting Countries in 1978	
Taiwan	2.4	1.8	Argentina (31%);	Chile (15%)
Hong Kong	1.9	. 0.8	Brazil (32%);	Argentina (20%)
Korea	0.4	1.1	Chile (24%);	Brazil (16%)
Singapore	1.6	0.9	Brazil (50%);	Argentina (27%)
All Asian ADCs	1.4	1.1	Brazil (30%)	Argentina (27%)
			Chile (14%)	

Source: IMF, *Directions of World Trade 1969-75,* 1978, Washington, D.C.

2. Latin American Perspective

The share of Latin American ADCs' exports to Asian ADCs is very low, being only eight-tenths of a percent in 1978, although that was a rapid increase from 1974 when it was only four-tenths of a percent. (See Table 6.) Therefore the Asian ADCs are much less important for Latin America as an export market than the reverse (0.8 percent as opposed to 2.4 percent of total exports in 1978). The same is true in relation to exports to LDCs only. Latin American exports to the Asian ADCs represent less than one-tenth of their sales to other LDCs, excluding the oil exporters and their neighbors in their own region. For the Asian ADCs that share was close to two-fifths.

The industrialized countries are more prominent export markets for Latin American ADCs, although their importance has been declining. Other nations in the same region are less important for Latin America than for the Asian ADCs but other LDCs are significantly more prominent. This may be related to the fact that Latin America's exports are relatively more concentrated in primary products.

Over the decade 1969 to 1978, Latin American exports to the Asian ADCs and to the world as a whole showed similar rates of growth per year of about 17 percent, much lower than the export growth of the Asian ADCs to Latin America which grew at about 30 percent. The value of Latin American exports to those countries reached only about $408 million in 1978, in contrast to $1,100 million by the Asian ADCs to Latin America, including Panama, and $700 million excluding it.

Table 6. *Latin America; Trend of Export Growth to Asian ADCs and Other Regions and Their Shares: 1969-78*

	Export Growth			Shares by Region		
	(rate per annum in current value)			(percentages)		
	1969-78[a]	1969-74	1974-78	1969	1974	1978
Asian ADCs	17.0 (19.6)	3.9	35.8 ·	0.8	0.7	0.83
Taiwan	22.9 (24.9)	13.1	36.4	0.2	0.1	0.35
Hong Kong	4.8 (3.6)	−5.3	18.9	0.4	0.1	0.14
Korea	46.3 (62.5)	41.4	52.5	..[b]	..[b]	0.15
Singapore	13.6 (25.1)	−4.8	41.9	0.2	0.1	0.15
DCs	16.3 (15.7)	22.8	8.6	74.4	71.2	69.0
Latin America	19.1 (16.0)	29.0	7.9	13.4	16.4	15.5
Oil exporters	43.4 (45.6)	49.3	25.7	0.8	2.8	4.9
Other LDCs	16.4 (16.3) ·	20.6	11.5	10.5	9.2	9.8
Total	17.3 (16.3)	23.9	9.5	100.0	100.0	100.0

Source: Table A.2 in the Appendix, from IMF, *Directions of World Trade,* Washington, D.C.

Notes: [a] Figures in parentheses indicate the rate of export growth of the Latin American ADCs only.

[b] Less than 0.05 percent.

Total Latin American exports have been growing faster to Korea, over 46 percent per annum, than to any other Asian ADC. As a result of this, the participation of Korea in Latin American exports has increased significantly, although it began from a very low base, and in absolute terms it is still quite low. There is a surprisingly low increase in exports to Hong Kong.

The poor performance of Latin America as an exporter to Asian ADCs is explained mainly by the behavior of Brazil, Venezuela and Mexico.[2] (See Table 7.) In all of them, exports to the Asian ADCs have grown much less than total exports. Therefore, their shares of sales to that region dropped considerably, but the impact of the performance of Brazil was more of a determinant in aggregate performance because it accounted for about a third of all the region's exports to the Asian ADCs in 1978. Venezuela and Mexico together represented about only 3 percent.

[2] The Latin American ADCs account for about four-fifths of all the region's exports to the Asian ADCs. That share was only about 45 percent in 1969.

Table 7. *Latin American ADCs; Share of Asian ADCs in Total Country Exports and Main Partners: 1969-78*

(in percent)

	1969	1978	Rate of Growth 1969-78	Main Asian Importing Partners in 1978 and Share of Total Exports to Asian ADCs			
Argentina	0.18	1.85	51.9	Taiwan	(51):	Korea	(19)
Brazil	2.21	1.14	12.5	Singapore	(40):	Hong Kong and Korea	(22)
Chile	—	2.65	72.0ᵃ	Korea	(50):	Taiwan	(45)
Mexico	0.36	0.14	5.4	Korea	(55):	Hong Kong	(33)
Venezuela	0.21	0.05	2.0	Taiwan	(80):	Hong Kong	(20)
(Panama)	—	4.35	53.3	Korea	(50):	Hong Kong	(44)
All LA ADCs	0.68	0.87	20.9	Taiwan	(42):	Singapore	(25)
						Korea	(15)

Source: Table A.2 in the Appendix, from IMF, *Directions of World Trade.*
Note: ᵃ This rate may be distorted by very low base. Growth per year between 1974 and 1978 was 47.8%.

The slow growth of exports to Asia by most Latin American countries was partly compensated for by rapid growth on the part of Chile and Argentina as well as Panama.[3] Chile is the Latin American ADC for which Asian ADCs represent a higher fraction of its own total exports (2.7 percent) and to which sales are increasing faster, especially to Korea. Argentinian exports also increased at a rate equal to over twice the average for Latin America as a whole. Its main market is Taiwan, supplying over 50 percent of all exports to Asia, mostly in the form of food. The Asian ADCs are an important market for Panama also, but mainly as a consequence of the very small value of that country's total exports which were about $430 million in 1978.

Taiwan accounts for over two-fifths of the total Latin American exports to the Asian ADCs. It is the single most important market for Argentina and Venezuela. Singapore is, on the aggregate, the second most important market for the Latin American ADCs but only as a result of its importance for Brazil. Korea is the third major purchaser

---

[3] Argentina and Chile accounted for 27 percent and 14 percent, respectively, of all Latin American exports to the Asian ADCs in 1978. Panama's share was only 4 percent.

of Latin American goods, and is the biggest single individual market for Chile, Mexico and Panama.

In looking at the import side, Table 8 shows that, for the Latin American ADCs, the Asian ADCs have been equally important, or unimportant, both as a source of imports and as a market for exports, because in 1978 the share of imports from that region was almost the same as the share of exports going to it, 1.0 percent.

This was not the case in the late 1960s; indeed, the amount of Latin American imports from Asian ADCs has more than doubled during the last 9 years. The main explanation of that result is the behavior of Chile, which increased the share of the Asian ADCs' in its total imports from virtually nil in 1969 to almost 3 percent in 1978. Only Argentina slightly reduced its share of imports coming from the Asian ADCs.

3. Trade Imbalances and Asymmetries

Latin America as a whole had a significant negative trade balance with the Asian ADCs in 1978, amounting to over $700 million, even when imports are measured FOB. Excluding the special case of Panama, the trade deficit falls to about $300 million, but this amount is still equivalent to about three-quarters of the value of the region's exports to Asian ADCs.[4] The Latin American ADCs alone also have a trade deficit with their Asian counterparts, but it is proportionately smaller than for the region as a whole. It is interesting to note that in the late 1960s Latin American-Asian trade generated a much smaller deficit for the former, and was roughly in balance excluding Panama from the analysis.

The Latin American countries are far from homogeneous in terms of their trade balance with the Asian ADCs. Venezuela and Mexico had relatively large deficits in 1978, between 6 and 20 times their level of exports, which, however, were very small. Chile had a small trade deficit in 1978 of about $16 million over total exports of $63 million. The Latin American country with the biggest surplus was Argentina, with $60 million in imports and $110 million in exports. Brazil had a surplus of $34 million. In aggregate, the Latin ADCs' deficit was equivalent to about a fifth of total exports in 1978.

---

[4] In other words, Panama accounts for almost a half of the aggregate Latin American trade deficit with the Asian ADCs.

Table 8. Latin American ADCs: Share of Imports from Asian ADCs by Countries and Main Partners

(in percent)

	1969	1978	Main Asian Partners in 1978			
Argentina	1.31	1.04	Singapore	(48):	Hong Kong	(25)
Brazil	0.44	0.62	Singapore	(72):	Hong Kong	(14)
Chile	—	2.63	Taiwan	(48):	Korea	(28)
Mexico	0.56	0.99	Singapore	(33):	Taiwan	(33)
Venezuela	0.83	1.20	Taiwan	(43):	Hong Kong	(30)
All LA ADCs	0.68	1.03	Taiwan	(32):	Singapore	(31)

Source: IMF, *Direction of World Trade,* 1969-75 and 1979.

The trade balance position of the Asian ADCs is very different, in the sense that all of them show surpluses of similar relative size. Naturally, the values change considerably whether one includes or excludes Panama. In both cases, Taiwan has the largest surplus, with about $230 and $70 million, respectively, followed by Hong Kong, $160 and $90 million, Singapore, $145 and $70 million, and Korea, $80 and $4 million.

Finally, in considering the prospects of trade in the future, it is useful to look again at what can be called "trade symmetries." This refers to differences between countries or regions of the shares of exports to and imports from another country or region. These coefficients give an idea of how important, in relative terms, the other region is as an export market or an import source. This influences the interest that a country or its government may have in deliberately influencing trade with a partner.

These trade symmetries (or asymmetries) differ according to balance of payments surpluses or deficits. The trade between most developing and developed countries show big asymmetries, although it may be balanced or show a surplus for the former. This is the case because exports to or imports from one another constitute a large fraction of the LDCs' total trade, while it represents a small fraction of the DCs' total exports or imports. This is the fundamental structural reason why LDCs are so interested in a New International Economic Order, while they make so little progress in attaining it; because their main counterpart, the DCs, are significantly less interested since their trade with the LDCs is a very small proportion of their total trade.

Trade relations between Asian and Latin American ADCs are, fortunately for their eventual cooperation prospects, relatively symmetrical. The exports of the former to their Latin partners are only marginally less significant in their total exports (0.9 percent) than in the case of the Latin American ADCs with respect to their own total imports (1.0 percent).[5] Something similar happens with the Asian ADCs' imports from Latin America. Obviously, the same symmetrical relationship does not necessarily hold at each individual country level. But considering them separately does not appear to be particularly relevant at this stage while reciprocal trade is still quite low.

To complete this overall picture of trade relations between Asian and Latin ADCs it is worth looking at the issue from another perspective which might help later to formulate an hypothesis about trade prospects. One of the most striking facts about trade relations between these countries is that some of the smaller Latin American countries like Chile have a much higher share of trade with the Asian ADCs than their larger neighbors. Chile imported as much from Asian ADCs as Mexico and Brazil which have export revenues two to five times bigger. Mexico and Venezuela exported to the Asian ADCs much less than what one would have expected from the significance of their exports to the world as a whole.

The Asian ADCs were, in 1978, much more homogeneous in terms of the distribution of their exports to the world as a whole and to the Latin American ADCs. Only Taiwan seems relatively biased in favor of Latin America, both as importer and as exporter while Korea was trailing as an exporter.

Before attempting to provide an explanation of that pattern of trade relations at least in the case of Latin America, it is necessary to analyze the commodity composition of trade.

4. Commodity Composition of Latin American-Asian Trade

In order to understand the previous pattern of exports and its likely development in the future it is vital to consider the composition of trade.

---

[5] Considering all Latin America, the situation is considerably different as a consequence of the big influence of the special Panamanian case. Including Panama, the preponderance of Latin America as an export market increases significantly for the Asian ADCs (to 2.4 percent of all their exports), while the share of LA's imports from them does not increase that much (to 1.5 percent only).

Table 9 shows that the composition of Latin American and Asian exports is very different, although unfortunately separate data for the Asian ADCs alone does not exist.[6] The table shows that manufactures constitute the bulk of Asian exports to Latin America (over 60 percent), while in the case of the latter only 12 percent of exports are manufactured products. On the other hand, primary products represent less than 40 percent of all Asian exports to Latin America, even though this includes exports by countries with very low levels of industrialization, while they represent almost 88 percent of Latin American exports to all Asia.

Some of the main categories of goods exported by Asia to Latin America are clothing which is 15 percent of the total; machinery and transport equipment which comprises 20 percent and other manufactures taking up 21 percent. Clothing and machinery and transport equipment have increased particularly quickly, at rates in excess of 50 percent per year between 1969 and 1977. Among the primary products, most Asian exports are crude raw materials.

In the case of Latin America, the main goods exported to Asia are food, comprising 38 percent of the total with cereals accounting for two-fifths of that percentage; crude raw materials taking up 20 percent, of which textile fibres account for over half; and animal and vegetable oils and fats which occupy 24 percent of the total.

It is interesting to note that Latin American exports of primary products to Asia have increased quite quickly. Between 1969 and 1977 they grew at a rate approximately 33 percent higher than the average rate of increase of those same exports to other regions of the world. Mainly as a consequence of this unusual performance, in comparison with world-wide trends in which manufactured exports grow much faster than primary exports, the share of primary products in Latin American sales to Asia have remained virtually constant over the last 8 years.

The Latin American ADCs area are also net exporters, and thus compete with the Asian ADCs in the world market, of clothing, fish, veneers and plywood, textiles and cotton fabrics, aside from the petroleum products mentioned earlier. But none of those commodities is a major export item for the Latin American ADCs, except in the

---

[6] These figures are not comparable with those presented in other tables. It is not possible to estimate how representative they are of the Asian-Latin American ADCs trade because there are differences in the definitions of the exporting as well as importing regions.

Table 9.   *Main Commodities Traded Between Asia and South America, 1969-77*

(in million dollars and percent)

SITC Classification	Exports from Asia[b] to SA[c]				Exports from SA to Asia			
	1969 million dollars	1977 million dollars	1977 (%)	1969-77 Growth Rate (%)	1969 million dollars	1977 million dollars	1977 (%)	1969-77 Growth Rate (%)
Primary Products[a]	68	193	39.1	13.9	125	512	87.5	19.2
0-1 Food, beverages and Tobacco	5	21	4.3	19.6	75	222	38.0	14.5
041-045	–	(8)	(1.6)	–	(9)	(87)	(14.9)	(32.8)
2 Raw materials excluding fuels, and vegetables	55	170	34.3	15.2	48	119	20.3	12.0
26 Textile fibers	(1)	(1)	(0.2)	–	(47)	(70)	(12.0)	(5.1)
28 Ores and metal scrap	(6)	(16)	(3.2)	(13.0)	–	(23)	(3.9)	–
4 Animal & vegetable oil	–	1	0.2	–	2	141	24.1	40.3
68 Non-ferrous metals	8	0	–	–	–	30	5.1	–
Fuels	3	3	0.6	–	18	1.2	–	–
Manufactured products	55	298	60.3	23.5	55	66	11.3	17.6
5 Chemicals	3	19	3.9	26.0	5	18	3.1	17.4
7 Machinery & transport equipment	3	99	20.0	54.8	4	17	2.9	19.8
6-8 Other manufactured goods	38	180	36.4	21.5	9	31	5.3	16.7
65 Textile yarn and fabric	(16)	(29)	(5.6)	7.7	6	13	2.2	10.1
73 Other manufactured metal products	(2)	(12)	(2.4)	25.1	–	–	–	–
84 Clothing	(2)	(74)	(15.0)	57.0	–	–	–	–
Total	126	493	100.0	18.6	145	585	100.0	19.0

Source: United Nations, *Yearbook of International Trade Statistics,* Vol. 1, 1974 and 1979, Special Table B.

Notes: [a] Primary products are SITC 0 to 2 plus 4 and 68 (includes non-ferrous metals). Fuels is SITC 3 and manufactures is SITC 5 to 8 excluding 68.

[b] Asia includes the four ADCs plus Afganistan, Brunei, Burma, India, Indonesia, Cambodia, Laos, Vietnam, Macao, Pakistan, Philippines, Sri Lanka and Thailand.

[c] South America (SA) includes all Latin America except Central America and the Caribbean.

case of petroleum. The most significant Latin American products competing with the Asian ADCs major export items are fish, with the Latin Americans having exports valued at $29 million as compared with $258 million worth from Asian ADCs at 1977 figures, textile garments, with the Latin Americans exporting $237 million and the Asian ADCs $264 million, and cotton fabrics, where the respective export totals were $115 million and $237 million. In the case of clothing, Latin America exports amount to about only $60 million as compared to $3,200 million exported by the Asian ADCs.

Analyzing future trade prospects for the two regions considered in this paper poses serious methodological problems. Trade does not only depend on GDP growth rates and purely static comparative advantages, but also on the competitors that each region faces; that is, the extent to which other Asian, African or Pacific countries could supply the Asian ADCs' import needs and to which the DCs could supply the Latin American import needs.

A careful consideration of this latter factor is certainly beyond the scope of this paper. But a modest attempt has been made to obtain a broad overview of comparative advantages at least in a static sense.

Tables 10 and 11 show the 5 main commodities exported by each of the Asian and Latin American ADCs respectively, together with the levels of imports and exports of the same commodities by each of the regions as a group.

At a first level of generality, looking at the 3-digit spectrum of commodities, the two economies considered look considerably more complementary than competitive. Within the list of 30 main commodities exported by each region at a world-wide level, 12 exported by the Asian ADCs and 18 by the Latin American, there is only one product that appears in both lists as a major export item. That is petroleum, which is heavily concentrated in a couple of countries: Singapore, in Asia, and Venezuela in Latin America. All the other main commodities exported by the Asian ADCs were not among the main exports of Latin America and vice-versa.

The complementarity of the trade structures of both regions is also apparent, although it is not as striking at a second level; that is, on a commodity by commodity basis. In the case of the Asian ADCs, Latin America is a net importer of 6 of its 12 main export items at the world level: ships, telecommunication equipment, crude rubber, electrical machinery, toys and woven textiles in that order of importance as measured by absolute value of imports. (See Table 10.)

Table 10. Asian ADCs: Main Goods Exported and Their Level of Exports and Imports by Latin American ADCs (1976)

(in million dollars)

| | Asian ADCs Exports | | | | Latin American ADCs Imports and Exports | | | | | | | | | | | |
| | Korea | Sin-gapore | Hong Kong | Total Asian ADCs | LA ADCs | | Argentina[a] | | Brazil[b] | | Chile[c] | | Mexico | | Venezuela | |
SITC					X	M	X	M	X	M	X	M	X	M	X	M
841 Clothing	1,132	117	1,964	3,213	191	130	49	—	109	—	—	27	33	40	—	63
332 Petrol. prod.	95	1,768	—	1,863	3,293	531	25	91	153	172	13	33	12	222	3,010	13
729 Electr. mach.	242	375	198	815	180	359	16	97	136	—	—	30	28	125	—	107
724 Telecom. equip.	138	169	300	607	140	459	—	40	132	146	—	12	8	110	—	151
231 Rubber crude	—	557	—	566	3	250	3	49	—	107	—	11	—	—	—	32
653 Wooven textile	272	—	78	350	48	70	—	12	48	27	—	2	—	51	—	29
694 Toys, sporting goods, etc.	—	—	324	324	—	32	—	—	—	—	—	—	—	—	—	32
631 Plywoods	208	79	—	287	67	—	—	—	53	—	—	—	14	—	—	—
735 Ships and boats	138	130	—	268	121	595	6	6,227	115	303	—	1	—	38	—	26
651 Wearing Apparel	204	—	60	264	266	29	24	—	181	—	—	2	61	—	—	27
031 Fish (fresh)	322	—	—	258	355	64	82	—	91	64	4	—	178	—	—	—
652 Cotton fabrics	—	—	237	237	115	—	—	—	69	—	—	—	46	—	—	—

Source: UNCTAD, *Handbook of International Trade and Development Statistics*, Table 43 (D) p. 132, and UN, *Yearbook of International Trade Statistics*.
Notes: [a] 1977 [b] 1978 [c] 1974.

Table 11. *Latin American ADCs: Main Goods Exported and Their Level of Imports and Exports by Asian ADCs*

(in million dollars)

SITC	Latin American ADCs Exports (1976)						Asian ADCs Imports and Exports (1978)							
	Argentina	Brazil	Chile	Mexico	Venezuela	Total	Total[a]		Hong Kong		Korea		Singapore	
							X	M	X	M	X	M	X	M
331 Crude oil	—	—	—	438	5,904	6,342	10	4,946	—	—	—	2,187	10	2,759
061 Sugar	131	1,148	—	170	—	1,449	27	241	24	33	—	177	3	31
281 Iron	—	921	132	—	283	1,336	—	56	—	—	—	56	—	—
071 Coffee	—	934	—	174	19	1,127	104	45	10	10	—	—	94	35
682 Copper	—	—	890	—	—	890	—	55	—	55	—	58	—	37
221 Oil seeds, nuts	—	718	—	—	—	718	—	—	—	—	—	78	—	63
81 Animal feeding stuff	142	508	33	—	—	683	80	138	—	52	—	—	80	86
044 Maize	518	150	—	—	—	668	—	325	—	32	—	231	—	62
732 Road motor vehicles	114	272	—	—	—	393	260	981	36	274	79	380	145	327
041 Wheat	301	—	—	—	—	301	—	289	—	20	—	235	—	34
332 Petrol products	—	—	—	—	—	243	2,906	1,018	41	646	30	12	2,835	360
851 Footwear	—	165	—	68	—	233	733	48	101	48	686	—	73	—
045 Cereal, nes, unmilled	225	—	—	—	—	225	101	47	—	47	28	—	—	—
283 Non-ferrous metal	—	—	181	—	—	181	39	294	—	145	39	102	—	47
011 Meat fresh or frozen	172	—	—	—	—	172	48	156	—	101	48	—	—	55
054 Vegetables	—	—	—	164	—	164	—	73	—	—	—	73	—	—
271 Fertilizers	—	43	—	—	—	43	—	—	—	—	—	—	—	—
251 Pulp and waste paper	—	78	—	—	—	78	—	181	—	—	—	181	—	—

Source: UNCTAD, *ibid.*, Table 4.3 (D), and UN, *ibid.*
Note: [a] There is no data published for Taiwan.

On balance, and excluding the special case of crude oil, there would still be a case for the hypothesis of complementarity at an aggregate level, in the sense that the aggregate value of Latin American imports is higher than its exports of the main Asian exported goods by a considerable margin.[7]

If the best prospects for increased exports exist in those goods in which Latin American net imports are already large relative to the Asian exports, then the main candidates are ships, telecommunication equipment and electrical machinery. But the prospects for clothing cannot be dismissed if the Latin American countries reduce their levels of import protection as several of them have started to do.

The complementarity of the Asian and Latin American economies is reinforced when trade structures are observed from the latter's perspective as exporter. Indeed, the Asian ADCs are net importers of 13 of the 18 main commodities exported by Latin America. It is a net importer of all but one of the 10 main Latin American export items. Crude petroleum, vehicles, maize, wheat, meat, sugar and pulp are the principal goods as measured by the value of their imports. It is interesting to see that all except one are primary products.

The major items in which the two regions are competitive at a world level are petroleum products, footwear, coffee and non-ferrous metals. Within these markets each region has very different shares: Latin America dominates in the exports of coffee and non-ferrous metals, while the Asian ADCs sell three times as much footwear and over seven times as much petroleum products. The aggregate value of Asian imports of the main Latin American export commodities exceed the value of the latter by a factor that ranges between 2 and 3 depending on whether one includes or excludes oil.

Apparently, the best prospects for increased exports from the Latin American to the Asian ADCs exist in food items, especially meat, wheat, sugar, feeding stuff and vegetables, and pulp. There is also a potential for very significant exports of crude oil, especially after the entry of Mexico into that market. The case of the expansion of motor vehicle exports is more questionable. It would be necessary to examine this case more carefully.

Complementarity is clearly greater between the Asian ADCs and two particular countries: Argentina, the major food exporter in

---

[7] On the other hand, that complementarity is considerably greater between subsets of countries.

the region and Chile. But all countries have some opportunities. At a regional level it is significant that Asian net imports of the main Latin American export goods amount to about $1.8 billion excluding oil. This figure represents over one fifth of the value of Latin American exports of those products. This would be the magnitude of what could be called the gross market potential of the Asian ADCs for Latin American exports.[8]

In synthesis, the disaggregated analysis by commodities confirms the a priori hypothesis that from the point of view of the Asian ADCs, the major interest for developing trade with Latin America would be to have a source of supply of food and raw material imports, and not predominantly as a key export market. To the extent that Latin America is also interested in developing its primary exports, there are good prospects for a significant expansion of trade between the two regions.

IV. Latin America's Commodity Exports

In the previous sections it has been shown that most exports from Latin America to the Asian ADCs are made up of primary products. Given the policy trends in the former region and the needs of the latter, it is likely that trade in these type of commodities will present the most promising prospects for Latin America in the future.

That situation may have some negative welfare implications for Latin America. It could reproduce the traditional pattern of trade that this region has had with the developed countries, and from which it tried to escape in the past. This issue will be addressed in the final section of the paper, and means of avoiding some of the negative aspects of it will be suggested.

In this section, however, the purely factual prospect of this trade will be examined and some background information on the characteristics of Latin America's commodity exports will be provided. Initially the importance of Latin American primary exports in the

---

[8] It is interesting to note that the equivalent values from the point of view of the Asian ADCs are much lower. Latin American's net imports of the main Asian export goods amount to only about $500 million, which represent merely 7 percent of the value of the main Asian ADCs' exports. But these figures are heavily influenced by the high value of Asian clothing exports. Excluding this item, the ratio doubles.

world's total will be examined, and then the competitive position of the region with regard to its main export commodities will be scrutinized.

1. Primary Exports at the World and Regional Levels

First of all, it should be noted that Latin America obviously is not the only possible source of natural resources or commodity exports available for the Asian ADCs; but it is one of the most important ones. It is seldom realized that the developing countries as a whole are not the main exporters of primary products in the world.[9] Indeed, they account for only about a third of all primary exports.

Notwithstanding, Latin America is the main source of primary exports from developing countries. It accounted for 40 percent of them in 1977, compared to 36 percent for Asia and 22 percent for Africa (IBRD, 1979, Table 1).[10]

Secondly the significance of Latin America's position as a primary products exporting region in the world is reinforced by its situation as an importer. It is the region with relatively the lowest imports of primary products and is therefore the largest net exporter in the world. Its net exports in 1977 amounted to almost $20 billion as compared to only $1 billion in the case of Asia and $6 billion in that of Africa. The developed countries, on the other hand, notwithstanding their significance as primary exporters, are still net importers at the rate of over $23 billion in 1977 (IBRD, 1979, Table 2).

The list of main primary products exported by Latin America at the worldwide level contains virtually the same goods that are exported most heavily to Asia. The only significant items which are not sold in Asia are tropical fruits, mainly bananas and cacao, cotton and some less important goods among the Latin American exports, that is, those representing less than 0.6 percent of the region's sales abroad, such as bauxite, zinc, tin and wool. What have been defined as the Latin American ADCs are the most important exporters of all the principal primary products sold to the Asian ADCs.

---

[9] All references to primary products in this paper exclude crude oil, unless it is explicitly stated otherwise.

[10] This implies 28, 25 and 15 percent, respectively, of the world's exports of primary products.

2. Competitive Position of Latin America in Its Main Exported Primary Products

As mentioned repeatedly in this study, an important factor influencing past and future trade trends is the availability of alternative import sources. At least for the case of Asia as an importer and of Latin America as exporter this issue can be studied in both a general and an aggregate fashion.

Table 12 presents the share held by Latin America, other LDCs and the developed countries in the worldwide exports of each of a selection of 7 of the principal Latin American commodities exported to the Asian ADCs. The main conclusion derived from Table 12 is that the Latin American competitive edge is not considerable in any commodity except coffee. In all the remaining commodities, it is the developed countries who account for the largest share of the world's exports. But among the LDCs, Latin America is the larger supplier of all primary commodities, except crude oil and copper.

Nevertheless, individual Latin American countries still have significiant shares of the world market. Brazil is the major exporter of 3 of the 7 selected commodities, with shares ranging from 10 percent to 23 percent of world exports. Chile and Argentina are also big exporters of copper and beef, respectively, in the world. This fact could give some Latin American countries the possibility of acting as market leaders to negotiate effectively some new forms of trade cooperation among LDCs within a New International Economic Order.

V. Trade Prospects and Other Concluding Remarks

The main conclusion that emerges from this study is that, so far, trade relations between Latin America and the Asian ADCs have been rather limited. The share of each group's exports to or imports from the other region have fluctuated between only 1 and 2.5 percent.

Notwithstanding its past performance, the outlook of future trade is promising; it is very likely that trade between the two regions studied here will expand faster than with any of their other partners in the future. The key reason is that Latin America is shifting progressively towards a more free trade development strategy. This will imply an expansion of exports and imports based on their natural

Table 12. Regional Shares in the World's Total Exports of the Main Latin
           American Exported Commodities: 1974-76

(in percent)

Commodities[a]	Latin America	Other LDCs	DCs	Ranking of main worldwide exporting countries[b]
Petroleum (17.8)	6.7	84.5	8.8	S. Arabia (25); Iran & Nigeria (47)
Sugar (5.4)	27.4	23.7	48.8	Brazil (10);Philip. & Dom.Rep. (21)
Iron ore (2.7)	21.9	18.3	59.8	Brazil (16); Liberia & Ven. (27)
Coffee (7.1)	58.9	33.9	7.2	Brazil (23); Colom. & Ivory C. (43)
Copper (3.2)	20.5	32.3	47.2	Chile (17); Zambia & Zaire (39)
Oil seeds (*)	38.7	14.6	46.7	n.a.
Beef (1.0)	12.2	1.5	86.3	n.a.

Source: IBRD, *Commodity Trade and Price Trends*, 1978 Edition, Washington,
D.C., 1978.

Notes: [a] The figures in parentheses represents the share of each commodity in Latin
America's total exports (* = less than 0.3%)

[b] Figures in parentheses are the commulative shares in world markets.

comparative advantages; and both regions have advantages in very
different products. Furthermore, the expected faster income growth
of the Asian and Latin American ADCs, as compared to the world as
a whole, introduces an additional dynamic factor that should tend to
increase reciprocal trade relations. However, this is a hypothesis
rather than a definite statement. It could obviously be an interesting
topic for further research and, thus, a few remarks on it may be in
order.

First, to test that hypothesis it would be necessary to resort to more
disaggregated data and to consider the domestic productive structures
in both regions, rather than trade alone. The scattered empirical
evidence presented here is too aggregated, in the sense of considering
roughly only two sets of goods: primary products and manufactures.
But it must be noted that Latin America could also concentrate
relatively more on exporting manufactures and still be complementary
with the trade structure of Asian ADCs.

Secondly, the hypothesis implies a very definite theoretical explanation of why trade has not been greater between the Latin
American and Asian ADCs. It is because exports of light manufactures from the latter countries were prevented from entering the
former countries' markets by very high trade barriers. Precisely for
that reason the elimination of those restrictions is likely to foster

trade. There are obviously other factors involved too, such as high transport costs.

Thirdly, the factors mentioned previously may explain why trade with the Asian ADCs is relatively more important for the smaller than for the larger Latin American countries. The latter have been in a better position to produce domestically the light manufactured goods exported by the Asian ADCs. They have also avoided reducing their tariff protection as well.

Finally, in analyzing future trade prospects, it would be interesting to study the experience of trade relations between Latin America and Japan since the late 1950s, when the latter was at the stage of development of the present ADCs. If Japan is a relevant model, the odds are that trade between Latin America and the Asian ADCs will expand significantly in the future, because trade has grown quickly between Latin America and Japan over the last two decades.

During the second half of the 1970s, some indications of the expected rise in Asian-Latin American trade started to materialize. The Latin American ADCs have taken the lead in this period: between 1974 and 1978 their exports to their Asian equivalents have increased at an annual rate of 45 percent, four times more than to the rest of the world. As a result of this, they reversed past trends and increased their share of exports going to the Asian ADCs from 0.7 to 1.5 percent in only four years. Argentina and Chile have in fact been the pioneers in this movement, with the rest far behind. A liberalization of trade in the other Latin American countries, as well as the beginning of Mexico's oil exports, could accelerate that trend considerably. On the buyer's side, Korea and Singapore have been the main importers, sustaining the expansion of Latin American sales to that region.

Korea, as well as Taiwan, have been the most dynamic exporters to Latin America in the second half of the 1970s. Chile and Venezuela have been the buyers taking most of those sales. The case of the latter is a clear result of the income rise coming from the oil bonanza, while that of the former is the result of the trade liberalization that has taken place in the country. There is no doubt that the 1979 trade figures will show that Argentina has dramatically increased her imports from the Asian ADCs as a result of the same process.[11]

---

[11] In fact, as this paper was being revised, the IMF came out with trade figures for 1979. They show that Argentina's imports from the Asian ADCs (excluding Taiwan) grew from $33 million in 1978 to almost $98 million the following year. As expected,

As for the future, it should be stressed that the trade liberalization that is taking place in Latin America does not imply opening the borders to the entry of cheap Asian consumer goods which are elsewhere invading world markets. Rather, it should act as a stimulus to exports on the part of Latin America. The export goods which were relatively more discriminated against in the past in Latin America and which will, therefore, expand faster in the future, are primary products. They are, in turn, the goods which most Asian ADCs need to import, in order to sustain their industrial growth and to satisfy the growing needs of their populations as their incomes rise. One can observe clearly this trade pattern emerging in the case of Chile and Korea.

Concentration on primary exports may pose political problems for some Latin American countries, who are particularly sensitive about this issue. In this case, there is scope for official cooperation between governments of the Latin American and Asian ADCs in order to reach trade agreements favorable to both. In particular, the Asian ADCs should consider reducing their tariff and non-tariff restrictions on the import of processed raw materials from LDCs. This has not been the case, for instance, with copper products, to which several Asian ADCs apply escalating tariffs in the same fashion as the developed countries do; Korea has even built a large copper refinery, which can be made profitable only if tariffs on refined copper are much higher than on unwrought mineral. This is probably the case with many other processed raw materials.

The latter type of agreement should be more feasible between primary exporters and countries in the rapid process of industrialization such as the Asian ADCs, precisely because they have not yet fully industrialized backwards as the present rich countries have. Therefore, often they do not already have vested interests in maintaining a raw material processing industry. What is needed, however, are long run agreements and careful joint industrial planning, because it is necessary to "jump" over several processing stages, rather than aim taking at small steps. The reason for this is that transport costs usually become an important impediment to profitable trade in more processed primary products. But in this field there may be substantial externalities as new transport routes are opened.

---

most of the increase is with Korea; imports from it increased from $2.3 million in 1978 to $23.7 million in 1979. Exports did not grow as fast (they "only" doubled to $82 million). Chilean exports to and imports from Hong Kong and Korea also doubled. (There is no data about the other ADCs.)

Finally, the concentration on fostering reciprocal trade relations should not preclude more joint cooperation at the world level. There are several areas of common problems with respect to exports to third countries, and especially to the rich ones. Further research is needed to identify the specific industries in which the Latin American and Asian ADCs are competing against each other in the developed countries. Rather than continue to undercut each other in those markets, they could coordinate their efforts to reduce protection on them in the developed countries. Greater cooperation between the two most significant groups of LDCs in world trade could certainly be enhanced through the development of more reciprocal trade relations. Such actions are also likely to open new options to other developing countries, contributing to effectively implementing a new International Economic Order.

REFERENCES

IBRD, *Commodity Trade and Price Trends*, 1978 Edition, Washington, D.C., 1978.

IMF, *Directions of World Trade, 1979*, Washington, D.C., 1980.

Tironi, E., "National Policies Towards Commodity Exports," French-Davis and Tironi (eds.), *America Latina y el Nuevo Orden Economico Internacional*, FCE, Mexico, 1980. (Forthcoming also in English, Macmillan, London.)

United Nations, *Yearbook of International Trade Statistics*, New York, 1979.

World Bank, *World Development Report*, Washington, D.C., 1979.

APPENDIX

Table A.1. Asian ADCs Value of Exports to Latin America and Other Regions: 1969-78.

(in million dollars)

Exports from / to	Hong Kong			Taiwan			Korea		
	1969	1974	1978	1969	1974	1978	1969	1974	1978[a]
LA ADCs	18	49	88	1	24	132	—[b]	17	68
Argentina	2	5	10	—	2	6	—	7	6
Brazil	2	14	13	—[b]	9	7	—	—	6
Chile	..[c]	1	11	..[b]	1	38	—	—	22
Mexico	6	10	15	1	1	25	—	10	11
Panama	10	36	76	—[b]	22	165	2	20	91
Venezuela	8	19	39	..	11	56	—	—	23
Others	22	38	74	5	42	109	3	48	69
All LA	50	123	238	6	89	406	5	85	228
DCs	1,516	4,152	8,033	696	3,895	8,511	515	3,684	9,482
Asia	319	976	1,812	261	857	1,780	78	357	1,104
Oil exporters	104	368	897	38	280	964	5	168	1,364
Other LDCs[c]	188	339	528	37	390	1,021	20	166	544
Total	2,177	5,958	11,498	1,038	5,510	12,682	623	4,460	12,722

Table A. 1. (Continued)

Exports to \ from	Singapore 1969	Singapore 1974	Singapore 1978a	Total Asian ADCs 1969	Total Asian ADCs 1974	Total Asian ADCs 1978
LA ADCs	21	91	128	40	181	416
Argentina	8	19	20	10	33	42
Brazil	3	43	65	5	66	91
Chile	1	4	8	1	6	79
Mexico	6	16	26	13	37	77
Panama	3	39	72	15	117	404
Venezuela	3	9	98	11	39	127
Others	9	26	39	39	154	291
All LA	33	156	239	94	452	1,111
DCs	519	2,754	4,590	3,246	14,485	30,616
Asia	704	2,197	3,951	1,362	4,387	8,647
Oil exporters	17	166	537	164	982	3,752
Other LDCs[c]	276	542	815	521	1,437	2,908
Total	1,549	5,815	10,132	5,387	21,743	47,034

Source: IMF, *Direction of Trade 1969-75 and 1979*, Washington, D.C.
Notes: [a] Estimates.
[b] Values less than $1 million.
[c] Other LDCs includes Middle East and Africa.

Table A.2. Latin America; Value of Exports to Asian ADCs and Other Regions: 1969-78

(in million dollars)

Exports from / to	Argentina			Brazil			Chile			Mexico			Venezuela		
	1969	1974	1978ᵃ	1969	1974	1978	1969	1974	1978ᵃ	1969	1974	1978	1969	1974ᵃ	1978
Taiwan	1	6	70	13	12	23	—	5	29	3	—	—	—	2	4
Hong Kong	2	4	15	34	19	30	—	—	2	1	2	3	—	1	1
Korea	..ᵇ	2	15	—	4	24	—	9	32	1	1	8	—	—	—
Singapore	..ᶜ	1	11	2	10	48	—	..ᵇ	—	—	..ᵇ	1	6	—	—
Total ADCs	3	13	111	49	45	125	—	14	63	5	3	12	6	3	5
DCs	998	2,060	3,569	1,677	5,415	8,279	921	1,793	1,515	1,057	2,369	4,866	1,734	7,220	5,554
LA	361	893	1,418	256	962	1,568	113	404	565	112	373	448	1,078	3,062	3,325
Oil exporters	21	181	288	7	558	905	3	9	99	16	45	151	2	—	1
Others LDCsᶜ	229	784	1,016	322	973	1,773	38	259	141	240	203	477	77	787	106
Total	1,612	3,931	6,402	2,311	7,953	12,650	1,075	2,479	2,383	1,430	2,993	5,954	2,894	11,072	8,991

Table A. 2. (Continued)

Exports from / to	LA ADCs			Panama			Total LA		
	1969	1974	1978	1969	1974	1978[a]	1969	1974	1978
Taiwan	17	25	126	:[b]	—	1	27	50	173
Hong Kong	37	26	51	:[b]	—	—[b]	46	35	70
Korea	1	16	79	—	:[b]	:[b]	3	17	92
Singapore	8	11	60	—	—	—	23	18	73
Total ADCs	63	78	316	—	—	1	99	120	408
DCs	6,387	18,857	23,783	97	146	160	8,709	24,315	33,811
LA	1,920	5,694	7,324	11	53	72	1,569	5,604	7,583
Oil exporters	49	793	1,444	:[b]	1	8	93	953	2,381
Other LDCs[c]	906	3,006	3,513	1	1	4	1,232	3,140	4,850
Total	9,325	28,428	36,380	109	201	245	11,702	34,132	40,033

Source: IMF, *Director of Trade 1969-75, 1979*, Washington, D.C.
Notes: [a] Estimates.
[b] Values less than $1 million.
[c] Includes Africa and Middle East.

• COMMENT _____

Mohamed Ariff,   *University of Malaya*

Tironi begins his analysis by noting down the major differences and similarities between the Latin American and the Asian ADCs, and concludes by emphasizing the enormous scope for trade co-operation between the two groups of ADCs. His main thesis is that the economies of the Asian and the Latin American ADCs are complementary rather than competitive.

The main shortcoming of the paper stems from the lack of a consistent grouping of countries, which has rendered comparison somewhat hazardous. Comparisons between various grouping frequently resorted to by the author tend to distort the picture somewhat. Neither the ADCs of Asia nor those of Latin America are by any means a homogenous lot. They are indeed too heterogenous to permit any meaningful analysis at the aggregate level. The author is not unaware of this, as shown by his attempt to disaggregate at a later stage. His attempt however is thwarted by the lack of adequate data. But, the fact remains that his conclusions based on highly aggregated sets of data should be treated with extreme caution.

It is very clear that the ADCs of Asia are very different from those of Latin America, although they are more or less at the same stage of development, as shown by their per capita income levels. In terms of factor endowments, population size, aggregate incomes, distribution of income, trade bias, composition of exports, and ratios of investment to GNP, the Latin American and the Asian ADCs are distinctly dissimilar. These dissimilarities, however, do not necessarily suggest that the economies of the Latin American and the Asian ADCs are inherently complementary and not competitive.

The author has pointed out that while the exports of the Latin American ADCs consist mainly of primary products, those of the Asian ADCs consist largely of manufactured goods. The author has also drawn attention to the fact that the Asian ADCs are net importers of 13 of the 18 main Latin American export commodities,

while the Latin American ADCs are net importers of 6 of the 16
main export items of the Asian ADCs, which, according to the
author, reflects the underlying complementarity of the economies of
the Latin American and the Asian ADCs. At the same time, the
author has not failed to observe that, in spite of this complementarity,
the trade flows between the two groups of ADCs have been rather
negligible. The author has provided no valid explanation for this
divergence between his a priori expectations and empirical observations. His explanation is simply mechanistic in terms of the differential performances of individual countries. Nonetheless, one may
venture to attribute the sluggish trade flows between the ADCs of
Asia and Latin America to the absence of historical ties and the
presence of formidable physical distances between them and the
availability of alternative sources of imports and markets for exports.

While the trade pattern between the two regions might suggest
some complementarity, the structures of trade between individual
countries of the two regions seem to question it. Thus, Hong Kong
and Taiwan, which are resource-poor, import very little from the
resource-rich Latin American ADCs. In any case, it would be incorrect
to infer anything about the complementarity or competitiveness of a
pair of countries or regions from the pattern of trade flows alone.
Trade in the real world is often distorted by policy interventions.

To ascertain the nature of the inter-regional relationship, one needs
to examine the structure of production in both export and non-export
sectors, in addition to the pattern of trade flows both between the two
groups and between them and the rest of the world. The author has
made an analysis of the trade figures, but he has failed to investigate
the structure of production. Thus, for example, it may be inferred
from the paper that only a few Latin American ADC manufactures
compete with the manufactured exports of the Asian ADCs in international markets. However, it is not known how many of the Asian
ADC manufactured exports would compete with local manufactures
in the domestic markets of the Latin American ADCs in the absence
of tariff and non-tariff barriers. It would be revealing to compare the
development and trade strategies and policies in general and the
structure of protection in particular of the Asian ADCs with those of
the Latin American ADCs. Perhaps all these fall beyond the scope of
Tironi's seminal paper, but at least the author could have qualified
his conclusions.

It appears from casual empiricism that the industrialization strategies of the Latin American ADCs are quite different from those of the Asian ADCs. The former seem to be rather 'inward-looking,' while the latter are clearly 'outward-looking.' As a result, there has been no direct competition between the two groups of countries in international markets. However, import-competing industrialization in the Latin American ADCs would not provide a viable basis for a complementary relationship with their Asian counterparts. A lot more serious work needs to be done on a product-by-product basis before this can be considered definitive.

The author asserts that the comparative advantage of the Latin American ADCs lies in primary production. This represents no more than a static view point. Moreover, this solution may not be acceptable to the Latin American regimes which have been highly critical of 'overspecialization' in primary production. Besides, the Latin American ADCs possess a variety of natural resources which may provide a strong basis for forward linkages. In other words, the Latin American ADCs may well develop a comparative advantage for a wide range of manufactures. Indeed, they may emulate the Asian ADCs whose dynamism has become a source of inspiration and envy for many a developing country. Thus, it is not only possible but also highly probable that the Latin American ADCs will soon follow in the footsteps of their Asian counterparts and go into export-oriented manufacturing production in a big way. However, it does not necessarily follow that this demonstration effect will lead to increased rivalry between the Asian and the Latin American ADCs in the international arena. The latter may have a competitive edge over the former in resource-based industries, while the former may concentrate on technology-intensive and skill-intensive manufactures. The Asian ADCs in particular have demonstrated their capacity for adaptation and transformation, which will ensure greater efficiency in international resource allocation in a dynamic world.

One may therefore argue that complementarity between the ADCs of Asia and Latin America need not necessarily partake of the character of the former specializing in manufactures and the latter in primary or food production. It is quite possible for these ADCs to go into export-oriented manufacturing and still maintain the complementarity necessary for inter-regional cooperation.

Tironi ends his paper on an optimistic note concerning the outlook for future trade between the Asian and the Latin American ADCs, notwithstanding the past dismal performance. It is clear from the statistics that the Latin American ADCs are more important to the Asian ADCs as a source of raw material imports than the Asian ADCs are to the Latin American ADCs as a source of manufactured imports. Future trade relations will have to be based on increased interdependence and this calls for the breaking down of the trade barriers. Tariffs on raw material imports are negligible or non-existent in most Asian ADCs. The Latin American tariffs on the imports of manufactures do not appear to be too formidable for the Asian ADCs to overcome. Yet, trade flows have been sluggish. Perhaps it is the non-tariff barriers, the absence of historical ties, sheer physical distance and ignorance of opportunities which explain the low volume of trade flows. Economic distance, measured in terms of the ratio of the costs of freight and insurance to total sales, may be reduced via scale economies by increasing the volume of trade flows. Economic distance is both the cause and the consequence of poor. trade flows. There is a need to study this aspect, and find ways and means of breaking this vicious circle.

Two other aspects also deserve special attention. One is the differential rates of inflation in the Latin American and the Asian ADCs, and the other the rise of regionalism in Latin America and Asia. The Latin American countries are known to experience runaway inflation while the inflationary rates in the Asian ADCs in general and for Japan in particular are mild by Latin American standards. The implications of this for trade flows, terms of trade, and balance of payment should be studied. The rising tide of regionalism may also affect the composition and direction of trade flows of the ADCs in the Pacific Basin. The implications of the emergence of LAFTA and Andean Common market in Latin America and ASEAN in Southeast Asia for inter-regional trade will have to be studied carefully. It is not at all clear at this stage how these various sub-regional groupings will fit into the broader Pacific basin concept of economic cooperation.

Ben Smith, *Australian National University*

Tironi has looked at the overall patterns of trade of the Asian and Latin American ADCs and found that they are reasonably complementary in that the Asian ADCs are predominantly exporters of manufactures while the Latin American countries are predominantly primary producers. On the basis of this difference he forms the hypothesis that trade between the two areas should be relatively intense, but of course formation of the hypothesis on that basis alone ignores the role of an important set of trade resistances of which distance is the most obvious in the present context.

Tironi finds that the intensity of trade between Asian ADCs and Latin America is relatively low, though it's higher for the export flow from Asia to Latin America than for the reverse. Asian ADC exports to Latin America have been growing more rapidly than their exports overall, while Latin American exports to the Asian ADCs have grown marginally more rapidly than their overall exports. Tironi makes little attempt to indicate what factors have brought about these results, but perhaps the level of aggregation here is too great to allow anything useful to be said.

At a more disaggregated level, Tironi shows that the largest Latin American country, Brazil, is a relatively unimportant market for Asian ADCs while the smaller country, Chile, is relatively important. However, the paper does not reveal whether this is because of differing relative factor endowments between Chile and Brazil, because of different biases in the trade policies of those two countries, or simply because Chile is closer to Asia than is Brazil.

A similar sort of variation appears if the reverse trade flow is examined where Brazil and Argentina are relatively important import sources for Singapore and Hong Kong, and Chile is a relatively important import source of Korea and Taiwan. Again it would be helpful to have some analysis of the underlying factors generating those results.

Tironi concludes his paper by suggesting that there is significant scope for increased intensity of trade between the Asian ADCs and the Latin American developing countries, because of the basic complementarity of the two sets of economies and because of expected increased openness of the Latin American economies in future. Though this judgment may well be correct, it can only considered tentative on the basis of Tironi's analysis. Tironi seems to suggest further that the anticipated expansion of trade is likely to be relatively balanced in the two directions, and that must be considered even more tentative.

There are two main directions in which research needs to be

extended before a confident picture of likely future trade relations between Asian ADCs and Latin American countries can be obtained. First, greater account needs to be taken of differences between the Latin American countries, both in relation to their basic comparative advantage structures and in relation to the relative importance of distance in respect of trade with Asia. A more comprehensive picture is needed, at a more disaggregated level, of the potential supply capacity of the Latin American countries as exported to Asia, and of their potential as export markets for Asian ADCs.

Secondly, one cannot really draw any conclusions about the potential trade relationship between the Asian ADCs and the relatively resource-rich developing countries of Latin America without also considering the position of the resource-rich developing countries of the Asian region itself. While there may be a high degree of complementarity between the trade structures of Asian ADCs and Latin American countries, the trade structures of ASEAN countries other than Singapore and Latin American economies are essentially competitive. Examination of the nature of the competitiveness, and of the importance of the greater distance between Latin America and Asian ADCs than between the latter and ASEAN, is crucial to determining the likely future flows of exports from Latin America. It may well be that greater openness of the Latin American economies will result in increased intensity of export trade from Asian ADCs to Latin America, but that the competitive nature of the closer resource-rich developing countries in Asia will inhibit a symmetrical increase in intensity of the reverse trade flow. That possibility is, of course, increased by the greater transport cost resistance to trade in primary products than in manufactures.

What seems to be needed is a broad study of the relationships between the resource-poor ADCs of the Pacific and the resource-rich developing countries, including both Asian and Latin American economics. One of the unfortunate aspects of the fact that this Conference has not included such a study is that the relationship between the ASEAN countries other than Singapore and the Asian ADCs has not been given any serious attention.

Finally, it may be that one could obtain some insight into potential trade flows between Latin American economies and the Asian ADCs by examining the trade patterns established between the former countries and Japan, making suitable adjustment for likely differences between the development patterns of the ADCs and the

Japanese experience. In particular, if the areas in which Latin American countries have successfully competed with resource-rich Asian ADCs for access to markets in Japan were examined, it might be possible to draw some tentative conclusions about export prospects to the ADCs as they continue to develop. Probably the main success of Latin American economies in Japan has been as suppliers of basic industrial raw materials for industries which will form a less important part of the ADCs development pattern than they did in Japan. Then, export prospects for the Latin American countries in Asian ADCs may depend heavily on the comparative advantage position of the former in the processing of primary products, where they would be likely to face competition from Australia and other resource-rich developed countries of the region as well as from ASEAN.

GENERAL DISCUSSION

One might argue that Latin American countries should not promote export expansion of agricultural and mineral products because they are not very labor-intensive, and hence would not contribute much to reduce unemployment. However, although primary production may not directly expand employment very much, its export earnings can finance the imports of investment goods that can be used for labor-intensive manufacturing, either for export or for import substi- tution. Thus, expansion of primary exports can lead to expansion of manufacturing and employment in Latin American countries.

The growth rates of primary exports will depend on world demand conditions, including growth of world income and income elasticities, which look good. Sweden, for instance, has gone through the stages of primary exporter and exporter of processed primary goods and is now exporting sophisticated manufactures. Japan also exported raw silk in the early stages. One does not have to believe that take-off can only come from manufactures exports.

Th Latin American advanced developing countries may have to be separated further into three groups depending on their level of industrialization: the most advanced group may consist of Brazil and Mexico which can export highly advanced industrial products, the less advanced one consisting of Argentina and Chile which are still exporting large amounts of raw materials, and the least advanced one may consist of countries like Venezuela. These different groups may have different trade relationships with Asian ADCs. It is probably there would be competition between Mexico and Brazil on the one hand and Korea and Taiwan on the other in exports of heavy industrial products such as ships. Furthermore, there may be competition between Latin American primary goods exporters and Oceanian countries.

The apparent lack of any substantial trading between Latin American ADCs and Asian ADCs might be explained by competitive economic structures, or it might be explained by the fact that Mexican exports are so heavily oriented towards U.S. market and Brazilian exports to the U.S., Japan, the EC and Africa that these Latin American ADCs do not have much incentive to diversify their markets geographically and to extend them to Asian ADCs.

On the other hand, the apparent lack of trade between Latin American ADCs and Asian ADCs might be explained in terms of import-substitution policies in Latin America. For instance, since Chile and Argentina eased their import-substitution policies, their imports from Asian ADCs have substantially increased. Because of the inherently complementary nature of resource endowments between Chile and Argentina on the one hand, with production of raw material and processed primary products, and Asian ADCs on the other, with labor and skilled labor-intensive manufactures, the trade volume between these two regions should expand rapidly in the future. In the past, the import-substitution policies of Latin American countries tended to reduce the volume of primary exports. As Latin American countries adopt more liberal trade policies, their primary exports will increase. The demand for raw materials by Asian ADCs will keep expanding rapidly.

Import-substitution policies of Latin American countries encouraged domestic production of the entire range of consumer goods. After the liberalization of import restrictions in Chile, imports of light consumer goods have expanded most rapidly. Capital goods are not subject to severe import restriction, and hence imports of capital goods by some Latin American ADCs from Asian ADCs may grow rapidly as the latter countries shift their export pattern towards investment goods in the future.

Latin American ADCs should not continue import-substitution

policies, nor should they try to imitate the export pattern of Asian ADCs. They have to promote the exports of natural-resource intensive goods more actively.

PART V

ADJUSTMENT TO ADCs IN ADVANCED COUNTRIES

AN ANALYSIS OF STRUCTURAL DEPENDENCE BETWEEN KOREA AND JAPAN

*Toshio Watanabe**

I. Introduction

Trade between Korea and Japan is vertical and one-sided because of the unilateral dependence of the former on the latter. The purpose of the present study is to portray the basic structure of this vertical trade pattern (Section II), to relate the pattern to the contrasting industrial structures of the two countries (Section III), and to analyze the vertical and unilateral industrial relationship of Korea and Japan by means of international input-output tables (Section IV). In the concluding section, an attempt will be made to indicate future prospects in the trade relationship between the two countries by comparing it with Japan's trade patterns vis-a-vis other Asian advanced developing countries (ADCs), ASEAN countries and the United States (Section V).

II. The Basic Structure of Industrial Specialization between Korea and Japan

Trade between Korea and Japan is vertical in the sense that Korea imports producer goods from Japan, while exporting light industrial consumer goods. In 1978, 82.7 percent of Japan's total exports to

* Associate Professor of Asian Studies, University of Tsukuba, Japan.

Korea were composed of such heavy and chemical industry products as machinery, metal products and chemicals. The exports from Korea to Japan in the same year were largely foodstuffs, raw materials and light industrial products, with textiles and textile articles accounting for 43.1 percent of the total.

The balance of trade by industry between Korea and Japan for the year 1978, as shown in Figure 1, shows the vertical inter-industry trade between the two countries. Of 22 industrial sub-sectors listed, net exports from Japan are dominated by such products as general machinery (22), electrical and electronic machinery (23), transport equipment (24), primary iron (19) and chemical products (14), while the trade balance favors Korea in textile products (09), food products (05) and fiber yarns (08).

Excluding tobacco (07), beverages (05), printing (12) and coal products (16), for which trade between Korea and Japan is insignificant in value, only two industrial categories, miscellaneous manufactures (26) and textile products (09), imply horizontal industrial specialization between the two countries. Textile products are of greatest importance and, together with fiber yarns (08), account for 56.5 percent of the total Korean exports to Japan. It has to be noted, however, that the greater horizontal specialization in textiles and textile articles is actually only apparent when scrutinized more closely.

Figure 2 shows the breakdown by 4-digit CCCN classification of the intra-industry trade index for all textiles and textile articles between Japan and Korea in the year 1977. As shown in the figure, Korea specializes in exports of various apparel products (CCCN categories 60, 61, and 62) in addition to silk and waste silk (50) and cotton yarns (55-05). With respect to such input materials as synthetic and man-made fiber yarns and woven fabrics (56), which require capital- and technology-intensive large-scale production systems, Korea mostly depends on imports from Japan. Furthermore, the intra-industry trade indexes shown in the figure are for the most part close to either $+1$ or -1, unmistakably indicating specialization between the two countries. Apropos of further upstream products such as ethylene glycol, caprolactum, and acrylonitrile, and of textile machinery, Korea is entirely dependent on imports from Japan.

Excluding food products (05) from consideration, electrical and electronic machinery (23) is second in importance only to textile products in Korea's exports to Japan. The vertical specialization is also evident in this intra-industry trade; Japan engages in technologi-

Figure 1. Japan's Net Exports to Korea by Industry and Intra-industry Trade Index [a] (1978)

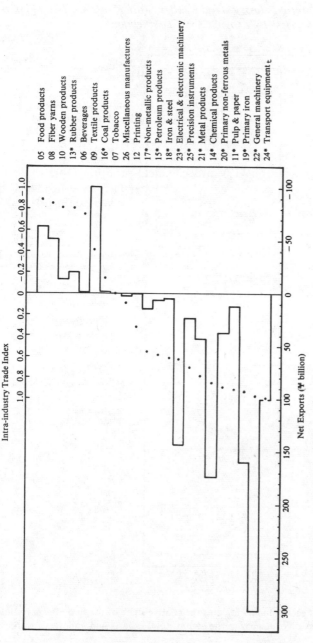

Source: Japan Tariff Association, *Japan Exports and Imports: Country by Commodity,* Tokyo, December 1979.

Notes: * Asterisks indicate heavy and chemical industries.

[a] The intra-industry trade index is shown by the formula $(E_{ij} - M_{ij})/(E_{ij} + M_{ij})$, where E_{ij} represents Japan's export of i commodity category to j country and M_{ij} her import of i commodity category from j country. When Japan's export of commodities in a particular industrial category to a country is equal to her import of the same category of commodities from the country, the trade between Japan and the country is considered completely horizontal and the intra-industry trade index is zero. If Japan entirely specializes in export to, or import from, another country with respect to a commodity category, the intra-industry trade index is either plus 1 or minus 1 respectively. Closer the index to zero in both signs, more horizontal is the industrial specialization between the two countries.

Figure 2.   Japan's Intra-industry Trade Index with Korea in Textiles and Textile Articles: 1977 (by CCCN Classification)

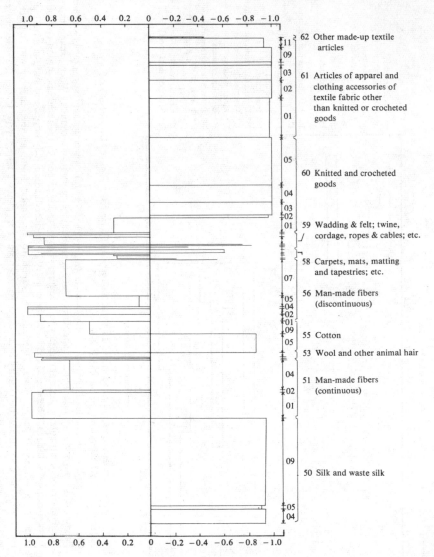

Source: *Ibid.*
Note: The width of each column indicates the relative share of the sum of export and import for each commodity category in the sum of total exports and imports of textiles and textile articles.

cally advanced production processes and Korea in standardized processes. Specifically, in relation to electronic machinery, which comprises the three categories of industrial machinery, household appliances and electronic parts, Korea's exports to Japan are substantial in the area of household electronic appliances such as radios, TVs, clocks and watches, and pocket calculators, for which the country has a comparative advantage, as their production processes are labor-intensive, mostly consisting of assemblage. The intra-industry trade index of Japan vis-a-vis Korea in household electronic appliances was therefore already low in 1977 at 0.25. Electronic parts are further classified into nine sub-categories: batteries, resistors, transducers, acoustic parts, device parts, electron tubes, semiconductor components, integrated circuits and other electronic parts. Japan is a net importer vis-a-vis Korea of batteries and integrated circuits, for which production technologies are highly standardized. Although Japan was still a net exporter of resistors, electron tubes and semiconductor components to Korea in 1977, the intra-industry trade indexes for these electronic parts were low at 0.23, 0.11 and 0.06 respectively, implying more horizontal specialization between the two countries. However, Japan's exports of transducers, device parts and acoustic parts to Korea were large, and their respective intra-industry trade indexes were 1.00, 0.84 and 0.72. The index for industrial electronic machinery was also high at 0.81. Here again Japan and Korea stand in a clear-cut vertical intra-industry trade relationship.

The vertical trade relationship in electrical and electronic machinery, rather than reflecting only the industrial specialization of the two countries, indicates that the Korean enterprises in this sphere of industrial activity were originally developed by the parent companies in Japan or the United States with the express purpose of taking advantage of international subcontracting. As long as a certain country is chosen by a parent company to serve as a base for exporting some "mature product cycle" goods, the country is bound to export such goods and moreover to depend heavily on imported upstream input materials. For instance, the export dependence of the Korean electronics industry was 49.6 percent in 1970 and 63.0 percent in 1977, while its import dependence was 61.8 percent and 61.2 percent respectively in the same years. It is noteworthy that the industry's import dependence remained practically unchanged over seven years.

Trade between Japan and Korea is characterized by wheels within wheels, of inter- and intra-industry, and intra-enterprise vertical division of labor. However, the ramifications of this vertical relationship does not mean complementary industrial interdependence between the two countries. Rather, it epitomizes the unilateral dependence of Korea on Japan, wherein the latter's exports of producer goods greatly outdistance the former's exports of consumer goods. As seen in Figure 1, Japan's net imports of consumer goods from Korea are more than offset by her net exports of producer goods to Korea, generating a large and growing commodity trade surplus for Japan. Korea's total balance of trade deficit vis-a-vis Japan increased more than six-fold from $589 million in 1970 to $3,412 million in 1978. Moreover, Japan's trade surplus relative to Korea amounts to only 0.31 percent of her GNP, while it is equivalent to 6.04 percent of GNP in Korea. The vertical and unilateral trade relationship between Japan and Korea is a manifestation of the interplay between their contrasting industrial structures.

III. Contrast in Industrial Structure between Korea and Japan

The difference in industrial structure between Korea and Japan can be immediately seen from the skyline maps in Figure 3. Japan is very dependent on imports of such resource-intensive products as foodstuffs (05) and wooden products (10), but self-sufficient in industrial structure with respect to nearly all the other industrial subsectors. Japan's large exports of iron and steel (18), primary iron (19), general machinery (22), electrical and electronic machinery (23), and transport equipment (24), have been generated on the basis of this largely self-sufficient structure. The industrial sector of Japan is characterized, in other words, by the "full-range industrialization" which ensures self-sufficiency of the economy and by the export-dependent growth of heavy and chemical industries.[1]

Korea has an industrial structure strikingly different from Japan's. As shown in Figure 3, the skyline of 22 subsectors is jagged, indicating the outward orientation of the industrial structure. In addition to foodstuffs (05), pulp and paper products (10) and other resource-intensive industrial products, Korea is heavily dependent on imports

---

[1]The term "full-range industrialization" was coined by Kiyoshi Kojima. For details, see Kojima (1979).

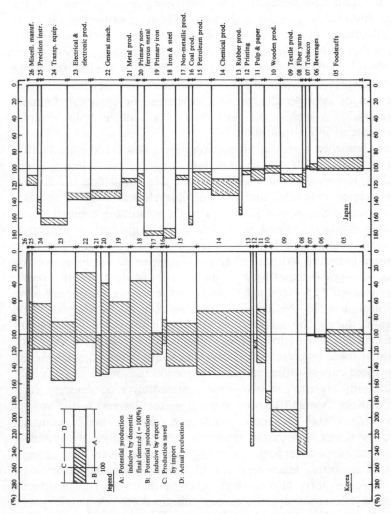

Figure 3. Skyline Maps of Japanese and Korean Industries (1975)

legend

A: Potential production
   inducive by domestic
   final demand (= 100%)
B: Potential production
   inducive by export
C: Production saved
   by import
D: Actual production

26 Miscell. manuf.
25 Precision instr.
24 Transp. equip.
23 Electrical &
   electronic prod.
22 General mach.
21 Metal prod.
20 Primary non-
   ferrous metal
19 Primary iron
18 Iron & steel
17 Non-metallic prod.
16 Coal prod.
15 Petroleum prod.
14 Chemical prod.
13 Rubber prod.
12 Printing
11 Pulp & paper
10 Wooden prod.
09 Textile prod.
08 Fiber yarns
07 Tobacco
06 Beverages
05 Foodstuffs

Japan

Korea

Source: Govt. of Japan, Administrative Management Agency, *Input-Output Tables 1975*, Tokyo, June 1980 and Bank of Korea, *1975 Input-Output Tables*, Seoul, 1978.

Note: The width of each column indicates the relative share of the respective industrial subsector in the total value of production from 05 through 26.

in the heavy and chemical industries, although some of these industries are to a substantial degree dependent on exports as well. The
export dependence is extremely high in fiber yarns (08) and textile
products (09), and the value of their exports is considerably larger
than the domestic demand. The overriding characteristic of the
Korean industrial structure is that the industries exporting far more
than 50 percent of the total output are juxtaposed with those industries, such as general machinery and primary metals, whose output
falls short of the domestic demand. In contrast to the full-range
industrialization in Japan, the more specialized industrial structure of
Korea can be considered a product of partial or "truncated industrialization,"[2] or simply the reflection of a smaller country at an
earlier stage of industrialization.

Korea launched a serious promotion of manufactured exports after
the mid-1960s when the production capacity of primary input
materials, intermediate and capital goods was small and the linkage
among related industries limited and undeveloped. Major manufactured commodities which Korea currently exports are mostly final
consumer goods at the end of the round-about production processes,
and consequently their import content is extremely high. The most
specialized industrial structure in Korea is determined by the promotion
of processed goods exports with a high import content. Table 1 shows
the breakdown of Korean net exports by use during the period from
1972 through 1978. Net exports of consumer goods show a rapid
expansion during the six-year period but there was a concomitant
increase in imports of intermediate products and capital goods. The
balance of trade by commodity category clearly points to the progress
of processed-exports-oriented industrialization in Korea.

As already stated, the two most representative commodity categories of Korea's manufactured exports are textiles and textile articles
and electrical and electronic machinery, and in these industrial
subsectors Korea and Japan represent a vertical division of labor.
Japan specializes in exports of man-made fiber yarns and fabrics,
industrial electronic machinery and high-technology electronic parts,
while Korea exports apparel and other secondary textile products,
household electronic appliances and standardized electronic parts.
This indicates that the expansion of Korea's manufactured exports
necessarily induces increased imports of input materials from Japan,

---

[2] See Kojima (1979).

Table 1. *Korea's Net Exports by Use (1972-78)*

(in thousand dollars)

		1972	1973	1974	1975	1976	1977	1978
I.	Food and beverages	-228,018	-306,873	-472,280	-280,534	-49,609	339,329	177,513
II.	Industrial supplies n.e.s.	-492,398	-830,198	-1,349,050	-1,288,131	-1,439,935	-1,501,547	-2,089,217
III.	Fuels and lubricants	-196,355	-273,423	-946,303	-1,280,251	-1,597,645	02,058,075	-2,404,129
IV.	Capital goods (except transport equipment) and parts and accessories thereof	-438,821	-565,018	-732,571	-871,214	-1,273,058	-1,441,752	-2,713,379
	1. Capital goods	-419,066	-543,264	-706,740	-862,557	-538,209	-1,137,417	-2,146,712
	2. Parts and accessories	-19,754	-21,754	-25,831	-8,657	-428,592	-304,335	-566,672
V.	Transport equipment and parts and accessories thereof	-159,260	-224,142	-453,130	-332,233	-146,891	-228,688	-390,360
VI.	Consumer goods n.e.s.	616,664	1,160,767	1,557,685	1,838,659	3,073,968	3,793,113	4,924,182
VII.	Goods n.e.s.	273	23,635	4,171	20,286	68,389	333,537	240,576
	Capital goods	-545,610	-727,097	-1,152,465	-1,165,385	-701,690	-1,262,903	-2,412,348
	Intermediate goods	-1,054,919	-1,651,585	-3,005,114	-3,425,210	-3,931,559	-4,491,754	-5,770,009
	Consumer goods	669,342	1,339,795	1,761,930	2,376,891	3,506,336	4,647,036	5,691,961
	Total	-897,914	-1,015,252	-2,391,478	-2,193,418	-1,058,523	-764,081	-2,249,814

Source: National Bureau of Statistics, Economic Planning Board, *Korea Statistics Yearbook 1979*, Seoul.

Figure 4. *Imported Input Dependence of Household Electronic Appliances Industries in Japan and Korea (1975)*

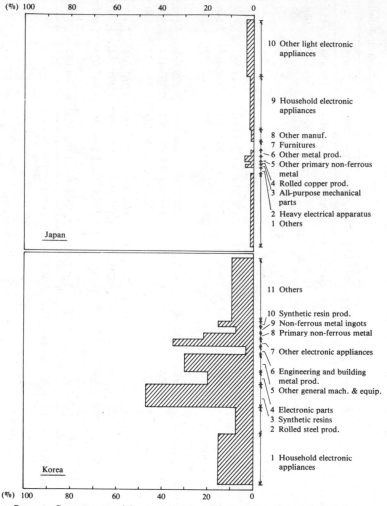

Source: Government of Japan, Ministry of International Trade and Industry, *White Paper on International Trade 1979,* Tokyo, 1980.

Notes: a) The vertical width of each component category indicates its relative share in the total value of inputs used in the entire household appliances industry.

b) Shaded areas indicate the percentages of imported inputs.

c) Excludes services, transportation and other inputs provided from without the manufacturing industries.

especially with respect to secondary textile products and household electronic appliances with higher import content. Figure 4 compares household electronic appliances industries in Japan and Korea in terms of their dependence on imported input materials. As Figure 4 shows, the industries in Korea have a much higher import content than their Japanese counterparts, indicating a linkage among the related industries. The industrialization in Korea in this sphere of activities is specialized and structured to generate processed-goods exports.

Although Korea's exports are highly import-inducive, the exports to Japan in particular are not large enough to secure a trade surplus. A large and growing balance of trade deficit for Korea vis-a-vis Japan indicates that the trade relations between the two countries are vertical but not complementary. There are a number of major factors which have prevented their vertical trade relationship from developing into a complementary interdependence. One is that Japan's import control over Korea's exports is insignificant in its impact. According to the survey conducted by the Industrial Bank of Korea, the share of restricted commodities in Korea's total exports by country of destination amounted to 18.9 percent relative to Japan, compared with 34.1 percent and 27.4 percent for the United States and the EC, respectively.[3] The slower growth of Korea's exports to Japan is not by any means due to the latter's strict import restriction, but to the selfsufficient full-range industrial structure of Japan, wherein a nearly complete set of domestic industries has grown to become capable of sustaining the whole streams of various production cycles.

The industrial structure of Japan which has been fostered since the end of the Second World War has a marked predilection for selfsufficiency compared with some other developed countries in the world. Self-sufficiency is the overriding premise pursued in Japan's industrial subsectors, ranging from such labor-intensive final goods as textile articles and wooden manufactures and intermediate materials and products such as iron and steel, nonferrous metals and basic chemicals, to capital goods like general machinery.[4] Because Japan

---

[3] Industrial Bank of Korea, *Monthly Survey Report,* No. 281, April 1979.

[4] For more detailed discussions on the self-sufficiency of the Japanese economy, see Ministry of International Trade and Industry, *White Paper on International Trade 1978,* Part III, Chapter I; Association of National Accounts Analysis, *Japan's Industrial Structure in the 1990s: Changing Trade Patterns and Industrial Adjustment [1990-nen no sangyo-kozo: boeki no henka to sangyo-chosei],* September 1978; and

runs almost the entire gamut of downstream and upstream industries within the round-about production process, the induced import per unit of additional output of a particular commodity does not amount to very much in any industrial subsector.

The industrial structure in Korea is essentially geared to generate processed-goods exports and consequently depends on imports of producer goods from Japan. Final goods assembled or processed in Korea are exported in larger quantities to the United States and the EC, rather than to Japan. As a consequence, Korea's balance of trade is in surplus relative to the United States and the EC. Korea's increased exports to these countries have contributed to reducing Japan's shares in these markets, and this gradual market takeover by an advanced developing country might be considered alarming from the Japanese viewpoint. It has to be emphasized, however, that Korea's expanding manufactured exports elsewhere in the world market directly generate increased imports of producer goods from Japan.

In order to give a more comprehensive view of the industrial relationship between Japan and Korea, the vertical but strongly unilateral trade between the two countries will be subjected to a quantitative analysis in the following section.

IV. Industrial Interdependence between Korea and Japan

The interdependence among domestic industries within a country can be analyzed by means of the inter-industry input-output tables. In order to study the industrial interdependence between two countries, it is necessary to link two sets of input-output tables through adjusting trade statistics between these countries.[5]

The linkage between input-output tables of two countries designated as A and B can be shown in the following simplified form:

Toshio Watanabe, *Challenge from Asian NICs [Ajia-chushin-koku no chosen]*, Nihon Keizai Shimbun Press, Chapter IV, Section 4.

[5] Major references are: I. Ozaki and Kozo Ishida (1970); I. Ozaki (1977); K. Ishida (1977); K. Ishida (1978); I. Ozaki (1978) IDE/KEIO Joint Product (1970); R.J. Wonnacott (1961); R.J. Wonnacott (1967).

		Intermediate Demand		Final Demand		Exports to 3rd Countries	Total Output
		A	B	A	B		
Intermediate Input	A	X^{AA}	X^{AB}	F^{AA}	F^{AB}	E^{AR}	$X^A(=X^{AA}\ X^{AB}+F^{AA}+F^{AB}+E^{AR})$
	B	X^{BA}	X^{BB}	F^{BA}	F^{BB}	E^{BR}	$X^B(=X^{BA}+X^{BB}+F^{BA}+F^{BB}+E^{BR})$

X^{AA} and X^{BB} indicate the flow of intermediate goods respectively within countries A and B, while F^{AA} and F^{BB} similarly signify the flow of final goods within each country. X^{AB}, X^{BA}, F^{AB} and F^{BA}, on the other hand, indicate the two-way inter-country flow of inter-mediate and final goods, while E^{AR} and E^{BR} represent the exports from the respective countries A and B to the rest of the world. It is possible to identify the whereabouts of the inter-country interde-pendence in terms of X^{AB} and X^{BA}, that is to say, exports of inter-mediate goods from A and B and from B to A, and F^{AB} and F^{BA}, namely exports of final goods from A to B and from B to A. In particular, the larger the values of X^{AB} and X^{BA}, the closer the inter-dependence between the two countries. The input-output tables so linked can effectively evince the pattern of interdependence between the two economies. Figures 5 through 10 are obtained by linking the most recent input-output tables of Korea and Japan, which were for the year 1975. Although the tables covered 33 industrial subsectors, only 22 among them, ranging from foodstuffs (05) through miscellaneous manufactures (26), are represented in the figures.[6]

Figure 5 shows induced production coefficients (B^{JK}) of the industrial subsectors in Korea. That is to say, a coefficient indicates the increase in the total domestic output in Japan per additional unit of final demand generated in a particular industrial subsector in Korea. For instance, a unit increase in final demand for electrical and electronic machinery (23) and textile products (09) in Korea has a coefficient of 0.3715 and 0.2348, respectively, in inducing the increase of total domestic output in the Japanese economy. The coefficient covers both direct and indirect induced output. Twenty-two industrial subsectors are ordered along the vertical axis as shown in the figures in accordance with the size of subsectoral per capita value added, decreasing from the bottom upwards. Figure 6 presents induced

---

[6] See T. Nagasaka, H. Ihara and H. Masuno (1979).

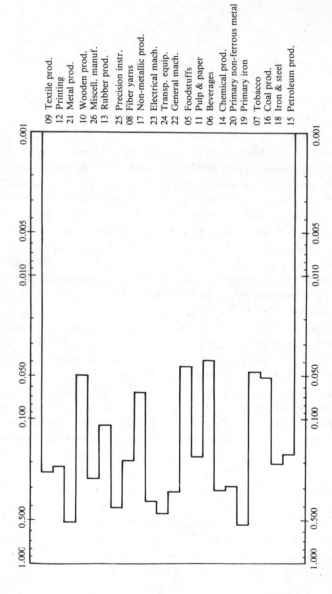

Figure 5. Induced Production Coefficients of Korean Industries Relative to Japan

Sources: Government of Japan, Administrative Management Agency, *Input-Output Tables 1975*; and Bank of Korea, *1975 Input-Output Tables*.

Figure 6. *Induced Production Coefficient of Japanese Industries Relative to Korea*

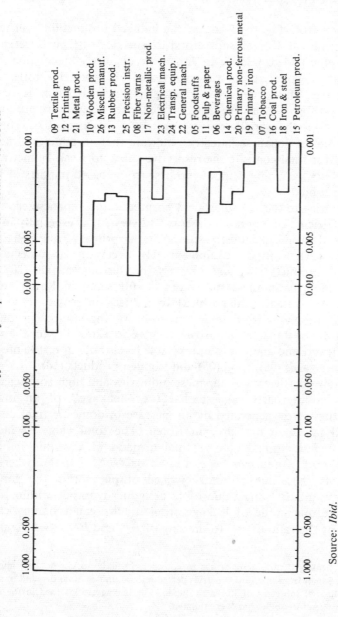

Source: *Ibid.*

production coefficients (B^{KJ}) of demand increase in the respective subsectors of Japan relative to the total output of the Korean economy.

As seen from Figures 5 and 6, the induced production coefficients of practically all Korean subsectors, irrespective of their different per capita value added, relative to Japan are distinctly higher than those of Japanese counterparts vis-a-vis Korea. In part this reflects the relative size of the two economies. The coefficients in Korea are roughly on the order of one-tenth, while those in Japan are around the order of one-thousandth except for textile products (09). The low coefficients of Japanese industries indicate that an additional unit of demand for final goods in the respective subsectors can be met within the domestic economy without recourse to increased imports of intermediate goods.

In contrast to the self-sufficiency ensured in the Japanese economy, the coefficients of Korean industries are very high, especially in such heavy and chemical industry subsectors as primary iron (19), metal products (21), transport equipment (24), precision instruments (25), chemical products (14) and primary nonferrous metals (20). The supply capacity in these subsectors is still small in Korea and an expansion in final demand directly induces increased imports of intermediate goods from Japan. In contrast, the induced production coefficients of Japanese industries relative to Korea are on the whole insignificant, and amount to appreciable levels only in textile products (09), fiber yarns (08), food (05) and wooden products (10).

The low coefficients of Japanese industries and high coefficients of Korean counterparts suggest that the "leakage" of an induced production effect generated by an increase in domestic final demand is small in Japan but large in Korea. The total value of induced output per additional unit of final demand in a certain industrial subsector of Korea can be expressed as ($B^{JK} + B^{KK}$), where B^{JK} represents the value of total induced output within the Japanese economy and B^{KK} the value of total induced output within Korea. Then the magnitude of leakage from the Korean economy can be shown by the ratio of B^{JK} to the sum of B^{JK} and B^{KK}. (See Figure 7.)[7]

---

[7] The "leakage" ratio actually has to consider, in addition, an induced import of Korea or Japan from the third countries per additional unit of final demand in a particular industrial subsector of Korea or Japan. The leakage ratios used in the present paper are therefore somewhat overestimated.

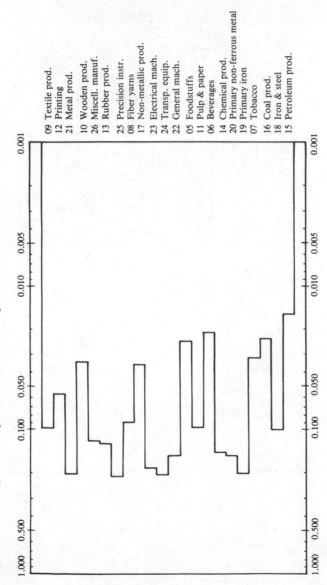

Figure 7.   Leakage Ratios of Induced Production for Korean Industries

Source: *Ibid.*

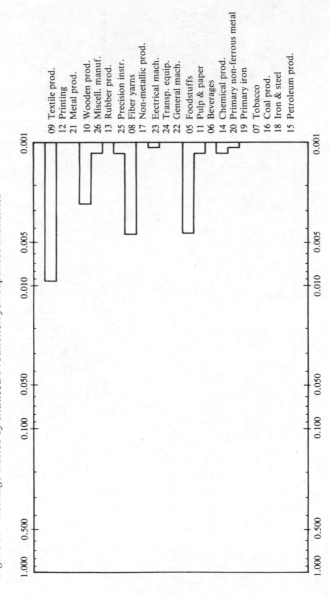

Figure 8.　Leakage Ratios of Induced Production for Japanese Industries

Source: *Ibid.*

Similarly, the leakage of an induced production effect with respect to Japanese industrial subsectors can be indicated by $B^{KJ} / (B^{KJ} + B^{JJ})$, where B^{KJ} represents the value of total induced output within the Korean economy and B^{JJ} the value of total induced output within the Japanese economy. (See Figure 7.)

As shown in Figure 7, the ratio of leakage is extremely high in the Korean industries, notably in heavy and chemical industry subsectors, amounting to more than 20 percent in transport equipment (24), primary iron (19), metal products (21) and precision instruments (25), and over 15 percent in general machinery (22), primary nonferrous metals (20) and electrical and electronic machinery (23). On the contrary, the leakage is negligible with respect to Japanese industries; the largest ratio for textile products amounts to less than 1 percent.

This approach is effective to put in proper perspective the question of the so-called catch-up by advanced developing countries (ADCs) with Japan. As shown in the leakage ratios in Figures 7 and 8, the induced production effects from increased Korean exports to the U.S.A. on the Japanese economy are quite substantial. The leakage is definitely beneficial to Japan. In contrast, the induced production effects from increased Japanese exports to the U.S.A. are mostly absorbed in the domestic economy and the leakage to Korea is small. It has to be noted that Korea's catch-up in the U.S. export market in competition with Japan is increasing the country's imports of inter- mediate goods from Japan and even strengthening its unilateral dependence on the Japanese economy.

The one-sided dependence of Korea on Japan also has to do with a large gap in the scale of national economy between the two countries. The inter-relationship between Korea and Japan can be examined from this angle. In the preceding paragraphs, attention has been drawn to the effect on total output in one country from a unit increase of final demand in an industrial subsector of the other country. In addition to this manner of approach, it is possible to gauge the effect on output in a particular industrial subsector of one country from an increase of total final demand in the other country. Based on the same linked input-output tables, Figures 9 and 10 are prepared to show such reciprocal effects with respect to Korea and Japan. The ratios are obtained by dividing the value of induced output in each industrial subsector of one country by the value of total output of the subsector. The ratios indicate, in other words, the magnitude of impact on the respective industries in one country from the increased

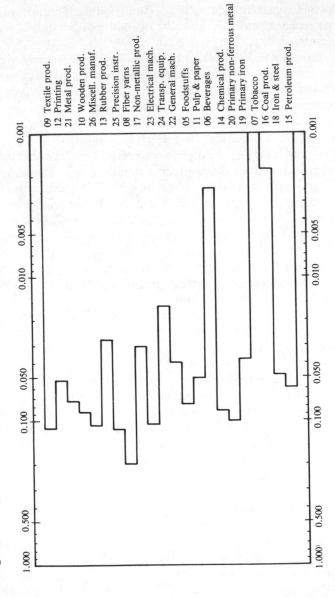

Figure 9.   Impact Ratios of Japan's Increased Total Output on Korean Industries

Source: *op. cit.*

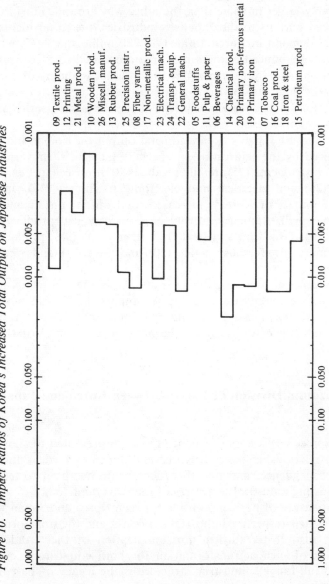

Figure 10. Impact Ratios of Korea's Increased Total Output on Japanese Industries

Source: *op. cit.*

total output in the other country.

The induced outputs of the respective subsectors in Japan are considerably larger in value than the other way around. For instance, the induced outputs in the Japanese industries due to an increase of total final demand in Korea totaled $3,780 million in 1975, whereas the conversely induced outputs in Korea amounted to $1,612 million in total in the same year. However, the national economy of Japan is much larger than that of Korea. Consequently, the ratio of induced output to total output in an industrial subsector is necessarily smaller in Japan than in Korea.

The impact of Japan's expanded total output on Korean industries as measured by the said ratios is especially large in fiber yarns (08), precision instruments (25), textile products (09), miscellaneous manufactures (26) and electrical and electronic machinery (23). In contrast, the impact of Korea's increased total output on Japanese industries is small, though relatively large in chemical products (14), coal products (16), iron and steel (18), fiber yarns (08), primary iron (19), primary nonferrous metals (20) and electrical and electronic machinery (23).

The evidence in the preceding paragraphs is that an expansion of the Japanese economy exerts a greater impact on Korean industries than the other way around, and that the difference in impact is due to a large disparity in the scale of the national economies of the two countries.

V. Horizontal Division of Labor between Korea and Japan

In the preceding sections evidence has been presented to show that the trade relationship between Korea and Japan is vertical and one-sided in dependence, and that this relationship has been fostered by the contrasting industrial structures of the two countries.

The expansion of horizontal trade between Korea and Japan would transform their respective industrial structures and the transformation would in turn foster further horizontalization of their trade. The desirability of such a transformation for both countries is evident. Japan's "full-range" industrial structure is the legacy of past industrialization which was geared primarily to overcoming the geographical and historical circumstances of being the first country to take off in the then-underdeveloped region. However, it is no longer justifiable on the basis of the principle of comparative advantage. Moreover, one of the consequences of her present industrial structure is an increasing trade surplus imbalance, another the trade frictions which have developed with the U.S.A., the EC, and the ADCs, including Korea. It is urgently necessary for Japan to rectify her industrial structure.

The processed-export-oriented industrial structure of Korea necessarily involves a substantial leakage of production effects induced by her own industries and impairs the possibility of improving her trade balance. Such openness of the industrial structure relative to outside forces indicates the pronounced "external vulnerability" of the Korean economy. Horizontalization of trade between Korea and Japan would increase the self-reliance and resilience of the former's economy and improve the efficiency of the industrial structure in the latter.

It is expected that the economic relations between the two countries will become increasingly horizontal in the future and approach more balanced interdependence. Indeed, the growth of heavy and chemical industries has been accelerating in Korea since the mid-1970s, with increasing domestic self-sufficiency and, to a lesser extent, exports of intermediate goods in these subsectors.[8] The processed-export-oriented industrialization of Korea is clearly undergoing its due transformation. On the other hand, the undervaluation of the Japanese yen was corrected after the Smithonian multilateral currency realignment of 1971 and Japan's self-sufficient industrial structure has become increasingly unwieldy in the newly emerging international monetary and economic situation. Throughout the 1970s, Japan's import quotas and tariffs were successively liberalized to accommodate the intensified trade frictions, notably with the U.S.A. and the EC countries, and Japan's direct foreign investment in manufacturing industries in Asian ADCs was rapidly stepped up. These trends will no doubt contribute to the eventual correction of Japan's industrial structure.

In order to discuss future prospects, it is useful to compare the existing patterns of specialization of Japan and other countries.[9] Figure 11 presents Japan's intra-industry export indexes vis-a-vis

[8] Watanabe (1978)

[9] See B. Balassa (1966), H.G. Grubel (1967), H.G. Grubel and P.J. Lloyd (1975), Y. Sazanami and N. Hamaguchi (1976) and L.N. Willmore (1972).

Korea for some 200 industrial subsectors by ordering them from +1 through −1 from left to right. For the purpose of comparison, three other series of indexes with respect to Asian ADCs (Korea, Taiwan, Hong Kong and Singapore), other ASEAN countries (Thailand, Malaysia, Indonesia and the Philippines), and the United States are shown in the same figure.

As can be seen from Figure 11, the trade between Japan and Korea is clearly vertical as mentioned previously, but less vertical than Japan's trade with ASEAN countries. Japan is nearly a 100 percent net exporter, or has intra-industry export indexes very close to +1, in more than 50 percent of the listed industrial subsectors with respect to ASEAN countries. Export indexes ranging from +0.5 through −0.5, which indicate more or less horizontal division of labor, are found in only 20 subsectors. In other words, Japan's trade with ASEAN countries is distinctly more vertical than her trade with Korea. Four Asian ADCs are more industrialized than the ASEAN countries. Consequently, vis-a-vis these countries, Japan is a 100 percent net exporter in a smaller number of subsectors, while subsectors which have intra-industry export indexes of +0.5/−0.5 are larger in number. Among Asian ADCs, moreover, Korea has the most horizontal relationship with Japan. In contrast, Japan's intra-industry export indexes vis-a-vis U.S.A. are evenly balanced as seen from their more or less diagonal distribution in Figure 11. The trade pattern between Japan and the U.S.A. indicates the horizontal specialization between the two countries.

Figure 12 shows Japan's intra-industry export indexes relative to Korea for the years 1965, 1970 and 1978. For the purpose of comparison, three sets of export indexes in the same years vis-a-vis Asian ADCs, ASEAN countries and the U.S.A. are presented respectively in Figures 13, 14, and 15. Although the trade relationship between Japan and Korea remains essentially vertical, it has undergone rapid changes over twelve years as shown in Figure 12. The industrial subsectors which have the indexes of +0.5/−0.5 numbered 14 in 1965 but increased to 25 in 1970 and 33 in 1978. With respect to Asian ADCs and ASEAN countries, the number of such subsectors increased from 12 to 33 and 26 for the former and from 5 to 8 and 20 for the latter. In contrast, the number of subsectors with indexes of +0.5/−0.5 with respect to the U.S.A. shows only slight changes over the years, with virtually no shift in Japan's intra-industry export indexes. Trade between the two countries remained almost exactly in

Figure 11. Japan's Intra-industry Export Indexes (1978)

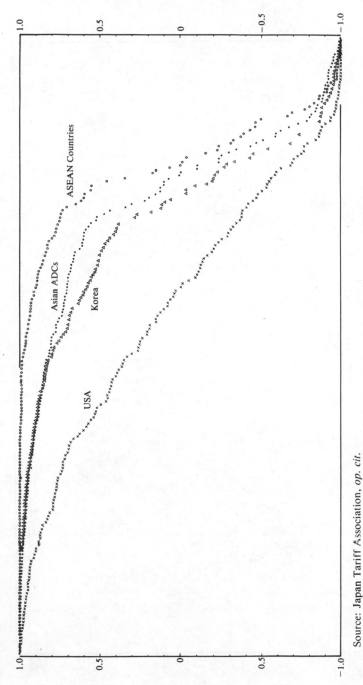

Source: **Japan Tariff A**ssociation, *op. cit.*

Note: Excludes those commodity categories for which the sum of export and import is less than ¥ 500 million.

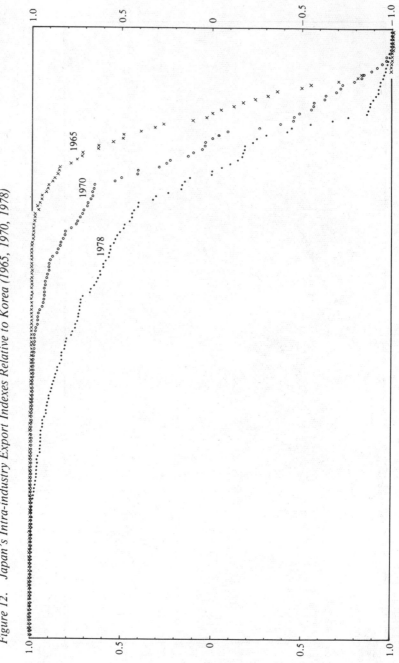

Figure 12. Japan's Intra-industry Export Indexes Relative to Korea (1965, 1970, 1978)

Source: Japan Tariff Association, *op. cit.*
Note: Excludes those commodity categories for which the sum of export and import is less than ¥ 500 million.

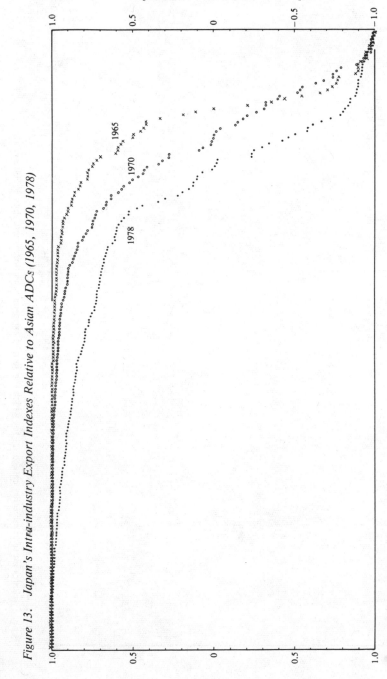

Figure 13. Japan's Intra-industry Export Indexes Relative to Asian ADCs (1965, 1970, 1978)

Source: Japan Tariff Association, *op. cit.*
Note: Excludes those commodity categories for which the sum of export and import is less than ¥ 500 million.

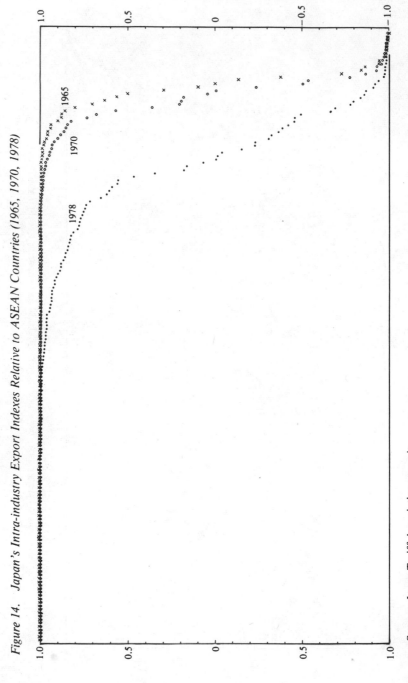

Figure 14. Japan's Intra-industry Export Indexes Relative to ASEAN Countries (1965, 1970, 1978)

Source: Japan Tariff Association, *op. cit.*

Note: Excludes those commodity categories for which the sum of export and import is less than ¥ 500 million.

Figure 15. Japan's Intra-industry Export Indexes Relative to USA (1965, 1970, 1978)

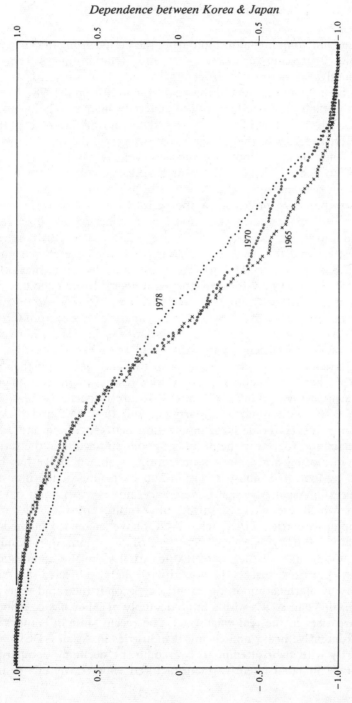

1978

1970

1965

Source: Japan Tariff Association, *op. cit.*

Note: Excludes those commodity categories for which the sum of export and import is less than ¥ 500 million.

the same horizontal relationship during the period from 1965 to 1978.

Table   2 presents Japan's varying trade relationships in terms of horizontal specialization coefficients by industrial subsector for the respective trading partners in the years 1965, 1970 and 1978. As seen from the table, the coefficients are generally high in relation to the U.S.A. but low for Korea, Asian ADCs and ASEAN countries. However, in terms of the changes over the years, the coefficients for heavy and chemical industry subsectors have risen sharply with respect to Korea, Asian ADCs and ASEAN countries, but only slightly in relation to the U.S.A. The rise has been especially rapid in many of the heavy and chemical industries vis-a-vis Asian ADCs. The shift to a more horizontal division of labor has been most pronounced in Japan's trade with Korea. The coefficients rose from 1.1 in 1965 and 0.6 in 1970 to 9.7 in 1978 for general machinery, from 2.8 and 13.2 to 34.9 for electrical and electronic machinery, from 2.2 and 1.1 to 7.7 for transport equipment, from 0 and 0 to 83.4 for coal products, from 14.8 and 7.9 to 22.5 for non-metallic products, from 0.1 and 5.3 to 23.7 for primary iron, and from 0.3 and 2.2 to 23.0 for metal products. Apropos of Asian ADCs, horizontal specialization coefficients with Japan had been high in textiles and textile articles and wooden products in the mid-1960s and their rise after 1965 has been slight. Especially with respect to Korea, the coefficients in the years 1965, 1970 and 1978 are respectively 27.4, 31.2 and 28.9 for textiles and textile articles, and 19.9, 36.5 and 17.1 for wooden products. Trade horizontalization between Korea and Japan is expected to progress in the producer-goods subsectors in the future.

The increasing horizontal specialization as shown above has been caused by the rapid industrialization and deepening of the industrial structures in Asian ADCs. It is necessary, however, to point out two factors which are likely to affect the futures of these advanced developing countries. First, Asian ADCs have succeeded in shedding the status of being marginal exporters of labor-intensive manufactured goods like textiles and textile articles in the international market, but this success is now increasingly subjected to closer scrutiny by alarmed importing countries. Second, the rapid economic growth of Asian ADCs with a limited supply of labor has contributed to sharp rises in the real wage rate. The recent shift in emphasis to capital-intensive heavy and chemical industries in Asian ADCs has to do partly with their attempt to overcome the declining comparative advantage in labor-intensive manufactured exports. In this respect, the catch-up by ADCs in heavy and chemical industries will undoubtedly accelerate in the coming years.

Horizontalization has also proceeded apace in trade between Japan and ASEAN countries in such industries as pulp and paper products (the horizontal specialization coefficient increasing from 1.4 in 1965 to 11.2 in 1970 and 9.5 in 1978), rubber products (0.3, 0.1 and 17.6 respectively), iron and steel (0, 0 and 6.0), electrical and electronic machinery (0, 0 and 6.4), precision instruments (0, 0 and 21.5), textile products (4.8, 19.0 and 30.7) and wooden products (4.5, 21.4 and 21.7). Especially notable is the increased horizontal division of labor in textile and wooden products, where coefficients are highest, when the horizontalization of trade in those commodities between Japan and Asian ADCs, especially Korea, has been clearly slowing down in recent years. While Asian ADCs are edging into export markets of heavy and chemical industry products in response to a slackening in exports of labor-intensive manufactures, ASEAN countries have now started to catch up in their turn in labor-intensive manufactured exports. Although still marginal exporters, ASEAN countries with their enormous labor surplus and lower real wages are likely to increase their market shares further. Their horizontal specialization vis-a-vis Japan is expected to progress through their trades of textile products and other labor-intensive processed goods.

As shown in Figure 11 and Figure 16, Korea's horizontal specialization coefficients and speed of horizontalization with respect to Japan are highest among Asian ADCs. Korea also has the largest population, GNP and total trade among them. Her exports to Japan are especially large compared with other Asian ADCs. In addition, the growth potential of Korea is probably largest. In this respect, the trade with Korea is likely to play a major role in shaping Japan's horizontal industrial specialization with neighboring countries. Increased horizontalization in heavy and chemical industries will be of utmost importance for Korea which aims to deepen her industrial structure through promoting heavy and chemical industries.

Table 2. *Japan's Horizontal Specialization Coefficients by Country and Industrial Subsector (1965, 1970, 1978)*

		Korea			Asian ADCs			ASEAN			U.S.A.		
		1965	1970	1978	1965	1970	1978	1965	1970	1978	1965	1970	1978
05	Foodstuffs	12.9	14.0	11.9	16.7	15.9	24.9	16.6	18.0	16.3	23.6	35.9	21.3
06	Beverages	—	—	—	—	—	—	0	0	0.3	12.6	19.0	45.1
07	Tobacco	—	—	—	—	—	—	—	—	—	0	0	0
08	Fiber yarns	0.4	32.3	34.3	11.5	39.6	41.9	2.1	0.6	32.8	0.7	1.3	45.7
09	Textile products	27.4	31.2	28.9	24.1	31.6	25.8	4.8	19.0	30.7	9.6	14.4	34.6
10	Wooden products	19.9	36.5	17.1	18.2	27.8	21.6	4.5	21.4	21.7	23.0	6.1	22.5
11*	Pulp and paper	0	2.4	12.1	6.4	17.5	9.2	1.4	11.2	9.5	33.8	34.4	28.7
12	Printing	15.1	9.5	67.5	13.7	14.3	90.2	7.5	1.8	93.5	16.9	23.6	30.7
13*	Rubber products	2.8	27.6	41.2	20.7	37.7	37.8	0.3	0.1	17.6	21.1	12.6	29.9
14*	Chemical products	6.9	13.8	11.2	7.9	14.9	19.1	4.9	4.7	9.4	31.4	35.6	44.6
15*	Petroleum products	0	89.8	52.0	10.4	36.7	19.8	27.1	31.5	8.6	6.9	3.9	2.7
16*	Coal products	0	0	83.4	0	47.8	99.5	0	0	0	0	0	28.4
17*	Non-metallic products	14.8	7.9	22.5	3.7	11.1	19.0	0	0.1	0.8	29.0	35.3	52.8
18*	Iron and steel	50.0	10.6	65.0	21.5	23.5	28.0	0	0	6.0	40.7	16.9	51.5
19*	Primary iron	0.1	5.3	23.7	0	7.3	13.0	0	0.3	4.6	11.4	2.8	1.5
20*	Primary non-ferrous metal	6.2	19.5	15.3	12.7	15.0	20.9	1.0	1.5	3.6	34.9	36.6	22.0
21*	Metal products	0.3	2.2	23.0	0.3	12.2	21.3	0.1	0.2	0.9	28.0	15.7	24.4
22*	General machinery	1.1	0.6	9.7	1.6	1.3	6.0	0.3	0.2	1.6	37.4	43.9	47.0
23*	Electrical & electronic machinery	2.8	13.2	34.9	3.8	20.4	22.4	0	0	6.4	52.4	50.6	55.9
24*	Transport equipment	2.2	1.1	7.7	0.5	6.8	10.6	0	0	0.4	23.9	17.2	13.7
25*	Precision instruments	6.4	1.8	28.2	2.5	3.3	16.5	0	0	21.5	42.3	44.2	44.0
26	Miscellaneous manufactures	21.2	56.9	53.4	24.4	44.0	51.0	18.0	30.0	38.4	29.3	30.6	53.0
	Total manufactures	8.7	17.1	32.4	8.7	16.3	27.4	3.9	5.9	15.2	33.4	31.0	35.7

Source: Japan Tariff Association, *op. cit.*

Notes: a) Asterisks indicate producers goods subsectors.

b) A horizontal specialization coefficient is defined as $\dfrac{1}{n}\displaystyle\sum_{i=1}^{n}\left[\dfrac{E_{ij}+M_{ij}-|E_{ij}-M_{ij}|}{E_{ij}+M_{ij}}\right]\times100$,   where E_{ij} represents Japan's export of i commodity to j country and M_{ij} her import of i commodity from j country. If commodities in a industrial subsector number n, the coefficient of the subsector as a whole is defined as the arithmetic average of coefficients of the respective commodities. When Japan's exports of commodities in a particular industrial subsector are equal to her imports of the same commodity category from the trading partner, the horizontal coefficient is 100. When Japan is either a 100% exporter or importer with respect to the other country, the coefficient is zero.

VI. Conclusion

Trade between Korea and Japan is characterized by its vertical relationship lacking in complementary interdependence. Korea's imports of producer goods from Japan are much greater than her exports of consumer goods to Japan. Consequently, Korea is unilaterally dependent on Japan, as evidenced by her large and growing balance-of-trade deficit. This vertical relationship of one-sided dependence has been fostered by the trade between the contrasting industrial structures of the two countries, one with a complete and self-sufficient set of industries and the other centered around a number of industries geared to export processed goods with high import content.

The vertical relationship between the two economies has been examined in detail by analyzing the international input-output tables. It has been found that the induced production coefficients of expanded outputs in Korean industries relative to the Japanese economy are much larger than the other way around, especially in producer-goods subsectors. This is due to the larger leakage to Japan of induced production effects generated in Korean industries. In contrast to Japan's self-sufficient full-range industrial structure which is capable of absorbing most of the induced production effects generated in her industries, industrialization in Korea is not yet self-sufficient and is incapable of benefiting wholly from the induced effects fostered in her own industries. Even though Korea's increased exports to the U.S.A. reduce Japan's market share, it should not be overlooked that they directly contribute to the expansion of output in the Japanese economy by way of leakage of their induced production effects.

Korea, however, is promoting heavy and chemical industries under the current Fourth Five-Year Development Plan and thereby aims to effect import substitution of intermediate goods and eventually to export some of them. This will duly serve to change the existing vertical trade relationship to one of more horizontal and interdependent specialization. Japan's horizontal specialization coefficients are predictably high in relation to developed countries but low vis-a-vis developing countries. However, horizontalization has been gaining speed in recent years relative to developing regions, most notably Asian ADCs. The progress of horizontal specialization vis-a-vis Asian ADCs is. now noticeably rapid in such subsectors as machinery, metals and chemicals, but is losing momentum in labor-intensive subsectors. Increased horizontal division of labor with Asian ADCs, centering on heavy and chemical industries, is expected to play a decisive role in expanding Japan's sphere of horizontal inter-dependence.

REFERENCES

Balassa, B., "Tariff Reduction and Trade in Manufacture among the Industrial Countries," *American Economic Review,* Vol. LVI, June 1966.

Grubel, H.G., "Intra-Industry Specialization and the Pattern of Trade," *Canadian Journal of Economics and Political Science,* Vol. XXXIII, August 1967.

Grubel, H.G. and P.J. Lloyd, *Intra-Industry Trade: The Theory and Measurement of International Trade in Differentiated Products,* Macmillan, 1975.

IDE/KEIO Joint Project, *International Input-Output Table: Japan-U.S.A. 1970,* IDE Statistical Data Series, No. 24.

Industrial Bank of Korea, *Monthly Survey Report,* No. 281, April 1979.

Ishida, K., "Economic Interdependence between Japan and U.S.A.," *Economic Quarterly [Keizai-gaku Kiho],* Rissho University, November 1977.

_____, "An Analysis of Employment Interdependence between Japan and U.S.A.," *Quarterly Labor Law [Kikan Rodo-ho],* Special Issue No. 2, April 1978.

Kojima, Kiyoshi, "Newly Industrializing Countries," *Monthly Report,* The Institute of Overseas Investment [Kaigai-toshi Kenkyu-jo], November 1979.

Nagasaka, T. and H. Ihara and H. Masuno, "Industrialization in Asian NICs and Japanese Industrial Structure," *Overseas Marketing Monthly [Kaigai Shijo],* June 1979.

Ozaki, Iwaw and Kozo Ishida, "The Determination of Economic Fundamental Structure: Part 1," *Journal of Mita Academic Association [Mita-gakkai Zasshi],* Keio University, June 1970.

Ozaki, I., "The Japanese Economy and Inter-DC Trades," *Economic*

Seminar [Keizai Semina], Special Issue, January 1977.

_____ , "Japanese Economy: Its Structure for Development," *Economic Review [Keizai Hyoron],* May 1977.

Ozaki, I. and K. Ishida, "Future Prospects of Industrial Structures in Japan and U.S.A.," *Weekly Eastern Economies [Shu-kan Toyo Keizai],* April 26, 1978.

Sazanami, Y. and N. Hamaguchi, "Intra-industry Specialization and International Trade," *Journal of Mita Academic Association,* Keio University, May 1976.

Watanabe, T., "Heavy and Chemical Industrialization and Economic Development in the Republic of Korea," *The Developing Economies,* Institute of Developing Economies, XVI-4, December 1978.

Willmore, L.N., "Free Trade in Manufactures among Developing Countries: The Central American Experience," *Journal of Economic Development and Cultural Change,* July 1972.

Wonnacott, R.J., *Canadian-American Dependence: Inter-industry Analysis of Production and Price,* North-Holland, 1961.

Wonnacott, R.J. and P. Wonnacott, *Free Trade between the United States and Canada,* Harvard University Press, 1967.

• COMMENT

Romeo M. Bautista, *National Economic and Development
                        Authority, Republic of the Philippines*

Watanabe's thorough documentation of the recent trade relationship between Japan and Korea and his analysis of likely prospects
represent a serious effort to relate the evolution of bilateral trade
patterns to existing industrial structures, an approach which contrasts
with the casual empiricism so prevalent in the literature on this subject.
There can be little disagreement with his analyses and findings but on
specific aspects of the paper some qualifications and clarifications can
be made.

In Section I it is shown that, in the bilateral trade between Japan
and Korea, the former specializes in heavy and chemical industry
products, and the latter in consumer goods of light industries. This
finding is of course not surprising, given the capital and technology-
intensive character of the former products and Japan's more mature
industrial economy. Even in product categories where much intra-
industry trade is evident, specialization is found to be based on a
distinction between technologically advanced production processes in
which Japan has a presumed comparative advantage and standardized
processes in which Korea specializes.

Much is made in the paper of the "unilateral dependence of Korea
on Japan, wherein the latter's exports of producer goods greatly
outdistance the former's exports of consumer goods." One cannot
attach much economic significance to this finding. Japan is surely not
the only supplier of Korea's producer good imports. If Korea had
imported more producer goods from other developed countries
resulting in a bilateral trade deficit for Japan, Japan would not be
characterized as unilaterally dependent on Korea. It is no particular
disadvantage for Korea to have a trade deficit with Japan, except in
the unlikely case of zero substitutability among the country's
destination markets of exports and among sources of import supply.

Section II of the paper makes an interesting contrast between the
industrial structures of Japan and Korea. Japan's industrial sector is

shown to be "self-sufficient" in the sense that, except for some resource-intensive products, it produces the entire range of industrial goods, in particular the intermediate inputs from the heavy and chemical industries. On the other hand, Korea heavily imports the latter products, to a significant degree, from Japan, but is highly export-dependent on some consumer products; its industrial structure is therefore "nonself-sufficient" and its exports highly "import-conducive." Manufacturing production in either country is of course not self-sufficient in the real sense of the word, in view of the heavy reliance on imports for natural resource-based inputs, including energy.

Two different industrial development paths taken by the two countries are indicated. Japan's manufacturing sector developed on a broad front, producing both consumer and producer goods, allegedly made necessary by the lack of proximity to the more advanced economies that could have supplied heavy and chemical industry products. Korea's industrial development, on the other hand, had been oriented toward production and exports of light consumer goods, drawing on foreign sources, especially Japan, for much of its requirements of industrial intermediate and capital goods. At least as perceived by Korean policymakers, shifting comparative advantage warranted the development of heavy and chemical industries in recent years; Watanabe gives no judgment on the view expressed that government promotion efforts were too much and too soon.

For Asian ADCs generally, there is clearly no necessity for a "full-range industrialization" of the kind that Japan pursued. It may not even make economic sense as a long-run objective for such small economies as Hong Kong and Singapore. As Anderson and Smith suggest, comparative advantage for these city-states would be likely to be in human capital-intensive industries and services, rather than physical capital-intensive industries.

One may note in this connection that developing country governments are frequently motivated by considerations of national autonomy and prestige in the uneconomic promotion of large-scale industries. This has effectively biased resource allocation against other industries, including export industries dependent on imports for material input, although they may have lower domestic resource costs. Until recently, as has been amply documented in a number of studies, Korean trade and industrialization policies on the whole have avoided this common pitfall among developing countries which might have spelled the difference between rapid and slow industrial growth.

Section III of the paper gives quantitative estimates of "the 'leakage' of the induced production effect generated by an increase in domestic final demand" in Korea and Japan based on the linked input-output tables of the two countries for 1975. Calculated values of the so-called induced production coefficient of Korea's manufacturing industries are shown to be consistently much higher than those of the corresponding industries in Japan, indicating a much greater production effect in Japan of a unit increase in manufacturing final demand in Korea rather than the other way around. These numbers should be viewed with more than the usual caution given to the standard input-output coefficients since not only production relationships but also, and more unrealistically, bilateral trade relationships are assumed to be fixed; following standard practice, the coefficients have been calculated as average coefficients but are used in the analysis as incremental coefficients.

But even taking these qualifications into account, the two major inferences made in the paper would seem tenable. One is that the accelerated expansion of Korea's manufactured exports in the last two decades, which in part displaced some of Japan's own exports of similar products, has had the effect of sharply increasing its imports of producer goods from Japan. Secondly, the rapid growth of Korea's heavy and chemical industries in recent years is bound to alter the existing vertical trade relationship with Japan to a more horizontal and interdependent specialization with increased intra-industry trade. This is given empirical support in Section IV by a very illuminating comparison of Japan's intra-industry trade indices with the United States, Korea, the Asian ADCs and ASEAN countries, except Singapore, over the years 1965, 1970 and 1978.

Finally, to return to the question of "full range" versus "truncated" industrialization which, the paper seems to suggest, are two alternative strategies for developing countries generally, it would not seem advisable for industrial planners and policymakers to blindly pursue either of these two industrialization strategies. A better approach would be to provide a distortion-free policy climate and infrastructure in which the choice of industries is determined primarily by private decision-makers, who are, after all, better qualified than government bureaucrats to evaluate the economic viability of industrial projects. This might be supplemented by a careful assessment of the social costs of, and social benefits from, the selective promotion of particular industries in the capital goods sector (among other strategic industries), taking into consideration inter-industry linkages, externalities and scale economies. The identification of industries for government promotion is generally frowned upon by academic economists, but by the nature of producer goods industries the perceptions of profitability by private producers may not reflect, especially in a long-run context, the social desirability of their development. On this ground the widely observed propensity of developing country governments to identify certain priority industries, which invariably include some heavy and chemical industries, as targets for promotional efforts, can at least in theory be rationalized.

Ronald Findlay, *Columbia University*

Watanabe's paper puts forward a systematic theoretical framework within which the structure and evolution of trade patterns can be analyzed quantitatively. Although his paper is about trade between Japan and Korea, the methodology of linked input-output tables that he employs is of considerable general interest.

The terminology of Watanabe's paper is very "Austrian" in flavor. The process of production is conceived of as a sequence of "stages," ranging from primary raw materials through intermediate goods and capital goods to final consumer goods at the end of the process. The concept of a sequence of stages of production would break down if there were irreducible circular interdependence between the sectors of an input-output table. For it to apply it must be possible for the sectors to be arranged in such a way that the input-output matrix is "triangular" or approximately so, with zero entries above the main diagonal. I assume that the matrices for Japan and Korea exhibit this triangular property.

International trade is "horizontal" when goods at the same stage of production are exchanged and "vertical" when it involves exchange of goods at different stages. Thus the "horizontal" trade in Watanabe's terminology corresponds to what is called "intra-industry" trade by Grubel, Lloyd and others, while his "vertical" trade corresponds to exchange of raw materials and labor-intensive manufactures for capital-intensive manufactures and technologically sophisticated products. This latter trade corresponds to the Heckscher-Ohlin pattern, based on differences in factor proportions, while the horizontal or intra-industry trade would have to be explained by economies of scale and product differentiation as in the recent theoretical work of Lancaster, Krugman and others. Watanabe's input-output framework is very useful in showing the relative importance of these two distinct types of international trade at any point in time, and how they change over time. The secular trend seems to be strongly towards the increasing relative importance of horizontal or intra-industry trade.

The findings for Japan-Korea trade are interesting and conform to what one would expect. Korean industrialization appears to have begun assembling final consumer goods with components and capital goods imported from Japan but is evolving to "higher" stages of production as capital accumulation and technological progress proceeds. Similar patterns are detectable in the comparative data for Japan and the ASEAN economies, while trade between Japan and the U.S. is much more "horizontal" in nature.

One criticism of Watanabe's paper is that he frequently uses normative expressions when his entire analysis is strictly positive in character. The reader might get the impression that "vertical" trade is inferior to "horizontal." The expression "unilateral and one-sided" to characterize the past Japan-Korea trade pattern has a strongly pejorative flavor that seems entirely unwarranted.

GENERAL DISCUSSION

One may raise a question as to how far government should intervene in order to maintain an optimal pattern of industrialization. In many developing countries government intervention often quickens the growth process. For the technologically most advanced countries, it may be very difficult to select promising industries to be promoted and it might be much easier to determine losing industries not to be promoted. However, for less developed countries, like present-day Korea or Japan in its early phase of growth, it may not be very difficult to choose industries which are promising. For instance, in the case of Korea, it may be relatively easy and safe to suggest a movement from simple labor-intensive industries such as textiles and footwear to more skill-intensive industries such as light machinery. This may explain why government intervention has worked to a greater extent in Korea and Japan.

Japan maintained heavy protectionist policies throughout the 1950s and 1960s in order to establish a "full-range self-sufficient" industrial structure. As a result, Japan has industrialized too broadly, including many industries in which Japan does not have any particular comparative advantage such as aluminum refining. This peculiar Japanese industrial structure led to chronic balance of payments (BOP) surplus problem in its trading with other advanced developing countries. Japan exports all kinds of investment and intermediate goods to ADCs but does not allow the ADCs to have access to the Japanese domestic market in sufficient volume. Consequently, countries like Korea and Taiwan have to maintain huge BOP deficits in their trade with Japan.

Watanabe says that countries like Korea have a "truncated" industrial structure, implying a heavy dependence on Japanese intermediate and capital goods and non-optimal industrial structure. However, one may rather argue that it is the Japanese pattern of industrialization which is not optimal and which represents a strong deviation from the principle of international division of labor. The Japanese economy seems to be too self-sufficient and has remained so far too long to be regarded as optimal.

Korea and Taiwan may not have to follow the Japanese pattern by promoting, for example, metal processing industries. A supply of processed metals may be secured in coordination with resource-rich countries. There may be no reason to believe that a "horizontal division of labor" between Korea and Japan, which implies trade of heavy and chemical products, would be more desirable than a "vertical division of labor," implying exports of labor-intensive consumer goods from Korea in return for Japanese intermediate and capital goods. Japan may have to move out of labor-intensive and energy-intensive industries and narrow down its industrial base as soon as possible.

As Korea develops heavy and chemical industries, there may emerge more room to trade with Japan and reduce its BOP deficits with respect to Japan. However, there is nothing inherently optimal in a horizontal division of labor if it should be based on the Japanese style "self-sufficient full-range industrialization." Although Korea. might have ended up only with a so-called truncated industrial structure without benefiting greatly from a vertical division of labor in its trade with Japan until now, a "vertical division of labor based on truncated industrialization" might still be closer to the principle of division of labor and international specialization.

ADJUSTING TO THE ADCs IN
THE FACE OF STRUCTURALLY DEPRESSED
INDUSTRIES: JAPAN

*Ippei Yamazawa**

I. Introduction

The Japanese economy underwent its most serious depression since World War II in 1974-75. While many manufacturing industries recovered after 1976, some industries continued to be depressed, with low capacity utilization, accumulated deficits, and spreading insolvency. Eleven of these industries were designated as "structurally depressed" and given government assistance under the newly enacted Structural Depression Act.

Recession cartels were permitted to extend under the Act and the continued recovery of domestic demand helped the industries to increase capacity utilization and reduce accumulated deficits, although leaving the underlying causes of structural depression unresolved. The Structural Depression Act represents a typical pattern of adjustment assistance by the Japanese government, but the adjustment to the ADCs was not so much represented by these industries as by textile and other labor-intensive industries.

The Japanese textile industry has long been adjusting to an increasing wage rate at home, the increasing competitiveness of the ADCs, and changes in trade policy. While some of the Japanese textile products still remain competitive in the world market, imports of lower quality goods have increased significantly under trade liberali-

* Hitotsubashi University, Japan. The author benefited from Professors G. Helleiner, E. Chen, H. Patrick, N. Plessz and other participants at the conference.

zation since the late 1960s. The adjustment of the Japanese textile industry has been characterized by a liberal import policy combined with adjustment assistance to domestic producers.

Although adjustment assistance in the past has not always been very efficient and consistent, thus leaving room for further improvement, the Japanese textile industry has so far been adjusting appropriately under the pressure of import increase. It has been successful in giving up lower quality, less sophisticated textile products and in upgrading its products as well as modernizing its equipment. The adjustment, however, involves the restructuring of the production system in traditional "textile areas," and requires another decade for its completion while waiting for a generation change in a number of small family factories staffed by elderly workers with no successors.

The main purpose of this paper is to survey the structural adjustment of the Japanese industries to major changes in economic conditions in the 1970s and to evaluate the adjustment assistance given by the Japanese government to the seriously affected industries. Section II introduces the Structural Depression Act and Section III analyzes in detail the adjustment of "structurally depressed industries" under this Act.

The remainder of the paper is devoted to an analysis of the textile industry adjustment to the ADCs. Section IV deals with the increasing competition the Japanese textile industry is facing from ADCs and the comparative advantage in structure Japan possesses at present. Section V explains the increase in textile imports under trade liberalization, and brief reference will be made to problems regarding the Japanese marketing and distribution system.

Section VI describes in detail the adjustment of the Japanese textile production of both larger and smaller firms in "textile areas," and predicts their future prospects. The last section confirms the appropriateness of the Japanese policy combination, that is, domestic adjustment assistance combined with a liberal import policy, in spite of the mounting demand for import restriction, in the context of the inherent characteristics of the Japanese textile industry and its proximity to other Asian textile producers.

II. The Structural Depression Act

In 1974-75 the Japanese economy encountered its most serious depression since World War II. Total manufacturing production has recovered since 1976 but several manufacturing industries continued to be depressed with low capacity utilization and low profit rates for individual firms within the industry. The Structural Depression Act (The Law for Provisional Measures for Stabilizing Designated Depressed Industries) was put into effect in May 1978 in order to relieve those "structurally depressed industries." Eleven manufacturing industries were designated as "structurally depressed" by the Act. They were electric furnace steel making, ferro-silicon manufacturing, aluminum smelting, synthetic fiber making, spinning, ammonia and urea fertilizer production, phosphatic acid production, vinyl chloride production, paperboard making and shipbuilding.

The requirements for designation were that the industry concerned was affected by large and sudden changes in both domestic and foreign economic conditions and had undergone a prolonged depression, that excess capacity existed and would continue to exist for a lengthy period, and that it was feared that the majority of firms in the industry would suffer because of the existing instability. Further, the requirements for designation as a structurally depressed industry included the need for the abolition of excess capacity as a prerequisite for overcoming the depression.

The relief program had three principal planks. A basic stabilization plan was prepared by MITI, in consultation with the advisory board concerned, for individual "structurally depressed" industries. The program aimed to restore a demand/supply equilibrium within three to five years and to control the abolition of excess capacity and new installation. If MITI found inadequate autonomous adjustment by private firms, those firms were to be instructed to form a cartel in order to abolish excess capacity and restrict new installations. Although the cartel is prohibited under the Anti-Trust Law, an exemption was made in this situation, through MITI's intervention. The abolition of excess capacity and business switchover to other industries was financed at low interest rates by the Development Bank. To relieve the employment difficulty caused by the abolition of excess capacity, a subsidy was to be given to firms for their within-firm replacement program. Furthermore, programs sponsored by

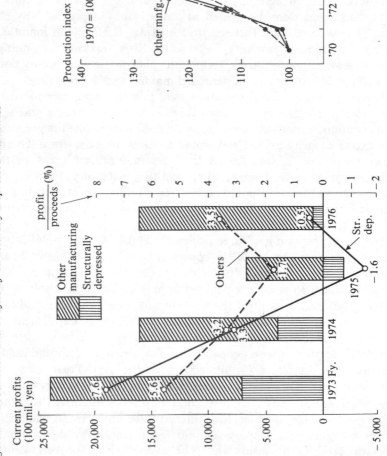

Figure 1.   Production and Profits of Structurally Depressed Industries

Source: MITI, *Management Analysis of Japanese Enterprises.*

both the central and prefectural governments to retrain and re-employ displaced laborers were to be strengthened.

The Japanese economy encountered big changes in its environment during the 1970s, such as rapid increases in the price of energy and raw materials, a shift to slower growth, and rapid appreciation of the yen. The "structurally depressed" industries were delayed in adjusting to those changes. Figure 1 shows the movement of production and profits of those industries in comparison with others. The percentage share of the former in total manufacturing was 14.3 percent in 1970. The figures indicate their worsening situation against overall recovery after 1975.

The justification for the relief program was that the structural depression of those industries would induce a chain reaction of insolvency and unemployment among related industries if they were left unaided. Other relief programs were introduced under the newly enacted Smaller Enterprise Business Switchover Act (1976), the Depressed District Act (1978), Industrial Area Smaller Enterprise Act (1979), and the Higher Yen Rate Act (1978). The first three focus on assistance to small and medium-size firms either individually or as a group in industrial areas. The last one was enacted in a rush to assist these firms through emergency loans or decreased interest rates, because of the rapid appreciation of the yen in 1977 and 1978 (55 percent in 12 months).

III. Adjustment of Structurally Depressed Industries

Each of the ten industries designated as structurally depressed are summarized in Table 1 in terms of demand and supply, capacity utilization and the financial situation of major firms during the years 1973 to 1977. To assist in interpreting the figures in the table, it may be helpful to offer a brief explanation of the structural depression of the individual industries.

Medium-size firms with 200-500 employees deal more efficiently with the production of a variety of small bars and rods, each in small lots, than do the large integrated steelmakers. With rapid economic growth and expanding construction demand, small bar production continued to increase so that new firms and severe competition for capacity expansion resulted. However, because sluggish investment in

Table 1. Indicators of Structurally Depressed Industries

	Electric-furnace made-steel	Ferro-silicon	Alminium	Synthetic fiber	Spun yarn
Production (1000 ton)					
1973	11,666	347.6	1,082	1,327	1,563
1975	9,313	306.1	988	1,142	1,261
1977	9,633	286.7	1,188	1,340	1,146
Production capacity (1000 ton)					
1973	15,900	500	1,238	3,831	14,722
1975	19,300	454	1,447	3,929	14,200
1977	20,950	498	1,641	5,030	13,699
Capacity utilization (%)					
1973	87.9	69.5	87.4	94.9	94.6
1975	54.0	67.4	68.3	79.7	84.2
1977	50.2	57.6	72.4	73.0	80.9
Domestic consumption (1000 ton)					
1973	11,050	399.9	1,624	947	1,556
1975	6,963	313.2	1,270	745	1,194
1977	8,366	327.8	1,386	975	1,089
Imports (1000 ton)					
1973	—	53.5	473	16.8	346
1975	—	26.1	358	6.6	159
1977	—	44.8	472	12.6	185
Exports (1000 ton)					
1973	513	1.7	2	392	240
1975	1,971	21.5	73	400	273
1977	1,577	3.4	176	383	326
Factory price (1000 yen per ton)					
1973	47.0-100.0	90.0-180.0	290	787	337.1
1975	41.5-62.0	190.5-230.5	272	654	284.8
1977	59.0	135.0-205.5	303	504	316.5
Current profits total of principal firms (million yen)					
1973	33,660	997	1,450	155,173	172,532
1975	▲ 33,323	▲ 2,389	▲ 13,160	▲ 41,487	▲ 104,451
1977	▲ 22,084	▲ 5,930	▲ 20,500	▲ 22,732	▲ 33,997
Number of employees (persons)					
1973	—	23,140	18,583	39,629	178,190
1975	—	29,273	18,287	38,377	135,159
1977	35,000	26,124	13,409	30,373	103,592
Number of firms (s & m firms)[a]					
1973	—	16 (8)	5 (0)	33 (7)	—
1975	—	17 (8)	6 (0)	33 (7)	—
1977	68 (29)	16 (7)	7 (0)	35 (9)	870 (681)

Source: MITI, *Kozo Fukyo-ho no Kaisetsu* [Explanation of Structurally Depressed Industry Act], 1978.
Notes: [a] Small and medium-size firms are defined as manufacturing firms employing less than 300 persons.
[b] Figures for 1976.

Table 1. (Continued)

		Ammonia fertilizer	Urea fertilizer	Phosphatic fertilizer	Vinyl chloride	Paper-board
Production (1000 ton)	1973	3,874	3,384	663	1,380	5,162
	1975	2,982	2,127	525	1,091	4,037
	1977	2,779	2,002	547	1,024	4,694
Production capacity (1000 ton)	1973	4,434	3,831	850	1,608	5,363
	1975	4,434	3,870	881	1,656	7,038
	1977	4,552	3,936	911	1,890	7,429
Capacity utilization (%)	1973	87.4	88.7	78	85.8	96.3
	1975	67.3	55.0	60	65.9	57.4
	1977	61.0	51.0	60	54.2	63.2
Domestic consumption (1000 ton)	1973	3,836	1,112	663	1,354	5,084
	1975	2,922	851	525	992	3,962
	1977	2,762	935	582	957	4,596
Imports (1000 ton)	1973	0	0	—	77	33
	1975	0	0	—	8	13
	1977	0	0	56	11	49
Exports (1000 ton)	1973	38	2,151	—	108	113
	1975	101	1,280	—	131	171
	1977	68	1,242	—	81	144
Factory price (1000 yen per ton)	1973	27	33	48,740	109	55-57
	1975	52	43	121,080	141	72-77
	1977	53	49	99,100	154	90-92
Current profits total of principal firms (million yen)	1973	▲ 4,141	▲ 4,141	▲ 224	99,802	6,391
	1975	16,844	16,844	▲ 9,163	▲ 13,124	▲ 16,814
	1977	▲ 11,934b	▲ 11,934b			
Number of employees (person)	1973	940	605	523	—	13,000
	1975		624	523	—	12,000
	1977	784	461	498	4,680	11,000
Number of firms (s & m firms)	1973	18 (0)	12 (0)	22 (2)	18 (−)	94 (71)
	1975	18 (0)	12 (0)	22 (2)	18 (−)	88 (65)
	1977	18 (0)	12 (0)	22 (2)	18 (−)	88 (65)

plant and equipment began to reduce the domestic demand for these steel products in 1974, when new equipment built at the end of the rapid expansion period started operation, capacity utilization declined to 50 percent. The firms either became insolvent or stopped production while the price of their products continued to fall short of their cost.

The rapid expansion of steel production increased the domestic demand for ferro-silicon, an input into steel making, and attracted new entrants to the business. After 1974, however, a big reduction in steel production decreased domestic demand, and higher electricity prices in Japan seriously affected the international competitiveness of this electricity-intensive product. Import pressure mounted and further reduced capacity utilization.

Oil price increases and higher electricity prices in Japan hit aluminum smelting, another electricity-consuming activity. Electricity costs increased from 24 percent to 35 percent of the total production cost and Japan's competitiveness deteriorated rapidly. Increased imports, combined with sluggish domestic demand, caused financial difficulty and the slow-down of production.

The increased price of naphtha, a product derived from crude petroleum, in Japan and the increasing competitiveness of the ADC producers, combined with stagnant domestic demand, are often pointed out as the direct cause of the difficulties of the synthetic fiber making and spinning industries. Many firms suffered from low capacity utilization and accumulated loss; and six spinning firms of medium size went bankrupt from 1975 to 1977. However, the maintenance of excess capacity, prolonged since the early 1960s, underlay these difficulties, which will be analyzed in the following section.

Major firms produce two types of chemical fertilizer, urea and ammonium, and are heavily dependent on export. Export decreased due to long-term changes such as self-sufficiency in Chinese and Indian markets, new entry by oil-producing countries, and higher material costs after the oil price increase. Decreased exports, combined with sluggish domestic demand, reduced capacity utilization to 50 to 60 percent. Seven factories stopped operation in 1976 and 1977.

The increased cost of domestic production of ammonium phosphate because of the higher price for imported phosphate ore was accompanied by an import rush of cheaper ammonium phosphate from the U.S., forcing many firms to a 60 percent level of operation and shipment at a loss. Two firms closed down and three others suspended operations during the years 1975 to 1977.

In spite of higher prices for naphtha and chloride, two major inputs into vinyl chloride production, sluggish domestic demand prevented a rise in the output price and forced shipment at a loss. A reduction of paperboard production at a loss was brought about by higher chip and energy prices and increased production costs on the one hand and sluggish domestic demand, aggravated by the prevailing practice of simple packing, on the other. Three firms became insolvent during the fiscal year 1976.

Shipbuilding, which is not included in Table I, was reduced to less than 40 percent because of sluggish exports which were caused by increasing competitiveness of the ADC producers and deteriorating competitiveness in some production lines of less sophisticated ships as well as by the depressed world demand for tankers. Depression in this industry was most worrisome because of its broad transmission to related industries and regional economies.

Excess capacity, accumulated loss, and increasing insolvency were common to those industries designated as "structurally depressed." MITI, worried about the transmission of financial difficulties to related industries and the general feeling of depression, moved to enact the Act. However, there were various factors causing excess capacity and two or more factors were at work in some industries.

Every industry suffered from sluggish demand both at home and abroad during the period of slower economic growth in Japan and in the world as a whole. However, such a big reduction in demand as in shipbuilding, and the active entry and severe competition for capacity investment, as found in electric furnace steel making and ferro-silicon production, delayed individual firms' adjustment to the sluggish demand situation.

Secondly, industries heavily dependent on cheap imports of petroleum and other raw materials or on low energy costs rapidly lost their cost advantage and became less competitive against products from other sources. Aluminum smelting, chemical fertilizers, synthetic fibers, vinyl chloride, and paperboard have all been affected by this factor.

The third factor was the increasing industrialization of the ADCs and LDCs. As they achieved import substitution and exported their products abroad, Japanese exports tended to decrease and imports to the Japanese market started to increase. This factor was typically reflected in the areas of textiles, chemical fertilizers, and ship-building.

These factors represent big and sudden changes in economic conditions in the 1970s and the "structurally depressed" industries designated above were most seriously affected by them, thus delaying their adjustment long after other manufacturing industries had completed their adjustment and had started to recover.

The reduction of employment was common to all industries in the table, as was the case in all other manufacturing industries from 1974 to 1976. Employment adjustment was severe in the midst of the depression but methods for coping with it contributed greatly to the financial improvement of the firms. Success was achieved mainly by stopping recruitment of mid-career workers, restraining over-time, and transferring employees within firms or to subsidiaries rather than laying off regular employees.[1] This explains why Japan had less acute employment difficulties than other developed countries.

The adjustment assistance program under this act was scheduled to be completed by 1983 and it may be too early to evaluate the performance of those industries partway through the program. Nevertheless, it seems that those industries have been protected from "structural depression" for the moment, thanks to the following two factors.[2] First, excess capacity has been partly abolished or sealed off under the recession cartel in seven industries, thus relieving firms of the financial burden of maintaining them. Aiming to achieve balance at a reduced level of production, the shipbuilding industry has effected a 39 percent production cut, a reduction of 85 thousand employees, and a cutback of 35 percent of its capacity. Similarly, 30 to 45 percent of ammonia and urea production equipment and 14 to 19 percent of synthetic fiber-making capacity had been abolished by the end of 1979.

Second, the continued recovery of the domestic economy has helped all industries to recover from the depression. Electric furnace steel makers and ferro-silicon producers benefited from a steel boom in 1979. The aluminum, chemical fertilizer and shipbuilding industries have also been supported by the recent depreciation of the yen and have recovered exports. The aluminum price was raised five times, a

---

[1] Shimada, Haruo. "The Japanese Labor Market After the Oil Crisis," *Keio Economic Studies*, Vol. xiv, No. I., 1977.

[2] *The Japan Economic Journal*, Industrial Review of Japan: 1980, March 1980; *Kozo-fukyo-sangyo no Genkyo to Kongo no Kadai* [Present Situation and Future Problems of Structurally Depressed Industries], Tokutei-fukyo-sangyo Shinyo Kikin, March 1980.

total increase of 50 percent, by January of 1980 in the tightened world market situation. No serious insolvency has occurred since 1979 and total employment in Japan has returned to the pre-1974 level.

The present recovery, however, tends to obscure temporarily the need for long-term adjustment. Industries which have had their comparative advantage deteriorate will find their adjustment delayed until the onset of the next recession when the structural depression problems will arise again. Either the replacement of a substantial part of domestic production overseas or the switchover to other promising lines of production will be needed to prevent the return of the problem in the long run.

The preceding review of the Structural Depression Act clarifies typical characteristics of industrial adjustment assistance in Japan. The increasing competitiveness of the ADCs, however, is only one of the factors necessitating the adjustment of "structurally depressed" industries. It is textile and other labor-intensive manufacturing industries that face an acute need for adjustment to the ADCs' development. The New Textile Industry Act of 1974, which was extended for another four years in 1978, gives weaving and other parts of the textile industry adjustment assistance similar to that given under the Structural Depression Act. Section III will analyze the adjustment of the textile industry to explain the Japanese adjustment to the ADCs.

IV. The Japanese Textile Industry and the ADCs

The adjustment problem of the Japanese textile industry is better understood in the context of its history during the post-war period. Japan was the sole exporter of textile products in the region in the early 1950s, but Asian ADCs have caught up with her as a bloc of textile exporters to the world market, and these in turn, are being pursued by China and the ASEAN countries in the 1980s. Competition between Japan and her Asian neighbors commenced in their home markets in the 1950s. It was intensified in the U.S. and other third world markets in the 1960s and has begun to be felt in her own domestic market in the 1970s.

However, it does not mean that the Japanese textile industry has been declining for the past thirty years. On the contrary, it has developed the synthetic textile sector as the new core of the industry,

Table 2. Demand-Supply Balance of Japan's Textile Industry: 1955-85

(in thousand M/T and percent)

	Domestic demand (D)	Exports (X)	Domestic output (S)	Imports (M)	X/S (%)	M/D (%)
1955	546	341	872	4	39.1	0.7
1960	743	487	1,270	4	38.3	0.5
1965	1,050	495	1,566	6	31.6	0.6
1970	1,444	610	2,036	63	30.0	4.3
1971	1,496	735	2,175	87	33.8	5.8
1972	1,528	719	2,130	143	33.8	9.4
1973	1,932	550	2,248	343	24.5	17.8
1974	1,431	622	1,948	211	31.9	14.7
1975	1,404	639	1,879	141	34.0	10.0
1976	1,533	637	2,000	169	31.8	11.0
1977	1,411	710	1,854	167	38.5	10.8
1978	1,738	568	1,975	317	28.8	18.2
1979	1,887	508	2,072	339	24.5	18.0
1980	1,898	595	2,213	281	26.9	14.8
1985	2,143	546	2,311	378	23.6	17.6

Source: MITI, *Toward New Textile Industry,* Sept. 1977; and *Long-Range Vision of Industrial Structure,* 1979.

Notes: a) Includes all textiles for both clothing and industrial use, converted to a yard basis.

b) Projected figures for 1980 and 1985.

c) $D + X = S + M$ does not necessarily hold because of the change in inventory stock.

its production has increased threefold, and it has undertaken actively capacity investment overseas during the same period. Although its expansion may not be comparable with that of steel and automobile production, nevertheless it continued to expand steadily until the early 1970s.

The steady expansion in output is partly attributed to the steady growth of domestic demand. Table 2 shows the aggregate demand and supply of all textile products, both for clothing and industrial use, converted on a yard basis.[3] The early 1970s marked the turning

---

[3] Textile materials are excluded from this table. If included, the overall textile trade balance has been decreasing from a big surplus to as small as 36 million dollar surplus (0.7 percent of total export) in 1978.

point after which domestic output stagnated and exports declined, while imports increased rapidly, even if one disregards the import rush of 1973.[4] Exports still exceeded imports and maintained a small net surplus, reflecting high export competitiveness in some lines of textile production. The 1980 and 1985 figures are the forecast made by MITI in 1978. Domestic demand is expected to remain unchanged, while both exports and production will turn downward as imports continue to increase.[5] If, however, the 1977-78 trend continues, imports will easily exceed the forecast in the table.

The textile industry still occupies a big share of the Japanese economy. The number of enterprises totals 310 thousand, 150 thousand for manufacturing and 160 thousand for the distribution sector. The number of employees totals 2.56 million, 1.47 and 1.06 million for manufacturing and distribution sectors respectively. If their families are included, ten million Japanese may be counted as still depending on this industry.[6]

Many lines of textile production are labor-intensive and the Japanese competitive advantage in these lines has been lost as her labor costs have risen much faster than that of her neighbors. The deterioration in competitiveness was clearly reflected in the replacement of Japanese textile products by those from the Asian ADCs in the U.S. market. During the five years 1969 to 1974, the Japanese share of cotton fabric and clothing declined from 29.4 percent and 23.0 percent to 8.2 percent and 7.8 percent respectively, whereas the Asian ADCs' share expanded from 37.7 percent and 45.3 percent to 52.5 percent and 62.0 percent respectively.[7] This tendency has accelerated in recent years. The Japanese share of cotton and synthetic fabrics in the U.S. market decreased by almost 40 percent (5.2 percent to 3.0 percent and 26.7 percent to 16.3 percent, respectively) in the years 1977 to 1979.[8]

The long-term trend of deteriorating competitiveness differs among various lines of textile production. Labor-intensive lines of standardized quality have lost competitiveness rapidly in the midst of such

---

[4] The sporadic import increase in 1973-74 will be investigated in Section V.

[5] They are based on the hearing from individual textile firms associations.

[6] MITI, *Toward New Textile Industry*, September 1977. Figures are for 1974. The 1973 numbers of enterprises and persons engaged in textile manufacturing are 150 and 1,470 thousand respectively.

[7] U.S. Department of Commerce, *Highlights of Export and Import Trade,* 1975.

[8] U.S. Department of Commerce, *TQ Series.*

drastic changes as the yen revaluation and continued wage increases in the 1970s and they will continue to lose competitiveness in the future. On the other hand, other lines of textile production are still competitive and maintain high export-output ratios. There remains plenty of room for upgrading and differentiating the present products.

Table 3 gives the demand-supply trend for major textile products including forecasts for 1980 and 1985. Increasing import-demand ratio (M/D) and declining export-output ratio (X/S) are commonly observed for all products as well as for the aggregated textile products in Table 3. However, the level of M/D and X/S differ greatly among the products.

The increasing M/D is evident for cotton yarn and fabric and clothing. Domestic production has already been replaced by imports in the case of low count cotton yarn and plain white shirts. The 1979 M/D of cotton textiles as a whole reached a 30.2 percent level. Decreasing X/S and increasing M/D are also expected for synthetic yarn under higher oil prices, while a high X/S and a low M/D are expected to be maintained in synthetic fabric where the increase in raw material price is offset by high technology and superior quality.

For example, Japan provided 82.6 percent of the U.S imports of polyester filament fabrics in 1978, far exceeding West European and Korean shares. In particular, thin silk-like fabrics for ladies' wear are produced using a special technology and are only available from Japanese producers. These remain competitive in the U.S. market at a higher retail price due to the yen revaluation. Deteriorated price competitiveness has so far been offset by such non-price competitive factors as superior quality and design, as well as reliable supply at specified delivery dates. On the contrary, standardized synthetic fabric has been dominated by Taiwanese products in the Philippine market where price competition prevails.[9]

The decreasing exports and increasing imports are also attributed to changes in trade policy. The Japanese textile industry has encountered various changes in trade policy since the early 1960s. Three trade agreements, the Long Term Agreement on cotton textiles (LTA) in 1961, the voluntary restraint of export of synthetic and woolen textiles to the U.S. in 1971, and the Multi-Fiber Agreement (MFA) in 1974, tended to affect unfavorably Japanese export to the U.S.

---

[9] Japan External Trade organization, *Overseas Markets,* Vol. 29, No. 335, September 1979.

Table 3. *Demand and Supply of Individual Textile Products*

		Domestic Demand (D)	Export (X)	Domestic Production (S)	Import (M)	M/D (%)	X/S (%)
(1) Cotton yarn (thousand ton)	1970	437	112	526	33	7.6	21.3
	1975	465	75	461	67	14.4	16.3
	1980	603	69	508	164	27.2	13.6
	1985	641	62	503	200	31.2	12.3
(2) Synthetic yarn (staple) (thousand ton)	1970	248	184	442	6	2.3	41.7
	1975	329	162	452	24	7.3	35.8
	1980	502	132	530	104	20.7	24.9
	1985	617	113	572	158	25.5	19.7
(3) Filament fabric of synthetic & regenerated fiber (million sq. meter)	1970	1,305	644	1,982	3	0.2	32.5
	1975	1,497	1,059	2,545	11	0.7	41.6
	1980	890	1,131	1,983	38	4.2	57.0
	1985	1,135	1,003	2,080	58	5.1	48.2
(4) Fabric of synthetic staple fiber (million sq. meter)	1970	658	750	1,461	10	1.6	51.3
	1975	628	624	1,141	40	6.3	54.7
	1980	683	567	1,210	40	5.8	46.9
(5) Cotton fabrics (million sq. meter)	1970	2,215	431	2,617	72	3.3	16.5
	1975	2,101	283	2,125	159	7.6	13.3
	1980	2,263	322	2,334	226	10.0	13.8
(6) Outer garment (million piece)	1970	251	85	326	19	7.5	26.1
	1975	327	53	325	55	16.9	16.3
	1980	456	60	424	95	20.8	14.2
	1985	618	66	533	154	25.0	12.4
(7) Underwear (million piece)	1970	479	13	493	5	1.1	2.6
	1975	427	40	391	36	8.4	10.2
	1980	539	50	480	64	11.9	10.4
	1985	567	60	459	113	20.0	13.1

Source: MITI, *Toward New Textile Industry*, September 1977.
Note: Projected figures for 1980 and 1985.

market. On the other hand, textile imports have been encouraged by a series of tariff reductions, as will be discussed in the next section.

Those policy changes have been regarded by many textile producers as pressure from outside. One of them was related to a political decision of the government and the other was attributed to the failure of government policy, although adjustment assistance was given to textile producers in order to compensate for those policy changes. The former was the voluntary restraint of export to the U.S. which was a compromise reached in exchange for the return of Okinawa, while the latter was the rapid appreciation of the yen after the government tried in vain to maintain cheap yen rates.

V. Textile Import and Trade Liberalization

Table 4 shows the increase in imports of textile products, excluding textile materials, to Japan, classified by country. Total import value increased by 450 percent from 1966 to 1971, by 340 percent from 1971 to 1976, and by 60 percent for the two years following 1976. In terms of annual growth rate at constant prices, they are 28 percent, 18 percent, and 15 percent respectively. Imports from developed countries occupied three quarters of total textile imports in 1966, 40 percent in 1971 and a quarter in 1976-78. The increasing share of the ADCs was remarkable during the decade 1966-76. Korea supplied 38 percent of textile imports to Japan in 1978, while China was the second largest single supplier. Imports from Singapore and other ASEAN countries increased rapidly but their combined share was still as small as 2.5 percent in 1978.

The sporadic increase in imports in 1973-74 deserves some explanation. It should be regarded as an abnormal divergence from the steadily growing trend since the late 1960s. It was induced by speculative demand in the middle of the world-wide commodity boom before the oil shock, and was aggravated by the complicated distribution system in the Japanese textile market. The various elements in the system have been linked with each other by a multi-layered distribution system so that there is a weak connection between producers and final consumers. Producers tend to be led, not directly by final consumption, but by speculative demand induced by market prospect. The maintenance of obsolete but still functioning spindles and looms

Table 4. *Japan's Imports of Textile Products by Countries*

(in thousand dollars)

Imports from	1966	1971	1976	1978
Total	68,721	382,934	1,699,240	2,730,815
1. Developed countries	49,778	152,701	411,165	745,899
	(72.4)	(39.9)	(24.2)	(27.3)
Asian ADCs (2-5)	7,252	146,732	956,261	1,470,470
	(10.6)	(38.3)	(56.3)	(53.8)
2. Korea	4,597	80,400	681,012	1,035,147
3. Taiwan	596	39,757	158,673	281,883
4. Hong Kong	2,018	26,031	108,342	144,076
5. Singapore	14	544	8,185	9,364
Other ASEAN (6-9)	222	3,803	37,144	54,945
	(0.3)	(1.0)	(2.2)	(2.0)
6. Thailand	147	2,722	22,518	29,291
7. Philippines	14	591	10,250	7,492
8. Malaysia	1	104	2,518	12,289
9. Indonesia	60	386	1,858	5,873
10. India	583	6,232	20,940	40,546
11. Pakistan	—	10,564	32,191	40,666
12. China	4,597	32,050	166,740	307,029
	(6.7)	(8.4)	(9.8)	(11.2)

Source: MITI, *White Paper on International Trade.*

Note: Includes only SITC 65 & 84. Figures in parentheses represent percentage shares of total imports.

by small and medium firms, in excess of the number called for by final demand easily leads to over-production and financial burden on those firms.

The sporadic import increase was an undesirable occurrence both for importers and exporters. Many importers, after rushing to rake in supplies from various overseas sources, suffered losses in the big pile-up of inventory and were discouraged from expanding imports further. Exporters in the developing countries, on the other hand, were buffeted by a sudden boom and a quick setback. Import increase in the late 1970s is regarded as a return to a steadier long-term tendency.

The increase in textile imports, especially from the Asian ADCs, is attributed to the liberal import policy of the Japanese government as well as to the rapid expansion of supply capacity in the Asian ADCs. Quota restriction was introduced on imports of silk and silk fabrics, mainly from Korea and China, in 1975 but it is regarded as an extension of sericulture protection and should therefore be distinguished from a generally liberal import policy in other manufactures.

Japanese tariffs were reduced on three occasions. Tariffs on most manufactures were reduced by 35 percent on average under the Kennedy Round (1967-71) and they were reduced unilaterally by 20 percent in 1972. They will be further reduced under the Tokyo Round (1980-87) according to a harmonization formula so that higher tariffs will be reduced more than lower ones.

Figure 2 compares changes in the distribution of tariffs on textiles under the TR between Japan, U.S. and the EC. Tariffs on textiles are higher than those on other products in general but a clear downward shift of the distribution is observed for each country. The pre-TR distribution of EC was concentrated narrowly within 5 to 20 percent with a peak in the 10 to 15 percent class. It shifts leftward so as to be included within 0 to 15 percent with a peak in the 5 to 10 percent class. The U.S. tariff distribution contrasts with the EC's by its wide dispersion over 0 to 45 percent with a broad peak in the 10 to 25 percent classes. It moves leftward, and will be close to the EC's pre-TR distribution by 1987.

The pre-TR distribution of Japan was between those of the EC and the U.S., but its post-TR distribution resembles the post-TR distribution of EC more closely, with a peak in the 5 to 10 percent class and with three quarters of tariffs included within the 5 to 15 percent classes. It is worth noting that in Japan a substantial portion of the TR reduction has been accomplished in advance by the 1972 unilateral reduction. That is, Japanese textile tariffs had been reduced to the pre-TR EC level by the early 1970s, and Japan maintained the lowest tariffs on major textile products among the three through the 1970s.

Textile imports to Japan have increased through the 1970s, so that in 1977 they occupied 20 percent of synthetic fabric imports and about 10 percent of cotton fabric and clothing imports from the ADCs to developed countries combined. The Japanese share was about a quarter or a third that of the EC and the U.S. The difference is attributed to the relative size of the Japanese market and severe competition there, as will be discussed below, rather than to the trade policy of the Japanese government. Greater shares for Korea and Taiwan (in Table 5) are not so much due to any favorable discrimina-

Figure 2. Distribution of Tariffs on Textiles under Tokyo Round Tariff Reduction (Distribution by Number of Tariff Items)

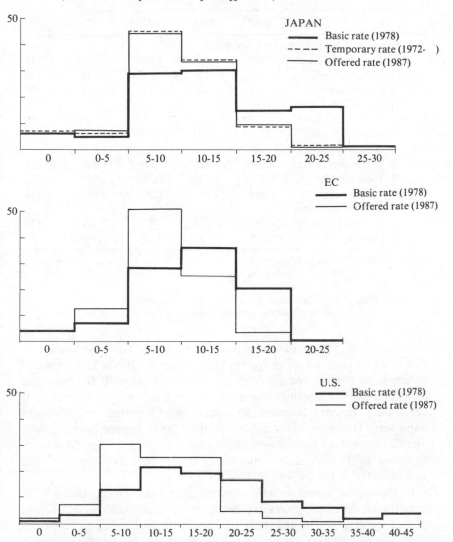

Note: Under the TR, the reduction formula is applied to the basic tariff rates of each country in 1973. Japanese tariffs have been reduced temporarily but their basic rates kept unchanged since 1972. The TR reduces the basic rates to what are close to the temporary rates already achieved in 1972. The Japanese government has decided to maintain the temporary rates until the basic rates are reduced to their level in 1987.

*Table 5. Numbers of Establishments and Employees in Textile Industry:
1960-77*

	1960	1965	1970	1975	1977
(A) Number of Establishments (thousand)					
1) Total manufactures	487	558	653	734	714
2) Total textiles[a]	102	119	146	157	150
3) Textile mills	83	100	113	114	107
4) Apparel and other finished products	19	19	33	43	42
5) Man-made fiber[b]	(38)	(51)	(77)	(76)	(76)
(B) Number of employees (thousand persons)[c]					
1) Total manufactures	8,169	9,921	11,680	11,296	10,874
2) Total textiles[a]	1,551	1,720	1,750	1,589	1,470
3) Textile mills	1,264	1,327	1,264	996	892
4) Apparel and other finished products	210	311	414	531	529
5) Man-made fiber	76	82	72	63	50

Source: MITI, *Census of Manufactures.*
Notes: [a] All figures are rounded numbers so that the sum of 3) + 4) + 5) does not make 2).

[b] Figures in parentheses are in simple numbers (not thousand).

[c] They include owners of the firms and their family workers as well as employees.

tion but simply reflect their competitiveness in the Japanese market.

It is often contended, however, that export to Japan is dominated by Japanese trading companies, thus making it difficult for outsiders to penetrate the Japanese market. It is true that a majority of developing country exports to Japan are handled by Japanese importers. However, there are more than 2000 importers in Japan's Textile Importer Association and each of them tries to realize whatever profitable trade opportunity it can find anywhere, as was well reflected in the import rush of 1973.

It should be noted in this context that the recent increase in imports of developing country products to Japan has been accompanied by changes in channels of importing and domestic distribution. The distribution system in the Japanese market has traditionally been characterized by "long and narrow" channels and high distribution costs resulting from small-scale retailers and multi-layered wholesalers. These complicated distribution channels have tended to prevent European and American exporters from penetrating the

Japanese market. Recently, however, large-scale retailers such as department stores and big supermarkets have grown so much as to be able to bypass existing channels and to import directly from abroad. Thirty-two percent of imported consumer goods purchased by department stores and 20 percent of those by big supermarkets are imported directly and these figures are expected to increase in the future. These changes provide "broad and short" channels, thereby reducing distribution costs and promoting competition, and providing more chances for foreign exporters if they are competitive enough to penetrate the Japanese markets. Asian ADCs have already taken advantage of the change in expanding the shares of their products in the Japanese market.

VI. Adjustment of the Japanese Textile Industry

Japanese textile manufacturing is composed of scores of big firms specializing in fiber-making and spinning on the one hand, and of a great number of small and medium firms specializing in weaving under subcontract to big spinners or trading companies on the other. Both fiber makers and spinners have been suffering from deteriorating competitiveness and prolonged maintenance of excess capacity. Cotton spinners have given up the domestic production of some lower-count yarn in the face of wage increases and the ADCs' increasing competitiveness. Synthetic fiber makers have suffered from higher material prices (10 to 18 percent higher than in the U.S.) and self-sufficiency in the ADCs and ASEAN.

However, there are several alternatives available for these big firms to take in adjusting to deteriorating competitiveness. Joint abolition of excess capacities can be made, utilizing the recession cartel and modernization of machines and equipment undertaken to enhance competitiveness with labor-intensive production in the ADCs. Firms could merge marketing and other activities to avoid duplicated investment and to improve their efficiency in these areas. Vertical integration of weaving and apparel-making through closer ties with medium-size firms at the middle and lower end of the spectrum of the industry could be carried out so as to exploit the possibility of increased value-added upgrading and differentiation. Domestic production could be relocated abroad through direct overseas investment and business activities diversified through extending into other areas such as fine chemicals and food processing.

Those alternatives differ in their effects on adjustment and individual firms have different access to each of them. Abolition of excess capacity is promoted as a temporary measure under the Structural Depression Act (1978-83). Some cotton spinning factories are competitive with fully automated, labor-saving production systems. Two groups of firms have been preparing for establishing joint marketing firms. A few firms have been investing overseas extensively since the mid-1960s, while other firms have been oriented more towards diversifying their activities. The percentage share of nontextile proceeds to total proceeds ranges from 54 percent for a fibermaker, 25 to 38 percent for six firms of both fiber making and spinning, to less than 8 percent for other spinning firms.

The latter group forms small industrial areas in which individual firms specialize both in different processes of weaving, dyeing, and finishing and in different varieties of textiles. A majority of them are small and medium-size firms with neither sufficient marketing nor credit facilities. They are not integrated vertically so as to produce integrated textile firm groups but they are linked under subcontract by trading companies which provide credit and marketing facilities. There are 64 textile areas producing cotton and synthetic-spun fabrics and they have organized the Association of Cotton Fabric Weavers, which altogether produced 82.8 percent in 1975 of the total output of Japan.[10] Therefore, it is necessary to understand the textile area organization to predict how it will adjust to increasing competitiveness from ADCs.[11]

The features which characterize Japanese textile production in textile areas, as contrasted with the integrated production of all processes of larger firms in the Asian ADCs, include an accumulation of skill and knowhow in weaving, dyeing and finishing specialization by many competent small firms suited to the production of many

---

[10] Other major organizations within the textile industry are The Association of Silk Fabric Weavers which is also composed of small and medium weavers of silk, artificial silk, and synthetic filament fabrics, The Association of Spinning Firms, and The Association of Chemical Fiber Producers.

[11] The author has benefited for the rest of this section from his visits to three textile reas, Mikawa, Banshu, and Tochio and meeting with people in textile business there in 1979 and 1980. He has also benefited from his access to a questionnaire survey of weaving firms conducted in 1976 by the Small and Medium Firm Promotion Agency.

varieties of quality goods in small lots and the capability of adjusting to changes in textile materials, from silk to cotton to synthetics, in types of products and in export markets. There is a strong dependence on exports, averaging 40 to 60 percent, but in some areas reaching 80 percent.

Adjustment assistance by the Japanese government has taken various forms, ranging from the abolition of excess capacity, modernization of machines and equipment, and switching-over to other lines of business, to more general retraining programs for displaced textile workers.

MITI and the Textile Industry Advisory Board have long been concerned with small and medium firms in textile areas. The problem of excess capacity and implementation of the abolition program has been addressed in a series of textile industry acts since 1956. Abolition based on individual firm's initiative has been the MITI's purchase-and-scrap program. A subsidy totaling 52.5 billion yen was spent on this program under the first through the fifth acts, of which 48.9 billion yen was given in return for the industry's acceptance of a voluntary restraint on textile exports to the U.S.

On the other hand, MITI started a series of structural improvement programs in 1967 (Special Textile Act). Under the guidance of prefectural governments, the weavers' association in each textile area submitted a plan in which the optimum capacity of its own area was specified and the building of new modern looms was undertaken together with the scrapping of obsolete ones of equivalent capacity. The number of looms scrapped and built was allocated among individual firms on the basis of the firms' application and their prospective competence. The Development Bank of Japan and the Small Business Promotion Corporation provided individual firms with low-interest long-term loans equivalent to 50 to 70 percent of required expenditure under the guarantee of the weaver's association. Almost 70 percent of the planned figure was achieved between 1967 and 1971. The program was extended until 1974. The program was renewed under the New Structural Improvement Act for 1974-79 and again extended for another five years in 1979. The program has contributed to the modernization of machines and equipment and new emphasis on assistance to R&D activities and the promotion of the modern apparel industry has been added since 1974.

However, the switching-over to other business has been less successful. Both loans and subsidies were given to small and medium weavers in order to promote the switchover as compensation for voluntary export restraint in 1971, but only 10 percent of the planned figure was realized. A major shift of small weaving firms was also continued over to related industries such as apparel-making and paper products.

Unlike the big textile firms mentioned earlier, small and medium firms in textile areas have only a limited access to other alternatives. They cannot afford foreign investment independently and the introduction of a new industry to their areas is too big a job for individual firms.

Table 5 shows the changes in the number of factories and persons engaged in the textile industry as a whole for the past two decades, including owners and their family workers as well as employees. The number of persons engaged in both textile mills carrying out spinning and weaving and man-made fiber-making decreased by one third between 1965 and 1978 while apparel-makers continued to increase until recently. In contrast, the number of factories decreased only slightly.

The change in firm structure underlying the aggregated change mentioned above is given in Tables 7 and 8. Although confined to small and medium weaving firms producing cotton and synthetic spun fabrics in textile areas, it shows a clear tendency in the 1970s. Medium-size firms with more than 100 looms and more than 30 persons decreased drastically in number, while small firms with 11 to 30 looms and 4 to 9 persons increased both in number of factories and looms. Family labor factories with 1 to 10 looms and less than 4 persons did not change greatly.

The prime moving force underlying this change is the increasing difficulty in recruiting young female employees. Only competent firms of medium size could maintain their scale of operation by introducing automatic, labor-saving looms as well as reducing their employees. Small firms mentioned above could manage to keep their employees comprised of family labor plus a few from the outside and maintain their traditional production. The structural change in the weaving sector appears to contradict the aim of structural improvement programs to increase the scale of firms while reducing their number.

However, the aggregate figure does not tell much about changes in the textile industry. The groups should be identified among the large number of weaving firms in the textile areas. One consists of major

Table 6. *Size Distribution of Weaving Firms (by Number of Looms)*

Number of looms	Number of factories			Number of registered looms		
	1965	1970	1975	1965	1970	1975
1- 10	10,148	11,188	10,746	45,386	51,599	51,852
	(61.4)	(63.7)	(58.1)	(13.6)	(16.3)	(16.0)
11- 30	3,986	4,210	5,361	72,359	74,285	95,030
	(24.1)	(24.0)	(29.0)	(21.7)	(23.4)	(29.3)
31- 50	1,089	997	1,231	42,575	38,997	48,326
	(6.6)	(5.7)	(6.6)	(12.8)	(12.3)	(14.9)
51-100	757	698	775	52,815	49,294	53,807
	(4.6)	(4.0)	(4.2)	(15.8)	(15.5)	(16.6)
101-300	465	390	338	75,468	63,688	53,886
	(2.8)	(2.2)	(1.8)	(22.6)	(20.1)	(16.6)
301-	91	83	44	44,755	35,960	19,577
	(0.6)	(0.5)	(0.2)	(13.4)	(12.5)	(6.5)
Total	16,536	17,566	18,495	333,358	317,532	323,941
	(100.0)	(100.0)	(100.0)	(100.0)	(100.0)	(100.0)

Table 7. *Size Distribution of Weaving Firms (by Number of Employees)*

Number of employees	1965		1970		1975	
- 3	7,827	(57.5)	10,148	(61.3)	10,146	(58.3)
4- 9	3,511	(25.8)	3,976	(24.0)	4,961	(28.5)
10- 19	956	(7.0)	1,089	(6.6)	1,141	(6.6)
20- 29	705	(5.2)	757	(4.6)	763	(4.4)
30- 49	164	(1.2)	179	(1.1)	135	(0.8)
50- 99	265	(2.0)	271	(1.6)	203	(1.2)
100-199	130	(1.0)	82	(0.5)	30	(0.2)
200-299	21	(0.15)	23	(0.14)	7	(0.04)
300-499	12	(0.09)	9	(0.05)	7	(0.04)
500-	29	(0.21)	23	(0.14)	17	(0.10)
Total	13,620	(100.0)	16,557	(100.0)	17,410	(100.0)

Source: Weavers' Association of Cotton and Staple Fibers.

Notes: Figures include only member firms of the Association but exclude weavers of filament fabrics and spinning-weaving firms. Figures in parenthesis indicate percentage shares.

medium-scale firms, *i.e.,* those in the last two classes of Table 6. Each of these firms has a score of smaller subcontracting firms (in the second—fourth classes), and can be expected to survive competition from their ADC rivals and continue to supply to home and foreign markets. The other is typically represented by small family labor factories, the first class in Table 7, which will leave the industry sooner or later.

The competitiveness of the first group is based on the following grounds, although straightforward evidence for it is not available. Looms which are old-fashioned but still in working order have long been maintained in textile areas. The share of automatic machines, both automatic and super-automatic, was 36 percent in 1978 while at the same time, the share of automatic machines in ADCs was 80 percent or more. The structural improvement programs have promoted the scrapping of old machines and the building of modern ones in each textile area.

Table 8 shows the distribution of weaving looms in all textile areas, according to age and type. Thirty-eight percent of the looms were built during the first two four-year plans of the programs. The percentage of automatic machines has been increasing and super-automatic looms have been preferred to automatic looms recently, while ordinary looms are still needed. Participation in the programs is biased toward firms of larger size. In the Mikawa textile area almost 100 percent of the firms with more than 40 looms participated in the program, while 59 percent of the firms with 20 to 40 looms, 31 percent of the firms with 11 to 20 looms and only 9 percent of the smallest firms with less than 11 looms did so. Automatic machines are labor-saving so that the number of looms operated by one worker is more than doubled, thus enabling the bigger firms shown in Table 7 to rapidly reduce their employees so as to offset rising wages.

While introducing modern machinery, major firms maintained the subcontract relationship with a score of small weavers with high technology, allowing these to specialize in differentiated high-quality products in small lots, thus taking full advantage of long-accumulated skills and knowhow in textile areas. Ordinary looms are better fitted for some production lines of differentiated products in small lots.

A large market for high-quality goods at home will give this group of major firms an additional advantage in competition with their ADC rivals. They are shifting their sales from the foreign to the domestic market where full development of apparel-making will

Table 8. *Composition of Weaving Looms by Type and Age*

(number of looms & percent)

Age \ Type	Ordinary loom	Automatic loom	Super-automatic loom	Total
Built before 1960	117,661	22,838	0	140,499
	107,938	24,353	0	132,291
	(28.5)	(6.4)	(0)	(34.9)
1960-66	66,422	20,271	5,017	91,710
	64,063	22,401	7,988	94,452
	(16.9)	(5.9)	(2.1)	(24.9)
1967-70	27,822	22,836	19,946	70,604
	27,065	25,047	21,637	73,749
	(7.1)	(6.6)	(5.7)	(19.4)
1971-74	45,013	7,952	21,092	74,057
	39,131	8,692	24,129	71,952
	(10.3)	(2.3)	(6.4)	(19.0)
1975-76	3,451	1,001	1,733	6,185
	3,421	1,094	2,074	6,589
	(0.9)	(0.3)	(0.5)	(1.7)
Total	260,369	74,898	47,788	383,055
	241,618	81,587	55,828	379,033
	(63.7)	(21.5)	(14.7)	(100.0)

Source: Association of Cotton and Staple Fiber Weavers.

Notes: Figures in the first rows indicate simple numbers of existing looms classified by age and type, those in the second rows numbers of capacity equivalent looms, and those in parentheses their percentage distribution by age and type.

provide them with a growing demand for high-quality fabrics of differentiated design and finishing. They see a better opportunity for overcoming the disadvantage of higher labor costs in such non-price factors as high quality, differentiated finishing and prompt delivery in the home market.

A firm characteristic of the second group can be described as follows. It is a family-labor factory in a small remodeled barn equipped with ten old-fashioned looms operated by three workers, the owner himself, his wife and his daughter. His daughter's husband either works at the town office or commutes to a nearby big city for a stable long-term job. The owner himself had worked at a bigger weaving factory before he started his factory during the textile boom in 1953. He is now in his fifties or sixties, but does not expect his son-in-law to succeed him in his business. He has a small paddy field to grow rice, vegetable and fruits sufficient for his family's consumption plus a small cash revenue.

He is a skilled textile workman who can tell the exact cause of trouble with his machines just by listening to their sound and is never idle in maintaining his old machines in good condition. He weaves narrow "yukata" fabrics for the domestic market or simply designed yarn dyed fabrics for export under subcontract. Yarns and designs are provided by his parent firms, he finishes his job at a specified date and is paid a weaving wage per unit of fabric. If the wage is too low during the recession, he stops his machines and waits for another boom. He has not applied for the structural improvement program because he has no successor and he will not continue to work long enough to pay back the loan by himself. But he has no intention of quitting his life-long business so long as he can afford to take care of his machines, which might be for another five or ten years.

The family labor firms of this type occupy 60 percent of the total, in terms of both factory number and persons engaged (Tables 7 and 8). They cannot be expected to undertake any positive adjustment and they will gradually die out.

Firms of an intermediate scale can move in the direction of either the first or the second type of firms. But the scale is not the decisive factor for survival. Many smaller firms with high skills will survive together with the group of major competitive firms in differentiated, high quality products under subcontract relationship with the latter group. On the other hand, even a bigger firm will fail if it sticks to the traditional way of business in the face of weakened traditional leadership by trading companies and big spinning firms.

Displaced textile workers have been given adjustment assistance under the Reemployment Promotion Fund and Employment Stabilization Fund as mentioned in Section II. Governmental assistance, however, has been concentrated not so much on textile employees as on small and medium textile firms. It reflects the characteristics of the Japanese textile industry where young female workers have little difficulty in finding new jobs, whereas a large number of elderly workers, either employees or owners of small family firms, cannot change their business easily and the rescue of individual firms as a whole is considered to be the aim.

Increasing dependence on elderly workers also affects the future prospects of competitive medium firms. Accumulated high skill embodied in these elderly workers supports the present competitive production of Japan and it will continue to do so as long as they cannot change to other businesses and remain in their present jobs. However, since the unprofitable situation of the textile industry does not attract new human resources, the present competitiveness is bound to erode in the long run.

VII. Conclusion and Policy Implications

To conclude this study, two policy problems with regard to the Japanese industries need to be discussed. One is to evaluate whether past government assistance policy is consistent with the Positive Adjustment Policy (PAP) proposed by the OECD and to suggest the direction for improvement, while the other is to confirm the maintenance of a liberal import policy. The two will be combined to produce a desirable policy environment for the adjustment of the Japanese industry to the ADCs.

1. Adjustment Assistance by the Japanese Government

Adjustment assistance implemented in the Structural Depression Act and the Textile Industry Acts typically takes the form of intervention by MITI in the industry concerned, including the promotion of either hoarding or abolition of excess capacity and the reorientation of the industry in new directions. Large and sudden changes in economic conditions, the prevention of a chain-reaction of business difficulties, compensation for trade policy changes, and assistance to medium-and small-scale firms have been listed as the the justifications for such intervention. It was explained that collusive actions by individual firms, even if they are helpful, were prohibited under the Anti-Trust Law and that the MITI's initiative was needed to exempt those relief actions from the Anti-Trust law.

The government's assistance is limited to medium- and small-scale firms endowed with high skill and further development potential but equipped with obsolete machines and insufficient financial and managerial capability to make the necessary adjustment by themselves. Modernization takes the form of automation, saving on labor, and the upgrading and differentiating of existing products. Although process innovation is sometimes criticized as defensive adjustment, labor-saving and upgrading are sometimes jointly achieved and cannot be distinguished clearly. These firms can survive competition with the ADCs only if they are partly supported in their effort to move in the right direction, so that the program should be distinguished from a mere maintenance of uncompetitive firms under heavy government support. They will continue to be competitive mainly because of non-price factors operating in the market for quality products.

However, it should be pointed out that the way of giving assistance has so far tended to aggravate the problem of excessive reliance on government by individual firms and to discourage autonomous adjustment at their own risk and profit. The purchase and scrapping of weaving looms by the government has tended to discourage their autonomous abolition by private firms in advance of the government's initiative, thus encouraging a prolonged maintenance of excess looms in the industry. The disposal program at the time of voluntary restraint of exports to the U.S. was no more than compensation for the foregone vested interest and its adjustment effect was limited, relative to the amount of subsidy. The emphasis of government policy is better shifted from direct to indirect assistance such as the promotion of R & D activities as well as autonomous business adjustment undertaken at the firm's own risk and profit.

Nevertheless the emergence of a group of competitive firms is encouraging. It is promoted by competition in the domestic market, not so much competition with imported products as between domestic products. An interview survey reveals that textile firms are more concerned with products of rival firms than with imports. The competition in the domestic market has been intensified by the switch-over by domestic producers from exporting to the home market, although increasing imports contributed to maintaining competitive pressure there.

Another aspect of industrial adjustment involves the limited possibility of change in business or employment which exists realistically for the older generation working in the textile industry. The successful completion of industrial adjustment may have to await the gradual natural attrition of these workers.

2. Maintenance of a Liberal Import Policy

The demand for import restriction has mounted during the 1970s, as textile imports increased under the liberal import policy. The big import rush of 1973 intensified the demand for restriction, which then appeared to resume with the recent rapid expansion of textile imports. It was reported in September 1980 that the Japan Spinner's Association had started to investigate the "dumping import" of cotton yarn from Korea since 1980 and had requested the MITI to introduce a bilateral agreement with Korea under the MFA.[12] So far, the Japanese government has not changed its liberal policy.

The demand for import restriction was based on the following grounds.[13] Import increase tends to offset domestic efforts to abolish excess capacity. The rationalization of textile production and the re-orientation of displaced labor and capital may be better achieved under orderly import expansion as the U.S. textile industry did under L.T.A. and M.F.A. Lastly, excessive import competition may erode an important part of the textile industry organization and lead to the eventual collapse of the entire Japanese textile industry, including those elements of it with a potential competitive advantage.

These arguments appear to be persuasive at first glance, but they cannot be justified for a number of reasons. They attribute the prolonged maintenance of excess capacity not so much to import pressure as to the inherent characteristics of the Japanese textile industry. But in fact, the competitive pressure of imports has promoted capacity disposal by encouraging textile forms to adjust autonomously.

The Japanese textile industry will still continue to be competitive in many lines of textile production and it is not likely that another import rush will affect many domestic producers and cause high unemployment under a liberal import policy. If another disturbing import rush is to be avoided, the best policy is to restructure the present system of textile distribution and implement a selective safeguard system with strict rules of application.

It is true that the textile exports from developing countries are promoted by heavy subsidies and that their expansion with increasing subsidy expenditure will not be consistent with the efficient allocation

---

[12] *The Japan Economic Journal* (Japanese edition), September 10, 1980.

[13] The arguments for restriction of textile imports are neatly summarized in Emoto (1974) and Hirai (1978).

of resources. However, it is competition both in national and international markets which corrects those policy distortions and leads to their eventual removal. For developed countries to respond with quota restrictions would be to reverse this correcting force.

The recommendation stated above, that of dispersing domestic adjustment assistance on a more rational basis combined with maintaining a liberal import policy, has a different orientation from the administered system of textile trade under the present MFA. The adoption of quota restrictions by Japan will further reduce competition in the textile trade, working against emerging textile exporters in the ASEAN and South Asia. Although these countries' textile exports have increased to the U.S. and EC at the cost of quota restrictions on Korea, Taiwan and Hong Kong, they will soon reach their quota and export growth will slow down. Import restriction is thus not a wise policy for Japan to adopt in view of her geographical proximity to the Asian ADCs and her close trade relationship with them.

With the slow increase of imports under the MFA by European and North American countries and with the maintained competitiveness of textile industries in Japan and some other developed countries, the expansion of potential world imports appears to be limited and competition among the Asian ADC and LDC exporters will become more severe. But it is under this severe competition that the efficiency of textile production will be improved and specialized exports of textile products at different processing stages and of different quality will be promoted in the region. Yet, at the same time, a long-term projection of world demand for and supply of textile products would be helpful for textile exporters in their effort to diversify production lines and markets for their products so as to achieve the desirable inter-industry specialization mentioned above.

REFERENCES

Emoto, H., "Thinking Import Restriction Problems—Proposals to Japanese Textile Industry," *Kasen Geppo* [Monthly Report of Chemical Fiber's Association], November 1974.
Hirai, T., "The Impact of Textile Import Expansion from the ADCs," *Kanzei Chosa Geppo* [Monthly Tariff Review], Finance Ministry, Vol. 32, No. 1, 1978-79.

Shimada, H., "The Japanese Labor Market After the Oil Crisis," *Keio Economic Studies,* Vol. XIV, No. 1, 1977.

• COMMENT _____

E.K.Y. Chen, *University of Hong Kong*

Yamazawa's paper can be conveniently divided into 3 parts for the purpose of discussion. The first is the causes for the existence of structurally depressed industries, the second is the adjustment process of the textile industry, and the third is policy implications.

First, Yamazawa discusses the causes and background leading to the structurally depressed industries. He maintains that on the demand side there was a fall during 1974-75 and some industries simply failed to adjust smoothly after the recession. On the supply side, the cost of production has been pushed up by higher oil prices, and the market, abroad and at home, has been increasingly threatened by the catching up of the ADCs. Of particular interest to this conference is, of course, the catching up of the ADCs. Yamazawa discussed 11 structurally depressed industries, but it is only in the case of textiles that the catching up of the ADCs is relevant. In the discussion of the structurally depressed industries and specifically the depressed labor-intensive industries in Japan, it is perhaps appropriate to also bring in some long-term economic and social changes that have been taking place.

Yamazawa might have been expected to take up the issue of demographic changes. Such changes would include changes in the age structure and educational standard of the population in Japan. With a slowing down of the growth of population in the 1960s and 1970s, the labor force as a whole has shown and will show considerable aging. Specifically, there has been and will be a decline in the share of the labor force in the 15-34 age group. An older labor force is usually more sluggish in making adjustments. Under the seniority system in Japan, an older labor force also means a higher average wage rate for the workers. The shortage of younger workers will also contribute to pushing up wages in general, and higher costs of labor will certainly affect the long-run comparative advantage of Japan. It is therefore expected that Japan will lose out to the ADCs in the labor-intensive industries at an increasing rate in the future. An additional factor is the increasing level of education achieved by the labor force. The consequence is that fewer people would be willing to work in low-level or labor-intensive manufacturing jobs. This factor further changes the comparative advantage of Japan. Hong Kong would have been in the same position if not for the legal and illegal immigrants coming to Hong Kong.

Thus there seem to be fundamental reasons for Japan to lose out in the labor-intensive industries beyond those of the oil crisis and the catching up of the ADCs. In light of these considerations, it is perhaps appropriate for Japan not to try too hard to retain industries such as textiles and clothing. In the longer run, Japan might even lose out in other labor-intensive industries such as consumer electronics, toys and watches. At present, Japan only imports about 15 percent of its total demand in textiles. This does not seem to me to be in line with its comparative advantage.

The second issue that Yamazawa discusses is the ways in which the textile industry in Japan has been adjusting to changes in the face of the rise of ADCs. Yamazawa has made two observations in this connection. The first was that the textile industry of Japan can still maintain its competitive position in some lines of production. However, the competitive edge in any line of production is becoming smaller and smaller. At present, such a competitive edge can only be maintained in the domestic market. Even in this case, it is only due to the peculiar distribution and marketing system in Japan.

Secondly Yamazawa observes that the adjustment of the textile industry in Japan has not been moving in the desired direction in as much as the number of small firms has increased and that of medium and big firms decreased. This appears to contradict an aim of the structural improvements to increase the scale of firms but to reduce their number.

Some reservations can be voiced about this view of adjustment. The trend of increasing small firms might not be too bad for Japan in the period of transition. Four reasons can be cited to support this belief: as pointed out by Yamazawa, a way of survival in the face of competition from the ADCs is to have small firms specialize in different production processes and products and thus cater to specific needs in the domestic market. For large and medium firms, their response should be to divert their investment overseas so that the labor-intensive production processes are undertaken in lower-wage coun-

tries. This has so far been very successful for Japanese textile multinationals and direct foreign investors. The existence of small firms
will facilitate the subcontracting system by which the operation of
large and medium firms is made more flexible. Now Japanese textile
firms can not rely on scale and technology to out-sell textile firms in
the ADCs. In Hong Kong and perhaps in Taiwan and Korea as well,
the textile firms have already been using the most up-to-date technology and are equipped with the most sophisticated skills. What the
Japanese textile firms can do is no more than retain a group of small
firms which concentrate on paying attention to minor details and
special designs and take advantage of the peculiar distribution and
marketing system to which they are so accustomed. Eventually,
Japan will lose most if not all of its comparative advantage in textiles.
The existence of small rather than big firms will have less chain-reaction effect on the economy when the industry has to be reduced to a
very small size in the not-too-distant future.

The third important issue that Yamazawa discusses in his paper is
the appropriateness of the existing government policies towards the
structurally depressed industries. Yamazawa is correct in stating that
government assistance, if overdone, would discourage rather than encourage industrial adjustment and that "the emphasis of government
policy is better shifted from direct to indirect assistance." Unfortunately, Yamazawa has not pursued the discussion in this connection
for he gives no indication of what indirect assistance can be implemented or in what way it can be implemented.

Furthermore, a general equilibrium rather than partial equilibrium
approach may be better to take when considering government assistance. In the course of dealing with the declining industries, policies
should also be considered for the promotion of new industries so that
the re-employment of displaced resources can take place smoothly.
In the context of Japan, high-technology industries should be promoted and from a recent report it is known that the Japanese government
has launched some long-term policies in support of R & D activities.

Another important policy implication discussed by Yamazawa is
industrial adjustment and trade policy. Yamazawa asserts that to
facilitate adjustment a liberal trade policy should be adopted. This
appears to be great news to the ADCs. But such a liberal trade policy
is of little real significance to the export of ADCs. This is because the
obstacles to penetrating the Japanese market do not lie with trade
restrictions but with the type of distribution and marketing system

peculiar to Japan.

For two reasons, Japan has to adopt a liberal trade policy. The first is the pressure coming from the U.S. and EEC; the second is the long-time huge trade surpluses that Japan has been building up in its trade with ADCs in Asia. But, until there are drastic changes in the distribution and marketing system in Japan, trade liberalization policies will be of little or no assistance in relieving the pressure on the U.S. and the EEC in their importation of textiles and other labor-intensive products from ADCs. Nor will they be of assistance in reducing the trade surpluses that Japan has been accruing from its trade partners in Asia.

Under the existing system, importing in Japan is handled by Japanese general trading companies and there is a multi-layer wholesale system behind them. It is very difficult if not impossible for ADC exporters to establish direct contracts with large buying groups in Japan. On the contrary, for the U.S. and European markets, the ADC exporters have direct contracts with groups like Woolworths, Sears or C & A. Furthermore, with such a system and the consequent difficulty in penetrating the Japanese market, the orders from Japan at any one time are usually in small quantities and it is thus usually not worthwhile for firms in the ADCs to start a new production line just to meet the rather peculiar specifications required by the Japanese consumers.

It would be useful to have Yamazawa explore whether there are ways by which the peculiar Japanese marketing and distribution system can be changed and whether the retention of such a system has been consciously, sub-consciously or unconsciously a deliberate policy of Japan to protect its domestic market from external competitors.

G. Helleiner, *University of Toronto*

Yamazawa has presented a fascinating account of Japanese industrial adjustment policies and experiences in two quite different kinds of problem industries: those hit by reduced aggregate growth, increased energy and materials costs, or yen appreciation; and those hit by increasing competition from the ADCs, of which textiles is an example.

Implicit in Yamazawa's, and Japan's, approach to adjustment assistance given to "losers" is that they should be "positively" provided for in one way or another, regardless of the cause of their problems. With this refusal to isolate trade adjustment, most trade economists would now agree, apart from textiles and, to a lesser extent, synthetic fibres and shipbuilding, the ADCs are not the source of the problems he discusses. It might have been useful to attempt to quantify the relative roles of ADC pressure and the other influences upon the various problem industries he discusses, one by one, as others have done for other OECD members; but implicit in his account is the view that, generally speaking, in Japan as elsewhere, the ADCs have so far been relatively unimportant sources of adjustment problems in the industrial sector.

Relative to other OECD countries, Japanese adjustment assistance policies seem strikingly small and medium-size firm-directed rather than labor-directed, except for family labor in small family firms. Various reasons may be offered for this relative lack of attention either to "positive adjustment" or "compensation for losers" in the labor market. They include relatively full employment and therefore ease in finding new employment if displaced, an unusual degree of within-firm labor redeployment and re-employment and a politically weak trade union movement. The last is not in Yamazawa's paper.

The distinctive Japanese style of labor relations may have allowed for the effective redeployment of labor within firms. However, it may have wider relevance, providing a model for other OECD countries and a potential target for European and North American trade union pressure. Otherwise, labor-focussed government policies are still probably more equitable and more efficient than firm-focussed ones.

Japanese policies for "structurally depressed" industries may also be contrasted with European and North American policies for "structurally depressed" regions. On the face of it, Japan's relatively greater emphasis on the former has generated more "positive adjustment."

Yamazawa's criticism of the MITI "purchase and scrap" program in the textile industry is a little startling in view of the praise which it tends to attract from "free traders' elsewhere in the OECD. He argues that "autonomous abolition" of capacity by private firms is delayed as they wait for tne government to decide to compensate them for it. But such effects are of secondary importance relative to the costs of the alternative of inappropriate re-equipment assistance, or protectionism, and the wasteful lobbying activity surrounding efforts to achieve them. No doubt these "bribes" could be more efficiently administered. "If it were done, it were well it were done quickly." "Abandonment compensation" is still a useful way through the political thicket however undeserving the recipients and ultimately unnecessary it may be.

Yamazawa could make one very pessimistic point about the prospects for "autonomous" adjustments to permanent changes such as ADC competition and higher energy prices, in Japanese industry. First, he says that sharp reductions in demand and resulting "severe competition" delays individual firms' adjustment, though the mechanism by which this occurs is not totally clear. Then he says that "recovery... tends to obscure temporarily the need for long run adjustment." If adjustment doesn't occur when demand is falling, nor when it is rising, when exactly can it be expected?

Without necessarily applauding the device of the "recession cartel," it would be interesting to learn more of its actual operation. This would include the industrial organization of capacity cutback, and the efficiency implications of this, whether there were mergers and takeovers, whether "rationalization" took place, who decided the production allocations and the requirements for capacity cuts among firms, and on what basis these allocations and cuts were made. In the discussion on Hong Kong, some of the inefficiencies of the system of quota allocations in the case of "VER cartels" were considered. Japan may be more efficient at making such decisions than Hong Kong, European steel producers or shipbuilders. The question must be asked as to why this could be so.

Finally, and inevitably, the question as to how "liberal" Japanese importing—from the ADCs or anyone else, in textiles or in other products—really is; and what must be addressed is what is really meant by "free entry" to a national market. Yamazawa uses the conventional criteria of governmental tariffs and quotas to argue that the Japanese market has been "open" to ADC exports. If Japanese imports of textiles and textile products are not higher, this is, he argues, because of such marketing factors as product design and quality and reliability of delivery. Yasuba suggested that language might also be a factor in the differential capacities of countries to penetrate one another's markets. This is certainly part of the story but not necessarily all of it. In recent research on Korea, Westphal and others report (Oxford Bulletin of Economics and Statistics, November 1979: 381-2) that "exports of clothing to Japan are greatly facilitated if either the firms doing the exporting or those supplying the fabric are at least partially Japanese-owned. This may be for no reason other than to assure the precise style or quality desired by Japanese consumers, but it may also follow from the problems faced by non-Japanese in penetrating the domestic Japanese marketing network. Exports of textiles and apparel to other destinations have typically been unrelated to DFI." Probably Japan is like other OECD members in that its government does not feel the need to erect or maintain high trade barriers in sectors where its home firms already exercise adequate and orderly control over imports.

GENERAL DISCUSSION

The fact that the Japanese textile producers have actively invested abroad, especially in ADCs, must imply a reduced domestic political basis for protectionist pressure. Even if the peculiar Japanese distribution system interferes with textile imports, ADCs may enhance their access to the Japanese market through joint investment arrangements with Japanese textile firms. However, actual experience shows that joint investment with Japanese firms does not always enhance ADCs' access to Japanese home market. Japanese firms often do not provide key technology to make the product exportable to the Japanese market. For instance, they do not provide the technique of bleaching and dyeing in the case of textile production. Furthermore, the Japanese government can control the import flows by controlling the general trading companies. The statistics show that during 1973-78, the import/domestic-consumption ratio of textiles in Japan declined from about 18 percent to about 10 percent.

The structure of the Japanese textile industry seems very similar to that of the Italian textile industry: it is the small-size firm that is most competitive and contributes most to total exports. When there are many small-size firms in a declining industry, it may be much easier to adopt scrapping techniques than in the case when there are a few large-scale firms in a declining industry such as aluminum, steel or automobiles in the U.S. The adjustment problem in the U.S. and in Japan seems to differ regarding the type of adjustment techniques applicable. Furthermore, most of the Japanese labor-intensive industries use a great deal of young female labor with high turnover rates, and since industries are well dispersed in a small country the workers do not have to be relocated from their home base to shift their working place. A large country like the U.S. seems to have more difficult problems in adjustment. For most Japanese industries, import competition does not seem to give real problems.

Although there has been substantial assistance on a company basis, there was actually fairly extensive assistance to labor for adjustment in Japan. As Japan has vacated quite large portions of its textile export market, though little of its domestic market, to ADCs, the ADCs in turn have to vacate their textile export markets to other less developed countries in the near future. Then ADCs will have to face similar adjustment problems, and hence should be prepared for it.

ADCs' MANUFACTURED EXPORT GROWTH AND OECD ADJUSTMENT

Colin I. Bradford, Jr. *

I. Introduction[1]

Economic development in the post-war period has been characterized by rapid industrialization in the developing world, bringing a set of poorer countries into middle-income status. The rise in per capita income and concomitant change in the composition of output resulted in the capacity of these middle-income countries to engage in the export of manufactures. Indeed, as manufactured exports from developing countries have grown, their composition has shifted from labor-intensive resource-based processing and manufacturing to more skill-intensive, capital-using and higher technology goods, previously exported only from industrial countries. These shifts in industrial output and capacity to expand industrial exports have given rise to increasing concern in industrial countries not only that traditional industries, such as shoes and textiles, would be adversely affected by competition from industries in developing countries but that more basic shifts in global industrial production problems were afoot which could require major adjustments in industrial countries. Hence, the

---

* Yale University, Associate Director, Concilium on International and Area Studies, U.S.A.

[1] In another context, a different version of this paper is to serve as an introduction to a larger study financed by the German Marshall Fund and sponsored by the Royal Institute of International Affairs (Chatham House) in London and the National Planning Association of Washington on "the implications of newly industrializing countries (NICs) for OECD trade and adjustment policies."

problem of adjustment to the trade potential of the advanced developing countries has emerged as a significant preoccupation within the OECD, not only for what it is but for what it is perceived to portend.

The preoccupation seems to be more acute in part because of the historical perception of the nature of the evolution which has occurred. Industrialization seems to have been a vehicle for economic development for the OECD world. In the post-war period many developing countries adopted import-substitution industrialization strategies as a means of diversifying their economies and reducing excessive reliance on primary production by forcing investment that was not forthcoming without additional incentives. While this was costly by conventional efficient resource allocation criteria, import-substitution industrialization did lead to substantial capacity to produce and eventually, in several countries, to the ability to export manufactures as well. This transition from an inward-looking to an outward-looking development strategy and its success in a variety of countries seemed to justify the initial contrivances of comparative advantage.

The logic of the industrialization process now seems to move inexorably onward. The concern now is that the advanced developing countries may have a combination of natural resource endowments, institutional support and lower cost but nevertheless skilled labor which can place them at a competitive advantage in a set of industries which cause severe displacement and dislocations in the industrial world.

The ADC adjustment problem is perceived as a tip of the iceberg kind of problem: the current manifestations are not seen as isolated cases of successful entrepreneurship, marketing and export policy but part of an emerging trend that has far larger dimensions in the future than it does presently, larger in volume, growth, product coverage, and in the number of countries of origin. From this point of view, there is a sense in which history seems to be moving with the developing countries, favoring their industrial growth as productivity growth declines in the OECD and as advanced countries move more into services.

The ADC adjustment problem for the OECD is undoubtedly exacerbated by the fact that it is occurring simultaneously with a number of other adjustment problems, the most important being adjustment to rising oil prices. Rising oil prices are stimulating the

longer term restructuring of investment patterns to develop new
sources of energy and changes in the composition of consumption to
accommodate shifts in the real relative price of energy. These are substantial adjustments that OECD economies and, to be sure, most
ADCs are attempting to undertake, as they deal with the shorter term
problems of balance of payments deficits, unemployment, inflation
and sluggish growth.

If the outlook for the OECD for the 1980s were for high economic
growth and employment as these simultaneous short-run and longer
term economic adjustments problems are worked out, the problem of
accommodating the expansion of manufactured exports from the
advanced developing countries would not seem as pressing. The fact
that the ADC adjustment problem is occurring simultaneously with
the process of global economic adjustment required by stagflation
and energy prices makes the ADC adjustment problem a more
pressing public policy issue than it might otherwise be.

II. The Role of the ADCs in the World Economy

1. The Locus of OECD—LDC Trade in Manufactures

Before focusing more specifically on the ADCs, it is useful to get
some idea of the order of magnitude of the trade adjustment problem
posed by the developing countries as a whole, as compared to the
magnitude of intra-OECD trade and of OECD imports of manufactures from other sources. To do this, the locus of the main problem
has to be ascertained, the sectors and markets of lesser importance
have to be whittled away in order to identify the main channels through
which LDC-OECD trade flows and problems are presented.

Data on U.S., Japanese, and EC imports of manufactures (SITC 5-
8) by area of origin allows a comparison of the OECD countries and
LDCs as sources of supply of manufactures (Table 1). It is clear that
intra-OECD trade is the predominant pattern in chemicals and in
machinery. Between 84 and 88 percent of U.S., Japanese, and EC
imports of chemicals (77 percent for the EC) and machinery came
from OECD exporting countries. The developing countries supplied
between 8 and 13 percent of the imports of chemicals and machinery
to the OECD.

Table 1. Relative Importance of Intra-OECD Versus OECD/LDC Trade in Manufactured Imports into Principal OECD Markets: 1977

			(in percent)
	U.S.	Japan	EC[a] (net)
Intra-OECD Trade			
Chemicals	88	84	77
Manufactures	73	45	62
Machinery	87	87	88
Misc. Manufactures	48	55	56
OECD/LDC Trade			
Chemicals	11	11	9
Manufactures	22	40	24
Machinery	13	12	8
Misc. Manufactures	49	40	34

Source: OECD, *Trade by Commodities; Imports, 1977.* Calculations from value of imports.

Notes: [a] Net of Intra-EC Trade

EC = Belgium-Luxembourg, Denmark, France, Germany, Ireland, Italy, Netherlands, United Kingdom.

A strikingly different magnitude appears in miscellaneous manufactures, which includes clothing and shoes. Here, OECD countries supply slightly over 50 percent of U.S., Japanese, and EC imports whereas the developing countries supply roughly 40 percent. In particular, the U.S. import market for miscellaneous manufactures is supplied roughly equally by the OECD and the LDCs.

In manufactures based on raw materials, the picture is more mixed and less conclusive. For the U.S. and the EC, between 60 and 70 percent of imports are supplied by the OECD and between 20 and 25 percent by developing countries. The Japanese market is more evenly divided between OECD and LDC suppliers (45/40 percent).

Looking at the U.S., Japanese and EC import market for these four sectors as a whole (Table 2), it becomes apparent that the U.S. and the EC (net of intra-EC trade) account for over 90 percent of the market. From a volume point of view, Japan is a relatively minor market compared to the U.S. and the EC. Even though the Japanese share of the LDC import market in manufactures is not large in a global context, there are undoubtedly import adjustment problems in

Table 2. *Percentage Composition of Imports of Different Types of Manufactures into Principal OECD Markets: 1977*

				(in percent)
	U.S.	Japan	EC (net)	Total
Chemicals	3	2	5	10
Manufactures	12	3	17	32
Machinery	21	2	16	39
Misc. Manufactures	9	2	9	20
Total	45	9	47	101

Source: OECD, *Trade by Commodities: Imports, 1977.*
Note: Calculations from value of Imports.

Japan of significant interest in specific sectors and with individual countries, particularly Korea. Nevertheless, from a global perspective, Japan is more important as an exporter of manufactures to the OECD, accounting for 17 percent of U.S. and EC manufactured imports, than it is as an importer of manufactures. Secondly, again looking at the U.S., Japanese, and EC import market in manufactures as a whole, chemicals are a relatively small sector, accounting for only 10 percent of manufactured imports in these three countries in 1977. The bulk of total OECD manufactured imports are machinery and manufactures based on raw materials. Imports of miscellaneous manufactures by the U.S. and the EC are not as significant in volume, but substantial enough to warrant attention from an OECD vantage point.

Finally, looking at total imports from LDCs into the U.S., Japanese and EC markets (Table 3), we see that 85 percent of these imports are to the U.S. and EC markets and are concentrated in these non-chemical manufacturing sectors. Hence, whether from an OECD or an LDC vantage point, LDC-OECD trade flows in manufactures are concentrated in these three sectors and in the U.S. and EC markets.

2. Relative Market Shares

Having narrowed down the locus of OECD-LDC trade in manufactures, an examination of market shares by alternative sources of

Table 3. *Sector and Market Composition of Manufactured Imports from LDCs as a Percentage of Total U.S. and EC Manufactured Imports from LDCs: 1977*

(in percent)

	U.S.	EC	Total
Manufactures	13	19	32
Machinery	13	6	19
Misc. Manufactures	20	14	34
Total	46	39	85

Source: OECD, *Trade by Commodities: Imports, 1977.*
Note: Calculations from value of imports.

supply is necessary to gain a perspective on the relative importance of LDC penetration into the U.S. and EC markets. In evaluating the importance of the LDCs (and the advanced developing countries, ADCs, in particular) as factors in trade adjustment in the U.S. and the EC, the LDC market share of manufactured imports must be weighed against the market share of Japan, for example, and of the U.S. and the EC in each other's market. Furthermore, Eastern Europe and Spain, Portugal, and Greece in Southern Europe have become significant exporters of manufactured products to the EC.

Relative to these other sources of supply, the LDCs have obtained proportionately large market shares of miscellaneous manufactures in the United States (49 percent) and in the EC (34 percent). The LDCs also have the largest single share of the EC import market in manufactures based on raw materials (24 percent) (Table 4). These are the sectors and markets where the relative weight of the LDCs is particularly high.

In the U.S market, the LDCs, Japan, and the EC have almost equal market shares in manufactures based on raw materials (21-23 percent), whereas Japan and the EC outstrip the LDCs in the machinery sector. The Eastern and Southern European countries are not large suppliers to the U.S. market as yet. The only sector in which the LDCs are predominant in the U.S. import market is miscellaneous manufactures.

In the EC, the U.S. is a relatively small supplier of manufactures. The U.S. accounts for only 9 percent of EC imports of manufactures based on raw materials, roughly equivalent to the market share of

Table 4. *Relative Importance of Various Exporting Countries and Regions in U.S. and EC Manufacture Imports: 1977 (Percentage of U.S. and EC Total Imports of Manufactures)*

		(in percent)
	U.S.	EC (net)
Manufactures based on raw materials		
U.S.	—	9
EC	23	—
Japan	21	5
LDCs	22	24
E. Europe	..	8
S. Europe	..	7
Machinery		
U.S.	—	35
EC	23	—
Japan	29	17
LDCs	13	8
E. Europe	..	4
S. Europe	..	6
Misc. Manufactures		
U.S.	—	16
EC	19	—
Japan	18	12
LDCs	49	34
E. Europe	..	8
S. Europe	..	8

Source: OECD, *Trade by Commodities: Imports, 1977.*
Note: ·· = negligible.

Eastern or Southern Europe, and for 16 percent in miscellaneous manufactures, equal to the Eastern and Southern European shares together. By contrast the LDCs supplied 24 percent and 34 percent, respectively, of the EC market in each of these products, indicating that the LDCs are the major factor in these sectors. Relative to the LDCs, Japan is a smaller supplier of these manufactures to the EC.

On the other hand, the U.S. share of the EC market in machinery imports (35 percent) is equal to the market share of Japan, the LDCs and Eastern and Southern Europe together. The LDC share of the EC machinery import market is only 8 percent whereas the Japanese share is 17 percent and the Southern and Eastern European share is 10 percent.

Perhaps the most important point brought out by these figures is the relative weight of U.S.-EC trade in manufactures compared to the combined market share now accounted for by relative "new" exporters which are Japan, the LDCs, and the Eastern and Southern European exporters. The "new" exporters together account for almost half the imports of non-chemical manufactures by the U.S. and the EC while U.S.-EC trade in non-chemical manufactures accounts for slightly over 20 percent in each market.

Herein lies one of the major reasons for the rising concern over manufactured exports from developing countries in general and the ADCs in particular. The growth of LDC-ADC exports to the U.S. and the EC are not in isolation but part of a general expansion in world manufactured exports from "new" sources which are now penetrating the U.S. and EC markets which used to be the sole source of such goods. It is not the developing country exporters of manufactured products by themselves which are the cause of trade adjustment problems but rather a cumulative set of dynamic exporters that together pose a more fundamental challenge to the U.S. and EC market.

An increasing share of developing country manufactured exports has been going to developed country markets over time (Table 5). Looking at the period of more recent dynamic manufactured export growth, the developed country market share has increased between

Table 5. Percentage Share of Developing Country Manufactured Exports by Destination [a]

	Developing	Developed	of which			Total[b]
			Europe	U.S.	Japan	
1955	50.9	45.4	22.6	14.7	0.8	100.0
1965	38.6	56.7	26.0	23.5	1.7	100.0
1970	33.3	62.0	21.4	31.5	4.4	100.0
1973	27.4	68.7	22.5	29.8	10.0	100.0
1976	32.1	64.8	24.4	27.3	7.2	100.0

Source: UNCTAD, *Handbook of International Trade and Development Statistics,* 1976 and 1979.

Notes: [a] SITC 5 to 8 less (67 + 68).

[b] includes socialist countries not shown.

1965 and 1976 from 57 to 65 percent, due largely to the rising share of Japan and the United States, while the developing country market share has dropped from 39 percent to 32 percent. This provides some perspective on the previous set of figures, indicating that the developed economies were absorbing the bulk of the incremental growth of developing country manufactured exports, as these grew at highly dynamic rates, and indeed were in general increasing their market share. The LDC-OECD relationship was central to the expansion of ADC manufactured exports.

This is confirmed by the fact that manufactured export trade among developing countries had a real annual growth rate of 13.7 percent between 1965 and 1974 while industrial exports from developing countries to developed economies grew at 16.1 percent. In contrast, industrial export trade among developed economies (excluding trade within Western Europe) and exports from developed to developing countries each grew at only 10 percent. Hence, it is estimated that the share in the world trade in manufactures of developing countries' manufactured exports grew from 5 percent in 1965 to 8 percent in 1974, with LDC exports to developed country markets growing from 3 to 5 percent of world trade in manufactures during the same interval (World Bank, January 1979: 18).

This gives an indication of the relative role in world trade of manufactured exports from the developing countries. The important fact is that they constitute an increasing share of world trade in manufactures due to their rapid growth, as does trade among developing countries, particularly trade within regions. Nevertheless, trade within Western Europe accounts for 40 percent of world manufactured exports. Other trade among developed countries constitutes 30 percent of the total, and exports from developed to developing countries are about 22 percent. Hence, even though the rapid growth of LDC manufactured exports has increased their share in world trade in manufactures, trade within Western Europe, other trade among developed countries, and developed country manufactured exports to developing countries are each of much greater importance in terms of the order of magnitude.

3. OECD Export Markets and Export Adjustment

Thus far, economic adjustment from the import side has been considered in isolation without looking at the role of OECD exports in the adjustment process and the role of the ADCs as export markets. Not only can the structure of trade relations be such that the balance of trade be in surplus for an OECD country vis-a-vis the ADCs, despite significant ADC imports, but over time new OECD exports emerge to meet new import demand by the ADCs. In some cases, OECD export capacity in manufactures can not only offset the rise of imports from the ADCs but help finance higher oil bills as well. Hence, to complete the picture of OECD-ADC trade and to more fully comprehend the adjustment process, OECD exports to the ADCs have to be taken into account in a comparative static sense as well as a dynamic sense.

The OECD area as a whole has consistently run a net surplus in trade in manufactured goods with countries outside the OECD area. This surplus has grown consistently in real terms. Manufactured exports to the ADCs, for example, grew by $44 billion between 1963 and 1977 while imports increased by $32 billion.[2] The experience of individual OECD countries has varied. As Table 6 indicates, Japan and the major European countries have had a growing trade surplus in manufactures with the ADCs, whereas the United States and Canada have experienced trade deficits in the 1970s.

Japan and Germany are the countries which have managed to transform their trade relations with the ADCs in manufactures into substantial export surpluses to a sufficient extent to play a larger role in their balance of payments, whereas the export experience of the other

Table 6. Trade of OECD Countries with ADCs in Manufactures

(in billion dollars)

	1963	1973	1977
Canada	0.03	− 0.20	− 0.63
United States	0.92	0.06	− 2.62
Japan	0.62	4.94	10.63
France	0.43	1.32	1.35
Germany	0.71	3.23	3.30
Italy	0.36	1.42	1.96
United Kingdom	0.37	0.64	1.34

Source: OECD (1979), Table 10, p. 29.

[2] OECD (1979), p. 6. This OECD study includes Spain, Portugal, Greece and Yugoslavia along with Korea, Taiwan, Hong Kong, Singapore, Brazil and Mexico in its definition of the ADCs.

Table 7.   Net Change in the Balance of Trade by Commodity Sectors between 1973-78

(in billion dollars)

	Japan	Germany	U.S.	Canada
Petroleum	− 15.2	− 14.5	− 30.4	− 2.3
Manufactured Goods	+ 53.8	+ 23.9	− 3.5	− 4.6

Source: McMullen, N., "The Newly Industrializing Countries in the World Economy," British-North American Committee, National Planning Association, December 1980, Table III 3.2, p. III-11A.

European countries with the ADCs has been more in the nature of an offset to increased imports from them.

This would seem to indicate that greater structural adjustment has occurred in Japan and Germany than in the other major OECD countries. These different degrees of structural adjustment are further seen in Table 7.

These figures suggest that relative price changes have occurred and resources reallocated toward manufacturing in Japan and Germany to permit expanded production and exports of manufactured goods to finance increased oil imports, whereas this has not occurred in the United States and Canada. Japan and Germany illustrate the kind of response possible to the continued changes brought about by higher oil prices and new trading powers which capitalize on the higher capacity to import manufactures in the ADCs as part of an overall adjustment process. The United States has been less responsive to these continued challenges of the world economy, which has been one of the reasons why the U.S. has been more sensitive to ADC imports than other OECD countries.

4. The Specific Role of the ADCs

Whereas there is now a good deal of literature that documents the increasing role of developing countries in world trade in manufactures, general categories or regional classifications tend to blur rather than elucidate reality. In fact, only a small number of developing countries are important exporters of manufactures in terms of volume. They are also highly dynamic exporters in terms of growth.

In 1976, Taiwan, Korea, Hong Kong, and Singapore accounted for over 90 percent of manufactured exports from East Asia; India 75 percent of manufactured exports from South Asia; and Brazil, Mexico and Argentina 70 percent of Latin America's industrial exports. Together these countries account for over three quarters of the manufactured exports from the developing world.

In terms of growth, the real rate of growth in manufactured exports between 1965 and 1974 from East Asia and Latin America averaged just over 20 percent, whereas the real growth rates for North America, Western Europe, and Japan were 8.9 percent, 10.4 percent and 15.6 percent respectively. The larger developing countries propel the regional growth rates, with the average annual real rate of growth in manufactured exports from Korea being 36.6 percent, from Taiwan 28.8 percent, from Brazil 25.4 percent, and Mexico 21.2 percent between 1965 and 1975 (Table 8).

These are spectacular growth rates and have resulted in very substantial increases in manufactured exports as a proportion of total exports for these countries.

Taking the ADCs as a subset of developing country exporters

Table 8. *Volume, Growth and Composition of Manufactured Exports from the ADCs*

	Manufactured Exports (US Millions)		Real Average Growth (% per annum)	Manufactured Exports (As % of Total Exports)	
	1965	1976	1965-75	1960	1975
Taiwan	187	6,921	28.8	14	NA
Korea	104	6,747	36.6	14	82
Hong Kong	989[a]	6,480[b]	11.9[a]	80	97
Singapore	300	2,920	15.0[a]	26	43
Brazil	111	2,332	25.4	3	27
Mexico	166	2,327	21.2	12	52
Argentina	81	976	16.7	4	25
India	809	2,803	2.8	44	45

Sources: World Bank (1979), Annex B; and *The Changing Composition of Developing Country Export,* January 1979, Table 7; and *World Development Report,* 1978, Table 7.

Notes: [a] Includes reexports
[b] Excludes reexports.

within the LDCs, the eight ADCs focused on in this study account for a significant proportion of OECD manufactured imports from the LDCs except for EC imports of chemicals and manufactures based on raw materials (Table 9). These eight countries are the predominant LDC exporters to the OECD of miscellaneous manufactures and machinery.

Looking at these two sectors at the two digit SITC level, the highest proportions of OECD imports from LDCs are in clothing, footwear, and electrical machinery (Table 10).

The eight ADCs account for over 80 percent of U.S. and Japanese imports of these goods coming from developing countries in these sectors (Table 11).

Table 9. *ADCs as a Percentage of Imports into Principal OECD Markets from LDCs: 1977*

	U.S.	Japan	EC
Chemicals	42	70	25
Manufactures	55	43	35
Machinery	75	81	44
Misc. Manufactures	88	94	68

Source: OECD, *Trade by Commodities: Imports, 1977.*
Notes: Calculations from value of imports.
        ADCs = Taiwan, Korea, Hong Kong, Singapore, Brazil, Mexico, Argentina, and India.

Table 10. *Imports from LDCs as a Percent of Developed Country Imports in Selected Manufactures, 1975*

	SITC	U.S.	Japan	EC (excluding Intra-trade)
Clothing	84	81.0	65.3	74.1
Footwear	85	61.5	53.1	61.7
Textiles	65	43.3	42.0	50.5
Electrical Machinery	72	42.4	23.8	15.8
Nonelectrical Machinery	71	6.5	7.1	7.9
Transport Equipment	73	1.7	2.4	12.3
All Manufactures		19.9	20.1	21.4

Source: World Bank, *The Changing Composition of Developing Country Exports,* January 1979, p. 39.

Table 11. The Role of the ADCs in Selected OECD Manufactured Imports
from LDCs: 1975

(in percent)

	SITC	U.S.	Japan	EC
Clothing	84	82	96	64
Footwear	85	89	95	66
Textiles	65	70	86	67
Electrical Machinery	72	86	92	64

Source: OECD, *Trade by Commodities: Imports, 1975.*
Note: Calculations from value of imports.

Hence, the eight ADCs focused on in this study are the predominant sources of imports in sectors where the LDCs are important suppliers to the OECD market.

This concentration in the pattern of sources of supply of LDC manufactured exports on the advanced developing countries is further shown in the data on the increment in manufactured and semi-manufactured imports from developing countries by selected advanced countries. For example, 70 percent of the increment in manufactures and semi-manufactures from developing countries between 1970 and 1977, absorbed by the United States came from Korea, Hong Kong, Brazil and Mexico. Roughly 50 percent of the increment absorbed by Germany and the United Kingdom came from Korea, Hong Kong and Brazil. Fifty-eight percent of LDC incremental exports absorbed by Japan originated from Korea (Table 12).

This data also confirms the pattern of concentration on the import side, showing that the bulk of the increment in manufactured and semi-manufactured imports absorbed by advanced countries from the ADCs between 1970 and 1977 has been concentrated in the United States, Germany, United Kingdom, and Japan (Table 13). Seventy-five percent of this increment is focused on these four countries, with 45 percent being absorbed by the United States alone.[3] As indicated earlier, Japan is a substantial market only for Korean exports, whereas the U.K. is a significant market for a greater variety of countries.

---

[3] Note that data are not available for Taiwan and that Table 13 includes Malaysia, the next largest East Asian exporters of manufactures after Singapore.

Table 12. *Percentage of the Increment of Manufactured and Semi-Manufactured OECD Imports from Developing Countries Between 1970 and 1977 by Country of Origin*

	U.S.	Germany	Japan	U.K.	Total for all Developed Countries
Korea	24.8	15.2	58.0	14.0	23.5
Hong Kong	18.9	22.4	6.9	26.2	18.8
Brazil	9.6	9.2	4.2	11.8	9.1
Mexico	17.0	..	..	..	8.0
Total	70.3	46.8	69.1	52.0	59.4

Source: UNCTAD, *Handbook of International Trade and Development Statistics,* 1979.
Note: .. = negligible.

Table 13. *Percentage of the Increment in Manufactured and Semi-Manufactured OECD Imports from Developing Countries between 1970-1977 Absorbed by Individual Advnaced Countries*

	U.S.	Germany	Japan	U.K.	Sub-total
Korea	43.6	8.4	22.5	4.5	79.0
Hong Kong	41.5	15.5	3.3	10.6	70.9
Singapore	40.9	12.5	9.2	6.5	69.1
(Malaysia)	36.1	13.0	8.5	8.7	66.3
Brazil	43.3	13.1	4.2	9.8	70.4
Mexico	87.7	2.6	0.8	0.7	91.8
Argentina	29.8	19.0	7.1	10.2	66.1
India	18.8	18.3	3.4	17.8	58.3
Total	45.2	11.6	9.9	7.6	74.3
All other Developing Countries	28.6	17.8	6.5	7.6	60.5

Source: UNCTAD, *Handbook of International Trade and Development Statistics,* 1979, p. 328.
(Data not available for Taiwan; Malaysia is included as the next largest East Asian exporter of manufactures).

The pattern of market shares for the East Asian and Latin American ADCs is roughly similar, with the exception of Mexico which is primarily oriented to the U.S. market. However, the pattern for all other developing countries is quite different, with a greater spread in import markets in which France and Italy account for 18.7 percent of the increment from all other developing countries as opposed to only 6 percent of the ADC increment. This more diverse pattern is quite similar to that of India, in that there is less concentration in the U.S. market. This seems to suggest some association of export dynamism with market concentration rather than with market spread.

III. What Constitutes an ADC?

The large LDC-OECD trade adjustment problem boils down to a rather specific set of relations between the ADCs and the United States and the EC countries and, to a lesser extent, Japan, which is itself, of course, a major exporter. The question emerges immediately as to why these particular countries are capable of exporting manufactured products at such remarkably dynamic growth rates. Are there a set of unique conditions prevailing in these countries which allow them to penetrate OECD markets in manufactures or are the developing country ADCs simply the first wave of a trend in the pattern of world industrialization which will bring other developing countries into world markets as exporters of manufactures in due course?

It seems clear that there is no single set of variables or conditions which, once achieved, assures that a country will enter upon a stage of exporting manufactures. Correlations of per capita income with the share of manufactures in total exports or exports per capita do not seem to yield any deterministic relationship.[4] Labor costs do not appear to provide a systematic guide to defining a country's competitiveness (OECD, 1979: 49-50). There is mixed experience in the degree of labor intensity in manufactured exports across different countries. Korea's export experience in the 1960s seems to have been concentrated in labor-intensive manufactures.[5] Mexico's trade

---

[4] Foreign and Commonwealth Office (1979), p. 10.
[5] Larry E. Westphal and Kwang Suk Kim (1977), pp. 4-43 through 4-51.

experience through 1975 seems to "suggest that Mexican manufacturing performs well in products that are capital-intensive, high-technology and/or based on mineral resources, while it performs less well in traditional, low-technology, labor-intensive processes" (World Bank, March 1979: 93 ff).

Instead of being determined by a set of preconditions or thresholds of economic variables, the countries focused on in this study—particularly Korea, Taiwan, Hong Kong, Singapore, Brazil, and Mexico—each seemed to have embarked on highly dynamic export experience because of a variety of historical circumstances, policy conditions, and physical characteristics which have combined to enable such performance.

These circumstances, conditions, and characteristics do not appear to be the same for each of these countries. In fact, there is tremendous variety among them. What appears to distinguish this group of countries is the fact that a number of promising factors seemed to have come together in a moment in time to facilitate dynamic performance in manufactured exports in the last two decades.

In the case of Hong Kong and Singapore, the nature of their physical characteristics, location, and history seems to have dovetailed to make them centers of manufactured exports. Indeed, these circumstances almost require that Hong Kong and Singapore engage in trade in manufactures as there appears to be little alternative. As Ted Geiger has written: "Hong Kong and Singapore are almost totally lacking in natural resources; their arable land can provide only a small portion of their food supply; nor do they have domestic markets large enough to serve as the initial base for industrialization. Hence, their very existence depends on their ability to import, which in turn rests upon their capacity to earn the necessary foreign exchange by exporting goods and services to competitive regional and world markets" (Geiger & Geiger, 1973: 8).

The geographic characteristics were reinforced by the historical development of Hong Kong and Singapore as entrepots, which in part grew out of their location. The financial, communications, and distributional skills associated with entrepot functions made Hong Kong and Singapore alert to developments in the world economy which facilitated their transition in recent years to manufacturing centers focused on export markets.

In the case of Korea, a set of initial conditions created by relatively high education levels making for a more skilled work force combined with a commitment in the early 1960s to an export-oriented growth strategy with full and continuous government support have led to Korea's rapid industrialization and spectacular performance in manufactured exports. Larry Westphal concluded that Korea's export-oriented growth strategy "was predicated on the relatively small size of the domestic market . . . and on Korea's very poor natural resource base" (Westphal, 1979: 58 ff).

Policy makers became aware that import-substitution industrialization would reach an exhaustion point within the limited Korean market and that growth would have to be based on an external thrust. A historic commitment was made to an externally oriented, growth strategy and was translated into fiscal, monetary and exchange rate policies which increased savings and placed the Korean economy on a competitive open footing with the rest of the world. Export incentives were generalized so that comparative advantage could be realized. The policy shift was permanent, due to the nature of the political commitment, so that the element of uncertainty was removed.

Taiwan appears to be similar to Korea in its development, industrialization, and export of manufactures. Japanese occupation of Taiwan from 1895 to 1945 provided a substantial injection of investment and human capital, establishing the basis for modern growth in Taiwan. The movement of numerous talented Chinese from the mainland to Taiwan after the Second World War furthered this development. A successful period of agricultural development and exports led rather naturally to and facilitated industrialization and manufactured exports. Policy reforms in 1960 reducing protectionist tariffs, unifying and adjusting the exchange rate and relaxing exchange controls were of fundamental importance in placing the economy on an outward-looking export-oriented growth path on a competitive basis with the rest of the world. Again, similar to Korea, the priority and permanence of these reforms removed elements of uncertainty and engaged other sectors in the endeavor making it a national enterprise rather than simply another government program (Fei, Ranis & Kuo, 1979: 21-53).

By contrast, the Mexican experience is much more mixed in terms of degree of protection and distortion and the success of its export drive. An overvalued exchange rate over a period of years, import restrictions and uncertainty concerning the duration of export incentives have limited Mexico's exports of manufactures. In the Mexican case, market size is sufficient to provide a stimulus to industry and the political structure has been open to internal protectionist pressures. Hence, the export drive appears to have been weakened and significantly smaller in per capita terms than manufactured exports from the East Asian ADCs.

It is interesting to note that, against this background, Mexico's success in manufactured exports is closely tied to the U.S. market. Almost half of Mexico's manufactured exports are products from assembly plants that are based at least in part on imported inputs from the U.S. market. Another 25 percent of Mexican manufactured exports consists of machinery exports, most of which are parts and components, largely for automobiles destined for the U.S. market. Hence, to a very substantial degree, Mexico's presence in world trade in manufactures is based on its proximity to the United States and special arrangements worked out between the Mexican government and auto parts manufacturers. Special provisions in U.S. import codes, which limit duties to value added outside the U.S., facilitate trade in assembly production industries (World Bank, March 1979: 11 ff).

Brazil's pattern of industrialization has followed a rather logical sequence from import-substitution industrialization in the post-war period through the early 1960s. A military coup in 1964 led to a complete change in economic policy which at first stressed economic stabilization from 1964 to 1967 and then, from 1968 through 1973, made export-oriented growth, with high priority on manufactured exports, the centerpiece of Brazilian development strategy. This shift in policy met with great success: Brazilian manufactured exports grew at an average rate of 25 percent per annum, not only leading the export drive but also stimulating Brazilian economic growth which averaged 10 percent per annum for the period.

This export-oriented growth phase was in large measure the result of deliberate policy changes in 1968. The Brazilian government shifted to a crawling peg exchange rate and established an elaborate system of export subsidies, tax exemptions and export credits designed to promote exports. These met with great success and the 1968-1973 period is now known as the "boom" period in Brazilian economic development.

The "boom" peaked in 1973 as productive capacity became fully utilized.[6] The oil crisis imposed greater constraints on Brazil due to dependence on foreign sources for 85 percent of her oil requirements.

These effects dampened Brazil's export drive and economic growth. Nevertheless, the "boom" period showed that Brazil has the capacity for dynamic manufactured export growth and brought Brazil into the ranks of the advanced developing countries.

What emerges from this brief overview of the ADCs is that their capacity to break into world markets in manufactures in large volume and at high growth rates follows from a diverse set of historical circumstances, markets sizes, and economic conditions. The manufactured export-oriented thrust of Hong Kong, Singapore and Korea resulted in part from the smallness of these economies which limited the growth trajectory of import-substitution industrialization. By contrast, the large size of the Mexican and Brazilian economies undoubtedly facilitated export competitiveness through economies of scale realized during the import-substitution phase. Mexico's proximity to the United States has been a major factor in its manufactured export growth, whereas seasoned observers conclude that Korea's relationship to Japan and the United States has not been responsible for its "phenomenal performance."

Despite this diversity, it appears that common to the Asian ADCs and Brazil is the experience of a historic shift in public policy which not only gave emphasis to manufactured exports but made them the central focus of economic policy and development strategy at a critical point in time. It is clear that the nature of Hong Kong and Singapore as city-states forced a similar kind of historic commitment. The policy reforms in Taiwan in 1960, in Korea in 1964-1965 and in Brazil in 1967-68 seem to have been similar in kind and were essential for the successful export drives that ensued. "Brazil's conversion to export status . . . has involved nothing less than a complete realignment of development strategy that has provided the same assurances of policy consistency that the import-substitution impetus of the 1950s satisfied."[7] In the case of Korea, "the changes in export incentive policies during the first half of the 1960s provided assurance of stable profits on exports and were the concomitance of the government's decision to adopt a strategy of export expansion" (Westphal, 1979: 61).

---

[6] Pedro Malan and Regis Bonelli, "The Brazilian Economy in the Mid-Seventies: Old and New Developments," and Edmar Bacha, "Issues and Evidence on Recent Brazilian Economic Growth," *World Development*, Vol. 5, No. 1 and 2, 1977.

[7] Albert Fishlow, *Foreign Trade Regimes and Economic Development in Brazil*, mimeographed, p. 89.

Hence, the Asian ADCs and Brazil seem to be characterized by a set of historical developments which created favorable conditions in which an export-oriented growth strategy could take hold. Importantly, in each instance such a strategy was launched as a central thrust of policy and became part of the domestic political orientation of these governments. This fundamental orientation of policy would not necessarily have been successful by itself but bore fruit in combination with initial conditions which were propitious for the dynamic growth of manufactured exports on a significant scale. On the other hand, in the absence of the political commitment to an export-led growth strategy, it seems unlikely that these countries would have become significant exporters of manufactures on a global scale.

If the absence of natural resources in the case of Hong Kong and Singapore were instrumental in launching them toward a manufactured export growth strategy, it raises the question of whether rich natural resource endowments might not inhibit the movement of other LDCs toward such a strategy. For example, the export drives of resource-rich Brazil, Mexico and Argentina are less intensive than those of the East Asian ADCs. India, Indonesia, and Malaysia have significant natural resource-based exports and have yet to emerge as highly dynamic exporters of manufactures. One wonders whether the more diversified economic structures of such countries do not allow a country the luxury of a more diversified export strategy. In these cases, comparative advantage exists in natural resource-based production which permits foreign exchange needs to be met without the internal transformation of economic structure and economic policy which successful manufactured export performance requires. "The availability of ample natural resources and/or foreign capital can thus be viewed as permitting the system to continue in its old tracks, thus avoiding the political and, at least short-term, economic pain of having to move to a different policy package. Growth rates can be maintained—just by adding more fuel to the engine—and difficult decisions postponed. The contrast (of the Latin American cases) with the East Asian cases which could not afford to pay for a prolongation of import substitution, but were forced by necessity to turn to the utilization of their human resources, is clear.[8]

---

[8] See Gustav Ranis, "Challenges and Opportunities posed by Asia's Super-Exporters: Implications for Manufactured Exports from Latin America," Paper for NBER/

IV. The Future

Throughout this analysis of the role of the ADCs in the world economy, two contradictory themes have been struck. One is that there is a historical process at work common to all countries in their economic development which brings about changes in comparative advantage over time, leading to shifts in the composition of output and eventually to changes in the pattern of exports. This view sees the emergence of the ADCs as part of a changing world economic structure corresponding to shifts in the international division of labor between countries. These changes are seen as a generalized historical movement in which industrial countries vacate intermediate sectors in industrial production in which advanced developing countries are currently more competitive and advanced developing countries, in turn, vacate more basic industrial sectors in which the next tier of developing countries have a relative advantage. This view, then, sees "the ADC adjustment problem" as a tip of the iceberg kind of problem, one in which the historical process of industrialization will continue to spread and the number of ADCs will continue to increase.

The other view sees the emergence of the ADCs as a process of concentration of industrial capacity in selected countries, characterized by special circumstances that make high volume, and dynamic expansion of manufactured exports feasible. This view suggests that the development of substantial industrial capacity of significance in the global structure of production and exports occurs only in unusual circumstances which lead to a major thrust toward the world market in manufactures. This process is essentially one of concentration in a limited number of countries rather than of spread to a wide variety of countries. The implication for the future of this view is that the ADC adjustment problem, as it has emerged in the 1970s, has stabilized in terms of the number of advanced developing countries capable of playing a global role in world trade in manufactures. The real issue for the future is not how to cope with the increasing number of developing country ADCs, but how to relate to those already on the scene and to the diversification of industrial capacity within them.

As with all complex problems, neither of these views of the issue

---

FIPE/BEBR Conference on Trade Prospects Among the Americas, March 24-26, 1980, San Paulo, Brazil.

have an exclusive hold on the truth. In fact, to a very considerable extent, both processes seem to be going on simultaneously. Nevertheless, it is useful to highlight the differentiation of these two views, so that in looking to the future, judgments can be reached as to the relative weight of these various forces affecting the shape of LDC-OECD trade relations in manufactures in the early to mid-1980s. To a certain extent, the relative weight that one would assign to the forces toward country concentration as compared to those toward country spread would be determined by the degree to which one is taking a global perspective, for which the term ADC by definition is a country of significance in world markets in terms of volume and growth, or, conversely, the degree to which one is taking a sectoral of industry perspective concerned with disruption and displacement derived from the cumulative penetration of foreign imports from whatever source. Both perspectives are relevant to the assessment and management of the issue in the 1980s. A judgment call is needed to orient both thought and policy.

The forces moving toward the concentration of industrial capacity in a limited number of countries is relatively more important in defining industrial trade adjustment between the OECD and developing countries than the more generalized historical forces for industrial spread. From a global perspective, the eight developing country ADCs—Korea, Taiwan, Hong Kong, Singapore, Brazil, Mexico, Argentina and India—are currently the predominant new actors among developing country exporters of manufactured products. As Table 14 indicates, the magnitude of manufactured exports from the next tier of developing countries is quite small relative to the ADCs. For example, manufactured exports from the five countries in the next tier in East Asia, which includes some of the most promising newcomers—Malaysia, Thailand, the Philippines, and Indonesia— together comprised less than 10 percent of the volume from the East Asian ADCs in 1976. The 22 countries in the next tier taken together constituted less than 20 percent of total ADC manufactured exports in 1976. It would take a growth rate of 20 percent per annum over a nine-year period in these countries to attain the volume of manufactured exports in nominal terms in 1985 that the eight ADCs achieved in 1976. Even if the manufactured exports of the eight developing country ADCs grew at only 15 percent during the 1976-1985 period compared to 20 percent for the next tier, ADC exports would be over $110 billion in 1985, over three and a half times as large as exports from

Table 14. *Manufactured Exports from the ADCs and the Next Tier of Developing Countries: 1976*

(in million dollars)

East Asia						
ADCs	Hong Kong	6,480[a]				
	Korea	6,747				
	Taiwan	6,921				
	Singapore	2,920				
			23,068			
Next Tier	Malaysia	799				
	Thailand	511				
	Philippines	397				
	Macau	207				
	Indonesia	119				
			2,033			
Latin America						
ADCs	Brazil	2,332				
	Mexico	2,327				
	Argentina	976				
			5,635			
Next Tier	Jamaica	345		Guatelmala	155	
	Columbia	384		El Salvador	200[b]	
	Venezuela	150[b]		Dominican Republic	120	
	Trinidad: Tobago	122		Costa Rica	119	
	Uruguay	170		Chile	150[b]	
				+20%	149	
						2,064
Africa						
Next Tier	Morocco	202				
	Tunisia	203				
	Bahrain	200				
	Senegal	200[b]				
	Ivory Coast	134				
			939			
South Asia						
ADCs	India	2,803				
			2,803			
Next Tier	Pakistan	677				
	Bangladesh	220				
			897			
ADC Total			31,506			
Next Tier Total			5,933			

Source: Donald B. Keesing, *World Trade and Output of Manufactures: Structural Trends and Developing Country Exports,* World Bank, January 1979, Annex B.

Notes: Countries in the "Next Tier" are determined by the amount of manufactured exports in 1976 in value terms.

[a] Excludes reexports.

[b] Estimates based on figures in previous years.

the next tier as compared to five times as large in 1976. In reality, of course, it is unlikely that ADC manufactured exports will grow more slowly than exports from the next tier, but even if they did, the ADCs would remain the predominant exporters among developing countries in 1985. In this sense, it would seem that the ADCs are the base of the iceberg rather than the tip. Without the eight ADCs, the issue of manufactured exports from developing countries would pale as a global issue.

From an industry or sectoral perspective, the difficulty of adjustment to expanded imports is derived from their rapid growth. The dynamism of manufactured exports from the ADCs has been generated, as has been seen, by a combination of circumstances and conditions which dovetailed in an unusual way to bring about a major thrust by these countries toward world markets. This surge in manufactured exports was, in each case, in part the result of a highly deliberate national effort. In these cases, economic forces and conditions favorable to rapid industrialization and the export of manufactures were present, more in the nature of necessary rather than sufficient conditions. The key elements in the emergence of the ADCs—particularly the four East Asian ADCs and Brazil—seem to have been political and social in character, leading to a societal commitment to an export-oriented growth strategy based on manufactured exports.

These trends would suggest that the dovetailing of favorable economic conditions with externally-oriented political and social forces is not likely to be a generalized phenomenon over a dozen or more additional countries in the future but rather will be limited to a few unusual countries. Secondly, they suggest that the internal history of individual countries is more powerful in generating the kind of national commitment required to become an ADC than the external historical forces behind the generalized spread of industrialization globally.

Finally, the fact that the rise of manufactured exports from developing countries has been due thus far largely to the dynamism of a few countries has not yet led to very much discussion of the self-reinforcing nature of the process itself. These reinforcing qualities would appear to operate both internally and externally. First, the managerial, marketing, design and entrepreneurship qualities needed for successful exports of manufactures are of the learning-by-doing variety and would tend to spin off from one set of activities to another. Once Korean manufacturers learned how to penetrate the U.S. market for electronic calculators in a major way, they could move on to color television sets with greater ease than other countries who have been marginal exporters. The importance of these qualitative capabilities to operate cumulatively in generating dynamic, externally-oriented activities at the level of the firm has to be a factor enhancing the tendency for country concentration in manufactured exports.

Secondly, foreign investors, international banks and multinational corporations tend to gravitate to countries with bright economic prospects. It is a curious conundrum of the creditworthiness syndrome that favorable foreign financial flows go to countries already doing well, permitting them to do better, while countries doing poorly, needing the external resources more, have difficulty attracting foreign funds. Hence, both internal and external factors tend to operate in a way which concentrates resources on countries in a self-reinforcing fashion, creating a dynamic climate in which success breeds success.

The implications of these points for the future are that the ADC adjustment problem in the first half of the 1980s, at least, will retain roughly the same form in terms of the country composition of LDC manufactured exports as it has currently. The problem for OECD industrial adjustment is less the spread of the industrialization process to increasing numbers of developing countries and their inexorable emergence as new exporters in a major way than it is the continuing dynamism in export growth from the ADCs and the diversification of industrial production and export capacity within them.

From a negotiating standpoint, trade adjustment in manufactured exports is not so much a matter of North-South relations involving the Third World as a whole as it is a matter between the OECD and the ADCs as well as an intra-OECD problem. The more concentrated nature of the problem makes it less a question of changing the international economic system to accommodate progressively greater numbers of industrializing countries than a set of more detailed sectoral and country-specific problems that need to be worked out.

Hence, the ADC adjustment problem is due more to an eclectic group of middle income countries gaining status in world industrial trade resulting from a combination of factors favoring their successful export thrust than it is due to a more generalized historical process in which industrial capacity and advantage are shifting from advanced countries to the developing countries as a whole. There seems to be a move from a monopsonistic world in which industrial countries used to be the exclusive source of manufactured goods to an oligopolistic world of a limited number of differentiated producers of significance in world trade rather than to a world of many small producers characteristic of a free market. Despite the eclectic nature of this limited group of producers, the adjustment to the industrial import problems posed by the ADCs in the future appear to be more manageable than the diffusionist notion of the problem would suggest.

The ability of OECD countries to absorb ADC imports in the early 1980s depends on OECD capcity to manage different types of adjustment pressures originating from a variety of sources.

V. The ADCs and Global Adjustment

There are four different kinds of economic adjustment that nations experience in adapting to exogenous pressures and forces. Balance of payments adjustment is perhaps the form of adjustment most frequently focused upon in international discussions, due to the role of the IMF in monitoring and advising governments on policies affecting their external accounts. Economic adjustment also refers to the domestic macroeconomic policies and processes needed to adapt to or offset the inflationary and recessionary effects of an external shock. In addition, the term refers to the longer-run structural changes required in an economy to shift resources in response to changes in relative prices, such as the gradual evolution of new technologies and new sources of energy supply. Fourth, trade adjustment refers to the response of sectors and industries to increasing competition from imported goods and the emergence of new offsetting export capacity.

Balance of payments and domestic economic adjustment commonly involve monetary and fiscal policies, whereas structural and trade adjustments commonly involve investment, pricing and productivity policies and programs. The former adjustment processes are decidedly macroeconomic in character, whereas the latter are microeconomic and sectoral.

The differences in the character of these policy responses have their origins in the differences in the character of the problems. The inflationary pressures, which predated the initial price rise in late

1973 but have been spurred further by continuous increases in oil prices, sweep across the entire economic landscape and require a broad policy response. Efforts to correct balance of payments deficits, to be successful, go beyond exchange rate and trade policies and must include monetary and fiscal policy to dampen demand. The generation of alternative sources of energy supply is a technological and development problem first, and secondly, investment and resource allocation problem. Import adjustment problems, on the other hand, are highly focused, manifesting themselves in specific industries and localities which must be dealt with in individualized ways.

Import adjustment problems are sometimes considered to have broader economic origins and, by extension, to require a broader economic response. But the fact that dynamism in manufactured exports from the ADCs has resulted in part from macroeconomic policy orientations and policy conditions in a particular set of developing countries does not mean that the impact of imports into developed economies have macroeconomic dimensions. The scope and nature of the ADC trade adjustment problem are fundamentally different on the OECD import side than they are on the LDC export side.

Trade adjustment is also different from the balance of payments and domestic economic policy adjustment problems posed by increases in oil prices since 1973. Whereas the scope and impact of balance of payments and stagflation problems resulting from oil price increases are societal and the response necessarily macroeconomic, trade adjustment problems are sectoral and the response microeconomic or, at most, intersectoral involving the import industry and the rise of new exporting industries and output.

The nature of these different forms of adjustment problems also differ in their degree of intensity. Inflationary and recessionary effects caused by exogenous forces and by macroeconomic adjustment policies have their impact through marginal changes in rates of inflation and growth which represent changes in degree. Displacement and unemployment in industries adversely affected by competition from imports can be changes in the fundamental existence of industries and the survival of firms. Hence, the intensity of the impact is sharper than it is for the broader kinds of adjustment problems. The response, on the other hand, is more difficult to rationalize in societal terms because of the more concentrated nature of the problem.

The process of trade adjustment within the OECD to the growth in imports of manufactured goods from the ADCs is exacerbated by the fact that the economic climate in the early 1980s is one in which the OECD economies are struggling with all four forms of economic adjustment simultaneously. The capacity of OECD policymakers to deal "positively" with the adjustment problems caused by ADC imports is constrained by the pressure on investment resources imposed by the energy problem in its longer-run manifestation and the challenge posed to macroeconomic policy by the conflicting directions of the stagflation impact of rising energy costs as they ripple through the balance of payments.

The ADC trade adjustment problem is exacerbated because it adds to the adjustment burdens of the OECD countries, taxing their capacity to adapt to economic change across a broad set of issues, stretching resources, and reducing maneuverability. It also is heightened by the trend at the onset of the 1980s to give greater priority to inflation over growth in macroeconomic policy. This will have two adverse effects: restrictive demand management policies will reduce demand for ADC exports in OECD markets; and they will tend to increase unemployment in the OECD, reducing the tolerance level for incremental unemployment in industries adversely affected by ADC imports. Additionally, those OECD countries which are also facing continuing balance of payments problems will be undertaking further contractionary demand management policies to cope with external adjustment.

Thus, the tendency to engage in restrictive macroeconomic policies does not bode well for the ADCs. In the 1970s, the ADCs benefited from an upward cycle in which their economic performance and creditworthiness enabled them to borrow to finance added growth. This fueled manufactured export growth through relieving the import bottleneck for both intermediate inputs and capital goods. As a result, of course, the ADCs now hold much of the world's debt. If credit tightens and export prospects dim, it is likely that this re-inforcing growth cycle could work in reverse: high debt payments, less new credit, and lower export earnings leading to restricted imports, less growth, worsening the creditworthiness outlook and reducing further the availability of credit. A key point, perhaps, is that the international banks themselves have an interest in seeing that a downward tendency does not become a downward spiral. Neverthe-less, the scenario is one which has enough elements of reality in it to illustrate the interrelationship of macroeconomic adjustment and trade adjustment and the degree to which they could work against each other on the export side of the problem. Of course, if the early 1980s bring a concerted effort at economic recovery, then these forces would work in the opposite direction. At the moment, this seems less likely.

Hence, the fact that global economic adjustment in the 1980s consists of a long agenda for the OECD — dealing with inflationary pressures which have their origin in some instances in the late 1960s, adapting to the economic repercussions of continuing oil price increases, coping with recurrent balance of payments deficits and high international debt, generating longer-run solutions to higher cost energy, engaging in trade adjustment to manufactured imports among OECD countries, from Eastern and Southern Europe and finally, from the ADCs — seems to mean that, from the OECD import side, the process of absorption of ADC imports will be more difficult because of the simultaneous nature of global adjustment and that, from the ADC export side, the deflationary tilt of OECD policy priorities at the onset of the 1980s will tend to dampen export prospects, constraining their economic growth and balance of payments outlook. From this perspective, it seems that the difficulties for the OECD posed by the ADC trade adjustment problem and the difficulties for the ADCs posed by the resulting effects of attempts by the OECD to deal with the myriad of adjustment problems facing them as a result of diverse historical trends coming to a head simultaneously in the early 1980s are equivalent and interdependent global problems which require global attention if one problem is not to make another problem worse by dealing with each separately.

REFERENCES

Bacha, Edmar, "Issues and Evidence on Recent Brazilian Economic Growth," *World Development*, Vol. 5, No. 2, 1977.

Fei, John C.H., Gustav Ranis, Shirley W.Y. Kuo, *Growth with Equity: The Taiwan Case*, Oxford University Press, 1979.

Foreign and Commonwealth Office, "The Newly Industrializing Countries and the Adjustment problem," Government Economic Service Working Paper, No. 18, January 1979.

Geiger, Theodore, and Frances M. Geiger, *Tales of Two City-States:*

The Development Progress of Hong Kong and Singapore, Washington, D.C.: National Planning Association, 1973.

Malan, Pedro and Regis Bonelli, "The Brazilian Economy in the Mid-Seventies: Old and New Developments," *World Development*, Vol. 5, No. 1, 1977.

OECD, *The Impact of the Newly Industrializing Countries on Production and Trade in Manufactures*, Paris, 1979.

Westphal, Larry E., "Korea's Experience with Export-Led Industrial Development," *Export Promotion Policies*, World Bank, January 1979.

Westphal, Larry E., and Kwang Suk Kim, *Industrial Policy and Development in Korea*, World Bank, August 1977.

World Bank, *Mexico: Manufacturing Sector: Situation, Prospects and Policies*, March 1979.

World Bank, *World Trade and Output of Manufactures: Structural Trends and Developing Countries' Exports*, January 1979.

• COMMENT

Narongchai Akrasanee, *UN ESCAP, Thailand*

As Bradford suggests, the adjustment problem is a very important one, and deserves special attention. In global perspective the problem is important in several ways. To the OECD countries, as the author has pointed out, the ADC adjustment problem is occurring simultaneously with a number of other adjustment problems. To the ADCs, they have to be able to continue to export manufactured goods and to import industrial raw materials and other primary goods and to the less industrialized countries (LICs), how the OECD and the ADCs adjust will affect them. The LICs are, therefore, very concerned with the ADC adjustment problem. To see how important the problem is to the LICs the trade deficit and debt of LICs have to be examined. This year's deficits for the LDCs is expected to be about $70 billion and the foreign debt will be about $300 billion. The capacity of LDCs to obtain credit to pay for the deficit and to service the debt depends upon their ability to expand exports, most of which go to the OECD countries.

If the problem is defined in global perspective as above, then the analysis will encompass more than what is presented in the paper.

First, the significance of the LDC trade in the OECD countries has to be identified in terms of commodity groups and specific countries, and then the ADC trade has to be identified. The conclusions reached are that the LDC trade is significant in the miscellaneous manufactures, especially in the U.S. This LDC trade is not significant in volume when considering individual OECD members. But it is substantial enough to warrant attention from an OECD vantage point. Another conclusion is that OECD-LDC trade flows in manufactures based on materials, machinery, and miscellaneous manufactures, and these imports have mainly penetrated the U.S. and EEC markets. Japan has not provided a significant market. The author then looked at relative share by alternative sources of supply in the U.S. to EEC markets, and found that they have been penetrated by

Japan rather than by LDCs. But leaving Japan aside because it is a member of the OECD, LDCs which have caused the problem are then grouped as ADCs. The author then asks whether there will be more ADCs that will cause more problems. Having examined the economic history of the ADCs, the author concludes that, because circumstances in the ADCs were so peculiar, it is unlikely that other LDCs will become ADCs in the near future. But the ADC adjustment problem is serious because OECD countries have many other adjustment problems at the same time leading the author to conclude that ADCs and the OECD have interdependent problems which should be solved together. In other words the ADCs are invited to join the OECD.

ADCs want to know why they cannot sell more to the OECD. To answer this question the analysis would have had to concentrate on which countries and which products have provided problems for which OECD countries.

The OECD countries most troubled would be those which have lost dynamism. They could be called the Newly Declining Countries, or NDCs, and they would be few in number. These countries may have relatively less of an oil energy problem than other OECD countries, but may have serious human energy problems. Their characteristics are easily distinguishable in terms of goods and services, namely they are very expensive relative to their quality. The NDCs and the LDCs are different in the sense that in the LDCs goods and services may be of low quality but they are cheap.

Looking at OECD countries, West Germany is not likely to cause problems but will continue to produce goods of higher quality. Japan will do the same, and will adjust to world trade. Other European countries also should not cause the ADCs much problem. Many OECD countries are well aware of the significiance of the ADCs to their exports and the employment creation associated with it. For example, the OECD Secretariat has estimated that during 1973-77 the net positive employment content of OECD trade with the ADCs was close to 200,000 annually.

Another dimension of the ADC adjustment problem is imports. The ADCs will have to adjust to the new resource constraint in the 1980s, as a result of resource nationalism and growing ability to use resources. The LDCs with natural resources will sell them at much higher prices or in processed form. This is already happening. For instance, a major Korean plywood firm had to close down recently because ASEAN countries refused to sell raw materials to it. As far as the

East Asian ADCs are concerned, their problems are just as dependent on other developing countries in the Pacific as with the OECD countries. In the future Hong Kong and Singapore may become the centers for services rather than manufacturing. They are already moving in that direction.

In 1976 the Asian ADC trade with the advanced Pacific countries was $30 billion; its trade with ASEAN was $6 billion. Since 1978 Korea has overtaken Japan as the biggest textile exporter to Indonesia. ASEAN will be a growing market for the ADCs manufactures, as well as a major supplier of processed industrial materials. If the ADCs plan for industrial expansion with the ASEAN market in mind, as they are doing now, then the adjustment problem may not be serious. But a problem which has often occurred is that Taiwan and Korea produce goods to sell elsewhere and when they cannot sell all of them, they dump the goods in one country. In many cases these goods are import substitutes. This adjustment problem created difficulties for those who have been advocating trade liberalization.

Apart from implicitly suggesting that the ADCs should join the OECD in order to solve adjustment problems the paper has not discussed other policy issues which are relevant for the overall theme of this conference. It would be useful to see discussion on several policy recommendations and institutional arrangements which have been made, which are meant to lessen the ADC adjustment problems. These would include efforts to restore economic growth in the OECD countries: maintenance of resource flow to the South; trade adjustment policies which may be short, medium and long term; results of the MTNs; and the establishment of a regional organization like OPTAD or a trade adjustment fund.

Peter Drysdale, *Australian National University*

Bradford's paper contains a great deal of interesting trade data which bear on the assessment of the position of the ADCs in global perspective. It is generally quite aggregative in nature, at the commodity level, and it does not include production data, no doubt because comparable data are difficult to collate, particularly on a consistent basis. A more important limitation of the data presented for analysis in the paper is that it is mostly snapshot data. Of the twelve very useful tables in the paper, only three make comparisons over time and only one contains information allowing the reader to obtain some perspective on the quantitative impact of the change in ADC trade shares over time. It would be helpful to bring the data together in a more compact and comprehensible form.

In brief, the focus of the paper is on the scale of the adjustment problem in the OECD countries to ADC export expansion and how these problems might be managed. The data in the paper do not allow ready assessment of these questions. Bradford notes two competing hypotheses: 'the tip of the iceberg hypothesis' and 'the concentrated trade growth' hypothesis; but neither is developed sufficiently clearly, it seems, from the viewpoint of informing policy judgment.

It is important to note again, in this context, that a major feature of the transformation of trade in labor-intensive manufactures, 'miscellaneous manufactures' in the paper, has in the last several years been the successive vacating of those, in aggregate relatively slowly growing international markets, by Japan and other industrial country export suppliers, not an extremely rapid vacating of the field by import-competing suppliers in OECD countries, however desirable that would have been in Australia, the EEC or North America.

Viewed in this perspective, the adjustment to the trade transformation in which the Northeast Asian ADCs have participated, for example, is more heavily focused on the export sectors of countries further along in the chain of trade and economic development, that has been explicitly acknowledged during the conference so far. This observation leads one to shift the emphasis in policy study and policy concern considerably.

Most importantly this observation underlines the importance of non-discrimination in the commercial policy approach for all potential ADCs. Trade policy arrangements of the kind which discriminate against rapidly growing suppliers, such as have been very prevalent, assume priority in policy attention over policies which encourage the scrapping of import-competing capacity in OECD countries, although of course both elements are desirable.

The critical difference between the response to the trade growth and adjustment process with regard to Japan's emergence as a major supplier of labor-intensive manufactured products on the international market in the inter-war period, and the response to

Japan's trade growth in the post-war period so far, hinges importantly on the constraint of international commercial diplomacy upon discriminatory trading arrangements, however imperfectly it has operated in some areas and however shakily it began. This is the major achievement of American commercial policy leadership in the post-war period.

ADCs and potential ADCs are well-represented in the Asian and Pacific area and Japan and her Western Pacific neighbors would seem to have a special responsibility to support the principle of non-discrimination in commercial diplomacy over the coming years. It is useful and important to develop a new coalition to maintain committment to a liberal trade regime in the Pacific community.

In a way this conclusion derives from the argument in Bradford's paper that the trade problems of the ADCs are heavily concentrated in particular trading relationships. However, it does not follow from that fact that the framework for managing those problems, especially in view of the third country exporter interests which have been stressed, is confined to those particular relationships. All forms remain relevant: in GATT there is the ongoing battle over safeguards; the principle of non-discrimination against newcomers is important to entrench in the Group of 77; and there are obviously substantial gains to be striven for, from the evidence provided in some of the papers prepared for this Conference, from MTN trade liberalization within the Western Pacific region itself.

GENERAL DISCUSSION

In dealing with the problem associated with ADCs' penetration of the import market of advanced countries, one may yet have to decide whether to classify Japan as an advanced, albeit very advanced, developing country or as another fully developed country. The author seems to have very much underestimated the prospect of other less developed countries emerging as a new generation of ADCs in the near future. For instance, one may have to take account of the potential represented by mainland China as a new exporter of manufactures in replacing the current ADCs.

Not only was the paper written purely from the OECD perspective, but it also overemphasized the growth of ADC exports to OECD countries and almost ignored the fact that imports of ADCs from OECD countries have been very rapidly increasing, so much so that the current balance of trade is in favor of OECD countries, rather than ADCs. The author must have used time series data, instead of cross-section data.

One could not argue that quantitative import restrictions by the advanced countries gave any direct benefit to ADCs. One might argue that such restrictions gave some indirect benefits by pushing ADCs into more skill-intensive lines of production. However, such unintentional benefits could arise only because of the dynamism of ADC economies.

Labor market distortions and stagflation in advanced countries interfere with any movement towards reduced protectionism. The prospect of protectionist trade policies in advanced countries may depend upon their ability to overcome the stagflation problem and to restrain labor union activities to reduce labor market distortions. At the same time, one may wonder whether the ADCs would not lose flexibility in real wage rates and, as a result, would be unable to maintain dynamism.

PART VI

GLOBAL PROTECTIONISM AND ADCs' TRADE STRATEGIES

U.S. POLITICAL PRESSURES AGAINST ADJUSTMENT TO GREATER IMPORTS

Robert E. Baldwin *

I. Introduction

Most economists would agree that one of the most important U.S. economic goals for the 1980s should be to devise more effective means of adapting the structure of industry to increasing exports of manufactures from both the developing economies and the more rapidly growing industrial countries. However, these economists would also have said the same thing about the 1970s, the 1960s, and even earlier postwar decades. Yet despite the persistent urgings of economists over the years for better adjustment assistance measures, there has been little change in U.S. adjustment since the 1950s. This policy consists of responses to domestic adjustment pressures resulting from a rise in imports of a particular type by temporarily restricting those imports. The expectation is that market forces will handle the required industrial adaptation. Changes which have been made in this approach since the 1950s have actually tended to thwart needed adjustment.

One modification introduced in 1962 and extended in 1974 was to provide special temporary aid to the domestic workers and firms faced with injurious import competition.[1] The effects of the program

* Professor of Economics, University of Wisconsin, U.S.A. This paper is part of a larger study for the World Bank. The author wishes to thank the Office of Foreign Economic Research, U.S. Department of Labor, for financial support for part of the research underlying the paper.

[1] The major form of assistance to workers was expanded and extended unemploy-

in facilitating adjustment have not been very satisfactory. A 1978-79 survey of worker experience under the 1974 program indicates that it was utilized mainly to finance temporarily laid-off workers who later return to their former firm and even their former job (Richardson, 1980: 15). Richardson suggests that the existence of general benefits coupled with the lack of penalties to employers who lay off workers under the program actually may have brought about a perverse expansion in the number of workers needing to be compensated (*ibid*: 16). In addition both permanently and temporarily displaced workers receiving aid under the 1974 trade adjustment program remained unemployed for longer than workers receiving aid under standard unemployment insurance programs, indicating that the special benefits may have encouraged unemployment (*ibid*: 30). Finally, the scheme has failed to provide much help to those who need it most, namely the permanently displaced.

Another important change in the early postwar adjustment policy of the United States has been the gradual abandonment of the idea that restrictions introduced in response to increased imports should only be temporary. Starting with voluntary export restraints in the mid-1950s, the textile industry, for example, has gradually moved into a position where it is being protected against significant import increases on a more or less permanent basis. The footwear and steel industries seem to be moving toward a similarly privileged position.

The temporary-protection approach to industrial adjustment has often been criticized for operating too slowly and being too blunt a policy instrument. An example of a more selective alternative that would speed up the re-employment of displaced workers is a wage subsidy paid to employers who would hire these workers (Neuman, 1979). However, rather than meeting the criticisms of the temporary-protection approach, the actual changes in U.S. adjustment policy have made it an even more imperfect and ineffective means of achieving industrial adaptation to shifts in comparative advantage positions among countries.

Policy-oriented economists have to ask why these unfavorable changes have occurred and how it has been possible for particular interest groups, using the political process, to secure policy changes which economists regard as detrimental to the nation's welfare. Until

---

ment compensation. The aid designed to promote movement to new industries, which included training, counselling, job-search, and relocation allowances, has been largely negotiated.

the interaction of political and economic forces in the determination of public policies is better understood, using economic criteria only as a basis for devising adjustment schemes may be only an exercise in irrelevancy as far as their implementation is concerned.

In line with these points, the purpose of this paper is to analyze the political-economic pressures exerted on the U.S. President with regard to the import-policy decisions over which he has control. The first section outlines the powers of the President to control imports and indicates how these powers have changed since the 1930s. The following three sections analyze specific areas of Presidential policy making. The first of these investigates the influence of various economic and political factors in the decisions reached by the President on affirmative recommendations for import relief by the International Trade Commission. In the next section the formulation of the trigger-price mechanism for steel imports is explored as an example of informal but very significant protectionist pressures exerted on the President. Finally, the nature of the duty reductions that the United States was prepared to make in the Tokyo Round of trade negotiations is analyzed for the purpose of testing various hypotheses about the political economy of trade policy.

II. Presidential Powers to Regulate Imports

Recent history in the area of import policy has been characterized by the greater utilization on the part of Congress of its constitutional powers to regulate international trade. Nevertheless, the President's delegated authority to regulate imports is still enormous. Moreover, it has mainly been his power to reduce import barriers that has been curtailed; his authority to limit imports has been increased in some respects. This section will briefly summarize these powers and how they have changed over time.

The extent of the President's tariff-reducing authority has varied in an almost cyclical manner. Periods in which the executive branch utilized a significant grant of tariff-cutting authority from the Congress, that is in 1934-39, 1945-48, 1962-67, and 1975-79, have usually been followed by periods of very little or no duty-reducing authority. While there has also been a fluctuating element in the degree of restraint on the presidential use of any duty-cutting authority, as, for example, in the enactment in 1948 and repeat in 1949 of a "peril point" clause, followed by its re-introduction in 1955 and removal again in 1962, a trend toward the dilution of the power of the executive branch in this area is evident since the 1962 trade act. An example of this was the establishment of a more formal framework for receiving advice from the private sector during trade negotiations and the strengthening of congressional liaison with the negotiators. This has restricted somewhat the degree of independence the President has in selecting the items eligible for reduction of duty and the degree of reduction. But more important have been the changes making it less difficult to set aside presidential rejections of affirmative ITC decisions concerning import relief.

Similar reductions in executive powers have occurred in the area of non-tariff trade distortions. Up until 1954 the Secretary of the Treasury determined both whether dumping had occurred and whether it had caused injury. However, the latter function was transferred to the ITC in that year. Under the new countervailing duty law the determination of injury in subsidy cases has also been made a responsibility of the Commission. In both instances Congress viewed the assignment of this function to the Commission as offsetting a tendency of the executive branch to be too liberal in its policy-implementing role. Imposing tighter time limits under the 1974 trade act for decisions of the Treasury in these fields was another manifestation of the dissatisfaction of Congress with this department's performance. More recently, under the threat that Congress itself would act to reorganize the administrative machinery for implementing trade policy, the President in 1979 shifted the administration of the anti-dumping and countervailing duty laws from the Treasury to the Commerce Department. The manner in which the law on unfair import practices (Section 337 of the Tariff Act of 1930) has changed further illustrates how the President's powers have been weakened because Congress felt he was too lenient in his administration of the law. Under the acts of 1922 and 1930 the President was given the power to exclude articles from entry if unfair methods of import competition, primarily patent infringements, were being practiced. The International Trade Commission assisted the President by undertaking the investigation and making recommendations but the decision of the President was final. However, with the enactment of the 1974 trade bill the Commission itself was given the authority to exclude imports of affected articles or issue cease and desist orders with regard to such practices. The President's role was reduced to being able to overturn these decisions within a 60-day period "for policy reasons."

At the same time that Congress has been diluting the presidential power to reduce trade barriers and especially to resist ITC recommendations for import-restricting actions, it has also been giving the President new powers to limit imports. The 1930 tariff act gave the President authority to deal with foreign discrimination against U.S. commerce by imposing new or additional duties on imports from countries that discriminate. The authority extended to excluding their goods if U.S. goods were excluded from these foreign markets.[2] The Trade Act of 1974 expanded this power to cover: "unjustifiable or unreasonable tariff or other import restrictions which impair the value of trade commitments made to the United States or which burden, restrict or discriminate against United States commerce"; "discrimination or other acts or policies which are unjustifiable or unreasonable and which burden or restrict United States commerce"; "subsidies (or other incentives having the effect of subsidies) on [a foreign country's] exports... to the United States or in foreign markets which have the effect of substantially reducing sales of the competitive United States product or products in the United States or in foreign markets"; and "unjustifiable or unreasonable restrictions on access to supplies of food, raw materials, or manufactured or semimanufactured products which burden or restrict United States commerce." In his efforts to eliminate these foreign practices the President could suspend benefits of trade agreements and impose duties, fees or other restrictions on both the products and the services of the appropriate foreign countries.[3] However, Congress could veto any actions taken by the President. In amending this provision, the 1979 trade act stressed the President's responsibility for enforcing U.S. rights under any trade agreement and simplified the list of foreign practices against which he is directed to take action.[4] In-

---

[2] The ITC was charged with being aware of foreign discrimination and making recommendations to the President in such cases.

[3] Before taking action against subsidized foreign exports the President required an affirmative decision from the Treasury that the subsidy existed and from the ITC that such exports substantially reduced U.S. sales.

[4] With the changes in the countervailing duties law the item dealing with subsidies was dropped, as was the final item dealing with restrictions on access to materials. The new language is similar to that in the second item above and simply directs the

terestingly, by a majority vote of both houses, this act also eliminated the power of Congress to nullify presidential actions taken under this provision within 90 days.

III. Presidential Actions on ITC Import-Relief Cases

Prior to 1974 there was no mention in the law of any set of criteria that the President should follow in deciding whether to accept or reject an affirmative import-relief finding by the International Trade Commission. The 1951 and 1962 trade acts merely state that the President "may" implement the recommendations of the Commission. Presumably, in granting the President this authority, Congress intended that the final decision should include a consideration of the foreign policy implications of withdrawing tariff concessions as well as of the impact of the increased imports on the competing domestic industry. However, the 1974 trade act states that the President "shall provide import relief..., unless he determines that provision of such relief is not in the national economic interest of the United States." Furthermore, the President is directed to take into account several criteria in determining whether to grant import relief. These include: the effect of import relief on the price to consumers of the imported article and its domestic substitute; the effect of import relief on the international economic interests of the United States; the impact on other U.S. industries as a result of any compensation or retaliation; the probable effectiveness of import relief as a means to promote adjustment; and the economic and social costs incurred by tax-payers, communities, and workers in the event relief is not granted.

In addition to these economic criteria enumerated in the law, certain other political factors seem likely to be important in shaping the President's actions on ITC cases. For example, it is more likely that the President would act favorably if the injured industry employed many rather than few. Cases in which labor was a petitioner or in which the Senate Finance Committee or House Ways and Means Committee recommended the investigation would also seem to have a higher than average chance of Presidential approval. Furthermore,

---

President to take appropriate action against a foreign action that "is unjustifiable, unreasonable, or discriminatory, and burdens or restricts United States commerce."

the President is likely to be more receptive to import-relief if his decision on a case must be made just before a presidential or congressional election. Still another likely period of high vulnerability on the part of a President to protectionist pressures is when he is in the concluding stages of multilateral trade negotiations. Finally, the President is not likely to grant import relief if doing so appears to run counter to a major policy goal that he is actively pursuing. For example, if he is trying to restrain general inflationary pressures, he is likely to be reluctant to grant import relief and thereby be accused of fostering further inflation.

Table I gives the results of relating presidential import-relief decisions (the dependent variable) from 1974-79 to various economic and political factors. Decisions in which the President granted import relief either by accepting the substance of an ITC recommendation, by negotiating an orderly marketing agreement, or by taking some other restrictive action are coded (1) in the logit analysis, while decisions rejecting import relief are coded (0). Various independent dummy variables are coded in the same manner. If an ITC decision or the initiation of the investigation occurred within August, September, or October of 1976 or 1978, periods just before an election, the case was coded (1), whereas if it occurred outside these time periods, it was coded (0). Thus, one would expect a positive coefficient between these variables and the dependent variable. Cases in which labor was a petitioner for the investigation were coded (1) and when that was not so cases were coded (0) as were those in which either Ways and Means or Senate Finance did (1) or did not (0) request the investigation. A positive relationship between these two independent variables and the dependent variable is expected. One also expects a positive correlation between the dependent variable and whether the President's decision occurred after the MTN "statements of understanding" in July (coded (1)) or before that date (coded (0)).

The basic continuous variables used to "explain" presidential decisions are the percentage of the ITC voting membership who reached a positive injury finding, the rate of inflation in the quarter preceding the ITC decision, and the national unemployment rate in that quarter. Since one would expect that the higher the percentage of Commissioners voting in the affirmative the more likely the President is to accept their injury finding and to conclude that the economic and social costs to workers will be high if relief is not granted, a positive relationship between the ITC variable and the dependent

Table 1. Factors Influencing Presidential Decisions on Affirmative ITC Import-Relief Cases, 1975-79

Equation	ITC	INFL	DUNAV3	D1	D2	D3	Likelihood Statistics
1.	6.5	−1.1	—	5.6	—	—	—
	(1.65)ᵃ	(−1.80)ᶜ	—	(1.70)ᵃ	—	—	(−10.1)ᵇ
2.	6.4	−1.0	—	—	—	4.9	—
	(1.67)ᵃ	(−1.79)ᶜ	—	—	—	(1.61)ᵃ	(7.9)ᶜ
3.	—	—	2.4	—	2.2	—	—
	—	—	(1.77)ᶜ	—	(1.72)ᶜ	—	(6.7)ᶜ
4.	—	−0.3	—	3.3	3.0	—	—
	—	(−2.24)ᵇ	—	(1.80)ᶜ	(2.09)ᶜ	—	(10.8)ᵇ

Notes: [a, b, c] significant at the 10%, 5%, and 1% levels, respectively.
Dependent variable = whether the President granted import relief (1) or did not (0).

ITC   = percentage of commissioners favoring import relief.
INFL   = annual inflation rate (GNP deflator) in quarter preceding *ITC* decision.
DUNAV3 = change in inflation rate between the two quarters preceding the *ITC* decision.
D1   = whether presidential decision was after (1) or before (0) July 1978.
D2   = whether initiation of *ITC* investigation was in August, September, or October in the years 1974, 1976, or 1978 (1) or not (0)
D3   = whether the *ITC* decision was within these election periods (1) or not (0).

variable should be revealed. The same is true with respect to the recent rate of unemployment. On the other hand, a negative correlation between the dependent variable and the recent inflation rate is likely.

As equations (1) and (2) in Table 1 indicate, the ITC variable is not quite significant at the 10 percent level when introduced together with the rate of inflation and either the stage of the MTN negotiations or the proximity in time of the ITC decision to a presidential or congressional election.[5] On the other hand, although the following information is not shown in the table, the inflation rate or change in this

---

[5] The ITC variable also is not significant either alone or in combination with any of the other variables tried.

rate always turned up as significant in the various runs tried with two or three variables. The unemployment variable invariably appeared with the wrong sign, and occasionally was even significant. However, the change in unemployment was significant in the expected direction. The level of industry employment was never significant. Neither were the dummy variables indicating whether the President's decision occurred close to the time of an election or during the concluding stages of the Tokyo Round negotiations were significant.

It thus appears that political factors do influence presidential decisions in ITC cases. However, rather than being influenced by the voting strength of the injured industry, the President seems more concerned with creating the impression of being generally sympathetic to industry's import problems during periods when he or his congressional colleagues are running for office or when he wishes to gain congressional acceptance of a particular piece of trade legislation. Also, it is not too surprising that he apparently sees a closer relationship between his anti-inflation programs and ITC decisions than between his full employment efforts and these decisions. However, an unexpected result that raises basic questions about the entire ITC import-relief process is the lack of a strong positive correlation between the degree of agreement among the Commissioners and the President's acceptance of the Commission's recommendation.

IV. Implementation of the Trigger-Price Mechanism for the Steel Industry

Because of the national nature of his electoral constituency, a President must be highly sensitive to the interpersonal utility effects of granting import protection to any particular industry in the economy. If those outside the assisted sector perceive the President's action as unfairly favoring its members, he risks the loss of many more voters than he gains by helping a single industry. Consequently, a President is unlikely to provide industry-specific protection unless he is convinced that the general public will support it. The events leading to the introduction of the so-called "trigger price" system to deal with the import problem faced by the steel industry in 1977 provides an excellent illustration of the type of political and informational effort required by an industry before a President is likely to act on its behalf.

Since the concern here is primarily with describing the various means used to convince President Carter that he should help the steel industry, neither the causes of the economic difficulties faced by the industry nor the nature of the trigger price system will be analyzed in detail. Briefly, as the economy continued its recovery in 1977, the increase in steel output fell short of its predicted level and employment actually fell slightly.[6] At the same time the volume of imports rose 35 percent with the result that the ratio of imports to domestic consumption increased from 14.1 percent to 17.8 percent. Most important, however, was the fact that net income before taxes and before taking account of losses on discontinued operations fell from $2.1 billion in 1976 to $1.1 billion in 1977.[7]

The industry viewed the surge in imports as the major cause of its unsatisfactory performance and, in turn, blamed the rapid import rise on subsidization of steel imports by foreign governments and on unfair pricing practices, namely dumping, by these producers.[8] Pressing for countervailing duties to offset foreign subsidies had the attraction of wide public appeal but had the practical disadvantage that the Administration had exercised the option under the 1974 trade act to waive the countervailing duties during the period of negotiation on a new subsidies code. It was highly unlikely that the President would jeopardize the entire negotiations by reversing this policy. Moreover, the chances of obtaining government assistance by focussing on the charge of foreign dumping, a practice that the American public could also be counted on to condemn, had been improved by changes in the anti-dumping law under the the Trade Act of 1974. The basic legal condition for dumping is the sale of an article for export at a price less than market value of the article in the exporter's home market. However the 1974 amendment in effect enlarges the definition of dumping to include sales at less than long-

---

[6] Steel shipments increased only 1.9 percent in 1977 whereas increases ranging from 7 percent to 12 percent had been predicted, and industrial production in general rose 5.6 percent. Similarly, employment in the steel industry dropped 0.4 percent compared to a rise of 3.7 percent for total nonagricultural employment. See American Iron and Steel Institute, *Annual Statistical Report,* 1977 and *Economic Report of the President,* January 1979.

[7] American Iron and Steel Institute, *Annual Statistical Report,* 1977.

[8] Required capital expenditures for pollution control facilities also were mentioned by the industry as an important source of its difficulties. These jumped from about $250 annually in the early 1970s to over $500 in 1977.

run average costs even if the domestic and export price do not differ.[9] Since pricing at less than average costs is typical during recession periods in industries with large fixed costs, the world steel situation at that time provided an excellent oppurtunity for American producers to utilize the new dumping law to their protective advantage.

The campaign to convince the public and the Administration that some form of restraint on imports was needed involved the use of almost all the techniques of a modern lobbying effort. It began in earnest in late May 1977 with the release of a study for the American Iron and Steel Institute (AISI) by an economic consulting firm that supported the industry's contentions that foreign subsidization and unfair competitive practice did exist and were causing injury to U.S. steel firms. During the AISI national convention held at the same time, industry leaders attracted further press coverage by stressing the industry's concern about the domestic impact of rising steel imports. That even these initial efforts were effective is evident from the immediate response of Budget Director Lance that the Administration was interested in the industry's problems as well as the reaction shortly thereafter from the Chairman of the British steel industry that U.S. countervailing duties on European steel would create utter chaos. Furthermore, by July, Japanese steelmakers had come up with another American-authored study disputing the AISI study's charge that Japan was selling steel below its production costs.

Perhaps the most effective means by which public attention was directed to the industry's problems were the well-publicized series of layoffs beginning in July and culminating in September with the permanent closing of an old but important steel works in Youngstown, Ohio. In mid-August, for example, Bethlehem Steel announced plans to layoff 7,300 workers in New York and Pennsylvania including 3,500 in Lackawanna, New York. This was quickly followed by statements from U.S. Steel, Armco Steel, and Lukens Steel stressing the need to release workers in Illinois, Indiana, and Ohio because of competition from foreign steel producers. Then in September Youngstown Sheet and Tube Company announced the permanent closing of the Campbell Works plant in Youngstown and the displacement of 5,000 workers. During this two-month period not a week went by without a

---

[9] Specifically, if the Secretary of Commerce determines that sales are being made at less than the cost of production, he is directed to construct the home market value of the article from cost data.

series of articles on the lay-off problems in all the major newspapers and weekly news magazines. They not only emphasized the plight of the displaced workers but, for areas such as Lackawanna and Youngstown, included interviews with community leaders who stressed the economic damage to the entire community. The president of the United Steelworkers Union also cooperated in the public relations effort by charging that 60,000 U.S. steelworkers had lost their jobs during the year as a result of increased imports.[10]

The Youngstown closing was further exploited when 250 workers from the area protested in front of the White House and claimed they had a petition with over 100,000 signatures urging curbs on imports of steel. Moreover, by closing the Youngstown facility and parts of the Lackawanna plant permanently, company officials not only were able to eliminate these high cost facilities in a manner that turned the bitterness of the affected workers toward foreign producers rather than toward to management but to dramatize their problems even more by recording significant once-and-for-all losses on their financial statements. Even the administration of the worker adjustment assistance program tended to validate the claims of the steel industry. Because the 1974 trade act transferred the determination of eligibility to the Labor Department, a government agency whose function is to promote labor's interests, and made it very easy for labor groups to satisfy the criteria for assistance, most of the workers displaced at Youngstown and elsewhere were declared to be eligible for special benefits on the grounds that they were threatened by increased steel imports.

Another important element in any effort to obtain presidential action is a demand from Congress for such action. The steel industry is one of the industries able to obtain the allegiance of a significant number of Congressmen and Senators. It was the steel industry's problems at this time that led to a formalization of this commitment by the formation of a Steel Caucus in Congress. This group, initially consisting of 25 Senators and 125 Congressmen, complained publicly about excessive steel imports and called for vigorous enforcement of the unfair competition laws against foreign steel producers.

Besides using a range of techniques to publicize their problem, the

---

[10] In fact, average employment in the industry fell only from 454,000 in 1976 to 452,000 in 1977 and total hours worked from 876.7 million hours to 875.9 million hours. AISI, *Annual Statistical Report,* 1977.

steel companies sought import protection by initiating complaints against foreign producers under various provisions of existing law. Earlier efforts to seek assistance in this way had not proved very successful. For example, in late 1976 various steel producers used a "shot-gun" approach in seeking import-restraining actions by the government under both the traditional and new unfair trading practices provisions (Section 337 of the 1930 Tariff Act, and Section 301 of the 1974 Trade Act), under the countervailing duty law, and under the anti-dumping law. None of the actions resulted in the import restraints desired by the steel companies.[11] However, a dumping complaint against carbon steel plate from Japan filed by a division of Gilmore Steel in March 1977 did result in a decision by the Treasury in September that the steel was being sold below Japanese costs. Moreover, the ITC subsequently made an affirmative injury finding. Shortly before this decision U.S. Steel had also filed dumping charges against Japan on a wide variety of products, but the Gilmore decision brought a flood of new dumping complaints. Between that decision and the end of the year charges of dumping were filed on nearly $1 billion worth of steel imports from Japan, all the major European producers, and India.

By the end of September the campaign to attract presidential attention to the industry's import problem had succeeded. Senator John Heinz reported on the 22nd of September that President Carter told Republican Senators that he was worried about the shutdowns and layoffs, although saw no immediate need to grant the industry's demands for import restraints.[12] At a news conference on the 30th the President stated that layoffs could not be attributed solely to foreign imports and he described the problems of the industry as

---

[11] Allegheny Ludlum Steel, Armco Steel, and six other companies filed charges of both unfair import practices under Section 337 and dumping under the 1921 anti-dumping law in the case of certain welded stainless steel pipe and tube; the American Iron and Steel Institute claimed under Section 301 that a bilateral agreement between Japan and the Community diverted steel from Japan into the U.S. market; and Armco filed subsidization charges on silicon steel from Italy under the countervailing duty law. The ITC issued a cease and desist order under Section 337 but this was disapproved by the President. The Treasury decided that the same products were also being dumped but the ITC made a negative determination on injury. In the countervailing duty case the Treasury came up with a negative decision on the subsidy issue. No action was taken in the Section 301 market diversion case but it may have had some effect on the decision in early 1978 to continue the quotas on specialty steel.

[12] *New York Times,* September 22, IV, 6:6.

"chronic."[13] But another news story the next day stated that the Administration was considering negotiating temporary steel import quotas.[14] Moreover, this article mentioned for the first time the existence of an inter-agency group headed by the Undersecretary of the Treasury that was considering various import-restraining alternatives. On October 13 Robert Strauss, the Special Trade Representative, chaired a White House conference of management, labor, and government officials that was also attended by the President. The previous day Strauss had reported that he and the President would seek to ease the steel industry's adjustment to import competition, and at the conference itself the President pledged a more vigorous enforcement of the fair trade laws to protect U.S. industry from dumping. More specifically, he informed the group that within the next month "there will be actions... taken to ensure that the present concern about the steel industry is alleviated, not by words or promises but by actions and decisions."[15]

From this and other accounts of what was happening around this time it appears that the decision had already been made to restrain imports on the grounds that foreign producers were dumping steel. Just how to implement such an action raised obvious problems, however, since levying anti-dumping duties is a second-best outcome for all the parties most concerned. Governments are fearful that the unilateral imposition of anti-dumping duties will touch off foreign retaliations and disrupt any ongoing trade negotiations. Domestic firms affected by dumping are not happy with the uncertain impact of countervailing duties, since foreign exporters may still be able to export a substantial volume of the product despite the extra duty. Foreign producers also prefer some other form of import controls. Since they possess monopoly power, without which they would not have been able to engage in price discrimination in the first place, these producers would prefer to charge the higher duty-inclusive domestic price themselves rather than see the countervailing government collect the extra duty revenue. Because of these incentives to seek an alternative policy solution to the problem, most dumping cases are not pursued to the stage of actually imposing countervailing duties. Either the complainant or the alleged dumper works out a

---

[13] *New York Times,* September 30, 19:3.
[14] *New York Times,* October 1, 31:4.
[15] *New York Times,* October 14, 1:3.

mutually agreeable pricing policy whereby the former withdraws his complaint or some market-sharing arrangement is settled upon with the assistance of the government. The anti-dumping law usually merely serves as a vehicle for exerting pressure to bring about one of these outcomes.

In this particular case the solution finally agreed upon by all parties was, in effect, the establishment of minimum prices for steel imports. More specifically, so-called "reference prices" were established for steel products based upon the production costs of the lowest-cost producer (Japan) and including various mark-ups on these costs. Imports entering the country below these prices trigger an expedited dumping investigation. In other words, under the arrangement there is a presumption that dumping is taking place if imports came into the country at prices below the reference or trigger levels.

For a while the trigger price system worked out extremely well for the steel industry. Its formal implementation on February 1, 1978 coincided with a significant increase in economic activity within the country so that by May of 1978 the capacity-utilization rate within the country was at 94 percent compared with only 75 percent in December, 1977, while the import penetration ratio fell from 20 percent to 14 percent during this period. A small number of cases arose in which exporters were accused of shipping at prices below the reference levels but, by and large, foreign producers respected the minimum prices and adjusted their output accordingly. The European Community even introduced a somewhat similar system to deal with its own import problem. However, in early 1980 the periodic increases in the reference prices that were being made supposedly to offset cost increase began to conflict with President Carter's declaration that inflation was now the major economic problem faced by the country. When the Administration failed to raise these prices in February of 1980 the U.S. Steel Corporation formally filed broad dumping charges against European producers. The government responded by dismantling the trigger-price scheme but it remains to be seen whether an accommodation will be reached with these producers before the case is finally decided by the ITC.

The introduction of a trigger-price mechanism for steel imports represents a highly successful lobbying effort on the part of the steel industry. There is no doubt that rapidly rising imports were worsening the industry's economic problems in 1977, and management was very concerned about the long-run implications of the import surge. However, the industry brilliantly took advantage of these difficulties through a series of announcements of layoffs that seemed to involve some adjustments to long-run trends as well as to the immediate import problem. It was also able to mobilize substantial support in Congress. Thus, when the President moved to assist the industry, it was in a period when public opinion appeared to "demand" that he act rather than at a time when he might appear to be taking steps to give special treatment to a particular industry.

There does not seem to be anything unique about the steel industry's effort that could not be duplicated by other major U.S. industries faced with similar circumstances, though perhaps not with such rapid results. But it also seems evident from this episode that the small industries that typically use the ITC import-relief mechanism, for example clothespins, mushrooms, and stainless steel flatware, cannot utilize this approach successfully. The number and geographic dispersion of firms as well as the size of the labor force is simply not sufficiently large to gain presidential action. Nor do such industries have the financial or voting power to be able to induce a substantial number of congressmen to pursue the industries' interests in a vigorous manner.

V. U.S. Tariff Reductions in the Tokyo Rounds

1. The Negotiating Framework

The Trade Act of 1974 provided the President with the authority to reduce import duties by up to 60 percent and to eliminate completely duties of 5 percent or less. However, in granting this authority, Congress not only specified that a small number of products be excluded from duty cuts but required the President to obtain advice both from various government agencies and private groups prior to entering into duty-reducing negotiations on the remaining tariff-line items. The mandated exceptions were items on which import relief had been given under Sections 201-203 of the Act which included some ceramic dinnerware, certain ballbearings, stainless and alloy-tool steel, nonrubber footwear, color TVs, industrial fasteners and CB radios, and on which protection had been granted on national security grounds, such as petroleum. At the governmental level the

President was directed to furnish the International Trade Commission with the list of articles on which duty concessions were being considered and to make offers on these items only after obtaining the advice of the Commission regarding the probable economic effects on domestic industries of modifications in these duties. Public hearings enabling any interested parties to present their views concerning tariff reductions on the items under consideration were also necessary prior to making offers to foreign countries. Finally, before entering into any trade agreement the President had to seek information and advice from the Departments of Agriculture, Commerce, Defense, Interior, Labor, State, and Treasury as well as from the Office of the United States Trade Representative.

A substantial input from the private sector was also mandated in the Act. The President was required to establish an advisory Committee for Trade Negotiations composed of no more than 45 representatives of government, labor, industry, agriculture, small business, service industries, retailers, consumer interests, and the general public for the purpose of providing overall policy advice on any trade agreement. In addition, he could establish both general advisory committees for industry, labor, and agriculture and sector advisory committees designed to give technical advice on various aspects of the trade negotiations. Presidents Nixon and Carter both took advantage of this latter authority and created an elaborate set of private sector advisory committees.

As this formal advisory framework makes evident, tariff-reducing decisions at the Presidential level are subject to a wide variety of domestic economic and political pressures. Moreover, besides these established mechanisms for bringing to bear the viewpoints of various groups, there are a host of informal means of trying to influence the outcome. For example, various individuals and groups representing particular economic interests often meet with officials in the different agencies concerned with trade matters to explain in detail their concerns. They also press their views on members of Congress who, in turn, may urge these upon the President and key members of his administration.

The objectives of other negotiating partners, that is to say foreign countries, also play an important part in shaping the nature of duty reductions, especially in the process of deciding upon the average depth of the duty cut. As in the Kennedy Round of negotiations (1962-67), negotiators in the Tokyo Round agreed upon a specific duty-cutting formula to be followed by all the major participants, but from which specific exceptions were permitted. In the Kennedy Round the rule was simply a 50 percent, across-the-board duty reduction. In the last negotiations, however, the European Community successfully pressed for a formula that would result in higher percentage cuts in high duties than in low duties. Although the average tariff levels on dutiable manufactures were approximately the same in the European Community and the United States, there were many more high duties in the United States, and Community officials wanted a duty-cutting formula that would harmonize the distribution of rates in the two trading blocs. The compromise formula finally settled on was proposed by the Swiss. Letting t be the duty rate and $\triangle t$ the change in this duty, the formula was. $\frac{\triangle t}{t} = \frac{t}{t+.14}$. Thus, a 14 percent duty was cut 50 percent under the formula, whereas a duty of 20 percent was cut 59 percent.[16]

Besides helping to determine the general tariff-cutting rule, other countries influence the pattern of exceptions to this rule. For example, if an important foreign participant presses vigorously for a concession on a particular item, a country may grant a reduction greater than the formula on this item, if there is no significant domestic opposition to such an action, or at least the country may resist domestic pressures not to cut on the item at all. Still another way in which foreign countries affect the pattern of duty cuts is their willingness to provide reciprocity in the tariff-cutting package. Sometimes a particular participant is unable, for domestic political reasons, to match the extent of the duty cuts that other countries offer on the country's exports. In that case the other countries generally pull back on their duty-cutting offers on items of particular export interest to that country in order to achieve a rough balance of concessions. Often the withdrawals are on products where the domestic pressures against cutting are considerable but sometimes it is necessary to achieve reciprocity by not cutting on items where there are no special economic or political problems domestically.

---

[16] Since the President was not permitted under law to cut more than 60 percent, the formula became a linear one of 60 percent for the United States above a duty level of 21 percent, the lowest rate at which the formula yields a cut of 60 percent.

2. Expected Relationships

The various economic-political characteristics that reflect the domestic pressures shaping the industrial pattern of duty reductions in a multi-lateral trade negotiation can be divided into two groups: those which indicate the ability and willingness of productive factors employed in an industry to provide funds and other resources for lobbying efforts, representing the demand for protection, and those that reflect the willingness of the President and the voters he represents to grant protection from an internationally agreed-upon tariff cutting rule, which represents the supply of protection.[17]

Even though a President might be willing to protect a particular sector because he believes a majority of voters would support this policy if they were made aware of the industry's situation, he may in fact not take this action if the industry itself does not explain its case well both to the President and the general public. In other words, an industry must be well-organized to be effective in the political market-place. However, because of the free-rider problem associated with voluntary lobbying contributions some industries may be unable to form effective lobbying organizations. The first category of industry characteristics attempts to capture differences among industries in lobbying ability and effort. As Olson (1965) notes, the ability to over-come the free-rider problem and form a common-interest group should be positively correlated with the degree of industry concentration and negatively with the size of the industry in terms of number of firms. Pincus (1975) argues that a geographically-concentrated industry should also be more effective in overcoming the free-rider problem due to better intraindustry communications. However, Brock and Magee (1974) maintain that geographically dispersed industries are more effective politically because of the greater number of political jurisdictions they represent. Another point made by Olson (1979) is that a lobbying organization is not usually formed immediately or, if it exists already, resources are not forthcoming in large amounts, upon the emergence of a new common interest for a group. A crisis or repeated series of crises may be necessary to shock members of the group into joining the group's lobbying organization or into increasing their contributions to this unit. To capture this

---

[17] For the analytical basis of this type of division, see Baldwin (1980). Also see the references in that paper for writings by other authors on this subject.

effect, such variables as the growth of industry output or employment and the change in the import penetration ratio seem appropriate. Another factor affecting the willingness to respond to import pressures is the ability of the productive agents and input suppliers to find alternative uses for their services and goods. The more immobile labor and capital are in the short run, the greater their relative losses and thus the harder they are likely to resist duty cuts. Individuals whose income contains a large element of "rent" due to such factors as the industry-specific or firm-specific nature of their skills, their age and seniority, the monopolistic efforts of their union or employee association, few alternative employment opportunities in the community, and the employment of their spouse in the same locality tend to be tied to one firm, industry, or community. Variables like the average age of the employees in an industry, the extent to which an industry is located in small communities, and the proportion of women employees quite clearly reflect the degree of worker mobility but it is not clear just how wage and formal training levels are correlated with mobility. On the management side, it seems likely that firms producing a range of goods covering several different industries are best able to adapt to import pressures.

It has also been suggested that protectionist efforts should be negatively related to the share of value added in the total value of an industry's output, since a given change in the price of an industry's output leads to a large percentage change in the value added when the value added share is small.[18] Moreover, if labor is more mobile than capital so that the latter factor bears the brunt of duty reductions, one might also expect the resistance to such cuts to be greater in those industries where capital's share of value added was small.

Aside from the ability of an industry to undertake effective lobbying activities, the degree of protection from duty cuts is affected by the President's perception of voter support for such protection. If voters are particularly sympathetic toward low income workers who suffer income losses and who have difficulty in obtaining alternative employment, the depth of duty reductions should be positively related to such industry characteristics as the average wage and the proportion of skilled workers, and negatively correlated with an industry's growth rate and profit performance as well as with the various

---

[18] This "effective protection" notion depends upon the assumption of fixed prices for goods used as intermediate inputs.

immobility proxies mentioned earlier. On the other hand, if the reason a majority of voters support protection for an industry is for selfish long-run insurance purposes, one would expect protection in industries that are similar to those in which the average voter is employed, that is to say industries where wages and skill levels, among other things, are near the median.

Attitudes of "fairness" on the part of voters as well as their concerns about national goals related to specific industries, such as national defense or the promotion of high technology, may also lead the President to grant less than formula duty cuts to industries where there is evidence of foreign dumping and subsidization or where some desirable national goal may be jeopardized. A high level of import penetration may also be regarded by the general public as unfair or at least as indicating that an industry has endured severe import competition in the past and now desires sympathetic consideration for assistance.

The absolute size of an industry is another important influence on the willingness of the President and general voters to support less-than-formula tariff cuts. Obviously, to some extent, the larger an industry and those industries that depend upon it, the more likely the President is to grant protection on the grounds of significant voter support from these industries. Other voters are also more likely to learn about the economic difficulties faced by a large industry than a small one simply because it attracts more attention in the media. The fact that large industries also tend to be ones whose output make up a large part of the voters' budget is not likely, in most instances, to offset this protective advantage since consumers are generally unable to form effective lobbying organizations.

The various factors described thus far are likely to influence the pattern of protectionism in most representative democracies, even though there are wide differences among such nations in their political, social and economic institutions.[19] For a detailed analysis of protectionism in a specific country it would be necessary to take into account just how the country's unique set of institutional relationships further affects the nature of protection across industries. For example, this pattern of protection could be influenced by such

---

[19] A paper by Anderson and Baldwin (1980) summarizing statistical studies of protectionism in Australia, Belgium, Canada, France, Japan, the United Kingdom, the United States, and Germany confirms this expectation.

factors as the precise nature of the division of responsibility for trade policy within the government, the unique economic and political relationships existing between key government leaders and various industries, the particular set of trade-offs desired by voters among different economic and social goals, and the special timing of certain political and economic events. Some of these factors could be incorporated into the statistical analysis through the use of dummy variables, though there is a danger that this procedure can turn into a statistical hunting exercise based on little more than anecdotal evidence. However, this approach is not followed here, since the analysis focusses on broad forces that shape the nature of protectionism over many countries. By analyzing a situation where a general tariff-cutting rule was applicable to all manufactured items, with a few mandated exceptions, the effects of these general factors should not be offset by special circumstances applicable to selected tariff items.

3. Empirical Results

The tariff cuts used to test the various hypothesized relationships just outlined are those that the United States offered in the Tokyo Round. They are not the actual reductions finally agreed upon, thus excluding final "pull-backs" for reciprocity reasons, but they do take into consideration the initial requests of other countries for specific concessions. The tariff cuts offered on the approximately 5,000 manufactured tariff-line items were classified into 292 4-digit industries on the basis of the Standard Industrial Classification (SIC) system of the United States.[20] Three different variations of the tariff cut were employed as dependent variables: the rate of decline in duties collected; the rate of decrease in the price of the domestically produced good, assuming a completely elastic import supply curve and perfect substitution between imports and domestic output; and the difference in the tariff rate given by the agreed-upon Swiss formula and the actual 1976 rate.[21] The various industry charac-

---

[20] In order to utilize the Databank of industry characteristics assembled by the staff of the U.S. International Trade Commission the tariff cuts were grouped into a slightly modified form of the pure SIC developed by the Commission staff.

[21] Letting t_i^0 and t_i^1 be the initial and proposed tariff rate on any item; M_i^0 the 1976 value of imports for that item; and n the number of TSUS items in a particular industry, the first cut equals

teristics utilized as proxies for the different types of economic-political variables discussed above were either taken from the Databank of the International Trade Commission[22] and other sources or constructed from data presented in government documents.[23] It proved possible to obtain information on many but not all of the variables mentioned in the discussion of expected relationships.

The results of regressing various industry characteristics on tariff cuts 1 and 2 are reported in Tables 1 and 2, while the regressions for cut 3 and the tariff level itself are listed in Table 4.[24] One surprising feature of the Cut 1 results is that the sign on the initial tariff level is usually negative and in any case, not significant. U.S. negotiators agreed to a formula under which high duties were to be cut more than low tariffs but in fact offered a set of cuts that had the opposite result.[25] This outcome should not be unexpected. As Kennedy Round

$$(1)\ \text{Cut 1}\ =\ \frac{\sum_{1}^{n}(t_i^o M_i^o - t_i^1 M_i^o)}{\sum_{1}^{n}(t_i^o M_i^o)}$$

the second cut equals

$$(2)\ \text{Cut 2}\ =\ \frac{\sum_{1}^{n}\left\{M_i^o\left[1-\left(\frac{1+t_i^1}{1+t_i^o}\right)\right]\right\}}{\sum_{1}^{n}M_i^o}$$

while the third is

$$(3)\ \text{Cut 3}\ =\ \frac{\sum_{1}^{n}\left[M_i^o\left(\left\{t_i^o\left[1-\left(\frac{t_i^o}{t_i^o+.14}\right)\right]\right\}-t_i^o\right)\right]}{\sum_{1}^{n}M_i^o}$$

[22] Office of Economic Research, U.S. International Trade Commission, *The U.S. International Trade Commission's Industrial Characteristic and Trade Performance Databank* (Washington: June 1975, xeroxed).

[23] A list of the variables used as well as their source is presented in Table 4.

[24] The average tariff level for dutiable manufactures has decreased very significantly in the United States. For example, the ratio of duties collected to the value of dutiable imports declined from 59 percent in 1932 to 10 percent in 1970. Consequently, existing interindustry differences in duties are closely related to the varying success among industries in resisting duty cuts over the last 40 years or so. In the tariff level regressions the expected signs on the different variables discussed are just the opposite of those for the three forms of duty reductions.

[25] The simple correlation coefficient is $-.19$, while the unweighted mean of the cut 1 offers in the 292 industries is .46.

Table 2.   *Relationship between U.S. Tariff Cuts in the Tokyo Round and Various Industry Characteristics*

Independent Variables[a]	Dependent Variable : CUT 1				
	All t's	All t's	$t > .05$	$t > .05$	$t > .05$
Constant	.81	.81	.11	.23	.45
TLEVEL	.13 (.40)	−.15 (−.38)	—	—	—
NTBUS	−.30 (−1)* (−1.75)	−.59 (−1)*** (−2.95)	—	−.17 (−1)*** (−3.24)	−.17 (−1)*** (−3.17)
SKUNSK70	−.97 *** (−3.19)	−13 (+1)*** (−2.39)	—	—	−.25* (−1.80)
CONR8L70	.65 (−3) (.79)	—	—	—	—
DP7076	−.27 (−1) (.79)	.80 (−1)* (1.84)	—	—	—
LNIMPENR	−.54 (−2) (−.44)	−.40 (−1)* (−1.69)	−.30 (−1)*** (−4.40)	−34 (−1)*** (−4.52)	−.27 (−1)*** (−3.38)
IMPENRAC	−.26 (−.65)	−.73 (−1.63)	—	—	−.42 * (−1.74)
TOTCAP70	−.62 (−.93)	—	—	—	—

	(1)	(2)	(3)	(4)	(5)
LO76	—	.54 (+1)** (1.97)	—	—	—
VSH76	—	-.25 (-1.22)	.14 (1.34)	—	—
FD13	—	—	—	-.27 (-1) (-.60)	-.49 (-2) (-.24)
FD11	-.99 (+1)** (-2.05)	-.70 (+1) (.95)	—	—	—
NOFIRMS	—	—	.14 (-4) (1.48)	—	—
TEMPL70	—	—	-.51 (-3)*** (-2.66)	—	—
PAY76	—	—	.13 *** (2.87)	.81 (-2)* (1.81)	—
DTEMPL	—	—	.11 * (1.77)	—	—
Adjusted R^2	.10	.14	.18	.09	.17
F Ratio	3.42	2.80	6.91	9.54	8.41

Note: [a] See Table 4 for list of explanation and source of independent variable (t-statistics in parenthesis).
* significant at 10% level   ** significant at 5% level   *** significant at 1% level

Table 3. Relationship between U.S. Tariff Cuts in the Tokyo Round and Various Industry Characteristics

Independent Variables[a]	Dependent Variable : CUT 2				
	All *t*'s	*t* > .05	All *t*'s	All *t*'s	All *t*'s
Constant	.19 ***	.14 (.1)	.82	.34 (−1)	.55 (−1)
IMPENRAC	—	—	—	.14 (−.48)	—
TLEVEL	.30 *** (16.83)	.28 *** (10.95)	—	.31 *** (12.89)	—
LNIMPENR	−.16 (−2)** (−2.54)	−.30 (−2)*** (−3.29)	−.19 (−2) (−.67)	−.87 (−3) (−1.02)	—
PRODWK70	−.22 (−1.31)	−.42 (−4)* (−1.84)	—	—	—
NTBUS	−14 (−2)*** (−2.79)	−.13 (−2)** (−2.03)	—	−.16 (−2)** (−2.14)	—
SKUNSK70	−.47 ** (−3.47)	−.37 (−1)** (−2.04)	—	.80 (−1)** (3.04)	—
LO76	—	—	—	−.15 (1.03)	—
TEMPL70	—	—	−.25 (−4) (−.70)	—	—
PAY76	—	—	−.47 (−2)*** (−3.84)	—	—

DP7076	—	—	—	.15 (2) (.63)	-.25 (-2)*** (-4.36)
VSH76	—	—	-.27 (-1) (-1.29)	-.93 (-.80)	-.80 (-3) (-.95)
LABINT70	—	—	-.21 (-1) (-.76)	—	.21 (-1) (1.52)
DTEMPL	—	—	.32 (-1)** (2.53)	—	—
XDV70	—	—	-.14 (-1) (.29)	—	—
CONR4L70	—	—	-.16 (-3) (-.99)	—	—
CONR8L70	—	—	—	-.18 (-4) (-.30)	—
DTEM7076	—	—	—	—	.39 (-2)*** (4.02)
NOFIRMS	—	—	—	—	-.04 (-6) (-1.41)
SPEC	—	—	—	—	-.36 (-4) (-.24)
Adjusted R^2	.53	.435	.20	.51	.19
F Ratio	66.52	29.93	4.29	25.46	9.19

Notes: [a] See Table 4 for list of explanation and source of independent variables (t-statistics in parentheses).
* significant at 10% level   ** significant at 5% level   *** significant at 1% level.

Table 4. *Relationship between Tokyo Round Cuts and pre-Tokyo Round Tariff Levels and Various Industry Characteristics*

Independent Variable[a]	Dependent Variable: CUT 3			Dependent Variable: TLEVEL		
	All *t*	All *t*	*t* > .05	All *t*	All Manufacturing except foodstuffs	All Manufacturing
Constant	−.20 (−2)	−.19 (−2)	.13 (−1)	.47 (−1)	−.21 (−2)	.26
TLEVEL	−.30 *** (−13.52)	−.32 *** (−12.44)	−.41 *** (−10.41)	−.28 *** (−10.67)	—	—
PRODWK70	−.26 (−4) (−1.19)	—	—	—	—	—
SKILLD70	−.49 (−1)*** (−2.93)	.16 (−1)*** (2.93)	.46 (−1) (1.48)	—	—	—
NTBUS	−.16 (−2)** (−2.37)	.46 (−2)*** (−3.58)	−.33 (−2) (−1.50)	−.24 (−2)*** (−3.12)	.12 (+1)*** (2.86)	.46 (−2)** (2.24)
LNIMPENR	−.27 (−2)*** (−3.61)	−.23 (−2)*** (−2.94)	−.26 (−2)* (−1.93)	−.14 (−2) (−1.58)	—	.32 (−2) (1.60)
SKUNSK70	—	—	—	−.73 (−1)*** (−3.46)	—	—
FDI2	—	−.17 (−5) (−.98)	−.94 (−1) (−.34)	—	—	—
PRODWK76	—	—	—	.39 (−4) (1.60)	—	—
CONR4L70	—	—	—	(−.50)	.11 (−1)* (1.72)	(.74)
DP7076	—	—	—	.39 (−4) (.0)	—	—

	(1)	(2)	(3)	(4)	(5)	(6)
LO76	—	—	—	—	—	.25 (+1)*** (6.04)
NOFIRMS	—	—	—	—	—	-.46 (-5)* (-2.13)
TEMPL70	—	—	—	—	—	.94 (-4)* (1.73)
PAY76	—	—	—	—	-.30 (-2) (-1.30)	-.16 (-1)* (-10.95)
VSH76	—	—	—	—	.45 (-1) (1.27)	-.41 (-2) (-1.87)
LABINT70	—	—	—	—	—	.19 (-1) (.57)
DTEMPL	—	—	—	—	-.41 (-1) (-.98)	.84 (-2) (.51)
XDV70	—	—	—	—	—	.34 (-1) (.52)
FD11	—	—	—	—	.93 (-1) (.08)	—
CONR8L70	—	—	—	—	.22 (-3) (1.29)	—
Adjusted R^2	.56	.61	.65	.56	.53	.37
F Ratio	45.33	74.97	58.08	44.01	26.84	16.29

Notes: [a] See following page for list of explanation and source of independent variables (*t*-statistics in parentheses).
  * significant at 10% level   ** significant at 5%   *** significant at 1% level.

Table 4. (Continued)

Definition and Sources of Independent Variables

*A. From the U.S. International Trade Commission's "Industrial
   Characteristics and Trade Performance" Data Bank:*

NTBUS   : Index of incidence of non-tariff barriers in the U.S., 1970.
SKUNSK70 : Basic labor ratio, 1970. Ratio of ($2,669 times total employ-
             ment) to total payroll, where $2,669 is the average wage of
             persons with less than 8 years education.
CONR4L70 : Concentration ratio, 1970 (percentage of shipments accounted
             for by the four largest firms in the industry).
IMPENR70 : Import penetration ratio, 1970: Imports divided by (shipments
             plus exports munus imports).
SKILLD70 : Skills measure, 1970: professional and kindred workers,
             plus managers and administrators (except farm), plus crafts-
             men and kindred workers, as percent of total employment.
             Based on 3-digit SIC data with values repeated at 4-digit levels.
PRODWK70 : Production workers, 1970 (thousands of persons).
PRODWK76 : Production workers, 1976 (thousands of persons).
TEMPL70   : Total employment, 1970 (thousands of persons).
LAVINT70   : Labor intensity ratio, 1970: payroll divided by value added.
XDV70   : Ratio of U.S. exports to value of shipments, 1970.
IMPENRAC : Absolute change in import penetration ratio, 1965-70.
TOTCAP70 : Total capital stock, 1970 (millions of dollars).

B. Variables Constructed from ITC Data Bank:

$LNIMPENR = \ln(IMPENR70)$
$LO70 = PRODWK70/VALADD70$ where $VALADD70$ is value added, 1970
                                (millions of dollars).
$LO76 = PRODWK76/VALADD76$
$VAL76 = (VALADD76\text{-}TPAYRL76)/TEMPL76$
                                where $TPAYRL76$ is total payroll, 1976
                                (millions of dollars) and $TEMPL76$ is
                                total employment, 1976 (thousands of
                                persons).
$PAY76 = TPAYRL76/TEMPL76$
$VSH76 = VALADD76/TSHIP76$ where $TSHIP76$ is value of shipments,
                                1976 (millions of dollars).
$DP7076 = [(VALADD76\text{-}PRODWG76)\text{-}(VALADD70\text{-}PRODWG70)]/$
          $TOTCAP70$ where $PRODWG76$ and $PRODWG70$

are production worker wage bills, 1976 and 1970, respectively.

$DTEMPL = (TEMPL70 - TEMPL65)/TEMPL65$

where $TEMPL70$ and $TEMPL65$ are total employment, 1970 and 1965 (thousands of persons).

$DTEM7076 = (TEMPL76 - TEMPL70)/TEMPL70$

$DVAL7076 = VAL76 - VAL70$ — where $VAL70$ is defined analogously to $VAL76$

$MH7076 = (PRODMH76 - PRODMH70)/PRODMH70$

where $PRODMH76$ and $PRODMH70$ are production worker manhours, 1976 and 1970 (millions).

C. Other Variables:

TLEVEL : Tariff level before Tokyo Round Cuts (Source: U.S. Government).

FTAX74 : Foreign tax credits in 1974 (Dept. of the Treasury, *Statistics of Income 1974*), thousands of dollars.

FD11 : FTAX74 divided by total assets, 1974 (*Statistics of Income 1974*).

FD12 : *FTAX74* divided by depreciable assets, 1974 (*Statistics of Income 1974*).

FD13 : (Foreign dividends plus foreign tax credits) divided by total assets, averaged over the years 1965-71 (Source: Horst, Thomas, "The Impact of American Investments Abroad on U.S. Exports, Imports, Employment," in U.S. Department of Labor, *The Impact of International Trade on Investment and Employment,* 1978).

NOFIPMS : Number of firms in the industry, 1977 (Source: *1977 Census of Manufactures).*

SPEC : Specialization ratio, 1977. Value of primary product shipments divided by value of primary and secondary product shipments. (Source: *1977 Census of Manufactures*).

negotiators had successfully argued when the harmonization issue came up during the 1960s, even a uniform across-the-board percentage cut is likely to put greater competitive pressure on high duty industries than low duty ones. (See Baldwin, 1965.) Not only will the domestic price decline more, assuming infinitely elastic import supply curves, but many high duty industries are declining and face highly elastic import demand curves.[26] Consequently, high duty industries can be expected to resist duty reductions more than low duty sectors under a proportional tariff-cutting arrangement and even more so under a progressive one. U.S. negotiators either did not fully realize the domestic political implications of yielding to the European Community's pressure for harmonization or counted upon dealing with the problem in the manner they finally followed, namely, by cutting low duties, especially some of those which were less than 5 percent, much more than high duties. Not only does domestic resistance to reductions on low duty items tend to be weak, due to the small decline in price, but because of the high import volume in many of these products, negotiators are able to achieve a fairly deep weighted average duty reduction by concentrating high percentage cuts on low duty items. Because of this negotiating tactic, regression results for various cuts are reported both for all industries and just for those industries where the average duty is above 5 percent. It should also be noted that, since the sign on the coefficient of t in the cut 1 case is not significantly different from zero, the sign on t in the cut 2 and cut 3 cases will be positive and negative, respectively.[27]

Characteristics indicating the ability of an industry to organize, including industry concentration, number of firms and geographic concentration do not perform well in the various duty-cut equations. Concentration and number of firms both have the expected negative signs but are not significant. A nine-region geographic concentration

---

[26] As the equation for tariff cut 2 indicates, the price decline associated with a 50 percent cut on a 50 percent duty is 16.7 percent whereas the price fall resulting from a 50 percent cut in a 25 percent tariff is only 10 percent.

[27] As equation (2) indicates, if the average duty cut does not vary as the duty level changes, then the average reduction in a product's price will be low for low duties and high for high tariffs. Similarly, the difference between the tariffs given the Swiss formula (subject to a 60 percent maximum cut) and those given by a formula that yields a linear cut will be positive at low tariff levels but become increasingly negative at higher tariff rates, i.e., the relationship between those differences and the tariff level will be a negative.

ratio (not shown) that was constructed was positive and significant but the equations in which it was included were not significant as a whole. Two variables that reflect the relative change in a group's incomes as a result of a duty cut, namely the share of value added in total value and labor's share of value added are also not significant. However, economic changes that supposedly tend to shock a group into organizing and actively opposing trade liberalization behave as expected. The changes in industry employment between 1965 and 1970, and between 1970 and 1976 are positively (and significantly) correlated with the duty cut variables as is the 1970-76 change in the ratio of non-wage value added divided by industry shipments, which is a rough measure of the change in the profit rate on sales. However, the change in manhours of employment between 1970 and 1976, though positive, is not significant. The change in the import penetration ratio is negative, as expected, but not always significantly so.

The set of variables performing best in the various duty-cut regressions' are those that reflect industry conditions where the typical voter, and thus the President, is likely to be sympathetic toward protection. As expected, the coefficients for average wage and the labor/value-added ratio are positively and significantly related to the tariff cut, while the coefficient on the ratio of unskilled workers to skilled workers in negatively significant. The level of the import penetration ratio is also usually significant in the expected direction. In addition, the consistently negative and significant sign of the non-tariff barrier measure may indicate a willingness of voters, and thus the President, to give protection against the full cuts agreed upon because of an industry's past, and perhaps present, competitive difficulties that led to the imposition of non-tariff barriers to imports.

Another variable that behaves in the expected manner is total employment, or the number of production workers in an industry. However, although always negative, this measure of political power was only significant in industries with duty rates greater than 5 percent. The magnitude of an industry's capital stock, an additional proxy for political clout, is not significant. Two measures that should reflect interests that benefit from a liberal trade policy, namely the proportion of earnings derived from foreign investments and the ratio of exports to industry shipments, are not significant.[28] Finally, a

---

[28] In a few regressions (not shown) the foreign investment variable was significant in the unexpected direction, *i.e.*, it was negative.

measure of the extent to which an industry specializes in the products of that industry is negative, as expected, but not significant.

As noted, in regressions of the different variables discussed on the level of the protective tariff in each industry one expects the signs of the coefficients to be just the opposite of those in the same regressions on the extent of duty cuts by industry, that is to say cuts 1, 2, and 3. The regression results in Table 4 indicate that this is generally the case. Tariff levels invariably tend to be high in industries where wages are low, production is labor-intensive, non-tariff barriers are used extensively for protective purposes, and the number of firms is low. In addition, the import-penetration ratio is generally high. Although the coefficient on this variable is not quite significant at the 10 percent level in the equation listed, the level of employment is high, and sometimes significant, and the value-added share is low, and only occasionally significant.

In summary, the ability of an industry to resist the full duty reduction ágreed upon by U.S. negotiators in the Tokyo Round of multilateral trade negotiations depended, not unexpectedly, upon such indications of current economic difficulties as sluggish employment growth, a poor profit performance, and a rising import penetration ratio and upon such past evidence of competitive problems as the existence of non-tariff measures of protection and a high import penetration ratio. However, two other variables that are not highly correlated with these measures of current or past performance are also significantly related to the depth of industry tariff cuts. These are the level of human capital possessed by workers in an industry and the industry's level of employment. The significance of the human capital variable is consistent with the notion that equity or altruistic considerations play a role in protectionism, as well as other forms of government assistance, while the employment variable suggests the importance of the voting power of large groups. Characteristics serving as proxies for the ability to form a pressure group, the relative gains from protection, and the country's export interests did not seem to be related to an industry's resistance to tariff reductions.

The variables that appear to be the most influential when examining the degree of tariff cuts also generally are the most significant variables in accounting for the level of tariffs by industry. However, in addition, there is evidence indicating that some "pressure group" factors, including number of firms and value-added share, influence protection levels in the expected direction. Furthermore, the extent of industry variability in tariff levels that can be accounted for by the various characteristics is considerably higher than for changes in these levels, particularly when the tariff level itself is excluded from these latter regressions.

REFERENCES

American Iron and Steel Institute, *Annual Statistical Report,* 1977.

Anderson, Kym and Robert E. Baldwin, "The Political Market for Protectionism in Industrial Countries: A Survey of Empirical Evidence," Paper presented at World Bank Conference on Market Penetration in Industrial Countries, Brussels, November 13-15, 1980.

Baldwin, Robert E., "Tariff-Cutting Techniques in the Kennedy Round," R.E. Caves, H.G. Johnson, and P.B. Kennen (eds.), *Trade, Growth, and the Balance of Payments,* Chicago: Rand McNally, 1965.

_____, "The Political Economy of Protection," National Bureau Conference on Import Competition and Adjustment: Theory and Policy, May 8-11, 1980, Cambridge, Massachusetts. (xeroxed)

Brock, William A. and Stephen P. Magee, *An Economic Theory of Politics: The Case of Tariffs,* 1974. (mimeographed manuscript)

Neumann, George R., "Adjustment Assistance for Trade-Displaced Workers" *The New International Economic Order: A U.S. Response,* David D.H. Denoon (ed.), New York: New York University Press, 1979.

New York Times, September and October issues, 1977.

Olson, Mancur, *The Logic of Collective Action: Public Goods and the Theory of Groups,* Cambridge: Harvard University Press, 1965.

_____, "The Political Economy of Comparative Growth Rates," 1979. (mimeographed)

Pincus, Jonathan, "Pressure Groups and the Pattern of Tariffs," *Journal of Political Economy,* August 1975, pp. 83-84., pp. 757-78.

Richardson, J. David, "Trade Adjustment Assistance under the

Trade Act of 1974: An Analytical Examination and Worker Survey,'' National Bureau Conference on Import Competition and Adjustment: Theory and Policy, May 8-11, 1980, Cambridge, Massachusetts.   (xeroxed)

• COMMENT _____

Kiyoshi Kojima, *Hitotsubashi University*

Baldwin's paper is an informative examination of the relationship, process and timing of pressure groups, and the U.S. President's political decision-making activities. It demonstrates that U.S. trade policy has been irrational, highly politicized and without any sound economic principle.

Economists should analyze whether or not the pressures as well as the presidential decisions were sound. In order to determine their soundness or irrationality, various kinds of lobbying groups should be looked at, including consumers, export industries, business and labor. Even within a depressed industry, the interests of business and labor are different and as regards the car industry even contradictory. Labor unions may wish to invite Japanese investment while business may not welcome it and, instead, as GM and Ford have done, invest abroad. Baldwin's paper does not analyze the conflict between these different interest groups. It may be that the U.S. external trade policy is not only lacking in principle but also may be pursuing an unsound 'fair-trade' strategy.

Economists continue to use the term "free trade" but the U.S. Government and Congress have invented the term "open and fair trade" and use it officially. One can query why they invented the term and what is meant by it. The free trade principle is based upon the idea that "imports are gains." To exchange or trade goods which were already produced and offered to the market with no artificial barriers is beneficial and contributes to raising the welfare of consumers and users. The free trade principle has, therefore, universal truth. Liberalizing imports is undertaken for the benefit of the importing country and should be done unilaterally whether or not partner countries do the same. The U.S. has been insisting on "reciprocity." The fair trade concept is bound up with the principle. The U.S. requests and forces partner countries to open their economies or to liberalize imports with the the aim of making the opportunity for exports between the U.S. and partner countries equal. Fair trade is requested for the sake of American export promotion but not for the other partner's benefit. American pressures have been beneficial to Japan which was led towards free trade due to American pressures. Fair trade does not involve liberalization of imports in the importing country's own interests—which should be properly called "free trade"—but involves pressure on trading partners by the U.S. Therefore, the U.S. has changed the term free trade to open trade and requests that openness should be fair, that is, equal, equivalent and non-discriminatory. Briefly, fair trade is based upon the idea that exports are gains; it is a negotiating or bargaining strategy for the U.S. when requesting fair or equal opportunity for export promotion. Its success depends upon the other partner's reaction, not America's own measures.

The U.S. policy of allowing equal opportunity for exporting countries worked very much in its favor until the mid-1960s because of the strong competitive position the U.S. held. However, this competitiveness subsequently declined, mainly because of relative neglect of domestic investment in modernizing industrial plant and huge direct investments abroad. The U.S. emphasis then shifted to a 'defensive' fair trade strategy which now encompasses various meanings.

The notion of 'fair trade' has a long history dating back to the 1930s. Under it, dumping and export subsidies are condemned. Voluntary export restraints or orderly marketing agreements are required.

The concept of fair or unfair is introduced into the transaction costs area. An example is fair terms of export credit. Japanese trading firms are said to be unfair because they are too efficient. Even undervaluation of the yen or German mark is said to be unfair. Slow adjustment of balance of payments is also condemned. These concerns aim to make the modality of export competition equal. These cannot be condemned on the basis of the "free trade principle" since to supply goods as cheaply as possible meets the free trade principle. American pursuit of this "defensive fair trade" policy works against free trade.

More vague and unreasonable condemnation in terms of fair trade comes from the old "pauper labor" argument. U.S. labor unions request that other countries should adopt fair labor standards. Japan is blamed because they work too hard while living in rabbit hutches. Criticism is also made of Japan for not undertaking much direct investment in America, for instance in the automobile industry.

The U.S. demand seems to be that competitive conditions as regards the production of commodities for export should equate with those in the U.S. Actually, these weaken other countries' competitive power as they are being asked to imitate inefficient American practices.

Theoretically, since there are differences of factor endowments, production function and tastes and value systems, comparative advantages appear and international trade is opened and expanded. To make competitive conditions equal means the negotiating of international divisions of labor and international trade.

What is most needed for the U.S. is to revitalize the competitive power of her industries and to strengthen export promotion efforts. When the U.S. undertakes this, it is doing precisely what it blamed other countries for doing. This creates a dilemma with regard to the fair trade strategy and probably would lead to its demise.

The difficult situation of the American economy, with a huge trade deficit, unemployment and inflation is readily understood. Even Japan may face similar difficulty not far in the future. However, the fair trade principle is not the correct answer to the problem. American scholars should instruct government and Congress in the proper theory of free trade.

Michael G. Porter, *Monash University*

Baldwin's paper offers a fascinating analysis of the political and economic pressures exerted on U.S. Presidential policy with respect to import restraints. The paper is one of an increasing number of quantitative approaches to political economy. (See also Pincus, 1975; Anderson, 1980.) The paper brings together a great deal of information on cycles and trends in U.S. pressure for protection and the increased power of the President to restrict trade and his reduced scope for cutting tariffs. Baldwin also provides some analysis touching on "the theory of lobby groups" as it applies to tariffs, econometric tests of variables "explaining" Presidential decisions on import relief and tests of the relationship between Tokyo Round tariff cuts and various industry characteristics such as skill ratios, import penetration and employment levels.

The author notes that the powers of the President to cut tariffs and moderate other trade restrictions have varied cyclically, with cuts occurring over the periods 1934-38, 1945-48, 1962-67 and 1975-79. In each case these cuts have been followed by periods of relatively stable degrees of protection. Superimposed on this cyclical story has been a steady erosion of the independent powers of the President to select items for tariff cuts and to choose the extent of such cuts. Congress has continued to dilute the trade expanding powers of the President, while increasing his trade-restricting role. The 1974 Trade Act, for example, empowered the President to suspend the benefits of trade agreements and to impose duties, fees and other restrictions in response to certain trade conditions. These "certain conditions" would appear to include every circumstance except thunderstorms and amount to a license to suspend the gains from trade when there are small localized disruptions on the one hand or generally unfavorable price and employment effects on the other.

Indeed, in assigning new powers to the President, Congress would not seem to be sharply distinguishing the "structural" from the "general," as is evident in the situation following the steel decline in the slump of 1975-77. Whereas the steel industry went down with the rest of the economy, and came up over this period, the situation regarding steel was seen as reflecting structural difficulty. This is not to say there were no structural difficulties, but it is merely to say that the decline and subsequent rise in the steel industry mirrored that of the rest of the economy, as measured by its industrial production. If these difficulties are accepted as structural then strong contra-cyclical surges in protection must be expected.

The paper includes a survey of United States anti-dumping regulations and highlights the 1974 amendment by which dumping was defined to include sales below long-run average cost. This modification of the anti-dumping regulations rules out most of the competitive pricing which, quite appropriately, characterizes industrial recessions. If such definitions of dumping were widespread this factor would also reinforce the linkage between a world economic downturn and protectionism. In analyzing the particular success of the steel industry in achieving anti-dumping regulations, Baldwin notes that there are some pro-protection characteristics of this industry, in particular the clout which results because steel employs most of its workers in certain key towns. Australian history in the area of tariffs on textiles provides a similar story of power based on concentrations of worker groups in key towns.

The paper contains a useful discussion of issues relating to the lobbying efforts of various groups in the community, noting for example that if capital is more mobile than labor then in a situation of economic decline lobbying activity may tend to be more intensive in those industries which are labor-intensive, given the higher proportion of labor released when industry contracts. This particular paper of Baldwin's does not go on to discuss the more general issues regarding lobby theory, that being covered in a separate paper "The Political Economy of Protection."

The paper incorporates two sets of tests; one relating to factors influencing Presidential decisions in International Trade Commission import relief cases; the other relating to tariff cuts in the Tokyo Round. The first set of results indicates that inflation, or changes in the rate of inflation, are more significant in explaining Presidential tariff decisions than are unemployment variables. Baldwin also finds that the President appears more sympathetic to import relief at times when his congressional colleagues are running for office. Overall, politicians are found to act like politicians, perhaps to the disappointment of some other members of the species, for example, economists. If it is accepted that protection policies are brought on by a combination of inflation and a desire to win votes in an election year then this may make a yet stronger case for a "fight-inflation-first" plank in economic platforms.

The second set of results relates to the Tokyo round and includes a longer list of explanatory variables and also allows tariff cuts to be measured in three different ways. A surprising negative finding appears to be that industry concentration ratios, the number of firms and geographical concentration are not important. These are some of the factors analyzed by Pincus in his 1975 study. Baldwin finds that changes in industrial employment, the ratio of unskilled to skilled workers, the average wage and labor value added ratios are important explanations of Tokyo Round cuts. Baldwin also finds that there is some weak negative statistical relationship between the growth in the import penetration ratio and the extent of tariff cuts. Perhaps the only surprise here is that so many factors are found significant— since one would expect co-linearity to strike out some factors known to be important.

Perhaps it will suffice to note that overall the results confirm the
view that political capacity to resist moves towards tariff reductions
depend on factors such as slow employment, poor profit performance, rising import penetration and a general history of competitive
problems.

One difference between the two sets of econometric results is that
in the former test, relating to Presidential I.T.C. decisions, 1975-79,
the inflation rate is found to be significant whereas in the tests of the
Tokyo Round cuts inflation is omitted, but a significant role is found
for employment conditions. Despite this slight difficulty of interpretation it remains clear that the pressure for tariff cuts is heavily
moderated by general inflationary conditions. Taking this point a
little further, it is possible to speculate that general concern with distributional issues, and with political payoffs to particular interest
groups in the community, leads back to a direct, and perhaps even an
overriding concern with macroeconomic conditions. Some of the
implications of this situation given a political system intent on achieving both distributional (or political) goals and conventional macroeconomic outcomes will be briefly sketched.

Figures 1 and 2 posit the existence of independent local of political
or distributional equilibrium and equilibrium with respect to a certain
level of demand in the import-competing sector. Both curves are
drawn with the extent of import constraints on one axis and the
degree of restraint applied to monetary and fiscal policy on the other
axis. If the two curves were coincident this would reflect a most satisfactory outcome in which international and domestic pressures have
induced the political process to respond in essentially the same
fashion as the economic system. However, in the more likely instance
in which the two curves have dissimilar slopes, there is a situation
akin to the classic Mundell-Fleming-Swan assignment problem in
which various decision rules regarding the adjustment of monetary
and fiscal policy on the one hand and protection on the other, may or
may not lead the system toward a stable outcome. In Figure 3 the
political locus has been drawn as flatter than the import equilibrium
locus and in this case the system converges to E from all points in the
space. However, in Figure 4 where a steep PP curve is assumed, that
is, a reduction in the degree of protection extracts a large price in
terms of weakening of monetary and fiscal resolve, the capacity of
the system to explode away from equilibrium is then seen. It is
obvious that one can have a great deal of fun demonstrating that

Figure 1.

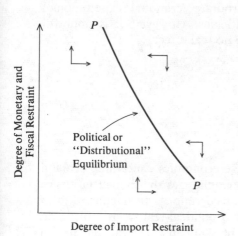

Figure 2.

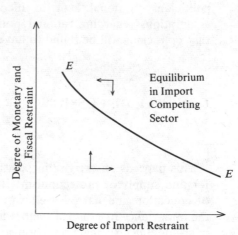

Figure 3.

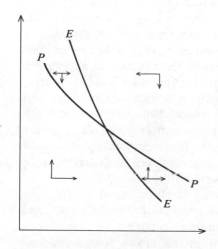

Figure 4.

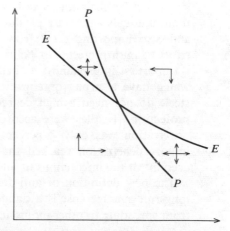

policy and politics can destabilize. It will be left for others to make politicians "rational," or to incorporate "rational expectations" assumptions regarding rational politicians. However, it is doubtful that politicians will be found to have no real effect.

GENERAL DISCUSSION

This paper is an exercise in positive economics concerning demand for and supply of protectionism. It emphasizes the limited influence of education and narrow welfare considerations. It emphasizes also the importance of political factors and political reality, as a first step in examining existing protectionist pressure in the U.S. and its interaction.

The timing of a presidential decision on an ITC recommendation does not seem to be related to a presidential election. The decisions on color TVs, steel and automobiles were taken long before the election date. Firm concentration and geographic concentration by themselves may not be important which would necessitate a consideration of their interaction with other factors. For instance, the multinationals which are producing certain commodities domestically and also importing them from abroad may not be active in their effort to push protectionist policy. That is, the structure of an industry is important in explaining its behavior. On the other hand, industries which have a strong organization such as textiles, automobiles and steel, do not need a high degree of import penetration to be given protection. Textiles were accorded protection in 1956 when import penetration was only 2 percent, while footwear had to wait until import penetration reached the 50 percent level. One has to take account of the interactions of all these variables.

The new definition of anti-dumping legislation based on declining long-run average cost is a dangerous concept. It should be stopped from spreading to other industries and other countries.

Foreign policy considerations such as the Tokyo Round negotiation, or export interest may be important for the U.S. Government in adopting protective measures. In the case of Japan, unions and small family enterprises are important factors in protection.

Japan was forced by U.S. interest groups to take actions which proved to be beneficial to the general public and the Japanese economy. However, the U.S. demand seems to go too far in asking for unreasonable adjustment in Japanese trade policy. An example of this is the U.S. pressure to reduce the tax rate on big passenger cars without considering Japanese road conditions. At the same time the U.S. itself freely adopts the so-called "fair trade practice" which really means a protectionist policy.

The implication for advanced developing countries is that they should not try to go into such highly visible items as automobiles, but rather into small and highly diversified products. That is, they have to play the game on the basis of the existing rules. On the other hand, if ADCs' exports are going to replace the existing Japanese market share which has already borne political burdens, they might be subject to less protectionist pressure.

RESPONDING TO THE "NEW PROTECTIONISM": STRATEGIES FOR THE ADVANCED DEVELOPING COUNTRIES IN THE PACIFIC BASIN

David B. Yoffie &
Robert O. Keohane*

I. Introduction

The advanced developing countries (ADCs) in the Pacific Basin have achieved astonishing rates of economic growth since the early 1960s, aided by rapid expansion of foreign trade. Korea, Hong Kong, Singapore and Taiwan as well as Japan in the 1950s and 1960s, have constructed foreign economic strategies consistent with their objectives, and have carried them out resolutely.

Yet international economic and political conditions are changing rapidly, with foreboding implications for the ADCs. The doubling of oil prices in 1979 is expected to contribute to an American recession in 1980, and at least to a slowing of growth elsewhere; the implications for the world financial system may be severe.[1] From the ADCs' perspective, political changes may be even more ominous. With the relative decline of American economic dominance in the capitalist world, the United States is less and less able or inclined to absorb the costs of maintaining an open trading system (Krasner 1979:491-531).

---

* Stanford University. The principal author of this paper, David B. Yoffie, wishes to record his appreciation to the Institute for the Study of World Politics for fellowship support and to the Jewish Federation of Cleveland for the Morris Abrams Award in International Relations.

[1] See Morgan Guaranty Trust Company, *World Financial Markets,* March 1980, for a careful and sober appraisal.

Future access to the U.S. market cannot therefore be guaranteed, and the likelihood seems high that protectionism will continue to increase during the 1980s. To make matters worse import restraints have been directed in a discriminatory way at the most successful ADCs. According to UNCTAD, for instance, "The erection of these restrictionist regimes is a grave threat to the trade and development of developing countries and would undermine their reliance on international trade" (UNCTAD, 1978: iii).

The most important policy tools of the "new protectionism" are Voluntary Export Restraints (VERs) and Orderly Marketing Agreements (OMAs), which are specifically designed to circumvent Most-Favored-Nation treatment. VERs have become so widespread that they now rank equally with tariffs and quantitative restrictions as the most widely used foreign commercial policies (Bergsten, 1975: 239). They are often viewed as especially worrisome to ADCs for four major reasons: they are directed at labor-intensive exports, concentrated in ADCs; they put the burden of implementation on the exporting country; they may lead to political tensions as a result of bargaining; and they involve bilateral negotiations, pitting each small ADC against a powerful developed country or the European Community.

The proliferation of OMAs and VERs therefore raises the question of whether the ADCs of the Pacific Basin can continue to follow successful foreign economic policies in an era of protectionism. Will the old bilateral strategies continue to be viable in the world of the 1980s, or is it more promising for these countries to develop new forms of multilateral collaboration, such as an Organization of Pacific Trade and Development (OPTAD)?

The question can only be answered if it is understood how the ADCs have succeeded in the past. In Part One, therefore, the bilateral politics of trade between the United States and the Pacific Basin ADCs are examined, beginning with Japan in the 1950s. Here the formulas for success employed by Japan, then by Hong Kong, Korea, Singapore, and Taiwan, in the textile, apparel and footwear sectors are explored. All of these have been persistent objects of protectionism. In Part Two, the question is raised as to whether these bilateral strategies, or variants of them, could still be viable for ADCs in the 1980s, and it is concluded that they are much more promising than the gloomy prognosis of many observers might lead one to believe.

Yet it remains possible that multilateral collaboration could further improve the prospects for ADC trade, or that this could have broader political advantages for these countries. In Part Three of the paper these issues are considered, first addressing the prospects for ambitious forms of collaboration, such as an Asian common market, then considering more limited forms of cooperation on trade bargaining, such as OPTAD. The argument is that only informal implicit forms of cooperation among the ADCs are likely to be helpful to their goals; high levels of institutionalization could well be counter-productive.

II. Bilateral Strategies: Requirements for Success

The ADCs in the Pacific Basin have been able to increase their gains from trade in all sectors, including protected ones, and to maintain political stability with their major trading partners. This has required that they recognize the political basis of trade and that they give priority to their long-term rather than immediate political and economic interests. Within the policy framework established by these two policy premises, they have been able to bargain for certain short-term benefits, circumvent or cheat on restrictive arrangements, and mobilize transnational and transgovernmental allies on their behalf. While no country has purposefully followed all of these strategies in a consistent or coherent manner, these policies are generally responsible for ADC success.

1. Understanding the Political Basis of Trade

An exporting country must understand the political basis of trade. Protectionism is frequently little more than an economic response to a political problem. An industrialized country's demands for import restraints may have less to do with "unfair" competition, "market disruptions," or a real threat to a domestic industry than to an electoral promise or an industry's political clout.

A prime example is the tension created in U.S.-Japanese trade relations over Japan's exports of cotton textiles and apparel in the mid-1950s. The VER that the U.S. negotiated with Japan in 1957 was not a response to a high level of market penetration: Japanese cotton textiles never amounted to over two percent of the U.S.

market. Rather, the VER was a reaction to the forceful entrance of American textile producers into U.S. politics. Not only were these organizations threatening to defeat the Eisenhower administration's efforts to renew the Reciprocal Trade Act, they also came close to sabotaging Japan's burgeoning trade with America. Boycotts of Japanese goods were widespread in southern states in 1956; and unless the administration had restrained the importation of Japanese cotton textiles, the U.S. textile industry might have pressured Congress for more severe action (Hunsberger, 1964).

This pattern has often been repeated since 1956, and is likely to continue. Trade is inherently political, and there is little that an ADC can do to alter this situation. But grasping the nature of the game is an important step toward manipulating the rules for one's own advantage. If the sole purpose of import restrictions is political appeasement, the ADC may be able to accommodate that purpose without reducing its rate of export growth. The importance of political symbols for the developed country's policy-makers may allow the ADC to exchange deference on politically salient questions for tangible economic benefits in less sensitive areas. The political nature of trade constitutes the first loophole in modern protectionism.

2. Pursuing Long-Run Gains from Trade

American protectionism has rarely been part of an integrated package for fostering an industry's "positive" adjustment. As a result, it has been filled with contradictions. It may provide immediate benefits to domestic groups, but it is a "short-run and ultimately self-defeating alternative to needed adjustment" (Blackhurst, 1978: 1). Often it comes very late, with import barriers being implemented only after a market has become stagnant or gone into decline.

ADCs need to respond to myopic protectionism, such as that of the United States, by focuses on long-term gains from trade. Such a response has two components, one political and defensive, the other economic and oriented toward increasing the gains from trade.

Politically, the best strategy is one of short-term compromise and willingness to make concessions. During the last 20 years, rapidly developing countries have successfully minimized large-scale trading problems with the United States when they made specific sectoral concessions; and they have exacerbated political tensions almost every time they refused to compromise. Maintaining broad market access is critical for all ADCs if they wish to continue their reliance on export trade. Since the executive branch of the U.S. Government has normally been hesitant to implement strong protectionist measures, it has required cooperation from the exporting country to avoid a choice between severe political dissatisfaction at home and overt protectionism. The latter would be inconsistent with international obligations or at least with the general policy of trade liberalism. Thus the ADC has some leverage. In 1957, for instance, Japanese agreement to voluntary export restraints led to the dropping of boycotts and a Presidential veto of more restrictive actions that had been recommended by the U.S. Tariff Commission. More recently, the Koreans and Taiwanese have avoided unilateral restrictions against their exports by agreeing to OMAs in footwear and color TVs.

A political strategy of compromise is a defensive strategy, designed not to achieve desirable new objectives as much as to minimize damage. The alternative, which is to reject protectionism forthrightly, has led to much worse results for exporting countries. This strategy promotes confrontation, which is likely to stimulate action by domestic protectionist groups. The American textile lobby, for instance, has held free trade legislation "hostage" in the past when its demands were not met.

Japanaese resistance to American demands for textile export restraints in the late 1960s provides a good example of the costs of confrontation. For almost three years, the Nixon Administration insisted that Japan, as well as Hong Kong, Korea, and Taiwan, limit its exports of synthetic and wool textiles. At times, the issue even dominated the agenda of U.S.-Japanese relations. It took a close defeat of a massive protectionist program (the 1970 Trade Act), a Nixon threat to invoke the "Trading with the Enemy Act," and implicit linkages to America's reversion of Okinawa to Japan, before the Japanese finally came to terms.[2]

If confrontation was necessary to preserve essential economic interests, it might be worthwhile for the exporting country. But this is in general not the case. Indeed, accepting certain forms of protectionism may in the long run be beneficial for the economic develop-

---

[2] The best single account of this episode can be found in I.M. Destler, H. Fukui, and H. Sato (1979).

ment of the ADC. Myopic protectionism, oriented toward short-term political problems, by the importing state can serve as a signal to the exporter to allocate resources more efficiently, diversify markets, and upgrade product lines. In the absence of protectionism, a profitable ADC manufacturer will normally continue production in established product lines until it has fully exploited the available productivity gains: there is little incentive to shift production in the short run. Yet if quantitative restrictions are imposed, exporters will need to sell fewer goods for more money, and will therefore need to improve the quality of their exports. "Trading up" is standard wisdom in international trading circles. This effect will be reinforced if controls are imposed on slowly growing market segments, but not on more dynamic sectors. In this case, ADC producers will have even stronger incentives rapidly to upgrade their exports, which will be in the long run beneficial to their continued growth. ADC governments, meanwhile, will be able to promote this upgrading by pointing to the protectionist measures making these steps necessary in the short run as well as desirable in the long run. The net result of the process in which the ADC focusses on long-term growth while the United States tries to avoid short-term adjustment costs is that the power of the United States to force others to change can be turned back on itself.[3]

Cases abound in which producers have adjusted successfully to restrictions by following such a strategy. The best illustration is the pattern of exports which followed the implementation of the Long Term Arrangement Regarding International Trade in Cotton Textiles (LTA). The common assumption about the LTA is that it was a very restrictive regime which severely damaged developing countries' economies. Upon closer scrutiny, however, a more complex picture emerges.

The cotton textile market was growing relatively slowly as early as

---

[3] In his classic work on *National Power and the Structure of Foreign Trade,* Albert Hirschman demonstrated this paradox from the opposite perspective. Hirschman showed that powerful states using *free trade* can actually limit the growth of LDCs. The essence of the strategy is the reverse of the one suggested here: importing countries could create dependence by forcing developing states to focus on "urgent demand" and short-term gains from trade, while at the same time *preventing adjustment*. The logic is identical: "Immediate loss" according to Hirschman, is "much greater than the ultimate loss for a developing state, after resources have been fully reallocated." See Hirschman (1945), p. 20.

the mid-fifties. Between 1955 and 1963, consumption of natural fibers increased by only 1.8 percent a year, while the rate of growth for synthetic fibers was 22.5 percent (Lynch, 1967: 178). Even though the LTA restrained exports in cotton products, it created an incentive for exporting countries to shift to man-made fibers which was the dynamic market segment. As a result, the imports of man-made fibers into the U.S. increased more than ten-fold between 1962 and 1970, with Japan, Taiwan, Korea, and Hong Kong accounting for almost 90 percent of the non-European total.[4] It is interesting to note that Hong Kong was among the slowest of these four to enter the synthetic market. This can largely be attributed to Hong Kong' substantial cotton quota and a relative lack of incentive to diversify. Thus, despite the supposed restrictiveness of the LTA, overall textile exports from these four countries increased dramatically in response to the restrictions. (See Table 1.)

The pattern of upgrading product lines and increasing gains in response to export restraints has also been exhibited in the shoe industry. In June of 1977, the U.S. negotiated Orderly Marketing Agreements with Taiwan and Korea in "non-rubber" footwear. For the year immediately preceding the agreements, Taiwan exported $395.2 million worth of shoes to the U.S., while Korea shipped exports worth $321.1 million. In the year ending December 1978, Taiwanese footwear exports rose to $589.9 million and Korean exports were valued at $437.1 million. In other words, within eighteen months Taiwan had increased the overall value of its exports 49 percent and Korea 36 percent, despite the restrictions. Part of the increase can be attributed to inflation and rising wage costs, but as Table 2 illustrates, a great deal of upgrading also occurred. The Korean government, in particular, took an active role in pushing up the value of its exports. When the restrictions were about to be implemented, they set up an incentive system to upgrade their existing product lines. Simultaneously, they established an export check price formula to ensure minimum prices on all shoes exported to the U.S.; and thereafter they increased the floor prices almost every three months.[5]

The strategy of focussing on long term gains from trade is not without risks. Accepting protectionism in one sector can establish a

---

[4] United States International Trade Commission, *The History and Current Status of the Multifiber Arrangement,* USITC Publication 859, January 1978, p. vi.

[5] *Korea Herald,* January 11, 1977.

Table 1.   U.S. Imports of Japanese, Taiwanese, Korean, and Hong Kong Textiles and Apparel under the LTA

(million of square yard equivalents)

	Japan		Hong Kong		Taiwan		Korea	
	Cotton	Man-made	Cotton	Man-made	Cotton	Man-made	Cotton	Man-made
1962	351	110	269	n.a.	85	n.a.	11	n.a.
1963	304	126	257	n.a.	35	n.a.	35	n.a.
1964	324	164	264	11	47	14	34	3
1965	404	310	293	19	52	25	26	18
1966	412	445	353	39	61	33	24	28
1967	376	352	354	74	69	60	30	64
1968	391	435	401	99	71	123	37	137
1969	395	585	413	145	61	238	36	212
1970	330	775	337	188	66	350	39	254

Source: U.S. International Trade Commission, *The History and Current Status of the Multifiber Arrangement,* January 1978.

Table 2.   Percentage of Total U.S. Non-Rubber Footwear Imports

(in percent)

	Taiwan		Korea		World	
Price Brackets	July '77	Dec. '78	July '77	Dec. '78	July '77	Dec. '78
Up to $1.25	39.9	0.8	11.5	0.05	24.1	9.6
$1.26 to $2.50	30.9	23.2	13.1	1.06	19.2	15.7
$2.51-$5.00	22.5	66.6	62.3	14.9	29.6	33.5
$5.01-$8.00	6.2	8.3	9.8	59.6	13.1	21.4
Over $8.00	0.02	1.1	3.2	24.4	13.7	19.8

Source: *Bulletin,* #7, Feb. 23, 1979, Volume Footwear Retailers of America publication.

precedent for restricting other sectors in the future. In addition, if restrictions become more comprehensive, as they have in textiles under the Multifiber Agreement (MFA), then the economic benefits over the longer run diminish; so there will no longer be a prospect of diversifying the product lines. These potential dangers, however, do not outweigh the direct benefits of the approach. It is critical that

ADCs maintain good relations with major importers. The costs to the ADCs of the collapse of trade regimes are extremely high. Furthermore, over the long run ADCs must be prepared to follow the course of Japan, giving up their market shares in labor-intensive protected sectors. If their economic growth is to continue, they cannot indefinitely rely on textiles, footwear, and similar products in their foreign trade.

3. Bargaining for Short-Term Benefits

A long-run orientation is consistent with Schumpeter's conception of industrial growth as involving "creative destruction." Economies must continually adjust, supplanting the old with the new. Yet long-term plans must be consistent with short-term needs. The dilemma is how to achieve one without jeopardizing the other. Even when an ADC decides that it has to accept a VER or an OMA, it can try to obtain its short-run objectives through the bargaining process. Bargaining allows an ADC to influence the nature of an agreement, and thereby reduce the severity of its short-run impact. Bilateral negotiations usually lead to higher import levels, greater flexibility, and more growth than unilaterally imposed programs. Moreover, protectionism can be more restrictive in form than in substance, and effective negotiating can help to assure this result.

Nevertheless, the ADC's leverage is limited. It will often have the least control over the most basic questions, such as the aggregate levels of imports or the scope of protection. ADCs have occasionally been able to stall the negotiations to provide time to raise their export levels and/or stockpile future supplies. But in most instances, aggregate numbers are highly visible, and are the most obvious target of attack for dissatisfied domestic interests.

Within these constraints, three bargaining tactics can be employed, separately or in combination, to reduce the restrictiveness of protection and meet an ADC's short-term requirements. Under some conditions, ADCs may be able to link unrelated issues to the negotiation at hand, to compensate for possible losses. Whether or not this is possible, the ADC can try to foster ambiguity in the agreement as well as to bargain for flexibility. Finally, in the process of accepting an agreement, an ADC may try to capture potential scarcity gains by obtaining guaranteed market shares.

a. Issue Linkage

ADCs have sometimes attempted to broaden negotiations over import restraints to other issue-areas, hoping to use leverage from other areas to counterbalance weakness in trade. Yet a linkage strategy is risky. As an ADC broadens the bargaining agenda, a Pandora's Box is potentially opened wherein both sides have the opportunity to introduce new issues into the negotiations. Thus linkages can only be profitably pursued under certain conditions. All other things being equal, the more broadly the importing country defines its interests, outside of narrow protectionist ones, the greater the developing state's potential leverage. The best linkage opportunities exist when the importing state has strong bilateral ties to the ADC. The United States, for example, has military bases, intelligence operations, and other important stakes all over the world. If an ADC has a relatively narrow range of interests, and controls one of these vital assets, its bargaining power is increased. Furthermore, as ADCs grow economically, they become increasingly interdependent, albeit asymmetrically, with the U.S. Export-oriented sectors in America have a great interest in increasing trade with a rapidly developing country, not restricting it. These types of crosscutting pressures can also provide a linkage possibility.

Historically, several types of linkages, many of them implicit, have been employed by ADCs confronted with protectionist demands. In 1956, the Japanese insisted, before the substantive negotiations, that bilateral relations would be damaged if the U.S. did not promise to end the boycotts of Japanese goods and prevent further restrictionist actions. During the 1960s, one of the reasons that the U.S. was unwilling to push Hong Kong harder on textile limits was the American need for an intelligence post used to monitor the PRC. And the most successful known case of linkage was devised by the Koreans in 1971. As part of the ROK's agreement to limit multifiber textiles, the U.S. promised Korea over $700 million in P.L. 480 agricultural aid. This was an explicit trade-off to offset Korea's projected costs. According to the principal negotiator, David Kennedy, some P.L. 480 aid was planned before the Korean linkage but the amount was subsequently increased. When there was a chance a few years later that all of the aid would not be delivered, the Koreans reversed the linkage to textiles. They insisted that their quotas be readjusted upward if the promise could not be fulfilled.[6]

Although linkages can have highly profitable payoffs, it must be remembered that linkages are hazardous. In most instances, it requires a developing state to practice brinkmanship. Moreover, the conditions for linkages are no longer as favorable as they once were. With American hegemony declining, and the U.S. global and bilateral commitments shrinking, there is a greater likelihood that the U.S. will use its own linkage strategies if an ADC helped to create the opportunity. Hence, linkages are best used selectively and only as a last resort.

b. Ambiguity and Flexibility

For the exporting state, ambiguity is desirable: precision should be avoided like the plague. Ambiguity can conceal substantive differences between governments as well as allow the exporter to ship more goods than interest groups in the importing country are led to expect at the time of an agreement. A developing country should seek an accord that is impermeable and restrictive in form, thus satisfying potential political problems, but porous and unrestrictive in substance.

Fortunately for the Pacific Basin ADCs, ambiguity is often easy to achieve, particularly in agreements with the United States. The negotiation of trade pacts usually involves the struggle of conflicting interests on both sides of the table, not merely between the two countries involved. Many issues, particularly technical and complex ones, are easily clouded in such a process. The first time that a treaty is negotiated in a manufacturing sector, therefore, it tends to be loosely worded and poorly designed. Furthermore, definitions of products can provide sizable loopholes for exporters. U.S. Customs definitions are often so antiquated or so complicated that they are nearly useless. Thus, classifying a shoe as rubber or nonrubber, a fabric as cotton or synthetic, or a television set as a subassembly or less than a subassembly can be as important to the eventual export figures as the base levels, growth rates, or numerous other clauses which an ADC cannot control.

Under the LTA, textiles had to be at least 50 percent cotton by weight to be restricted. As mentioned earlier, this allowed for gains far above what could have been realized with higher cotton quotas.

---

[6] Documents obtained from the Department of Agriculture through the Freedom of Information Act; and interview with David Kennedy, by David Yoffie, November 11, 1979.

Similar loopholes were also apparent in the recent footwear OMAs. Only "non-rubber" shoes were included under the arrangements. By adding rubber to footwear sales or making other minor alterations, shoes could become "rubber" and thus legally outside the jurisdiction of the quota.

Flexibility provisions can have advantages similar to ambiguity. In textiles, for example, category switching, borrowing against future quotas, and carryover provisions to future quotas can provide an exporter with a much larger increase than the five or six percent supposedly allowed under the LTA and the MFA. In 1976, Korea used its flexibility to ship 74 million square yards of textiles and apparel over its assigned aggregate limit.[7] Korea's overshipments were larger than most countries' total quotas.

In the footwear OMAs, both Korea and Taiwan were able to negotiate for significant flexibility in their accords. American compromises included a pipeline clause which allowed each country an additional 27 percent of the first year's restraint to enter the U.S. without being considered in violation of the quota, shorter duration for the treaties, and late starting dates for enacting the agreements, above and beyond borrowing and carryover clauses. The pipeline and carryover provisions, plus an ambiguity concerning the definition of the exporting dates, severely lessened the quotas' short-run impact. A few statistics will illustrate the point. In 1976, Koreans exported 44 million pairs of non-rubber shoes to the U.S., and they stated in January of 1977 that their total export capacity for that year was 60 million pairs. The U.S. sought to roll back Korea's 1976 total as far as possible, and in fact, reduced Korea's quota level to 33 million pairs for the year ending June 1978. However, by using their various flexibility clauses, the Koreans were able to export 58 million pairs of shoes during 1977.[8]

c. Scarcity Gains

A third element of the bargaining strategy has been to assure that the exporting country captures any scarcity gains that might be generated by protection. Under an export restraint arrangement and other types of quantitative restrictions, prices usually increase because

---

[7] United States International Trade Commission (1978), p. 40.

[8] U.S. Department of Commerce, *Footwear Industry Revitalization Program: First Annual Progress Report*, 1978, pp. 26-27.

of forces or anticipated reduction in supply. Unlike the situation under a tariff, windfall profits are not automatically absorbed by the importing government. Who captures the scarcity gains will partly depend upon the relative concentration of market power between exporters and importers, partly upon the market-sharing arrangements the exporting nation can make with the U.S., and partly upon any abnormal shifts in supply and demand that may occur.

Figure 1 depicts the situation in formal terms. A tariff of (P_2-P_1) would transfer a sum equal to area *"A"* to the importing government. A quota of Q_1 Q_3 will, given the domestic supply and demand curves, have the same effect on the price of the goods, but the scarcity rent, *"A"*, will not accrue to the government. If the foreign producers do not fear a loss of market share from other suppliers, they can be expected to raise prices to absorb the rent for themselves. If the exporters fear such a loss from other foreign suppliers, and the U.S. importers are relatively concentrated, the importers will absorb the rent.[9] If a government such as Taiwan or Japan takes an active role in fostering exporters' concentration or bargaining with importers, this will tend to transfer more of the windfall gains to the exporters, even in a market characterized by a high degree of importers' concentration.[10]

In the first restraint arrangements, the Japanese made no provision in their agreement with the U.S. to assure their market position. As a result, Japan's share of the U.S. fabric market dropped from over 70 percent in 1956 to 35 percent in 1961 (Lynch, 1967: 173). Hong Kong, in particular, was able to capitalize on the slack in Japanese exports. Since that experience, all ADCs have helped assure their market shares by insisting that a clause in the bilateral accords guarantee that an ADC will not be put at a disadvantage vis-a-vis other parties. This has become a standard feature of all textile accords. In addition, when the U.S. negotiated the footwear OMA, both Taiwan and Korea made this the first issue on the bargaining table.

The point of this discussion is that a variety of opportunities for

---

[9] It is possible, of course, that both foreign producers and importers will be worried about a loss of market shares from the possible entry of new domestic producers. In such a situation, prices are likely to remain low. The diagram in Figure 1 does not encompass such a possibility, which would have to be reflected in a shift in the supply curve down and to the right.

[10] William Cline *Imports and Consumer Prices: A Survey Analysis,* prepared for the American Retail Federation, 1979; and Bergsten, *op. cit.*

Figure 1.

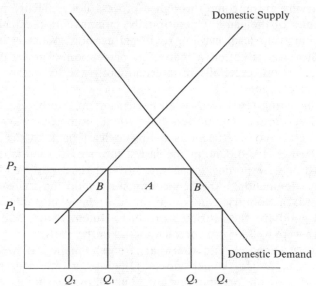

Q_2Q_4 : imports before quota
Q_1Q_3 : imports after quota
P_1 : price of imports before quota
P_2 : price of imports after quota
A : scarcity rent as a result of quota (or tariff of P_2-P_1)
B : deadweight loss
   Source: C. Fred Bergsten, "On the Non-Equivalence of Import Quotas and Voluntary Export Restraints," C. Fred Bergsten (ed.), *Towards A New World Trade Policy: The Maidenhead Papers,* N.Y.: D.C. Heath & Co., 1975.

ADCs are built into the bargaining process. The developing country should bargain tenaciously for loopholes. Such bargaining, which is necessary to avoid short-term losses, does not jeopardize long-term interests. It is part of the rules of the game.

4. Circumvention

After an ADC signs an agreement with an importing country, the phase of implementation begins. At this point, exporting countries may attempt to circumvent the restrictions, either legally or illegally.

Circumvention can be defined as the evasion of regulations, that is to say achieving an outcome through a process not explicitly permitted by the rules of the game. Operationally, circumvention extends along a spectrum from legal evasion to illegal evasion. What is legal and illegal, however, is often a matter of perception. The legality of a particular action, especially in international trade, is easy to identify only at the extremes.

Circumventing restrictions is an ancient art in, international trading circles. Exporters and importers have found numerous ways to side-step bilateral quota restrictions dating at least back to the interwar period (Heuser, 1939). One of the easiest forms of evasion is transshipment, which is, exporting to an uncontrolled third party en route to the final destination. Another common method has already been mentioned: a country can substitute a freely exportable or half-finished good for the restricted product. Dutch, Swiss, and Belgian exporters were well known for such tactics in the 1930s.

In textiles, apparel, and footwear, transshipment has become the classic quota dodge. Under global QRs or tariffs, transshipments would be difficult or unimportant, but with a string of bilateral arrangements, they are virtually impossible to prevent. Hard data on the extent of transshipment is unavailable. Yet in a series of articles recently published by the U.S. textile and apparel industry newspaper, it was suggested that hundreds of thousands of dozens of various categories of apparel worth millions of dollars are shipped every year from Asia in direct violation of U.S. quotas.[11] The cost of buying false papers in Hong Kong, for example, is only about one-third the cost of buying legitimate quotas. Goods can then be shipped in massive quantities to Indonesia or Sri Lanka, which are quota-free ports, and relabeled before sending them off to the United States. Transshipment was also immediately apparent after implementation of the footwear OMAs. Taiwanese companies shipped footwear parts to Hong Kong for assembly, which resulted in Hong Kong's shoe exports jumping 225 percent in 1978.

Exporting half-finished goods and freely-exportables are equally familiar among modern ADC circumvention techniques. While the opportunity to export synthetic textiles in place of cotton was removed with the negotiation of multifiber agreements, Taiwan, Korea, and Hong Kong frequently export piecework to countries such

---

[11] *Daily News Record,* October 29, 1979.

as the Philippines or even Japan, allow these states to assemble the apparel, and then ship them to the U.S. In footwear, both Taiwan and Korea fully exploited the "rubber" loophole mentioned earlier. In the first year of the OMA (July 1977-June 1978), rubber increased from 28 percent of Taiwan's overall footwear exports to almost 38 percent; and for Korean exports, the percentages went from 39 percent to over 50 percent. During the first quarter of 1979, the Koreans were exporting 200 percent more rubber footwear than non-rubber, as compared to only one-half as much rubber as non-rubber in the first quarter of 1977.[12]

Under some conditions, exporters may have little incentive to circumvent quotas. As mentioned previously, prices generally increase under a quota, and the net results may benefit exporters, particularly if these firms have other markets available or can switch to more sophisticated products not covered by import restrictions. Incentives to cheat arise when losses from quotas exceed price benefits. Low quotas may lead to underutilized capacity in the short run, inducing firms to cheat temporarily while restructuring production. If there is concern about elasticity of supply, exporters may not receive high enough prices as a result of quotas. In this case, both importers and exporters will have a strong incentive to cheat. Finally, when restrictions become comprehensive, as they have in textiles, cheating may be the only way to avoid surplus capacity.

Yet ADCs and multinational corporations are not the only responsible parties. In many cases, circumvention is encouraged or tacitly approved by the United States. At one stage during the Vietnam War, overshipments were readily accepted because domestic production was lagging behind demand.[13] In addition, American bureaucrats often recognize that the agreements are somewhat restrictive, but that cooperation is needed to make a pact work. Therefore, permitting circumvention can satisfy some of the restricted party's legitimate grievances, and simultaneously keep the protectionist regime intact. Furthermore, the U.S. has never implemented an effective system of sanctions. The most any importer has ever paid for illegal circumvention of a quota is $10,000, a trivial sum compared to the potential profits.[14]

---

[12] *Trends in the Demand and the Supply of Non-Rubber Footwear,* Brimmer and Company, Inc., July 1979, Table 4, p. 13.

[13] *Daily News Record,* May 12, 1966.

[14] *Daily News Record,* October 31, 1979.

While some cheating is necessary and beneficial to both the restricted and restricting nations, cheating in large doses can be dysfunctional. If an ADC attempts to circumvent quotas too often or too much, a breakdown in the system is likely to occur. Moderate circumvention can keep a protectionist arrangement within politically acceptable bounds, but excessive cheating can lead to such rapid losses that the U.S. has little choice but to crack down. Instead of reinforcing short-term profits, too much circumvention can result in a more restrictive system. In 1972, Hong Kong threatened to sabotage its recently negotiated multifiber agreement when it overshipped man-made fiber knit textiles.[15] This led to a mini-crisis in U.S.-Hong Kong trade relations, which was not settled for several months. Treaties and laws no longer function as a guide to behavior when circumvention goes beyond tolerable levels.

The most prominent constraint against cheating and circumvention in world trade is reputation. A reputation as a cheater can have severe political consequences for some developing states. A great deal of emotionalism characterizes the debates over protectionism, especially in the U.S. There, claims of exploiting cheap labor and unfair competition pervade the arguments. If protectionism is accepted under these conditions to avoid a spillover into other sectors, a reputation for honesty may be critical in preserving economic peace. Circumventing agreements, even in small amounts, can upset a precarious political balance, bringing short-term and long-term strategies directly into conflict.

Japan, for instance, had a powerful reputation for illegal and unfair trade practices between the wars. Among its most frequently cited transgressions were "violating copyright laws and patent rights, using false marks of origin, and 'sudden flooding' of markets for the purpose of destroying competition" (Patterson, 1966: 274). The result was widespread discrimination against Japanese goods for nearly twenty years following World War II. Not surprisingly, Japanese decision makers were highly sensitive to charges of cheating, and the government imposed heavy penalties on transshippers and other evaders in its efforts to change its image. During the late 50s and early 60s, the Japanese acquired a reputation for honesty that was

---

[15] *Daily News Record,* May 5, 1972; Interviews by David Yoffie with Ron Levin, and Don Foote, Department of Commerce, Textile Division, October 12, 1979; Interview with Stanley Nehmer, former Deputy Assistant Secretary of Commerce for Resources, October 11, 1979.

unsurpassed in Asia.

A cheater's reputation, however, is not without advantages. Known cheaters are not always held accountable for their actions. American officials frequently note that Taiwan and Korea are incapable of controlling what goes in and out of their ports. This has meant that these countries can doubly benefit: they obtain the gains from additional trade, but they are not politically liable. Known successful cheaters may also attract business. Importers unable to find producers with quota allocations are most likely to seek out a cheater to obtain the products.

The greatest practical problem with circumventing quotas is that the efficacy of the strategy declines over time.[16] The textile lobbies in the U.S. have put increasing pressure on the American administration to prevent transshipment and to tighten loopholes. The Special Trade Representative's Office responded to this pressure in March of 1979 with a statement now known as the Textile White Paper. Under the heading of "Law Enforcement," the government stated its intention to "dramatically improve the administration's enforcement of all our textile agreements."[17] This included improved monitoring of transshipments, stronger regulations on certificates of origin, and fewer exceptions to allowing overshipments. The ability of the U.S. to achieve these goals is questionable; but its renewed efforts in this realm signal a need for reevaluation.

5. Transnational and Transgovernmental Ties

In its struggle to shape the form of protectionism, an ADC is not limited to formal diplomatic channels. This is particularly true in the United States, since the American Government is rarely united on protectionist issues, and the U.S. bureaucracy is relatively open to transnational and transgovernmental contacts. The State Department and Treasury will usually argue for free trade; Labor and Commerce normally insist on import restraints, and when the special Trade Representative's Office is involved, it often takes a middle ground.

---

[16] Interesting moral issues are also raised by cheating, since some people might be inclined to justify the practice on the grounds that ADCs are poor relative to importing countries, or that they have been denied, through the exercise of power, their "natural right" to free trade.

[17] Office of the Special Representative for Trade Negotiations, *Press Release*, #302, pp. 3-4.

Strong lobbying with sympathetic agencies can reinforce bureaucratic splits. Such lobbying can be particularly effective if the ADCs form coalitions with organized domestic interest groups such as trading associations, or with multinational corporations.[18]

Transnational and transgovernmental allies may provide useful information and support during negotiations. In 1977, for instance, the chief negotiator for the footwear agreements, Stephen Lande, allegedly leaked the U.S. negotiating instructions to the American Importers Association, which passed them on to Korea and Taiwan. Lande had hoped that knowledge of the American position by the ADCs would make the negotiations easier. In fact, this allowed both countries to push the United States negotiators to the limit of their instructions, and even beyond on certain points.[19]

Transnational and transgovernmental connections can also ease some burdens of implementation. Friends in high places can warn of impending crackdowns, thus warding off costly embargoes. The American Textile Manufacturers Institute, the most prominent textile lobby in Washington, has accused the State Department of notifying Asian governments that their quotas are about to reach their limits. The State Department then supposedly makes an arrangement for these nations to submit requests for quota adjustments that are to be reviewed favorably.[20]

Transnational and transgovernmental lobbying efforts, however, cannot be pushed too far. Dramatic efforts, such as those pursued by Japan, Hong Kong, and others late in the 1971 textile negotiations, are likely to politicize an issue, strengthening the resolve of higher-level officials. A transnational and transgovernmental approach is best viewed as a supplementary means to other tactics for subtly influencing America's domestic policy process.

---

[18] For a discussion of transgovernmental coalition-building, see Robert O. Keohane and Joseph S. Nye, "Transgovernmental Relations and International Organizations," *World Politics*, 27-1, October 1974, pp. 39-62.

[19] Interview by David Yoffie with Thomas Graham, former Deputy General Counsel, STR, and Negotiator of the OMAs with Korea and Taiwan, September 4, 1979.

[20] Interview by David Yoffie with American Textile Manufacturers Institute officials, June 22, 1979.

III. Are Bilateral Strategies for ADCs Still Viable?

The success formula for ADC exporters in the past has required that they recognize the political basis of trade. Part of this recognition is the awareness that in any direct test of strength, the ADC will be in a weak position vis-a-vis the United States or the European Community. Interdependence between exporters and importers is highly asymmetrical: the ADC requires markets for its goods more than the industrialized importer needs the goods. In the last resort, the importer can allocate or withhold market shares as it believes its interests demand.[21] Hence confrontation must be avoided, and linkage strategies must be used with care.

The increasing industrial base of the Pacific Basin ADCs has not necessarily increased their political power vis-a-vis importers. Indeed, the ADCs may find themselves in worse bargaining positions in the 1980s than they did in the 1970s, as a result of their very success. In the short run, OMAs and VERs may have seemed to have dealt successfully with the political problems raised by ADC exports, but over a period of time, the ADCs have increased their exports and American industries have continued their decline, in sectors such as textiles, footwear, apparel, and color TVs. American decision-makers are slowly learning that some of their protectionist policies are counterproductive. This does not lead them toward freer trade but toward more effective restrictions. The evolution of· the international regime in textiles is a case in point: as international arrangements and bilateral accords are renegotiated, they become more sophisticated and restrictive. Another example is provided by the increasingly selective nature of protectionist policies: according to the IMF, industrial nations have implemented over 30 restrictive measures against Taiwan since 1976; and Korea has been affected by over 70 such actions since the early 1970s (Nowzad, 1978: 108 & 110).

This changing political environment makes some parts of the success formula more important than ever. ADCs must continue to recognize the political basis of trade and to emphasize long-term gains. They must also bargain for as much ambiguity as possible, and they should

---

[21] Susan Strange has stressed the importance of control over markets as a source of power. See "What is Economic Power, and Who Has It?" *International Journal,* 30-2, Spring, 1975, pp. 207-224.

continue to seek to capture scarcity rents. Their diplomats will need, even more than in the past, to lobby effectively with various branches of the United States Government while maintaining a low public profile to avoid politicized confrontations. The search for loopholes must go on.

The increased economic capabilities of the ADCs will create liabilities as well as assets for them in the 1980s. On the negative side, the magnitude of ADC exports, especially to the United States, ensures that increasingly they will be targets of political attack in the importing countries. Between 1963 and 1976, the share of world exports in manufactured goods held by Korea, Taiwan and Hong Kong tripled from 1.35 percent to 4.1 percent, and in selected sectors such as footwear, their market shares are much greater (OECD, 1979: 19). In 1977, Taiwan and Korea alone accounted for 61.2 percent of all shoe imports into the U.S., close to 30 percent of the entire American footwear supply.[22] The size and concentration of ADC exports will make it increasingly difficult for countries such as Korea and Taiwan to cheat on agreements in the 1980s without facing retaliation.

Yet the increasing size and sophistication of the ADC economies will also confer advantages that can be exploited with a bilateral, long-term-oriented, loophole-seeking strategy. With a diversified export base, loopholes can be exploited more quickly. And even though agreements necessarily become more complex and comprehensive, loopholes are always likely to exist. Thus a bilateral strategy continues to offer the promise of gains, although some of the political obstacles will probably become more severe during the next decade.

Yet to say that bilateral strategies need not be abandoned is not to imply that new attempts at multilateral action are unnecessary. It is quite conceivable that the ADCs could combine bilateralism and multilateralism to improve their situation further, or to resist deterioration as a result of political changes. Therefore, multilateral options for the ADCs should be considered.

---

[22] U.S. Department of Commerce, *op. cit.*

IV. Prospects for Multilateral Cooperation

Multilateral cooperation could, under proper conditions, contribute greatly to the effectiveness of ADC international economic strategies. At the most ambitious level, one can imagine a common market for Asia, in which trade within the region would expand, producers in relatively small countries could produce more efficiently for a wider market, and progressive harmonization of national policies would take place. Cooperation could also be more limited, being restricted, for instance, to cooperation in bargaining with large importers such as the United States and the European Community. This more limited cooperation could take several forms: a formal exporters' organization, an organization including both importers and exporters, or implicit collaboration among producers, or between exporting countries and some elements in the importing states. Both the more and the less ambitious forms of cooperation will be considered.

1. A Common Market in Asia?

Students of regional integration in general agree that certain preconditions are necessary for the formation of effective regional organizations such as the European Common Market. These preconditions are conveniently divided into two categories: structural conditions, and perceptual conditions (Keohane & Nye, 1975: 379-382). Structurally, it seems clear that three conditions must be met for regional integration schemes to have a good chance: governmental elites must hold complementary values; governments must be adaptable, that is, capable of responding effectively to new demands; and societies must be pluralistic, with participation by a number of modern association groups. Perceptually, the major conditions seem to be: that elites must perceive that integration will have substantial benefits and that these benefits will be distributed equitably; regional cooperation must be seen as a cogent response to the external situation; and the initial costs of integration must appear low, or at least exportable to others outside the scheme.

It seems clear that the Pacific Basin region as a whole does not meet the structural conditions for integration. The diversity of ideologies, cultural orientations, and political regimes is much too great. Even if one excluded the   countries of Indochina, the People's

Republic of China, and Taiwan, the diversity of Pacific Basin members is much greater than that of any successful or even partially successful integration scheme.[23] It is not surprising, therefore, that within the Pacific Basin, the greatest progress in multilateral political and economic collaboration has been made in ASEAN, which includes only five countries, Indonesia, the Philippines, Thailand, Malaysia and Singapore, which are much more similar economically, culturally, and politically to each other than to most other Pacific Basin countries. ASEAN, furthermore, had a special advantage at the time of its formation: it was seen by regional leaders as a cogent response to a threatening external situation.[24] Thus it had an initial political impetus. Despite this, its accomplishments have been modest.

In light of these conditions, it is not surprising that Asian intergovernmental cooperation has largely taken place on a micro-regional basis. As James N. Schubert points out, "of thirteen Asian intergovernmental organizations formed (in 1967-75), six are exclusively Southeast Asian in membership, four are Southeast Asian with one or two other Asian members, one is Southeast Asian-Western, one is East-Southeast Asian, and one is South Asian." (Schubert, 1978: 455). Specific and fragmented functionalist approaches to regional cooperation in Asia have proven much more successful than grand schemes in the past, and there seems little reason to expect this to change in the 1980s. It would be very surprising if an Asian common market developed in the course of this century.

2. Cooperation for Trade Bargaining

Politically, it is easier for states with common interests to collaborate on particular issues than for them to establish a comprehensive regional agreement. The OPEC states, for instance, would be unable to meet the basic conditions for regional integration, yet they are able to maintain a rather loose quasi-cartel arrangement in oil in a highly favorable political and economic environment. Even if a common

---

[23] Apart from Europe, the Central American Common Market and the Andean Group have probably been the most successful attempts, although both have had serious and sometimes debilitating problems. Various integration schemes in Africa have had at most modest success. But none of these groupings is nearly as diverse as the Pacific Basin taken as a whole.

[24] Saw Swee-Hock and N.L. Sirisena, "Economic Framework of ASEAN Countries," Saw Swee-Hock and Lee Soo Ann (ed.), *Economic Problems and Prospects in ASEAN Countries,* Singapore: Applied Research Corporation, 1977, pp. 1-27.

market arrangement is infeasible in Asia, more limited cooperation could be practical.

The OPEC model of a formal exporters' organization is clearly not sensible for the ADCs of the Pacific Basin. They need to secure access to the markets of developed countries, more than the developed countries need their goods. Substitutes could always be found for ADC exports, at slightly higher cost and with some relatively mild inconvenience. Thus the first and most basic condition for an OPEC-type cartel is not met.

A more realistic alternative would seem to be a regional arrangement involving both advanced industrialized countries and developing countries, perhaps institutionalized in an Organization for Pacific Trade and Development. This proposal has been discussed in various Pacific Trade and Development conferences since 1968, and therefore deserves some comment here, in the light of the analysis of bilateral strategies of ADCs.[25]

From a political standpoint, the value of an OPTAD would crucially depend on how it was structured, and the degree to which an institutionalized organization, with formal rules, was sought. It would be unwise to develop OPTAD as a formally structured, highly institutionalized entity. Such an organization would increase the salience of ADC-U.S. trade relations, and reduce flexibility by introducing more rules. Even if the United States were to agree to such a highly institutionalized OPTAD, the rules that the U.S. would agree to in the 1980s would be very different from the liberal GATT rules of the 1940s and 1950s. Indeed, the very magnitude of the undertaking, and the possibility that permanent or quasi-permanent loopholes for huge imports to the U.S. could be established, would make the United States very conservative in making agreements. The ADCs have an interest in keeping trade low-key, minimizing the significance of any

---

[25] Peter Drysdale, "An Organization for Pacific Trade, Aid, and Development: Regional Arrangements and the Resource Trade," Lawrence B. Krause and Hugh Patrick (eds.), *Mineral Resources in the Pacific Area,* Proceedings of the Ninth Pacific Trade and Development Conference, Federal Reserve Bank of San Francisco, 1978; Peter A. Drysdale and Hugh Patrick, "Evaluation of a Proposed Asian-Pacific Regional Economic Organization," *An Asian-Pacific Regional Economic Organization: An Exploratory Concept Paper,* Committee Print, prepared by the Congressional Research Service, Library of Congress, for the Senate Committee on Foreign Relations, 96th Congress, first session, GPO, 1979; Lawrence B. Krause and Sueo Sekiguchi (ed.), *Economic Interaction in the Pacific Basin,* Washington: Brookings Institution, 1980, pp. 259-262.

particular agreement, maintaining flexibility, and trying to keep the
United States Government from adopting a coherent and comprehensive long-term trade policy. Since under present international and
domestic conditions, any long-run U.S. trade policy would most likely
be protectionist, none of the ADC objectives would be well-served by
a new, highly salient, Pacific Basin trade organization.

International organizations are not essentially persuasive entities.
They are important insofar as they affect the political processes of
intergovernmental relation, and they should be analyzed realistically
in this light. The impact of international organizations on national
policymaking processes takes place largely through their effect on
international negotiations among diplomats or between bureaucracies.
Some organizations facilitate cooperation by promoting transgovernmental ties among bureaucrats, out of the glare of publicity.[26] Others,
such as some UN-affiliated organizations, often accentuate conflict
by publicizing controversy and adopting what appear to people in
certain influential countries to be absurd or biased positions. A
highly institutionalized OPTAD would be of little positive value, and
could even worsen the existing situation by making issues more
subject to political controversy and by making rules more rigid.

Rejecting formal institutionalized arrangements does not, however,
imply that an informal, low-profile OPTAD would be undesirable.
There is a good deal to be said for informal exchanges of information, both among private citizens and among government officials.
Multilateral contacts among bureaucrats on specific issues of mutual
interest can be extremely valuable. Some of the most significant
attempts to bring cohesion and good sense to international relations
occur through relatively informal contacts, either loosely within the
framework of an international organization or outside of one entirely.
Thus the principal difficulty with plans for OPTAD is not the idea
that multilateral discussions of common problems should be
encouraged, but the implication in some formulations that these discussions should take place within a formally constituted organization.

From the point of view of the advanced developing countries, there
is a good deal to be said for collusion among themselves. This
cooperation, however, should also be implicit, rather than formalized

---

[26] For a positive assessment of the International Energy Agency along these lines, see
Robert O. Keohane, "The International Energy Agency: State Influence and Transgovernmental Politics," *International Organization,* 32-4, Autumn, 1978, pp. 929-951.

in an organization that could become a target for criticism as an attempted cartel. ADCs should quietly seek to exchange information and even to agree on minimum bargaining positions, thus making it less likely that the United States could use a favorable agreement with one ADC to bring the others to terms. Information is crucial to bargaining success. From an information point of view, ADCs already have an advantage deriving from the greater coherence of their governmental structures, and the greater relative attention that they pay to U.S.-ADC trade issues. Their liabilities, however, derive from the fact that they are separate from and compete with, one another. To some extent, compensation for these liabilities could be found in informal cooperation and information exchange.

Throughout the late 60's and 70's, Taiwan, Korea, Hong Kong, and Japan have generally benefited from limited exchanges of information. Sino-Korean Cooperation Conferences, for example, have provided forums to discuss trade strategies and to coordinate bargaining positions. During the 1971 textile crisis, this type of cooperation helped to reduce some of the uncertainty associated with compromising with the United States. Similarly, Taiwan and Korea benefited from their communications in the early stages of the negotiations over footwear in 1977. Informal cooperation allowed these ADCs to establish a tough minimum bargaining stance for their confrontations with the United States. Although the ultimate agreement is always based on individual national needs, multilateral coordination is advantageous if it can provide a baseline on which bilateral agreements can be built.

Informal patterns of collusion among the ADCs might, in some cases, be extended to American negotiators, or elements within the U.S. policy, that could be brought into transgovernmental and transnational coalitions on a wider basis. ADCs that quietly worked together could be more effective in working with potential coalition partners within the United States, since these actors could benefit from knowing what the positions of all ADCs would be, rather than being linked only with one or two. In 1971, for instance, U.S. Ambassador-at-large David Kennedy encouraged cooperative strategies among the textile exporters. Although Kennedy's principal objective was to get an agreement, he was sympathetic to ADC interests; he also wanted to help the ADCs avoid the confrontation that ultimately occurred. Kennedy reasoned that each state might gain confidence in itself and the United States as well as show a willingness to compromise if it shared information with its competitors.[27]

Thus informal patterns of transnational and transgovernmental bargaining can be more effective than institutionalized organizations. The latter may carry with them the comforting illusion of rules on which participants can count: but rules in world politics are often broken. Strong working relationships with other producers, and with sympathetic elements in the United States, are more valuable for the ADCs than formal rules, even if those rules were favorable to ADC objectives. A close knowledge of importing countries' political processes, and the establishment of many points of access, are the most important prerequisites to reducing uncertainty and providing a basis upon which ADCs can plan effective long-run strategies. The advantages of ADCs lie precisely in their abilities to foresee and adapt to change. No strategy should be followed that fosters the illusion that change may be unnecessary.

Here the example of Japanese errors in the late 1960s, on the textile issue, becomes relevant once again. Between 1969 and 1971, Japan attempted to defend an established position in textiles, and resisted opening up its own market, revaluing its currency, or otherwise responding to the changed situation where it was no longer a small, poor state but a major trading power. Japan took refuge behind legalisms and static formalisms and suffered the Nixon Shock as a result. This was particularly ironic and senseless because the Japanese were bargaining for an industry with little substantive future, as Japanese textile producers were losing their competitiveness in the late 1960s and early 1970s. Within a few years, Japan could not even come close to filling its hard-bargained quotas. A major danger of forming an OPTAD, even if initially it was favorable to the ADCs, is that it would become a legalistic barrier behind which they would be tempted to hide, resisting change until it was too late.

V. Conclusion

One cannot be overly sanguine about the prospects for Pacific Basin ADCs in the 1980s. If the consequences of the oil price increases are as severe as pessimists expect, the economies of Hong Kong, Korea, Taiwan, and Singapore may be hurt very badly and

---

[27] Interview with David Kennedy, cited footnote 12.

there may be little that their governments can do about it. The decline of American political and economic power is bad for the ADCs in a variety of ways. It makes them more vulnerable to political-military threats, and also jeopardizes the American leadership orientation that kept U.S. markets relatively open to ADC products. Furthermore, it has also created the conditions for other disruptions in the world political economy, including the oil crisis, which have severe effects on the ADCs.

The focus in this paper has not been so much on world political and economic conditions that affect the ADCs, but on ADC strategies themselves. Here the continued appropriateness of the basic lines of ADC strategy can be observed. The focus on long-term gains, coupled with the search for loopholes, must continue to be the basis for ADC policy. The principal orientation of policy should continue to be bilateral, although this approach could be supplemented with implicit, low-profile cooperation among the ADCs, and with sympathetic elements within the importing countries. In a perilous world, no strategy followed by small and weak countries can guarantee success. Yet as far as can be seen, Pacific Basin ADCs have fashioned a strategy that takes advantage of their strengths and minimizes the consequences of weakness. They should continue to follow it into the 1980s.

REFERENCES

Bergsten, C. Fred, "On the Non-Equivalence of Import Quotas and Voluntary Export Restraints," C.F. Bergsten (ed.), *Toward A New World Trade Policy: The Maidenhead Papers,* New York: Health & Co., 1975.

Blackhurst, Richard, Nicholas Marian, and Jan Tumlir, *Adjustment, Trade and Growth in Developed and Developing Countries,* GATT Studies in International Trade, No. 6, Geneva: GATT, 1978.

Destler, I.M., H. Fukui, and H. Sato, *The Textile Wrangle: Conflict in Japanese-American Relations, 1969-71,* Ithaca: Cornell University Press, 1979.

Drysdale, Peter, "An Organization for Pacific Trade, Aid, and Development: Regional Arrangements and the Resource Trade,"

Lawrence B. Krause, and Hugh Patrick (eds.), *Mineral Resources in the Pacific Area, Proceedings of the Ninth Pacific Trade and Development Conference,* Federal Reserve Bank of San Francisco, 1978.

Heuser, Heinrich, *Control of International Trade,* Philadelphia: Blackstone's Sons & Co., 1939.

Hirschman, Albert O., *National Power and the Structure of Foreign Trade,* Berkeley: University of California Press, 1945.

Hunsberger, Warren, *The United States and Japan in World Trade,* New York: Harper & Row, 1964.

Keohane, Robert. O., and Joseph S. Nye, "Transgovernmental Relations and International Organizations," *World Politics,* October 1974.

Keohane, Robert O., and Joseph S. Nye, Jr. "International Interdependence and Integration," Nelson W. Polsby, and Fred I. Greenstein (eds.), *Handbook of Political Science, Volume 8, International Politics,* Reading, Mass: Adison-Wesley, 1975.

Keohane, Robert O., "The International Energy Agency: State Influence and Transgovernment Politics," *International Organization,* Autumn, 1978.

Krause, Lawrence B., and Sueo Sekiguchi, (ed.), *Economic Interaction in Pacific Basin,* Washington, D.C.: Brookings Institution 1980.

Krasner, Stephen, "The Tokyo Round: Particularistic Interests and Prospects for Stability in the Global Trading System," *International Studies Quarterly,* December 1979.

Lynch, John, *Toward an Orderly Market,* Tokyo: Sophia University Press, 1967.

Morgan Guaranty Trust Company, *World Financial Markets,* March 1980.

Nowzad, Babram, *The Rise of Protectionalism,* Washington D.C.: International Monetary Fund, 1978.

OECD, *The Impact of the Newly Industrializing Countries on Production and Trade in Manufactures,* Paris: OECD, 1979.

Patterson, Garner, *Discrimination in International Trade: The Policy Issues, 1945-65,* Princeton: Princeton University Press, 1966.

Schubert, James N., "Toward a Working Peace System in Asia: Organizational Growth and State Participation in Asian Regionalism," *International Organization,* Spring, 1978.

Swee-Hock, Saw, and N.L. Sirisena, "Economic Framework of

ASEAN Countries,'' Saw Swee-Hock and Lee Soo Ann (ed.), *Economic Problems and Prospects in ASEAN Countries,* Singapore: Applied Research Corporation, 1977.

Strange, Susan, "What is Economic Power, and Who Has It," *International Journal,* Spring, 1975.

United Nations Conference on Trade and Development, *Growing Protectionalism and the Standstill on Trade Barriers against Imports from Developing Countries,* TD/B/C., 2/194, 1978.

U.S. Department of Commerce, *Footwear Industry Revitalization Program:* First Annual Progress Report, 1978.

United States International Trade Commission, *The History and Current Status of the Multifiber Arrangement,* USITC Publication 859, January 1978.

• COMMENT _____

Seung-Joo Han, *Korea University*

The Keohane-Yoffie paper presents a cogent and persuasive argument concerning the strategy of the ADCs against protectionism in the United States. It is a thoughtful and provocative paper.

It assumes that protectionism is a political reality that is not necessarily rational or desirable, but which cannot be avoided, much less ignored. It also observes that the ADCs are in a very weak position vis-a-vis the United States inasmuch as their need to export their goods is far greater and more urgent than is the U.S. need to import them. However, according to the paper, the ADCs during the past decade or so have done quite well in minimizing the losses that could have resulted from rising protectionism in the U.S. Learning from the past mistakes of their own and Japan, they have generally succeeded in making the most of what is an undesirable situation.

"Successful" ADC response to U.S. protectionism has consisted in part in comfort in the thought that short-term export loss is not really bad in the long run because it forces the exporting country to restructure its industry and upgrade its merchandise. The ADCs have used whatever bargaining chips they can muster including security relations and trade concessions. They have circumvented restrictions by taking advantage of loopholes, ambiguities, interpretive flexibilities, and have even cheated. In most cases, each ADC has dealt with the problem in a bilateral context, in a low-key and inconspicuous way, and in an acquiescent and passive manner. The paper then argues that, since methods such as the ADCs employed have worked, there is no need to risk a new approach such as creating an OPTAD. In fact, according to the paper, multilaterialization and institutionalization of efforts on behalf of open trade will be counterproductive; it will only result in mobilizing and solidifying the protectionist forces in the United States and making it more difficult for the ADCs to circumvent trade restrictions.

The paper has done a superb job of conceptualizing the ways in which the ADCs have responded to export restrictions imposed upon them by the United States. However, there are some questions about a few assumptions that the paper makes in presenting its case. First, it assumes that protectionist pressures by certain interest groups in the United States are so overwhelmingly powerful that the U.S. government has no choice but to cater to them. This seems an exaggerated picture. As some earlier papers presented in this conference, particularly by Baldwin, have indicated, the government has a considerable leeway in protecting the "public interest" against what is obviously a sectional interest even within a highly pluralistic political setting such as the United States. One cannot argue that this "political reality" is inevitable and that nothing can effectively alter it. In fact, a regional institution such as the proposed OPTAD could be extremely useful for the U.S. government in its effort, if it chooses, to resist sectional protectionist pressures. The same thing can be said about not only other developed countries but also in connection with the ADCs and LDCs which in their own obvious and extensive ways practice various measures of protectionism. OPTAD, for example, would provide advocates of open economic relations throughout the region with the ammunition needed in arguing for liberalization and against protection in their respective countries.

Second, the paper makes the double assumption that the ADCs have come through the U.S. protectionist measures of the 1970s relatively unscathed and that the nature of threats to open trade will remain more or less the same in the years to come. The validity of these assumptions can be discussed much more thoroughly and effectively by an economist. On the whole, however, one can argue that international trade in general and trade by the ADCs in particular have been quite adversely affected by the protectionist trends in the developed countries and that the 1980s will present a greater and more difficult challenge to the exporting countries due to a number of factors such as economic stagnation in the developed countries, resource problems, competition from the second generation ADCs, and competition among the ADCs themselves. The OPTAD proposal is being made in response to the difficulties of the past and in anticipation of new problems in the future.

A third assumption of the paper is that the merit of the OPTAD proposal very much depends upon its presumed ability to deal with the trade question. Certainly, trade is the most important issue in the whole scheme. But OPTAD is more than a free trade plan. Furthermore, the trade issue itself is not unrelated to other important issues such as investment, finance, and industrial restructuring. At present, few people contemplate the possibility of coping with the trade problem by forming a regional common market. However, multilateral efforts can be made, for example, in establishing a trade fund which can serve as a source of long-term finance for the LDCs and ADCs as well as a means for financing short- and medium-term foreign exchange shortfalls. Attempts can slso be made to achieve coordination between and among the DCs, LDCs and ADCs in promoting and regulating foreign direct investment. These activities, furthermore, need not foreclose the possibilities of bilateral arrangements that apparently have been quite effective in safeguarding, at least to some extent, the exporter interests.

Finally, the paper seems to be saying that, since there is no chance that the United States, particularly with its protectionist forces, will accept an arrangement such as OPTAD, there is no need for trying to bring it about. Such an attitude may indeed end up as a self-fulfilling prophesy. A regional cooperation scheme seems to be a concept worth pursuing. Proponents of the OPTAD approach should be thankful that this paper has raised questions which they should be prepared to answer.

Hisao Kanamori,   *Japan Economic Research Center*

It is appropriate that Yoffie and Keohane emphasize that advanced developing countries (ADCs) should recognize the political base of international trade and attach importance to long-term interest. It is also persuasive that they point out that there are many paths for ADCs to evade the protectionism of advanced nations through bilateral strategies.

However, on the other hand, it is also a fact that there are various limits to a solution of the problem through such bilateral strategies. As the authors point out, these limits are that there is a difference in power between a developed country and an ADC with the result that the latter may be compelled to accept an arbitrary decision made by the former, that limitless concessions or compromises may bring humiliation upon the people, that a solution of the issue through bilateral strategies is in danger of conflicting with the interests of other ADCs, and that a solution such as searching for loopholes will affect the reputation of ADCs.

It may be true that the new protectionism which developed countries adopt against ADCs would actually take the form of voluntary export restraints on the part of ADCs or conclusion of orderly marketing agreements, and these may be required in certain cases in order to provide time for industrially advanced countries to adjust their industries to a changed situation. It is, however, not advisable for ADCs to make limitless concessions or to compromise, because they are apt to become permanent systems instead of short-term adjustment policies as is evidenced by the cases of steel products and textiles.

The authors are negative concerning OPTAD and it is true that there have been examples of multilateral organizations sometimes making the solution of issues more difficult. However, international organizations such as the OECD have gone a long way toward coordinating economic policies among the nations of the world. It is foolhardy to place great hopes on these multilateral organizations, but it cannot be denied that they can play some role in the solution of international economic issues. A solution of an actual international issue may require bilateral negotiations or informal cooperation between the countries which are specifically involved in the issues. However, it seems more desirable to prepare an international forum to discuss the means of solution in advance than to press ADCs arbitrarily for voluntary export restraints or conclusion of orderly marketing agreements.

GENERAL DISCUSSION

There is an alternative way to explain the ADCs successful expansion of their exports in the U.S. market other than simply saying that benevolent U.S. bureaucrats knowingly or unknowingly helped to create loopholes in U.S. protectionist measures. It is rather that there are rewards in finding ways to get around protectionist measures, and hence resources are spent to expand imports from ADCs. Such market responses cost resources but still reduce the possible impact of full implementation of protectionist measures. Therefore, instead of suggesting sabotage by bureaucrats, one may have to emphasize the power of market forces and the limit of what the government can do. Because of market forces the protectionist efforts of the U.S. government may have been, to a significant extent, futile.

In the past, perhaps the ADCs gained by playing the game. However, if the ADCs keep yielding to the protectionist measures of the U.S. and other advanced countries instead of resisting them from the beginning, not only by undertaking legal battles in the U.S. but also by going to GATT, the ADCs may have to pay a higher price than they need to pay. That is, an individualistic approach may inflict a more harmful effect in the long run. Instead of being satisfied by obtaining rent created by voluntary quota restrictions, ADCs may have to fight more vigorously to mobilize world opinion.

The author suggests that the quantitative import restrictions were beneficial to the ADCs because they forced ADCs to upgrade the quality of their exports. However, there is no reason why such upgrading cannot be done through the free market system.

In the future, the loopholes in protectionist measures may be completely closed. Then ADCs may achieve better bargaining power through collective action on a regional scale. Due to the increasing visibility of ADCs, the U.S. may become much tougher in its implementation of protectionist policies. Therefore the ADCs may have to seek better bargaining power and alternative strategic approaches through a regional organization like OPTAD to make it more difficult for the developed countries to justify their protectionist policies.

One can still be pessimistic as to whether another new international organization would make much difference. Due to the failure of leadership in advanced countries to resist domestic political challenge, it may become more difficult to circumvent political decisions on protection in the 1980s. In any case, a loose OECD type of organization which emphasizes more frequent contact may be more productive than an EC type of organization which emphasizes tight legalistic arrangements. UNCTAD seems to have been too large in size to accommodate various internal dissensions. If ADCs want to avoid being the simple taker of the protectionist policies of advanced countries, they have to take advantage of collective action.

SUMMARY AND COMMUNIQUE

SUMMARY OF THE ELEVENTH PACIFIC TRADE AND DEVELOPMENT CONFERENCE ON TRADE AND GROWTH OF THE ADVANCED DEVELOPING COUNTRIES

Lawrence B. Krause*

I. Introduction

The Eleventh Pacific Trade and Development Conference gave special attention to certain Advanced Developing Countries—Korea, Taiwan, Hong Kong, Singapore—and their economic relations with other countries in the Pacific Basin. These countries are also often referred to as Asian newly industrializing countries or ADCs. Quite early in the conference it became clear that two dimensions of policy were being discussed, namely optimality of trade and deviations therefrom and the degree of government interference in or direction of economies. These two dimensions are pictured in Diagram 1. The horizontal axis represents trade conditions; either free trade or deviations. It was noted that a deviation could either be trade-reducing and therefore to the left of the optimal point, if intensity of trade is measured on a horizontal scale—subsequently called a left-wing deviation—or trade-expanding so that trade is increased beyond the optimum point and called a right-wing deviation. A left-wing deviation will occur if either imports or exports are restricted by trade policies such as tariffs or quotas on imports or prohibitions on exports. A right-wing deviation will occur if either exports or imports are increased through such measures as excessive export subsidies or

*Senior Fellow, The Brookings Institution, U.S.A.

negative tariffs on imports. The second dimension represented on the vertical axis is the degree of government interference in the economy; either a policy of interventionism or laissez-faire.

II. Characterizing the Asian ADCs

It is quite clear where Hong Kong fits on Diagram 1. As indicated in the paper by T.B. Lin and Yin-Ping Ho, Hong Kong always followed a free trade policy and the government kept its direction of the economy to a bare minimum. Thus Hong Kong is a free trade/laissez-faire country.

Singapore has also adopted a free trade policy, but as the paper by K.P. Wong makes clear, government direction of the economy has been very extensive. Indeed, Singapore may have had the most intrusive government of any of the Asian ADCs and thus is classified as a free trade/interventionist country.

Korea is clearly a deviationist/interventionist country but it is unclear whether it is more trade-restraining through import restrictions, and therefore left wing, or more trade-expanding through export promotion, which would be characterized as right wing. The paper by Chong H. Nam contains measures of trade distortions. However, the net balance is indeterminant. Some participants felt that Korea was a right-wing deviationist based on the observation of very high export and import to GNP ratios and the particularly rapid rise of those ratios in recent years. Other participants noted that economic conditions both in Korea and in world markets were very favorable to the expansion of Korea's trade and thus high trade ratios did not necessarily signify a right-wing deviation.

Taiwan is another deviationist/interventionist country as described in the paper by K.S. Liang and C.H. Liang. Measurements of trade promotion indicate that Taiwan's trade is less distorted than that of Korea and that Taiwan seems to be moving toward a free trade position faster than Korea.

III. Why Is Export Promotion Growth-Promoting?

The first major question addressed at the conference was that of why export promotion is growth-promoting. This was the principal focus of the paper by A.O. Krueger. Three hypotheses were advanced. First, it was recognized that correcting or offsetting the left-wing distortions that often became extreme under a previously followed import-substitution strategy of development when a new strategy of export promotion was adopted yielded once-and-for-all static efficiency gains which would raise growth rates during the period while the gains are being captured. If this was all that was involved, the faster growth rates would soon recede. However, faster growth has persisted in countries following export promotion strategies so something more is believed to be involved.

A second hypothesis is that dynamic advantages are particularly attached to export promotion, some of which are measurable and others not. One important advantage comes from economies of scale arising from producing for world markets rather than narrow domestic markets. However, studies of industrial organization of both plant and firm economies of scale are not suggestive of extremely large efficiency gains. Other measurable dynamic advantages include improvements in technology provided by domestic and foreign firms and more and better training of workers. Other important advantages are believed to be improvement in entrepreneurial skills arising from having to compete in world markets, large profit expectations from the seemingly unbounded world market and extensive inter-industry linkages that radiate from export industries. These non-measurable gains may be peculiarly related to manufacturing, although the tie to manufacturing should not be exaggerated.

The third possible source of faster growth could come from the improvement of economic policies in general that usually accompany the adoption of an export-promotion strategy. This may be particularly important in Latin America. Thus governments stop trying to fight the market as they did with import-substitution strategies, but work with the market which yields continuing benefits. Better macroeconomic management would follow and yield faster growth. The three hypotheses are reinforcing and not mutually exclusive. However, the attribution of importance to particular factors and the policies that bring them about is necessary, but will require more research. Without such knowledge it will be impossible to attribute to its proper cause the reason for success or failure of an export-promotion strategy as it occurs in the future.

IV. Must Countries Follow the Japanese Model of Development?

The second major question examined was whether countries need to follow a Japanese model in order to have continued success in industrialization. There is a certain amount of ambiguity about what is meant by the Japanese model, but it clearly involves a significant amount of government planning and government guidance to the private sector as development advances, with increasingly more complex technologies being mastered.

The Lin and Ho paper made clear that Hong Kong has not followed the Japanese model in the past, but the authors suggest that more government direction to the economy may be needed in the future. They are concerned that Hong Kong may become too unstable because of world economic instability, because of competition from even newer advanced developing countries, (ADCs) and because of growing protectionism in developed countries. They favorably commented on the work of an investigative committee and its 1979 report that contained proposals for the diversification of the Hong Kong economy in both production and market structure, utilizing government action as a way of minimizing risk.

Portfolio theory does point to diversification as a way of handling risk, but the gains come from having a degree of independence among losses, as seen in co-variance matrixes. If, for instance, an economic slowdown affected all countries equally, it would not benefit a country to pay the cost of spreading its exports over a larger number of countries to avoid a cyclical slowdown.

It is instructive to review the recent economic history of Hong Kong. If the previously mentioned investigative committee had been convened ten years earlier and had somehow forecast that the decade of the 1970s would contain the oil shock, a significant slowdown of OECD countries, especially the United Kingdom, its most important customer in 1969, that Korea and Taiwan would become fierce competitors for labor-intensive manufactured products, and that protectionism in textiles, Hong Kong's most important export, would become worse and if the committee's analysis had suggested that in the absence of government action, Hong Kong would remain heavily dependent on selling textiles to Europe and North America, then surely they would have recommended that Hong Kong take steps to diversify its economy in 1970 and the recommendation would have been wrong in 1970 and may also be wrong for the 1980s. Hong Kong has continued to prosper despite adversity. One of the major factors in that success has been the ability of Hong Kong's entrepreneurs to adjust to new situations and sieze opportunities within existing industries and markets. Government direction may not rigidify the economy, but the risk is there and must be recognized as an offsetting cost of government interference.

The most important external factor influencing Hong Kong's economy in the 1980s is likely to be the emergence of Mainland China as an actor in Western markets. China will provide many opportunities and challenges for Hong Kong and it is unlikely that the government will foresee developments nor design appropriate actions better than Hong Kong's private entrepreneurs. Thus Hong Kong's strength may lie in its absence of government direction and regulation.

In the paper addressed to Latin America, Fernando Fajnzylber argues that strong government direction to advance industrialization is absolutely necessary. In particular he suggests that government must join with private interests to plan for and create the necessary conditions for self-sustaining industrial expansion, including exports of industrial products — called an internal nucleus of technological dynamization. This effort may require the development of domestic capital equipment producing industries and require the forging of a link between the advanced industrial sector and agriculture. He is doubtful that this will evolve under the alternative of free trade. He sees a need to control the operations of foreign transnational corporations within Latin America, possibly more severely than did Japan during its catch-up period. Whether governments would be better at devising and implementing a complex strategy to create a sophisticated industrial economy rather than an import-substitution program in Latin America in the past is highly doubtful. There are risks that the new strategy would degenerate into mere import-substitution of highly advanced equipment which would result in higher cost, inefficient industries. Some Latin American countries have now given up on the import-substitution approach and have endorsed export promotion as an alternative, with good results. Whether this strategy alone will be enough to assure self-sustained industrial growth is still uncertain.

The paper by Chong H. Nam on Korea suggests that a Japanese model was followed. However, he questioned whether Korea was wise to follow Japan so rapidly. In particular he criticized the degree to which heavy and chemical industries were stimulated at the expense of light industry. At a very minimum the shift in emphasis was probably excessive and the methods chosen too inefficient and arbitrary. Furthermore, Nam showed that Korea had been increasing its protection of agriculture in recent years, also following the Japanese example. The stressing of heavy and chemical industries primarily for home markets represents something of a reversion to import-substitution but it could be followed in turn by another round of export promotion when these industries become internationally competitive. Such a cycle of policies may even be quite effective in stimulating growth.

The paper by Toshio Watanabe on Korea-Japan trade which primarily was devoted to utilizing an imaginative empirical tool—interacting input-output analysis between pairs of countries—also touched on the question of the desirability of the Japanese model of development. He suggests that if Korea follows the Japanese model, it will develop a broad and less specialized industrial structure which in turn would lead to desirable horizontal trade between Korea and Japan between or within industries at the same level of industrial sophistication. The conference raised a number of questions concerning the normative part of the analysis in that horizontal trade does not appear to be inherently superior to vertical trade, but the empirical results were recognized as being of great interest.

The paper by Wong Kum-Poh indicates that Singapore is following a Japan-type model, but with major differences from Japan's actual economic history. Singapore, through its conscious policy of increasing low wages, is actually pushing labor-intensive manufacturing out of the country, while Japan permitted them to coexist. Also Singapore welcomes foreign direct investment for the purpose of transferring technology to it, bringing in capital and taking risks while Japan severely limited equity participation of foreign firms in its development.

The paper by the Liang team also indicated that Taiwan has been following a Japanese model. Indeed, Taiwan kept fairly close to the true spirit of the model by forcing domestic businesses to attain international competitiveness rather quickly. On the other hand,

Taiwan has been more liberal in permitting foreign firms to make direct investments in the country than did Japan.

In some of the discussion, the point was made that due to the required interdependencies of some large-scale investments, some government guidance to the private sector may be necessary and desirable to bring about the desired coordination of demand and supply. However, it was also suggested that the ADCs need not and should not follow Japan's example in protecting agriculture or mineral processing which might well be done better in raw material producing countries. Indeed, Japan at times seemed to want to be self-sufficient in every product they could produce.

V. Relation between a Strategy of Export Promotion and Income Distribution

Interest in income distribution at this conference arose in part because of expected linkages between income distribution and growth. As theory suggests, the distribution of income may influence growth through the rate of domestic saving since higher saving may arise from unequal income distribution. Also, unequal income distribution that occurs because of sharply different wages of workers due to skill differences may be a necessary market signaling device to direct educational resources where they are needed. Thus, increasing wage differentials may lead to faster growth through the process of correcting skill shortages.

However, the main concern over income distribution arose from its social, political, and equity implications. The link to growth may be indirect but important if an increasingly unequal distribution of income leads to social and political instability. The relationship between income distribution and social and political conditions may be quite complex, however, as implied by Japan's experience where rapid growth with growing income inequality was combined with political stability.

Wontack Hong addressed the question directly in his paper by examining the links between income distribution and export promotion. In Korea, export growth permitted an expansion of economic activity, a rise in employment and an increase in wages during the 1960s which led to more equal distribution of income as expected.

However, during the 1970s, income distribution deteriorated as measured by several indicators even as economic development proceeded. Because of the experience of Taiwan where export-led growth continued to improve income distribution in the 1970s, one can conclude that export expansion need not worsen income distribution.

Hong's principal explanation is that the particular instrument used for export promotion was responsible for the negative result in Korea. Exports were promoted through providing subsidized credit to firms that would export. The amount of credit provided was so substantial and the degree of the subsidy so great that it amounted to at least 8 percent of GNP. Since most of the subsidy was provided to a limited number of large firms, income distribution could become more unequal. This explanation is not fully satisfactory, however, since it is not clear who gave up the 8 percent of income that was transferred through the subsidy.

Three competing hypotheses were offered to explain developments in Korea. If Korea's emphasis on heavy and chemical industries during the 1970s was so significiant as to move Korea, on balance, back into an import-substitution strategy, then a part of the income distribution result is not surprising. From the experience of many countries, it appears that import-substitution is associated with a worsening of income distribution. Alternatively, it was noted that sharp increases in oil prices during the 1970s had an impact on different groups in society at different times. While there is no particular reason to expect a worsening of income distribution after all consequences of a rising relative energy price have worked themselves out, at any point in time that result may appear even though it will ultimately be reversed. Thus, it was argued that a finding that income distribution had worsened may be premature. A third explanation could be that the rise of inflation in Korea during the 1970s was responsible for the worsening of income distribution. This explanation may complement Hong's hypothesis if it can be shown that Korea's export-promotion strategy was the cause of the inflation. It seems clear that the issue cannot be settled with existing knowledge and will require more research.

VI. What Role Does Direct Foreign Investment Play in Export Promotion?

The conference addressed the question of what role foreign direct investment does have or should have in an export-promotion strategy, but clearly only scratched the surface of the issue. The point was made through citing the experience of a number of countries that Japanese foreign investment is highly desirable if a country wants to export to Japan. Indeed, the point was made that it may be a necessity in order to successfully work through the difficulties of the Japanese distribution system. Similarly, it was noted that Japanese trading companies have significant power to determine where raw materials are processed and thus have a strategic position which must be recognized.

It was noted that foreign direct investment in Mainland China will be particularly influential in determining the exports of manufactured products from that country. Links are being established between Hong Kong entrepreneurs and China which hold great promise for promoting exports. As was mentioned previously, Singapore also obtains access to world markets because of the significant investment of foreign enterprises.

A different link between direct investment and exports was examined in the paper by Kym Anderson and Ben Smith. They note that because of significant economies of scale in the exploitation of natural resources and the requirements of huge amounts of capital that is involved, new investments cannot be made economically attractive unless a secure market for most of the envisioned output is guaranteed. One way to bring that about would be to establish joint ownership of the resources including companies from countries that would utilize the output. By owning significant equity shares in the project, companies in importing countries could provide the assurance of a market needed to raise the required finance. Ownership ties also provide the assurance of supply desired by importing countries.

VII. Finance and Financial Institutions and Growth of ADCs

Another subject that requires greater in-depth attention than was provided by the conference is the role of finance and financial variables in the development of the ADCs. In the brief paper by Wong Kum-Poh directed to this question, it was noted that the public sector accounts for one-quarter to one-third of total gross domestic capital formation in Singapore and therefore government finances are a point of focus in the analysis. Government revenues were consistently greater than current expenditure, but insufficient to cover capital expenditures. The gap was financed by borrowing in the domestic market. Indeed, the government borrowed more than enough to cover its needs. The resulting government-induced shortfall in domestic financial markets was made good by private borrowing from abroad; that is, foreign borrowing was greater than required to cover deficits in the current account of the balance of payments. As a result, the monetary authority of Singapore accumulated foreign exchange reserves. Thus Singapore financed its development needs, maintained control over its money supply and prepared for foreign disturbances at the same time.

Singapore might have paid excessively to pre-borrow foreign capital, except that it also encouraged the creation of an offshore capital market. The locating of the Asian dollar market in Singapore permitted the country to tap it for its own needs at lesser cost. Many interesting lines of inquiry follow from the Wong analysis. Having an entrepot banking sector permits Singapore to earn service exports and create some lucrative jobs. This was also noted in the Ho and Lin paper on Hong Kong. The spread effects and linkages to other service activities suggest this could be an important activity for development, but it requires some investigation. Also the consequences of competition with other financial centers such as Hong Kong, Manila and even Tokyo and New York needs consideration.

Financial issues also briefly entered the analysis of Taiwan by the Liang team. They noted that operating firms in Taiwan went through a process of financial deepening as they developed. However, they did not tie the analysis to the evolution of financial institutions in the country. Clearly the function of financial intermediaries must be explored and linked to the development process.

In the paper on the balance of payments of Korea, Yung-Chul Park rejected the notion that financial variables were of great significance, that is, the monetary approach to the balance of payments would not help in the explanation of the link between export growth and the trade balance. However, it was noted that the current account and the capital account are determined simultaneously. Thus, monetary analysis can be a useful addition since it helps explain capital flows, although the major explanation may still come from a different analytical approach. Park did conclude that export growth did improve the balance of trade because it increased domestic saving and thus moderated domestic absorption in Korea. The enhancement of saving occurred through the increase of profit from export activities.

Finally, financial variables were discussed in relation to the choice of exchange rate behavior by Taiwan, but since the Taiwanese are still in a process of experimentation, little could be deduced as yet from the experience. From these various glimpses at the complex ties between finance and development, it would appear that the subject is worth an entire conference devoted to it alone.

VIII. Adjustment of Older Industrial Countries to the ADCs

The development of the ADCs and particularly their great success in exporting manufactured products to older industrial countries raise the question of how difficult an adjustment may be involved and how it may be accomplished. In the paper by Colin Bradford, the conclusion was reached that the dimensions of the problem have generally been exaggerated. This finding is based on the belief that those developing countries that are likely to be important in terms of world markets have already been identified rather than just being the first of many more to follow and that the process of their emergence has been one which depended more on internal political and public policy commitment, which occurs in relatively few countries at any given moment, than on the more generalized process of industrial spread. However, it was strongly suggested that the dynamic theory of comparative advantage would not support this rather comfortable conclusion for developed countries. In the absence of trade barriers, it is more likely that many more developing countries would be very competitive in many different industries in the future.

The paper on the United States by Robert Baldwin examined

adjustment in political economy terms since adjustment policy is seen as similar to a public good determined in a political market. The empirical analysis suffered from the absence of a structural model and thus it is difficult to interpret his statistical findings. A structural model of the United States needs to recognize that Congress is the source of protection in the U.S. Government since its members represent constituents rather than national interests, and commercial policy is also a tool of Congress in encroaching upon the President's discretion in foreign policy. Congress seeks political support from its constituents and the President needs the political support of Congress. Thus, when the President takes an action that affects constituents, it can only be interpreted as part of the political processes of Congress. Empirical investigation of protection is possible, but should not be confined to import barriers since the United States also restricts exports. Indeed, the United States restricts all exports to some countries, some commodities to all countries, and selected products to selected countries. These export restraints must also be seen in political terms since they must harm the economic interests of the United States and can be investigated within a structural model of Congress.

Japan has been reasonably successful in avoiding formal protectionist pressures and has promoted positive adjustment, as described in the paper by Ippei Yamazawa, although gaining access for foreign manufactured goods into Japan without the help of a Japanese trading company is still very difficult. The reason that Japan has been more successful in avoiding formal barriers than the United States in this regard may well be related to Japan's shortage of natural resources and the fact that informal barriers effectively protect Japanese domestic producers. Most Japanese constituents recognize that Japan is too dependent on other countries for their necessities of life to practice blatant protectionism, while many Americans fantasize that the Unied States could be self-sufficient with little loss of income. However, even in Japan when constituent pressure has been significant in demanding protection as in agriculture, formal protectionist policies have been followed.

The response of the ADCs to protectionist demands by the United States was examined in the paper by David Yoffie and Robert Keohane. They recognized that so long as the ADCs were prepared to provide the United States with a political victory so that constituent pressures would be appeased, the ADCs in return could obtain economic advantages including good access to the U.S. market. The paper also raised doubts as to whether the ADCs would benefit from efforts to create a new intergovernmental institution in the Pacific, but the conclusion is doubtful since it was addressed to a narrowly defined institution to negotiate trade problems rather than a broadly conceived institution to promote cooperation in many fields that would involve both private and government participants which is what is being discussed in the Pacific.

IX. Natural Resource Trade with the ADCs

The conference examined the question of how the absence of natural resources would affect the trade and development of the ADCs. It is clear that the shortage of land severely limits Hong Kong and Singapore in developing land-using industries such as heavy and chemical industries that are being promoted in Korea and Taiwan. Furthermore, the shortage of natural resources in all of these countries should make them importers of natural resource goods.

The trade relations between the ADCs and the resource-rich advanced countries were examined in the paper by Kym Anderson and Ben Smith. They developed the theory of trade specialization and examined trade data which they found consistent with the theory. The same theory should have applied to Japan at a somewhat earlier stage, but the trade pattern did not develop as fully as expected because of Japan's protection of agriculture and effective protection of processing of mineral ores. Such mistakes should be avoided by the ADCs.

The theory should also apply to the trade between the ADCs and resource-rich developing countries. In the paper by Ernesto Tironi, trade relations between Latin American and the Asian ADCs were examined and it was discovered that little trade has taken place. Tironi suggested a number of reasons for this including transportation costs which make Latin American resource goods too expensive in Asia, the lack of historical ties, and the absence of effective export promotion policies by the Latin Americans. Another reason can be found in the Watanabe paper analyzing trade relations between Korea and Japan. It may well be that Korea has been importing natural resources in the form of semi-processed manufactured goods from

Japan. While this trade pattern may not continue to make economic
sense given changing relative costs of energy since processing natural
resources is energy-intensive and expensive in Japan, the trade may
continue until other countries compete more effectively with Japanese
exports. Thus, there may be more room for Latin American exports
to the ADCs in the future if other barriers do not distort the pattern
of trade.

X. Relation between the 10th and 11th PAFTAD Conferences

In conclusion, it is interesting to relate this conference to the Sydney
Conference in 1979 on ASEAN countries. As seen in the top part of
Table 1, the rates of growth of GNP and of international trade for
the Asian ADCs have been very high. Indeed, it is just these measures,
including exports of manufactured goods to industrial countries,
which brought forth the name advanced developing countries.

However, it is also true, as has been stated at this conference, that
the ADCs cannot ignore the ASEAN countries. Obviously, the point is
superfluous for Singapore since it is part of ASEAN. When the
bottom half of Table 1 is examined, it appears that the economic
growth of the ASEAN countries and the ADCs are quite similar. Of
course, ASEAN export growth and import growth have been less than
the Asian ADCs', but this comparison is probably misleading. Since
the import content of exports is probably much less for ASEAN than
the ADCs, it may well be that the growth of domestic value added
being exported is not too dissimilar. A measure of net export growth
would be needed to test this proposition and would be of considerable
interest.

Because of the growth of both the ADCs and ASEAN, an interdependent relationship including trade of goods and services has
begun to develop between them. This is in addition to the growing
interdependence of all of them and the advanced countries in the
region. Thus the Pacific Basin has maintained its dynamism despite
world difficulties and can look forward to more of the same.

Diagram I.

	Free Trade	Deviation[a]	
Interventionism	Singapore	Taiwan	Korea
Laissez-faire	Hong Kong		

Note: [a] left-wing deviation—trade reducing
right-wing deviation—trade creating

Table 1. Average Annual Growth Rates of Real GNP and Value of Exports: Selected Pacific Basin Countries

(in percent)

Country	Real GNP Growth 1970-79	Exports Growth (current price) 1970-79
Hong Kong[a]	9.02	19.12
Korea	10.02	44.84
Singapore	8.98	23.13
Taiwan	8.66	28.10
Indonesia	7.29	42.35
Malaysia	7.96	18.70
Philippines	6.30	20.63
Thailand	7.90	24.73

Source: IMF, *International Financial Statistics;* IMF, *Direction of Trade*; Paper by Lin & Ho.
Note: [a] 1969-79.

COMMUNIQUE

The Eleventh Pacific Trade and Development Conference took place on September 1-4 at the Korea Development Institute in Seoul, Korea. The Conference theme was "Trade and Growth of the Advanced Developing Countries in the New International Economic Order." It was attended by over forty economists and others from universities, governments and research institutions. Fifteen countries were represented, including Australia, Canada, Chile, Hong Kong, Indonesia, Japan, Korea, Malaysia, Mexico, New Zealand, the Philippines, Singapore, Taiwan (Republic of China), Thailand, and the United States.

The Conference examined the factors that affect the success of export-oriented growth strategies, and in particular those of Korea, Taiwan, Hong Kong and Singapore. Participants called attention to the many differences among these countries, including the extent of government intervention to promote export activity; the size and nature of the protected sectors and how these sectors are affected by the shift of resources to exporting industries; the role of foreign investment, etc. The growth record of all these countries nevertheless provides strong support for the contribution of international trade to efficient development. Furthermore, these countries have set an example for more industrially advanced countries in their ability to adjust to changing market conditions.

The Conference also recognized that export-oriented development brings with it important problems. First, to what extent it is necessary and desirable for government to provide export incentives, rather than simply to remove protective import substitution policies? If export promotion policies are to be followed, then what is the appropriate extent, form and timing for such policies? Should export promotion policies attempt to identify particular industries as leading export sectors, or should they provide general incentives which will permit private entrepreneurs to develop export potential in any industry? How should protected sectors (e.g., agriculture) be treated so that sufficient resources can be transferred to export industries? What are the income distribution effects of export promotion and if necessary can export policies be modified to avoid contributing to greater inequality?

In general the Conference concluded that the advanced developing countries have moved strongly toward efficient development based on economically viable export potentials. In spite of the external shocks (e.g., oil price increases) of the 1970s their export-oriented strategies have continued to be successful. In so far as inefficiencies or inequalities prevail they would appear to be generated by uneven success in controlling inflation, excessive credit subsidies, the effect of agricultural protection and perhaps by a tendency to place emphasis on physical-capital-intensive goods rather than on a gradual shift into more skill-intensive goods. On balance, however, the export promotion strategy does not appear to date to have biased the pattern of industrialization in directions that will seriously handicap the future competitiveness of the economies of the advanced developing countries.

Considerable attention was also paid to the ability and willingness of the industrially more advanced countries to accommodate the exports of the advanced developing countries. The current and future economic and political circumstances of the "advanced" group of countries were considered. Tendencies toward more protectionist policies were noted in major developed countries (the EEC and other OECD countries), and the need for improved access to the Japanese market was stressed. It was recognized that the problem was exacerbated by the current slump in all the "advanced" economies, and by the particular difficulties of certain large industries (e.g., textiles, footwear, and other labor-intensive manufactures as well as automobiles and steel in the United States, and primary metals and agriculture in Japan). Furthermore, as slower growth may be expected to prevail over the next few years the problems will not soon disappear.

In the context of this problem, Conference participants stressed the central importance of the projected rapid rates of economic growth in the 1980s in East and Southeast Asia, and the consequent increasing value of access to these markets to growth in the whole Pacific area. Perception of this prospect should result in more active efforts toward Pacific area cooperation and the limitation of current tendencies toward protectionism. The importance of resource trade with Australia, Southeast Asia and other countries in the Pacific region was also stressed.

The next Pacific Trade and Development Conference will be held in later summer of 1981 in Vancouver, Canada. The theme for that meeting will be "The Renewable Resources of the Pacific Region."

INDEX